The Blue Sapphire of the Mind

The Blue Sapphire of the Mind

*Notes for a
Contemplative Ecology*

—◦⟨●⟩◦—

DOUGLAS E. CHRISTIE

OXFORD
UNIVERSITY PRESS

OXFORD
UNIVERSITY PRESS

Oxford University Press is a department of the University of Oxford.
It furthers the University's objective of excellence in research, scholarship,
and education by publishing worldwide.

Oxford   New York
Auckland   Cape Town   Dar es Salaam   Hong Kong   Karachi
Kuala Lumpur   Madrid   Melbourne   Mexico City   Nairobi
New Delhi   Shanghai   Taipei   Toronto

With offices in
Argentina   Austria   Brazil   Chile   Czech Republic   France   Greece
Guatemala   Hungary   Italy   Japan   Poland   Portugal   Singapore
South Korea   Switzerland   Thailand   Turkey   Ukraine   Vietnam

Oxford is a registered trademark of Oxford University Press in the UK and certain other
countries.

Published in the United States of America by
Oxford University Press
198 Madison Avenue, New York, NY 10016

Library of Congress Cataloging-in-Publication Data

Christie, Douglas E.
The blue sapphire of the mind: notes for a contemplative ecology / Douglas E. Christie.
p. cm.
Includes bibliographical references and index.
ISBN 978-0-19-981232-5 (alk. paper)
1. Nature—Religious aspects—Christianity.   2. Ecotheology.   3. Contemplation.
4. Spiritual life—Christianity.   I. Title.
BT695.5.C497 2013
261.8'8—dc23
2012019801

[ISBN: 978-0-19-981232-5]

1 3 5 7 9 8 6 4 2
Printed in the United States of America
on acid-free paper

When the mind has put off the old self and shall put on the one born of grace, then it will see its own state in the time of prayer resembling sapphire or the color of heaven; this state scripture calls the place of God that was seen by the elders on Mount Sinai.[1]

EVAGRIUS OF PONTUS

The world is blue at its edges and in its depths. This blue is the light that got lost. Light at the blue end of the spectrum does not travel the whole distance from the sun to us. It disperses among the molecules of the air, it scatters in water. Water is colorless, shallow water appears to be the color of whatever lies underneath it, but deep water is full of this unscattered light, the purer the water the deeper the blue. The sky is blue for the same reason, but the blue at the horizon, the blue of land that seems to be dissolving into the sky, is a deeper, dreamier, melancholy blue, the blue at the farthest reaches of the places where you see for miles, the blue of distance. This light that does not touch us, does not travel the whole distance, the light that gets lost, gives us the beauty of the world, so much of which is in the color blue.[2]

REBECCA SOLNIT

Contents

Preface

It may not mark the precise moment when the ideas at the heart of this book began to take shape, but it is the moment I remember most clearly: my friend Yizhar Hirschfeld, the gifted Israeli archaeologist, had invited me to accompany him to visit Khirbet ed-Deir, the ancient Christian monastic site in the Judean desert that he had helped to excavate and document. We drove south from Jerusalem, past Hebron, stopping for tea at a local Bedouin encampment, before pushing on down a narrow, rough dirt road to the site. The ancient monastic settlement was situated in a long, sloping bowl, with rock faces rising up on three sides. A narrow channel had been cut out of the rock face to collect water, which ran down to a large cistern. An old stone wheel, once used for making olive oil, leaned against the back wall, where the outlines of the original monastic dormitory and refectory were still visible. Yizhar pointed out a field nearby that had long ago been the site of an olive orchard. And in a cave cut into the hillside, we encountered the remains of the monastic church, the space inside dark and still, intricate byzantine mosaics gracing the floor, the pale blue sky just visible in the distance.

I had been studying ancient Christian monastic thought for some years already when I visited Khirbet ed-Deir. But until that day, I had not fully grasped the concrete, material context in which that thought had unfolded and flourished. Nor had I realized the complex and intricate character of the economy in which the monks participated, or how profoundly it depended on the particular geography of the places where they lived. Standing in the place itself, I began to sense the great ingenuity and care with which the monks had situated themselves in this landscape, and how intimately their thought was bound to the life in this place. I did not yet possess the language of "contemplative ecology." But here in this place, I began to feel the delicacy and beauty of a spiritual practice bound to a particular place and arising from it. My habitual tendency of privileging monastic thought over practice,

so-called interior life over the physical, embodied character of monastic practice gradually began to dissipate. I found myself thinking in new ways about
monastic life as a whole, about how spiritual thought and practice are shaped
by landscape and how the experience and perception of living in a place can
be deepened through spiritual practice.

It would be some years before I began to think about these questions in
relation to ecological concerns in a more explicit way. But already I was beginning to sense that the ancient Christian contemplative ideal of weaving the
inner and outer worlds into an integrated vision of the whole had the potential
to offer something important to us in the contemporary moment. My own
experience of growing up in the Catholic spiritual tradition had been decidedly mixed in this regard. On the one hand, there was the simple beauty of
the sacramental vision of reality, in which every particular thing in the physical world was seen as reflecting and revealing the sacred—and thus possessing
inherent dignity and value; I had absorbed this idea early on into my sense of
the world. But there was also the long tradition of dualism within Christian
thought, in which matter and spirit were separated into distinct and incompatible dimensions of experience, with matter, the body and the physical world
often being denigrated or undervalued. I also felt the burden of this tendency
within Christian thought and sensed its larger impact on the world around
me. And I could not really imagine how I might make sense of these competing and seemingly irreconcilable influences coursing through my tradition.

This is why, I think, I was continuously drawn toward the simple, concrete practices of ancient Christian monasticism (as they appeared both in
the earliest texts and in contemporary monastic communities). Here was an
approach to living that understood contemplative practice in terms of a fierce
commitment to paying attention, an encompassing, transformative work oriented toward remaking the self and community, a *healing* work inclusive of
everything and everyone. The breadth and inclusivity of this vision, including
its commitment to the work of social and political transformation, spoke to
my own hunger for a way of living that could penetrate beneath the surface of
things, that was more integrated and holistic than the often narrowly individual understanding of spiritual practice I found present in so much contemporary thought. Here I found a spiritual tradition that, at its deepest and most
creative, expressed an attitude of radical openness to the life of the other, to
the world as a whole.

I also came to see that the quality of attention the monks cultivated in
their contemplative practice—*prosoche* was one of the names given to this
practice—had a wider and deeper application that transcended the monastic

tradition. I began to notice a comparable commitment to paying attention, to seeing deeply into things, in the work of particular artists, poets, and writers, especially those for whom attention to the natural world—in its beauty and its brokenness—had emerged as a central concern. The spiritual character of paying attention, I realized, could not be easily distinguished from its aesthetic and moral character. To open oneself to seeing in this way was to risk being drawn into an utterly involving engagement with all that one beheld. It was to risk becoming vulnerable before the other, humble, open. I began to wonder: what would it mean to behold the living world with the same fierce attention the early monks gave to their lives? Could a commitment to enter into the life of the world and to practice this kind of regard and reciprocity contribute to its healing, help it thrive and flourish?

To raise such questions is, I realize, to risk confusing things. After all, can the early Christian contemplative tradition really be said to be *ecological* in its concerns? And can contemporary poetry and literature of nature truly be said to have a *contemplative* dimension? Perhaps not in any strict sense. But there is a way of considering these questions, I believe, that can help to illuminate the shared concerns that draw these apparently disparate traditions of thought and practice together. This is one of the primary values in trying to articulate the idea of *contemplative ecology*—an understanding of spiritual practice that places the well-being of the natural world at the center of its concerns, and an approach to ecology that understands the work of cultivating contemplative awareness as critical and necessary to its full meaning. Discerning the particular shape and texture of this vision of the world is not easy, especially in the present moment, when the character of our discussions about the relationship between religion, science, and the natural world is often so tense and fractious. But I have come to feel that it is important to try to do so, if for no other reason than that it might help us discover (or rediscover) our capacity to imagine, inhabit, and respond to the world as a whole. And perhaps inspire a renewed commitment to attend to and work for the healing of the fragmented communities and places that are increasingly coming to characterize our world. This book represents a modest contribution to that healing work: a rumination on the idea that our ecological commitments, if they are to reach mature and sustainable expression, need to be grounded in a sense of deep reciprocity with the living world. And that this sense of reciprocity must be cultivated over time, in a process of deepening awareness and growing ethical maturity rooted in practices akin to those long cherished in the great spiritual traditions of the world—*contemplative* practices, oriented toward helping us see and inhabit and tend to the world fully and deeply.

It is a great pleasure to thank those friends and colleagues who have accompanied me along the way and who have contributed so much to the creation of this book. I have been blessed with extraordinary teachers and mentors: Donald Nicholl and Sandra M. Schneiders helped me see early on what it meant to think of spirituality not as something separate and distinct from ordinary experience but as a fully embodied and encompassing dimension of life itself. Peter Brown introduced me to the strange, fascinating world of monks and philosophers in Late Antiquity, and helped me grasp the intimate relationship between their intense spiritual practice and the complex social meanings of that practice. H. Daniel Peck, through his generous and inspired leadership of the 1997 NEH Summer Institute "The Environmental Imagination" at Vassar College, made it possible for me to participate in a wildly stimulating six-week-long conversation on literature, nature, and spirit with Lawrence Buell, John Elder, Terry Tempest Williams, A. R. Ammons, Barry Lopez, Laurie Kutchins, Ralph Black, Gyorgyi Voros, Charles Bergman, Bonney MacDonald, Nancy Cook, Bill Fleming, and others, a conversation that has continued to deepen across the years. Mary Evelyn Tucker and John Grim, through their pioneering work at the Forum on Religion and Ecology, have been a source of continued inspiration to me; I am particularly grateful to them for inviting me to participate in two important gatherings at Harvard University's Center for the Study of World Religions: on Christianity and Ecology and on Nature Writing.

Contact with monastic places and communities, both ancient and contemporary, has had a significant impact on my ongoing efforts to understand and interpret traditions of Christian contemplative practice. I am grateful to Maximos El-Anthony and Dar Brooks-Hedstrom for hosting me during memorable visits to the Monastery of St. Antony and the White Monastery in Egypt; to Guido Dotti and Enzo Bianchi for their hospitality and conversation during an extended stay at Bose Monastery in Italy; to Sr. Cristina, the superior of the Poor Clares in Cortona, Italy, who welcomed me into her community and made space for me to think and write there during a critical period of the book's development; to Raniero Hoffman, Bede Healey, Daniel Manger and the community of New Camaldoli in Big Sur, California, for inviting me to give their annual retreat; to Luke Dysinger, of St. Andrew's Priory in Valyermo, California, for his continued support and friendship. And especially to Kathy DeVico, Abbess of Redwoods Monastery in Whitethorn, California, and to the entire community there—Veronique, Godelieve, Victoria, Annette, Ann Marie, Claire, Karen, Suz, Maricela, and Maurice; they have opened themselves to me so beautifully in friendship and hospitality over the years and have taught me so much about the meaning and significance of sustained contemplative practice.

Portions of this book were worked out in talks or conference presentations and in the conversations and exchanges that always arose from these encounters. I want to express my appreciation to Wendy Wright at Creighton University, H. Daniel Peck at Vassar College, Georgia Frank at Colgate University, Robert Toth of the Thomas Merton Center for Contemplative Living, and David Addiss of the Fetzer Institute for inviting me to give talks to their communities and for their gracious hospitality and their thoughtful, critical engagement with my work. I also want to thank Dena Merriam of the Global Peace Initiative of Women for inviting me to participate in the Contemplative Alliance Conference at Asilomar, California, in October, 2010.

I have also benefited a great deal from my long association with the fine community of scholars working on early Christian monasticism and asceticism. Conversations with James Goehring, Dar Brooks-Hedstrom, David Brakke, Richard Valantasis, Elizabeth R. O'Connell, Yizhar Hirschfeld, Georgia Frank, and Teresa Shaw have been particularly helpful in leading me to think more deeply and critically about the early Christian monastic world.

I want to thank those friends and colleagues whose reflections on the natural world, spirituality, and contemplative practice have inspired me in different ways (though perhaps without their always knowing it): Belden C. Lane, Philip Sheldrake, Gregory Boyle, SJ, Arthur Holder, Barbara Newman, Bernard McGinn, David Abram, Jenny Price, Martin Mosko, Michael Rotondi, Stephanie Kaza, Chet Raymo, Ann Taves, Robert Orsi, Mirabai Bush, Steven Chase, Pir Zia Inayat-Khan, John David Pleins, Mary Oliver, Pattiann Rogers, Richard Nelson, William Kittredge, Scott Slovic, Robert Hass, Dennis Apell, Tensie Hernandez, and Sharron Duggan. A special thanks goes my oldest and dearest friend, Peter Lynch, whose sharp wit and searching intellect continuously provoked in me a more subtle and clear understanding of the most fundamental questions.

My colleagues at Loyola Marymount University have not only humored me but have also been a source of continuous encouragement and support during the book's long gestation process. I am grateful to Charlotte Radler, Anna Harrison, Roberto Dell'Oro, Brian Treanor, and Paul Harris, who have engaged me and my work with such warmth, openness, and intelligence. I am particularly grateful to the late Howard Towner, a fine biologist and a good friend, who taught me as much as anyone has about what it means to behold the world. A big thanks also, to my Dean, Paul Zeleza, for awarding me a College Fellowship that allowed me to bring the book to completion. My colleague and friend Ruben Martinez—writer, performer, political agitator, and teacher extraordinaire—bravely agreed to team-teach a course with me on the desert (not once but twice), and has greatly expanded my understanding of what it means to engage that strange, beautiful landscape with courage and moral integrity.

"Would you mind having a look at this chapter?" Those words escaped my lips more than a few times, usually with some trepidation. Who has time? To my continued astonishment, this request almost always met with a generous response. I am grateful to Georgia Frank, Martin Laird, Columba Stewart, Jenny Price, Steven Chase, and William Gibson who read portions of the manuscript and who were both honest and kind in their assessments of the work. Lynda Sexson read almost every word and regularly sent detailed (and piquant) postings from Montana on what should stay and what should go. During a week-long stay together at Redwoods Monastery, Donald Grayston read the entire penultimate draft and at the end cheerfully pronounced himself (mostly) satisfied. Daniel Mendez and Linda Claros were extraordinarily helpful in reading and correcting the proofs. No one read the manuscript more carefully or perceptively than Jennifer Abe; her unfailing ability to distinguish what matters most from what is secondary made a huge difference in helping me maintain a clear sense of the central pulse of the book.

I received generous support during the course of researching and writing this book from the Louisville Institute and from the Association of Theological Schools and the Luce Foundation. I would like to thank James W. Lewis at the Louisville Institute; Stephen Graham and Daniel Aleshire of the Association of Theological Schools; and Michael Gilligan and Lynn Szwaja of the Luce Foundation for their faith in this work.

I am deeply appreciative to Cynthia Read at Oxford University Press— both for her unfailing professionalism as an editor and for her genuine enthusiasm for the book; it makes a difference. Lisbeth Redfield, who shepherded the book toward publication, was always gracious, perceptive, and intelligent in her observations about matters needing further attention. I am grateful also to the anonymous readers for the press, whose careful reading of the manuscript helped me go deeper and further in my thinking than would have been possible otherwise.

My family has been a continued source of support to me, and I want to thank my parents, my sister Barb, and my two brothers, Mike and Tim, for their loving presence in my life.

It is customary in this space to thank (and offer apologies to) one's partner and children for allowing one to be absent for the extended periods of time necessary for writing the book. With a precious few exceptions, I can honestly say that this book was composed hardly at all in the quiet space one usually considers necessary for careful, critical thought. Instead, it came into being in the vibrant, enlivening company of my wife Jennifer, and the wild, beautiful, never-predictable presence of the children in my life: Julia Rose, Samantha, Jessica, Bennett, and Adam. What a joy it has been to work on this book in their company and to be continuously reminded that the work itself has been undertaken in no small measure on their behalf.

June 2012

The Blue Sapphire of the Mind

Immersion in the Larger Whole: Toward a Contemplative Ecology

This living flowing land
Is all there is, forever

We *are* it
It sings through us[1]

GARY SNYDER

[B]y being attentive, by learning to listen (or recovering
the natural capacity to listen which cannot be learned any
more than breathing), we can find ourselves engulfed in
such happiness that it cannot be explained: the happiness
of being at one with everything in that hidden ground of
Love for which there can be no explanation.[2]

THOMAS MERTON

IT IS JUST before dawn at Redwoods Monastery, deep in the forest of
Northern California. Eight figures sit silently in a spacious, cinderblock chapel. Candles flicker against the wooden benches. As the light slowly fills the
space, the shape of a simple square altar emerges. Behind the altar, a wall of
glass twenty feet high. Just visible through the glass is another figure, tall,
graceful, silent: a huge redwood tree. Its presence is particularly strong this
morning. It is the Feast of the Exaltation of the Holy Cross. Since at least
the time of Constantine, Christians have been meditating on this great mystery, the saving wood of the cross, or as some would later call it, the verdant
cross. The tree on which salvation was won. Today, in this place, we approach
this mystery in silence. Also with some anxiety. In the distance, we can hear
the muffled roar of trucks moving through the forest, carrying felled trees
to the mill. The struggle over the fate of this forest is ongoing. Most of the
old growth Redwood trees that once blanketed this corner of California are
gone; the few that remain are under continuous threat. For the members

of the community at Redwoods Monastery, the Redwood forest is the space within which the whole of their contemplative life unfolds; not merely background, but ground. Tending to the forest and its ecosystem and resisting its callous destruction have become part of the contemplative spiritual practice that grounds their life in this place. This practice of paying careful attention to place is shared in various ways with many others here in the Matolle River watershed, and far beyond.

Later that day, I catch a glimpse of this as I travel fifty miles north to participate in a rally aimed at saving what is left of the Headwaters Forest, one of the few remnants of old growth trees in this entire ecosystem. I arrive to find the proceedings well underway. Several thousand people have gathered in this forest clearing, some having traveled here from as far away as Portland, San Francisco, and Los Angeles. A thundering rhythm echoes across the damp field, into the trees and back toward us, through us. The drummers have taken the stage. The mosh pit is starting to heat up. "Feel the pulse," one of the drummers cries out. "It's the pulse of the forest, the pulse of your heart." No one here needs much persuading. The Headwaters Forest is under frenzied assault from logging companies and the prospect of this loss hovers over this gathering. We are here to organize, to plan strategies of resistance, to show by our physical presence that we will not stand quietly by while these ancient trees are razed. But there is also something else in the air, difficult to describe but palpable: a longing to express our feeling of kinship with this place, these trees. This is perhaps why, late that afternoon, restless after hours of speeches, we happily relinquish ourselves to the rhythm of the drums. All around the field, people begin rising from the wet ground, begin dancing, swaying, laughing. Five thousand of us, embraced by the forest, dancing—to celebrate, to deepen our resolve, to rekindle our hope.

For a moment the world seems simple, whole. The prospect of losing these trees seems an illusion, an impossibility. On all sides of this damp field, we are surrounded, sustained by their presence. Nor does the clear-cut hillside that has unleashed tons of mud on the nearby town of Stafford seem real. Even the machinations of the corporation responsible for the logging, with its cynical practice of paying off junk-bond debts with assets gained from cutting down trees seem, for a moment, to have no weight or substance. There is only this pulse, this rhythm, this forest, and all of us, dancing and moving together in the soft afternoon light of this autumn day. There is only this wordless celebration of community, solidarity, ecstatic wonder. It feels sufficient in that moment to let the pulse of this wild place carry us, console us, renew us.

This moment eventually passes, and a sobering recognition of the hard work ahead returns. Preserving what remains of this forest will require sustained scientific research, community organizing, political action, legal maneuvering, and economic calculation. And yet, this does not tell the whole story. Something of the magic of this late afternoon in the forest remains with me long after I have returned home, as does the deep silence of that morning in the monastery chapel. I begin to see that such moments of simple attention are also part of the larger struggle of tending to our increasingly degraded world. Indeed, they may well be at the heart of what poet Gary Snyder calls "the real work," the cultivation of a simple awareness of the enduring beauty and significance of the natural world. What precisely is the character of this work? And how can it support the complex and wide-ranging project of ecological renewal? This book is an attempt to address these questions by articulating the shape and character of what I am calling a *contemplative ecology*.

Notice Everything: Toward a Contemplative Ecology

> Never in any case whatever is a genuine effort of the
> attention wasted.[3]
>
> SIMONE WEIL

Contemplative ecology can best be understood as an expression of the diverse and wide-ranging desire emerging within contemporary culture to identify our deepest feeling for the natural world as part of a spiritual longing. At a time when much contemporary discourse about the meaning of the ecological crisis is often framed almost exclusively in terms of biological, economic, or political necessities, sometimes in ways that deny the spiritual dimension of our relationship with nature altogether, the effort to integrate spiritual traditions into our understanding of the natural world, or to think of the natural world as having spiritual significance may appear quixotic. However, there is growing desire to find a language and sensibility that can help us ground our efforts to respond to and preserve an increasingly degraded natural world in more than simple, utilitarian terms. One of the primary goals of this book is to argue for the significance of spirituality in helping us think about the meaning and significance of the natural world in our lives and formulate a meaningful response to the growing erosion of the natural world. In particular, I want to argue for the importance of *contemplative spiritual traditions* in reshaping our way of imagining and living in the natural world. "Contemplative ecology" is a way of describing the effort to integrate these contemplative traditions into the larger work of ecological thought and renewal.

There is increasing attention in the present moment to what has been described variously as the "greening of religion," "spiritual ecology," or "ecological spirituality." At the heart of these phenomena are two related insights that are changing the way we conceive of both ecological and spiritual reality. The first is the growing awareness within religious communities of the necessity of retrieving from their own traditions of thought and practice their own deepest affinities for and commitment to the natural world. This is usually what is meant by the phrase "the greening of religion," and suggests the deepening commitment on the part of these communities to integrate feeling and concern for the natural world into the very fabric of religious thought and practice.[4] In some cases this means retrieving ideas and practices that have long been a part of the tradition, but have been lost or neglected. In other cases, it means reimagining the very heart of religious identity—including ethics, theology, ritual practice, and spirituality—in light of the growing awareness of the threat to and significance of the living world.

The depth and extent of these changes are difficult to assess accurately. But it seems clear from the proliferation of both official statements and grass-roots efforts that this process of the "greening of religion" is becoming both more pervasive and more deep-rooted within religious traditions. There are many possible explanations for these changes. Certainly one important factor is the growing awareness of the need for a more serious engagement on the part of religious communities to the worldwide ecological crisis. But there is also evidence to suggest that members of religious communities are discovering that the beauty and power of their own faith traditions is deepened when it is conceived of as more intimately related to the living world. In other words, the growing efforts to articulate a greener faith are rooted not simply in the perception of the potential instrumental value to be found in such a shift of emphasis, but also in the growing awareness of how much the experience of faith itself is embodied, deepened through being more firmly rooted in the earth. The "greening of religion" is in the first instance a way of understanding how religious traditions are being renewed by being reimagined in light of ecological reality.

The second insight, to which the term "spiritual ecology" gives expression, concerns the growing recognition that a full and adequate understanding of ecology requires the integration of spiritual insight and practice.[5] Given that the modern science of ecology came into being as part of an effort among biologists and other scientists to describe and interpret and theorize the complex interplay between living organisms and their environment, such a statement might well appear strange, even nonsensical. What can it possibly mean to suggest that ecology ought to be understood as having a spiritual dimension? One thing it does not mean is that the scientific study and analysis of organisms in their environment somehow requires reference to supernatural language and concepts to arrive at a complete understanding of the phenomenon under question. Not only would this undermine and contradict the scientific method upon which ecology is based, it would also mean falling prey to an "extrinsic supernaturalism"—a way of understanding the spiritual or supernatural that completely transcends this world—and imposing such an understanding on our experience of the natural world. To argue for a "spiritual ecology" means, rather, acknowledging that ecological understanding ought to be set within the widest possible framework, and include not only the effort to understand how organisms interact with their environment, but also how these ecological networks shape and are shaped by human culture and thought, including human emotion, reason, imagination, and yes, soul. To speak of ecology in this way is to acknowledge that the term itself is being extended beyond its original, strictly scientific meaning to encompass a much more extensive arena of thought and experience, as Gregory Bateson did many years ago in his influential book *Steps to an Ecology of Mind* and as many others are doing now.[6] The most thoughtful efforts of this kind do not advocate supplanting scientific ecology with a purely metaphorical ecology of mind or spirit. Rather, they suggest a way of understanding the living world that takes seriously both the ecology of organisms in their environment and the web of associations and meanings arising from careful attention to this ecological reality.[7]

This double insight—that spiritual thought and practice is immeasurably enriched through being situated within the natural world, and that ecological understanding is given added depth and meaning by extending the ecological field to include traditions of spiritual thought and practice—comprises the heart of the emerging spiritual ecology that I intend to examine here. But what makes such a spiritual ecology *contemplative*? What does it mean to speak of a *contemplative ecology*? And how can the articulation of a contemplative ecology contribute to the broader project of ecological renewal?

To address these questions, it is helpful to return for a moment to that monastery chapel, and to that clearing in the Headwaters Forest. In particular I want to focus on the kind of attention necessary for cultivating an awareness of the beauty and significance of the living world as well as its fragility. The nature of such awareness is mysterious. It can arise as a momentary and short-lived flash of recognition, or take root and endure as a permanent part of one's consciousness. Nor is the spiritual significance of such awareness easy to describe or categorize. In classic religious discourse, such as that of the ancient monastic tradition in which the Redwoods community stands, one would usually describe this as the awareness of the presence of God or Spirit. Yet, in the diverse, religiously eclectic context of the present historical moment, such explicitly religious language is not always meaningful. Still, the need to express what it means to dwell in the presence of something of enduring value and meaning remains. In some cases this means making explicit reference to God or Spirit. In other cases, it is enough to express a sense of the limitless beauty and vitality of the natural world itself and of the expanded (or transcendent) awareness of the self that arises in relation to this mysterious reality. And sometimes it means acknowledging the power of a not-yet-fully articulated communal reality that includes all of this and more. However one understands the precise focus of this awareness, the question of what it is to become aware of oneself as alive in the living world and how to cultivate this awareness for the sake of that world remains one of the most pressing spiritual concerns of our time.

In the tradition of ancient Christian monasticism, such awareness was called contemplation. *Theoria* in Greek; in Latin, *contemplatio*. Contemplation refers in the first instance to a particular way of seeing—arising from a pure heart—and is one of the primary ways in which the monks spoke of the ultimate aim of spiritual practice: the vision of God. But they did not limit their account of this heightened perception to the metaphor of sight. They also spoke of the need to listen attentively for the still small voice of the Spirit, to become sensitive to the delicate, often-erotic touch of the Divine, to learn how to taste, to savor God's presence, even to become attuned to the intoxicating fragrance of the Holy One.[8] These sensual metaphors paradoxically point to a kind of perception that transcends anything that can be expressed in ordinary language, indeed that transcends anything known to us in the physical world. However, it is also clear that, for the early Christian monks, the language of contemplation provided a way of perceiving existence that encompassed all of reality, that enabled one to attend to the most simple and mundane elements of existence and to see them as filled with significance, as sacred. It enabled one to notice and cherish the *koinonia* or community into which one had been invited to dwell, and to commit oneself to the life and health of the community. And while community usually referred in the first instance to the monastery and the monks with whom one lived, it also opened out onto a much wider horizon, inclusive of the entire cosmos. The contemplative was invited to *notice everything* and to experience all things as part of a sacred whole. The monks believed that this encompassing, penetrating way of seeing, while possible for everyone, must be cultivated, brought into the center of consciousness through disciplined practice. By means of such practice, they were convinced, consciousness could gradually be deepened, or—if viewed within the larger moral-spiritual framework within which they understood their lives—*healed*. One could learn to live in the world as a healing presence, attentive and responsive to the lives of other beings and capable of helping to reknit the torn fabric of existence.

"Some Affinities of Content"

It is not easy to live in that continuous awareness of
things that is alone truly living ... [9]

JOSEPH WOOD KRUTCH

The cultivation of this kind of contemplative awareness has long been central to the life of Christian monastic communities and finds analogous expression in many other religious traditions. It is also becoming an increasingly significant part of the contemporary experience of the natural world, especially among poets and naturalists. In her 1991 essay, "Some Affinities of Content," poet Denise Levertov describes the growing sense of affinity between the way we experience (and speak about) the natural world and the way we experience (and speak about) the sacred. As this sense of affinity grows and deepens, she says, we are beginning to see the reciprocal influence between poetic discourse and spiritual discourse grow and deepen. As an example, she notes how Chinese and Japanese poetry and Buddhist thought and practice have influenced certain Pacific Northwest poets, and how this has given rise in their work to what she calls "a more conscious attentiveness to the non-human and to a more or less conscious desire to immerse the self in that larger whole." It has given rise, in other words, to a kind of "spiritual quest." In reading this work, she claims, one is often taken beyond the level of a casual observer, "to a universal level that speaks to the inner life." Such poems, Levertov suggests, "communicate not just the appearance of phenomena but the presence of spirit *within* those phenomena."[10]

The pattern that Levertov notices among these poets of the Pacific Northwest, of a reciprocal and deepening affinity between the language of spirituality and the language of the natural world, finds echoes in the work of many other contemporary writers as well and is an important expression of the larger pattern of spiritual ecology emerging within contemporary culture. It is often distinguished by its contemplative character and as such has particular significance for illuminating the kind of contemplative ecology I am considering.[11] Two aspects of this contemplative orientation are particularly significant: first, what Levertov describes as the "more conscious attentiveness to the non-human;" and second, the "desire to immerse the self in that larger whole." To orient oneself toward the non-human, to give one's conscious attention fully and deeply to a place, an animal, a tree, or a river is already to open oneself to relationship and intimacy with another. It is to see and feel the presence of the Other not as an object, but as a living subject. To experience this Other as part of "a larger whole," part of a vibrant and complex ecology, and to seek to immerse oneself in that larger whole, is to open oneself to that larger whole completely and without reservation. It is to risk the kind of vulnerability and merging of identities that mystics sometimes refer to in relation to their experience of God. Language that expresses this kind of intimacy with the natural world can indeed take one beyond the level of the casual observer and mediate a deeper awareness of the "inner life," or the soul. Not as something that can be distinguished or separated completely from all that surrounds one, or from the distinctive life of what one beholds in a particular moment, but as a quality of awareness that enables one to enter in and respond to both the seen and unseen dimensions of one's embodied life in the world.

Levertov's own work often expresses such contemplative awareness of the natural world. Her poem "Settling," written not long after her arrival to live in the Pacific Northwest, evokes that sense of dawning awareness at entering into the presence of a new, still unfamiliar, but alluring, place.

> I was welcomed here—clear gold
> of late summer, of opening autumn,
> the dawn eagle sunning himself on the highest tree,
> the mountain revealing herself unclouded, her snow
> tinted apricot as she looked west,
> Tolerant, in her steadfastness, of the restless sun
> forever rising and setting.

The eye adjusts slowly—to the distinctive colors of the place in this season (gold, apricot), to the presence of other beings (the dawn eagle), to the great mountain in the distance (Rainier—Tahoma), for this moment, at least, visible. It is a luminous world, inviting: she "was welcomed here." But places have moods. And they do not all express the same sense of hospitality. When she looks again later, things have shifted, and she must now reckon with a different more challenging reality.

> Now I am given
> a taste of the grey foretold by all and sundry,
> a grey both heavy and chill. I've boasted I would not care,
> I'm London-born. And I won't. I'll dig in,
> into my days, having come here to live, not to visit.
> Grey is the price
> of neighboring with eagles, of knowing
> a mountain's vast presence, seen or unseen.[12]

Behind that "grey"—"heavy and chill"—the mountain disappears. Unstated, but implied: the place is not what it first appeared to be. Also, these long "grey" days (sometimes continuing for weeks) are not for the faint of heart. But "London-born," she is prepared to struggle with the place on its own terms. And so the work of entering in ("digging in") begins in earnest. She means to "live" here, not visit. And what of those presences that were so inviting upon her first arrival? They are still there. But they follow their own mysterious rhythm. The new inhabitant is invited not only to behold all the life unfolding before and around her, but also to learn how to behold the unseen and unknown.

I grew up in the Pacific Northwest and spent my early days moving under the shadow of this great mountain. It became imprinted on my childhood imagination, along with the sweet fragrance of fir trees, the cool, moist air drifting in off the North Pacific Ocean, and the muted colors of a world existing under an almost perpetual blanket of cloud. But I moved away when I was fifteen years old and lost hold of the place and the sensory pleasures that grounded my life there. Even the memory of these pleasures faded, although for a long time I was only vaguely aware of this loss or what it meant to me. Encountering this poem many years later, with its simple naming and evocation of the texture of the place—mountain, tree, sun, cloud, chill air, eagle—I suddenly felt the force of this loss in a new way. And I found myself wondering how much I had ever really noticed the place of my birth, why I did not notice more, why it slipped from my consciousness so easily. But I also felt moved by the unexpected gift of having this place, still dear to me, revealed to me anew in this poem, of feeling something of my own long-ago experience mirrored in its words, made present to me again through my encounter with those words. I experienced it as a gift, an invitation to renew my relationship with this place, to locate myself again within this particular "whole."

And so I do, turning my attention in a new way not only toward my native place, but also to the place in which I find myself living now—a desert landscape so utterly different from where I grew up. I consider (with the poet's help) the kind of struggle involved in learning to see a place, take it in, respond to it. The practice of attention, I begin to see, requires commitment and courage; also a willingness to reckon with oneself, to clarify and deepen one's own capacity to see and cherish the world. The place will not reveal itself all at once, but must be lived into in humility and openness, must become subject to a deep and abiding regard. In this way, it can become part of an unfolding relationship, one that includes all the particular phenomena of the place as well as the inner life of the poet or seeker. To perceive and give expression in language to what Levertov calls the "spirit *within* [the] phenomena" is an imaginative act born of a recognition that our relationship with the natural world is, as Robert Finch suggests, "more than strictly intellectual, biological, cultural, or even ethical... [that it] is, at its very heart, *an enduring mystery*."[13]

This intuition of the world as alive and vibrant and mysterious is something woven into the imaginative life of every child. Yet it is easily lost and once lost can only be reacquired through a renewal of the imagination and spirit.[14] My own experience of being reawakened to my native place through the gift of a poem suggests one of the ways this renewal can happen, and why the shared effort among contemporary poets and writers to describe and express our experience of the natural world is so important. Such language can reveal the world, can open human consciousness to a new way of perceiving and being in the world. But it is so easy to fall back into habits of inattention and torpor, to lose one's hold on the fragile thread of awareness that allows the world to be taken in and experienced as sacred. Writers working to see and express the natural world are not unaware of this challenge. Joseph Wood Krutch, that eloquent chronicler of the deserts of the American Southwest, once noted: "It is not easy to live in that continuous awareness of things that is alone truly living ... the faculty of wonder tires easily ... Really to see something once or twice a week is almost inevitably to have to try to make oneself a poet."[15] This plaintive remark reflects what is surely one of the most fundamental concerns among contemporary writers regarding the practical question of what it is to see and know the world, namely the ephemeral character of awareness itself. To cultivate and sustain the kind of "continuous awareness" that Krutch describes as "alone truly living" is immensely difficult. It requires disciplined practice. It means somehow learning to turn one's entire being toward the world with genuine regard, working to keep alive in ourselves that fundamental sense of openness and attention to the world we call wonder.

In her book *The Ecology of Imagination in Childhood,* Edith Cobb describes wonder as "a kind of expectancy of fulfillment." The child's primordial sense of wonder, she says, is most often "displayed as surprise and joy," and is "aroused as a response to the mystery of some external stimulus that promises 'more to come' or, better still, 'more to do'—the power of perceptual participation in the known and unknown." This capacity, Cobb suggests, can be cultivated long after the first naïveté of childhood has passed, long after that initial sense of "more" has begun to diminish. "When it is maintained as an attitude, or point of view, in later life," she says, "wonder permits a response of the nervous system to the universe that incites the mind to organize novelty of pattern and form out of incoming information. The ability of the adult to look upon the world with wonder is thus a technique and an essential instrument in the work of the poet, the artist, or the creative thinker."[16] Or, one might add, in the work of the contemplative.

"Contemplation," says Thomas Merton, "is essentially a listening in silence, an expectancy."[17] Here is another kind of expectancy, also born of wonder, that one might come to know what Merton describes elsewhere as "the happiness of being at one with everything in that hidden ground of Love for which there can be no explanation." It is here, perhaps, in the shared sense of wonder, that the common contemplative sensibility of the poet and the monk can be seen most clearly. It is here too that one can see the particular contribution the monastic tradition has to make to the cultivation of the contemplative ecological practice that I am considering here.

A Contemplative Sense of the Whole

Silk thread, you were drawn into the fabric. //Whatever
single image you made yourself part of ... feel how the
whole carpet is meant, its glorious weave.[18]

RAINER MARIA RILKE

This contribution can be seen most clearly in the monastic commitment to a continual process of conversion or change of heart in a particular place. *Conversatio morum* is the name given to this spiritual practice in the sixth century *Rule of St. Benedict.* This phrase is difficult to translate, but can be rendered roughly as "the commitment to a continual change of heart in relation to God." What is implied in this notion (and given partial expression through the vow and ethos of *stabilitas*) is the understanding that this change of heart or conversion entails a steady but gradual reorientation of one's entire being to the presence of God in a particular monastic community, that is in a particular place. This commitment to a particular place, to a deepening awareness of the life and spirit of this place as the ground of one's entire contemplative life, is one of the distinctive contributions the monastic traditions has to offer to the larger task of learning to see and dwell in the world as a sacred place.

The significance of this contemplative practice was first brought home to me many years ago during a stay at the monastery of Our Lady of Clairvaux near Vina in the Central Valley of California. It was the first time I had ever been to a monastery. I had come there in the hopes of learning from the monks what I could about the practice of contemplation, even though at that moment contemplative prayer was for me little more than an idea. Nothing in my religious upbringing had taught me to understand prayer as anything other than direct verbal communication with God. But I had begun learning about a different approach to prayer—simpler, less formulaic, more expansive—as this came to expression in the ancient Christian monastic tradition. Perhaps here in this place I might experience for myself how members of this particular monastic tradition cultivated the art of contemplative prayer. During my time there, I devoted myself assiduously to keeping the monastic *horarium*, rising in the dark at 3:30 a.m. for vigils to immerse myself in the deep rhythm of communal prayer—first the ground of silence, then arising out of that silence the slow, ruminative chanting of the psalms, and then a return once more to silence. And so it went, as I continued to enter with the monks into this charged space of prayer at regular intervals throughout the day. But this was a kind of prayer unlike any I had ever known. It was simple, rooted in silence, and opened out onto a vast horizon of mystery whose presence I had long sensed, but had never known how to attend to. Gradually, as the days passed, I learned to give myself over to the rhythmic movement of this contemplative practice, learned to enter into the stillness and silent expectancy that was at its heart. As I did so, I began to notice something else: that the place itself and attention to the place formed an integral part of the contemplative practice.

The back and forth rhythm between word and silence that comprises the heart of monastic prayer is itself situated within a larger pattern or rhythm that shapes the entire monastic life. This is the rhythm of *ora et labora*—prayer and work. St. Benedict, like the desert monks before him, long ago recognized that contemplative practice must be embodied, must avoid the dangers inherent in an exclusive or extreme emphasis on prayer alone. This is why the monastic day is structured around an alternating rhythm of work and prayer, time spent in the church or cloister and time spent working in the fields or orchard or kitchen or library. The Apostle Paul's injunction to "pray without ceasing" (I Thes 5:17) is to be realized in the monk's life not through an exclusive attention to prayer at the expense of everything else (as if prayer were a discrete and disembodied reality), but through a deft interweaving of the mundane elements of daily living into the space of contemplative awareness. During those days I spent at Vina, as I moved back and forth between the church and the fields beyond the church, I found myself increasingly aware of moving within a "larger whole" that included the sound of the creaking wooden benches of the monastic choir, the monks' work boots scuffling along the linoleum floor of the church, and voices raised in prayer; also fragrant incense, the faint winter light streaming in through the windows, as well as the long rows of prune and walnut trees, the slow moving Sacramento river at the edge of the monastery grounds, the distant sound of a train whistle, birdsong in the early morning, the glint of light shining off the water tower. Also the longings hidden within the hearts of all of us gathered in that place.

The longer I was there, the more difficult it became to discern the precise boundaries of the contemplative awareness within which I moved and through which I now perceived the world. And this difficulty, I began to see, revealed an important truth: that all of these elements are indeed woven together as part of a larger whole. I did not fully grasp the utterly integrative, sacramental character of this experience at the time, but I began to intuit even then that here was an approach to living that was whole and undivided. There *was* no inner life, no outer life, but simply a life lived in the presence of God in which everything was included, nothing excluded.

I speak of an ideal of course. Over the years, as I have come to know and participate in the life of different monastic communities, and given myself over to careful study of the classic texts of this tradition, I have realized more fully than I did at the time what it is to give oneself over to the contemplative life as a *project*, and how this project remains ever unfinished, always unfolding. Still, it is a vision of life that I continue to find immensely compelling, and I have devoted much of my life to the task of interpreting the contemplative traditions of Christianity in terms that can be retrieved and adapted for contemporary use. It has been a source of unending astonishment to me to discover how many and various are the possible adaptations of these contemplative traditions. Far from being of interest only to monks, the contemplative vision of life, I have discovered, speaks in a meaningful way to a wide range of persons seeking to live their lives with a greater sense of authenticity and purpose. To live contemplatively, in this sense, can be understood simply as a certain intense way of being alive, grounded in a conscious awareness of the depth and beauty of one's own soul and one's relationship to God and the whole of existence.

Still, the Christian contemplative tradition, in particular the primitive tradition of ancient Egyptian monasticism, is insistent that the acquisition of such awareness is a long, difficult process, requiring a disciplined attention to the sources of our own fragmentation and alienation and a commitment to a kind of therapeutic process whereby the soul can be remade in God, restored to its original image and likeness. Part of what makes the contemplative approach to spiritual renewal so significant is its honesty about the depth of our alienation and the effects of this alienation on our lives and on the world. Renewal is possible, the contemplative tradition maintains, but for it to be sustained and meaningful it must touch into the very roots of our being.

I confess that for a long time I understood this renewal process largely in personal, even individual terms. But through an ongoing participation in the lived experience of actual contemplative communities—initially with the monks at New Clairvaux, then with the Cistercian nuns at Redwoods monastery near the California coast, and eventually with monks on Mt. Athos in Greece, at St. Catherine's near Mt. Sinai and at St. Antony's monastery in the remote Red Sea desert of Egypt—my sense of the *wholeness* of contemplative experience began to grow and deepen. And I began to realize that this sense of wholeness was there from the beginning of the Christian monastic tradition. By wholeness, I mean not only the ancient contemplatives' feeling for the living world—although the stories evoking the monks' simple awareness of the beauty of the desert, or appreciation for its deep silence, or wonder at the prospect of kindling intimate reciprocity with other living beings bear important witness to the paradisal dream which was so central to their lives. I also mean the monks' intense commitment to *pay attention*, out of which emerged a sense of compassion and responsibility for the broken world.[19] The ancient desert monastic tradition understood the contemplative as one who opened himself to a long, difficult process of purification, not only for his own sake but for the sake of the larger community. Here I began to see, was an utterly convincing vision of *koinonia* or community, in which the work of personal renewal was inextricably bound up with a vision of renewal of the whole.[20]

The ancient monks had a sober and honest understanding of how extensively the fabric of their world had become torn and frayed. The harshness of the late Roman empire had reduced entire communities to fragmented, impoverished places and this apocalyptic reality profoundly shaped the monks' understanding of their contemplative vocation. To engage in an act of *anachoresis* or withdrawal was to seek in solitude not an escape, but a means of reconstituting a broken whole. The images that became so central to the early monastic vision—of monks engaged in a fierce struggle against nameless forces within and without, and of others dwelling joyously in a still-fresh paradise—suggest how encompassing their contemplative practice was for them and what it meant for them to work toward a genuine restoration, in their own lives, and in the life of the society and world of which they were a part. The monastic tradition has always emphasized the importance of ascetic practice—the work of relinquishment and purification by which the broken self is gradually healed, and brought to a new capacity to meet the broken world in openness and freedom and compassion.

My encounter with this particular expression of contemplative spiritual practice, both as a historical tradition and as a living reality, has helped open my eyes to the more diverse and wide-ranging expressions of contemplative thought and practice emerging in contemporary culture. One of the most important expressions of this contemplative sensibility is found in the work of contemporary writers, artists, ecologists, anthropologists, geographers, architects, and others who are reflecting in their own way on the spiritual significance of the natural world, including the question of whether we can learn again to apprehend and respond to an increasingly degraded and threatened world as sacred. This question has a profoundly ethical character: how can we learn to live differently so that we do not continue to visit our most destructive impulses upon the natural world? But it also touches into the very depths of what many are coming to see as a fundamental question of spiritual identity. Who *are* we in relation to the natural world, ultimately? And how does our self-understanding influence our sense of what it is to live in and tend to the wild world?

As the natural world becomes ever more deeply compromised, such questions are becoming increasingly urgent. But what can it mean, in a historical moment in which questions of spiritual identity are increasingly framed not only in relation to specific religious traditions but also in relation to a vast and eclectic array of non-religious symbols and ideas, to retrieve a common sense of the natural world as sacred? Can we discover and learn to stand in a vision of the world that takes seriously the diversity of experience while also recognizing real places of convergence and commonality? Can we learn to become sensitive to those "affinities of content" that signal a shared (if varied) awareness of the natural world as vital, precious, and yes, sacred? An orientation to spiritual identity that is contemplative in character can, I believe, provide a fruitful way of developing such a sensibility and help to create a bridge between and among many of the diverse expressions of reverence for the natural world emerging in contemporary discourse.

The Christian contemplative tradition has a distinctive contribution to make to our shared efforts to learn to live more attentively and responsibly in the natural world. Still, the true significance of this contribution will only be felt and appreciated by situating it in relation to comparable efforts to renew our sense of the sacredness of nature emerging throughout contemporary culture. This wider, shared expression of concern for the natural world, and the effort to articulate this concern in terms of a language of spiritual practice, provides the context within this contribution must be understood. And if the Christian contemplative tradition has a particular contribution to make to this shared work, as I believe it does, so too should the emerging ecological consciousness be understood as crucial to understanding what a contemplative ecology will look like in the present moment.

One way of understanding this book is to view it as an exercise in what theologian David Tracy has described as the work of "critical correlation" or what is sometimes called the work of "bricolage."[21] Tracy argues that any meaningful religious reflection—especially reflection within a particular tradition—must involve an effort to correlate classic spiritual texts or traditions and common human experience. Such work, he suggests, can be mutually illuminating and can extend the possibility of religious reflection far beyond what one can achieve through a singular focus on either the classics or contemporary experience. In this understanding, the classics, having been tested by the community and judged to have enduring significance, can provide valuable resources for interpreting and deepening contemporary experience. But they must also be subject to critical engagement in light of contemporary experience and their meaning must be capable of being renewed, deepened, and even altered in light of that experience. The ancient Christian monastic tradition, which first took root in the deserts of Egypt, Judea, Syria, and Asia Minor in a moment of profound social, political, and cultural crisis, gave expression to a moving spiritual vision and practice that offered its own response to that crisis. Rooted in a strong commitment to place and to a spiritual practice oriented toward a gradual transformation of the human person and the world itself, this spiritual tradition has enjoyed enduring influence not only in terms of its central ideas, but also as a way of life. The affinities between this tradition and the different visions of spiritual ecology coming to expression in the present moment are striking, and the benefits of thinking of them in relationship to one another are, I believe, noteworthy. Among the most significant of these affinities is the shared sense that the ecological crisis (which is also a cultural, social, and political crisis) we are facing in this moment is at its deepest level spiritual in character, and that our response to this crisis will require of us nothing less than a spiritual transformation. It is my conviction that bringing these distinct but complementary traditions of discourse and practice into dialogue with one another and articulating the vision of the world that emerges from this dialogue can help us better understand both the true character of the crisis we are facing and the path of spiritual transformation open before us.

The Natural World and Contemporary Spiritual Practice

Meaning making is wounding.[22]

ROBERT ORSI

What will such a dialogue look like? And what will it mean for us, intellectually, morally, and spiritually, to try to weave together a sense of the world as whole that takes seriously both the insights of ancient spiritual traditions and the understanding of the world born of modern ecological thought? Is this even possible? It seems important to pause and acknowledge some of the significant challenges involved in attempting to articulate and argue for the meaningfulness of a contemplative ecology. I want to note two such challenges that I believe have particular importance for this book. The first is the challenge of understanding how or whether the diverse and often divergent ideas of nature present in contemporary discourse about ecology and the environment can be situated in relation to efforts to articulate an ecological spirituality. The second is the challenge of thinking about how or whether the seemingly endless diversity of meanings attached to the terms "spiritual" and "spirituality" in the contemporary moment can inform careful thought about ecological concerns. The term "contemplative ecology" suggests that there is in fact a way of thinking about these two broad domains of knowledge or fields of discourse in relationship to one other, that there is a way of thinking about spiritual practice that has an ecological character, or a way of thinking about ecology that includes reflection on the moral or spiritual dimensions of experience. But what will it mean to do so? And what approach to the integration of these ideas will prove most fruitful? Much of this book is taken up with the attempt to address these questions. Still, it is worth pausing to describe the broad outlines of the approach I am proposing here.

Nature. The natural world. The living world. The physical world. The more than human world. The environment. The cosmos. The whole. These are but a few of the terms that have emerged in contemporary discourse to describe the living reality within which our lives unfold. The very plurality of terms says something important about the complexity of our ideas about and experience of this reality and the difficulties of arriving at anything like a simple clear understanding of it. Some of these terms refer to a reality that is primarily, if not solely, physical—something whose meaning can best be apprehended and described using the methods and theories of modern science. Others refer to a reality whose meaning can only be fully apprehended through attention to myth, story, art, and traditions of spiritual practice; nature in this understanding is inescapably physical and concrete, but it is also seen as numinous and mysterious, never completely knowable in its immensity and depth. There is also the question of the real difficulties, raised clearly and persuasively by William Cronon and others, arising from our tendency to think of nature as something utterly separate from us, as pristine, "out there," beyond the realm of human culture and thought, indeed in some ways as fundamentally opposed to it.[23] The need to arrive at a more subtle and fluid understanding of nature that is respectful of its wild otherness but also sees it as capable of being incorporated into the complex reality of human culture without being completely subsumed or defined by it is one of the real challenges before us.

Sometimes these different approaches to and understandings of nature can be reconciled with one another; other times a rapprochement between them is more difficult. The differences matter of course. Still, we find ourselves in the present moment struggling to discover a way of imagining and speaking of the whole of reality that neither privileges nor marginalize one or another of these dimensions of knowledge or experience. The fierce and often intractable debates between "science" and "religion" (two terms that have themselves become oversimplified and impoverished in the process) that are such a large part of the contemporary cultural moment often have just this effect. "Nature" in this context becomes a polarizing term, poised uneasily against "creation." Similarly, debates about the relative claims of nature (often characterized as remote or untouched wilderness) and human culture often result in an impasse that does little to help us navigate the very real challenges of learning to live in a diminished but still vibrant world. In such a polarized climate, it often becomes difficult if not impossible to arrive at an integrated understanding of the world in which we live that takes seriously its biological complexity, aesthetic beauty, and spiritual significance. I hope to avoid this kind of polarization here, and remain open and attentive to the many shifting meanings that we attach to the idea of nature in this particular historical moment and to the possibilities for situating these different meanings in closer and more fruitful relationship to one another.

This will mean, among other things, taking seriously the way the variegated and still-emerging field of ecology, defined in one recent account as "the spatial and temporal patterns of the distribution and abundance of organisms, including causes and consequences," conceives of its domain.[24] This admittedly spare definition of ecology nevertheless points to the fundamental insight that the study of ecology has contributed to our understanding of the world—namely that life is not a characteristic of individual organisms but rather of networks or webs. And that it is upon the health and strength of these webs of life that everything depends. As biologist Daniel Botkin notes, we have now come to understand that "life is sustained only by a group of organisms of many species … a certain kind of system composed of many individuals of different species—and their environment, making together a network of living and nonliving parts that can maintain the flow of energy and the cycling of chemical elements that, in turn, support life." Nor, as we now understand, is this network, or the life of particular ecological communities within the network, static and unchanging. Rather, they are fundamentally dynamic; the changes that occur continuously throughout the network are intrinsic to it and necessary for life. This "dynamic equilibrium" is a basic characteristic of the world we inhabit.[25] Our very sense of the world as well as our sense of responsibility for it depends on our capacity to understand and live within this reality.

In this moment of acute environmental degradation, this understanding of the character of ecological networks upon which life depends, and especially of the fragility of these networks, has become integral to our sense of the world. Human identity is itself becoming increasingly ecological. And no small part of that identity derives from the sense of the world that is emerging in the work of those who study, analyze, and tend to these fundamental life systems. Still, the question of how we can deepen our own feeling of regard for the world and our capacity to live responsibly in relationship with it requires a more wide-ranging inquiry into the meaning of this ecological identity. For some, this inquiry has come to be identified as a part of an effort to rethink the fundamental elements of our common existence, to imagine what it might mean to cultivate an awareness of ourselves as existing deeply and inescapably within this ecological reality—what Timothy Morton calls "thinking the mesh."[26] Taking seriously this "ecological thought" will of necessity mean learning to live into a deeper and more encompassing moral or ethical relationship with the living world, cultivating what Aldo Leopold long ago named as our "ecological conscience."[27] Implicit in such ideas, for many, is the growing sense that learning to imagine ourselves and the world in this way will require opening ourselves to self-conscious spiritual practices rooted in the desire to kindle a greater feeling and responsibility for other living organisms and for the world as a whole—practices that will help us feel and respond to the *claim* of the living world upon our lives. Such practices sometimes arise from within particular religious traditions; but often they come into being from outside of such traditions, or in an eclectic blending of old and new traditions. To speak of an ecological spirituality or a spirituality that is informed by intimate contact with and feeling for the natural world can and will mean many different things in the present cultural moment. But a common feature of such spirituality or spiritual practice is a deepening awareness of oneself as existing within and responsible for the larger whole of the living world.

Still, what does it mean to speak of spirituality in such a context? And, in particular, of a contemplative spirituality? The meaning of spirituality, which has become such a prominent part of contemporary discourse about the world, remains wildly fluid and often opaque. Sometimes it refers, as it has often done historically, to a mode of experience of the Divine or tran-scendent that occurs within the context of a recognizable religious tradition. But its meaning in the present moment is often broader, and more diffuse than this. The increasingly common distinction between spirituality and religion (the former usually referring to personal dimensions of experience and the latter referring to an experience rooted in more structured, institu-tional forms of religious life) suggests that many of the most profound and important expressions of spiritual experience are now occurring outside the bounds of traditional religious forms and structures.[28] One attempt to express this broad and diffuse understanding of spirituality defines it as: "the expe-rience of conscious involvement in the project of life-integration through self-transcendence toward the ultimate value one perceives."[29] Such an under-standing of spirituality is fundamentally open, especially in terms of the ulti-mate value that underlies it. Conscious involvement and self-transcendence are its defining features; but the object or aim of such self-transcendence is left undetermined. Understood in this way, spirituality can be situated within a religious framework and have an explicitly theistic character. But it can also exist beyond or outside of such a framework and remain agnostic about the ground of transcendent meaning. Here, the meaning of the transcendent or the holy or the ultimate is less bounded than it often is when it is closely associated with particular religious symbols; it is more open to a plurality of possible meanings.[30]

Something similar can be said about the notion of "lived religion," an idea that is coming to have increasing importance for helping us understand the creative and eclectic strategies which human beings employ to discover and express spiritual or religious meaning in their lives. In practice, such strategies often reflect an open and flexible relationship to religious traditions, a willingness to hold apparently conflicting or paradoxical views in tension in the search for a meaningful way of being in the world.[31] The longing to articulate a meaningful spiritual practice that draws upon but also transcends or reimagines the language and symbols of particular religious traditions, that in some cases is hardly recognizable as religious at all, is one of the most prominent features of the contemporary cultural landscape. It is within this unbounded, fluid, open space that the increasingly common expression "I am spiritual but not religious" has arisen and has come to have such poignancy and significance in the present moment. This fluid, open way of imagining and inhabiting spiritual identity and practice has particular importance for helping us understand the emerging contemplative ecological spirituality that is the subject of this book.[32]

Still, in spite of the growing significance of such eclectic, "trans-religious" or "non-religious" spiritualities, any effort to understand how spiritual practice can inform greater ecological awareness as well as a commitment to environmental renewal must also reckon with the contribution that historical spiritual traditions can make to this larger work. The ancient Christian contemplative traditions upon which I draw in this book offer one example of the continuing significance of historical expressions of spiritual practice in the contemporary moment. These contemplative traditions have not only shaped the life and thought of generations of monastic practitioners, but have also become important in the lives of a broader and more diverse group of seekers in the contemporary moment.[33] During its long history, both the understandings of contemplative practice and the forms of life arising from these traditions have undergone continuous evolution and development as contemplatives have sought to situate and resituate themselves meaningfully in the world. But there are also striking continuities of thought, practice, symbols, and rituals that have informed this way of life from the beginning and continue to do so in the present moment. Learning from this way of life and drawing upon it to help us with our own questions will mean opening ourselves to the power of these traditions, and to the spiritual practices and modes of discourse honed over centuries—not blindly or uncritically but with a certain curiosity and trust that they can help facilitate the discovery of an openness and freedom that can contribute significantly to our capacity to notice and care for the world.

In the context of the environmental crisis, the question inevitably emerges: can such contemplative traditions help us reimagine our place in the world and enliven our capacity to care for it? I believe they can do so and will elaborate upon this conviction further in the pages that follow. For now, I wish only to suggest the importance, in this particular historical moment, of remaining open to and curious about the wide diversity of ways we are learning to express our deepest feeling of regard for the natural world, and of attending in particular to the way ancient spiritual traditions can inform this common work. From within the particular tradition of contemplative practice that is my focus in this book, I look outward toward other, kindred forms of spiritual practice, seeking useful points of correspondence between and among them that can help us learn how to imagine and tend to the larger whole.

Such common contemplative work raises other questions as well. One of the most important of these has to do with whether the inescapably personal and intimate character of contemplative practice can be understood as having the capacity to inform and inspire critical social action. Spirituality and spiritual practice have often been perceived and characterized as detached from and uninterested in the concrete, embodied, social-political realities of the world. The intensely inward-looking character of spiritual disciplines, with their insistent attention on the transformation of the self, has certainly contributed to this perception. So too have the tendencies of certain ascetic practices within contemplative traditions—practices that often reflect a suspicion of the body, human sexuality, and the physical world—contributed to this perception. There is some truth to these perceptions; the Christian contemplative tradition has had its own long, and complicated struggle with these questions. But there is also another truth, namely that spiritual practices are often undertaken by persons and communities in order to achieve freedom from harmful, compromising attachments and to create the climate in which it becomes possible to adopt a more open, loving disposition toward others and the world. Such practices often lead to a serious engagement with and critique of fundamental social, cultural, and economic values that are perceived as tearing at the very fabric of life and community. In our own time, there has been a growing recognition of how important traditions of spiritual practice can be to the larger work of social and political liberation and in particular to the struggle to achieve environmental restoration.[34] Still, the impulse behind such work is not new; it can be traced far back into the roots of our great spiritual traditions, including the ancient Christian contemplative traditions upon which I am drawing in this book. The critical retrieval of these traditions can, I believe, help to inform a deep and wide-ranging social-political-ecological critique. In particular, it can inform and contribute to a renewal of the kind of *tactical practices* that Michel de Certeau has argued are so necessary for helping us resist the often-harmful claims made upon us by dominant structures of power.[35] In short, this work of retrieval can inform and enliven our own efforts to articulate an alternative vision and way of living that honors the integrity of the living world and our own spiritual lives.

These observations lead, almost inevitably, to a recognition of the engaged, participatory character of this work, to the element of risk involved in learning to see and inhabit the world in this way. If there is a necessarily descriptive, analytic character to the work of articulating a contemplative ecology, there is also something potentially costly and self-implicating about it. One does not stand aloof from such work, but enters in, often deeply. In recent years, there has been growing attention to the question of how if at all one can simultaneously *describe and analyze* a religious or spiritual practice with careful scholarly rigor and *participate* in it. The so-called "participatory turn" in the study of religion and spirituality suggests one possible response to this question, namely that participation and engagement in the subject is sometimes the most honest and open way of representing its particular character.[36] But participation and the search for meaning and understanding can be ambiguous, even dangerous for the participant. I am thinking here of Robert Orsi's observation regarding the search for meaning and the risk of interpretation in scholarship on religion and spirituality: "Meaning making begins in wounding," he says, "and the process of meaning making is wounding."[37] There is, in other words, no safe position when it comes to engaging fundamental questions of religious and spiritual meaning; one must be prepared to risk everything. Certainly this is a characteristic feature of the ancient Christian contemplative traditions. There, the work of cultivating an encompassing, utterly involving gaze leads to the most intense experience of vulnerability and risk. As my own work on these traditions has deepened, I have become increasingly aware that I could not and did not wish to remain at a safe distance from them. Over time, I have become more involved, more open, more vulnerable. And I have chosen to proceed here in a manner that reflects this contemplative process. It seems to me that if the idea of contemplative ecology is to gain purchase on our imaginations and contribute something significant to our way of living in the world, it will of necessity have to find its way into the places where we are most vulnerable, especially in relation to the natural world. This will mean, I think, learning to open ourselves not only to the fragility and vulnerability of the world, but also to how profoundly it lives in us and matters to us.

Common Ground, Ultimate Ground

God's ground is my ground and my ground is God's ground.[38]

MEISTER ECKHART

Many of those I encounter on that wet September day in the Headwaters Forest seem to take it as axiomatic that the natural world is shot through with Spirit and that our efforts to respond and tend to it effectively will require us to pay attention to this dimension of the world. All around me I see evidence of a heartfelt and spontaneous response to the call to "immerse the self in that larger whole." And not only for personal reasons, for the feeling of belonging that comes from that immersion, but also for the *sake* of the larger whole. This imaginative reweaving of self and living world, in *all* its dimensions—eco-logical, literary, ritual, political—is characteristic of an emerging poetics of sacred place. The retrieval of ancient religious images and symbols is a crucial element of this poetics. But the significance of these symbols, what they actu-ally *mean* to us, is being transformed by our contemporary experience—by our experience of an increasingly diminished natural world, and by a climate of almost irreducible religious diversity.

What James Joyce once said in reference to the crazy-quilt ethnic and religious inclusivity of popular, grass-roots Irish Catholicism—"here comes everybody"—seems an apt description of this Headwaters gathering. Visible by their signs, badges, or presence on stage are members of the Buddhist Peace Fellowship, representatives of the North American Conference on Christianity and Ecology, neopagans, Native American elders, Presbyterians for Ecological Justice, a rabbi representing the local Jewish community, and many others who might best be described in terms that river rafters and rock climbers sometimes use: "beyond category."

The religious rhetoric and imagery is equally eclectic: there is recurring appeal to the biblical ethos of stewardship, to the idea that we have been given a "sacred trust" and need to be caretakers of the earth. Starhawk appeals to the ancient and enduring connections known to the Wicca traditions that bind us to the natural world. A Buddhist monk leads us in meditation, calling to mind the sacredness of all sentient beings. And a rabbi chants, first in Hebrew, then in English, the haunting words of the psalm: "I lift up my eyes to the hills, from whence will my help come? My help will come from the maker of earth, stars, and sun (Ps 121)."

There is an altar dedicated to Judi Bari (the environmental activist injured in a mysterious car bombing) who is for many here a martyr. Perhaps the most striking reinvention of an ancient sacred form is the large altarpiece, a triptych modeled after medieval Christian examples, with a towering redwood tree visible on the central panel, images of threatened animal species native to this habitat displayed along the two side panels and, all along the bottom, images of habitat destroyed by clear-cutting. This transposition of sacred symbolism is striking and meaningful for many gathered here. As I stand pondering these images I notice many others pausing before these shrines and descending for a moment into a place of mourning and silent reverence. Given all that has been lost, there is an inescapable sadness surrounding these shrines. Yet they are also places of hope, where those who are mourning can and sometimes do give voice to their commitment to preserve the life that still remains. These improvised sacred symbols help to place the trees and the entire local biotic community at the center of a concern so deep and strong that it cannot—at least for many of those gathered here—be named without them.

Eventually, the drumming and dancing subside. Bonnie Raitt takes the stage for a final song. It is the old Blind Faith tune, "Can't Find My Way Home," a fitting coda to this day so filled with longing for home, so fraught with feelings of homelessness. Then we move on to the last ritual act of the day, a procession—from the place of worship to the site of desecration, the mudslide in Stafford. We make our way slowly out of the field and along the side of a small country road, passing a phalanx of police officers dressed in riot gear. We walk with our posters, giant puppets, drums, sacred objects, up the hill toward Stafford. It is part carnival, part protest march, part religious procession. It is at once a gesture of solidarity with the people of that town and an act of remembrance, a way of saying: this place, these people, this event will not be forgotten. Stafford will not be allowed to become an "unfortunate consequence" of careless, illegal logging practices. In an attempt to help secure what is left of the town against the next big slide, we fill thousands of sandbags and place them against the now-stripped hillside. Will it be enough? Almost certainly not. But as one resident tells us: "We desperately need help. The first slides cleaned off the mountain so it's slick as glass. Any new slides will be like bullets—much, much faster than the first ones. Living here now is like living in the barrel of a gun."

This too is part of the poetics of sacred place—the often disturbing metaphors of fear and anxiety that emerge as the desecration of the places we inhabit deepens and spreads. "Like living in the barrel of a gun." A harsh and frightening image of what it feels like to live under the shadow of this once forested, now slick-as-glass hillside, an image that captures only too well our current predicament. Even more ominous, and harder to find language for, is the sickening, fathomless sense of loss that affects many in this community and throughout this region. Rooted in the mounting accumulation of losses—first the trees, then the hillside, then individual homes (seven were lost in the slide)—it opens out onto something both more basic and more profound. It has to do with the growing sense that we are losing what Thomas Berry calls "intimate modes of divine presence." It touches on the sense that in a world made desolate, the presence of the sacred and life itself will be lost to us. And with it will be lost our capacity for intimacy, delight, and wonder.

These are ultimate, necessary realities without which life itself is unimaginable. Gradually, it has begun to dawn on us that they arise from and are sustained by the living beings of this world, which are themselves ultimate and necessary. This sense of the *ultimacy* and *necessity* of what we are losing and what we still hope to preserve, is becoming increasingly integral to the meaning of the natural world in contemporary experience. Often, these ideas have no explicit religious meaning. But they are coming to be associated more and more with the sacredness of nature. And while we still do not have a shared language of the sacred that can ground and galvanize the work of community building, political resistance, and ecological preservation, I wonder whether the language of ultimacy and necessity might provide a place from which to begin.

How, for example, can we learn to express the deepest or most ultimate ground of our shared concern? The twelfth-century Dominican mystic Meister Eckhart famously employed the image of the *grunde* or ground to express the deepest dimension of the soul that enables human beings to recognize and dwell within the Divine. It is, Eckhart claimed, "the purest thing that the soul is capable of ... the noblest part ... indeed ... the very essence of the soul which is the soul's most secret part ... here God's ground is my ground and my ground is God's ground."[39] For Eckhart, the ground of the soul stands at the center of everything that exists, in us, in God and in the world. Contemplative living is nothing more or less than a simple awakening to this ground. This is a beautiful and capacious idea that can help us grasp the underlying unity of all being and the intimate relationship that exists between and among all living beings. Still, if we ask what it might mean to bring this classical spiritual ideal to bear upon our contemporary efforts to create a stronger and more enduring sense of connection with the living world, we may need to attend more carefully to the concrete reality of the ground in our lives, that is, the places where we actually live.

This is what Scott Russell Sanders attempts to do in his thoughtful meditation on place, *Staying Put,* offering a kind of bioregional reading of this ancient spiritual ideal. "The likeliest path to the *ultimate* ground," says Sanders, "leads through my local ground. I mean the land itself, with its creeks and rivers, its weather, seasons, stone outcroppings, and all the plants and animals that share it. I cannot have a spiritual center without having a geographical one.... If our interior journeys are cut loose entirely from ... place, then both we and the neighborhood will suffer."[40] There are clear echoes here of the old philosophical-mystical idea of the ground of being. But Sanders wants to extend and broaden the way we understand this ground, and invite us to reconsider where we look for it. There is always a danger among spiritual practitioners of detaching the soul's quest from the actual material world. Thinking about this ground in relation to our singular, embodied existence in place can help us reclaim the radical immanence of the Divine that was certainly implicit in Eckhart's teaching, even if it has not always been taken seriously in the subsequent contemplative tradition. Detach our ultimate concerns from the gritty details of our actual world, as we have too often done, and "both we and the neighborhood will suffer." Instead, this contemplative vision suggests, it is here in the life and texture of particular places—noticed, cherished, cared for—that this *ultimate* ground can and must be discovered.

Reorienting contemplative practice in this way toward the local and the particular can also help us retrieve a sense of the preciousness of the living world, its utter necessity. We are learning again how to value particular places, particular living beings, and how to consider more deeply what is essential and necessary in our lives. The ancient Christian contemplative tradition meditated long and hard on Jesus's teaching on the need to value and attend to what he called "the one thing necessary" (Luke 10:42). Indeed, acquiring the gift of discernment—learning to distinguish what is crucial or necessary from what is extraneous or secondary—has always been understood as one of the hallmarks of mature contemplative thought. But what is "the one thing necessary?" To what are we called to attend with our whole heart and soul? The classical response to this has always been "God" or "the soul." This is still a meaningful response. But in a historical moment of increasing spiritual diversity, in which a common understanding of neither "God" nor "soul" can always be assumed, we continue to struggle to find ways to account for the source of our deepest values and allegiances. The contemplative idiom is coming alive again in the present moment, but in surprising and unlikely forms that its ancient practitioners would hardly have imagined. But like them, we are coming to recognize in our own way the importance of the "one thing necessary," the cultivation of a simple, spacious awareness of the whole that may yet help us rediscover what it is to live in the world with purpose, meaning, and depth.

Montana writer William Kittredge touches on this question in his arrestingly simple consideration of the meaning of the sacred. "To me," he says, "sacred means necessary." At its root, he acknowledges, this necessity may be primarily biological or psychological. "We evolved in nature, with other animals.... Isolate us from nature too long, as individuals, as societies, and we start getting nervous, crazy, unmoored, inhabited by diseases we cannot name, driven to thoughtless ambitions and easy cruelties."[41] He echoes here the diagnosis of Paul Shepard, who argues in his book *Nature and Madness* for "the necessity of a rich nonhuman environment" as crucial to healthy psychological development in human beings.[42] But Shepard freely acknowledges the rich, inclusive character of the human relationship with the natural world, in particular its importance for helping us form a meaningful spiritual life, and a connection with the living world that is both deep and encompassing. "[E]cological reality (flowers-bees, bears-salmon) become satisfying otherness in their own right and metaphorical sign images or messages about the inner world, the binding forces of human society, and the invisible spiritual realm."[43] It is in response to this rich, relational reality, in profound poetic response, through play, storytelling, song, and dance that we come to know who we are in the world, that we come to know the ground of our own being, the ground of the world, ultimate ground. Becoming aware of this rich ecological reality, coming to feel it as part of one's own being and learning to live in reciprocal relationship to it is, to use Kittredge's term, so necessary. A sacred task.

"Never Weary of Gazing"

There are no unsacred places;
there are only sacred places
and desecrated places.[44]

WENDELL BERRY

I return to Redwoods Monastery in the early evening in time for Vespers. Entering again into the silence and stillness of this place, I am conscious of the presence of all those who gathered that day at Headwaters, as well as the trees and all those beings living in their shadows. They are all held within this contemplative space, a space that keeps expanding to include more and more varied beings. My awareness of their presence continues to deepen until it becomes almost impossible to distinguish the boundary between the self and this rich community. A new sense of community gradually emerges. But the work of cultivating such contemplative awareness, I begin to understand, entails a deepening commitment to tend to and take responsibility for this community. The habits of careless inattention that have put these trees and this ecosystem in jeopardy are so widespread and deep-seated that only a sustained practice of attention can help restore us to an awareness of who we are in relation to the larger whole that is rooted in authentic respect and reverence. Only such a renewed awareness can inform the kind of sustained action that will be required to realize lasting ecological restoration.

Sometime later, after the experience of that day had begun to settle, I came across a striking account of just such a practice in one of John Muir's descriptions of the trees he encountered during his first summer in the Sierra Nevada mountains in California. He notes carefully the distinctive qualities of particular specimens of goldcup oak, Douglas spruce, yellow pine, silver fir, and sequoia. But it is the sugar pine that seems to have caught and held his attention most deeply. He called it "an inexhaustible study and source of pleasure."

> I never weary of gazing at its grand tasseled cones, its perfectly round bole one hundred feet or more without a limb, the fine purplish color of its bark, and its magnificent outsweeping, down-curving feathery arms forming a crown always bold and striking and exhilarating . . . at the age of fifty to one hundred years it begins to acquire individuality, so that no two are alike in their prime or old age. Every tree calls for special admiration. I have been making many sketches, and regret that I cannot draw every needle.[45]

A little more than a half-century later, while considering a different tree, a candidate for governor of California was said to have made this now infamous observation: "If you've seen one redwood, you've seen them all."[46] An argument for trees as homogenous and uninteresting, one that has had considerable influence in this part of the world. It is an idea as far from Muir's careful attention to the particular as one can imagine and still, regrettably, too much with us. "Every tree calls for special admiration," Muir said, sitting before the old sugar pine, making sketch after sketch, full of regret that he could not draw every needle.

Such a sensibility was rare then and it is rare now. Still, I wonder whether it is possible even to begin imagining our way out of our current impasse unless we take more seriously than we have done Muir's challenge—echoed by so many contemporary writers, poets, artists, scientists, and religious thinkers—to notice and cherish the individual lives of wild beings. To do so will require opening ourselves to these wild beings, these Others, learning to take seriously their emotional, moral, and spiritual claim upon us. It will mean cultivating a habit of attention and regard that has for too long eluded us—a form of contemplative practice in which regard for the natural world occupies a central place.

Can the effort to notice and cherish the natural world be understood as part of a meaningful spiritual practice? If so, what will this practice look like? What will it mean to give oneself over to such a practice? And what might such a practice contribute to the larger, communal project of learning to live in the world with care and attention? These are the primary questions I wish to consider here. Framing these questions in light of the shared affinity for contemplative practice found in the contemporary literature and poetry of nature and in the Christian monastic tradition can, I believe, make a significant and distinctive contribution toward the articulation of a meaningful contemporary ecological spirituality. Central to this contribution is the possibility of developing a discourse—drawn from ancient spiritual traditions and from contemporary thought—that enables us to understand the practice of attention to and regard for the natural world as part of sustained spiritual discipline. As a concrete step toward realizing this possibility, I want to offer here a constructive vision of what a contemplative ecology can look like in relation to a particular spiritual tradition. To this end, I will consider how the contemplative traditions arising from the ancient Christian monastic world can help us frame and interpret our emerging sense of a contemplative ecological spirituality. In turn, I want to ask how the deepening sense of the natural world as sacred—especially as this is articulated in contemporary literature and poetry—can contribute to the reinvigoration of our traditions of contemplative spiritual discourse and practice.

As I consider the tumultuous, improvised ritual that unfolded in the Headwaters Forest that day, and the ongoing life of this monastic community, I begin to think this might actually be possible, that we might be on the verge of learning again how to see and imagine the wild world as alive and sacred and whole. After long years of struggle, led by a vibrant coalition of local and statewide environmental organizations, a historic agreement was finally worked out to save crucial parts of the Headwaters Forest. And the community at Redwoods Monastery, together with all those who sojourn with them in that place, persist in their own silent, contemplative witness on behalf of this place. In no small measure becaue of these efforts, certain parts of the forest remain whole, alive, vital biological communities: Sanctuary Forests, as one group calls them. But threats to this ancient and still-fragile habitat persist. The logging trucks rumble by on the road just beyond the monastery grounds. The question of whether the life and integrity of this place can be maintained in the years ahead remains uncertain.

"There are," suggests Wendell Berry, "no unsacred places; / there are only sacred places / and desecrated places."[47] I think about this as I enter again into the silence of this monastic space. It is the Feast of the Exaltation of the Holy Cross—the sacred, redemptive tree. I sit for a long time in that silence looking up at the giant redwood tree behind the altar. I never weary of looking at it. The light slowly bleeds from the evening sky, and the tree fades into the shadows. Finally it disappears completely, a hidden presence, a holy remnant.

2

Contact, or The Blue Sapphire of the Mind

See everything
and ourselves *in* everything
healed and whole
forever.[1]

RAINER MARIA RILKE

To crave and to have are as like as a thing and its shadow.
For when does a berry break upon the tongue as sweetly as
when one longs to taste it, and when is the taste refracted
into so many hues and savors of ripeness and earth, and
when do our senses know anything so utterly as when we
lack it? And here again is a foreshadowing—the world
will be made whole. For to wish for a hand on one's hair
is all but to feel it. So whatever we may lose, very craving
gives it back to us again. Though we dream and hardly
know it, longing, like an angel, fosters us, smooths our
hair, and brings us wild strawberries.[2]

MARILYNNE ROBINSON

IN HIS TREATISE *On Thoughts*, the fourth-century monastic writer Evagrius
of Pontus likens the experience of contemplation to dwelling in a kind of
place. "When the mind has put off the old self and shall put on the one born
of grace," says Evagrius, "then it will see its own state in the time of prayer
resembling sapphire or the color of heaven; this state scripture calls the place
of God that was seen by the elders on Mount Sinai."[3] This description of contemplation is, like many accounts of spiritual experience in early Christian
monastic literature, an approximation of something utterly mysterious and

ultimately beyond expression. And yet, as is so often the case in the Christian contemplative tradition, language and images are brought to bear upon the task of articulating what cannot, at least not fully, be said or imagined. One of Evagrius's most important contributions to the discourse of early monastic spirituality is his insistence that pure prayer is "imageless," an indication of how seriously he took the challenge of penetrating beyond ideas and images of God for the sake of God. In this account, however, he employs both geography and color to describe the true character of contemplation. These images are drawn from the Exodus account that describes the extraordinary experience of Moses and the Israelite elders on Mt. Sinai. There, we are told, they "beheld the God of Israel. Under his feet there appeared to be sapphire tilework, as clear as the sky itself" (Ex 24:10).

This account and others like it played a crucial role in shaping the early Christian understanding of contemplation. Evagrius, like his contemporary Gregory of Nyssa, configured the mountain as an imaginative space, a symbolic landscape capable of evoking and illuminating the contemplative's deepest experience of God. In transposing the geographical image of Moses's encounter with God on Mt. Sinai to the inner life of the monk, the "place of God" became almost indistinguishable from the "place of prayer."[4] And yet, in a move that reflects Evagrius' vigilance to guard against any literal reading of these images, he insisted that dwelling in this "place" required a radical renunciation of all images, even the image of the "place of God." This is the meaning of Evagrius' claim that: "The mind ... when it is in prayer ... is in a light without form, which is called the place of God."[5] Here and elsewhere in Evagrius's writings one encounters what feels like an impossible paradox: the experience of contemplation at its deepest level is utterly imageless; and yet the mind in prayer seems like a space saturated with light the color of sapphire or like a place—"the place of God." Still, this is a paradox that Evagrius insists must be accommodated if the monk is to remain open to an experience of prayer that is true and deep.

This vision of the monk completely subsumed into the life of God, living *in* God, is one of the most sublime and captivating expressions of contemplative experience in all of early monastic literature. Its specific character is rooted in Evagrius's particular perspective on the monastic journey, especially his insistence on the need to seek God in a place beyond all images and language. Still, it is consistent with the testimony about the ultimate end of monastic life that has come down to us from so much of the early Christian monastic tradition. And it is rooted in an image of place, a place that has existence both in the physical world and in the world within. It is a vision of the whole, suffused by a sense of God's presence, and it is consciousness of this whole that the early Christian monks sought to cultivate through their contemplative practice.

If we consider the sense of place out of which this contemplative vision arose, it becomes necessary to acknowledge two related truths. For Evagrius and many other early Christian monks, Mt. Sinai was less important as an actual place than it was as a symbol of a certain intimacy with God the contemplative might hope to realize on the inner journey. Even so, the evocation of the mountain and the sapphire-blue tiles remains an important reminder of the intricate relationship that exists between outer and inner landscapes, and of the way the physical landscape can spark thought, open the imagination, deepen awareness. The mountain became a place toward which the monk could direct his gaze, a point of orientation, an emblem of the awesome and charged space of his own inner life. Still, it was not only a symbol. Many of Evagrius's monastic contemporaries lived under the shadow of the great mountain. For them, Mt. Sinai existed not simply as a place of the imagination, part of an inner landscape, but also as a place of concrete specificity, the particular landscape in which their lives unfolded. It is here that they gave themselves over to the daily rhythm of monastic living that served as the ground out of which the contemplative vision articulated by Evagrius and others arose.

This contemplative vision arising from the ancient Christian monastic world expresses a hunger still present and familiar to us at the dawn of the twenty-first century: the longing to live with an awareness of the whole. And it speaks to the promise inherent in all great spiritual traditions of the world, that the human mind (or heart or soul) is capable of expanding and deepening to such an extent that it becomes possible to incorporate everything and to be incorporated into everything: to exist and know oneself as existing within the whole. To dwell in the place of God, as Evagrius puts it, is to live with a particular intense awareness of this reality, to know oneself not as a solitary, autonomous being but as one whose identity can only be conceived of as existing within an intricate web of encompassing relationships. The primary work of contemplative practice is to become more aware of this web of relationships, to learn to live within it fully and responsibly and to give expression to it in one's life. That such awareness is the fruit of long practice, a gradual transformation of consciousness that only comes about through sustained self-reflection and a gradual relinquishment of the ego's tenacious attachments, is one of the most valuable insights arising from contemplative traditions of spiritual practice. The potential contribution of such contemplative traditions to the work of reknitting a broken, fragmented world should not be underestimated. To retrieve a vision of the world as whole—through sustained attention to the underlying unity that connects all beings to one another and to the root causes in our thought and practice that contribute to the deepening fragmentation of self, community, and world—is necessary to the work of healing that is at the heart of any sustained ecological renewal.

We are now facing the very real possibility that such a vision of the whole has been rendered unimaginable and unrealizable by the sheer range and extent of the ecological degradation we have visited upon the world. One of the most potent and enduring images of our precarious condition to have emerged from the literature of ecology during the past twenty-five years—of the world as an archipelago of ecologically impoverished islands—suggests that fragmentation is a fundamental reality with which we must now contend.[6] This image of widespread ecological fragmentation—one that reflects the increasingly evident loss of biodiversity and ecological integrity throughout the world—raises serious questions about whether it is still meaningful to speak of cultivating a vision of the whole, and whether *any* spiritual practice can help to mend this torn fabric.

And yet, the contemplative tradition in which Evagrius and the other early Christian monks stand was itself formed in a historical moment of intense and widespread loss, in which the social and cultural fabric that had long bound life together in the ancient Mediterranean world had begun to fray to the breaking point. This particular tradition of spiritual practice emerged in part as a response to this tearing of the fabric, and represents a sustained effort to face it with courage and honesty, all the while remaining open to the possibility that paradise—a world whole and untarnished—might yet be rediscovered. The blue sapphire of the mind of which Evagrius speaks— that condition of graced and encompassing awareness of being immersed in the All—did not arise spontaneously in the life of the monk in a kind of blissful ignorance of suffering and loss, but emerged through long struggle, through a sustained practice of examining the sources of the alienation and fragmentation that afflicted the monks and their society. Contemplative practice meant opening oneself honestly to the whole of reality as it presents itself, and to the long, difficult process of relinquishing one's attachment to the ego's isolating and alienating power. Only in this way could one hope to realize in oneself a more encompassing, whole vision of reality. It was only by giving oneself wholeheartedly to this work, the monks believed, that one could contribute meaningfully toward the reknitting of the torn fabric of the world. This contemplative vision resonated profoundly among their contemporaries in the late fourth-century, for whom these contemplatives came to be known, according to one early account, simply as: "T[hose] by whom the world is kept in being."[7]

This is an audacious claim. But it echoes similar claims found in many other spiritual traditions regarding the significance to the wider community of those who devote themselves to such contemplative work. In its most profound expressions, such contemplative work can be understood as undertaken on behalf of the world and as contributing toward its healing and restoration. Indeed, the aim of contemplative living, in its widest application, is to address the fragmentation and alienation that haunts existence at the deepest possible level and, through sustained practice, come to realize a different, more integrated way of being in the world. Here, amidst the inevitable fragmentation of existence, the contemplative seeks to recover a vision of the whole and a new way of living in relationship to the whole.

The Torn Fabric

> I have come to feel that there is here in North America
> a hidden place obscured by what we have built upon it,
> and that whenever we penetrate the surface of the life
> around us that place and its spirit can be found.[8]
>
> JOHN HAINES

It appears like a flame, rising, then banking and gliding over the salt marsh, tracing a luminescent arc across the late autumn sky. *Casmerodius albus*, or Great Egret. Nearby, a jumbo jet from Los Angeles International Airport lifts off, engines whining, hurtling toward some unknown destination. Soon another follows in its wake. And another. I continue watching the egret as it circles, then drifts down and finally disappears behind a small ridge. For a moment it is quiet. Only the song of a meadowlark, the cry of gulls. The pickleweed shifts in the wind. Behind me, the jets continue their ritual procession. The low, steady roar of heavy machinery sounds in the distance. Out of the corner of my eye, I see a flash of white: the egret's head reappears over the top of the ridge, surveying the scene. Then it lifts and soars up over the salt marsh and the nearby cluster of houses and is gone.

The place where I stand today is a tiny remnant of what was once an enormous and vibrant stretch of coastal wetlands opening out onto the Pacific Ocean from the Los Angeles Basin. Egrets have a precarious hold on life here, as do most of the other species that call this place home. They are being pressured from all sides, as the same inexorable forces that have left

Southern California almost completely bereft of open space take hold here. That any part of the wetlands is being preserved at all has been seen as something of a miracle, given the usual, all-consuming pattern of development in Los Angeles. Still, the deal struck between local and state environmental groups and Playa Vista Development Corporation to enable a high-density housing complex to be constructed here has come as a blow to those who had hoped to see the entire wetlands preserved; a crucial opportunity to preserve and restore the much more extensive wetlands has now been lost forever. Only time will tell whether what remains will be able to survive as a viable habitat, or whether it will prove too small, too fragile to support life. Will it become incorporated in a meaningful way into the life and imagination of this huge metropolis, or simply become a kind of museum space, marginalized and forgotten? Increasingly, in urban places such as Los Angeles, as well as in remote rural places, the fate of wild places (and of wildness itself) will depend on whether we can feel, see, and tend to the whole life of the place, and whether such places can be seen and felt as part of the life of the whole.[9] This is one of the contributions that contemplative practice and awareness can make to the larger ecological project: helping to create a climate in which it becomes possible to imagine and tend to and dwell within the life of the whole.

But what is this vision of the whole? And is it really possible to imagine it, much less tend to it or dwell within it? As I consider what this might mean here in the Ballona Wetlands, I am confronted with the challenge of incorporating into a single vision of reality not only the relationships among the many organisms that inhabit this place in the present moment, but also the long history of the place and the stories that have come down to us (especially those of the Tongva people for whom this place has long been sacred), the emerging life of the community that now inhabits the mixed-use development known as Playa Vista, the ongoing political and biological challenges of ecological restoration in the open space that remains, as well as my own feelings for the place, for all that has been lost and for its still-unknown future. It sometimes seems, amidst the traffic and congestion and the growing expanse of pavement and condominiums, that there is no vision of the whole to be found here, only fragmentation, degradation, and competing, irreconcilable claims. But as the life of this place continues to unfold, as restoration work progresses and as the community struggles to better understand its own relationship with the place and what it will mean to remain attentive to the faint traces of wildness that still exist here, the question of whether the "place and its spirit can be found" grows ever more necessary and meaningful. It also opens out onto larger questions about the presence of spirit in a world whose fabric is becoming increasingly torn and frayed, and about our own will and capacity to tend to it.

Addressing these questions in a meaningful way will mean striving to understand the complex character of the places in which we dwell, something that can be discovered only by attending to the particular geographical, biological, historical, cultural, political, and economic realities that have formed and shaped them and in some cases threaten to undo them. But there is also a more personal dimension to this work that involves confronting our own deepest feelings for these places, our feelings about their continuing erosion and degradation, and the often-unconscious sources of our own neglect and apathy. All of this is included in the contemplative work of attending to what John Haines describes as the relationship between the "place and its spirit."

It is difficult to avoid the sense that, in our own time, such work often begins with reflection on the experience of loss. Such experience includes and often comes to consciousness initially through an encounter with extreme and devastating losses—of species, of wild places, and of human communities, especially poor communities who suffer disproportionately as ecosystems are diminished or destroyed.[10] Within this reality lie other losses, just as profound, but less easy to articulate: the loss of beauty, intimacy, the wild, even the loss of the sacred. With the natural world becoming ever more threatened and degraded and its rarity and fragility ever more apparent, the sense of the world as both sacred *and* threatened (or desecrated) has begun to coalesce in contemporary experience in a way that likely has no exact precedent. There is a sense of ultimacy to this experience of loss that I believe helps to account for the growing tendency to think of it as having a spiritual character. Part of what makes the experience of loss on a local scale like the Ballona Wetlands so poignant and troubling is that it reflects and gives particular and personal expression to a systemic crisis whose depth and extent almost defies comprehension. "We now have a sense," says E.O. Wilson, "that we are bringing life to a close. I mean, we're destroying life; we're reducing the natural world out there in an irreversible way."[11] There is a sense for many that we are not merely losing places and species; we are losing the "Beloved Other."

I think about this as I recall standing here with my young daughter and hearing her ask, in all innocence (though perhaps already conscious in her own way of all that is being lost): "Where will all the creatures go daddy?" Her question pierces me. And this is not only because I do not in fact know what will become of these creatures and can offer no real reassurances to her. It is also because her question touches on and exacerbates my own longstanding concern and anxiety about this and other comparable losses, for which I have not been able to formulate any meaningful response. Struggling with these feelings, searching for a way to hold and respond to them, has come to occupy an increasingly significant part of my inner life. So too has the practice of simple regard for what remains. I believe this is becoming increasingly common in the present historical moment—a sense of anxiety and longing bound up with a simultaneous love of and fear for the fate of the natural world.

Reflecting on the meaning of such loss and on the enduring sources of our feeling for the living world can, I believe, serve as a starting point for a larger ethical and spiritual project of renewal and healing. But this can only happen if the experience of loss and the sense of being bound to the natural world can be fully acknowledged, taken into our consciousness, brought into the center of our moral and spiritual awareness. Harold Searles has argued that our ability to meet the environmental crisis is hampered by "a severe and pervasive apathy which is based largely upon feelings and attitudes of which [we are] unconscious."[12] What are these feelings and attitudes? And why are we not more aware of them, more able to act in response to them? It is not easy to say. But Shierry Weber Nicholsen's *The Love of Nature and the End of the World* offers a particularly thoughtful and probing response to these questions, making a strong case for the utter necessity of the inner work that will enable us to face the true impact of the losses we are experiencing while also accessing the deeper sources of our enduring feeling for the living world.[13] So much of our emotional-psychological-spiritual affliction in the face of a rapidly diminishing world, she suggests, is buried, hidden from view. It must be teased out, brought to the surface, in a way that is analogous to the psychoanalytic process. If we are to discover the inner resources necessary to resist the increasing degradation of both the world and our souls, Nicholsen argues, we will have to acknowledge and face honestly the depth of our affliction and find the courage to bring together, imaginatively and affectively, the eroded world and the eroded self. This approach makes it possible to join the most intimate and personal experiences of loss—loss of the particular places, communities, and beings that matter to us personally—with the larger, more encompassing sense of the "loss of the world" or "loss of life," which runs like a hidden current through our lives.

This is not easy to do. In drawing these disparate experiences of loss together, says Nicholsen, we may begin to experience something approaching spiritual vertigo, as the fragility of the psychological structures holding us together becomes apparent. And yet this would seem to be an unavoidable part of what it means to acknowledge our true condition. Nicholsen draws upon the work of Robert Jay Lifton to suggest a way of understanding this condition: as a "loss of symbolic immortality," the loss of those symbolic structures of meaning and hope (such as those provided by classic Christian eschatological visions of the end that include renewal and rebirth) that help us to cope with the inevitable fact of mortality. One consequence of the erosion of these structures, which is such a pervasive part of our experience of ecological degradation, is a growing sense of psychological and spiritual precariousness, what Michael Ortiz Hill describes as the "stark, raw nakedness of the apocalyptic psyche."[14]

Such a portrait of our current condition may appear bleak, lacking in the one ingredient indispensable to any viable work of ecological renewal: hope. However, without such recognition of what it actually *feels* like to face the end—the end of one's own life or the end of the world—we may never be able to discover the resources for responding to and taking responsibility for our condition, for kindling hope out of an apparently hopeless situation. It may be that we are particularly vulnerable in this moment of our history to what Lifton calls "psychic numbing," a psychological dissociation that arises in response to events or experiences too painful to face or absorb. It is an understandable and sometimes necessary response, at least in the short term. But as Nicholsen argues, in the long term such psychic numbing can be dangerous; it can lead us to "shut off awareness of the destructive consequences of our acts, thus preventing ourselves from responding emotionally to the pain we cause [or experience]."[15] To pretend that we do not feel grief in the face of all we are losing and to avoid the hard work of facing our grief can only deepen our alienation from ourselves and from the living world.

But what possible response to this predicament can yield a more open, creative way of engaging the world? Is there a way to cultivate an awareness of who we are in the natural world that takes seriously both the depth and acuteness of our losses, and the still-vibrant feeling for the world that pulses within us? More than this, can such awareness be employed in service of a creative and thoughtful ecological ethic, a more responsible and open-hearted way of living in the world?

The great ecological thinker Aldo Leopold long ago saw the connection between our ability to access our deepest feeling for the living world and our capacity for developing a meaningful land ethic. "We can be ethical," he said, "only in relation to something we can see, feel, understand, love, or otherwise have faith in."[16] Leopold himself only arrived at this vision after a serious and sustained reckoning with the limits and gaps in his own perception of the natural world, expressed most memorably in his account of what happened to him after he killed a wolf in the high desert country of Arizona. I will consider this story in greater detail later in the chapter. For now I simply wish to note that for Leopold, this experience served as a catalyst that helped him begin to face honestly and deeply his own habits of carelessness and inattention toward the natural world; it also led him to recognize the larger pattern of moral blindness that had contributed so significantly to the ecological devastation already apparent to him during his life time. The work of searching out the deeper sources of our attitudes toward the natural world became crucial to the development of his ecological ethic, his vision of the whole.

Such contemplative reflection—the sustained practice of reckoning with who we are in relation to the natural world and what kind of response is asked of us—is indispensable to the work of ecological healing and renewal. Leopold's insight, that an ecological ethic capable of helping us repair the torn fabric of the world must be rooted in our deepest *feelings* for the world, has now come to occupy a central place in our understanding of what it means to live in a responsible and reciprocal relationship with the living world. But the question of what it means to *cultivate* such a transformed awareness remains. This question has increasingly come to the fore among writers and poets of the natural world, and represents one of the most significant "affinities of content" between their writing and the literature arising from contemplative traditions of spiritual practice. The question of how to cultivate a transformed awareness and live out of the center of that awareness has long occupied a central place in the understanding of what it is to embark on the path of contemplative living. The contemplative traditions have always taken seriously the question of how contemplative practice, by helping to heal and reconstitute the fragmented self, contributes to reknitting the entire fabric of being. They have developed their own understanding of the "ecological whole" and the work of contemplative practice is undertaken in no small measure in the hopes of restoring and renewing that whole.

The Inner Mountain

[For the one who] wishes to live in solitude in the desert, there is only one conflict ... and that is with the heart.[17]

ANTONY OF EGYPT

"[L]e baptême de la solitude" ... is a unique sensation
and has nothing to do with loneliness, for loneliness

presupposes memory. Here, in this wholly mineral landscape lighted by stars like flares, even memory disappears;
nothing is left but your own breathing and the sound of
your heart beating. A strange, and by no means pleasant,
process of reintegration begins inside you, and you have
the choice of fighting against it, and insisting on remaining the person you have always been, or letting it take its
course."[18]

PAUL BOWLES

"He fell in love with the place." This is how the *Life of Antony*, one of the most
influential texts from the ancient Christian monastic world, describes the
monk's response upon first laying eyes on the place in Egypt's eastern desert
known as the inner mountain. Many years earlier, Antony had left his home
in the Nile Valley to embark upon a long, arduous life of ascetic practice in
the desert. But after his dwelling became overrun with visitors and suppli-
cants, he felt compelled to seek an even more solitary place to live out his
monastic life. Responding to an inner prompting, he set out for the remote
desert region to the east. For three days and three nights, in the company of
"a band of Saracens," he made his way across the harsh open terrain of the
Galâla Plateau. Finally, he arrived at: "a very high hill. Below the hill there was
water—perfectly clear, sweet and quite cold, and beyond there were plains,
and a few untended date palms."[19] This was the monk's first encounter with
this wild, beautiful place and it captivated him completely. Antony found the
inner mountain so alluring that he "remained on the mountain alone," plant-
ing a garden, giving himself fully to the life of the place, and spending the rest
of his days there. The inner mountain became "his own home,"[20] the place
where he learned to keep his heart awake.[21] There Antony became: "one who
as Scripture says, having *trusted in the Lord, was like Mount Sion,* keeping his
mind unshaken and unruffled...."[22]

It is not easy to account for Antony's sudden, extravagant feeling for this
place or to understand all that it meant for him to have discovered it. But even
this brief account suggests the sense of recognition and affinity that he felt
upon arriving there and how his life would be changed by it. The account of
the experience related in the *Life of Antony*—of a monk living in the deepest
solitude of the desert, in perfect harmony with himself, God and the place
itself—became an emblem of the entire early Christian monastic quest.[23] Here
was a kind of paradise, the realization of a dream long cherished by the monks
of finding a home in the world, in themselves, and in God. Still, the sense of

ease and well-being in this account is deceptive, for it gives hardly any indication of what it cost the monk to get there, what it meant to face himself in the long, exacting ascetic work of the cell. Nor does it give any real sense of how this experience deepened his self-awareness and altered his orientation and commitment to the wider community. These elements of Antony's story are crucial to understanding the full meaning of the ascetic quest in early Christian monasticism. They help to account for why this particular image—of the monk living alone on the mountain, with a deep awareness of himself as part of a larger whole—remains one of the most significant expressions of the contemplative life to have emerged from the movement. And it suggests something about how significant *place* became to that unfolding contemplative vision.

Already in Antony's lifetime the inner mountain had become a kind of dreamscape, a mythic place made sacred by the strivings of the monk who inhabited it. And yet it was also an actual place in the physical landscape—stark, empty, beautiful—a place responsive and hospitable to the spiritual longings of Antony and the other monks who made it their home. This fluid, reciprocal relationship between place and spirit, the interior and exterior landscape, became a distinctive part of the world of the early Christian monks, the geographical particularity of the desert shaping their inner lives, even as their inner experience influenced how they imagined and inhabited the desert landscape. As a place—both actual and imagined—the inner mountain (along with the monastic cell and the desert as a whole) came to be seen as a symbol of the monk's deepest penetration into the place of silence and solitude where God is to be sought and found. It also came to stand as an emblem of the profound healing that contemplative practice could help to bring about—in the life of the individual monk and in the larger community.

The birth of Christian monasticism in the deserts of Egypt, Syria, Asia Minor, and Judea during the late third and early fourth centuries occurred during a period of tremendous cultural, religious, and social ferment. Ascetic movements of various kinds—Gnostics, Manicheans, neoplatonic philosophers, devotees of the Temple of Serapis and others—already existed by the time the first Christian monks embarked upon their own experiments in contemplative living.[24] The reasons for the growth and development of this widespread and diverse ascetic culture are complex and cannot be reduced to any single cause. Nor can the meaning of ascetic life for those who participated in it be accounted for in any simple way. Still, a significant factor in its rise and development was the widely shared sense of anxiety provoked by the growing political, economic and social instability in the late Roman empire. Historian

Peter Brown has made a persuasive case for understanding the rise of ascetic and monastic practice (both Christian and non-Christian) in Late Antiquity as a response to a "crisis in human relations" that had arisen amidst this instability and uncertainty.[25] To those groaning under the weight of the social and economic obligations that afflicted so many during this time, the impulse to withdraw to the margins of society, to seek a space of freedom and relief in the simple, spare life of the ascetic held real appeal.

Still, if such a life provided a genuine sense of relief from the growing social and economic pressures of life in the late Roman Empire, embarking on this ascetic path was anything but an escape. For those who set out on this path—whether as members of those small communities of ascetics that took hold in the towns and villages along the Nile Valley, or as part of the incipient communal expressions of monastic life that arose in the desert regions nearby, or in the more solitary expressions of monastic living undertaken by those rare souls who chose to withdraw on their own into the wildest and most remote places—it was an utterly involving and demanding undertaking requiring the willingness to subject oneself to a life of sustained ascetic practice. At the heart of this practice lay the hope that, amidst the fragmentation and alienation that threatened to undo life completely, a new, free, and authentic self might be born. This dream of freedom, which the monks conceived of as the recovery of paradise, was at the very heart of the monastic enterprise. And while there was an inescapable solitary dimension to the work, its true significance can only be grasped if it is placed within the social, communal reality in which the monastic project unfolded.

The contemplative ecology of early Christian monasticism reflects the acute crisis in which the movement was born. Those who took up the ascetic life during this period, devoting themselves to rediscovering in their own lives a semblance of the wholeness and freedom that was so sorely absent from the world, came to occupy a crucial role in the struggle to repair the torn fabric of the world. The great esteem in which these ascetic practitioners came to be held by their contemporaries, manifested in their growing status as mediators, arbiters, and healers, suggests that their particular response to the fragmentation that afflicted so many during this time was meaningful and captivating. To embark on the ascetic path was to open oneself to a relentless confrontation with a wounded, fragmented self and the often-painful process of relinquishment that could, eventually, lead to the possession of a genuine sense of freedom. The "autarkic man," the one who had achieved such freedom, became an emblem of hope for all who were struggling to become free, a genuine force for healing and renewal in a broken world. The hidden, often solitary work of the monk was understood as inseparable from the larger struggle of his contemporaries.

But what was the character of this work? And how precisely did it contribute to the reknitting of the whole? A closer look at the *Life of Antony* can shed light on these questions. Two related dimensions of this story give it particular importance to the project of articulating a contemplative ecology. The first, already noted, is the intricate and complex way the story depicts the monk's inner journey as unfolding within a particular geographical landscape. Equally significant is the portrayal of the monk's descent into the abyss of suffering and emptiness for the sake of the larger community; this experience of relinquishment and loss and the subsequent emergence into a place of reintegration and wholeness becomes a paradigmatic image for the contemplative life in general. Taken together, these two dimensions of the early monastic experience constitute a meaningful and compelling contemplative ecology, a sense of what it meant to face the deepest sources of fragmentation, in oneself and in the world, and to seek a genuine and lasting reintegration of the whole.

"Places are good to think with," says anthropologist Keith Basso.[26] For the desert monks, the place of the desert became a cherished landscape for thinking about what it meant to stand in the center of their own souls and to hold and connect everyone and everything in a single, complex experience of awareness. This process of thinking—or, to use a term commonly found in the monastic vocabulary, ruminating—became for the monks a continual exploration of a geography, at once physical and spiritual, in which they sought and sometimes discovered what Evagrius called "the place of God." To seek this place—a pure, simple awareness of oneself as alive in God—and learn to dwell there became central to the monastic quest to remake the self and create the conditions for realizing a more expansive and intimate relationship with the whole. But acquiring the depth of awareness capable of holding and responding to the whole was costly; it meant learning to relinquish the attachments and anxieties that kept the monk from becoming free. The monks' willingness to subject themselves to the grueling undoing and remaking of the self was crucial to their quest to stand with and live on behalf of the broken world.[27]

For Antony, this quest began in an unexpected moment of awakening that occurred when he was a young man living in his native village in the Nile Valley. He had grown up there with his parents and sister and had shown himself to be spiritually precocious as a child. When he was around twenty years old, both his parents died. In the aftermath of this loss, he found himself drawn into a careful and searching process of reflection about his life. One day, he entered a church and there heard the account of Jesus's challenge to the rich young man to sell his possessions and give the money to the poor (Mt 19:21). Hearing this text had a profound effect on him (he felt "as if ... the passage were read on his account") and he immediately went out and gave away most of his possessions, keeping only what he needed to live a simple, modest life with his sister. A little later, he heard another text, Jesus's exhortation not to be anxious about tomorrow (Mt 6:34), and he was moved to give away the rest of his possessions, withdraw from his life in the village and begin devoting himself to the ascetic quest in the solitude of the desert.

It is not easy to determine, based solely on this brief, highly stylized account, all the elements that led Antony to embark upon his ascetic journey into the desert. But the narrative makes clear that for Antony this was a moment of crisis, in which he suddenly found himself gripped by a new awareness of himself in relation to the absolute and new set of possibilities opening up before him. At the heart of this emerging vision for his life was a call to renounce everything for the sake of God. The simple naïveté of Antony's response—he retained nothing from his old life but gave himself with naked abandon to the life unfolding before him—likely masks a more complex reality. But it nevertheless points to a cherished and important moment in early Christian monastic experience: the realization that under the crushing weight of anxiety and care that marked the lives of so many living during this period, one could choose to cut the cord and through a simple act of renunciation reorient one's life around a new reality. And even if the ultimate consequences and meaning of such a choice could hardly be guessed at in that initial moment, the gesture of renunciation itself revealed much about the strength of the experience and the longing to which the monk was responding. The acts of *apotaxis* (renunciation) and *anachoresis* (withdrawal) became signs not only of all the monk was leaving behind but also of all the monk was seeking. Still, these dramatic gestures marked only the beginning of a much longer and more demanding process of renunciation that the monk would enact in the daily struggle of ascetic life. In Athanasius's narrative, this is described in terms of Antony's dynamic movement through space and time to a place of freedom. So the monk moves, initially renouncing village, home (*oikos*), and the entire domestic sphere, for the sake of an as-yet-undetermined life on the margins of the village, at the edge of the desert (*eremos*). After a time, he sets off again, traveling deeper into the wilderness, into the precarious space of solitude. He walks a path (*hodos*), concretely and metaphorically, filled with challenges and temptations with which he must reckon, eventually settling down in an old fortress and then moving into an abandoned tomb. The tomb becomes a crucible in which Antony opens himself little by little to the work of purification and renewal. It is here in the lonely solitude of the cell that the true meaning of the desert in the life of the monk becomes clear.

"Sit in your cell and your cell will teach you everything," said Abba Moses, evoking simply and clearly the power and authority of the cell in the early monastic imagination.[28] Antony took this call seriously, giving himself over to a solitary regimen of ascetic practice for more than twenty years. At the heart of Antony's regimen, which consisted of a range of practices such as silence, keeping vigil, fasting, reading, and prayer, was a sustained struggle with his own conscience, an effort to acquire self-knowledge. The *Life of Antony* describes this as the work of *prosoche* or paying attention. Entering into the silence of the desert, Antony "began paying attention to himself."[29] The struggle with the self was hardly simple. It meant grappling continuously with those parts of the self the monks called the passions, those anomalous, unhealed parts of the soul, and the demons who brought them into the monks' conscious and unconscious awareness.

The way into those depths could be terrifying. Athanasius's detailed account of Antony's struggle with the demons makes this clear. When he tells us, describing Antony's initial encounter with the demons, that the devil "attempted to lead [Antony] away from the discipline, suggesting memories of his possessions, the guardianship of his sister, the bonds of kinship, love of money and of glory, the manifold pleasures of food, the relaxations of life, and finally, the rigors of virtue, and how great the labor is that earns it ... " we recognize immediately the doubts and fears arising in the mind of a person not yet fully resolved upon a new course of life. The mention of his struggle with *memories* suggests the profound depths at which these concerns occupy the ascetic; they are not merely peripheral concerns, but touch upon the things he cares and worries about the most, the places within him where he is most vulnerable. The devil, Athanasius tells us, "raised in [Antony's] mind a great dust cloud of considerations," a telling indication of the kind of confusion and anxiety the ascetic experienced as he struggled to live more deeply into this life.[30]

For Antony, the descent into the desert mirrored the descent into his own soul: as he moved further into the desert, his struggles increased in depth and complexity. Athanasius tells us that after Antony had taken up habitation in some tombs outside his village, his progress provoked the enemy to such an extent that "approaching one night with a multitude of demons he whipped him with such force that he lay on the earth, speechless from the tortures.

[Antony] contended that the pains were so severe as to lead one to say that the blows could not have been delivered by humans since they caused such agony."[31] What *were* these pains? Athanasius does not tell us. But the way they are described—"so severe as to lead one to say that the blows could not have been delivered by humans," suggests something of how bewildering and frightening this experience was for the monk. Here is an agony so great that it could not be accounted for by any simple reference to ordinary human experience. This is but one of many instances in early Christian monastic literature where one senses just what the confrontation with the demonic in solitude really involved: the most demanding and far-reaching struggle with the self.

The question of how, precisely, to understand this struggle in the life of the monk has long occupied historians of the early monastic world. Certainly, it is difficult to escape the sense that the demons can be understood on at least one level as representing elements of the monk's own psyche, expressed in vivid symbolic form. Peter Brown has argued that for the early monks, the demonic was "sensed as an extension of the self. A relationship with the demons," he suggests, "involved something more intimate than attack from the outside: to be 'tried by the demons' meant passing through a stage in the growth of awareness of the lower frontiers of the personality. The demonic stood not merely for all that was hostile *to* [the monk]; the demons summed up all that was anomalous and incomplete *in* [him]."[32] This acute psychological understanding of the encounter with the demons is confirmed by the monks' own testimony. One day Abba Abraham asked Abba Poemen: "How do the demons fight against me?" Poemen responded: "The demons fight *against* you? ... our own *wills* become the demons, and it is these which attack us in order that we may fulfill them."[33]

One senses here the terror that sometimes overcame the monks as they felt themselves being overwhelmed, even consumed by the power of the demonic. The willingness to allow oneself to become so vulnerable, to descend into the place of the greatest doubt and uncertainty was a crucial part of the monastic practice of *prosoche* or attention to self through which the monk eventually came to be transformed in Christ. The importance the monks attributed to this practice is expressed most clearly in the intricate and systematic taxonomy of the self found in the writings of Evagrius and Cassian, especially in their articulation and analysis of the "eight principal thoughts." Learning to be adept at recognizing and responding to these shifting and often treacherous *logismoi* or thoughts, which revealed so clearly the competing impulses within the monk's inner life, was critical to the monk's journey toward an integrated and free self, alive in God.

In the opening section of the *Praktikos*, Evagrius describes the eight principal thoughts this way: "All generic types of thoughts fall into eight categories
in which every sort of thought is included. First that of gluttony, then fornication, third avarice, fourth sadness, fifth anger, sixth acedia, seventh vainglory, eighth pride. Whether or not all these thoughts trouble the soul is not
within our power; but it is for us to decide if they are to linger within us or
not and whether or not they stir up the passions."[34] Here, Evagrius articulates
the underlying framework through which he will examine, with tremendous
subtlety and insight, the ever-shifting *logismoi* or thoughts that move through
the monk's soul and affect his capacity to know and love God. It was critical that the monk learn to understand the precise source of these thoughts,
how they worked to undermine his resolve and sense of purpose, even his
identity in God. This is because, as Peter Brown has argued: "Consent to evil
thoughts, many of which were occasioned, in the first instance, by the dull
creakings of the body—by its need for food and its organic, sexual drives—
implied a decision to collaborate with other invisible spirits, the demons ....
[Their] pervasive presence, close to the human person, was registered in the
'heart' in the form of inappropriate images, fantasies, and obsessions."[35] These
logismoi could be so potent and so debilitating that unless the monk cultivated the ability to identify, scrutinize and struggle against them, and even
eventually to resolve them, prayer, knowledge of God, and life in community
would become impossible.

"We have acquired a dark house full of war," says Antony in one of his letters.[36] This ominous declaration captures Antony's own sense of the general
condition of human beings caught in a web of compromising impulses and
habits they cannot control. But it also describes with haunting pathos his (and
so many other monks') experience of being so intensely vulnerable to the subtle and debilitating power of "The devils and their disciples... [who]," he says,
"sow in our hearts every day ... their hardness of heart and their numbness."
Antony also bemoans: "the many sufferings they bring us at every hour, the
weariness which causes our hearts to be weary at all times." Nor does Antony
give any comfort to those who wish to live with the illusion that these demonic
forces are somehow distant from us, not part of us. "We are their bodies," says
Antony, "and our soul receives their wickedness; and ... then it reveals them
through the body in which we dwell."[37] It would be difficult to imagine a more
difficult, entangled, compromised existence than this. And yet this is precisely
the world within which the monks engaged in their ascetic struggles.

The ascetic life in this sense meant something like annihilation, especially the willingness to scrutinize, struggle with, and finally renounce the

carefully constructed and defended self. What, if anything, emerges on the
other side of such annihilation? The monastic literature testifies, over and
over, that this harrowing emptying out the self, this baptism of solitude,
could and did sometimes lead to a place of genuine freedom and hope. But
only a sustained commitment to pay attention to oneself, to search out the
deep sources of the soul's chronic attachments could lead the monk to such
a place. Thus the importance of constant vigilance. Among Antony's last
words to his brothers were these: "Live as though dying daily, paying attention to yourselves ...."[38]

Only the closest of Antony's friends witnessed his terrifying solitary struggle. But many more came to know the person who emerged out of that space
of desolation, transformed and full of light. And that person was capable of
holding and tending to so much. When after twenty years Antony finally did
emerge from of his long solitude, "as though from some shrine, having been
led into the divine mysteries and inspired by God," the power of his presence
was palpable. He was recognized immediately as a healer, a person capable
of reconciling those who had become estranged from one another, someone
able to liberate those suffering from the terrible grip of the demons on their
lives, full of encouragement for those lost in grief or despondency, a bearer of
compassion.[39]

This same rhythm of contemplative practice—descending into the depths,
emerging to tend to the needs of the wider community—shaped Antony's long
solitary life on the inner mountain. It is here that we catch a glimpse of how
his contemplative practice became part of an intricate "economy of exchange,"
leading to the deepest and most intimate relationships with the wider community that Antony had ever known. Athanasius relates that Antony "loved
more than everything else his way of life in the mountain,"[40] and came to
regard it as "his own home." He often "remained on the mountain alone,"[41] for
the sake of the discipline and the "contemplation of divine realities."[42] Here
on the inner mountain Antony began to taste the reality of deep intimacy
with God. But the narrative also makes it clear that even in the depths of his
solitude, Antony remained intimately engaged with those living beyond the
mountain. Some of them provided him with material support, in exchange
for which he gave them "provisions from the mountain," that is, his words
and assistance, his healing presence.[43] This compassionate response to others
became a hallmark of his contemplative practice. He exhorted his followers:
"Let us treat one another with compassion, and let us bear one another's bur-
dens."[44] Such compassion came to expression not only through concrete acts,
but also through the mysterious power of his presence. Athanasius relates that

"While sitting in the mountain, [Antony] kept his heart alert."[45] In so doing he maintained a profound awareness of the struggles and suffering of those living far from the mountain. "With those who suffered he sympathized and prayed... [and] the ones who suffered therefore received the words of the old man as healing."[46]

This image of the monk, standing in the midst of a broken community, helping by his very presence to heal all that has been torn asunder, suggests the kind of spiritual power contemplative practice could yield in the life of one who embarked on this path. It also suggests the integral relationship between solitude and community, contemplation and action. Monastic *anachoresis* or withdrawal, which has often been construed as a simple refusal or abandonment of the world, should instead be seen as a strategy aimed at freeing the monk from the compulsions and anxieties that prevent him from seeing and engaging the world with simple awareness and compassion. The monks came to believe that it was only by acquiring a consciousness transformed through a long process of purification that they could hope to participate in healing the deeper wounds of the world.

Antony's story, indeed the story of early Christian monasticism as a whole, can serve as a rich cultural resource capable of supporting the work of developing a contemplative ecological vision. Of particular value to this effort is the ancient monastic vision of spiritual transformation—rooted in a commitment to sustained, embodied contemplative practice. At the heart of this practice was the effort to realize in their lives what the monks sometimes referred to as purity of heart (cf. Mt 5:8), a way of seeing oneself and the world as whole and undivided. The self was a cosmos unto itself, as rich and intricate and profound as the physical cosmos, and the monks believed their fates were intertwined with one another. They were also convinced that it was possible to recast one's relationship to the world and others in terms of genuine freedom and reciprocity, and in so doing come to reinhabit paradise. But achieving such freedom and seeing it bear fruit in the world required the will to struggle against the tyrannical force of the ego and make oneself vulnerable to the long, slow steady cleansing of one's consciousness. The healing of the world required healing of the self. To seek this healing meant risking everything, both for the sake of one's soul and for the sake of the wider community. It meant opening oneself to change so profound that the boundaries between oneself and God, oneself and others, oneself and the living world became utterly porous and fluid. It was for the sake of this transformed awareness that Antony embarked on the solitary journey that would eventually lead him to the inner mountain.

This careful attention to the work of seeing, healing, and restoring the whole—self, society, the world understood as a single, continuous fabric—is one of the most significant dimensions of the ancient Christian contemplative witness. It finds echoes in much contemporary spiritual thought and practice, expressed with particular force in those instances in which contemplative practice stands at the center of a witness oriented toward cultural, social, and political critique and renewal. In twentieth and early twenty-first centuries, one thinks of the witness of Dietrich Bonhoeffer, Simone Weil, Dorothy Day, Thomas Merton, Martin Luther King, Jr., Oscar Romero, Thich Nhat Hanh, the Dalai Lama, Aung San Suu Kyi, and the Trappist monks of Tibhirine, among others.[47] A common feature of these diverse witnesses is their careful attention to the need to integrate contemplative practice within a sustained response to the needs of the world. In this context, contemplative practice seems always to move, dialectically, in two directions at once—inward, into the depths of human consciousness and outward, toward a fuller engagement with one's fellow human beings and the wider world. This double movement requires everything a person can give of himself or herself—because the movement within almost always involves a harrowing confrontation with the unhealed parts of one's soul and because the movement outward calls forth an ever deeper sacrifice of oneself, a willingness to live beyond oneself, on behalf of others.

This fundamental tension, sometimes articulated in terms of the relationship between contemplation and action, points to the significance of *struggle* within contemplative practice, especially the struggle to stand in the midst of and hold in a compassionate embrace the reality of a broken world. Here one senses the immense complexity of mature contemplative practice, the way it strives to balance both seeking the Divine (or the transcendent) at the very center of one's life, and seeking the well-being of the whole of reality from within the unitive experience of this mystery. To open oneself to such practice means learning to live in the Divine *and* in and for the world as a single continuous gesture.

In the terms articulated by the ancient Christian contemplative tradition, this practice is rooted in the ability and willingness to learn to *see* differently, to see oneself not as detached or alienated from everyone and everything but as participating in and responsible for the whole. Such change does not happen simply by exchanging one set of ideas or perceptions for another; it occurs when the habits of mind that have contributed to one's isolation and blindness are allowed to be challenged at the deepest level of one's being. This is why the monks believed that the process of coming to see oneself as part of the whole required the most rigorous and sustained commitment to spiritual practice.

Such practice could and sometimes did yield a kind of clarified vision of reality that expressed itself in a renewed capacity for love, for life in community. That the cultivation of such a vision of the whole should have required the kind of radical retreat from the world characterized by Antony and the other ancient monks seems on the face of it a contradiction. But this retreat, this willingness to plumb the depths of the self in the expansive solitude of the desert, was in fact crucial to the larger work of healing and restoring community.

The Wild and the Sacred

We yearn to escape the demons of our subjectivity. We yearn to escape ourselves, into intimacy. We yearn to sense that we are in absolute touch with things; and we are of course.[48]

WILLIAM KITTREDGE

Is nothing sacred? Are there no natural phenomena—cells, organisms, ecosystems—before which we might stand in humble awe?[49]

STEPHANIE MILLS

The yearning to be "in absolute touch with things": in spite of everything, it remains undiminished. Yet we also recognize that the simple awareness of what it is to be alive in the world too often eludes us, and that our alienation from things, from the world, from ourselves, seems to permeate everything. Here in its simplest terms is the predicament that we face as we look out onto the broken world that we ourselves have created. As William Kittredge reminds us, "we are of course" in absolute touch with things. And yet we also feel the corrosive force of the "demons of our own subjectivity"—in our own souls and in nearly every aspect of our relationship with the world. Can we really hope to escape these demons? What would such freedom look like? And how might it help us to rekindle intimacy with the world, and enliven our efforts to repair it? As the erosion of the living world deepens and expands, these questions have become ever more pressing. So too has the challenge of understanding how to address them. The witness of the contemplative tradition suggests that our efforts to address the causes of our broken world will require us to face ourselves honestly and deeply, to engage in the hard work of healing in ourselves the fragmentation and alienation that we continuously visit upon the world. But what will it mean for us, living at the dawn of the twenty-first century, amidst an unprecedented ecological crisis, to engage in such contemplative work and to do so with an explicit consciousness of its ecological significance?

Part of our response, I believe, will involve discovering a contemplative idiom of our own that can help us make sense of our desire to honor both the vibrant physical world and the rich, imaginative inner life that enables us to cherish it. The contemplative witness represented by Antony, his contemporaries, and those who followed them in the subsequent monastic tradition can contribute to this work, especially by reminding us of how a sustained practice of attention can yield a radical transformation of consciousness. And by revealing how such a transformed consciousness can deepen our capacity for real contact with the natural world, for genuine intimacy. Such contemplative awareness, understood as part of a sustained practice of attention and reciprocity, can help us heal the wound that has opened up between our increasingly solipsistic and alienated selves and the natural world. Still, in our efforts to understand how such awareness is born in us, how it can be cultivated and deepened and made part of a meaningful contemporary environmental ethic, it is important to recognize how mysterious and delicate a process this is, how impossible it is to fathom it completely. The discovery of what Evagrius calls "the mind born of grace," an awareness of what it is to live in the presence of the All, arises in no small measure through the ascetic's careful, steady practice of attention—to his own soul and to the life of the world. Ultimately, though, it is a gift, unbidden and not entirely comprehensible. Still, the gift can be cultivated, brought to greater awareness, integrated more fully into our lives. This is the primary contemplative task.

Rainer Maria Rilke's early diaries reveal a person struggling to allow such contemplative awareness to be born in him. In the spring and summer of 1898, he traveled to Italy, ostensibly to study renaissance art. His experience of living in Florence opened him to a more profound awareness of the kind of sensitivity and reciprocity such beauty was calling forth from him. "I feel that I am on the way to becoming an intimate of everything that beauty preaches; that I am no longer a mere listener who receives its revelations like mute favors, that I am becoming more and more the things' disciple, someone who heightens their answers and confessions with discerning questions, who elicits from their hints and wisdoms and learns to return their generous love with the disciple's quiet devotion."[50] This sense of participation in an unfolding process of initiation continued to deepen throughout his time in Florence. The language of his diaries—in particular the increasing use of the language of kinship— reveals his growing awareness of a change in him that was gradually enabling him to enter into and feel part of the intricate, encompassing whole of the world. Practicing the "disciple's quiet devotion," (what he describes elsewhere as learning "to be reticent" in the presence of the natural world), he notices that "everything has come so much closer to me." To his friends, it seemed that this sense of close contact with nature was something that he had always felt. But he himself knew otherwise. "No … it is only very recently that I have gazed at it and savored it this way. For a long time we walked along next to each other in embarrassment, nature and I. It was as if I were at the side of a being whom I cherished but to whom I did dared not say: 'I love you.' Since then I must have finally said it; I don't know when it was but I feel that we have found each other."[51]

This sense of courtship and deep reciprocity with the natural world would gradually grow and deepen in him until it became one of the hallmarks of his mature poetic voice. But here, in these early diaries, one senses him standing at the edge of a threshold, just beginning to sense what it might mean for him to open himself to the world so fully. It is with a sense of chagrin that he realizes how long he has been living at a distance to the world and to his own experience. "When I think that I myself was once one of those who look on life with suspicion and mistrust its power. Now I would love it regardless—rich or poor, vast or narrow. However much belonged to me I would love tenderly and allow all that was latent in my possession to ripen in my innermost being."[52] The sense of his dynamic participation in something alive and powerful is palpable here. So is the ongoing cultivation of his own inner life—of his deepening capacity to "gaze," to "savor," to "love tenderly"—that enables him to take in this experience so that it can ripen within him. And if the precise cause of this awakening eludes him, the fact of its importance for his life does not.

A little more than two years later, in September 1900, Rilke records in his *Schmargendorf Diary* the effects on him of a walk with a friend across a heath in Worpswede. As usual there is animated conversation between the two friends. But eventually the wild wind cuts the conversation short and in that space of silence arises a sudden awareness that "So much is happening."

Beneath the vast skies the darkening colorful fields lie flat—wide hilly waves of rustling heather, bordering them stubble-fields and new-mown buckwheat, which with its stalk-red and the yellow of its leaves is like richest silk. And the way all this lies there, so close and strong and real that one can't possibly ignore or forget it. Every moment something is held up into the vivifying air, a tree, a house, a slowly turning mill, a man with black shoulders, a large cow or a hard-edged, jagged goat that walks into the sky. There are no conversations in which the land-scape doesn't take part, from all sides and with a hundred voices.[53]

Here, simple observation and description become woven into a rich inner experience of the world. The deepening capacity to gaze and savor alters the experience of what it is to move through the world, reordering the usual pos-ition of subject and object so that all is encountered as alive, all is taken in as part of single conversation.

Still, one wonders: what meaning and value is there in this way of seeing? Does it mean anything? Does it change anything? The answer to these ques-tions likely depends on the value one places in what it means to see the world "so close and strong and real that one can't possibly ignore or forget it." For Rilke, at least in these early diaries, the primary significance of such experience is aesthetic; however, it is difficult to miss the ethical and spiritual meaning embedded in this aesthetic response. Seeing the world in this way reveals a sensitivity to things, an awareness of their beauty and significance that is for Rilke close to the very heart of what it is to be spiritually alive. In this condition of radical receptivity and transparency, self and world unite. Describing his own emerging sense of this reality, Rilke says: "There is something like selfless-ness in this way of taking part in nature. I am gradually beginning to compre-hend this life that passes through large eyes into eternally waiting souls. This daily attentiveness, alertness, and eagerness of the senses turned outward, this thousandfold seeing and seeing always *away* from oneself ... this being only eye ... this purity of life, this always being joyful because something is always happening."[54]

The sense of vitality and joy in this account testifies to the effect of such deepening awareness on the one who has such an experience: it changes eve-rything. But does it do anything for the world? Rilke himself never drew any explicitly ecological conclusions from these observations. But it is clear that he believed such transformation of awareness *did* matter, did make a difference to the world. For the contemplative who is awake to the world in this way, aware that "something is always happening," it is not possible to live indiffer-ently or carelessly. The world can never disappear from view, never become merely a backdrop to the unfolding human drama. The contemplative's "daily attentiveness, alertness, and eagerness of the senses turned outward" help res-cue the world from oblivion, even as the contemplative is saved by the simple beauty of the world, by the recognition that the fabric *is* whole and we are woven deeply into it. This is how Rilke would express it years later in one of his *Sonnets to Orpheus*:

Sing the gardens, my heart, those you never knew; gardens
as if poured into glass: bright, unattainable.
Show, my heart, that you *aren't* without them.
That when their figs ripen, they have *you* in mind.
That when their winds grow almost visible
amid the flowering branches, it's *you* they embrace.
Silk thread, you were drawn into the fabric.
Whatever single image you made yourself part of

....

Feel how the whole carpet is meant, its glorious weave.[55]

This intuition regarding what it is to know oneself as part of an encompassing whole has the feeling of a deeply personal witness to the truth of an experience that may well have no other source of verification than the witness itself. Still, the evocation of the experience—of being remembered by the ripening figs, of being embraced by the almost visible winds, of being a "silk thread … drawn into the fabric," of "feeling how the whole carpet is meant," of knowing oneself to be part of "its glorious weave"—invites a serious consideration of the possibility that the experience might be true. In these gardens, in this rich imaginative space, the world comes alive in the soul. There is no separation, no distance. Everything is part of everything. We feel and know it to be true.

Still, the question of what kind of response this experience will call forth in us, and how we can transform an intuition, a moment of awareness, into a way of living, remains. This is not far from the central question with which Aldo Leopold struggled in his *Sand County Almanac*, a question he ultimately answered in a kind of credo. "We can be ethical," he said, "only in relation to something we can see, feel, understand, love, or otherwise have faith in."[56] Leopold shared Rilke's sense of the importance of coming to see and know a place intimately and deeply and became convinced that without a real effort to cultivate such intimacy, our efforts to learn how to live in the natural world thoughtfully and ethically will not be sustainable. He came to think of this as the work of cultivating what he called an "ecological conscience." In a 1947 essay, written a year before Leopold died, he described it this way: "Ecology is the science of communities, and the ecological conscience is therefore the ethics of community life."[57] This simple statement captures one of his most important and enduring insights, that ecology must include the human struggle to see and understand the world as part of an encompassing whole. For Leopold, this struggle meant not simply following an ethical code (as important as this is), but searching out the deepest sources of our relationship with the natural world, opening ourselves to a new awareness of who we are in the world. To achieve a deep and lasting change in our awareness and our practice, Leopold suggests, will require a willingness to engage in the equivalent of what certain spiritual traditions have commonly referred to as an "examination of conscience."

In a justly renowned section of the *Sand County Almanac* called "Thinking Like a Mountain," Leopold memorably recounts the painful experience as a young man that provoked in him a profound examination of conscience and brought him to the threshold of a new awareness of who he was in the world and of his own relationship to the whole. He was traveling with friends in the rimrock country of Arizona, when a wolf with several cubs suddenly appeared below them crossing a river. "In those days," he says, "we had never heard of a passing up a chance to kill a wolf. In a second, we were pumping lead into the pack ... when our rifles were empty, the old wolf was down, and a pup was dragging a leg into impassable slide rocks." What happened next changed everything.

> We reached the old wolf in time to watch a fierce green fire dying in her eyes. I realized then, and have known ever since, that there was something new to me in those eyes—something known only to her and to the mountain. I was young then, and full of trigger-itch; I thought that because fewer wolves meant more deer, that no wolves would mean hunter's paradise. But after seeing the green fire die, I sensed that neither the wolf nor the mountain agreed with such a view.[58]

The significance of this experience upon Leopold's emerging ecological awareness was profound. In what follows this brief account, he articulates the birth of his growing understanding of the intricacy of ecological relationships and of the blindness that had prevented him and others from seeing and respecting them. He had dreamed of a hunter's paradise. Instead, he came to see that the policy of the extirpation of wolves throughout the West had led to the rapid, unchecked growth of deer populations, the subsequent defoliation of entire mountains, and the impoverishment of whole ecosystems. He would devote much of his life to drawing out the implications of this insight, asking what it might mean to rethink not only our individual relationships with the natural world but also the values underlying our shared economic and political life. The "land ethic" that emerged from these reflections has become one of the most influential and enduring expressions of how a transformed awareness of our relationship with the world can lead to a more mindful way of living.

Leopold's own experience suggests how important the transformation of one's awareness can be to the work of cultivating a meaningful ecological ethic.[59] Also how mysterious it is. The unexpected force of the "fierce green fire" in the wolf's eyes seems to have unnerved him. But what did it mean? He could not say, at least not precisely. "There was something new to me in those eyes— something known only to her and to the mountain." Leopold takes care to honor the mystery of this encounter. And nothing in his subsequent reflections on the ecological significance of wolves in their environment undermines this sense of mystery. He wants to understand how the ecosystem works, and what intricate pattern enables wolves and deer and mountains and humans to exist and thrive together. But there is something in this pattern that eludes and will always elude precise explanation, something to do with its wild character. "Perhaps this is the hidden meaning in the howl of the wolf," suggests Leopold, "long known among the mountains, but seldom perceived among men." It cannot be fully known; it is too deep and mysterious. But Leopold makes it clear that we have a greater capacity to open ourselves to this mystery than we have acknowledged or expressed, and that until we learn to open ourselves more fully to wild world, until we learn to "think like a mountain," we will have nothing but "dustbowls, and rivers washing the future into the sea."[60]

To "think like a mountain." Few ideas have come to resonate more deeply in our emerging ecological consciousness than this one. This is in no small part, I believe, because of its imaginative reach, born of Leopold's conviction that we have a greater capacity to know and participate in the life of the beautiful, complex world within which we live and move than we have yet realized; also because of Leopold's insistence on the presence of mystery, the recognition of all that cannot be known, at the heart of our experience of the world. There is a relationship, he seems to suggest, between our desire to kindle intimacy with the living world and our intuitive awareness of its endless power and mystery; and a recognition of the need for this relationship to become enfolded within an ongoing practice. What Rilke calls the "thousand-fold seeing and seeing always *away* from oneself"—an orientation toward the world at once attentive to its particular life and open to its endlessness—must become a habit of mind, a habit of being. This will not mean, of course, turning our attention away from the fragmentation and loss that is increasingly becoming such a central part of the world we inhabit; this must be faced with both honesty and courage. Indeed, this deepening loss makes it even more imperative that we learn to cultivate an awareness of and appreciation for the life of particular beings and places in the world, even as we learn to open ourselves to the mysterious whole of which they are a part. Seen within the framework of contemplative thought and practice, this means acknowledging the dialectical tension between all that can be known and understood in our experience of the world and all that is and must remain unknowable.

But what does it mean to give such prominence to mystery, to that which cannot be known or grasped, especially in relation to our experience and understanding of the natural world? This seems on the face of it to be incompatible with the primary impulse within so much contemporary ecological thought to open up a space of understanding where the intricate relationships among and between different organisms in the natural world can be better described and known. Certainly such understanding is necessary if the work of conservation is to be undertaken with intelligence and care. Still, there is another persistent thread of concern that has become woven into much contemporary reflection on what it means to know and apprehend the natural world: the concern to protect and guard mystery. Often, this concern is rooted in a desire to protect and guard the irreducible otherness of natural world—its wildness—that will always exceed our capacity to know or understand or control. Certainly this is part of what Leopold speaks to in his testimony concerning his encounter with the dying wolf. There is "something known only to her and to the mountain" he says—an implicit acknowledgement of a dimension of the world beyond our capacity to know or understand. But this apparent lack or gap in our knowledge can be seen as a richness, an excess to which we are invited to attend and open ourselves.

This is why it is necessary to pause and consider, again and again, how the wild comes to us in the palpably particular:

In the blue night
frost haze, the sky glows
with the moon
pine tree tops
bend snow-blue, fade
into sky, frost, starlight,
the creak of boots,
rabbit tracks, deer tracks,
what do we know.[61]

What *do* we know? That question, arising at the end of Gary Snyder's "Pine Tree Tops," echoes for a long time afterwards in the silence of the night. It is an important, troubling question. What *do* we know—about the lives of wild animals, about rivers, trees, the wind? How much has our *assumption* of knowledge obscured our vision, prevented us from seeing, feeling, loving what is continually unfolding before us? How much arrogance is wrapped up in that assumption of knowledge? To struggle with these questions is, I think, to find ourselves confronted with a profound spiritual challenge. It is the challenge of discovering whether we have the capacity to adopt a posture of genuine humility before the ever elusive, ever mysterious wild. In this sense I agree with Stephanie Mills that the question of the wild ultimately "shakes out as a religious question." The question, suggests Mills, is this: "Is nothing sacred? Are there no natural phenomena—cells, organisms, ecosystems— before which we might stand in humble awe?"[62]

Humility. From *humus,* ground or soil. It is a word, an idea, whose meaning, it seems, we have hardly begun to understand. It suggests a kind of moral and spiritual disposition of lowliness, littleness. Not self-abnegation or self-loathing, but an honest acknowledgement of who we are, or who we might become: beings close to the earth, of the earth, aware of our kinship with other living beings, capable of looking out onto the world from below.

> I move among the ankles
> of forest Elders, tread
> their moist rugs of moss,
> duff of their soft brown carpets.
> Far above, their arms are held
> open wide to each other, or waving—
> what they know, what
> perplexities and wisdoms they exchange,
> unknown to me as were the thoughts
> of grownups when in infancy I wandered
> into a roofed clearing amidst
> human feet and legs and the massive
> carved legs of the table ...[63]

Such, Denise Levertov suggests, is the view from below, the child's view— the curious-crawling-around-under-the-dining-room-table-among-ankles-and-socks view. Like the view from the forest floor, it is intimate, but also strange and bewildering. So much is unknown, unknowable, hidden, secret, other. Here one moves close to the ground, *on* the ground. There is proximity, close contact with the soft mossy carpets, with all those feet and legs. But there is also a world beyond and above—"the minds of people, the minds of trees/equally remote" says the poet.

A world beckons, but refuses to disclose its meaning, at least not completely and not in terms that we ourselves control. The minds of trees are as
remote to us now, the poet suggests, as the minds of people (grownups) were
to us as children. Nor is this a gap that can or should be bridged. Instead, this
lack of certainty about who or what we behold begins to seem fruitful, important, necessary. We are invited to relinquish our assumption of knowledge,
adopt a position of humble awe and allow ourselves to be "drawn to upgaz-
ing," full of wonder.[64]

Humility. Awe. Wonder. Here are dispositions of mind, elements of a
sensibility that can help us learn to attend more carefully to the mystery of
the living world. Levertov's poem gives one expression to a sensibility that
is emerging with increasing frequency in contemporary ecological literature
and which bears striking similarity to a an attitude found in many traditions
of spiritual discourse. Fundamental to such a sensibility is a willingness to be
dispossessed of our knowledge of things, emptied of language and concep-
tions about the world that only serve to obscure what we are seeking.

Within ancient Christian contemplative practice, this habit of dispossession is crucial to the cultivation of a spiritual sensibility rooted in darkness
and unknowing.[65] In this "apophatic" way (or *via negativa* as it is sometimes
called), emptiness and silence are as important as thought and language to
the work of engaging and responding to the mystery unfolding within and
without. In this context, the work of radical relinquishment, of letting go
of all images and ideas about God, or "losing God for the sake of God" as
Meister Eckhart memorably expressed it, comes to be seen as the chief work
of the soul. This is also characteristic of Evagrius of Pontus's understanding of
imageless prayer, in which one comes to dwell in "the place of God" which is
no place, and behold what is beyond all beholding: the luminous blue sapphire of the mind. "If you long to practice prayer," says Evagrius, "renounce
absolutely all things, so that you may inherit the whole."[66] Here one senses the
power of relinquishment, of allowing oneself to become emptied, open, receptive to what can only be experienced and known beyond language, images and
thought. Here too one feels the importance and necessity of paradox, that
habit of mind so critical to traditions of spiritual thought and practice, in
which images and ideas are employed to evoke profound spiritual experience
even as the possibility of reading them literally or categorically is negated.
One enters the desert to lose everything in the immensity.

Thinking about how these questions took root in the ancient Christian
monastic imagination inevitably leads one to consider the character of the
places in which these monastic figures lived, and the landscapes that shaped

their imagination. This does not mean that one should assume a simple correspondence between the vast, open landscape in which their lives unfolded and the spirituality of emptiness that emerged from these monastic communities.[67] The desert was not a single, simple reality within early Christian monastic experience. For many of its inhabitants it was a deeply ambiguous space, alluring but also fearful and threatening. Still, one should not ignore the wild beauty into which these desert dwellers were drawn or what it might have meant for them to live out their days under that luminous sky and in such deep silence. The passage into that wild place, and the willingness to make oneself vulnerable, created the conditions for a radical undoing and remaking of the self that was also a rekindling of intimacy with the wider community: a dispossession that made possible a repossession of the whole.

The willingness to be dispossessed for the sake of the larger whole remains one of the most significant contributions of this ancient spiritual tradition to the larger project of social, cultural, and spiritual transformation. At the heart of this tradition is a longing for contact with an immensity that can never be named or completely known, but whose presence and transforming power can nevertheless be felt and experienced. It is for the sake of contact with this mysterious presence—wild and sacred—that one enters into the work of *apophasis*, emptiness, and silence, that one risks becoming lost, disoriented, dispossessed. Also for the sake of a rebirth or renewal that can take root and flourish nowhere else.

Contact

> What is this Titan that has possession of me? Talk of
> mysteries!—Think of our life in nature,—daily to be
> shown matter, to come in contact with it,—rocks, trees,
> wind on our cheeks! The *solid earth!* the *actual* world!
> The *common sense! Contact! Contact! Who* are we? *where*
> are we?[68]

HENRY DAVID THOREAU

Is it still possible for us to imagine undertaking such a dispossession for the sake of the whole in the present moment, especially in relation to all that is being lost to us in the natural world? And to conceive of what it might mean to make it part of a sustained contemplative practice? How we respond to these questions will depend in no small measure on how effectively idioms and practices from the past can be translated into meaningful contemporary discourse and practice. But it will also depend on our willingness to risk the kind of relinquishment that these contemplative traditions claim is necessary for real and lasting personal and social transformation. There is considerable evidence that this work is already being undertaken in the present moment; and much of the subsequent discussion in this book is devoted to engaging and responding to this work. But I want to conclude this chapter by casting a glance further back in time, to a case that I believe remains significant for helping us think about what the work of dispossession in relation to the natural world entails. I am referring to Henry David Thoreau's account of his journey up Mt. Ktaadn in 1846.

Few in the modern tradition have articulated the sense of what it is to lose oneself in the wild world as forcefully and persuasively as Henry David Thoreau. As critics such as Allan Hodder and David Robinson have argued, such ecstatic experience had a significant, if also complex and ambiguous, spiritual meaning for Thoreau.[69] His account of his journey up Mt. Ktaadn in 1846 occupies a distinctive place in this regard, primarily because of its dramatic evocation of an ecstatic experience of contact with the wild world that is also a descent into unknowing. Thoreau describes being brought to the very edge of himself, and beyond, in response to the radical otherness of the wild. His effort to express his sense of this immensity also leads him to the very edge of language, which bends and cracks and ultimately fails to encompass all that has happened to him, reflecting his acute recognition of the limits of what can be said about such experience. Still, the sense of having beheld and been seized by something powerful and mysterious remains. The fundamental tension reflected here—between what can be said of such experience and what is unsayable, what can be known and what must always remain beyond our capacity to know or comprehend—enables us to situate Thoreau's account meaningfully within that older and still-enduring conversation about such questions that first took hold for Christian contemplatives in wild deserts of Egypt, Asia Minor, Syria, and Judea, and offers suggestions for how we might think of these very different discourses together.

Still, there are elements of Thoreau's account that are distinctive and help to deepen and extend this conversation in important ways, not least of which is his sustained effort to understand what it is to live with an awareness of the wild, not simply as something that one encounters in discrete, dramatic moments, isolated both temporally and geographically from ordinary existence, but as a continuous dimension of everyday life. In this sense it is important not to isolate Thoreau's dramatic account of his experience near the summit of Mt. Ktaadn from the rest of his narrative (in which he gives careful attention to complexities of human interchange with the natural world), or for that matter from his other thinking about what it means to attend to and relinquish one-self to the power of the wild: it permeates everything. Nor should we overlook Thoreau's understanding of the integral relationship that exists between the depth of our experience and awareness of the wild and the possibility of social transformation. The radical dispossession and reorientation of the self that takes place in the presence of the wild is necessary, Thoreau is convinced, if we are to arrive at a more thoughtful and sustainable vision of our common social and political life.[70] Such relinquishment, he believed, leaves one less inclined to claim knowledge and power, more open to and curious about the life of the other, more capable of exchange, reciprocity, love. It is within this larger frame of reference, including his experiment at Walden Pond, that Thoreau's account of his experience on Mt. Ktaadn should be seen and understood: as part of a sustained effort to consider how our openness to becoming vulnerable to the encompassing power of the wild, our willingness to become lost in its immen-sity, can transform our very sense of what it is to be alive in the world.

The narrative of his journey to Ktaadn is framed in a way that enables us to sense what is coming and feel the significance of what happens to him near the summit of the mountain. But he does not rush; he moves through the landscape slowly, carefully, offering a sober, meticulous account of its com-plex, ambiguous character. He notes at the outset how few backwoodsmen and hunters have ever climbed Ktaadn, proudly locating himself among the few foolish or brave enough to try. Of the forest through which he is about to travel, he observes that the wild or unsettled parts of it are far more extensive than the settled regions, a simple reminder of how far removed this place is from the more domesticated land near Concord. Still, certain parts of the land have been settled and large swaths have been deeply scarred by logging, which has been so aggressive and extensive that it seems to Thoreau destined "to drive the forest all out of the country." And there also are stark remind-ers of: "the Indian's history, that is, the history of his extinction."[71] So: this place is hardly pristine or untouched by human history and interaction. And yet, as Thoreau moves further into the forest, he begins to become aware that he is indeed moving into a more remote place than he has ever been before, with few roads and ever fewer indications of human habitation: what he calls "a bran new country."[72] There are still "forest houses" and stumps of white pine to be seen. But he notes that he and his companions could "overlook an immense country of uninterrupted forest."[73] Eventually in the distance, they glimpse Ktaadn: "its summit veiled in clouds, like a dark Ithmus in that quar-ter, connecting the heavens and the earth."[74]

They were still thirty miles or so from the mountain, and it was increasingly difficult going. Thoreau relates, often in painstaking detail, the tremendous effort it took for them to make their way past rapids, across lakes, through ever deepening thickets of trees and underbrush. But there is also something else: the sheer remoteness of the place in which they now found themselves. "No face welcomed us," Thoreau says, noting the depth to which they had penetrated into the forest.[75] They are more and more alone.

The deepening wildness and emptiness of the terrain through which they travel is no small part of the story that Thoreau has to tell. The further they journey into the forest, the less certain they became of their bearings and of themselves. Thoreau does not adorn his account. He simply relates how it feels to move ever further from the known and familiar into the unknown and strange country in which they now find themselves. It is at once exhilarating and disorientating. Which means that by the time he reaches the field of giant boulders near the summit of the mountain—a place he describes as "an undone extremity of the globe"—we are not surprised to hear of his growing apprehension and bewilderment at what lay before him. It has been deepening already for some time. Nor does it feel exaggerated. On that particular day, the wind was strong and the clouds were rising and falling, obscuring his vision and ultimately blocking his ascent of the mountain. The place, he says, is: "vast, Titanic, and such as man never inhabits." And he recognizes that he cannot comprehend it. Later, he makes an attempt to describe what he felt that day: "Some part of the beholder, even some vital part, seems to escape through the loose grating of his ribs as he ascends. He is more lone than you can imagine. There is less of substantial thought and fair understanding in him, than in the plains where men inhabit. His reason is dispersed and shadowy, more thin and subtile like the air."[76] This is the first of two important passages in his narrative in which Thoreau relates what it felt like to gaze upon and be enveloped within the wildness of Mt. Ktaadn. The sense of psychological disorientation here is palpable: some vital part of the beholder, he says, "seems to escape through the loose grating of his ribs." His sense of solitude grows more acute. His thought becomes gradually less substantial. His reason becomes "dispersed and shadowy," as thin as air. The beholder grows less and less secure, more precarious though the mountain remains utterly solid and substantial. There is a kind of exchange or displacement, and the beholder, whether willingly or not, gives way before the wild otherness of the mountain. He yields himself to it and allows himself to be drawn into its wild, mysterious power.

There is little question that Thoreau hungered deeply for just this kind of strong experience. But did he guess how much it would cost him, how much of himself he would have to relinquish to acquire it? As David Robinson has suggested, Thoreau's entire account of the journey to Ktaadn can in some ways be understood as a response to the question posed by Ralph Waldo Emerson some time earlier in his essay on "Experience": "where do we find ourselves?" For Emerson, this was a complicated question arising from both his hope of discovering what Stanley Cavell has described as new beginnings and rediscovered foundations in life and experience and his uncertainty about whether this was possible. Thoreau carried just such a hope into his Walden experiment; and it seems also to have been a critical part of his motivation for embarking into the wild country of the Maine woods. But the narrative, especially the culminating section of his experience near the summit of Mt. Ktaadn, reveals an apparent confounding of expectations, especially in terms of Thoreau's ability to say what it is that has happened to him. He does not fall silent. But the experience is so strong and dense that he seems unable to grasp or express all that is in it. Some part of his very self "seems to escape" as he ascends the mountain. His thoughts lose substantiality, becoming like the clouds in which he finds himself immersed. He cannot arrive at an adequate account of the experience.

Still, he continues to try to do so. Especially significant in this regard is the justly celebrated account of his experience near the summit of Mt. Ktaadn that expresses all the ambiguity and uncertainty contained in Emerson's poignant question. The search for the self has now become bound inextricably to the question of whether one can open oneself to the deepest, wildest dimensions of the world itself. And the elusive, mysterious character of Thoreau's own experience of being overtaken by this wildness, as well as his recognition of the impossibility of giving a clear account of what has happened to him or what it means, now finds its way into this remarkable testimony.

What is it to be admitted to a museum, to see a myriad of particular things, compared with being shown some star's surface, some hard matter in its home! I stand in awe of my body, this matter to which I am bound has become so strange to me. I fear not spirits, ghosts, of which I am one,—*that* my body might,—but I fear bodies, I tremble to meet them. What is this Titan that has possession of me? Talk of mysteries!—Think of our life in nature,—daily to be shown matter, to come in contact with it,—rocks, trees, wind on our cheeks! The *solid earth!* the *actual* world! The *common sense! Contact! Contact! Who* are we? *where* are we?[77]

What is Thoreau after here? What if anything has he found? The sheer rush and density of his language makes it difficult to decipher either the tone or possible meaning of this account. A hunger for contact with the "actual world" seems to contend with skepticism about whether this is really possible. Hard matter is the fundamental reality; but the hard matter of his own body remains strange to him. Still, there is awe, mystery. He trembles to encounter other bodies, he marvels at "our life in nature," the daily contact with matter—"rocks, trees, wind on our cheeks!" And he exclaims, in a tone that feels at once bewildered and joyous, over what seems to him the most fundamental mystery of all: "The *solid earth*! the *actual* world!"

One senses the confused, conflicted character of the experience underlying this account, the sense of a person drawn right out to the edge of himself, uncertain about how to express the immensity of what he feels and knows. But there is also the sense of a person coming to an immediate and vital knowledge of something valuable and lasting that simply cannot be expressed in any other way: a knowledge that has come about through an unexpected and profound undoing of all that has been known before, a relinquishment that is also a new vulnerability to all that lay before him. It is probably important not to separate this account too sharply from Thoreau's long and sustained exploration of what it means for human beings to open themselves to the wild world. Or to elevate this particular encounter with the wild that took place deep in the Maine woods from the kind of experience Thoreau came to feel was accessible to us everywhere in the midst of our ordinary lives. "It is vain to dream of a wildness that is distant from ourselves. There is none such," he observed, ten years after his initial journey to Mt. Ktaadn.[78] Still, there is something important and instructive about this account that bears directly upon the central questions of this book. I am referring to the dimension of unknowing and dispossession that marks Thoreau's account. This became a prominent theme throughout his work. "At the same time that we are in earnest to explore and learn all things," he wrote in *Walden*, "we require that all things be mysterious and unexplorable."[79] No one was more curious about exploring and learning all things than Thoreau; but his sense of the mysterious and unexplorable character of all things remained fundamental to his feeling for the world. And he never stopped asking himself what it would mean for him to risk opening himself more and more fully to this wild, mysterious reality.

There is something comparable here, I think, to the way ancient Christian contemplatives speak of *apophatic* experience, especially the sense of radical dispossession born of excess and overflowing. The meaning of such dispossession is not always the same, of course. But the shared sense of reaching a limit in experience, beyond which language and concepts cannot take us, is striking. It invites further reflection on the importance of such experience to the work of seeing and experiencing the world, not on terms dictated and determined by us, but in response to what is given to us. The question of whether we still possess the capacity for risking ourselves in this way, of opening ourselves to such experience, remains important and necessary, especially in relation to the still-wild but rapidly diminishing world.[80] "In wildness is the preservation of the world," Thoreau famously wrote. This observation, repeated so often that it verges on becoming a cliché, still retains its power, its capacity to move, especially when seen as an evocation of that unutterably powerful dimension of the world that will always exceed our capacity to comprehend or express. Seen not as a lack or an incompleteness but as a gift, the contemplative traditions remind us that our willingness to open ourselves to this space of unknowing can help us rediscover something critical about the world and our place in it. One of Thoreau's most important contributions to this common work, I think, is his own willingness to stand in the darkness of unknowing and to see it as luminous, as a space full of potential for personal and social transformation.

"*Contact*! *Contact*! *Who* are we? *where* are we?" That exclamation, born of a palpable knowledge of one's own life as touched by and participating in the life of the whole. Those questions, reflecting an awareness that what we know and experience will always be exceeded by the immensity beyond and within. The sense that we possess the capacity for cultivating a more encompassing awareness of the wild world and of living from the center of this awareness is both alluring and hopeful. The task of integrating such awareness into our individual and collective lives clearly remains unfinished. But as a way of understanding what it might mean to inhabit the world more fully and thoughtfully, this contemplative vision has a particular contribution to make to the work of healing our broken, fragmented world. We are beginning to recover a sense that the simple act of gazing, of paying attention—one of the most ancient and enduring ways of understanding contemplative practice—can open up a space in the soul, a space in which the world may live and move in us. And that we are being called to renew our commitment to this work—for the sake of the world.

Penthos: *The Gift of Tears*

There are tears which pierce through the earth and rise as
stars in other skies. I wonder who has wept our stars?[1]

E.M. CIORAN

We must kindle the divine fire in ourselves through tears
and hard work.[2]

AMMA SYNCLETICA

"WE ONLY GRIEVE for what we know." So claims Aldo Leopold in his ecological masterpiece *The Sand County Almanac*.[3] The immediate context of this
remark is Leopold's reflection on the increasing rarity of a once-abundant
species of prairie wildflower, the cutleaf Silphium. How could this beautiful
plant have come so dangerously close to extinction, he wondered? Why did
its impending disappearance from the world not provoke a stronger response?
Why was there no expression of grief? More than fifty years later, amidst ecological degradation far more extensive than anything Leopold could have
envisioned, these questions still reverberate. Grief over losses in the natural
world has become a common part of our personal and collective emotional
landscape. At the same time, the very depth and extent of these losses has
produced, for many, a kind of psychic numbing, resulting in an inability or
unwillingness to acknowledge or respond to this loss lest it completely overwhelm and perhaps debilitate us. There is too much to grieve. Still, Leopold's
observation raises important questions about the role of grief in shaping our
feeling for the natural world, as well as its place within the larger effort to
develop a coherent and meaningful ecological ethic.

Can such an ethic be developed without serious attention to the felt sense
of loss that afflicts persons and communities as they face the disappearance
of species and the degradation of entire ecosystems? Leopold's connection
of knowledge and grief is instructive here. The ability to mourn such loss, he
suggests, is itself a reflection of our knowledge of and feeling for beings and

places in the natural world. "We only grieve for what we know." Similarly, the diminishment or loss of the capacity to mourn reflects a loss of knowledge, an unraveling of the ties of kinship that bind us to the lives of other beings. Leopold does not develop this idea at any length. But his brief attention to this matter suggests something important about the way grief in the face of loss in the natural world can take hold of us, and how it can transform our very sense of the world. The ability to mourn for the loss of other species is, in this sense, an expression of our sense of participation in and responsibility for the whole fabric of life of which we are a part. Understood in this way, grief and mourning can be seen not simply as an expression of private and personal loss, but as part of a restorative spiritual practice that can rekindle an awareness of the bonds that connect all life-forms to one another and to the larger ecological whole.

What would it mean to include mourning as part of a contemplative spiritual practice oriented toward deepening our sense of reciprocity and feeling for the natural world? How might openness to grief and mourning facilitate a more intricate and expansive knowledge of the whole and a greater awareness of the significance of our own relationship to that whole? Can a greater openness to grief and mourning contribute to a greater awareness of one's existence as woven into an intricate fabric of being?[4] The desire for such contemplative awareness, whether understood in explicitly religious terms or not, has come to occupy an increasingly important part of the contemporary cultural landscape, especially in relation to the challenge of deepening our relationship with the natural world. This is particularly important when grappling with the question of how to overcome a deeply ingrained habit of seeing the natural world as an object, a thing somehow detached from our own lives. Contemplative awareness, in the sense that I am using the term here, entails a more involved, intersubjective way of knowing, in which the boundaries between the self and the other are experienced as porous and fluid. Tears, born of grief, often signal the first spark of such awareness. To weep is to make oneself vulnerable to the other, to relinquish the illusion of detachment and control. Learning to apprehend the natural world in this way can open up a completely different and more encompassing ecological awareness.

But what does it mean to open oneself to grief, to consider it, as I believe Leopold does, as a critical part of the work of coming to know and care for the natural world? To address this question, I want to begin by situating Leopold's insight within the context of a larger conversation concerning the role of tears and mourning in the work of spiritual transformation. Many spiritual traditions place high value on the role of grief and mourning in facilitating both personal and communal transformation. One such tradition, arising from the world of ancient Christian monasticism, gives particular attention to how tears—understood as a gift—can open up the soul and create the possibility of a more authentic relationship to the Divine and to others. This tradition can, I believe, help illuminate our contemporary efforts to include mourning as part of a meaningful spiritual practice, one that has particular value in an age of ecological loss and destruction. But developing such a spiritual practice also requires reckoning honestly with the impediments to mourning that so often undermine our efforts to respond deeply and honestly to loss. Here, I want to draw upon the classic work of Alexander and Margarete Mitscherlich, *The Inability to Mourn*,[5] to consider the consequences, for persons and for entire societies, of the suppression of grief. This work, along with that of W.G. Sebald, reminds us that grief is not simply a private, personal response to loss, but also comes to expression, or fails to come to expression, within a broader social, cultural, political (and we would now add, ecological) fabric. Seen in this wider context, the ability to mourn becomes one of the most important signs of whether, in the face of devastating loss, persons and society as a whole can learn to act on behalf of genuine social, political, and ecological renewal. Finally, I want to consider what it might mean to integrate the practice of mourning more fully into our relationship with the natural world and how such practice might help us learn to see and respond to the world more honestly and deeply. The ancient contemplative traditions can help us in recovering a greater sense of intimate relatedness with the natural world; but so too can our own literary traditions help us to reclaim this sensibility. In spite of longstanding habits of evasion and denial, these diverse cultural resources can help us to acknowledge the place of grief in our experience of the natural world and to enter into that grief as part of the work of authentic and sustained ecological renewal.

The Gift of Tears

Weep. Truly, there is no other way but this.[6]

ABBA POEMEN

Grief and loss are becoming an ever more prevalent part of the contemporary experience of the natural world. Yet it is not easy to know how to respond to such feelings, or to know what meaning they may have. These questions became acute for me several years ago during a meeting on the natural world at Vassar College in upstate New York. I was sitting around a large table together with several colleagues who had spent most of that summer studying and reflecting on the place of the natural world in our teaching and writing. Our time together had nearly come to an end and, perhaps in response to our impending departure, we found ourselves talking more intimately and personally about the places in the natural world that had meant something to us in our lives. Stories came tumbling out about childhood places, wild places, ordinary backyard places, places where some intimate sense of connection with the living world had been born and nurtured. There was such delight, even joy, in naming and describing these places. But gradually the conversation turned to the feelings of loss that we also carried within us. Many of these places no longer existed. I found myself thinking about the ancient wetland near my home in southern California where once abundant populations of egrets, plovers, and great blue herons are rapidly diminishing as a huge housing complex slowly devours the space. Another person recalled a creek he had played in as a child in South Carolina, now mostly silted over from logging. And so it went, one place after another, paved over, plowed under, razed for one form of development or another. The mood in the room darkened. We found ourselves speaking to one another through tears, through an immense grief that, until that moment, had been moving beneath the surface of our conversations. But now it showed itself and it was strong and fierce. There was not a single person in that room who had not been touched by it. In that moment, our sense of shared loss became palpable, dense and sharp. It was like coming to an awareness of the enduring presence of an old wound.

It would be difficult to say all that was contained in those tears. Certainly loss was part of it, a sense that something crucial and irreplaceable had disappeared, or was on the verge of disappearing, forever. But there was also an intense affection and tenderness in the description and stories of particular places, a feeling for the world that still existed even though the places themselves had in some cases ceased to exist. I sensed also more than a little longing, perhaps for reparation and return, for the reconstitution of a world that might yet exist if we could rekindle in ourselves enough feeling and regard for it. It is striking how strong the memory of those tears remains for me, even though so much else from that time has long since faded from view. I suspect this has something to do with the honest, piercing character of the feelings that were expressed that day. In offering our simple accounts of those places that had shaped and formed us, their acute fragility, as well as their preciousness and importance to us, became clearer, more palpable. It seems too that something else, more difficult to describe or define, began to emerge in that moment: something like a new awareness of ourselves as beings alive in the world. That this awareness was so closely bound up with a sense of loss and grief is, for me, one of the most poignant and significant elements of the experience. The sense of being alive in the world and awakened to its fragility and beauty was mediated to us *through* our tears, through the unexpected but undeniable sense of being pierced by sharp feeling for places we had known and loved, places whose loss and diminishment we were in that very moment struggling to acknowledge and absorb.

Tears for lost places, for a whole lost world of possibilities. Also, tears born of gratitude for what has been, for what might yet be retrieved and restored. Tears as a source of renewal. Tears as gift.

This is how the Christian monastics of the fourth century Egyptian desert thought about tears. What they referred to as the "gift of tears" formed a distinctive and central part of their spirituality, helping to awaken the soul to the ultimate horizon against which the monk was living. But this practice was certainly not exclusive to them. Tears have occupied an important place in many spiritual traditions, serving as a crucial means by which persons and communities are able to seek healing for what has been broken asunder. Often, weeping helps to reknit the bonds broken by death, helping to open or renew a sense of relationship between the living and the dead. So too can ritual acts of mourning play an important role in restoring balance within society.[7] And in some cases, tears even have cosmological significance, helping to connect and reintegrate different planes of existence in the universe.[8] Tears, it turns out, often play a central role in helping persons and communities face crisis and respond creatively to it. Certainly this was true of the ancient Christian monastic tradition. The Christian monastic movement arose amidst a moment of acute crisis, in which the crushing weight of economic and social pressures were forcing many persons living in the Nile Valley to flee from towns and villages and seek refuge in the desert. There was a pervasive sense, shared and articulated in a particular way by the monks, that a new and more penetrating awareness of self and world would be required to help heal the rifts that were threatening their society and culture and sustain life and hope in the future.[9] The ascetic practices they cultivated were oriented toward precisely this end; and tears came to occupy a central place in this ascetic work.

The language used to describe this practice reveals both the power and mystery of the experience among the ancient monks. In Greek, the most common terms are *penthos* or *katanyxis*, both of which suggest a profound piercing of the heart that is the very source of the tears.[10] Such tears could not be manufactured or planned for; when they came, they came mysteriously, unexpectedly, as a gift. Yet, one could seek them, open oneself to them. Tears were highly valued in the ancient Christian monastic world, for they were believed to express and make possible an honest reckoning with one's life (especially one's fragility); a life-changing transformation; a reorientation to God and to the larger community. Still, while there was broad consensus among the early Christian monks regarding the importance of tears, the teaching itself was often presented with little comment or explanation. In one saying, "A brother asked an elder, 'What should I do?' And the old man said to him. 'We ought always to weep.'"[11] Abba Poemen reported that the elders, "put compunction as the beginning of every action."[12] "Let us weep," Abba Macarius counseled his disciples, "and let tears gush out of our eyes...."[13] And Abba Antony, widely regarded as the founder of the ancient Christian monastic movement, exhorted those who wished to follow the monastic way of life simply to: "weep, and groan in your heart."[14] In broad terms, these exhortations can be understood as reflecting a desire on the part of the monks to emulate and embody the Gospel teaching, "Blessed are those who weep, for they shall be comforted" (Mt 5:4). But in practice, both the reasons for tears and their meaning remained complex and often obscure. John Climacus, who wrote extensively on this matter, noted, "[T]ears can come about in various ways. Tears come from nature, from God, from suffering good and bad, from vainglory, from licentiousness, from love, from the remembrance of death, and from numerous other causes."[15] Although Climacus himself takes great pains to distinguish these different kinds of tears, elsewhere, especially in the earliest monastic traditions, such distinctions were not always made so clearly. Tears were difficult to interpret or understand. Their meaning, if it was to be found out, would emerge only through a long, patient process of rumination.

There were certain concerns that the monks returned to again and again and that formed the heart of their teaching on *penthos*. Mortality was one of the most important of these. At the most basic level, the monk was one who gave himself over to the practice of *memento mori*, a sustained reflection on mortality, not only his own but also that of every living thing. Abba Poemen is reported to have seen a woman sitting in a tomb "weeping bitterly. He said, 'If all the delights of the world were to come, they could not drive sorrow away from the soul of this woman. Even so the monk would always have compunction in himself.'"[16] On another occasion, Poemen witnessed a woman weeping in a graveyard for her dead husband, son, and brother. "This whole woman's life and soul are turned to compunction," he said.[17] These two stories—taken from the borders of the monastic world—contain images for the monk to hold in his consciousness as he considers the meaning and purpose of his own

life, images that can transform the horizon against which he is living and perhaps alter the way he is living. It is a matter, as Abba Matoes noted, of waking
up to the singular urgency of the present moment. Echoing the eschatological
teaching of Jesus in the New Testament, Matoes said: "weep, have compunction, for the time is drawing near."[18] Cultivating an awareness of one's mortality, turning the whole of one's life and soul to compunction, meant coming to
feel the fragility and preciousness of existence, learning to live continuously
against a horizon of ultimacy.

Compunction carried one across a threshold on the far side of which lay a
qualitatively different existence, one marked by freedom and openness. Abba
Poemen, one of the greatest of the monastic elders, said: "Whoever wishes to
be liberated from sins is liberated from them by shedding tears, and whoever
wishes to acquire the virtues acquires them by shedding tears. Tears are the
way which Scripture and our Fathers have handed down to us, saying Weep.
Truly, there is no other way but this."[19] Why is this "the only way?" Why must
one "always weep?" Poemen's saying provides a hint: because tears are a means
by which liberation from sins and the acquisition of virtues can be attained.
This language reflects the particular religious and cultural milieu of ancient
Christian monasticism, in which the ideas of sin and virtue framed the horizon against which the monk lived his life. But sin in this context was understood not primarily in terms of personal moral fault (although it sometimes
had its proximate roots in such an experience), but rather as a fundamental
condition of alienation that was reflected in both personal and communal
reality. The language of sin enabled the monks to grapple with the fractured
reality of their own lives and the life of the community and world within
which they lived; it helped them to see and acknowledge the tear in the fabric
of the whole. So too the language of virtue points to the hope that one could
gradually recover in oneself a sense of wholeness and freedom. Tears played a
central role in this process, helping to open up the soul to an honest and deep
reckoning with who one really is—in relation to everyone and everything—
and in the process lead toward a reknitting of the torn whole.

There is an undeniable dimension of sadness or grief woven into this
experience, for to wake up to one's moral, spiritual fragility (as well as that of
others) means facing, directly and without evasion, the harsh ambiguity of
existence itself, including all that is broken and in need of repair—in oneself
and in the world. Tears signaled a willingness to open oneself to this reality,
to mourn for what had been lost or was in danger of being lost, and to open
oneself to the possibility of renewal, regeneration. In the first instance, this
meant facing oneself. But as the desert monks understood it, this meant not

simply engaging in a momentary examination of one's life, but opening one-self to a sustained process of self-reflection, opening oneself to the possibility of change and renewal, a transformation of one's entire relationship to the world. As Philip Rousseau notes, "*Penthos,* or the experience of sorrow, mani-fested in tears, was not [for the early Christian monks]... an incidental ges-ture, but the symbol of a sustained inner change. The ascetic was not merely ... pricked with compunction, but set upon a path ... a journey that demanded spiritual growth and helped to achieve it."[20] Walking this path required one to scrutinize not only one's behavior, but also the deeper, more mysterious, often-inaccessible roots of motivation and desire. It was these deeper wells of unconscious motivation, the monks recognized, that determined behavior and revealed the extent of one's bondage (which is one of the ways the monks thought about sin). Tears, through the sheer force with which they moved through one's being, became a primary means through which one could be brought to face this bondage and motivated to seek release from it. The pierc-ing recognition of one's helplessness in the face of the debilitating habits of sloth or greed or pride or anger sometimes yielded a sense of release expressed in tears, whose illuminative and healing power no amount of conscious reflec-tion could ever hope to match.

The early Christian monks knew that tears could help break open the soul, kindling a deeper awareness of one's vulnerability and fragility, and one's capacity for intimacy with God and all living beings. But opening oneself in this way required courage, a willingness to face one's own fragility as well as the fragility and brokenness of the world. It meant refusing the temptation to evade the reality of those bonds that connect all beings to each another, and embracing the fact that one exists in a shared world. Weeping, when under-stood as part of a conscious spiritual practice, had the capacity to flood the soul with an awareness of the intricacy, beauty, and spiritual value of all exist-ence. Still, it was possible to ignore or refuse to acknowledge the truth of this reality. But doing so meant relinquishing oneself to a kind of moral and spir-itual blindness, an existence characterized by little possibility for intimacy or reciprocity with others. Hence the need to ask oneself continuously: am I capable of tears? Am I capable of opening myself to the beauty of my own soul, of the souls of others and of the world itself? These questions had tre-mendous significance for the early Christian monks and signaled a level of seriousness about their spiritual practice without which it would have been difficult to conceive of their lives.

And what if tears did not come, if one was not so moved? Was renewal still possible? The monks were not dogmatic about this, and never went so far as to suggest that tears were absolutely necessary for spiritual transformation and renewal. But they recognized how important it was to feel grief in the face of loss and brokenness. The inability to weep was something to be taken very seriously.

It is important to acknowledge that neither this particular spiritual practice nor the sensibility that underlies it can be simply or easily translated across the considerable temporal and cultural distance that separates the monks' world from our own. Still, I believe their insistence on the need for the kind of profound emotional and spiritual honesty embodied in tears can be instructive to us as we grapple with the challenge of what it is to see and feel and respond to the natural world in this moment of ecological destruction. It is worth considering whether something like the practice of *penthos*, the cultivation of tears, can help us rekindle our awareness of the beauty and fragility of our shared life within the natural world, and in the process help us deepen our sense of responsibility and care for the world.

The Inability to Mourn

We grieve only for what we know.[21]

ALDO LEOPOLD

[T]he defense against shame, guilt, and mourning leads
to emotional emptiness in the individual and, in consequence, to psychological and political immobility, to a
lack of ideas and imagination in society.[22]

MARGARETE MITSCHERLICH-NEILSON

Aldo Leopold's *A Sand County Almanac* is notable for its elegiac quality, its clear recognition of, and sadness in the face of, all that is already being lost. In the section entitled "Prairie Birthday," he examines the character of the North American prairie as well as the character of the human regard for the prairie's flora and fauna. He is clearly skeptical about how deep that regard runs. While exploring near his home in Dane County, Wisconsin, a certain graveyard catches his attention, mostly because it contains within it a "pin-point remnant of the native prairie on which the graveyard was established in the 1840's." Of particular interest to Leopold is a plant called the cutleaf Silphium—"spangled with saucer-sized yellow blooms resembling sunflowers"—which he thinks may well be the sole remnant of its kind in the western United States. He noticed the Silphium in bloom on July 24th when he first passed by the graveyard. When he returned on August 3rd, "the fence had been removed by a road crew, and the Silphium cut. It is easy now," Leopold notes, "to predict the future; for a few years my Silphium will try in vain to rise above the mowing machine, and then it will die. With it will die the prairie epoch." This is, suggests Leopold, "one little episode in the funeral of the native flora, which in turn is one episode in the funeral of the floras of the world."

This last phrase signals what for Leopold is clearly the seriousness of this loss. The loss of cutleaf Silphium is but a single instance of a phenomenon occurring with alarming frequency throughout the world. And it raises the question of why it is that such loss can occur with so little sense of grieving on our part. Leopold employs an analogy to get at what he sees as the fundamental moral failure behind our inability to mourn: "The erasure of a human subspecies," he suggests, "is largely painless—to us—if we know little enough about it.... We grieve only for what we know. The erasure of Silphium from western Dane County is no cause for grief if only one knows it only as a name in botany book.... Few grieved when the last buffalo left Wisconsin, and few will grieve when the last Silphium follows him to the lush prairies of the never-never land."[23]

Still, grief is not entirely absent. But the loss that now provokes grief is ultimate, final, irrevocable. This changes the character of grief itself, suggests Leopold. "We grieve," he says, commenting on the extinction of the passenger pigeon "because no living [person] will see again the onrushing phalanx of victorious birds, sweeping a path for spring across the March skies, chasing the defeated winter from all the woods and prairies of Wisconsin...."[24] Grief is born, Leopold suggests here, out of a vision of absence, the opening up in one's conscious awareness of a void where once there was a vast, abundant presence. For Leopold, the particularity of the loss matters. Nothing will or could ever replace these magnificent birds. They are gone forever. And this is at the root of the grief we feel. Yet the acute sense of loss that comes through reflecting on these particular birds also becomes a means of grasping the larger pattern of the fabric within which they once fit. "It is a century now since Darwin gave us the first glimpse of the origin of species. We know now what was unknown to all the preceding caravan of generations: that [we] are only fellow-voyagers with other creatures in the odyssey of evolution. This new knowledge should have given us, by this time, a sense of kinship with fellow-creatures; a wish to live and let live; a sense of wonder over the magnitude and duration of the biotic enterprise."[25] But we have not yet grasped—at least not in a way that matters or changes our behavior—the true significance of this knowledge.

The clearest evidence for this is the void that now exists in the biotic community where those beautiful birds once lived and moved. Nothing remains but a new and strangely empty grief. "For one species to mourn the death of another," Leopold notes, "is a new thing under the sun.... "[26]

To have arrived at a point where such mourning is even possible or necessary is a terrible reminder of the kind of losses we are facing, and the failures that have led us there. Grief surfaces, but is constrained by the very extent of the loss we now face. Perhaps more often though, as in the case of the cut-leaf Silphium or any number of other species that are disappearing from the world, the impulse to grieve never surfaces at all. We fail to grieve because we have no knowledge or feeling for these beings. They do not matter to us. Or, to anticipate part of the argument to come, because we have actively suppressed our feeling for them and especially our feeling about the endless loss and destruction we are currently witnessing, not to mention aiding and abetting. Our inability to mourn is, from this perspective, a telling, damning comment on our impaired moral condition. And it can be linked, directly or indirectly, to the inertia and impotence that afflicts us, as persons and as a society, when we consider the cost of facing the increasing environmental degradation all around us.

An analogous case, initially articulated by Alexander and Margarete Mitscherlich in their classic work *The Inability to Mourn*, can be seen in the German people's response to their experience of and complicity in the events of World War II.[27] I believe this case has tremendous relevance for helping us think through our current impasse with regard to the care and preservation of the natural world. It was precisely the intuition that Germans in the post-war period were afflicted with a nearly pathological inability to grapple with and mourn the loss and destruction they endured and inflicted on others that led the Mitscherlichs to formulate their theory regarding the inability to mourn. The Mitscherlichs define mourning as: "a psychological process in which the individual, by repeated and painful remembering, slowly learns to bear and to work through a loss. The alternative to the sorrow and pain of mourning for a past heavy with loss," they argue, "is a rapid shift to new objects, identifications and ideals. These then replace those that have been given up." This is precisely what happened in Germany in the years following World War II: "The manic effort to undo, the enormous collective effort to rebuild, a kind of national occupational therapy, made permanent denial and repression possible for the majority of Germans." Such denial and repression come at a high cost. There is, the Mitscherlichs argue, a "compulsion to repeat," a resurfacing in persons and society of the very ideals—in this case the ideals of the Nazi state—that have been officially denied but never fully reckoned with. But the Mitscherlichs point to another consequence of this mentality that is perhaps even more troubling: "the defense against shame, guilt, and mourning," they contend, "leads to emotional emptiness in the individual and, in consequence, to psychological and political immobility, to a lack of ideas and imagination in society."[28]

A significant expression of this phenomenon has been catalogued by W. G. Sebald in his book *On the Natural History of Destruction*.[29] Originally published in German as *Luftkrieg und Literatur* (*Air War and Literature*), the title of the English translation derives from the name British journalist Solly Zuckerman proposed for a report he was to write following his time investigating the destruction inflicted by the allied bombing of Cologne. Zuckerman was by all accounts so overwhelmed by the extent of the devastation he witnessed that he never wrote the report. Still, the haunting title remained and later became integral to Sebald's own reflective work on post-war Germany. The natural history of destruction that Sebald wishes to write concerns the vast losses incurred and inflicted by the German people during World War II. But he finds it almost impossible to do so, noting with astonishment the almost total absence from the German literary record of the late war and post-war period of anything approaching an honest, sober account of loss. This is especially true of the German people's own losses during the devastating air raids, during which time six hundred thousand Germans died, three and a half million homes were destroyed and seven and a half million people were left homeless. Given the vast and unprecedented scale of this destruction, it is difficult to fathom how it could have happened, as Sebald argues, that it "left scarcely a trace of pain behind in the collective consciousness." Or, as Alexander Kluge notes: "it never became an experience capable of public decipherment."[30]

The reasons for this erasure are many and complex and it is not my intention to examine all of them here. Still, I believe Sebald's work, in particular his sustained effort to understand how all this pain and loss could have disappeared so completely from public consciousness, is deserving of our serious attention. If we can understand better the dynamics of collective amnesia that afflicted post-war Germany, especially the inability of the German people to face and mourn the tremendous losses they experienced, perhaps we can begin to understand the collective amnesia regarding the destruction of life-forms that seems to be such a central part of our own experience of the natural world.

One of Sebald's most helpful insights, I believe, is his sense of the crucial relationship between the aesthetic and the moral; in other words, how our manner of representing reality both expresses and shapes how we experience it and respond to it. In the case of German literature during the post-war period, Sebald notes that with very few exceptions, writers were either afraid or unwilling to represent the loss and destruction simply and honestly. "There was a tacit agreement," says Sebald, "equally binding on everyone, that the true state of material and moral ruin in which the country found itself was not to be described."[31] It is not difficult to understand why this was so. In the face of horrific destruction and death, Sebald claims, "the need to know was at odds with a desire to close down the senses."[32] He is not unsympathetic to those who struggled with this terrible dilemma. In an essay he wrote attempting to incorporate responses to his initial lectures on this subject, he relates in excruciating detail fragments of recollections that were sent to him by survivors of this destruction, such as the account of a woman who witnessed a train arrive at the Stralsund railway station in the summer of 1943, carrying refugees from the Hamburg firestorm, "most of them still utterly beside themselves, unable to speak of what had happened, struck dumb or sobbing or weeping with despair." Some of them carried suitcases, inside which were their dead children who had suffocated in the smoke or died some other way. Nearly all of these persons subsequently disappeared into obscurity; we will never know what it meant for them to have endured such loss. They could not or would not speak. But Sebald recognizes that "the right to silence claimed by the majority of these people is as inviolable as that of the survivors of Hiroshima...."[33] There is nobility and courage in such silence; sometimes too, it possesses a revelatory quality, a reminder of how much one can never know about the depth of trauma that emerges from the heart of such a catastrophe.[34]

Still, there is another kind of silence that trauma can induce, the silence of evasion and denial. It is this haunting silence in the literature of the post war period that captures Sebald's particular attention. He notes the frequent recourse to clichés to describe the destruction, a habit of thought and speech that has the effect of silencing or obscuring the full weight and horror of what has been lost. The function of such clichés— such as "that fateful night," "all hell was let loose," "we were staring into the inferno"—"is," Sebald suggests, "to cover up and neutralize experiences beyond our ability to comprehend...." They are "no more than ... gesture[s] sketched to banish memory."[35] Such language is but a further expression of the inability to mourn, a clear sign that the serious work of mourning has not yet begun.

The question inevitably arises: what other recourse is open to us—aesthetically, morally, spiritually—if we are to face up to such devastating, overwhelming loss? Sebald himself recognizes the real difficulty in arriving at a meaningful response to this question. Citing examples from the work of those German writers who were courageous enough to "break the taboo on any mention of the inward and outward destruction"—Herman Kasack, Hans Erick Nossack, Heinrich Böll, and Peter de Mendelssohn—he notes that even these writers generally approached the subject "rather equivocally."[36] But there are moments in this literature when an honest, spare account of what has happened shines through the gloom of amnesia that settled over so much of the German populace after the war. In such moments, Sebald notes, we recognize that, "[t]he ideal of truth inherent in its entirely unpretentious objectivity proves itself the only legitimate reason to produce literature in the face of total destruction."[37]

Literature, in this sense, participates in a moral task of witnessing to and even repairing what we have destroyed. But it also reveals our moral condition. Sebald's forceful, uncompromising statement leaves unanswered the question of whether any literature can ever hope to achieve such moral and aesthetic clarity, and whether catastrophic loss of the kind that occurred at the end of World War II or of the kind that we are now witnessing in the natural world, can ever be given adequate literary expression. Can *A Natural History of Destruction* actually be written? Or is it more than language or our sensibilities can bear? However one answers this question, the moral task of pursuing "the ideal of truth inherent in its entirely unpretentious objectivity" remains. It may be that this pursuit is simply part of what is required of us if we are to overcome the habits of apathy and evasion that too often characterize our attitudes toward the losses we experience. However inadequate our descriptions and narratives of loss may be, it is difficult to imagine ever arriving at a place of real moral honesty in our relationship with the natural world without at least making the attempt to give voice to them.

It is in this sense that the analogy between the crisis in postwar Germany as described by Sebald and the Mitscherlichs and our current ecological crisis can be most helpful to us. We too live within a social-political reality in which silence and the rhetoric of evasion have become all too familiar. We deflect responsibility because we cannot or will not acknowledge that the rapidly deepening erosion of the natural world has to do with us. Those voices that do sound the note of urgent concern are often drowned out by other voices that deny the seriousness of ecological degradation and loss or its importance to us. A silence, like the silence of all those increasingly barren habitats, weighs heavily upon us. But if we hope to arrive at a deep and authentic response to this crisis, we will have to find a way to speak honestly about all we are losing and what this loss means to us. This is why the work of mourning is so important.

The Shadow of Grief

Our darkest grief has the bronze color of the moon
eclipsed.[38]

HENRY DAVID THOREAU

When the body lay, dressed and washed, in the coffin on
the table, everyone came to take leave of him and everyone cried. Nikolushka cried from agonizing bewilderment that was rending his heart. The countess and Sonya
cried from pity for Natasha, and from grief that he was
gone. The old count cried because he felt that he too
must soon take this terrible step.
Natasha and Princess Marya wept too now. But they did
not weep for their personal sorrow, they wept from the
emotion and awe that filled their souls before the simple
and solemn mystery of death that had been accomplished
before them.[39]

LEO TOLSTOY

Loss, especially the sudden, wrenching loss of someone beloved, often results in an unexpected and uncontrollable flood of tears. But as Tolstoy's account reminds us, it is often difficult if not impossible to understand our own tears, and how many different feelings lay behind them. Even facing death, we cry for different reasons, or for many reasons altogether. Nor is there any way of knowing how long such tears, once they begin to flow, will last. Common wisdom suggests it is good to be able to feel and express grief and loss, especially in the face of death, but that it is also good not to dwell there too long; a time comes for "moving on," for getting on with one's life. But who knows, really, how true this is, especially given how little control most of us have over the circumstances that bring us face to face with loss and death? Tears seem to move according to their own rhythm and pace. Equally mysterious is the knowledge and awareness that come to us through tears. The crushing weight of loss can overwhelm every attempt to derive meaning from the experience, leaving one dwelling in a mute darkness. But the piercing of the heart induced by loss can also have an unexpectedly sobering effect, lifting one out of complacency and sharpening one's awareness of the fragility and preciousness of one's life, and of life itself. Tears can open the soul to the world.

How does this happen? And why? It is not easy to say. The contemplative monastic literature offers one suggestion, namely that the practice of attending to the *end* of things—whether this is understood to be the end of the monk's own life or the end of all things (the day of judgment)—is so sobering that it could not help but provoke one to see one's existence more clearly and sharply. For the monks this practice was part of a larger process of moral reckoning that was rooted in maintaining a clear focus on one's mortality. "Always keep the day of your death before you," counseled Evagrius, "and you will have no fault in your soul."[40] Consciousness of the end, especially of one's mortality, could help create the conditions for paying more careful attention to every aspect of one's existence, and for living with a greater sense of purpose. Sometimes this sharpened awareness came through tears, piercing the soul with a felt sense of the limits of life, and of the crucial need to pay attention to what was unfolding before one in each moment. Tears helped the monk to see his own existence and the world more clearly and often signaled the beginning of a process of reckoning that could have far-reaching consequences.

Seeing the world through tears. Is perception truly deepened through the emotional-spiritual upheaval that tears reveal? Or do tears obscure one's vision of things? The witness of Leopold, Sebald, the Mitscherlichs, and others suggests that real moral honesty, openness to the shape and texture of one's own life and the life of the world, necessitates a certain emotional vulnerability, a capacity to notice and feel the beauty of things, a capacity to feel their loss. This seems a simple truth: the fragility and impermanence of things heightens our awareness of their value and preciousness. But it is not easy to waken to such awareness. It requires moral effort, a willingness to open oneself to notice and feel the weight of existence. Still, the monks cautioned against the temptation to seek tears, to make the presence or absence of tears too much of an object of one's concern. They understood that if and when tears did come, they should be seen as a gift, given to help deepen one's capacity for seeing, feeling, and responding to the world and the movement's of one's own soul. One finds a similar concern among certain North American poets and writers, for whom the effort to grapple with the experience of grief and loss is intricately bound up with the question of how we can know and love the natural world. In the work of Henry David Thoreau, for example, one finds strong evidence of how his sensitivity to loss and grief contributed to the development of his distinctly contemplative awareness of the natural world. Among contemporary writers, a comparable concern with the spiritual significance of grief can also be discerned, even if the proximate sources of grief involve more extensive and far-reaching loss than they did for Thoreau. At an historical moment when the habit of denying and evading our sense of grief over all that is being lost to us in the natural world seems as strong as ever, it is imperative that we seek out the kinds of cultural and spiritual resources that can help us retrieve our own deepest feeling for the natural world. The importance Thoreau attributed to what he referred to as the "shadow of grief" points toward one such resource. Here, grief and tears are seen as crucial to the work of spiritual renewal through which the soul can be awakened to a more profound awareness of nature's enduring beauty and value.

We have no record of whether Henry David Thoreau shed tears when his beloved brother John died, suddenly and unexpectedly, in January of 1842. But there is little doubt that this event, and his reflection on it for years afterwards, altered forever both his sense of himself and the way he viewed the natural world.[41] It would not be too much to say that his experience of grief and mourning opened up the world to him. Nor was this an isolated event, for not long after his brother John's death, Ralph Waldo Emerson's five-year-old son Waldo, for whom Thoreau had developed a strong affection, died. These two losses were devastating for Thoreau. David Robinson argues that in the aftermath of these terrible losses, Thoreau underwent a form of "symbolic death," losing the self he once was but also discovering, little by little, the resources necessary for undergoing an emotional and intellectual renewal. One of the most significant shifts in Thoreau's thinking at this moment was his insistence that one can find health only in nature and not in society, an idea whose poignancy can be felt with particular force in the aftermath of John's death. He was desperately seeking solace and meaning and began to sense that only nature could provide the kind of healing he needed. Robinson suggests that one way of reading Thoreau's works *A Week on the Concord and Merrimack Rivers* and *Walden* is as chronicles of his recovery. But even before these more mature works appeared, there is evidence that Thoreau was already working out these issues in his 1842 essay, "Natural History of Massachusetts."

This is a pivotal essay, especially if one reads it as reflecting Thoreau's attempt to work out the meaning of his own existence, and the meaning of existence itself, following John's death. It is generally regarded as the first work in which one can sense the emergence of Thoreau's gift for describing nature with luminous precision, a sensibility Thoreau would continue to hone and develop in subsequent works. So too one sees Thoreau expressing forcefully and clearly here his conviction that health is to be found above all in nature. "Unless our feet at least stood in the midst of nature, all our faces would be pale and livid. Society is always diseased, and the best is the most so. There is no scent in it so wholesome as that of the pines, nor any fragrance so penetrating and restorative as the life-everlasting of the high pastures."[42] The very forcefulness of Thoreau's emphatic declarations of nature's health and beauty, Robinson notes, must have required a tremendous effort of will at this moment of his life. What is more, he suggests, it is difficult to avoid the conclusion that they "mask the pain, fear, and despair that he was still fighting off...."[43] Thoreau knew that nature was not only healthy; he had seen disease carry away two of his most beloved life companions. And yet, he could not deny its fundamental vitality. His struggle to reconcile himself to this paradox was neither abstract nor impersonal. When Thoreau declares: "To the sick, indeed, nature is sick, but to the well, a fountain of health,"[44] one senses him working out this difficult paradox in his own emotional life. And even if there is no simple resolution possible, Thoreau, in characteristic fashion, opts for an understanding of life and nature that is fundamentally hopeful: "Surely joy is the condition of life."[45]

Thoreau's struggle to make sense of his own ongoing existence in the aftermath of his brother's death led him to reckon honestly with nature's profound ambiguity. His grief enabled him (perhaps required him) to consider the vitality and beauty of nature with new eyes, even as it brought home to him with new force what Robinson describes as "a deepened sense of life's fragility."[46] From this perspective, his developing quest to chronicle the beauty and vitality of the natural world can be understood as a deeply personal process, inextricably bound up with his own efforts to understand himself and his place in the world. There is nothing remarkable in this, except perhaps the extent to which we are able to see his awakening to the natural world as having been born in grief. Living into this deepening sense of the world's fragile beauty required of Thoreau an ongoing effort—to notice and cherish the world and to understand how his life and the life of the world might be understood in light of the profound loss he had experienced.

The record of this effort can be seen in Thoreau's diverse literary works, in which he undertook the work of chronicling both his evolving understanding of the natural world and his self-understanding. Although one can find traces of Thoreau's preoccupation with grief and loss in all his major works, it is in *A Week on the Concord and Merrimack Rivers*, which he conceived of as a kind of memorial narrative of the 1839 excursion he had taken with his brother John, that one can see him working out these concerns most directly.[47] Nor are Thoreau's concerns about loss in this work only personal. The profoundly elegiac quality of *A Week* seems to touch everything, encompassing Thoreau's still-raw experience of his brother's death, as well as the eclipse of cherished historical and cultural traditions, and the erosion of the natural world, all of which his voyage with his brother revealed to him and which he now weaves together in a single fabric of loss.

One catches a glimpse of how Thoreau's own personal sense of loss continued to haunt him in a passage from the "Friday" chapter, in which he describes a moment toward the end of the journey when he and his brother drifted together down the river. They pass Penichook Brook, then drift under "long rows of alders or groves of pines or oaks," then pass the mouth of the Nashua and after that Salmon Brook. He notes how "the shadows chased one another over wood and meadow, and their alternation harmonized with our mood. We could distinguish the clouds which cast each one, though never so high in the heavens." Then comes a strange and unexpected question: "When a shadow flits across the landscape of the soul, where is the substance?" The meaning of this question is not easy to determine. But it leads Thoreau into a meditation on the meaning of happiness and how it comes to a person and how the "constant abrasion and decay of our lives" affect us. Not only clouds cast shadows, suggests Thoreau. "Every man casts a shadow; not his body only, but his imperfectly mingled spirit. This is his grief." This shadow, he notes, is only visible to us because of the light that shines upon us. The suffusion of this light, he says, is sometimes such that "we are able to enlighten our shaded side." Nevertheless, he acknowledges that the shadow often remains: "[O]ur darkest grief has the bronze color of the moon eclipsed."[48]

One can discern here traces of the shadow cast by Thoreau's enduring grief over his brother's death. One can sense too Thoreau's struggle to find a place for this shadow amidst the landscape of his own soul and in his understanding of the natural world. His affirmations of nature's vitality and beauty, which surface throughout the narrative, continue to reflect the shadows of loss. How to acknowledge the reality of loss, the inevitability of time's passing, while also affirming the continuity and beauty of existence? This question becomes ever more resonant for Thoreau as he expands his reflections to include losses that run deeper and wider than his own personal experience.

Some of the most profound of these losses in the natural world, he notes, are also among the most subtle and delicate:

> Some have thought that the gales do not at present waft to the voyager the natural and original fragrance of the land, such as the early navigators described, and that the loss of many odoriferous native plants, sweet-scented grasses and medicinal herbs, which formerly sweetened the atmosphere, and rendered it salubrious,—by the grazing of cattle and the rooting of swine, is the source of many diseases which now prevail.[49]

The natural world is becoming a diminished place and so is our experience of the world. Thoreau makes no attempt to look away from this diminishment, nor to minimize its importance. Something crucial and irreplaceable is being lost from the world, and for Thoreau being alive and awake meant noticing and reckoning with this loss.

Thoreau's sensitivity to loss became inseparable from his heightened awareness of the fragile beauty of the world and his commitment to naming and describing it. In a sense, this was part of his work of mourning, something that helps to account for the particular poignancy of Thoreau's efforts in *A Week*. "Its dual and sometimes conflicting celebration of both immediate experience and memory," suggests Robinson, "reflects Thoreau's complex sense of the fragility and the miraculous continuance of life. He is alive while John is dead, the victim of a trivial accident. Yet, he and John shared the same experiences in their river trip, experiences which now demand that Thoreau recover and reconstruct them, and that he accept his own continuing life under the terms of a new wakefulness in the world."[50] Seen in this light, Thoreau's descriptions of the natural world in *A Week* (and in his other works as well) take on a heightened significance: they reflect a carefully cultivated practice of attention born at least in part from a deep and lasting grief. Yet it is not expressed *as* grief, but as a joyous affirmation of life.

In a passage from the "Friday" chapter that appears just after Thoreau's reflections on the "darkest grief [with the] bronze color of the moon eclipsed," he comments on the extraordinary sight of autumnal flowers that appeared before John and him as they arrived at Horseshoe Interval in Tyngsborough near the New Hampshire border.

> Asters and golden-rods ... alone expressed all the ripeness of the season, and shed their mellow luster over the fields, as if the now declining

summer's sun had bequeathed its hues to them. It is the floral solstice a little after midsummer, when the particles of golden light, the sundust, have, as it were, fallen like seeds on the earth, and produced these blossoms. On every hillside, and in every valley, stood countless asters, coreopsis, tansies, golden-rods, and the whole race of yellow flowers .... [51]

Descriptions of natural phenomena like this appear throughout *A Week*. Yet, this account, with its exuberant, even ecstatic tone, its proximity to some of Thoreau's most poignant meditations on grief and loss and its presence toward the very end of his account of his journey with his brother John, reverberates with unusual power. As an expression of Thoreau's "new wakefulness in the world," it reflects a sensibility not unlike what Japanese literature refers to as *mono no aware*, "beauty tinged with sadness." The perception of beauty is here bound up with and shaped by an awareness of sadness.

This way of seeing the world became increasingly integrated for Thoreau into a spiritual vision of existence he calls "natural life." But the fact that he describes it as "natural" does not mean it is either easily achieved or widely practiced. Thoreau complains that: "Men nowhere, east or west, live yet a *natural* life, round which the vine clings, and which the elm willingly shadows. Man would desecrate it by his touch, and so the beauty of the world remains veiled to him. He needs not only to be spiritualized, but *naturalized*, on the soil of the earth.... only the convalescent raise the veil of nature." [52] Becoming "naturalized" means allowing our fundamental capacity for perception of the world to be deepened, made sharper, more capacious. It means accepting our fragility and vulnerability, our condition as *convalescents*, perhaps as mourners. This is the only way we can lift the veil and learn to *see* the world.

The hope that we may yet learn to see the world in all its intricate beauty is central to Thoreau's understanding of "natural life." Yet he does not limit himself to hoping simply for a new *vision* of the world; he advocates a restoration of *all* the senses. This is the key to the extraordinary understanding of spiritual renewal that Thoreau articulates toward the end of *A Week*: "We need pray for no higher heaven than the pure senses can furnish, a *purely* sensuous life. Our present senses are but the rudiments of what they are destined to become ... The ears were made, not for such trivial uses as men are wont to suppose, but to hear celestial sounds. The eyes were not made for such groveling uses as they are now put to and worn out by, but to behold beauty now invisible. May we not *see* God?" [53] The audacity of that last question suggests just how far Thoreau wishes to extend his understanding of spiritual renewal. It includes everything. It is a fundamentally hopeful, light-filled vision of existence, one that is all the more poignant for arising out of the dark shadows of grief that long haunted Thoreau. Ultimately Thoreau's capacity to mourn his brother's death and for a diminished world opened him up to the world and helped him love and cherish it.

Memento Mori *and the Work of Mourning*

> This series of events caused horror, anguish and bittern-
> enss throughout the land; the whole nation was plunged
> into mourning and, until the end of time, or at least as
> long as a few of these people survive, they will not cease
> to tell and re-tell… this sad story of a massacre which
> wiped out their entire nobility, beloved and respected by
> them for generations and generations.[54]

BARTOLOMÉ DE LAS CASAS

> Great grief is a divine and terrible radiance which trans-
> figures the wretched.[55]

VICTOR HUGO

Thoreau's deeply personal experience of loss, along with his sustained effort to stand in it, grieve for it, and live a life worthy of it, remain instructive. His sensitivity to his own deepest feelings of sadness and loss—over the loss of his brother as well as over the gradual diminishment of the natural world and the disappearance of the indigenous peoples who had once inhabited the places through which he now moved—became part of his remarkable capacity to see and feel for the world. Mourning opened him to his own experience and to a more profound awareness of the vibrant, still-beautiful world. Still, it is worth noting that walking this path did not come without a cost: facing and reckoning with the presence of loss amidst ongoing life—his own life and the life of the world—required a more-or-less continuous attention to the harsh reality of death. Not a morbid preoccupation with death, but a recognition of its inescapable presence, and of the way awareness of its presence can shape experience and sometime contributes to a greater attention to life.

There are echoes here of the ancient spiritual practice of *memento mori*— always keeping in mind the day of your death—a practice that for the early Christian monks became integral to realizing the kind of sharpened self-awareness that made knowledge of God and a compassionate response to a suffering world possible. Seen in this light, the work of mourning or what the monks called the gift of tears can be understood as part of a profound moral effort to open oneself to existence, to accept responsibility for one's existence, one's place in the world. This sense of responsibility pervades all of Thoreau's work and is reflected not only in his ongoing sense of obligation to live wakefully for the sake of his now-lost brother John, but also in his ever deepening commitment to attend to and devote himself to the fragile, beautiful, increasingly threatened world.

Do we still have the capacity to mourn this deeply—over the fragility of existence or over the diminishment of the natural world that is becoming ever more deeply woven into our experience during this particular historical moment? As we struggle to find language and practices that can help us recover this capacity, it is worth reflecting again on Sebald's pointed question: does our contemporary literary record reflect a serious effort to engage the loss we are experiencing and to accept responsibility for it? Does it express real grief over all that we are losing, a grief strong and deep enough to awaken the soul to a renewed feeling for the natural world? Or does it more generally reflect our inability to mourn and thus reveal our incapacity to formulate a genuine affective response to the loss we are experiencing?

It seems clear that there is nothing like the pervasive silence and evasion that Sebald saw as characteristic of post-war German literature. Still, the sense of mourning that is embedded in our own contemporary literary record is often so dense or oblique that we sometimes miss its deep pathos. Retrieving these voices and acknowledging the significance of this work of mourning can help us to recover the sense of value that the natural world still holds for us. In the present context, this means opening ourselves to grieving for losses that are at once particular, local and personal *and* global. These losses are often, though not always, bound up together in our imaginations, the loss of local places and particular life-forms becoming part of a larger, more encompassing loss, so large that the imagination struggles to take it in or grieve for it. Yet our grief now includes the loss of something that is truly global in character, and possessing an almost unimaginable reach; the more particular losses we experience closer to home cannot, finally, be separated entirely from this more pervasive erosion of life. Increasingly, the work of mourning for a diminished world must take all of this into account, inviting us to name and describe and conceptualize the entire range of losses we experience.

Giving voice to the experience of loss is neither simple nor easy. In part, this is because it has so many faces: it includes and is often focused upon extreme and devastating losses—of species, of wild places, and of human communities, especially poor communities that suffer disproportionately as ecosystems become diminished or destroyed. Within this reality lay other losses, just as profound, but less easy to articulate: the loss of beauty, intimacy, the wild, even loss of the sacred. Reflecting on and describing such loss can, I believe, serve as a starting point for the larger ethical and spiritual project of renewal and healing. But only if the experience of loss can be taken into our consciousness, brought into the center of our moral and spiritual awareness. Harold Searles has argued that we are "hampered in [our] meeting of th[e] environmental crisis by a severe and pervasive apathy which is based largely upon feelings and attitudes of which [we are] unconscious."[56] This observation suggests that the work of ecological renewal will require not only an honest attempt to describe (and imagine) all that is being lost, but also a willingness to grapple with the unconscious forces (especially unconscious fears) that prevent us from acknowledging and responding to the destruction of life forms on the earth.

And so the question arises: can we find a way of expressing the loss we are experiencing in a way that enables us to face our situation, that perhaps helps us to grieve honestly and deeply? If literature is to contribute to this process, as I believe it can and must, it will need to meet the same high standard Sebald articulated as being necessary for post-war German literature: "[t]he ideal of truth inherent in its entirely unpretentious objectivity proves itself the only legitimate reason to produce literature in the face of total destruction." The destruction we face now has a different character than that which Sebald examines in his work, for it includes the unnecessary loss of human life, but also reaches beyond this to include the loss of animal and plant species, the loss of places, and the loss of something as fundamental and elusive as biodiversity. Naming and describing this loss, and acknowledging its impact upon us, may well be one of the most important spiritual practices we can engage in at this moment.

The work of mourning begins close to home, close to the ground. We do not mourn loss in general, but rather experiences of particular loss. It is in part because of this that we need accounts of loss that are firmly embedded in personal experience, in specific landscapes. But because of the scale of the loss we are currently experiencing, and because the loss is so fundamental and runs so deep, we need to discover language that can encompass the whole of this reality and in so doing make present to us the preciousness of what we are losing. It may be that by this means we may learn to weep for what has been lost to us, weep, and repent and begin to make reparation.

Turtle Island: this is one of the names indigenous peoples have traditionally given to the place known to us as North America. The term refers to no political entity, but it remains important as a way of imagining and gaining access to the original landscape, peoples, and cultural traditions of this place.

Also, as Gary Snyder notes, it is a name that can help us, "see ourselves more accurately on this continent of watersheds and life-communities—plant zones, physiographic provinces, culture areas; following natural boundaries."[57] This is an invitation to a different kind of moral relationship with the place we inhabit, one rooted less in habits of acquisition and ownership and more in a disposition of openness and reciprocity. Yet, part of learning to see ourselves accurately means attending carefully to those moments of our shared history in this place marked by carelessness and greed, when the destruction of peoples and places became chronic. And if mourning includes making reparation, there is a particular obligation to attend to the history of the destruction and displacement of indigenous peoples.

Nowhere in the literary record of the Americas is there a harsher and more honest account of the injuries inflicted on the peoples and land of this continent than in Bartolomeo de las Casas's *A Short Account of the Destruction of the Indies*, otherwise known as *The Tears of the Indians: Being an historical and true account of the cruel massacres and slaughters of above twenty millions of innocent people; committed by the Spaniards*, published in 1552. The title alone suggests the kind of story it has to tell. And in spite of the author's avowed attention to remain silent regarding the most vicious and brutal incidents, the work remains a horrifying catalogue of violence committed by the Spanish against the indigenous peoples of the Americas. In Hispaniola, las Casas relates, "I saw with my own eyes how the Spaniards burned countless local inhabitants alive or hacked them to pieces, or devised novel ways of torturing them to death, enslaving those they took alive. Indeed, they invented so many new methods of murder that it would be quite impossible to set them all down on paper and, however hard one tried to chronicle them, one could probably never list a thousandth part of what actually took place."[58] Nor was the destruction limited to the inhabitants of the region; the places were also left devastated. In Venezuela, he recounts how a group of German merchants, under the authority of the Spaniards, were responsible for "devastating over four hundred leagues of the most fertile and blessed land on earth and for killing all the people or driving them out of great provinces that once struck awe in the beholder: valleys forty leagues in extent, whole regions as delightful as one could desire...."[59] Las Casas's account of the devastation of the Americas by the Spanish is almost impossible for the imagination to absorb, so extreme and encompassing is the brutality and violence of the stories it tells.[60] Yet, in its stark, simple description of the atrocities committed by Europeans in their encounters with the peoples of the Americas, it remains one of our most important and early witnesses to a pattern of destruction that was to be repeated continuously in the new world. It demands that we consider the slaughter of indigenous peoples and the devastation of the landscape as bound together in the story of this place and to consider especially the moral implications of this story for us.

"The Tears of the Indians," the haunting title Las Casas gave to his work, provides a hint at the depth of the loss he recounts. But, ironically, we have relatively little access to these tears; the Indians described in his account are usually dispatched by their attackers so rapidly and with so little regard for their humanity that they disappear mostly in silence. Still, the terrible grief— of the victims themselves and of the writer who tells their story—is palpable on almost every page. One wonders: can "the tears of the Indians," buried deep within this catastrophic genocide, still reach us? Can they teach us anything? Can they become part of our own grief—for the destruction and loss recounted in Las Casas's work, and for the destruction and loss that has become so deeply woven into our own experience on this continent?

One response to this question, both pointed and eloquent, can be found in Barry Lopez's important essay, *The Rediscovery of North America*.[61] Published on the five hundredth anniversary of Columbus's arrival in the Americas, Lopez reflects on Las Casas's awful account and wonders what, if anything, we can still take from it. One thing that emerges is a renewed sense of the extent of what we have lost: "whole communities of people, plants, and animals ... languages, epistemologies, books, ceremonies, systems of logic and metaphysics—a long, hideous carnage."[62] But there is even more. We have also lost, to a very great degree anyway, our capacity to see and feel the world, to experience it not simply as a resource to be exploited but as a gift to be wondered at and cherished. The habits of violence, acquisition, and exploitation revealed with such bald honesty by Las Casas continue to shape our way of being in the world. "How then," wonders Lopez, "do we come to know the land, to discover what more may be there than merchantable timber, grazeable prairies, recoverable ores, dammable water, netable fish?" To pose such a question is part of the work that Lopez describes as seeing ourselves more accurately on this continent. Nor it would seem is it a question that one can address except through tears.

The early Christian monks spoke of being "pierced" to the depth of their souls, and of tears flowing in a moment of sudden recognition of an aspect of their own moral-spiritual life that was in need of healing or renewal. The tears themselves became the means of that healing, the medium through which a clearer, more honest awareness of oneself, the world and God became possible. The potential for something like this kind of moral-spiritual awakening, it seems, is present in Lopez' question. To consider "what more may be there" is as much a question about our own capacity to take in and respond to the world as it is about the world itself. This capacity may indeed have gone dormant, or diminished to the point where it seems lost to us completely. Asking how and why this has happened is to be brought face to face with a gap in the soul almost too painful to acknowledge; for it reveals our own culpability, our own neglect of responsibility for and consideration of the world, our complicity in its devastation. Still, such an examination of conscience can also lead to a moment of recognition that changes everything, a moment when one begins "looking at the land not as its possessor but as a companion." Such a shift of perception cannot be brought about by sheer force of will or determination. It is more like a wild seed that takes root in the ground and grows, little by little, until one realizes that it is no longer possible to see in the old way. Still, it is important to notice it, open oneself to it. This is what it means, Lopez suggests, to "cultivate intimacy." Naming, remembering, and weeping over what has been lost, and our own part in this loss, is part of this work. But so is learning to pay attention, allowing ourselves to wake up to the world: "We would have to memorize and remember the land, walk it, eat from its soils, and from the animals that ate its plants. We would have to know its winds, inhale its airs, observe the sequence of its flowers in the spring and the range of its birds." This is a simple, but demanding practice, for it entails a complete reconfiguring of our moral, spiritual ecology: "To be intimate with the land like this is to enclose it in the same moral universe we occupy, to include it in the meaning of community."[63]

The question of how to articulate such a vision of community and how to help bring it into being has come to occupy a central place in the contemporary literary imagination. This question cannot be separated from what it means to reckon with loss and our own culpability for this loss, with the need for tears. The reflections of Henry David Thoreau and Aldo Leopold stand as important reminders within the North American literary tradition of the importance of grief for deepening and expanding the moral imagination. But the concern to reimagine what it is to mourn for a broken world extends far beyond the work of these exemplary figures; indeed there is a growing chorus of writers exploring this crucial question.[64] And while the meanings of loss and grief in these works are as distinctive as the works themselves, the concern to identify the contours of this experience and to understand how it might help us deepen our feeling for the natural world belongs to a shared sensibility that has become an indispensable part of our contemporary spiritual struggle.

A striking example of how contemporary literature gives voice to the power of grief and how it can contribute to a significant moral and spiritual renewal is Richard Nelson's lyric account of the uninhabited (and unnamed) island near his home in Alaska, *The Island Within*. This work is noteworthy not only for its probing description of his growing intimacy with the natural world, but also for its honest evocation of accumulating losses that are also part of his experience of this place. Parts of the island are wounded, the legacy of years of clear-cutting, and he struggles to find language for the degraded landscape and for the feelings of grief, separation, and loss. He describes stumbling upon:

> A sudden, shorn edge where the trees and moss end, and where the dark, dour sky slumps down against a barren hillside strewn with slash and decay... [t]he road angles into a wasteland of hoary trunks and twisted wooden shards, pitched together in convulsed disarray, with knots of shoulder-high brush pressing in along both sides. Fans of mud and ash splay across the roadway beneath rilled cutbanks. In one place, the lower side has slumped away and left ten feet of culvert hanging in midair, spewing brown water over the naked bank and into a runnel thirty feet below.

He begins traversing the "field" ahead of him, but soon realizes that moving across a clear-cut is unlike anything he has ever tried before. "The ground is covered with a nearly impenetrable confusion of branches, roots, sticks, limbs, stumps, blocks, poles, and trunks, in every possible size, all gray and fibrous and rotting, thrown together in a chaotic mass and interwoven with a tangle of brittle bushes." It is, he says, a "whole forest of stumps," an "enormous graveyard, covered with weathered markers made from the remains of its own dead."[65]

This place, once filled with the music of winter wrens, is now almost completely silent. It has become a dead zone, and Nelson confesses feeling afflicted by a deep "sadness for what is lost...." It is an inescapable and painful part of his experience of this place. And sadness sometimes becomes mixed with anger and resentment toward those who have treated the island with such callous disregard. Still, he is careful not to demonize the loggers or to separate himself too completely from them and their motives and longings. Climbing up onto a huge stump to look out across the huge empty valley, he counts the rings and discovers it was 423 years old when it was felled. He pauses to dream his way back to the tree's beginnings and growth, to that moment when the seed fell to the ground, to its steady growth across four centuries to a height of some one hundred fifty feet and a weight of several dozen tons, to the moment a man approached it with a chainsaw in his hand. "I would like to believe he gave some consideration to the tree itself, to its death and his responsibilities toward it, as he pulled the cord that set the chainsaw blaring."[66] But whether or not any such consideration was ever shown to the tree, Nelson remains convinced that "a profound transgression was committed here." Who is responsible? Nelson does not excuse himself; instead, he grapples with his own complicity in the tree's and the entire valley's destruction. "Whatever judgment I make against those who cut it down I must also make against myself. I belong to the same nation, speak the same language, vote in the same elections, share many of the same values, avail myself of the same technology, and owe much of my existence to the same vast system of global exchange."[67] No one is innocent. But it is possible, he argues, to "strive towards a different kind of conscience, listen to an older and more tested wisdom" and learn to live with attention and care. But learning to do so will mean committing oneself, as Nelson does here, to the work of bearing witness to all that has been lost, naming and describing the precise character of that loss, and opening oneself to feel the loss as one's own. The practices of *penthos* and *memento mori* may need to be reimagined, as they are here, to include not only a consciousness of one's fragility and mortality, but also that of all living beings.

Can such a spiritual practice have any meaningful effect on the way we live in the world? It can if it helps open up a space in the imagination to feel the luminous presence of other beings. It is here that a genuine vision of renewal can be born. Nelson imagines this degraded landscape, left alone for a few centuries, gradually returning to life. "The whole community of dispossessed animals would return: red squirrel, marten, great horned owl, hairy woodpecker, golden-crowned kinglet, pin siskin, blue grouse, and the seed-shedding crossbills. In streams cleared of sediment by moss-filtered runoff, swarms of salmon would spawn once more, hunted by brown bears who emerged from the cool woods."[68] If we are to participate in and contribute to creating the conditions for such a return, even if this means leaving a place long enough so that it can recover, some kind of vision for renewal will need to underlie our efforts. And the vision will itself need to be supported by a deeply felt sense of belonging and relationship. This, finally, is what the work of mourning can contribute to ecological renewal: the creation of a moral-spiritual space that enables us to experience ourselves as part of a larger, more encompassing world.

Tears, the Criterion of Truth

In the world of feeling, tears are the criterion of truth.[69]

E. M. CIORAN

"We only grieve for what we know." Aldo Leopold's haunting observation can now be seen as even more far reaching in its implications than it first appears. This is especially true if one considers the profound moral significance implied in what it means to *know*. To know must include not only an acknowledgement of the deep and binding claim that the familiar and the dear have upon our moral imaginations, which is at least part of what Leopold means when he wonders why we grieve so little for what we are losing. It must also include a recognition of how pervasive is our habit of *evading knowing*, of refusing to see and take responsibility for our complicity in the destruction of the world. Our inability to mourn, seen from this perspective, is an expression—one of the most telling—of the profound moral emptiness that afflicts us.

Is our current situation really analogous to that of so many of the German people after World War II? One must acknowledge important differences: the full weight of the emerging ecological catastrophe has not yet settled itself upon us. We have not yet experienced the ecological version of the fire-storms that raged through Hamburg. Or perhaps it would be more accurate to say: the ecological destruction that we have already witnessed and experienced—much of it serious and alarming—has only recently come to be seen and understood as part of an emerging catastrophe. And certainly not universally. We continue to deflect responsibility because we cannot or will not acknowledge that it has to do with us. In this sense, we share in the same moral blindness that afflicted those whom Sebald and the Mitchelichs describe in their work. How else are we to understand the steady drum-beat of denials regarding the reality of global climate change that have characterized so much public political discourse in recent years? Or the seemingly endless cases of short-sighted, economically expedient decisions that have resulted in the sacrifice of sensitive and irreplaceable habitats? Such cases do not need much elaboration; they are already far too familiar to us. But what we do need to consider more deeply is the character of our response. In particular, especially in light of Sebald's challenge regarding the need to deepen the relationship between the aesthetic and the moral, how well do our literary traditions express the reality of loss we are facing and the need for mourning in the face of that loss?

Are we developing our own moral-spiritual vocabulary for dealing honestly with all we are losing?

One can point to any number of contemporary literary expressions that suggest that we are at least beginning to open ourselves to the work of mourning for all that is being lost to us. The emergence of such works reveal a growing concern with the moral-spiritual question of what it means to face up to and grieve—honestly and deeply—the accumulating losses in the natural world and cultivate a more open sense of relationship with and responsibility for the world in light of that grief. They can be seen as contributing in important ways to what Clifton Spargo calls an "ethics of mourning," in a way that reorients our understanding of mourning away from the question of the survivor's struggle for consolation and toward a more encompassing sense of the dialogical relationship between the living and the dead.[70]

Still, as Judith Butler notes in her book, *Precarious Life: The Powers of Mourning and Violence*, we are only at the initial stages of articulating a politics and ethics of mourning that can sustain our work in an ecologically fractured world. While her concerns are not explicitly ecological, her attention to the embodied, political character of authentic mourning provides a way forward to imagine mourning in an ecological context more richly than we have done thus far. "[E]ach of us," she notes, "is constituted politically in part by virtue of the social vulnerability of our bodies.... Loss and vulnerability seem to follow from our being socially constituted bodies, attached to others, at risk of losing those attachments, exposed to others, at risk of violence by virtue of that exposure."[71] This way of understanding the common ground of loss and vulnerability—and the shared mourning that emerges from it— perhaps makes the most sense in the context of the precariousness we share as human beings in the face of threats like the AIDS epidemic, genocide, global poverty, war, and terror. But it is not such a great leap from this insight to the recognition of a shared vulnerability rooted in our being *ecologically* constituted bodies. Nor is it difficult to imagine a shared commitment to mourning arising out of our common experience of ecological loss.

This is one of the great virtues of Elizabeth Kolbert's work, *Field Notes from a Catastrophe*.[72] In it, she simply, clearly, and courageously attends to the most basic facts of the already-unfolding catastrophe of global warming, describing them with what Sebald might call an "entirely unpretentious objectivity," so that we might begin to take into ourselves the full extent of the losses accumulating all around us. Here is one example of what it means to meditate long and hard on who we are as *ecologically* constituted bodies, bodies exposed and at risk to the violence emerging from *within* the world itself. The enormity of this threat has the potential to overwhelm any authentic impulse to mourn, much as Sebald and the Mitscherlichs observed in the case of the German people stunned into silence by the violence they had perpetrated and undergone. But we have seen in our own time the corrosive effect of suppressing mourning, artificially and prematurely, such as we witnessed in the post September 11th world, when barely ten days after the attack then-President Bush announced that we had finished grieving and now needed resolute action to take the place of grief.

We do need resolute action. But it is difficult to imagine how such action will bear real fruit—and avoid the "compulsion to repeat"—if it is not rooted in an authentic expression of mourning for our threatened world. The consequences of not-mourning—or pretending there is no need to mourn except briefly or briskly, or acting as though mourning is defeatist or a waste of time— are clear. We will continue to deny the full reality of the loss we are facing and we will be left utterly unable to respond to the challenge before us. Shierry Weber Nicholsen has observed that "loss not fully faced and mourned can lead one to fall under the spell of numbness and cruelty. It can lead to guilt and the wish to blot out the future … the consequences of a failure to mourn on the scale of the whole community are repression, apathy, deadness, and lethargy."[73]

This is one possible path open to us. But it is not the only one. A story told about one of the early Christian monks, Abba Arsenius, relates that "he had a hollow in his chest channeled out by the tears which fell from his eyes all his life while he sat at his manual work."[74] Here is a strange, even bewildering, image of a life given over to mourning. One senses that the monk's own body has become a site scarred by tears for a broken, fallen world—a kind of landscape, not destroyed by running water, but eroded and fashioned into a holy object.

In the ancient monastic tradition, the gift of tears was seen as crucial to healing the self and the world. Can such a spiritual practice have meaning for us in an age of ecological degradation, as we struggle to come to terms with losses so deep and extensive that we can barely acknowledge them, much less absorb them into our conscious lives or act in response to them? It seems to me that it can have meaning, especially if it helps reawaken us to our capacity to face and name and mourn all that is being lost, and restore us to a more honest and open knowledge of the living world. "In the world of feeling," suggests E.M. Cioran, "tears are the criterion of truth."[75] Real and sustainable ecological restoration may well depend on our rediscovery of this truth.

4

Topos: *At Home, Always a Stranger*

Where are we really going? Always home.[1]

NOVALIS

All the days of your life keep the frame of mind of the
stranger....[2]

ABBA AGATHON

SITTING NEAR THE threshold of his monastic cell in the Wadi Natrun, I listened as Fr. Wadid talked about what it meant for him to live the monastic life
in Egypt today. "The center of our life," he said, "is the practice of the Gospel.
This was true of primitive Christian monasticism and it is still what we aspire
to today. Monasticism at its deepest level is a lived response to the Gospel—a
Gospel life." He paused for a moment, letting the silence gather before proceeding. I paused too, trying to take in the meaning of what he had just said.
The idea itself was simple enough. I had encountered it often in my reading of
the literature of early Christian monasticism. "Whatever you do, do it according to the testimony of the Holy Scriptures," said Abba Antony, expressing
simply and directly a bedrock principle of the ancient monks. Still, sitting in
the open desert listening to Fr. Wadid express his own sense of this principle,
I found myself struck, for the first time really, by the *power* of this idea. Also
unnerved. Suddenly, I found myself in the grip of questions that until that
moment had only existed as half-formed ideas in my mind. What exactly did
it mean to live a gospel life? More to the point, how was one to do it? What
did it mean, personally and existentially, to attempt to fulfill the injunction
to live one's life according to the testimony of the scriptures? I wondered also
whether this monastic cell, hidden away in the Egyptian desert, and the life
of the monk living here might hold some clue about the possible realization
of this ideal?

For the next two hours we pursued these and other related questions in
a conversation that seemed only to gain in energy and momentum as we

proceeded. We paused from time to time to sip our tea or to drift for a moment within the immense silence of the surrounding desert. Then we would begin again, probing the questions before us. Haunting the edges of our conversation was the image of Antony standing at the threshold of a new life, suddenly being confronted by the words of the Gospel: "If you would be perfect, go, sell what you possess and give it to the poor, and you will have treasure in heaven" (Mt 19:21). That he responded as he did, leaving everything behind and embarking upon a long, harrowing struggle in the desert, remains one of the strangest and most compelling moments of the early Christian monastic story. There is no way of knowing, even now, all that lay behind that gesture and why Antony responded to this Gospel text in the way that he did. But one important part of his response seems to have been the impulse to cut through all the extraneous elements of his life for the sake of what the contemplative tradition described as "the one thing necessary." This impulse shaped the early monastic experience profoundly and continues to shape the Christian contemplative tradition today. In some senses, it is the only question that matters: how to strip away everything, how to open oneself without condition or hesitation to the infinite?

In response to this question, the monks sometimes embarked upon a path into the vast, unknown space of the "great desert." Or, in what seems like a very different kind of gesture, they sometimes spent their entire lives inhabiting the tiny space of a cell. "Sit in your cell and your cell will teach you everything," exhorted Abba Moses, in an eloquent evocation of the early monks' confidence in the power of long and deep commitment to place to form and shape one's consciousness.[3] But there was also recurring attention among the monks to the importance of being free from undue attachments to any place, free to move. "Blessed are they who go away for God's sake, having no other care," said Abba Agathon. "All the days of your life keep the frame of mind of the stranger..." he noted elsewhere.[4] Staying put and venturing forth. The wisdom that comes from living deeply into a place; and the kind of knowledge that can only be acquired by leaving one's place, and risking the unknown. The early Christian monks understood both of these "ways" or "paths" as potentially fruitful responses to the call to relinquish everything for the sake of the Gospel. Nor did they see them as contradictory to one other. Both were part of the unfolding character of their lives. But what did it mean in practice to give oneself over to "the work of the cell," or to "go away for God's sake?" What kind of life was this? Could I live it? Did I want to do so?

As my conversation with Fr. Wadid unfolded, I found myself turning these questions over in my mind. I wondered about why I myself had "gone away?"

And why had I come to this particular place? As I looked around at the tiny monastic cell where we now sat drinking tea and talking, I found myself moved by its eloquence and realized the place itself and all it represented had much to do with why I was here. It was a poor and simple dwelling, located perhaps a mile away from the Monastery of St. Macarius in the Wadi Natrun. Built like a make-shift bunker into the side of the hill, its rusting, corrugated steel roof sagged under the weight of sand deposited there by shifting winds. Fr. Wadid's few possessions—a couple of books, a small stove, and a pot for making tea, some blankets—were just visible through the low door. There was nothing superfluous here, only what was necessary to support him in the work to which he had given himself, the work of the cell. I was abashed by the humble character of the place and moved by the simple honesty of his life here. And I realized that the witness of his life in this place, so filled with integrity and purpose, might help me to understand something of what I had come here to discover: what it meant to "practice the gospel."

It was only later that I began to understand the significance of this experience at St. Macarius, and of this particular understanding of gospel living, for helping me address the question of what it means to cultivate a sense of place as part of a sustained contemplative practice. This had never really been a question for me. But I had begun to realize that I had no language or practice adequate for helping me integrating my so-called "interior experience" with my experience of the physical world. I had always read the early monastic literature primarily as a drama of the interior landscape. That was where my own interest lay and that is what I had always sought from the stories of the ancient Christian monks—guidance through the landscape of the soul. Indeed, I had given hardly any thought at all to the actual locus of their lives. Or to the locus of my life for that matter. But I had grown hungry for the palpable and was beginning to feel the need to ground my own religious experience in place, to let its particular texture inform and shape my soul. Also, I had begun to perceive a deeper and wider sense of alienation from place and from the natural world growing all around me. It was this, I think, that led me to notice something in ancient Christian monastic works that I had not seen before: the particular way of monks had of locating themselves in the world and the significance of the language of place and movement in their articulation of what it meant to live the contemplative life. I began to wonder whether this ancient monastic tradition might be able to contribute something to our own efforts to reclaim place as part of a sustained contemplative practice.

Can this ancient contemplative way of being in place contribute anything meaningful to the question of how to live in the highly mobile, technologized, and urban world increasing numbers of human beings inhabit today? It feels on the face of it impossibly anachronistic and ill-suited to helping us negotiate the challenge of rethinking our own ambiguous and conflicted relationships with place. Nowhere is this ambiguity more in evidence than in the sense of chronic placelessness that has come to characterize so much of our own contemporary experience of the world. Pervasive patterns of economic and political instability have forced growing numbers of human beings into a condition of perpetual homelessness or exile. The deepening degradation of the natural world is also contributing to this reality, with once-thriving places becoming so ecologically, socially, and culturally impoverished that they remain barely inhabitable. Increasingly, the sense of belonging to and feeling knit into the fabric of a place is becoming lost to us. And with it is arising a growing awareness of a deep alienation that can perhaps only be adequately described as a kind of "soul loss."

Amidst this deepening sense of displacement and homelessness, we are witnessing a newfound urgency to discover language and practices that can help us *situate* ourselves more carefully and thoughtfully within the world, to recover the art of what some have called "place-making," the imaginative work of beholding, inhabiting, and cherishing the particular places where we live. The ancient Christian monks cultivated their own distinctive approach to place-making, while also maintaining a clear awareness of themselves as exiles, as persons without a place. In an age when both displacement and the hunger for place are becoming ever more significant elements of our experience, I want to consider how this contemplative tradition of place-making might contribute to the kind of spiritual renewal that can help us cultivate a capacity for tending to an increasingly fragile world.

Exile as Soul Loss

Isn't [this] the age of the expatriate, the refugee, the stateless—and the wanderer?[5]

ELIE WIESEL

[E]veryone can…testify to another, less reckonable kind of homesickness, one having to do with unsettlements that cannot be located in spaces of geography or history…losses too private and reprehensible to be acknowledged to oneself, let alone to others."[6]

JOSEPH O'NEILL

It was many years ago that I first encountered Masaccio's great fresco *The Expulsion from Paradise* in the Brancacci chapel of the church of Santa Maria del Carmine in Florence. I had seen the image once in an art history class in college. But nothing could have prepared me for the force of the image as I stood gazing up at those two figures on the wall of that dimly lit chapel—Eve's head thrown back, her face a mask of agony, her hands covering her body in shame; Adam's hands drawn up over his eyes in a moment of sudden, convulsive grief. Behind them: the gate to paradise, from which they have been forever banished. I felt a visceral aversion to the image. I did not really want to open myself to its potent evocation of loss. I did not want to feel it so deeply. But I recognized it. I remembered the words of the *Salve Regina*, the ancient hymn that Cistercian monks have sung at Compline since the middle ages: "poor banished children of Eve, mourning and weeping in this valley of tears." Also that haunting observation of St. Augustine's toward the beginning of his *Confessions*: "Our hearts are restless until they rest in you, O God." That cry from the heart reveals what for Augustine is the true character of the soul's predicament: we have become exiled from our true home in God and will be forever restless until we find our way back. His own autobiographical account of loss, and of longing for restoration, sits nested within that quintessential account of loss and homecoming in the New Testament, the story of the prodigal son (Lk 15). Augustine evokes the pathos of the son's predicament deeply and sees his self-generated exile as a fundamental metaphor for our common condition: lost and alone and bereft. It is, for Augustine, the condition of every soul.

These questions about displacement and our hunger for home, which have long had strong purchase on the Christian religious imagination, continue to haunt us. But as the harsh realities of displacement, homelessness, and exile become ever more pervasive and chronic, the meaning of these questions and the possible responses we give to them are continuing to shift and deepen. We find ourselves reconsidering the fundamental character of our placelessness and our longing for place. Is it best understood, as it often has been understood in traditions of spiritual practice, primarily as a metaphysical or spiritual predicament, rooted in the unchanging realities of impermanence and mortality? And if so, is it possible to avoid the kind of detachment from the material character of existence that leads to a neglect or even a denigration of the physical world? A sharp distinction between the material and spiritual, this world and the world to come (or the world within) may well seem too simple; but it is a distinction that has had a profound effect not only on Christian thought and practice but on many other spiritual traditions as well.

Coming to an awareness of homelessness as a fundamental condition of existence, a reflection of personal and spiritual alienation too deep ever to be fully accounted for or resolved, is for many spiritual traditions at the very heart of the process of awakening that leads to genuine spiritual maturity. Still, we are more sensitive than we once were to the danger of thinking about this question in purely metaphorical or interior terms. Whatever the spiritual meaning of homelessness may be, it seems increasingly clear that it cannot be separated entirely from the precarious and fragile character of our material existence. Indeed, much of its meaning is to be found there. So it is also with the hunger for home. The dream of homecoming owes much to the longing for a place of stable and encompassing security. That this dream can never be fully realized amidst the impermanence of actual existence has often meant projecting it into another world—either beyond or within. But should this necessary reckoning with the fact of impermanence mean, as it so often has meant, sacrificing all hope of making a home in this world? Or is it possible to reconceive the very idea of homelessness and the desire for a spiritual home, so that they include the concrete and particular character of the actual world, and the possibility of learning to live with a deep and abiding affection for the world?

It has been over fifty years since Simone Weil, in the midst one of the most severe crises of displacement of the twentieth century, reflected on these questions in her book *The Need for Roots*. "To be rooted," she famously claimed, "is perhaps the most important and least recognized need of the human soul."[7] Tanks and troops were rolling across Europe leaving in their wake devastated landscapes and communities, and an enormous number of persons dead or made homeless. Rebuilding Europe, Weil was convinced, would require an honest reckoning with our chronic rootlessness, and a complete rethinking of what it means for human beings to belong to a place and take responsibility for it. In the half-century since Weil made her pointed observations, this question has only become more urgent. Elie Wiesel, who was himself uprooted and made an orphan by the events of World War II, looked back on the experience of the past century, and asked: "Isn't [this] the age of the expatriate, the refugee, the stateless—and the wanderer?"[8] Nor has the dawn of the twenty-first century seen any significant relief. Along with the ever-growing numbers of displaced persons, the destruction and disappearance of natural places is now contributing a new dimension to the sense of displacement; as we reach ever further into the wilderness, marshalling its "resources" for our use, it becomes more and more difficult to imagine the living world as home. Many of the basic patterns of so-called contemporary life are further eroding the loss of a sense of place. We spend increasing amounts of our time in what Marc Augé calls "non-places"—in supermarkets, airports, and hotels, on highways or in front of TVs, computers, and ATM machines.[9] Gradually, the sense of what it means to dwell within a particular place and community, to become intimate with the landscape, to enter into and be shaped by the stories and the culture of the place is becoming attenuated. We are losing our sense of place. It is not easy to calculate the costs of such loss, or its effects on our sense of well-being, on our sense of involvement in and commitment to the places we call home, on our sense of the sacred or on the world itself. But, as an ever-growing body of evidence suggests, the costs are immense.

The condition that Peter Berger described over thirty years ago as a kind of "metaphysical homelessness" seems to have become in our own time even more pervasive. Berger associated this condition with the effects of secularization and the increasing pluralization—especially as manifested in the multiple, shifting, and often-conflicting places that persons and communities must constantly negotiate—that has come to define postmodern society: "The secularizing effect of pluralization has gone hand in hand with other secularizing forces in modern society. The final consequence of all this can be put very simply (though the simplicity is deceptive): modern man [sic] has suffered from a deepening condition of 'homelessness.' The correlate of the migratory character of his experience of society and of self has been what might be called a metaphysical loss of 'home.' It goes without saying that this condition is psychologically hard to bear."[10]

We are beginning to reach a clearer understanding, thanks to the careful work of cultural geographers and anthropologists, of the particular character of this homelessness and of the serious, if also often ambiguous, effects of chronic movement and uprootedness on both human communities and places.[11] We are also beginning to understand more clearly than we once did how deeply social well-being can be eroded by a loss of rootedness in place.[12] Nor can we any longer ignore the often-contested character of places, and the way the hunger for a home is often realized or thwarted by the way local and global power relations unfold.[13] Commenting on this trend, Steven Feld and Keith Basso note: "Whatever else may be involved, this development surely reflects the now acute world conditions of exile, displacement, diasporas, and inflamed borders, to say nothing of the increasingly tumultuous struggles by indigenous peoples and cultural minorities for ancestral homelands, land rights, and retention of sacred places."[14] In light of this, we are learning more and more to frame our understanding of place in dynamic, cultural and political terms that take seriously the notion of places as contested sites.[15] And we are coming to see with new clarity the significance of place and the loss of place among historically displaced peoples, in particular what it means to experience loss of place as a kind of "soul loss."[16]

A heartbreaking contemporary example of this phenomenon can be seen in the experience of the Hmong people's displacement from their home in the highlands of northwest Laos after the Vietnam war and their fitful attempts to make a place for themselves in the United States. Upwards of 150,000 members of the Hmong community were forced by persecution—because they had cooperated with U.S. forces in Vietnam and Laos—to flee their homeland, many of them ending up in the Central Valley of California. In Anne Fadiman's moving account of their experience, *The Spirit Catches You and You Fall Down*, it becomes clear that for the Hmong loss of place was almost always also an experience of what they called "soul loss." Often "soul loss" manifested itself as physical illness, a sickness of the soul that pervaded every aspect of a person's life. This was baffling to most of the North American physicians who were asked to care for the Hmong in California. For them, what the Hmong considered the most significant underlying causes of their diseases simply did not exist; these were not diagnosable using the categories of Western medicine. But for the Hmong, the underlying causes, which they understood to be spiritual in nature, were at the root of everything. Consider for example one of the most commonly reported diseases among the Hmong in North America, *Nyab Siab*, or "difficult liver." The causes were believed to include: loss of family, status, home, country or any important item that has a high emotional value. The symptoms? Excessive worry; crying; confusion; disjointed speech; loss of sleep and appetite; delusions.

Bill Selvidge, a North American physician who worked with the Hmong in Central California, describes the first Hmong patient he had ever seen as suffering from what seemed to him to be a broken heart. In Hmong terminology, he would have been diagnosed as having a difficult liver. He relates his impression this way: "Mr. Thao was a man in his fifties. He told me through an interpreter that he had a bad back, but after I listened for a while I realized that he's really come in because of depression. It turned out he was an agoraphobe. He was afraid to leave his house because he thought if he walked more than a couple of blocks he'd get lost and never find his way back home again. What a metaphor! He'd seen his entire immediate family die in Laos, he'd seen his country collapse, and he *was* never going to find his way home again. All I could do was prescribe anti-depressants." Mr. Thao was the first of many Hmong patients whom Bill Selvidge would treat over the years who suffered from what could only be described as a "profound loss of 'home.'"[17] Everything in America was unfamiliar to them; this was an especially acute problem for newcomers who in their initial attempts to find a place in America, "wore pajamas as street clothes; poured water on electric stoves to extinguish them; lit charcoal fires in their living rooms; stored blankets in their refrigerators; washed rice in their toilets; washed their clothes in swimming pools; washed their hair with Lesotil; cooked with motor oil and furniture polish; drank Clorox; ate cat food; planted crops in public parks; shot and ate skunks, porcupines, woodpeckers, robins, egrets, sparrows, and a bald eagle; and hunted pigeons with crossbows in the streets of Philadelphia."[18] But loss of home was not only about the inability to interpret and fit into what were for the Hmong baffling new social mores; it went deeper, touching on the unfamiliarity of "the sound of every birdsong, the shape of every tree and flower, the smell of the air, and the very texture of the earth." Fadiman notes that for many, "the ache of homesickness [could] be incapacitating."[19]

The severity of the affliction the Hmong have endured in their displacement is inextricably bound up with their strong sense of its spiritual significance. Rooted in actual losses that are concrete and particular, the feelings associated with these losses nonetheless extend outward toward the far horizon and down into the darkest reaches of the soul. There is here an intricate "ecology of loss." No one element can be considered apart from the whole. The soul's well-being cannot be separated from its relationship to place. Nor is this an isolated or singular instance of homelessness. But it points to the need to name and face all the losses we have endured (even they are irreparable) if we are to have any chance of recovering a meaningful relationship with the places in which we live.

I recall the river of my youth, the great Columbia, and consider the intricacy of what was lost within the Columbia River watershed—all the particular biological, social, and cultural losses—when the river was dammed. Gone is the wild, powerful, unpredictable river that used to rise twenty feet at Vancouver, Washington and fifty feet at the Dalles (the river's flow and level is now carefully controlled by engineers). Gone are the deep canyons and enormous towers of basalt that once marked the Columbia's path to the ocean, "broad bars of flood-washed boulders, gray sand beaches lined with cedar canoes, bright white water rapids where waves mounded higher than a man." Gone are the rapids and waterfalls, Redgrave Canyon, Surprise Rapids, Kitchen Rapids, Kettle Falls, Gualquil Rapids, Priest Rapids, Celio Falls, The Dalles—over 109 all told as recently as 1921. Gone are the native grasses that once thrived in the Columbia basin: bunch grass, wild rye, Idaho fescue, Sandberg blue grass, sand grass, needle grass, Indian millet, bearded wheat grass. Gone (almost completely) are the salmon that once choked the river from bank to bank.[20] Gone—flooded by the construction of the Grand Coulee Dam—are 21,000 acres of prime bottom land where indigenous communities had been living for nearly 10,000 years, the best hunting, farming, and root gathering places, most of the tribal burial grounds. Nearly gone is an entire indigenous culture oriented around the river and the salmon; around the Grand Coulee Dam it is the Colville people who have felt this loss most acutely.[21]

This is not, unfortunately, an isolated case. The inundation and erasure of life and memory through the seemingly endless damming of the world's rivers may represent only one instance of a much wider pattern of ecological devastation that has left in its wake untold spiritual loss. But reflecting on this particular case can help us understand how extensive and intricate the fabric of this loss is. In her novel *The Winter Vault*, Canadian writer Anne Michaels attends with astonishing care and detail to the cumulative losses left in the wake of the creation of the Aswan dam in Egypt and the St. Lawrence Seaway in Canada. In both cases, everything that could be moved was moved—houses, personal artifacts, animals. But there was so much that could not be moved, including the life and feeling of places that would soon exist no longer. How could these be moved? And if they could not be moved, what then? How can one even begin to calculate such loss? Michaels tells of a woman living near the St. Lawrence Seaway who is distraught at the thought that the graveyard where her husband's body is buried will soon be inundated by the huge engineering project. Soon, she realizes, both he and the place will be utterly lost to her. She pleads with an engineer working on the project for some redress. But all he can offer her is what he has been authorized to do by the company: "[T]hey can move your husband's body…the company will pay the expenses." After a long silence, she responds:

> If you move the body then you'll have to move the hill. You'll have to move the fields around him. You'll have to move the view from the top of the hill and the trees he planted, one for each of our six children. You'll have to move the sun because it sets among those trees. And move his mother and his father and his younger sister—she was the most admired girl in the county, but all the men died in the first war, so she never married and was laid to rest next to her mother. They're all company for one another and those graves are old, so you'll have to move the earth with them to make sure nothing of anyone is left behind. Can you promise me that? Do you know what it means to miss a man for twenty years? You think about death the way a young

man thinks about death. You'd have to move my promise to him that I'd keep coming to his grave to describe that every place as I used to when we were first married and he hurt his back and had to stay in bed for three months—every night I described the view from the hill above the farm and it was a bit of sweetness—for forty years—between us. Can you move that promise? Can you move what was consecrated? Can you move that exact empty place in the earth I was to lie in next to him for eternity? It's the loneliness of eternity I'm talking about! Can you move all those things?[22]

Some things can be moved. Many others can never be moved, not without incalculable loss. The loss described here is utterly singular and personal, one might even say small. And yet, its significance can hardly begin to be measured. And it touches into and reveals a web of loss that is much more immense and far-reaching, for which we are still struggling to find language.

Still, there is deep ambiguity woven into such loss. It is impossible to overstate how deeply it can cut, how lasting its impact can be on the soul, on the community; but there is also the danger of imagining that the loss of a place means the loss of all memory and feeling for that place. This question of whether such memory and feeling can endure even after a place is gone surfaces in the correspondence between the Laguna writer Leslie Marmon Silko and the poet James Wright. He had written to her about her novel *Ceremony*, expressing his admiration for how powerfully it conveys the importance of the Pueblo people's relationship to the land, how "it was as if the land were telling the stories in the novel." Silko relates how "when I was writing *Ceremony* I was so terribly devastated by being away from Laguna country that writing was my way of re-making that place, the Laguna country, for myself." She likens her work to sand paintings where "all things in creation are traced out in sand." There they have another life, connected to but distinct from their actual life in the world. The question of how such imaginative work contributes to our ability to respond to and live with the losses we experience, especially lost places, is only becoming more acute. Silko frames her own response to this question in an unexpected way:

Didn't [Plato] talk about the idea of the tree being more real or important than the actual physical tree itself? Well, I don't exactly agree with *that* either, but I think there is a materialistic impulse in Western thought which says that if you don't have "the real thing—untouched and unchanged" then you don't have anything of value/meaning.

When the Army Corps of Engineers flooded the sacred shrines and land near Cochita Pueblo, many non-Indian people (and Indians as well) said, "Well, it is all ruined. Why do they (the Cochitas) even go near those places?" But here it seems is an instance where this quasi-Platonic idea works well: the strong feelings, the love, the regard which the Cochita people had for those places that were flooded, those feelings and the importance of those feelings, memories and beliefs are much more important than the physical locations. Which isn't to say that a great hurt and loss didn't occur when the shrines were flooded, but the idea or memory or feeling—whatever you want to call it—is more powerful and important than any damage or destruction humans may commit.[23]

One may feel moved to demur from such a sweeping affirmation of the power of memory and feeling to overcome the reality of the loss that confronts us; there is already too much callous disregard of things and places lost from the world. Still, Silko offers an important reminder of the significance of the work of remembering and keeping alive within us the feeling associated with places now lost to us; the significance of the imaginative life, through which we may yet learn to rekindle a feeling for the world.

There is, however, no way of avoiding the enduring effects of place-loss on our souls. Perhaps this is why we return to the question of our common condition of exile so frequently, turning it over and over in our minds, touching the scar where a certain knowledge of place once stood, wondering who we are when it fades or is lost to us altogether. Joseph O'Neill traces ponders these questions in his novel *Netherland* in relation to the shadow world of expatriates from India, Pakistan, Trinidad, Jamaica, South Africa—even Holland—who meet to play cricket in obscure green fields in and around New York City. "I've heard that social scientists like to explain such a scene—a patch of America sprinkled with the foreign-born strangely at play—in terms of the immigrant's quest for subcommunities. How true this is: we're all far away from Tipperary, and clubbing together mitigates this unfair fact. But surely everyone can also testify to another, less reckonable kind of homesickness, one having to do with unsettlements that cannot be located in spaces of geography or history; and accordingly it's my belief that the communal, contractual phenomenon of New York cricket is underwritten, there where the print is finest, by the same agglomeration of unspeakable individual longings that underwrites cricket played anywhere—longings concerned with horizons and potentials sighted or hallucinated and in any event lost long ago, tantalisms that touch on the undoing of losses too private and reprehensible to be acknowledged to oneself, let alone to others."[24]

What are those "unsettlements" that we feel so strongly, but which "cannot be located in spaces of geography or history?" And what is the character of the longings that arise in response to them? There may be no adequate way to completely account for or explain these elements of our experience. But the continuing efforts at naming and describing them offer a meaningful way to begin reckoning seriously with the condition of homelessness that has come to affect us so profoundly. And they offer us an opportunity to reflect on why our longing for home runs so deep, and how renewed attention to place might help us rekindle a living sense of home.

Place-making as Contemplative Practice

We *are* in a sense, the place-worlds we imagine.[25]

KEITH BASSO

The ancient Christian monks felt the sense of primordial homelessness deeply and employed the language of exile to express their own sense of what it was to be on the way, seeking God as a lost soul seeks its home. For the early monks, this was a potent metaphor that captured their deep ambivalence about the extent to which they were willing to allow the world to gain purchase on their souls; but exile, homelessness, and the longing for home also had a more concrete meaning for many of those living in the late fourth century, including the early Christian monks. Enforced movement, driven by chaotic social, political, and economic forces had become increasingly common; persons, indeed whole communities were being turned, sometimes overnight, into chronic wanderers. To be homeless, or in exile, or on the way: these were often embodied social and political realities before they became images for the spiritual quest. So too the question of what it meant to seek or find a home was profoundly shaped by the reality of actual homelessness and displacement. It is hardly surprising, then, that both place and movement should have figured so prominently in shaping the understanding and practice of Christian contemplative life. In reflecting on these matters as part of their contemplative practice, the early Christian monks contributed something distinctive to the work that anthropologist Keith Basso calls "place-making."

For the monks, the work of place-making meant attending carefully both to the often-unpredictable and precarious character of their movement through the world and to the poignancy of coming to know particular places in the world as significant and meaningful. It also meant becoming sensitive to the way these concrete realities formed and remained bound to their inner experience, that is, how place and movement shaped their contemplative awareness and practice. The knowledge of self and God that emerged through their contemplative practice involved a deepening sense of place and an awareness that no place, finally, could claim them completely. Living within the tension of this apparent paradox enabled them to cultivate a remarkable capacity for inhabiting the world and tending to it with openness, freedom, and reciprocity. I want to examine more closely the testimony of these early monastic figures, as well as some of their later followers, on the question of what it means to consider place-making as a form of contemplative practice. But first it will be useful to consider how place-making has come to figure so prominently in contemporary discourse about place.

Keith Basso, who has worked on mapping the place-names of the Western Apache people near Cibeque, Arizona for over thirty years, describes place-making as "retrospective world-building,... [a form of cultural activity] a universal tool of the historical imagination." In the Western Apache world, places and place names are dense with meaning, holding and bodying forth the entire history of the people. To say the name of a place, to tell a story about a place is to waken memory, conjure up everything that ever happened there, and make it present again to the community. For the Western Apache, this is more than mere reminiscence; remembering what happened in a given place becomes woven into the personal and collective identity of the people. "[W]hat people make of their places," Basso suggests, "is closely connected to what they make of themselves as members of society and inhabitants of the earth.... We *are* in a sense, the place-worlds we imagine."[26] In Western Apache culture, the land, and each particular place in the landscape, teaches, imparts lessons, through the remembered stories of what happened in these places. The landscape holds and embodies the accumulated memory and experience of the community. As one Apache elder memorably expressed it: "Wisdom sits in places."[27]

This is a bold claim for the power of place to shape human identity, and for the capacity of human beings to imagine "place-worlds" that they can subsequently inhabit. One might wish to raise questions about such a close identification between place and self; surely I am more than the sum total of the places in which I have lived. Still, these insights about the power of place arising from the Western Apache world have a deep resonance and have much to teach us about what it is to be a human being alive and aware in the world. In this sense, place-making can be understood as a deeply contemplative work.

This is because, as Basso notes: "... places possess a marked capacity for trig-gering acts of self-reflection, inspiring thoughts about who one presently is, or memories of who one used to be, or musings on who one might become. And that is not all. Place-based thoughts about the self lead commonly to the thoughts of other things—other places, other people, other times, whole net-works of associations that ramify unaccountably within the expanding spheres of awareness that they themselves engender."[28] Neither Basso nor the Western Apache peoples use the language of contemplative practice to describe this work. But the attention given to what the Western Apache refer to as "work-ing on one's mind" or what Basso refers to as the "expanding spheres of aware-ness" arising from such work bears a striking resemblance to what the early Christian monks described as the work of rumination, that long, thoughtful chewing-over of experience aimed at helping to bring the contemplative to a more lucid and expansive awareness of the presence of God. For the Western Apache, suggests Basso, this work of self-reflection becomes most fruitful when it is incorporated into a disciplined, sustained practice. It is, he says, "understood to be a drawn-out affair that becomes less and less difficult as it becomes increasingly habitual.... Disciplined mental effort, diligently sus-tained, will eventually give rise to a permanent state of mind."[29] This, I believe, is a lucid description of how contemplative practice deepens and transforms awareness over time. Here, the wisdom found in places gradually becomes part of a "permanent state of mind," part of an expanding awareness of what places are and what they mean to persons and to the community.

The contemplative work of place-making—of seeking and finding the wis-dom of places—is complex and delicate. As Basso's work among the Western Apache makes clear, it involves a subtle interplay of diverse elements of reality and experience that, if artificially or prematurely separated from one another, can diminish the potential meaning of place. The American photographer Robert Adams, in his description of what makes for compelling photographs of the landscape, offers what I think is a helpful framework for understanding this work of place-making. "Landscape pictures," he notes, "can offer us three verities—geography, autobiography, and metaphor. Geography is, if taken alone, sometimes boring, autobiography is frequently trivial, and metaphor can be dubious. But taken together, as in the best work of people like Alfred Stieglitz and Edward Weston, the three kinds of information strengthen each other and reinforce what we all work to keep intact—an affection for life."[30]

This elegant and economical account of the multiple ways of seeing and knowing a place reflects the kind of self-conscious awareness of place as constructed and ever-shifting in its meanings that has come to define much contemporary thought on this subject. Seamus Heaney, in his essay "The Sense of Place," offers a comparable assessment of the delicate relationship between geography and imagination: "It is the feeling, assenting, equable marriage between the geographical country and the country of the mind,... that constitutes the sense of place in its richest possible manifestation."[31] In a similar way, Lawrence Buell notes that, "place is something we are always in the process of finding, and always perforce creating in some degree as we find it...." Buell distinguishes between what he calls "map knowledge," the concrete, particular knowledge of a place, including its ecological character, and "experiential place sense," the imaginative, affective response to a place that allows it to become significant for a person or community, arguing that both are necessary if the meaning of place is to achieve both weight and depth within human experience.[32]

Geography, autobiography, and metaphor: why do they have such little power when considered separately? And how does their integration help deepen our perception of place, and of our own experience? Beginning with geography, Adams acknowledges that taken by itself it can be boring, even banal; but he recognizes also that it provides us with "a record of place...a certainty that is a relief from the shadow world of romantic egoism." That is, in gazing upon and reflecting upon a particular place, we are compelled to reckon with the place as it presents itself, in all its concreteness and specificity, not as we imagine it or wish it to be. And in so doing we are, if only for a moment, drawn out of the often-stultifying atmosphere of our own preoccupations and asked to confront the otherness of the place. Still, Adams argues that "[m]aking photographs [of place] has to be...a personal matter; when it is not, the results are not persuasive. Only the artist's presence in the work can convince us that its affirmation resulted from and has been tested by human experience." So, even as geography acts to check the all-consuming force of the ego's concerns, truly to see a place and to give artistic expression to this vision requires deep personal engagement. A landscape photograph (or any meaningful work of art for that matter), if it is to move us, must arise from and be informed by *experience*. It must somehow express this experience. And what of metaphor? Here we are invited to consider the work of imaginative meaning-making that Basso describes in terms of "networks of associations" that emerge as we reflect on wider meaning of a given experience of place. Adams observes that, "If a view of geography does not imply something more enduring than a specific piece of terrain, then the picture will hold us only briefly." That is, while we do want and need a sober and honest "record of place," we want more than this. We want to understand who we are in this place, what it means for us, why it matters. "What we hope for from the artist," says Adams, "is help in discovering the significance of a place. In this sense," he says, "we would in most respects choose thirty minutes with Edward Hopper's painting *Sunday Morning* to thirty minutes on the street that was his subject; with Hopper's vision we see more."[33]

We see more. I want to note and hold onto that tantalizing phrase, for I think it points to what is perhaps the central feature of place-making when understood as a contemplative work. It is a way of seeing the world, a way of being in the world that allows us to cherish it with all the feeling we are capable of. It is a way of seeing that enables us to gauge the true significance of what we gaze upon. This kind of seeing is akin to what the early Christians meant when they spoke of *theoria*, that way of seeing into the heart of reality that sometimes revealed the very face of the Divine. Or like what the poet Gerard Manley Hopkins meant when he spoke of "inscape," the luminous, utterly singular texture of a thing that emerges with blazing clarity when a person actually looks upon that thing with care and sensitivity. A capacity to "see into" all that is there.

Becoming a Stranger

In whatever place you live, do not easily leave it.[34]

ABBA ANTONY

Always I must wander, in order to finish my course.[35]

ABBA BESSARION

A week before his death in December 1968, the Cistercian monk and writer Thomas Merton stood, barefoot and alone, gazing up at the great Buddhas at Polonnaruwa in Sri Lanka. This is how he described the experience: "Looking at these figures, I was suddenly, almost forcibly, jerked clean out of the habitual, half-tied vision of things, and an inner clearness, clarity, as if exploding from the rocks themselves, became evident and obvious . . . all problems are resolved and everything is clear, simply because what matters is clear. The rock, all matter, all life, is charged with *dharmakaya*—everything is emptiness and everything is compassion. I don't know when in my life I have ever had such a sense of beauty and spiritual validity running through one aesthetic illumination. Surely, with Mahabalipuram and Polonnaruwa my Asian pilgrimage has come clear and purified itself. I mean, I know and have seen what I was obscurely looking for. I don't know what else remains. . . ."[36]

This account leaves little doubt about the power and profundity of this experience and has been justly celebrated as a singular moment of awakening in Merton's life, a breakthrough that left him unalterably transformed. Still, it is maddeningly dense, its meaning elusive. *Something* important about his own spiritual identity clearly shifted as he stood there, gazing up at the faces of the Buddhas. But apart from a sense of deepened *clarity*, it is difficult to say, really, what this experience meant for him. Nor do we have the benefit of further reflections on the experience from Merton himself: six days later, he lay dead on the floor of his room in the Red Cross center outside of Bangkok, Thailand.

I want to respect the mystery of this experience and even the silence that surrounds it. Still, I think this strange and unexpected moment at the end of Thomas Merton's life can help us understand something important about the significance of place within contemplative practice. For, whatever else may be said about Merton's experience with the Buddhas at Polonnaruwa, it was without question a profound encounter with a *place*, and a subtle, mysterious expression of contemplative place-making. If one were to press further and ask what kind of an experience of place it was, I would say it was among other things an experience of homecoming, a sense of having arrived home after a lifetime of restless wandering. But it was also, paradoxically, a moment of intense displacement: the encounter occurs far from home, as he beholds and responds to a powerful symbol of a religious tradition not his own and begins to sense and feel a release from some of the constraints that had kept him from coming home to himself and to God during his long monastic life. In the time leading up to his journey to Asia, Merton had begun to waken to a longing to "become a stranger."[37] This was for him part of a yearning to experience and express more fully his own solidarity with all those marginalized and homeless beings for whom a sense of place and belonging had long remained a distant dream. At the same time, this longing expressed a desire that had been growing within him during his entire monastic life—to enter more deeply into a place of unknowing and dispossession where he could perhaps begin to behold God beyond language, beyond concepts, in darkness. Yet, during the years preceding this journey to Asia, Merton had begun to find, especially in the contemplative practice in his hermitage at the monastery of Gethsemani in Kentucky, a deeper sense of belonging and rootedness than he had ever known in his life. In a paradox well-known to his monastic forebears, he had begun to reckon with the recognition that relinquishment of all security, all knowledge, all claim to belonging was utterly bound up with what it meant to find his way home.

At the heart of his encounter at Polonnaruwa was an experience of see-ing; or as Merton himself described it, a moment of *recognition* that until that moment, he had not been able to see at all: "I was suddenly, almost forc-ibly, jerked clean out of the habitual, half-tied vision of things, and an inner clearness, clarity, as if exploding from the rocks themselves, became evident and obvious." He is looking at the rocks, at the subtle, beautiful shape of the Buddhas. But while Merton claims that the light, the illumination, the emerg-ing clarity, seems to be "exploding from the rocks themselves," it is in fact bursting forth from his own consciousness. *He* is the one who has been liv-ing with the "habitual, half-tied vision of things;" *he* is the one who has been seeking liberation from this narrow, conventional way of seeing; and it is *he* who is in that moment, freed to see things as they truly are. In Robert Adams' terms: *autobiography*.

Still, there is no question that the rocks themselves—those 12th-century Buddhas carved into that granite ridge at Polonnaruwa—mediate this break-through. A reminder of the importance of *geography*, even if it is in this case a culturally and spiritually dense geography, a deeply aesthetic expression of place. And what of metaphor? The entire experience spins inwards with tre-mendous centripetal force to touch on a central question of meaning: "The rock, all matter, all life, is charged with *dharmakaya*—everything is emptiness and everything is compassion." Here Merton is seen to arrive at an experien-tial awareness, a felt sense of a truth about existence that had, up until this very moment, eluded him. It is not possible to grasp the full significance of this experience, in part because Merton himself offers us no further reflections about it, and in part because of the elusive, expansive character of the expe-rience itself. But it seems clear that this is for Merton a moment of profound recognition, in which he comes to see who he is most deeply in the world, and comes to understand something new and important about the mystery that has long been unfolding within and around him. "I know and have seen what I was obscurely looking for," he says. Nothing else remained.

These final, cryptic comments leave unanswered the question of what exactly Thomas Merton was looking for in Asia, or why this particular experi-ence seems to have represented such a definitive moment of arrival for him. But it is less important here to try to answer that question than to ask about the seeking itself, the longing, the restlessness and the hope that characterized both his journey to Asia and his entire monastic life. For nearly twenty-seven years, this restless yearning had been worked out in a single place, the Abbey of our Lady of Gethsemani in Kentucky, a place he had come to know intimately and to consider his home. Now, toward the end of his life, that same yearning had led him to leave Gethsemani and travel halfway around the world, to discover in a foreign land and amidst a different religious tradition an even deeper sense of belonging than he had known before. Yet, if his journey to Asia and his experience at Polonnaruwa in particular represented for him a kind of homecoming, it also revealed to him the true extent of his condition as an exile and wanderer and stranger.

Merton's encounter at Polonnaruwa is emblematic of a long-standing paradox in the Christian contemplative tradition: that to discover one's place in the world, one has to be prepared to become a stranger. And it points to what I think is one of the most significant aspects of contemplative place-making, namely the commitment on the part of the contemplative to struggle with the way both place and loss of place shape and form us. The Christian contemplative tradition affirms simultaneously that contemplative practice is at once bound to place and free of its claims, rooted but always moving toward an immense, limitless horizon. In the ancient monastic tradition, the monk was one who lived in a monastery or a cell, seeking in stability and commitment to a place a way of practicing attention to self and God—an idea that was influentially codified in *The Rule of St. Benedict* as the "vow of stability."[38] But the monk's search for God also included and often consciously fostered a certain restlessness, a recognition that setting off for a new place, even having no permanent dwelling, was often necessary to the work of attending with honesty and integrity to "the one thing necessary." Moreover, these fundamental, if sometimes contradictory, impulses also contributed importantly to the way the ancient monks *imagined* the contemplative life. For Evagrius and other Christian monks, the highest level of contemplative awareness of divine presence was imagined as a kind of place, not bound by space and time or ever fully knowable, but a place to seek out and live into all the same. But for others, the fundamental task was to leave behind all places, to learn what it meant to inhabit "the frame of mind of the stranger. . . ." The early monastic tradition was not at all consistent in its attitudes toward the question of how place and the movement through place should inform the contemplative quest. Rather, it seemed to relish the paradox that the "place of God" could only be sought and discovered by the one who was prepared to become a stranger.[39]

In their commitment to living within this paradox, the early Christian monks cultivated an approach to place-making that has much to teach us about the integral character of place within contemplative practice, and about the role contemplative practice can play in helping us recover a sense of place as charged with spiritual significance. Perhaps the single most important contribution of this tradition is its sustained effort to *integrate* those elements of place-making that Robert Adams refers to as geography, autobiography, and metaphor. Thus, early monastic literature does in fact give careful attention to the actual places that shaped the monks lives (geography). So too does it reveal a conscious awareness on the part of the monks of the significance of the questions and struggles they brought to these places from their own experience (autobiography). And it points to the persistent impulse among the monks to frame the most important questions about the meaning of contemplative practice and the apprehension of divine presence in terms of place and movement, rootedness and exile (metaphor).

Still, the tendency that Adams noted as being common to much landscape photography—of privileging one or another of these elements and neglecting the others—can also be seen in the literature of early Christian monasticism. Early monastic literature reveals that the monks were in fact sensitive to the places in which they lived and took note of their importance for their lives; references to the desert, to mountains, monastic cells, roads and paths, the town, among other places, recur frequently in the stories and sayings of the early monks. Often these places are carefully named and described, their characteristic features noted. But just as often the monks mythologize both these places and their movement through them, employing the language of place primarily to express the deepest longings and struggles of their lives. This emphasis on place as a kind of interior landscape was in some sense inevitable. In their particular understanding of what it meant to live the Gospel life, the monks wanted above all else to discover how to acquire what they described variously as purity of heart or stillness or inner freedom. Their ruminations on place almost always reflected this abiding concern, and places gained in value and meaning for the monks to the extent that they helped them realize this dream. So, the desert, the cell, the mountain, the road or way, exile and wandering, as well as particular places, such as Kellia, Mt. Sinai, and the inner mountain, all became crucial elements of a monastic vocabulary centered on the question of how to open oneself fully and deeply to God. In the process, the geography of the early monastic world became integrated into a sustained conversation about what it meant to practice the contemplative life with integrity and freedom. But did geography itself matter? Did the landscape itself figure into the imaginative lives of the early monks? Or did the metaphorical or autobiographical dimension of their experience of place always take precedence over the gritty, concrete, particular character of the place?

In some respects it seems unfair even to frame the questions this way. After all, the early monks can hardly be expected to have embodied in their lives the kind of sensitivity to place that has come to characterize contemporary ecological thought and practice. But the specter of idealism has long haunted our thinking about how place signifies in our lives, and the effort to retrieve a feeling for the particular and palpable character of our ecosystems, bioregions, and watersheds has been crucial to helping us reclaim a more embodied and intricate sense of what a place is and how to live in a place. None of this, of course, is to be found in the literature of the ancient Christian monastic tradition. Still, it is clear that whatever inner or transcendent meaning the monks assigned to place and the movement between and among places, it was bound to the palpable reality of their lives in those places.[40]

The monks did not speak often about the light, the air, or the geographical terrain in which they lived. But we know from the literature that they were sensitive to the landscape and responded to it in different ways. We know for example that they took up habitation in caves and abandoned tombs, in wadis and in the shadow of mountains where there was water and protection from the sun and wind. We know they made use of what was able to grow in these regions, crushing olives for oil, weaving reeds into baskets, and trading for other basic necessities. And we know that some monks moved more or less continuously across the landscape, living a poor, itinerant life. It has become increasingly clear that some of the fundamental dimensions of monastic spiritual identity—the call to relinquish one's possessions and withdraw to the margins, the belief in the power of stability and of dwelling in the cell, the impulse to wander—were not simply disembodied ideals but owed much of their meaning to the concrete material and social conditions of the monks' lives.

We now understand better than we once did, for example, how deeply the place of the monk, rooted in the practice of *anachoresis* or withdrawal, was dependent for its meaning on the social, political, and economic crisis engulfing the towns and villages of the Nile Valley. Withdrawal was sometimes an act of survival amidst the increasingly heavy burden of Roman imperial power; it also came to be understood as an act of defiance and resistance. The cell or monastery was a place of refuge in the most concrete sense imaginable. Still, the cell soon came to acquire huge metaphorical significance, as the place where the monk underwent an arduous process of purification and transformation. And to the extent that the monk was understood to have undertaken this struggle not only for his own sake, but on behalf of all those still groaning under the crushing weight of social and economic pressures in the village, the social and even political meaning of *anachoresis* came to be bound up inextricably with its spiritual meaning. The place of the monk was charged with significance, not as an isolated place, but as part of a complex social and geographical network of meaning.[41]

One can see something similar at work in accounts of early monastic wandering. It is tempting to read these accounts of wandering and movement primarily in terms of the idea of pilgrimage. While there is little question that the impulse to travel often had a religious or spiritual meaning associated with it (one whose value and meaning was much debated among early Christians), it is also clear that travel and movement in the late antique world also arose in no small measure from social and political forces that impelled people into the often-precarious and perilous conditions of the open road. "Many late antique travelers were on the road not by their own choice, but in flight from the urban upheaval resulting from German migrations," notes Maribel Dietz. "As refugees headed first into Africa, and later, after the Vandal invasions, eastward to Egypt, Palestine, Syria, Greece, and Asia Minor, which were still under Roman control, long-distance travel increased dramatically, and upheaval and displacement became a way of life in the late empire."[42] It was under these conditions, suggests Dietz, that many Christians, including Christian monks, began to experience travel and dislocation as increasingly commonplace. And it was "these very conditions," Dietz argues, that "created the opportunity for infusing travel with religious significance. It was in this world that monastic men and women began to explore the ascetic qualities of wandering itself."[43] It is difficult to know for certain the extent to which the reality of itinerancy among early Christian monks was influenced by this broader phenomenon of movement and instability. But it is difficult to avoid the conclusion that the fact of itinerancy among early Christian monks and the significance of the language of movement—exile, wandering, of becoming a stranger—within Christian contemplative practice owes at least something to the reality of chronic mobility that had become a fact of life for so many in the late antique world. Before exile became a spiritual ideal, it was a fact of life. And while its subsequent meaning for the monks cannot be attributed solely to this fact, neither can it be entirely dissociated from it.

These concrete social and political realities can help us better understand, I think, how both place and movement became such critical elements of the monastic vocabulary and why they came to have such deep resonance for the monks in their ongoing conversation about the meaning of contemplative life. But they hardly begin to account for the complexity of the monastic struggle to live at once "in place" and "on the way." Consider this exchange between a brother and Abba Poemen about how best to live in a particular place. The brother asked Poemen: "'How should I behave in the place where I live?' The old man said, 'Have the mentality of an exile in the place where you live, do not desire to be listened to and you will have peace.'"[44] The underlying assumption here is that the brother should in fact stay put and not move. But there is more to it than that. Everything depends on how he chooses to live in the place, especially his willingness to cultivate the "mentality of an exile." What this means precisely we are not told. But for Poemen it is clearly associated with the relinquishment of ego ("do not desire to be listened to"). Only this will enable the brother to inhabit the place with true peace (*hesychia*). The complexity of this exchange points to the early monks' acute attention to the meaning of place and what it meant to inhabit it with integrity. It points also to the fact that as often as not dwelling in place was a social reality, in which one's own life in that place was bound to the lives of others, whether physically present or present in memory and feeling.

We see evidence of this in another saying in which Abba Longinus questioned Abba Lucius about his thoughts: "'I want to go into exile,' [said Abba Longinus]. The old man said to him, 'If you cannot control your tongue, you will not be an exile anywhere. Therefore control your tongue here, and you will be an exile.'"[45] One senses here an underlying subtext: the longing to escape a difficult or challenging situation. But Abba Lucius challenges the monk to go deeper, to practice entering into exile in his own place, by relinquishing his attachment to gossip and careless talk. By maintaining silence. Apparently the temptation to flee trouble was commonplace among the monks. Amma Theodora tells the story of a monk, "who, because of the great number of his temptations said, 'I will go away from here.' As he was putting on his sandals, he saw another man who was also putting on his sandals and this other monk said to him, 'Is it on my account that you are going away? Because I go before you wherever you are going.'"[46] Exile, in other words, could not be achieved by so simple a gesture as flight. It required rather learning to stay put, reckoning honestly with oneself. It required opening oneself to the possibility of a deep, inner transformation.

It is for this reason that the monks often cautioned those who were tempted to flee from the place where they lived to pause and consider their motives and what they might lose in moving so easily. Amma Syncletica counseled: "If you find yourself in a monastery do not go to another place, for that will harm you a great deal. Just as the bird who abandons the eggs she was sitting on prevents them from hatching, so the monk or the nun grows cold and their faith dies, when they go from one place to another."[47] For Abba Antony, the matter could be stated even more simply: "In whatever place you live," he exhorted his hearers, "do not easily leave it."[48] Still, simply dwelling in place was not considered sufficient in itself. Nor could a place save a person if the life he or she lived there lacked integrity or purpose. "See how I have walked before you" said Abba Isaac of Cells. "If you want to follow me and keep the commandments of God, God will send you his grace and protect this place; but if you do not keep his commandments, you cannot remain in this place."[49] There is no magic in place itself, only the purity of intention one brings to it. To live faithfully in a place, to open one's heart to the simple practice of listening to and following "the commandments" (or the teaching of the Elder), was to begin to learn what the place might teach you. But to ignore this simple practice was to forgo the possibility of learning all that one's life in that place might teach and reveal. It was to break the bonds of reciprocity that could hold a person and a place together. As one of the anonymous sayings puts it, "If a [person] settles in a certain place and does not bring forth the fruit of that place, the place itself casts him out."[50]

These sayings are consistent in affirming that choosing the right place and dwelling there conscientiously could have a significant impact on the well-being of the one who lived there. However, it was the *way* one chose to engage the place, respond to it, and live in it that allowed it to become spiritually meaningful and, as the saying puts it, "bear fruit." It is because of this that the monks also struggled to understand when and under what circumstances it was acceptable, even necessary, to move. They recognized that the cell could become a kind of fetish. When this happened, one must be prepared to flee for the sake of one's soul. "If you find yourself growing strongly attached to your cell," said Abba Evagrius, "leave it, do not cling to it, be ruthless. Do everything possible to attain stillness and freedom from distraction, and struggle to live according to God's will, battling against invisible enemies. If you cannot attain stillness where you now live, consider living in exile, and try to make up your mind to go…make stillness your criterion for testing the value of everything, and choose always what contributes to it."[51] Evagrius was one of the fiercest advocates of this radical freedom and believed the monk should be ever-vigilant regarding anything that would hinder this freedom from taking hold in his soul. Interestingly, he uses the same criterion as other monastic teachers do when advocating for the importance of stability—seeking stillness (*hesychia*)—to judge when living in exile might be necessary. *Hesychia*, which is close to the heart of the monastic ideal of integrity, was not tied strictly to either place or movement. Still, the monks were sensitive to the way that attachment to place could become corrupted and undermine one's fundamental commitment to seeking this deep peace. Because of this, Evagrius urged those who were serious about contemplative life to "welcome exile. It frees you from all the entanglements of your own locality, and allows you to enjoy the blessings of stillness undistracted." He even offered practical advice: "Do not stay in a town, but persevere in the wilderness. 'Lo,' says the Psalm, 'then would I wander far off, and remain in the wilderness' (Ps 55:7). If possible, do not stay in a town at all…seek out places that are free from distraction and solitary…endure fearlessly, and you will see the great things of God…."[52]

This polemic against "staying in town," is but one expression of a consistent monastic rhetoric about the importance of seeking out the right place. For Evagrius, as for Antony, the wilderness is the place par excellence for contemplative living, for it is there above all that one can struggle to "live according to God's will," and discover the presence of *hesychia* in one's life. Still, even given its obvious advantages as a place of relative quiet and solitude, there was a danger that monks would fall prey to the "cult of the desert." Instead of recognizing the desert as one of many places that could help the monk discover the stillness and freedom at the heart of contemplative life, the monks sometimes literalized that wild, open landscape, fetishizing it every bit as much as they did the monastic cell. A story of an old man who questioned Abba Ammonas suggests the difficulty of maintaining perspective when it came to the question of where to live one's life: "'Three thoughts occupy me, either, should I wander in the deserts, or should I go to a foreign land where no-one knows me, or should I shut myself up in a cell without opening the door to anyone, eating only every second day.' Abba Ammonas replied, 'It is not right for you to do any of these three things. Rather sit in your cell and eat a little every day, keeping the world of the publican always in your heart, and you may be saved.'"[53] Ammonas's response points to the consistent attention the monks gave to the character of one's motivations in doing anything at all. Here the question of where best to live is addressed with reference to the story in Luke's gospel of the Pharisee and the Publican (Lk 18). Again, we find ourselves facing the question of what it means to live the Gospel life. For Ammonas, this is far less dependent upon where one lives than it is on the realization in one's own being of the truth of the Gospel, in this case the quest for a deep humility and recognition of one's need for God. This is what it means to "sit in one's cell," to "become an exile." In any given situation, one may in fact be called to stay put, or to wander; but the truth and meaning of these gestures will, suggests Ammonas, depend completely on one's ability to enter deeply into the "world of the publican"—a world characterized by simple need, humility, openness, and freedom.

This is the world the monks sought to inhabit above all else. They understood that they could inhabit this world in different places, or in no place at all. But whether they lived alone in a cell, or together with others in a coenobium, or wandering on the open road, they knew they could only hope to inhabit this world by being completely faithful and honest to their way of life. Perhaps this helps to account for the continuous dialogue between those who advocated in the fiercest possible terms the need for dwelling deeply in a place and those who believed that only by leaving all places behind and becoming an exile could one hope to realize the truth of the Gospel in one's life. The dream of paradise that so occupied the early monastic imagination seemed to require both of these realities. The story of Antony beholding the inner mountain for the first time and "falling in love with the place," treating it "as his own home," and dwelling deeply there, "as if on Mt. Sion with his mind unruffled," represents one emblematic image of that dream; a transformed soul in a landscape made luminous by his striving. But one must also include here the stories of those like Abba Bessarion, whose life we are told, "had been like that of the bird of the air, or a fish, or an animal living on earth, passing all the time in his life without trouble or disquiet." We are told that, "the care of a dwelling did not trouble him, and the desire for a particular place never seemed to dominate his soul . . . he always lived in the open air, afflicting himself on the edge of the desert like a vagabond . . . 'I cannot live under a roof so long as I have not found again the riches of my house.' . . . For always I must wander, in order to finish my course.'"[54]

These images resonate with the power of other, older images: Adam in the Garden, the New Testament vision of the one who has learned what it means to live "free from care." For the early monks, these echoes were significant, for they sought above all else to inhabit a world modeled for them by their biblical forbears. Their own sense of the truth that "wisdom sits in places" led them to notice and attend to places while also moving freely through the world. To be at home and on the way was woven deeply into the contemplative practice of the early monks. And if this paradox seems often to have pulled the early Christian contemplatives in opposite directions, it also led them continuously back to the question of what it meant to open oneself and respond to the deepest sense of the call that brought them to this life in the first place. Honesty, depth, integrity: these are the values that consistently informed the ancient Christian contemplative practice of place-making.

The Work of the Cell

There is no place left.[55]

THOMAS MERTON

To find a way to reach the island, we must assume on principle, as we have always done, the possibility and even the *necessity* of doing so. The only admissible hypothesis is

that the "shell of the curvature" that surrounds the island
is not *absolutely* impenetrable—that is, *not always, everywhere*, and *for everyone. At a certain moment*, and *a certain place, certain people* (those who know how to and
wish to do so) can enter.[56]

RENÉE DAUMAL

I think often of that day spent with Fr. Wadid in the Wadi Natrun. The
utter obscurity of the place, the simplicity and focus of his life there, and
the expansive character of the vision that informs it continue to haunt me.
Certainly it is not the only way to respond to the call to live for the sake of
"the one thing necessary." But as one particular response to this call, it offers
an important witness to what it means to live into this ideal. At the heart of
this witness is that essential contemplative practice Thomas Merton referred
to as "the work of the cell." For Merton, as for the ancient Christian monks,
engaging in this work entails learning to dwell deeply in the place to which
one has been called, and trusting that the place itself, in all its distinctive
particularity, will reveal the meaning of that call. But it also means striving
to remain open to every subsequent call to move deeper and relinquishing
any claim to a particular place or an identity rooted in that place. The work
of the cell requires in other words a capacity to inhabit a space of fluidity
and paradox, always seeking a place to dwell and never ceasing to take upon
oneself the mind of an exile.[57] This distinctively contemplative approach to
place-making, rooted in the Christian monastic tradition, finds echoes in
many other traditions of spiritual practice and in much contemporary ecological thought and practice. These traditions of contemplative place-making
share a common concern to understand what it means to attend carefully to
where one is in the world and how to cultivate a genuine sensitivity to and
regard for place. But they are also sensitive to what it means to be without
a place, to be a stranger, a wanderer, or an exile.[58] There is a growing awareness that particular stories and practices of place-making have the power
to ground contemplative practice and that the retrieval of such stories can
make a significant contribution to the work of ecological renewal. I want
to return here to one such story—Thomas Merton's journey to Asia in the
fall of 1968—that I believe has particular significance for helping us think
more carefully about what it might mean to integrate place-making into a
sustained contemplative practice.

During the summer of 1968, while preparing for his trip to Asia, Merton
found himself struggling with the question of how he might live out his
monastic vocation with greater depth and integrity at this particular moment.

One of the critical questions facing him was whether he should remain at the Abbey of Gethsemani in Kentucky, or leave to find a place where he could commit himself more fully to the solitary life he felt himself being called to live. He had struggled with this question for many years, and on several earlier occasions had come close to leaving Gethsemani. Still, he had also gradually come to appreciate what it meant to be a monk of that particular place and, especially during the decade of the 1950s, had come to know and love the place deeply, learning the names of the trees and the birds, becoming attuned to the subtle rhythms of weather and the seasons, and committing himself more and more deeply to the life of the community. When, in the early 1960s, he was given an opportunity to begin spending time alone at a newly constructed dwelling on the monastery property, it seemed only to confirm his sense of being in precisely the place he was meant to be. "If I have any desire left in the world," he noted in the autumn of 1960, "it is to live and die here."[59] Merton soon came to think of this as his hermitage and he began to spend long afternoons there, prompting this observation: "Places and situations are not supposed to matter. This one makes a tremendous difference."[60] On the day after Christmas that year, in a journal entry that has the feel of a kind of year-end examination of conscience, he speaks of his sense of "a journey ended, of wandering at an end. *The first time in my life* I ever really felt I had come home and that my waiting and looking were ended."[51] It is difficult to miss the significance of this statement, coming from a person who had been orphaned at age sixteen and had been haunted his entire life by a hunger for a place to call home. But the sense of finality is deceptive; Merton would live eight more years, and his "waiting and looking" would continue unabated.

By 1968, this waiting and looking had begun to take on a new form. His journal entry for January 6th, the feast of Epiphany, registers a deep if unspecified sense of foreboding: "Last night curious dreams, perhaps about death. I am caught suddenly in a flood which has risen and cut off my way of escape—not *all* escape, but my way to where I want to go. Can go back to some unfamiliar place over here—where? Fields, snow, upriver, a road, a possible bridge left over from some other dream. (Sudden recollection and as it were a voice: '*It is not a bridge…no bridge necessary!*')."[62] A month later, he found himself suddenly recalling a moment in his life years earlier when he had faced a critical juncture: "Perhaps now I am returning to some such moment of breakthrough. I hope I am. I won't have many more chances!"[63]By the following autumn, as he was preparing to embark on the first leg of his momentous journey to Asia, he was ruminating on *The Tibetan Book of the*

Dead and expressing his hope that he might be on the verge of a "'clean passage,' direct, into a new space or area of existence—even in one's 'this present' life—clean unclogged steps into more maturity."[64]

There is evidence throughout the last year of Merton's life that he was indeed moving closer to a kind of breakthrough into a "new space or area of existence." However, the passage itself was anything but clean. He found himself struggling, as never before, with the question of where it was he belonged and how, in the time that was left to him, he might live out his monastic vocation with real honesty and integrity. Learning to do so might require him to recommit himself more fully to his monastic life at Gethsemani Abbey in Kentucky. Or it might mean leaving for another place, perhaps even becoming an itinerant, a wanderer. These practical questions also increasingly shaped the way Merton thought and spoke about the contemplative life during this period, as homecoming and exile entered more and more fully into his contemplative vocabulary—sometimes representing two utterly different ways of conceptualizing contemplative life, other times pointing toward a deeply integrated vision and practice that included both. What did it mean to look for a place to dwell? Or to set off on a journey whose precise aim must always remain shrouded in mystery? These questions emerged with new force during the final period of Merton's life, and his attempts to address them mark one of the most significant contributions of his late writing.

From his earliest years as a monk, Merton had developed a deep and abiding love for Gethsemani Abbey and the woods and the knobs surrounding the monastery. Over time, he had cultivated a sense of intimate relationship with the birds and animals that lived there, with the stars and planets overhead, with so many elements of that very particular place. His journals from the late 1940s onward reflect an ever-more exacting habit of attention to the place. And in spite of the questions that had arisen from time to time about whether Gethsemani was the right place for him to live out his monastic vocation, this feeling for the place never diminished. By late 1967 and early 1968, one senses in his journal entries an affection for the place that is almost completely pure, unsullied by feelings of discontentment or restlessness. On October 18, 1967, he records this impression:

> There was an eclipse of the moon about 4 to 5 this morning. The clouds cleared a little and I was able to see it begin. Then after I said Mass I went out and the eclipse was closer to full, the clouds had almost completely gone. The moon was beautiful, dimly red, like a globe of almost

transparent amber, with a shapeless foetus or darkness curled in the midst of it. It hung there between two tall pines, silent, unexplained, small, with a modest suggestion of bloodiness, an omen without fierceness and without comment, pure.[65]

But it is not only extraordinary events like this that catch his attention. He is aware and routinely makes note in his journal of the waning and waxing of the moon, for example. On January 26, 1968, he records this observation: "Two nights ago—early morning, before dawn; the old moon—dying crescent—hung in the South with Antares (of Scorpius) almost caught in the crescent...." Then, less than a week later (on his fifty-third birthday): "Clear, thin new moon appearing and disappearing between slow slate, blue clouds—and the living black skeletons of the trees against the evening sky."[66]

These simple, lyric descriptions of the movements of the moon and the stars are hardly remarkable in themselves; yet they suggest the importance Merton had come to attribute to paying attention to where he was, to noticing the minute particulars of his place. Reading carefully through his late journals, one gains a strikingly detailed sense of the living world around the monastery. In one relatively brief section of his late journal, for example, Merton notes the presence of golden crowned kinglets; wild ducks; crows (which he says he is learning to esteem more now after having received poet Haydn Caruth's reprimand); cardinals; a towhee (he calls it "*my* towhee"); a "solitary mockingbird, apparently with no mate, that patrols the whole length of the rose hedge" (later, the mate appears); crocuses "bunched together in the cold wet grass"; "at night, with the rains softly falling, a frog...singing in the waterhole behind the hermitage"; and "a big doe, [flying] down the field in the bottoms head up, white-flag of tail erect...."[67] And that does not even include the many accounts of fragrance or color or music. Or, as here, after a long afternoon spent at the farm of John Jacob Niles, of light and silence: "The thing that struck me most—the wonderful pale fall light of Kentucky on the stones and the quiet of the Kentucky hollow."[68]

Such moments of simple awareness became increasingly important to Merton's sense of the sacred, helping him ground his own unfolding narrative of faith in a particular place, a place that held within it so much of his own history. Walking outside by St. Bernard's lake on an unseasonably warm day in November, 1967, he was surprised by a sense of the richly layered character of the place and its continued impact on him: "the sky, hills, trees kept taking on an air of clarity and freshness that took me back to spring twenty years ago when Lents were hard and I was new in the monastery. Strange feeling!

Recapturing the freshness of those days when my whole monastic life was still ahead of me...."[69] Coming at a moment when he was once again seeking to retrieve the truth of his own monastic vocation, this sudden reminder of the power of the place to kindle self-knowledge carried unexpected weight. A little more than a month later, on January 4th of the new year, Merton reflected once again on his life at Gethsemani, and on his still-frequent feelings of restlessness and desire to find some place better. "Evening—new moon—snow hard crackling and squealing under my rubber boots. The dark pines over the hermitage. The graceful black fans and branches of the tall oaks between the field and the monastery. I said Compline and looked at the cold valley and tasted its peace. Who is entitled to such peace? I don't know. But I would be foolish to leave it for no reason."[70]

Still, he *did* have his reasons. There were increasing numbers of visitors coming to see him at the monastery, the amount of noise (from machinery and hunting in the next valley) was growing, and the monastery itself was becoming a much busier and less quiet place. And, after several long years of giving himself fully and deeply, in his contemplative practice and his writing, to the effort to resist war, violence, and racism, he had begun seeking a way to recover a greater stillness and renew his contemplative vocation. All of this left him wondering about whether or not the time had come for him to "disappear," to drop off the map. During June of 1968, while reading Sautideva on solitude, he began to arrive at a clearer understanding of what he was seeking in his contemplative life: not escape but a deeper, more authentic way of engaging the world: "What impresses me most at this reading of Sautideva is not only the emphasis on solitude but the idea of solitude as part of the clarification which includes living for others: dissolution of the self in 'belonging to everyone' and regarding everyone's suffering as one's own.... To be 'homeless' is to abandon one's attachment to a particular ego—and yet to care for one's own life (in the highest sense) in the service of others. A deep and beautiful idea."[71] This was not a new idea for Merton. He had worked for much of his monastic life to find a way to bring his deep commitment to contemplative practice to expression in honest, open engagement with the larger community. Yet, the idea spoke to him now with new force, and seemed to capture what he himself ought to be about as he gazed out onto the horizon of his life unfolding before him.

There are strong echoes here of the ancient Christian contemplative ideal of seeking one's place through becoming an exile, a stranger, a wanderer. And yet, in the tradition of contemplative practice within which Merton stood, this ideal could be realized in different ways—by dwelling deeply in a place or by abandoning oneself to the unknown. In Merton's work, this ideal comes to expression in a distinctively contemporary idiom that can, I believe, help to create a bridge between that distant world and our own and in the process help us to grapple with what a contemplative approach to place-making might look like for us. No small part of the potential value of Merton's witness lay in its context and in the way he engaged the critical issues of his time: he lived through a century that endured the Holocaust, the bombings of Hiroshima and Nagasaki, the continuing violence of racism, the Vietnam War, and the growing threat of environmental degradation. To "become a stranger," a "homeless wanderer," meant above all opening oneself to the suffering and alienation of those most vulnerable to the corrosive forces of war, racism, and poverty, and seeking a way to bear some part of that suffering for their sake. It also meant resisting, both actively and in a more hidden way, the destructive forces that lay behind that suffering—something that became integral to Merton's own practice of the contemplative vocation during the last few years of his life.[72]

Embracing this precarious position consciously and thoughtfully became a crucial part of what it meant for Merton to engage in "the work of the cell," a part of the contemplative vocation he also referred to at times as "the work of loneliness." Writing to his Muslim friend Abdul Aziz in January, 1961, Merton articulated his own sense of what it meant for him to live as a monk of the monastery of Gethsemani, the place where "Christ was abandoned by all who loved Him.... I think then that this means our life as monks lived especially under the sign of a kind of inner solitude and dereliction, and I know from experience that this is true. But it is in this solitude and dereliction we are united with others who are alone and solitary and poor."[73] To open oneself to this solitude and dereliction was part of what it meant to participate in what he called, "The absolute aloneness of Christ...the total loneliness of Christ," something he had come to believe was central to his own vocation as a monk and a Christian. "...[T]he way one begins to make sense out of life," he said, "is taking upon oneself the lostness of everyone."[74] This became for him a deeply personal task, and yet also a work undertaken for the sake of the healing of the larger community. This was the work of the cell.

Would he be able to continue to undertake this work where he was currently living? Or would he need to move? One senses during this season of his life that Merton was seeking not so much a new or different *place* (at least not for its own sake) as a renewed sense of his own deepest center. If a change of place could help him to find this, he would consider moving to a new place, or at least leaving Gethsemani for an extended sojourn elsewhere. But it was the *interior* change and renewal that mattered most. This perhaps helps to account for why his response to the places he encountered during the last months of his life are so fundamentally equivocal, why his heart and imagination seemed to leap at the sight of these new places as if he were rediscovering some long-lost parts of himself. Traveling through the landscapes of California, New Mexico, and Alaska in the summer and fall of 1968 seems to have opened up a new space of freedom within him. Or perhaps one should say it allowed him to recover that sense of freedom which had long been at the center of his monastic vocation but which, for a variety of reasons, had become obscured. This I think is how one ought to read his often-rapturous responses to the places through which he was traveling at this moment: as responses to the possibilities of spiritual renewal that these places seemed to promise. Not that the places themselves were incidental. But they were clearly part of a larger complex of questions occupying Merton at this moment, centering upon the elusive but necessary task of clarifying and deepening his quest for God.

"I dream every night of the west." He recorded these words on May 22, 1968 upon his return to Gethsemani Abbey from his first trip to California and New Mexico. Of what was he dreaming? Recalling a day spent in the hills overlooking the black sand beaches of Needle Rock on the Pacific Ocean in Northern California, Merton notes: "It was a bright day and the sea was calm, and I looked out over the glittering blue water, realizing more and more that this was where I really belonged. I shall never forget it. I need the sound of those waves, that desolation, that emptiness." Then a little later, he adds: "I need the silence and the emptying. Radical change in my ideas out there." One cannot help but noticing here, as elsewhere during this period, the complex reciprocal interplay between the landscape itself and the felt effects of the landscape on Merton's interior life. The place itself—the sound of the waves, its desolation and emptiness—catches his attention and he takes pains to describe it as simply and clearly as possible. But there is also the mysterious force of the place on his mind, his sense of himself, what he describes as: "the emptying...[the] radical change in my ideas out there." Why is this so? Why does *this* place move him so, seem to open up such a vast new space within him? It is difficult to say. But it seems clear that it is this entire complex reality—the particular character of the place itself, its capacity to take life within him and kindle his imagination, his sense of new horizons of meaning opening up within this particular landscape—that accounts for his insistent attention to place during the last months of his life.

Still, one catches glimpses in these late journal entries of a fundamental, perhaps irresolvable tension in Merton's attitude toward place. On the one hand, particular places, in all their complexity, speak to him ever more deeply of the possibility of finding a real home in the world. On the other hand, such places become part of an increasingly resonant metaphorical or symbolic language, pointing to and providing access to an elusive interior place Merton seeks to inhabit. In a journal entry dated May 30, 1968, written shortly after his return from California, he recalls: "The worshipful cold spring light on the sandbanks of Eel River, the immense silent redwoods. Who can see such trees and bear to be away from them? I must go back. It is not right that I should die under lesser trees." But he also acknowledges "the country which is nowhere is the real home; only it seems that the Pacific Shore at Needle Rock is more nowhere than this, and Bear Harbor is more nowhere still."[75] These observations express a particular longing for the Pacific Coast. They suggest, at least implicitly, that this place is a place better suited to him (at least at this point in his life) than Kentucky. Yet the first reflects a feeling of deep affinity for a particular place, while the second, with its evocation of the "country which is nowhere," subtly undermines that idea. It is true that particular places (Needle Rock and Bear Harbor) are seen to be "more nowhere" than others. Still, the language of place bends and stretches here to suggest a spiritual awareness both embedded in a particular place but also transcending it.[76]

These ruminations on the "real home" that is "nowhere," arise at precisely the moment when Merton's imaginative life is becoming more and more taken up with the possibility that he may be moving toward a condition of permanent homelessness. Not only, perhaps not even primarily in physical terms, but rather toward a radical, internal homelessness, borne of a renewed commitment to a renunciation of all that is known and familiar to him. While in New Mexico, Merton was reading the *Bhagavad Gita,* and was reflecting on its depiction of "the states of life." He was beginning to see clearly that his present life was that of *Vanaprastha*, "the forest life...a life of privacy and quasi retirement." But in a journal entry dated May 16, 1968, he acknowledged the sense of attraction he is beginning to feel toward the last stage of *Sanyasa*: "Total renunciation. Homelessness, begging. The Sanyasin lives only on food given to him. He is freed from all ritual obligation. The sacred fire is kindled only within. No household shrine. No temple. He is entirely turned to deliverance, renouncing all activity and attachment, all fear, all greed, all care, without home, without roof, without place, without name, without office, without function, without reputation, without care for reputation, without being known."[77] As an ideal, this extreme vision of ascetic practice had real appeal for Merton at this moment of his life, corresponding as it did to his desire for a more radical renunciation and a deeper practice of solitude. As a practical form of life, it is more difficult to imagine how it could be realized. And while it was a deep, inner change he was seeking above all else, increasingly he found himself unable to dissociate this longing from the question of where and how he was to live. Merton's attention was clearly focused on "a new path … opening up." But it was a path whose direction and trajectory remained mostly unknown to him. Ultimately, it seems, the hunger for home, for a safe place to dwell, could not be separated from the desire to keep moving ever deeper into the mystery that was beckoning him forward.[78]

On October 15, 1968, shortly after his plane took off from San Francisco on its way to Asia, Merton wrote: "The moment of take-off was ecstatic. The dewy wing was suddenly covered with rivers of cold sweat running backward. The window wept jagged shining courses of tears. Joy. We left the ground—I with Christian mantras and a great sense of destiny, of being at last on my true way after years of waiting and wondering and fooling around. May I not come back without having settled the great affair. And found also the great compassion, *mahakaruna* … I am going home, to the home where I have never been in this body.…"[79] What a strange idea: going home to a place where one has never been, at least in the body. And yet this is how Merton framed his journey to Asia: as a homecoming to an as-yet-unknown place. This comment reveals much about Merton's shifting interior landscape during the last years of his life, and his growing sense that his own Christian monastic vocation could only be understood fully in light of insights from Asian spiritual traditions. He felt at home there, more so than he often felt within his own Catholic tradition and he sensed that his journey to Asia might reveal to him the full meaning of this intuition.

Yet, only a month before leaving for Asia, while staying at Christ in the Desert Monastery in New Mexico, Merton had reflected in very different terms about his upcoming journey. "A journey is a bad death," he noted, "if you ingeniously grasp or remove all that you had and were before you started, so that in the end you do not change in the least. The stimulation enables you to grasp more raffishly at the same, familiar, distorted illusions. You come home only confirmed in greater greed—with new skills (real or imaginary) for satisfying it. I am not going 'home.' The purpose of this death is to become truly homeless.… There is," he said "no place left."[80] No place left. One senses here a deep reckoning with the old monastic question of relinquishment:

was he prepared to relinquish his identity, his entire life, for the sake of the "one thing necessary?" On his trip to Asia, this would mean remaining vigilant against the temptation to become a tourist and turn the journey—and the landscape of Asia—into an object, or a kind of currency to be hoarded. Whatever the journey might hold for him, he was beginning to realize the need to let go of attachment to any particular outcome, any ideal image of what the trip should mean. He had to let himself go into the unknown, "become truly homeless."[81]

On November 16, less than a month before he died, Merton found himself staying at the Mim Tea Estate in Darjeeling. A little more than a week earlier, he had concluded the last of three momentous encounters with the Dalai Lama. Now he was resting, recovering from a chronic, lingering cold, and struggling to absorb the meaning of those encounters. It was from here that he set out to meet Chatral *rinpoche,* whom he described as "the greatest *rinpoche* I have met so far." They met at *ani gompa,* a small nunnery near Chatral's hermitage above the village of Ghoom near Darjeeling in the Himalayan hill region of West Bengal, India. Merton's account of his encounter with Chatral reveals him as having been intensely conscious of both where he was and of the immensity of what was unfolding before and within him.

> [We spoke of] *dharmakaya*—the Risen Christ, suffering, compassion for all creatures, motives for 'helping others'—but all leading back to *dzogchen,* the ultimate emptiness, the unity of *sunyata* and *karuna,* going 'beyond the *dharmakaya*,' and 'beyond God' to the ultimate perfect emptiness. He said he had meditated in solitude for thirty years or more and had not attained to perfect emptiness and I said I hadn't either.
>
> The unspoken or half-spoken message of the talk was our complete understanding of each other as people who were somehow on the edge of great realization and knew it and were trying, somehow or other, to go out and get lost in it....[82]

This encounter was for Merton perhaps the most significant experience of his entire Asian trip, save his great moment of awakening at Polonnaruwa. It shares with that later experience a sense of deepening clarity (his sense of being "somehow on the edge of a great realization") as well as a growing recognition of all that lay beyond his understanding and conscious awareness. This encounter was both intensely particular—he recalls Chatral as looking "like a vigorous old peasant in a Bhutanese jacket tied at the neck with thongs and a red woolen cap on his head"; and the nunnery as, "two or three cottages just down behind the parapet of the road"—and capacious beyond his ability to express. He was going home; and he was hoping to get lost.

By now home and homelessness had become powerful and necessary metaphors in Merton's contemplative vocabulary, metaphors he could not do without when engaging the deepest concerns of his life. And yet, I think there are also traces of geography and autobiography hidden within these comments, and that these trace elements can help us understand better the power these metaphors had for Merton, and the power they can have for us in helping us understand the role of place in contemplative living. Merton's journals reveal a deep preoccupation with the meaning of place, a preoccupation that seems to have been rooted to a great degree in painful memories of his own rootless childhood. His reflections on place required him to face these wounded places in himself as part of the larger work of opening himself to the healing work of God. As such, they were crucial to his growth and development as a contemplative. But it seems clear that he also experienced healing and deep joy in learning to pay attention to and cherish the places to which he believed God had providentially guided him. In so doing he learned to cherish the world itself, to feel at home there, even as he continued more and more taking on the mind of an exile.

In the end Thomas Merton did make it home. A simple white cross marks the place of his burial among his brother monks at Gethsemani Abbey. But his journey home was anything but simple. Following his sudden death (likely by accidental electrocution) at Suwanganiwas, a Red Cross Center outside of Bangkok, his body was placed on a United States Air Force jet carrying the bodies of American soldiers killed in Vietnam back to the United States. His final passage home seems a fittingly ambiguous symbol for one who expressed so eloquently in his own life and writing such deep solidarity and compassion for the suffering and marginalized. At the end, he seemed, like the soldiers he accompanied, strangely homeless.

"Where are we really going? Always home." So claims the poet Novalis. On his final journey to Asia, Thomas Merton was convinced that he was "going home, to the home where I have never been in this body...."[83] Is this geography? Autobiography? Metaphor? It is difficult to say. These elements of experience, it turns out, are so intricately bound up together that it seems hardly possible to think of them separately. So it is with our efforts at place-making. We want, as Robert Adams suggests, to "see more." To do so means learning to trace the contours of our lives as they are shaped by the particular places in which we have lived, as well as by the places we have lost. We are also called to see and notice and cherish the places themselves in all their intricate complexity. And we are invited to inhabit a rich interior landscape, rooted in the concrete particularities of our lives, but expanding outward toward a metaphorically resonant, endlessly receding horizon.

5

Prosoche: *The Art of Attention*

The highest ecstasy is … attention at its fullest.[1]

SIMONE WEIL

Nothing is more essential to prayer than attentiveness.[2]

EVAGRIUS OF PONTUS

"THE SALMON ARE back. I saw them yesterday." Sr. Claire whispers these words to me at breakfast on New Year's morning. She offers this report to me in her usual, straightforward manner. Yet there is more than a little excitement in her voice. The salmon in the Mattole River watershed here in Northern California have been struggling for survival. Their habitat has been so severely compromised by logging that fewer and fewer of them have been making it upstream each year to their spawning grounds. There is concern that soon they may stop coming altogether. So, their return this year is cause for celebration. And word of their presence has now become part of our New Year's celebration at Redwoods Monastery. Soon, I am standing on the bank of Thompson Creek gazing down into the rushing water below. But I do not see them. Not immediately anyway. I laugh at my own impatience. Then I take a deep breath and settle in to wait and watch. I am joined in this vigil by Claire and by my daughter Julia. It is cool and dark under the canopy of redwood, alder, and maple trees, silent, except for the sound of the wind and the water. I shift my weight from one foot to the other and continue scanning the water below. Still nothing. Perhaps I am not looking in the right place. But it has been so long since I have seen salmon in the wild. Would I recognize them even if I saw them? I am not sure.

It is a familiar feeling, this uncertainty about what I am looking for and how to look for it. And it pertains not only to salmon but to almost everything that matters most to me. This concern with learning how to look, how to pay attention, how to see—learning to avoid missing, through carelessness or inattention, that which is most precious and valuable—is, I think, at the heart of what first brought me to this monastery over thirty years ago. And it is what draws me here still. The previous evening, I had gathered with the members of the Redwoods Monastery community and with other friends of the community who had joined them for the New Years-Epiphany celebration, to sit in the darkness of the monastery chapel, waiting, watching, keeping vigil. Standing on the edge of the riverbank this morning is, I begin to see, another way of keeping vigil, part of the essential spiritual practice of paying attention.

In the Christian spiritual tradition, the practice of watchfulness or keeping vigil traces its roots back to at least the late third and early fourth centuries, when Christian monastics first entered into the silence and solitude of the Egyptian desert to search for God. The early monks spoke of the value of *prosoche* or attention, of *nepsis* or vigilance, and of *hesychia* or stillness in their quest for an encompassing, contemplative awareness of the Divine. At its deepest level, the contemplative life was understood by the ancient monastics as a way of seeing (or to extend the metaphor as the monks often did, a way of listening or touching or tasting or smelling). *Theoria*, the word most often used to describe this contemplative awareness, refers to a way of seeing that includes but also transcends what is visible on the surface. It is a way of seeing deeply into the *whole* of reality, God, the world, everything, and situating oneself with integrity in relation to this whole.

But what does it mean to see and apprehend the whole? What does it mean to see in a way that honors both what is visible to the eyes as well as what is not visible? In an age of ecological crisis, addressing these questions has become both more crucial and more problematic than ever. As the very fabric of life continues to fray and tear, the need for us to be able to apprehend the whole, to see all things as existing in intimate relationship with one another, has never been more necessary. In spite of this, some of our most characteristic ways of thinking about and imagining the world have made it increasingly difficult for us to do so. Nowhere is this more apparent than in the oft-noted bifurcation and antagonism between scientific and religious ways of apprehending reality. Although both science and religion have a deep investment in being able to apprehend the whole of reality, the radical materialism and reductionism that underlies so much contemporary scientific thought and the radical transcendence and dualism at the heart of so much contemporary religious thought and practice makes a rapprochement between them seem, at times, impossible. And in the present cultural moment, at least in North America, the often-aggressive sense of antagonism between Darwinian determinism and classical religious thought and practice (in particular, though not exclusively, fundamentalist Christian thought and practice) only seems to be deepening. We are being encouraged to see reality not as whole, but as bifurcated or fragmented, as rooted either in matter or in spirit, as guided either by biological forces or by an unseen, divine hand.[3]

That this fragmented vision of reality seems so transparently thin and inadequate has done little to undermine its imaginative and even programmatic power in the present moment. Nor can one avoid the sense that it is contributing profoundly to our deepening feeling of alienation from the living world, to what some have referred to as the disenchantment of the world.[4] Still, there are other ways of seeing and apprehending reality that are more subtle and more deeply rooted in our intuitive feeling for the whole, and that are not as susceptible to such simple reductions. The ancient Christian contemplative tradition, with its deep commitment to the simple practice of *prosoche* or attention, offers one important resource for helping us recover a more encompassing vision of the whole. One also finds a striking commitment to the practice of attention in modern and contemporary traditions of reflection on the natural world. And while the precise meaning of what it is to pay attention varies considerably among and between these traditions, there are compelling reasons for considering them together. Perhaps the most significant reason is their shared sense of what it means to cultivate the art of attention as part of a serious, disciplined practice. The precise shape of this discipline came to mean one thing for the monk, and another for the poet and naturalist. But one can often discern a shared sense of the value of the *practice* itself, of all that can come from learning to be still and pay attention—to oneself, to the world, and yes, to the mysterious sense of the whole that sometimes emerges from such practice. The recovery of such practice can, I believe, help us heal some of the imaginative rifts that have prevented us from seeing and living in the world with a sense of its integrity, beauty, and mystery. Learning to pay attention, in such a way that we can begin to perceive and become responsive to what Wordsworth called "the life of things," may well be one of the most important contributions we can make to the work of ecological renewal.

Cleansing the Doors of Perception

To *think* of a thing is different from to *perceive it* as 'to
walk' is from 'to feel the ground under you.'[5]

SAMUEL TAYLOR COLERIDGE

Standing on the banks of Thompson Creek at Redwoods Monastery that morning, scanning the water for the returning salmon, I found myself suddenly aware of another moment years earlier when I stood looking out onto the Columbia River near my childhood home in Washington. Or rather, looking out onto the enormous Grand Coulee Dam that spanned its banks. And blocked its flow. I remember how the sheer enormity of the dam staggered my ten-year-old imagination. I felt dwarfed by it, reduced to something small and fragile and insignificant. My stomach pitched and churned as I gazed out onto its immensity. I thought: if it wanted to, this thing could engulf me. It was 1964. I was traveling through Eastern Washington on vacation with my family and we had made a detour on our journey back home to Seattle just to see the dam. It did not disappoint. I stood there a long time looking out onto that vast expanse of concrete (enough to bury the state of Texas a foot deep, I was told), listening to the roar of the water as it tumbled down, down, down into the abyss. I thought about the turbines, hidden deep inside the dam. They were especially fascinating to me. I did not even understand altogether what they were, how they worked, only that by some strange alchemy involving water, gravity, and the churning of those turbines, a massive amount of energy came coursing out of that Dam. Power. Electricity: enough to run everything—the lights in our home, my electric train, the entire city of Seattle where I lived. My father worked for a lighting company at the time; those were his light bulbs (I imagined) lighting up the skyscrapers in downtown Seattle. I had just done a third-grade report on light bulbs, tracing the intricate path of those frail filaments along which a vast, unseen source of energy coursed and emerged, eventually, as light. Standing there that day on the Grand Coulee Dam, it all came together for me: the wonderworld of technology, the seemingly infinite promise of the future, all that we, I, could do to change the world.

Another thing I realize as I reflect back on that day: I hardly noticed the river—the mighty Columbia—at all. It was an afterthought. So were the salmon. Nor did I think to ask who had lived there before the dam was constructed, or what had become of their home and their culture. No, I was mesmerized by this technological colossus, unable to see anything beyond its mass and weight. It had created a cosmos all its own and for the moment I stood within it.

It is troubling for me, more than forty years later, to have to reckon with this experience. It so clearly expresses the character of my life in that place at the time—detachment and alienation from the natural world—and my own complicity in its impoverishment. Certainly, I had a strong sense of the beauty of the Pacific Northwest, something that lives deeply within me even now. But I had no particular sense that my relationship with the place had a moral or spiritual character, that it involved reciprocity or responsibility. Nothing in my Catholic school education had led me to think in these terms—not even the sacramental tradition in which I had been raised (and to which I devoted myself for many years as an altar boy). Nor had I been taught to think this way at home. I was in this respect typical of many of those living at the time in my home place: appreciative of the physical beauty of our home, but unaware of and unprepared to take responsibility for the effects of our lives upon the world around us. The damming of the Columbia by then had already drastically depleted the salmon run. It had also flooded the dwellings and sacred sites of the native peoples, and helped accelerate their displacement from the shore of the Columbia to distant reservations. But there were formidable economic interests that ensured that this and other dams would be built, that the wild Columbia would be reduced to what it has now become: a cluster of lakes.

That all of this could have unfolded without serious resistance or even comment by the large majority of those living in the Pacific Northwest, and that I myself should have been so completely unaware of these realities, is to me both astonishing and shameful. I was only a child. But still I wonder: why was it so difficult for me, for us, to *see* the river, or for that matter the world through which it coursed? I have since come to realize that the fate of the Columbia is hardly remarkable at all and that a similar fate has befallen wild rivers all across the West. At the root of these developments is the widespread acceptance of the notion that rivers are to be thought of (seen) fundamentally as natural resources—that is, as elements within a complex socio-economic calculus that determines how wealth is defined and understood in our society. Gradually, this sense of things is beginning to change, as more and more inhabitants of this region (and beyond) have begun to ask about the health and well-being of their rivers and of the possibility of reimagining and restoring impoverished, degraded watersheds. There are more and more cases, such as in the Klamath river watershed on the California-Oregon border, where the particular economic-ecological-moral calculus that has led to the degradation of so many watersheds and ecosystems is beginning to change, where the dams are beginning to come down and the salmon are starting to return. We are learning to see these places more fully, and to reorient our lives in relation to them.

Still, the challenge of learning to see the places we inhabit in all their vibrancy, beauty, and power, and to value them in other than purely utilitarian terms, remains. There are still too many instances where our inability or unwillingness to see has resulted in the most callous disregard and destruction of the natural world. It is here, it seems to me, that the contemplative traditions, with their deep commitment to cultivating both a sharply focused attention and an encompassing awareness, can be of such great help to us. For the contemplative traditions (by which I mean to include here not only monastic traditions of thought and practice but also kindred religious, poetic, and ecological traditions) invite us to consider not only what it means to see the world, but also what it means to see and know the self *within* the world. Indeed, they are bound up together. From this perspective, learning to see anything truly cannot occur without a significant deepening of self-knowledge. Nor can one hope to acquire any significant knowledge of the self if one does not experience a cleansing of what poet and visionary William Blake called the "doors of perception." In his work *The Marriage of Heaven and Hell,* Blake memorably asserted: "If the doors of perception were cleansed, everything would appear to us as it is, infinite. For we have closed ourselves up, 'til we see all through the narrow chinks of our cavern."[6] This statement expresses with haunting clarity an insight one encounters continuously in the contemplative traditions of thought and practice: that the true significance of what we see and experience is often obscured by a kind of moral-spiritual blindness. Our vision of the world is incomplete, distorted. We still possess the capacity for living within a fuller, more encompassing vision of reality. But it must be *retrieved.* The imagination itself must be made whole.

The great English poet Samuel Taylor Coleridge points to something similar in his reflection on what it means to *perceive* a thing: "To *think* of a thing is [as] different from to *perceive it*," he noted, "as 'to walk' is from 'to feel the ground under you.'" What is it to perceive a thing, in the sense that Coleridge means it here? It is, I believe, to allow it to enter into one's imaginative life so that it becomes part of the fabric of one's being. Certainly, perception, understood in this sense, involves thinking. But it is a certain kind of thinking that is sensitive to nuance, hungry for meaning, open to ambiguity. It often proceeds slowly, carefully, allowing experience and awareness to accrue gradually. It is thinking that wants to enter into lively relationship with the thing about which one is thinking, perhaps become immersed in it. In one of this notebook entries, Coleridge noted: "There have been times when looking up beneath the shelt[e]ring Tree, I could Invest every leaf with Awe."[7] Here, perhaps, one catches a glimpse of that cleansing of the doors of perception to which Blake alludes. And if it is fleeting in character, such perception is nevertheless real, and can gradually become woven into a growing awareness of what Wordsworth describes as "the deep power of Joy…[by which]…We see into the *Life* of Things."[8]

Joy. Awe. The capacity to see into the *life* of things. Everything appearing to us as it is: infinite. Here are elements of a vocabulary of contemplative practice that point to a different and fuller way of seeing and living in the world.

Thinking about all of this in the context of my experience at Redwoods Monastery, especially the practice of keeping vigil (both the long vigil in the monastery chapel on New Year's Eve and the vigil on the banks of Thompson Creek on New Year's Day), I find myself considering again the meaning of our collective, if varied, efforts to cultivate a habit of attention that takes seriously the deep connection between what some have referred to as the interior and exterior landscapes. Even this language of two landscapes, I realize, risks perpetuating the kind of fragmented way of apprehending reality that has already done so much harm—to us and to the world. What we need most at this moment is a language and a way of living supple and fluid enough to allow us to dwell deeply within the liminal space or penumbral region where the imagination and the living world meet and move together.[9] The two landscapes, if one wishes to speak in these terms, need to be seen and apprehended as dimensions of a single, whole, indivisible reality. But how to find such a language? How to cultivate such a way of living? In what follows, I want to focus my attention on these two fundamental questions by considering how the ancient spiritual practice of watchfulness or attention, and its contemporary poetic, artistic, and ecological expressions might help us reimagine what it is to live in the world with genuine regard.

Cultivating a Habit of Regard

Live as though you were dying every day.[10]

ABBA ANTONY

I look at the world; this world that I quite often feel as though I were seeing for the first time.[11]

SENECA

Abba Poemen, one of the most highly respected of the early Christian monks, once said: "Vigilance, attention to the self, and discernment; these are the guides of the soul."[12] Among the ancient Christian monks and among many of their non-Christian contemporaries, the cultivation of the habit of *prosoche* or attention—to the self, to others, to the world, and to God—was close to the heart of what it meant to practice the spiritual life. "Pay attention to yourself," was often the first word of counsel a monk would receive upon embarking on the ascetic path. But its importance endured throughout the life of those seeking to live this way of life with integrity and awareness, gaining new significance and meaning as one's life and experienced deepened. Toward the beginning of Athanasius's *Life of Antony*, the conversion to the monastic way of life of Antony is described in these simple terms: "He began to pay attention to himself."[13] At the end of his life, Antony is reported to have exhorted his disciples: "Live as though you were dying every day, paying attention to yourselves and remembering what you heard from my preaching."[14] Such statements make clear the centrality of *prosoche* for the life of the monk. But what exactly did such attention entail? What was its meaning in the life of the one who undertook this way of life? And how did it contribute to the monk's capacity to see and live in the world more fully?

One response to these questions is to note the importance of the connection, as the saying of Abba Poemen indicates, between the practice of *prosoche* and the work of *diakrisis* or discernment. Indeed, in some respects, these can be considered almost equivalents. Both ideas point to the notion that the cultivation of the self is a profound, moral-spiritual project apart from which no real understanding of anything is possible. Discernment here refers to the capacity, rooted in deep experience, for making subtle judgments about the questions that matter most. In the desert monastic tradition, discernment came to be considered one of the characteristic features of one possessing spiritual maturity or wisdom. The one possessing discernment could sort through the myriad thoughts and impulses flowing through the mind and distinguish between those most likely to feed the ego or otherwise blind the soul and those that would lead one to become more deeply grounded in the true center of his own identity in God. The lack of discernment in the life of the monk was likewise considered fatal. "Without discernment we are lost," said one of the elders. This was no small problem among those who undertook this life, for as so many of the stories emanating from this tradition suggest, the tendency toward self-deception and moral blindness was (then as now) pervasive. Engaging in the long, slow process of learning to pay attention to oneself and to cultivate discernment was crucial if one was to have any hope of realizing in one's life a genuine sense of openness, honesty, and freedom. It was the key to acquiring something the monks valued above all else: the ability to see and live with a pure heart.

For the monks, realizing this ideal in their lives meant above all learning to live with an intense awareness of the present moment. This is the significance of Antony's statement, "Live as though you were dying every day." Live, in other words, with a continuous awareness of your mortality and hence of the unutterable preciousness of every moment. As philosopher Pierre Hadot has demonstrated, the practice of *prosoche* figured importantly not only within early Christian monasticism but also for many non-Christian philosophers, especially those from the Stoic and Epicurean schools. Here also, *prosoche* was understood as a fundamental spiritual exercise, the primary aim of which was to alter one's very consciousness of time, leading one to an intense, encompassing awareness of what it is to live in the present moment. "It is a continuous vigilance and presence of mind, self consciousness which never sleeps, and a constant tension of the spirit," says Hadot.[15] Marcus Aurelius gives eloquent expression to the practice of *prosoche* as it was understood within the Stoic tradition: "Everywhere and at all times, it is up to you to rejoice piously at what is occurring *at the present moment*, to conduct yourself with justice towards the people who are *present here and now*, and to apply rules of discernment to your *present* representations...."[16] The monastic tradition had its own analogous understanding of what it meant to live with an open, free awareness of the present moment. Athanasius relates that Antony used to make no attempt to remember the time he had already spent at his ascetic efforts, but rather made a new effort each day, as if beginning afresh each moment. "He observed that in saying *today* he was not counting the time passed, but as one always establishing a beginning, he endeavored each day to present himself as the sort of person ready to appear before God—that is, pure of heart and prepared to obey his will, and no other."[17] Evagrius of Pontus, one of the great monastic teachers of contemplative practice, noted that prayer, by which he meant the profound communion of the mind with God, was only possible for one who knew what it meant to pay attention: "If you seek prayer attentively you will find it," says Evagrius, "for nothing is more essential to prayer than attentiveness."[18] To pay attention to one's own existence so carefully that each moment carried with it a sense of living within eternity could have a significant impact on one's very sense of what it meant to be alive. But such heightened awareness of the present moment was not limited to the personal or even interpersonal dimension of one's life. It extended, potentially, to one's very sense of what it is be alive in the world.

In an important essay entitled "The Sage and the World," Hadot suggests how the practice of *prosoche*, in particular this acute attention to the present moment, could contribute to a growing sensitivity in the life of the sage to an awareness of the world as a whole and to what it meant to be alive in the world. Indeed, for the sage as for the monk, awareness of the present moment was inescapably bound up with an awareness of existence itself. The first-century Roman Stoic philosopher Seneca reflects on this mystery in one of his *Letters to Lucilius*, commenting: "As for me, I usually spend a great deal of time in the contemplation of wisdom. I look at it with the same stupefaction with which, on other occasions, I look at the world; this world that I quite often feel as though I were seeing for the first time."[19] Here we see the kind of dramatic deepening of perception that could and sometimes did occur, according to Seneca, when one learned to pay attention. The habitual way of seeing things—that is, looking with a glancing or cursory attention—suddenly falls away in favor of a sense of astonishment, or as Seneca puts it, stupefaction, in the face of what one appears to be seeing for the first time. It is noteworthy also that Seneca makes hardly any distinction here between the power of one's perception of wisdom, that is the inner life of the sage, and the power of one's perception of the life of the world. These were seen and experienced as elements of a single, continuous awareness of the whole of reality. To see "as if for the first time," was to be alive and awake to oneself and the world.

The Christian contemplative tradition struggled deeply with what it meant to learn to pay attention, to live with a simple awareness of the whole. The monks recognized how easy it was to become distracted, how various and complex and powerful were the impulses and thoughts that drew and held and obscured the mind, that prevented one from acquiring the simple, honest awareness of the self and of God that was at the heart of contemplative living. They knew that unless one could learn to attend to and eventually master the myriad conflicting "thoughts" that arose continuously in one's mind, one's consciousness would never be clear enough or free enough to enable one to pay attention to the things that matter most—the truth of one's own life, the needs of one's fellow human beings, the luminosity of the living world, or the abiding presence of God. The ascetic work oriented toward clearing space in the mind became the necessary ground out of which the very possibility of a more encompassing awareness of the whole could arise and take root in one's life. Still, the realization of this ideal in the life of the monk was immensely difficult, for the effort to practice attention in relation to any particular aspect of one's life inevitably raised more searching questions arising out of the deeper currents of one's life, often rooted in feelings and experiences of which the monk had no conscious awareness.

Why, for example, were anger and judgment and pride so tenacious, so difficult to overcome? Why was it often so difficult to pray? Why was it so challenging to live with others in community, so difficult to express simple affection or love toward another? These fundamental questions often had a deeply personal character, touching on the most intimate and hidden dimensions of a monk's life. But they also possessed very often a relational, social, even ecological character, touching on the monk's capacity to engage others and the world as a whole, not in a condition of perpetual anxiety and blindness (i.e., not beholden to the power of the passions or thoughts) but openly and freely. The early monastic literature bears witness to the monks' conviction that it was indeed possible to learn to live this way; but it also suggests how long and difficult the struggle to achieve such freedom could be. All the crucial spiritual exercises—solitude, stillness, fasting, attention to one's thoughts, meditation on scripture, submission to the authority of an elder—were oriented toward helping the monk realize this freedom and express it in relation to God and others. And all of them depended on the ability of the monk to cultivate the capacity for paying attention, for resisting the inclination to give way to habitual distraction. Mature contemplative practice, understood as the capacity to live with a simple awareness of the presence of God at the heart of everything, was itself the fruit of such attention.

Sometimes one needed to attend to and resist or struggle against a particular thought or impulse, as for example the temptation to succumb to or act out of lust or pride or anger. If given enough room to fester in the soul, such thoughts could consume one entirely, often leading to a condition of chronic anxiety or even despair. The upwelling of such thoughts in the mind (or as the monks often imagined them, as attacks from the demons) could be utterly debilitating and demoralizing; but attending to them carefully also provided the monk with an opportunity to scrutinize the complex character of his desires and the wounded, anomalous places in his soul to which such thoughts appealed. Bringing these thoughts to conscious awareness and struggling to understand oneself in relationship to them could help to initiate a gradual transformation in which their particular power gradually dissipated and the mind could regain its own original freedom.

An important example of this work can be seen in the monks' struggle to practice true detachment. Captured emblematically in Antony's response to the radical call to discipleship of Matthew 19:21, the ascetic impulse toward detachment gave crucial expression to the desire for a single-minded existence focused on God. At the most fundamental level, this meant simplifying one's life, letting go of everything that might prevent one from opening oneself fully and freely to God—one's possessions, one's place in the world, one's family even; but more than this, it meant relinquishing the very identity that one had built upon these things. Clearly, such radical renunciation was a profoundly liberating gesture for many of the early Christian monks; but it could also be destabilizing and disorienting, provoking fears and anxieties that could utterly overwhelm the one who had initially made such a gesture in faith and hope. The practice of attention, in this context, involved learning to notice and respond to the particular thoughts and fears that most directly threatened to undermine one's purity of intention or the thoughts that tended to arise when one failed to live into this intention with honesty or integrity. Paying attention to such thoughts could be immensely painful, for doing so could and often did lead the monk toward an utterly debilitating "loss of nerve," a discouragement so deep that his very sense of the presence of God and of the grounding truth of his own life might be undone completely. Yet, for anyone who hoped to arrive eventually at a place of true freedom, it was critical to learn to pay attention to all those thoughts and thought streams arising in the soul.

The "great dust cloud of considerations" that Antony described as having blinded his vision in the early stages of his ascetic journey was in fact comprised of very particular thoughts and feelings that needed to be sorted through and distinguished from one another if the monk was to have any hope of arriving at a clearer vision of his life. For the one struggling to practice detachment, for example, there was a particular need to pay attention to the sense of sadness (*lupe*) that sometimes arose in the mind as one considered all one was leaving behind. This, at least, is how Evagrius of Pontus framed the question. "The monk with many possessions," says Evagrius, "carries around the memories of possessions as a heavy burden and a useless weight; he is stung with sadness and is mightily pained in his thoughts. He has abandoned his possessions and is lashed with sadness."[20] *Lupe* or sadness occupied a central place in Evagrius's taxonomy of the eight principal thoughts with which the monk must struggle. And as with all the other principal thoughts, the power of sadness lay in the particular way it acts upon the mind, allowing certain latent fears and anxieties to take hold of one and determine how one understands one's experience, indeed one's entire existence. The persistent presence of sadness in the soul could, Evagrius suggests, lead one eventually to be overcome with doubt and regret about the fundamental choice to open oneself to the monastic path. Feelings of sadness about one's lost possessions are the primary expression of this doubt and regret; they are experienced, Evagrius suggests, sometimes as a kind of weight, other times as a stinging whip. The images themselves suggest what is really at issue: that one has not truly let go of these things or one's feelings about all they represent for one's life. They are still present in the mind as a heavy, tormenting presence. It is for this reason that the work of attending to and struggling to understand and overcome the debilitating hold of such thoughts on the mind is so crucial in the life of the monk. Evagrius describes the serious consequences of failing to do so: "When certain thoughts gain the advantage, they bring the soul to remember home and parents and one's former life. And when they observe that the soul does not resist but rather follows right along and disperses itself among thoughts of pleasures, then with a hold on it they plunge it into sadness with the realization that former things are no more and cannot be again because of the present way of life. And the miserable soul, the more it allowed itself to be dispersed among the former thoughts, the more it has now become hemmed in and humiliated by these latter ones."[21] This simple, phenomenological account of the monk's predicament forcefully conveys the sense of growing, deepening loss and disorientation that can take hold of one who has allowed thoughts to go unexamined and unchecked. The psychological complexity of the experience is striking; such thoughts, to the extent that they are ignored or misdiagnosed, only grow in number and subtlety and power the longer they inhabit the soul. The monk who does not attend to or learn to understand them may well come to experience himself as bound in a kind of web—humiliated, discouraged, unable to see anything, unable to pray.

This was, in Evagrius's understanding, the most devastating effect of this dispersion of thoughts: contemplation, that pure, unfettered apprehension of the presence of God at the center of one's life, became impossible. "Sunlight does not penetrate a great depth of water; the light of contemplation does not illuminate a heart overcome by sadness."[22] One could also say the same of a heart overcome by anger, pride, gluttony, or any of the other *logismoi* or thoughts that threatened to colonize the soul. This is why the monastic tradition placed such emphasis on the need to purify and transform one's mind or heart: for the monk to experience the profound and abiding sense of God's presence that was the great hope of monastic life, it was necessary to have arrived at a place of genuine freedom. Only a sustained commitment to pay attention to oneself and search out the deep sources of the soul's chronic attachments could lead the monk to such a place.

The mysterious process of reshaping one's consciousness, which is fundamentally what the practice of attention to one's thoughts was understood to facilitate, was at the very heart of the monastic practice of *prosoche*. But practicing *prosoche* meant more than simply attending to and resisting those obsessive preoccupations symbolized by the *logismoi* or thoughts. It also meant learning to recognize and open oneself to those intimations of the presence of God always close to hand in the life of the monk. It meant learning to see—oneself, God and the world—with a full, free, encompassing vision. The specific practices understood to help one realize this vision—silence, solitude, dialogue with an elder, and rumination upon scripture, among others—both narrowed and sharpened the focus of the mind and opened it little by little to the widest possible horizon. The practice of rumination or meditation on scripture, nearly ubiquitous among the ancient Christian monks, provides a useful lens for considering how the practice of *prosoche* not only protected the monk from the kind of mental dissipation that made contemplation impossible, but also opened up a space where one's perceptive capacities became ever more refined and one could begin to sense oneself as dwelling in relation to the infinite.

The sustained practice of meditation on the Word of God was a foundational element in the daily round of communal prayer practiced by the ancient monks. Attending to the Word, turning it over carefully and reverently in the mind, was believed to provide protection and solace in the monk's continuous struggle against the demons, while also gradually opening up a space in the mind in which imageless or pure prayer could begin to take hold in one's life.[23] Part of what made the practice of rumination on the Word so important was precisely its facility for focusing the monk's attention on the simple awareness of God. A saying from the *Apophthegmata Patrum* tells of a brother who, while reciting Scripture at the *synaxis* with one of the elders, "forgot and lost track of a word of the psalm." The elder noticed this, and when the *synaxis* finished, described to the brother his own practice. "When I recite the *synaxis,* I think of myself as being on top of a burning fire: my thoughts cannot stray right or left." He then asked the brother: "where were your thoughts, when we were saying the *synaxis*, that the word of the psalm escaped you? Don't you know that you are standing in the presence of God and speaking to God?"[24] Here one catches a glimpse of how critical the simple capacity for paying attention was in the spiritual experience of the ancient monk. To allow one's attention to wander and to "lose track" of the psalm was, it seems, tantamount to losing track of the presence of God. Such a view perhaps says as much about the power the ancient monks attributed to the Word of God as it does about the power of attention itself. But there is a clear sense here that they are bound up together, that attention is not only an ascetic practice, but a disposition or orientation that is necessary for anyone who hoped to apprehend the Divine. Inattention or carelessness in one's practice of meditating on scripture could open the door to a stream of *logismoi* and cause one to become oblivious to the presence of God mediated through those words. It was this concern that led one elder to affirm: "if God reproaches us for carelessness in our prayers and distractions in our psalmody, we cannot be saved."[25]

The monks recognized that without a clear and abiding awareness of God's presence at the heart of one's life, there could be neither meaningful resistance to the many *logismoi* that constantly threatened to dissipate one's consciousness, nor a recognition of one's true identity in relation to the Divine. If to consent to *logismoi* meant, as has been suggested already, consecrating oneself to demonic partners, then attainment of the kind of tranquility of mind and purity of heart that came as a result of the practice of *prosoche* meant consecrating oneself to the One whose presence is revealed through the Word. Perhaps this helps to account for the monks' willingness to reduce the scope of their attention so radically, and for their commitment to seek and cultivate such profound simplicity of regard in their contemplative practice. In one of John Cassian's *Conferences*, Abba Isaac advocates the continual repetition of a single verse from scripture (Ps 70) as the key to opening up the consciousness to the presence of God. He claims that: "the verse ('O God, make haste to save me, O Lord, make haste to help me') is an impregnable battlement, a shield and a coat of mail which no spear can pierce ... it will be a saving formula in your heart."[26] This verse, with its concise, urgent expression of need and its hope that one will indeed be saved from whatever trouble one is facing, became particularly beloved of the ancient monks; indeed, it is still uttered in Christian monastic communities today at the beginning of gatherings for communal prayer.

Why were early monks prepared to put such trust in the simple repetition of a single verse from the Psalms? And how did such practice become part of the "saving" work of the contemplative? A clue is provided in Abba Isaac's allusion to the inner disposition one should cultivate in reciting and ruminating upon the text. He contends that "a person who perseveres [in such practice] in *simplicity and innocence* ... is protected."[27] The precise character of this disposition is not described here in any detail, but its basic meaning is not difficult to discern. The person who meditates in this way, Isaac suggests, has already begun to move beyond the condition of habitual distraction that characterizes the mind of the one who is still tyrannized by thoughts and impulses beyond his control. He is *protected* from them— that is, from the distraction and dissipation that comes from allowing them room to fester in the soul—by the simplicity and innocence with which he opens himself to the presence of God manifested in the Word. But it is more than simple protection; the acquisition of such simplicity and innocence is itself understood to be an expression of the soul's growing purification and openness, the *means* through which one could know and stand in the truth of God. Reciting the text in a condition of openness, vulnerability and trust, "ceaselessly revolving it" within oneself, would eventually lead one, the monks believed, to a place where "continual meditation becomes finally impregnated in [y]our soul."[28]

The practice of *prosoche* here entailed a steady deepening and simplification of the mind, as one moved from the recitation of a text with the lips—a physical, embodied act often undertaken in the company of others—to a largely internal and hidden process in which one's consciousness gradually became both capacious and simple enough to behold the Divine. While the precise manner in which this shift of awareness happened could not always be perceived or fully understood, the monks testify that through sustained practice the Word did sometimes become an "interior possession," so deeply absorbed into the monk's consciousness that it was no longer possible to discern any distance between the text, the One revealed in the text, and the person ruminating on the text. There was only an expansive awareness of oneself as living in the presence of God. Abba Nestoros, in another of Cassian's *Conferences,* describes the mysterious process of transformation this way: "If these things [from scripture] have been carefully taken in and stored up in the recesses of the soul and stamped with the seal of silence, afterwards they will be brought forth from the jar of your heart with great fragrance and like some perennial fountain will flow from the veins of experience and irrigate channels of virtue and will pour forth copious streams as if from some deep well in your heart."[29] It is difficult to miss here the sense of profound inner transformation that was, for the early monks, at the heart of their practice of simple attention to the Word. Nor should one underestimate the sense in which such attention became the ground of an encompassing awareness of the whole.

The *Conference* of Abba Isaac cited above provides further insight into how this process of rumination worked and why the particular quality of attention required for practicing it came to mean so much to the early monks. Above all, it was because of their conviction that the power and presence of God could be encountered and experienced only through such sharply focused attention. Abba Isaac claims that this verse from Psalm 70: "... Carries within it all the feelings of which human nature is capable. It can be adapted to every condition and can usefully deployed against every temptation ... this verse keeps us from despairing of our salvation since it reveals to us the One to whom we call...."[30] It is striking to note how capacious scripture was seen to be, a single verse carrying within it and calling forth from the one who recites it "all the feelings of which human nature is capable." A complex array of emotions is compressed into and carried by this briefest of utterances: a cry for help; humility; watchfulness (born of unending worry and fear); a sense of frailty; assurance; confidence; desire; love; terror. The spiritual *potency* this work is clear: it reveals, Abba Isaac claims, "the *One* to whom we call."

The early Christian monks were convinced that the practice of holding the Word at the center of one's consciousness would lead gradually toward a living *encounter* with the One speaking in and through the text. Abba Isaac suggests that to engage in meditation on the Word in this way would lead the monk beyond the wealth of thoughts that constantly threatened to undermine his sense of God's presence and toward a place of simplicity or poverty of intention. The mind will go on grasping this single verse of scripture "until it can cast away the wealth and multiplicity of other thoughts, and restrict itself to the poverty of a single verse."[31] When it does so, the monk may well find himself in that sublime place that Abba Isaac claims one can come to know when the experiential grasp of the Word becomes fused with the experience of pure prayer—"contemplation of God alone."

There is a clear bias in this teaching toward simplicity: God is the simple one *par excellent* and the one who wishes to know God must become simple, at least in the sense of allowing the mind to regain its capacity for simple, focused attention and awareness. Complexity, especially the baffling and often-chaotic complexity of the *logismoi,* is a clear source of pain and trouble in the monk's life; and the one who would gain access to the inner stillness that makes "contemplation of God alone" possible must learn to rein in and ultimately overcome the tyranny of this particular complexity. But what of the beautiful complexity of the world itself, especially the natural world? Is this also to be overcome and transcended? Or does it call in its own way for the monk's attention? Certainly there is ample testimony in this tradition to the need for the monk to overcome the temptations of the world. Indeed *fuga mundi* or flight from the world is one of the great themes of early Christian monastic teaching. But this ideal is more ambiguous and subtle than it often appears. Yes, certain aspects of life in the physical world—especially sexuality, material wealth, and inordinate attachment to home and family are often portrayed as particularly fraught with potential trouble for the one who seeks the deep freedom promised by monastic life. But as often as not, it is the inner disposition of the monk, the tendency to become enslaved by certain habits or practices that comes in for closest scrutiny, not the things themselves. And the force of eschatological awareness among the monks—their sense of living against the horizon of eternity—often led them to call into question the ultimate value of things that were judged to be, in comparison to the life of the world to come, inherently ephemeral. Such ideas certainly contributed, in parts of the monastic tradition at least, to the sense that "the things of this world" were not to be valued as highly as the ultimate realities rooted in the life of God. Evagrius, for example, believed that "If the intellect has not risen above the contemplation of the created world, it has not yet beheld the realm of God perfectly. For it may be occupied with the knowledge of intelligible things and so involved in their multiplicity."[32] This comment reveals the ongoing struggle the early monks often experienced in their attempts to affirm the transcendent and encompassing mystery of God that could be encountered in created things but not completely contained by them.

There are recurring voices within this contemplative tradition that insist that the highest forms of contemplation will always involve cultivating an openness or movement toward radical transcendence—toward a divine mystery beyond language, beyond images, and even beyond this world. Still, there is also evidence for the persistence of a tradition of thought and practice that came to be known as *theoria physike* or natural contemplation. In this approach to contemplative practice, attention to the natural world became a means of attending to the Divine; and awareness of the presence of the Divine unfolding within the mind could lead to a heightened sensitivity to the created world. Abba Moses, whose teaching is recorded in one of John Cassian's *Conferences*, comments on the immense difficulty for any embodied being of acquiring the kind of pure knowledge of God to which Evagrius refers. "To look upon God at all times and to be inseparable from Him, in the manner which you envisage, is impossible for a man still in the flesh and enslaved to weakness. In another way, however, it is possible to look upon God, for the manner of contemplating God may be conceived and understood in many ways. God is not only to be known in His blessed and incomprehensible being, for this is something which is reserved for saints in the age to come. He is also to be known from the grandeur and beauty of His creatures . . . ."[33] This idea, which would later develop into the notion of the "two books" (scripture and creation) by which God is known to human beings, suggests the importance the early monastic tradition attached to the practice of apprehending the Divine through the created world. If the practice of paying attention to the created world in this way was sometimes ambiguous or fraught with tension, there was nevertheless a clear sense in this tradition that authentic contemplative practice could and often did involve learning to see deeply into the created world.

Peter of Damaskos, an eleventh-century Eastern Christian writer, gives eloquent expression to this ideal, and points to the subtlety and depth involved in paying attention to the created world:

> By ... contemplating dispassionately the beauty and use of each thing, he who is illumined is filled with love for the Creator. He surveys all visible things in the upper and lower worlds: the sky, the sun, the moon, stars and clouds, water-spouts and rain, snow and hail, how in great heat liquids coagulate, thunder, lightning, the winds and breezes and the way they change, the seasons, the years, the days, the nights, the hours, the minutes, the earth, the sea, the countless flocks, the four-legged animals, the wild beasts and reptiles, all the kinds of bird[s], the springs and rivers, the many varieties of plant and herb, both wild and cultivated. He sees in all things the order, the equilibrium, the proportion, the beauty, the rhythm, the union, the harmony, the usefulness, the concordance, the variety... contemplating thus all created realities, he is filled with wonder.[34]

Such expressions of wonder in the midst of the created world are not uncommon in the Christian contemplative tradition. Still, this account presents a striking phenomenology of what it meant for the contemplative to learn to cultivate such wonder in response to the created world. A crucial dimension of this work, according to this particular witness, involved learning to contemplate the created world *dispassionately*. In English, this word has many different connotations, almost none of which capture the particular meaning it had in the ancient Christian contemplative tradition. There, as the work of Evagrius, Cassian, and others makes clear, it meant learning to see beyond or free from the passions, those anomalous thoughts and feelings that often clouded the mind and prevented it from apprehending reality freely and openly. To "contemplate dispassionately the beauty and use of each thing" is, in this sense, to see things clearly—unencumbered by the clinging, egoic mind. It is to be free and open enough in oneself to see things for what they are, to appreciate their particular qualities, and to see them as part of a whole. In the context of the Christian contemplative tradition, this means seeing them *in God*. Peter's account helps us to see this how intimately this contemplative experience of illumination—a strong recurring motif of spiritual awakening in the Eastern Christian tradition—is connected to a sense of deeper apprehension of the beauty and harmony of the created world. To wake up in this way is a single, integrated experience; it is to come alive and learn to see everything, oneself, God, the world, as part of a whole.

Attention as Ecological Practice

> [Darwin's] manner of deep watchfulness [allowed]
> the ordinary ground of life to become sanctified, to be
> brought into *sensus plenior*—a "fuller sense"—through
> the offering of simple attention.[35]
>
> LYANDA LYNN HAUPT

Can these ancient contemplative traditions help us in our efforts to learn to see and cherish the world more deeply? I confess that this question has come to have real personal importance for me. Over time, I have come to feel that the often-hidden work of contemplative practice—rooted in a simple, open-hearted attention—does have enormous meaning and significance. And that the deepening of awareness that occurs through this practice really can change the quality of being, not only one's own being but also the being of the world as a whole. This, I realize, is an audacious claim, and one that cannot be proven. Still, there is ample testimony from the contemplative traditions that such practice can and often does yield a deep sense of freedom and openness—to oneself, others, God, and the world as a whole. And that this shift in awareness has meaning not simply for the one engaging in such practice but also for the larger community, however that community is understood. The contemplative undertakes this work not only for himself or herself but also for the sake of the larger whole. My own experience of sitting in stillness, of waiting, listening, struggling in the silence of such contemplative space—whether in the company of my friends at Redwoods Monastery or as part of a more solitary practice—has given me glimpses into the kind of clarified awareness and deepened reciprocity that can arise when such simple attention takes root in the soul. It can soften the hard edges of one's habitual perceptions, so that what previously seemed utterly distinct or separate from one's own life now appears as intimately woven into the fabric of one's very being.

As I consider again my own experience growing up amidst the wild beauty of the Pacific Northwest, and how little I saw or felt the world around me, such contemplative practice takes on new meaning. I begin to see it as part of the work of reparation, part of my attempt to create in myself a more fluid and open space in which the world can live and breathe and move. Also a way of reckoning with my own deep sense of loss. Perhaps, I think, my own deepened regard for the world, *our* deepened regard, born of sustained contemplative practice, may contribute to its healing.

Still, I wonder: what would it mean for contemplative practice—in particular the practice of *prosoche* or attention—to be considered an integral part of a deepening *ecological* awareness? What shift or expansion in our very sense of contemplation would need to occur for us to include the living world as part of our contemplative practice? What kind of shift or expansion in our very understanding of contemplation would need to occur for us to include the living world as part of our shared contemplative practice? And how might such a reconceived understanding of contemplative practice—for example, a retrieval and renewal of the old idea of *theoria physike* or natural contemplation—contribute to actual ecological renewal? One such direction would be to apprentice ourselves to those who have realized in their own lives something of this holistic and integrating way of seeing the world. It is especially important in our own time, I believe, that we find a way of overcoming the kind of corrosive dichotomies that have prevented us from seeing the world as whole. At a moment when the very fabric of the world is fraying to the point of utter dissolution, it is more than a little dispiriting to behold the specter of militant Darwinism contending with equally dogmatic religious ideologies for cultural supremacy. Too often, this discourse is haunted by the old, reductive dualisms that do little to contribute to our capacity to reimagine the world as at once biologically complex, aesthetically rich, and spiritually significant. But one also finds work arising from a range of different discourses—science, literature, spirituality, and art—contributing to a less reductive, more nuanced and whole way of perceiving and living in the world. To consider the contemplative character of such work, to ask how our emerging efforts to notice, understand, and appreciate the living world more inclusively can help us heal both our divided imaginations and our increasingly fragmented world, is an important and necessary task.

Recent work on the origins of western science and on the work of early naturalists suggests that some of our assumptions about the fundamental differences distinguishing so-called "religious" from "scientific" ways of apprehending the natural world may need to be revised. This is particularly true if one focuses less on the explicit question of the possibility of the existence of God (in light of scientific discovery and thought) and more on the distinctive manner in which certain scientists and naturalists learned to look at the natural world.[36] In spite of many thoughtful attempts to find common ground between the respective positions of science and religion, the former question has often yielded a sense of radical incompatibility or incommensurability between two competing and ultimately alien positions. But if one pauses to examine carefully the particular manner in which many scientists and naturalists have trained themselves to gaze at the world, and to consider the language they use to describe their experience of the natural world, a very different sense of things emerges. Here one often finds a deeply contemplative sensibility that reveals a reverence and even a love for the world that often cannot be accounted for by employing the limited vocabulary of science. Such testimony ought to give us pause about making overly simple assessments about the absence of spiritual thought and practice, including contemplative practice, amidst the scientific community. This has led at least one observer to suggest that we need to begin thinking about the meaning of a "contemplative science."[37] While such practice of contemplative attention to the world cannot always be translated into an explicitly theistic worldview (indeed those who look at the world in this way often remain skeptical about traditional religious belief), it nevertheless suggests fruitful possibilities for considering anew the spiritual significance of the practice of looking carefully at the natural world.

Richard Holmes's book, *The Age of Wonder: How the Romantic Generation Discovered the Beauty and Terror of Science*, offers a marvelous starting point for helping us rethink what it means to attend to and value the natural world—on its own terms and as a source of spiritual meaning and wonder. Holmes points to the contemporaneous developments of science and romanticism in late-eighteenth- and early-nineteenth-century Europe and demonstrates that, contrary to the common perception of a deep antagonism between them, they should be understood as having developed symbiotically and as having continuously informed and challenged one another. The magnificent discoveries by Joseph Banks in geography and anthropology, Humphrey Davies and Antoine Lavoisier in chemistry, and William and Caroline Hershel in astronomy, for example, unfolded within a rich cultural-intellectual milieu in which the literary work of Samuel Taylor Coleridge, Lord Byron, John Keats, and Mary Shelley was also seen as contributing significantly to the search for a more complete understanding of the living world. The longing to see and understand the world fully and deeply characterized the work of both scientists and poets, and they participated in what came to be understood as a shared project. At the center of this shared project was a passion for looking carefully at things. But it was a particular way of looking at things. Evidence for this is especially apparent in the private journals and letters of, among others, Joseph Banks, Gilbert White, Samuel Taylor Coleridge, Dorothy Wordsworth, and William Herschel. Holmes points to the "precise, even reverent contemplation of nature ...an (almost sacred) attention to things simply and precisely observed" as one of the hallmarks of this age.[38]

Consider this account from Coleridge's journal from November, 1803, in which he describes what he beheld upon waking early one morning on a coach ride to London:

> It was a rich Orange Sky like that of a winter Evening save that the fleecy dark blue Clouds that rippled above it, shewed it to be Morning[—] these soon became of a glowing Brass Colour, brassy Fleeces, wool packs in shape/rising high up into the Sky. The Sun at length rose upon the flat Plan, like a Hill of Fire in the distance, rose wholly, & in the water that flooded part of the Flat a deep column of Light. — But as the Coach went on, a Hill rose and intercepted the Sun—and the Sun in a few minutes *rose* over it, a compleat 2nd rising, thro' other clouds and with a different Glory. Soon after this I saw Starlings in vast Flights, borne along like smoke, mist—like a body unindued with voluntary Power / — now it shaped itself into a circular area, inclined — now they formed a Square —now a Globe — now from complete orb into an Ellipse — then oblongated into a Balloon ...now a concave Semicircle; still expanding, or contracting, thinning or condensing, now glimmering and shivering, now thickening, deepening, blackening![39]

One senses here something of the sense of stupefaction in the face of existence in the world to which Seneca earlier alluded. And yet the mind is not clouded, but rather intensely alert to the intricate shape and texture of things, to their strange beauty, to their wondrous power. There is a desire to perceive in all these different elements moving *together* the very dynamism and life of the world. Such intense preoccupation with seeing and describing things— whether the shape and movement of the world before one's eyes, the chemistry of invisible gasses, or the subtle pattern of the stars in the heavens—was at the same time an effort to *imagine the world*, to feel and understand the world and one's place in it in a new way. To be sure, the opportunity to probe the intricate workings of the natural world so closely sometimes had a disturbing, destabilizing, effect on the imagination. It could be terrifying to look out onto a world so new, so strange. But the struggle to learn to stand within a world of such power and intricate beauty was understood as a whole, inclusive work—one with a deep contemplative character—in which scientists and poets were engaged together.

Still, one of the undeniable effects of the scientific discoveries of this age was to call into question many of the old certitudes, in particular certain classical religious and theological ideas. The very meaning of the world was changing and the question of whether this emerging vision could still support a meaningful theological response became one of the great and troubling questions of the time. Nowhere, perhaps, did this question come to more acute expression than in response to the work of Charles Darwin. More than one hundred fifty years after the publication of his revolutionary *Origin of Species*, the questions are still with us. Whether we can even read Darwin clearly through the distorting lens of our own culture wars remains an open question. The common perception of Darwin—embraced both by scientists for whom Darwin's understanding of evolution has become a foundational truth and by those Christian believers for whom Darwin's ideas represent a threat to a theistic worldview—is that he saw the natural world as bereft of spirit. The challenge of rethinking this perception is immense, not least because we must do so through the filter of our own increasingly hardened cultural and religious assumptions. Still, there is another way of thinking about Darwin's contribution, and it involves—surprisingly perhaps—attending carefully to the *contemplative* character of his work as a naturalist. Lyanda Lynn Haupt has recently argued that, if we focus less exclusively on Darwin's theory of natural selection and its possible theological implications, and examine more carefully his remarkable development as a naturalist as chronicled in his early notebooks and diaries, we may begin to grasp more clearly than we have done before the distinctive contemplative sensibility that grounded his work. In her beautiful and original book, *Pilgrim on the Great Bird Continent: The Importance of Everything and Other Lessons from Darwin's Lost Notebooks*, Haupt suggests that Darwin's own complex and intricate way of paying attention to the world can and perhaps ought to be understood as a significant form of contemplative practice.[40]

Haupt uncovers this important element of Darwin's work by focusing her attention on Darwin's little-known "Ornithological Notes," which she reads alongside Darwin's *Beagle Diary*.[41] Based on a notebook Darwin kept during his five-year voyage on the Beagle from 1831 to 1836, the "Ornithological Notes" offer us an important window into understanding how Darwin grew as a naturalist during his years on the Beagle, and how his capacity to see and feel and interpret the natural world deepened and matured. In Darwin's more mature works, which he carefully prepared for publication, we find, says Haupt, "the polished results of his ornithological study and contemplation." But in the "Notes," she suggests, "we find the study and contemplation themselves, and they are wonderful—quirky, zealous, irreverent, and humble." The "Notes," together with the *Beagle Diary*, she argues, "reveal not only the seeds of Darwin's thoughts on evolution but also his deep sensitivity regarding the behavior and ecological study of animals in their natural, wild places." They reveal, in other words, how Darwin learned to "watch, how to think, how to twine beauty with science, and objectivity with empathy."[42] These are qualities of mind and habits of being he did not possess when he embarked on the *Beagle*. He had to learn them, practice them, grow into them. Yet he did so, and to an astonishing degree.

It is this growth and deepening of Darwin's own awareness of the world that Haupt finds most striking and which leads her to make one of the boldest claims of her book: "Over time [Darwin] grew as a watcher of birds, and he was elevated in mind, in imagination, and—this is a word rarely used in connection with Darwin, but I will argue for it strongly—in spirit."[43] One almost never hears talk of Darwin's spirituality, or of his spiritual vision. This is in no small measure due, I would suggest, to the limitations we often place on such language. If describing Darwin's vision of the world as spiritual requires us to locate him firmly within a recognized historical, creedal expression of faith, such as that which in he grew up as a member of the Church of England, we may well have to disavow any such language in speaking of his view of the natural world. But if we mean by such language what Haupt does when she speaks of Darwin's slow "conversion to a particular way of seeing—a biological vision that is relentless, patient and steeped in a naturalist's faith that small things matter," then we may be compelled to reconsider both Darwin's view of the world and our understanding of spirituality.[44] Through Haupt's careful, patient attention to Darwin's growth as a naturalist, she helps us to see and feel Darwin's way of engaging the world for what it was: a kind of contemplative awareness. "His manner of deep watchfulness," she suggests, allowed "the ordinary ground of life to become sanctified, to be brought into *sensus plenior*—a 'fuller sense'—through the offering of simple attention."[45]

This is Haupt's language, not Darwin's. But it is an intriguing and illuminating choice of words for describing what she believes to be Darwin's fundamentally contemplative orientation to the natural world. This phrase *sensus plenior* is most commonly associated with a notion common among early and medieval Christians that careful, prayerful attention to the sacred text often leads from a mostly literal understanding of the text to something fuller, richer, more imaginatively and spiritually expansive. The possibility for this *sensus plenior* was believed to be inherent in the text itself, which mediates a mystery beyond itself—the very presence of the Divine. But as we saw earlier with the example of the early Christian monks, it requires a perceptive reader to draw forth this fuller sense, to make it real in the life of the reader. This contemplative approach to reading, in which one becomes more and more sensitive to the infinitely capacious power of the Word, and is gradually transformed by it, provides a useful analogy for understanding the gradual process through which Darwin learned to become sensitive to the fuller sense of the natural world. And it allows us to hold in the imagination the kindred character of distinct contemplative practices arising from widely varying traditions and contexts.

Darwin had important models that shaped how he oriented himself in and thought about the natural world, including the work of the great naturalist Alexander von Humboldt. Haupt suggests that Darwin's initial way of framing his observations in South America was, if anything, still modeled too closely on Humboldt's example. He had yet to find his own voice. However, the "Ornithological Notes" allow us to witness Darwin working his way through what Haupt describes as "the imposed transcendence of Humboldt's influence to the more honest, personal transcendence located in the true, everyday things of the earth." Here, she suggests, we encounter not simply the seeds of Darwin's later theories, but more importantly the very font of Darwin's creativity as a naturalist. In his growing capacity to see and describe and take in the world, we begin to perceive what she describes as "the beauty of that which is still being formed."[46] Haupt is referring here to a still-being-formed *awareness*, in particular the delicate, mysterious process by which Darwin became attentive to the life-forms around him and to the meaning of his own relationship with these life-forms. Darwin's early descriptions of bird-life in Brazil reveal a still-narrow and thin awareness of the world around him. Moving through an ecosystem widely acknowledged to possess the highest avian diversity in the world, Darwin noted: "I was surprised at the scarceness of birds."[47] His eyes and ears were not yet attuned to this particular place, to the subtle movement of life-forms in the rainforest. And when he did see birds, his ability to notice or describe their differences or particularity was severely limited; the word he uses most often to describe the birds he sees in those early entries is simply "beautiful." But within a year, Darwin's notebook came to be filled with detailed morphological and behavioral patterns born of his growing capacity for patient observation. He was beginning to learn how to pay attention, and in paying attention to feel himself drawn into the world he observed. It is in this kindling of relationship, Haupt suggests, that we can best appreciate Darwin's emerging contemplative vision.

There is a telling moment early on in Darwin's time in Brazil when one senses his awareness of the world through which he is moving already beginning to deepen. He is still learning to know the place, and his ability to see and feel what is around him is not yet mature. Yet, he is beginning to open himself to and allow himself to be moved by the distinctive and particular life of the place. On February 29th, 1832, he wrote: "I have been wandering by myself in a Brazilian forest." Haupt notes the importance of those three simple words: wandering, myself, forest. Here and elsewhere in the *Notes*, she says, one can see evidence of Darwin's increasing ability to "calm himself, to see into things on his own." He describes the delight he experienced (though he notes that "delight is ...a weak term for such transports of pleasure") from the elegance of the grasses, the distinctive gloss of the foliage, and the strange paradox of the way sound and silence enfold one another in the forest. Commenting on this phenomenon, Darwin observed: "Within the recesses of the forest when in the midst of it [the deafening noise of the insects] a universal stillness appears to reign."[48] This was still early in his time in South America, and one does not yet see evidence of the kind of careful observation of minute variations in the appearance and habits of different species that would become a habitual part of Darwin's engagement with the natural world. Still, one sees here something perhaps just as important, his growing awareness of all that simple, careful attention could yield.

It is not easy to determine how or whether Darwin's cultivation of this capacity for contemplative awareness of the natural world contributed to his eventual formulation of the theory of natural selection. Haupt makes a persuasive case that Darwin's time sense of *engagement* with and *participation* in the natural world was crucial to his ability to discern the intricate patterns and relationships that he later incorporated into his theory of natural selection. But the practice itself, the careful work of noticing, describing, and responding to the natural world, something Haupt claims reflects Darwin's "conversion"—from student to pilgrim—remains among the most important legacies of Darwin's journey in South America. Darwin's time in Maldonado, southern Uruguay, in April 1833, marked a particularly important turning point. It was a year and a half into his journey, a moment when his long, steady practice of carefully attending to birds in the wild had begun to yield new insight and appreciation, and a heightened sense of intimacy with the birds of this region. His attention to the Chucao Tapacolo, a shy forest species not at all easy to see, reveals his changing sensibility. They are small birds, and as Haupt notes, "to observe them closely, Darwin made himself small, and quiet, and patient." He comments in his notebook: "This bird frequents the most gloomy & retired spots in the humid forests ...and at some times, although its cry may be heard, it cannot with the greatest attention be seen;

but generally by standing motionless, in the wood, it will approach within a few feet, in the most familiar manner."⁴⁹ Compared with Darwin's later, momentous encounters with finches on the Galapagos Islands, this simple description of an encounter with a small, elusive bird hardly seems worth mentioning. Still the note of familiarity that Darwin sounds here suggests the extent to which he was gradually coming to occupy what Haupt describes as "the center of [his] natural insight." The "simple warmth," toward his subjects, the "quiet intimacy" of his encounters with birds is noticeable and striking. So is Darwin's growing capacity for patience and stillness in the presence of other living beings. This sense of Darwin's deepening capacity to see and feel the life of the world around him is one of the most significant elements to emerge from his "Ornithological Notes."

Darwin's deepening capacity to see and feel the intricate particulars of the life of the world around him would eventually contribute significantly to his ability to perceive the pattern of the whole, something that would only come to full expression in his later, more mature works of natural history. Yet, in his work in South America, we witness him coming alive to the presence of animals and beginning to feel something of their mysterious power. "Here, in patience, in stillness," Haupt notes of Darwin's approach in the "Ornithological Notes," "the birds show themselves and tell their secrets. Their stories are not shaken out of them beneath a microscope but revealed, animal to animal, with a kind of earthen *familiarity*, on the forest soil."⁵⁰ It is Darwin's growing attention to this mysterious, complex reality, his deepening habit of "expectant familiarity" as he observed the lives and habits of animals, that shines through so clearly in the "Notes"; also his growing habit of what Nora Barlow has called "sympathetic participation" in the lives of these animals, something that transformed his thinking about the natural world and helped him (and eventually all of us with him) to see the intricate patterns underlying and sustaining it.

Darwin became increasingly bold in inquiring into animal consciousness, something that would later bring him under suspicion of engaging in a kind of reckless anthropomorphism. But Haupt questions whether he is really guilty of this, and suggests instead that Darwin was beginning to imagine the world with an intimacy and humility and creativity that took him far beyond anything most of his contemporaries at that time had begun to conceive of. "In his observations of seals and birds and other animals, in his often playful musings about their thoughts and behaviors, Darwin utterly, and even joyfully, abandoned his privileged human status. He threw his own thoughts and behaviors right into the animal mix, putting all creatures, including humans, on the same continuum of consciousness. Rather than imposing human consciousness upon animal behaviors, he animalized consciousness in general." And in so doing, something began to change in him. As Haupt puts it: "he embraced a new kind of humility—a radical humility that made him strangely slender, able to peer into the wilderness through doors only slightly ajar, to see, in a new and small and gracious way, the movement of life."[51] This is a beautiful but unexpected image, especially when applied to the practice of a naturalist whose work would ultimately become such a large, even dominating presence in the scientific community. Yet, Darwin's thinking about the natural world as a whole, and about the evolution of species in particular, depended, crucially, on his increasingly refined capacity to disappear, to enter quietly into the intimate and hidden lives of the animals in whose presence he moved daily. His *experience* of noticing and feeling the life of the world around him, of learning to make ever more subtle distinctions in the behavior and appearance and even thought of animals, his sense of the sheer richness and complexity of the ecological reality within which he found himself moving—*this* was the ground out of which his thinking and his increasingly bold theorizing about the natural world emerged.

This intuition about Darwin's shifting sensibilities, gleaned from a careful reading of the "Ornithological Notes," leads Haupt to an unconventional but fascinating insight regarding Darwin's time on the Galapagos Islands, a time that many have pointed to as crucial to his development of the theory of natural selection. It would be many years before Darwin himself made the conceptual leaps enabling him to articulate his mature theoretical thinking on this subject. But here on the Galapagos Islands, Haupt notes, Darwin "experienced his most radical intimacy with wild beings ... a closeness to animals that surpassed anything he had yet known."[52] How, precisely, did this experience shape Darwin's later thinking about evolution? It is impossible to say for certain. But Haupt invites us to consider how the patterns emerging in Darwin's felt sense of the world, especially his sense of "wild intimacy" with the living beings among whom he moved, may have contributed to his deepening understanding of the character of relationships within and among species. Darwin's mature vision would eventually reveal what Haupt describes as "a natural order that refuses to mark humans as separate or exceptional or beyond the reach of wildness."[53] This, of course, is part of what made his theories so controversial. It still does. But there is something noble and beautiful in this way of seeing the world. And if this reading of Darwin's work as a naturalist is correct, it means that this vision of the world arose in no small part from his own personal sense of profound participation in, and intimacy with the natural order. Attention to Darwin's contemplative practice as a naturalist suggests how his actual experience of intimacy within the natural world may have contributed to his ability to see and imagine the natural world as a place of endless intimacy among and between species.

"Immense and wonderful" is how Darwin described the wild life of the world around him late in his life.[54] This simple exclamation belies, of course, the long hard years of patient observation that informed this sensibility. Nor can it be understood apart from the painful questions about the coherence of the universe that haunted him for most of his life; Darwin would never arrive at anything like a simple affirmation of a theistic worldview. Still, the habitual tendency to view Darwin's work as undermining our capacity for apprehending the natural world as a source of spiritual wonder is misleading. Darwin's own lifelong practice of attending carefully to the natural world yielded a sense of the world as beautifully and intricately patterned. As he articulated in the *Origin of Species*: "When I view all beings not as special creations, but as the lineal descendants of some few beings which lived long before the first bed of the Cambrian system was deposited, they seem to me to become ennobled."[55] This observation is capable of many varied interpretations; it has been and will continue to be seen by many (happily or unhappily) as clear evidence of the utterly materialist underpinnings of Darwin's thought. But there is also something else here worth pausing over: Darwin's sense of the "ennobling" character of the larger pattern of unfolding life to which his own painstaking observations of the world, first apparent in his "Ornithological Notes," led him. When one considers how ennobled the world appeared to him through the lens of his mature theory of natural selection, and the extent to which his brilliant apprehension of the whole depended on his long cultivation of a capacity to see and respond to the intricate character of living beings, one feels a sense of renewed appreciation for the power of simple attention to yield a synthetic, integrated understanding of the world. By attending to Darwin's development as a naturalist, it becomes possible to view him as having been not only a scientist of extraordinary originality and theoretical range, but also an uncommonly perceptive contemplative. And it points toward a growing awareness that has come to mark so much of our own emerging sensibility regarding the natural world— that long, patient attention to the world is a meaningful and significant form of contemplative practice, and that our capacity to deepen and sustain such practice may well prove crucial to the work of tending to and helping repair the world.

Looking Deeper into the World

The question is not what you look at but what you see.[56]

HENRY DAVID THOREAU

My ambition reaches no further than a few clods of earth,
sprouting wheat, an olive grove, a cypress....[57]

VINCENT VAN GOGH

In the American wing of the Chicago Art Institute hangs a painting by George
Inness called *The Home of the Heron*. Inness painted it toward the end of his
life when he was living in Tarpon Springs, Florida, and it is without question
one of his most beautiful and fully realized works. During the last few years,
Inness's work and this painting in particular have become important to me.
Whenever I am in Chicago, I make a point of going to see it. I never tire of
looking at it. At the center of the canvas, rising up out of the mist, is the small
but recognizable profile of a heron. The eye moves toward it immediately. But
then one notices the grove of trees above and around the heron—their slender trunks and soft, bronze foliage framing the bird as it rises from the water.
The geometry of the painting is meticulously constructed, with the horizontal and vertical planes balanced in perfect proportion to one another—
something that helps one behold and respond to the painting as a whole. And
yet nothing is fixed. There are no clear boundaries. Everything moves and is
bound together within a kind of gentle haze. One senses this almost immediately. And yet it is not simply or easily apprehended. There is a depth and
dimensionality to Inness's work, especially his late work, that keeps drawing
one further in. It holds the eye and the imagination even as it recedes before
you. It opens up and out, moving endlessly beyond itself. Like the heron, rising up out of the mist and into the world.

The longing to see and perceive the whole, even as one notices and
responds to the distinctive character of this or that particular facet of the
whole: this is something that characterizes both the contemplative and the
aesthetic gaze. The contemplative gaze often draws upon an aesthetic intuition in which combinations of color, form, texture, and dimension help to
conjure an image of the Divine or an image of the space in which one encounters the Divine. Such images work, paradoxically, to open the imagination to
a certain way of seeing and to signal the limits of images and the imagination
in helping us apprehend the Divine. Evagrius's blue sapphire works exactly
like this, presenting the mind with a particular image through which one can

begin to sense and feel the expansiveness of prayer, all the while pointing to an immensity far greater than the mind can grasp. The blue sapphire draws one in and sends one forth into the endlessness of the divine mystery. It holds the contemplative gaze even as it releases it. The mind grasps and is grasped by the particular even as it empties itself to dwell within the whole.

One sees something analogous at work in certain expressions of land-scape painting. Here the fashioning of color, form, texture, and dimension become a means of seeing and taking in both the minute particularities and the mysterious whole, both the "outer world" perceptible to the senses and the "inner world" mediated by the senses but infused by Spirit. Certainly this was true for George Inness, who was influenced, as Henry David Thoreau and other American transcendentalists were, by Emmanuel Swedenborg's idea of "correspondence"—the belief that there is a spiritual world that cor-responds to the world we know and perceive in our senses. These worlds are not separate and distinct from one another; rather they are interwoven, part of a single fabric. As Adrienne Baxter Bell notes of Swedenborg's vision of the spiritual world: "This world is not above the natural world in space but is an *interior* world, lying within the realm of the natural...."[58] Inness found this idea immensely helpful in developing an aesthetic-contemplative vision capa-ble of taking in the whole complex fabric of the world—its material particu-larity inseparable from its spiritual meaning.[59] He gave eloquent expression to this vision in his work, especially in the softness of tone that characterizes his mature landscapes. He shared this manner of "painting softly" with a number of his contemporaries—James McNeill Whistler, John Henry Twatchman, Thomas Wilmer Dewing, and others—in whose work one can also sense the fluidity of relationship between and among things, the impermanence of boundaries, the subtle fusion of worlds.[60] Here one encounters a sustained if varied effort to behold and represent things in their utter singularity, in their ever-shifting relationship to every other thing, and in their relationship to the whole.

The effort it takes to look at things this carefully, deeply, and inclusively and to represent them truly and honestly can hardly be overstated. Other art-ists from this period have left us their own accounts of what it meant to try to behold the world this way and why it mattered. In a letter written to his son on September 8, 1906, near the end of his life, Paul Cezanne describes the immense difficulty he feels in trying to represent what he sees: "I must tell you that a as painter I am becoming more clear-sighted before nature, but that with me the realization of my sensations is always painful. I cannot attain the intensity that is unfolded before my sense. I have not the magnificent richness of colouring that animates nature. Here on the bank of the river the motifs multiply, the same subject seen from a different angle offers subject for study of the most powerful interest and so varied that I think I could occupy myself for months without changing place, by turning now more to the right, now more to the left."[61] There is tremendous pathos in this old man's reflections on his work, especially regarding the gap he experiences between what he sees and feels (or more broadly what comes to him through his "sensations") and what he is able to express. It is painful for him to reckon with this gap and with his awareness of how far he is from being able to realize and express his true subject.

But there is also something beautiful and hopeful in this reflection, especially in Cezanne's sense of the endlessness of all that lay before him, its fathomless mystery. And the allure he feels in the face of the ever-shifting, always emerging, never completely describable motifs along this riverbank. He is becoming more clear-sighted before nature. But he is also becoming more aware of its endless complexity and intricacy, the shifting moods of a place depending on the time of day and season. It cannot be grasped or known, not completely. It can only be seen, partially and provisionally. Then seen again. And yet again. Here one senses the recognition of the need for a kind of *ruminatio* in which one can be drawn ever deeper into the mystery of what one beholds, and forward in search of the forms that can best express what one sees. In a letter written to Emile Bernard sometime earlier, Cezanne explains why in these latter years he found himself increasingly drawn toward abstraction. Again it has to do with color. "Now, being old, nearly 70 years, the sensations of colour, which give the light, are for me the reasons for the abstractions which do not allow me to cover my canvas entirely nor to pursue the delimitations of the objects where their points of contact are fine and delicate...."[62] There is something akin here to the softness of expression toward which Inness and the tonalist painters found themselves drawn, which allowed them to express the subtle movement and relationship between and among things. For Cezanne it is abstraction that makes this possible, especially the *empty spaces* on the canvas that enable one to sense the fine and delicate points of contact between and among particular objects. How carefully one must look to see and notice these points of contact and the spaces between them; how much it helps in the work of cultivating awareness of the relationships between and among things and between those things and the larger whole.

Some years earlier Vincent van Gogh found himself struggling with similar questions, including the question of how to capture and represent the way particular colors present themselves in the landscape. In a long, detailed letter to his brother Theo written in September 1882, van Gogh describes his preoccupation with "the question of the depth of color," especially in relation to the color effects seen in autumnal woods. He tells his brother that he has not seen such effects represented in Dutch paintings, and he longs to do so in his own work. But once he embarks upon his own attempt, he encounters unexpected difficulties. He realizes he has not looked closely enough.

> Yesterday evening I was working on a slightly rising woodland slope covered with dry, mouldering beech leaves. The ground was light and dark reddish-brown, emphasized by the weaker and stronger shadows of trees casting half-obliterated stripes across it. The problem, and I found it a very difficult one, was to get the depth of colour, the enormous power and solidity of that ground—and yet it was only while I was painting it that I noticed how much light there was still in the dusk—to retain the light as well as the glow, the depth of that rich colour, for there is no carpet imaginable as splendid as that deep brownish-red in the low of an autumn evening sun, however toned down by the trees.

Here, the artist struggles to convey the full complexity and delicacy of what he sees and with the uncertainty he feels about how to give life to what he sees on his canvas. His subject is simple: a grove of beech trees at dusk on an autumn day. Yet, there is so much that must be accounted for if one is to give life to this particular scene. The light and dark reddish-brown of the ground. The lighter and darker "half-obliterated" shadows cast upon it by the trees. The "enormous power and solidity" of the ground. The sudden realization while painting (while the day is draining away) of how much light remained in the dusk. The need to "retain" this—the light, the glow, the rich color—all of it. Even as it is disappearing from view.

He has not noticed all of this before, certainly not with the subtlety and precision with which he now beholds what is before him. But now that he begins to see in this way, he sees even more. And he describes it for Theo.

> Behind those saplings, behind that brownish-red ground, is a sky of a very delicate blue-grey, warm, hardly blue at all, sparkling. And against it there is a hazy border of greenness and a network of saplings and yellowish leaves. A few figures of wood gatherers are foraging about, dark masses of mysterious shadows. The white bonnet of a woman bending down to pick up a dry branch stands out suddenly against the deep

reddish-brown of the ground. A skirt catches the light, a shadow is cast, the dark silhouette of a man appears above the wooded slope. A white bonnet, a cap, a shoulder, the bust of a woman show up against the sky. These figures, which are large and full of poetry, appear in the twilight of the deep shadowy tone like enormous *terres cuites* [terracottas] taking shape in a studio.

The entire, complex life of the scene begins to emerge in this written account, even as it is taking form on the canvas. One can sense van Gogh's delight in his growing awareness of all that is unfolding before him, the distinctive particularity of objects and figures, the shifting movement of light and shadow, the depth and complexity of color. We who stand before his finished work sometimes feel, perhaps without always knowing what it is we are feeling, the intensity of the gaze that brought this work into being. From his letters, we can sense that this gaze was rooted in the desire to see everything, to miss nothing and to perceive as far as possible not only the distinctive character of individual things but the whole pulsing life of what was unfolding before him. The relations between and among things. The movement and play of light and shadows, of time passing. And to gather this into a single aesthetic expression that holds and reflects the life of the subject.

Van Gogh complained to Theo what a "hard job" it was painting this particular scene. "The ground used up one and a half large tubes of white—even though the ground is very dark—and for the rest red, yellow, brown, ochre, black, sienna, bistre, and the result is a reddish-brown, but one ranging from bistre to deep wine-red and to a pale, golden ruddiness. Then there are still the mosses and a border of fresh grass which catches the light and glitters brightly and is very difficult to capture." One smiles to read this account, the artist's technical account of pigments and the amount of paint required revealing more than he knows about the depth of his own commitment to see and tend to the world before his eyes. A hard job. Yes.

But his complaints feel a little half-hearted, for he seems to sense already the importance of what he is struggling to say in his work—its importance to him, certainly, but not only him. "I said to myself while I was doing it: don't let me leave before there is something of the autumnal evening in it, something mysterious, something important."[63]

I confess I find this expression of regard for the world immensely moving: "Don't let me leave before there is something of the autumnal evening in it." For me, this captures simply and beautifully what it means to commit oneself to the work of sustained attention to the living world. What would it mean, I wonder, to hold this observation at the center of our own efforts to live with greater attention and awareness? To be able to say: "Don't let me leave before my eyes become sensitive and responsive to the life unfolding around me. Don't let me leave before the life of this particular place that I now inhabit begins to enter into and take hold of me body and soul. Don't let *us* leave before the luminous world becomes woven into the center of our consciousness, our concerns."

We are still struggling to understand how the practice of attention to the subtle workings of the natural world can be integrated into a unified spiritual vision and how such a vision can contribute to a more thoughtful, respectful way of inhabiting the world. Part of this work will surely involve giving more careful attention to the aesthetic dimensions of our experience—the way light, color, texture, and form appear before us in the world and enter into our consciousness. Such attention can and often does open out onto a wider and deeper sympathy for the life of particular places and a concern for their well-being. And it can inform a decidedly ecological sensibility as the awareness of oneself as inhabiting a distinct watershed or ecosystem begins to take hold and flourish. But just as important to this larger work will be the effort to understand how the kind of attention the ancient monks referred to as vigilance, watchfulness, and *prosoche* can expand and deepen our capacity for noticing and dwelling within the whole. Entering into the space of contemplative prayer has always been understood as being rooted in an attention that is at once focused and capacious. In a way that is analogous to the landscape artist who attends carefully to the life of a particular thing while also remaining open to the wider field of being all around, the contemplative practitioner gives himself or herself to an intensely focused gaze upon a single thing (envisioned in the Christian contemplative tradition as "the one thing necessary"; or "the pearl of great price"; or "the narrow gate") that is understood to be a doorway into a world of endless communion. The mind reduces its scope of attention in order to discover that it already inhabits this more expansive space, and participates in a larger whole. The stillness into which one descends in contemplative practice is the climate in which attention, which initially cannot alight on anything, gradually becomes simple, open, receptive. The mystery at the heart of such stillness begins to reveal itself, in particular moments of insight and understanding about the self and the world, and in the emergence of an awareness so capacious and wide-ranging that it cannot bounded by anything. Or even named. It is noteworthy that Evagrius, who bequeathed to us the beautiful image of the blue sapphire as an emblem for the nature of authentic contemplative experience, also suggests that true prayer is at its deepest level, imageless. It includes and encompasses everything but cannot be contained by anything.

"The song of a river," Aldo Leopold once noted, "is audible to every ear, but there is other music ...by no means audible to all. To hear even a few notes of it you must first live here for a long time, and you must know the speech of hills and rivers. Then on a still night, when the campfire is low and the Pleiades have climbed over rimrocks, sit quietly and listen for a wolf to howl, and think hard of everything you have seen and tried to understand. Then you may hear it—a vast pulsing harmony—its score inscribed on a thousand hills, its notes the lives and deaths of plants and animals, its rhythms spanning the seconds and centuries."[64] I ponder this as I think about that morning on the banks of Thompson Creek near Redwoods Monastery when I stood searching for the returning salmon. And I recall too that moment years earlier when I stood atop the Grand Coulee Dam, stunned by its technological wonder, blind to the presence of the Columbia River and the salmon moving through its waters. Perhaps I was too young to know how to listen for the song of that river, or the vast pulsing harmony within and beyond it. I had not yet discovered in myself a space capacious enough to receive and hold that harmony. Little by little, through long years of practice, this has begun to change.

For me that morning on the banks of Thompson Creek possessed (and possesses still) deep poignancy. I had longed to see these creatures. Not only for the simple pleasure of encountering them, but also because of what their presence would mean for the possible return to health of the local watershed, to this place I had come to love so deeply. I realized too that I was seeking to recover something in myself, a healing of my own imagination, my own long-dormant capacity to see and feel the living world. There was a time when I would not have considered these salmon or the place itself worthy of my attention, when my ability to fit them into a recognizable world was almost non-existent. My own path toward a more "sympathetic participation" in the world has been long and slow. Gradually I have come to understand that the practice of attention—whether rooted in the ancient monastic practice of *prosoche* or in an even older tradition of watchfulness born of anticipation at the wonder one might behold in looking out into the living world—is crucial to the path I must walk. Little by little I am learning again to see and yes, love the world.

That morning, I stood for a long while looking down into the water with my daughter and my friends from the monastery. Would they come? Would they? "There!" someone cried out, pointing to a bend in the creek. And then I saw them, a pair of salmon moving slowly upstream, their dappled, gleaming bodies undulating in the current. Straining to find their way home. I watched them for several long moments and did not turn away. I did not want to miss anything: the music of the river, the dark green moss on the rock, the branches of the alders quaking in the morning breeze, my companions beside me, these beautiful wild beings moving in the water below. In that moment, there was only this whole, this vast pulsing harmony, and I was in it. After a few moments the salmon moved further upstream and eventually disappeared from view. But the sight of them moving in the water remains etched in my mind. I behold them still.

6

Logos: *The Song of the World*

In the beginning was the Word.[1]

THE GOSPEL OF JOHN

The Word did not come into being, but *it was*. It did not
break upon the silence, but *it was older than the silence
and the silence was made of it*.[2]

N. SCOTT MOMADAY

DEEP IN THE heart of a sandstone canyon, in what is now southern Utah,
an unknown artist daubs pigment against the stone. Again and again until a
slender, ghostly figure emerges, its deep auburn hues radiant, its gaunt silhouette gesturing forth. Soon other figures emerge to join the first. Eventually
there is a host of them arrayed along the canyon wall. Thousands of miles
away, at almost the same moment, an old man on the island of Patmos in
Greece pauses to wonder at the marks drying on the parchment before him:
"When all things began, the Word already was. The Word dwelt with God,
and what God was, the Word was...through the Word, all things came into
being (Jn 1:1)." Of those mysterious figures in Barrier Canyon, Kiowa writer
N. Scott Momaday has noted: "They are invested with the very essence of
language, the language of story and myth and primal song."[3] Of what do they
sing? Perhaps more than anything, they sing of the world. Or rather they
sing the world. Here, the gesture of language arises through the shape of the
canyon, the rise and fall of bird song, the play of sun and moonlight among
the cottonwoods, the shifting currents of floodwater, the wind. The world
is encountered, known, expressed through a word. A similar intuition can
be found among the earliest expressions of Christian faith. The evangelist
makes this clear: "Through the Word, all things (*panta*) came into being." *All
things*. Apart from the Word, "not one thing came into being." Here, close
to the source of Christian life, one encounters another primal song, giving

expression to the intricate dance between word and world. It is a song full of wonder and amazement at the notion that God has been speaking from all eternity through everything that exists. Wonder too that the creative Word through whom the cosmos came into being has taken on human flesh and dwelt among us (Jn 1:14), has made all things whole again.

Does the world have a voice? Does it beckon to us, call us toward an intimate encounter, toward a response of reciprocity, even love? Can we learn to listen and respond to this call, orient ourselves toward the world in a way that reflects a renewed sense of responsibility and care for the world? Such questions might seem either hopelessly romantic or anthropomorphic, or both. Yet the impulse to frame our questions about the potential meaning of the natural world in terms of what Momaday calls "the language of story and myth and primal song" has long been woven into the human community's sense of the world's expressive power. However we understand this language—its origins, its syntax, its intelligibility, its possible spiritual meaning—its significance in mediating our encounter with the natural world can hardly be disputed. Still, we are living at a moment when our sense of the world's expressive power and of our capacity to hear and respond to this speech is being slowly eroded. There are many reasons for this, some having to do with dramatic changes in the natural world itself, others having more to do with our changing perceptions of nature and the cosmos and still others having to do with significant shifts in how we inhabit the world. Whether we can continue to find meaning in the idea of a world created and sustained by a Word or in the stories and songs arising from particular places on the earth or in the gestural power of animals, plants, and landforms will depend in no small measure on how we respond to these emerging challenges—both in practical terms and in terms of the rehabilitation of our imaginations.[4]

The potential cost to us in losing our capacity to feel and respond to the voice of the world—or what Jean Giono has described simply as "le chant du monde," the "song of the world"—is enormous. But the cost is not borne simply by us. Something fundamental in the very life of the world is being lost. Consider for example the growing number of places around the world that, through chronic ecological degradation, are now falling utterly silent. This is not a silence rooted in tranquility or peace; it is the silence of death. Our awareness of this threat has been growing steadily during the last fifty years, ever since Rachel Carson published her astonishing and disturbing account of the effects of pesticides on living species, *Silent Spring*. The force of her language resonated then and resonates still.[5] Still, if anything, the silence we face now is more acute and pervasive than that which provoked Carson's fierce response. Once vibrant ecosystems have become so compromised that the particular sounds and music of those places have been reduced to a whisper or a hollow echo of our own mechanical presence. What kind of Word can such places speak? What songs and stories can arise here? In the face of this deepening silence, it has become more difficult than ever to know what it might mean to attend to the voice of the living world. Even if we learn to sharpen the acuity of our hearing, are the voices we hope to hear still speaking? Or will we discover that the life of the world and its expressive character have become so severely diminished that all that is left for us to hear is an ominous silence?

In light of this growing threat, the question of how we might learn to cultivate a capacity to listen to the voice of the world can be seen not simply as a matter of personal preference or aesthetic pleasure, but rather as a critical ethical-spiritual challenge. Yet, even as the world grows more silent and the effort to listen to its diminished life becomes more strained, we find ourselves reckoning with the strangely paradoxical realization that the relentless assault of noise within which we live is rendering our efforts to listen more deeply to the voice of the world fruitless. As I write these words, I can hear outside my window the roar of a lawnmower along with a weed-eater's whining cry; a moment ago, the garbage truck rumbled by; before that the ringing of the telephone; also the faint hiss of a jet passing overhead. I live in a large metropolis. These sounds—along with those of sirens, screeching tires, honking horns, the hum of the refrigerator—form part of the acoustical ground or soundscape of my life. There is also life here—the rich abundance of languages that flow through the streets of Los Angeles, the music, poetry, and art arising steadily from nearly every neighborhood of the city. And one can, if one listens carefully, hear the sound of birdsong, or the wind whispering in the trees. But it is increasingly difficult to attune one's ear to the subtler music of the place. The built environment, especially here, has extended to the point that only a few small empty spaces remain. Everything is filled. Calculating the often-ambiguous effects of such unrelenting noise upon our lives is not easy; but it is becoming increasingly evident that the effects are real, often pernicious, and must be reckoned with.[6] For some, these questions have come to be understood as having a fundamental spiritual character—the loss of silence being felt as a significant expression of a more pervasive and growing impoverishment of spirit, and the "practice of silence" being seen as a means of retrieving our capacity to hear the deeper rhythms of language arising in and through the living world.[7]

This strange paradox—born of living in a world at once unbearably cacophonous and nearly empty of sound—points to the particular difficulty we face in the present moment in reckoning with the question of how or whether the living world can be considered expressive. Also whether our ongoing efforts to learn how to listen and respond to the living world still have meaning or purpose. Nor can one ignore a dimension of this question that has long haunted human consciousness and which appears to be growing more pronounced in the present moment. I am referring to the fundamental existential or religious question regarding whether the world we inhabit has any voice at all, whether it has any meaningful center or purpose. Pascal, in the face of the cosmological revolutions of the seventeenth century, famously expressed the growing sense of unease regarding the reliability or hospitality of the universe; considering the endless expanse of the heavens, he declared: "The eternal silence of those infinite spaces strikes me with terror." This perception of the universe as a cold, empty place bereft of any pattern or meaning (or at least not any meaning decipherable by us) has, if anything, become even more deeply woven into the fabric of modern and post-modern existence, making it increasingly difficult for many to conceive of any kind of voice or presence arising out of the life of the world.

What then are we to make of these older forms of knowledge, reflective of an intuition that the world is and always has been expressing itself, and that our own speech and capacity to communicate arises from a prior word spoken by the world? Can we still make sense of what the ancients sensed when they spoke of the "music of the spheres?" Or what Teilhard de Chardin has described more recently as the "hymn of the universe?" Can we retrieve and learn to inhabit again stories that take seriously our profound incorporation in the living world? It is perhaps true that we can no longer approach these questions with the same naïveté we once did. But I want to consider here whether it is still meaningful to conceive of the world as expressive of speech, and whether we still possess the capacity to hear and respond to it. And whether the traditions of contemplative thought and practice—both those rooted in explicitly religious and spiritual traditions and those arising within the ecological and literary discourse of the present moment—can help us retrieve a meaningful sense of the world as rich with speech.

In terms of the questions I am considering in this book, I want to ask whether a thoughtful retrieval of the Christian contemplative sense of the Word—in all its cosmological and sacramental fullness—can contribute to a richer and stronger sense of what it is to inhabit a world that is, at the level of its deepest structure, an expression, a voice, a song. Similarly, I want to ask whether the contemporary literary and poetic expressions arising in response to the living world can help us feel and sense more fully the gritty texture of the world's expressive power—and perhaps help us rethink the meaning of the Christian idea of the Word incarnate. This theopoetic work seems not only possible but necessary if we hope to rediscover the living world as charged with the presence of the Holy. To realize this may well require us to learn again how to listen. But listen for what? To whom? It is not easy to say. Nor is it easy to imagine how, in a world suffused in white noise, what we might hear if we did learn to listen more carefully. I think again of the words of Alaska writer John Haines regarding the challenge of paying attention to the life of this particular place: "I have come to feel," he says, "that there is here in North America a hidden place obscured by what we have built upon it, and that whenever we penetrate the surface of the life around us that place and its spirit can be found."[8] What might it mean to listen with such care and attention that the life and spirit of the world became audible, perhaps even intelligible? What would it mean to respond to this "word" so fully and deeply? Such questions, rooted in the sense that a dialogue between ourselves and the living world might be reimagined, suggest the possibility that we may yet come to hear the words beckoning to us from that hidden place.

Interlude: Word and World

Perfect silence alone proclaims [God].[9]

MAXIMUS THE CONFESSOR

Seeee sitli-sitli te-te-te-te-te-zrrrr.

WHITE-CROWNED SPARROW

It has been over twenty-five years since I first encountered the remote, wild place on the Northern California coast known as the Sinkyone Wilderness. I was spending a week at Redwoods Monastery and decided to brave the steep, narrow, winding road that led down to the bluff overlooking the Pacific Ocean. That particular day, the entire coast was shrouded in thick fog. I could hardly see anything; only the muted outlines of trees and shrubs, and the swirling movement of the mist itself. I stood there a long while, feeling the strange wonder of being utterly immersed inside that thick, dense world of cloud. Gradually, I began to notice the sounds of the place: the rhythmic pulse of waves pounding against the cliffs; gulls crying; then the faint, sweet sound of bird song, rising and falling, rising and falling, rising and falling. What creature was this? I had no idea. For the next few hours, I wandered through the fields and along the cliff's edge. Eventually, the cold cutting through me,

I made myself move from that spot and began my journey back up the road to the monastery.

It was some years before I returned to the Sinkyone Wilderness. This time I had come to live for a month in the old 1920s ranch house that serves as the visitors' center. After unpacking my bags, I walked again out into the field where I had stood before amidst the fog and bird song. On this day, it was bright and clear, the ocean luminous, the grass field like burnt gold. Swallows circling overhead, moving back and forth from the field to their mud nests against the house. A raft of pelicans gliding out over the water. Terns diving. Once again, I was entering into the life of that place. Then I heard it: the faint sound of bird song. Once, twice, a third time. I was only just beginning to notice birds at the time, and still could not easily identify them in the field, either by song or appearance. But the song of this particular bird delighted me and I learned to recognize it early on during my stay at the Sinkyone. Later, with the help of a field guide, I discovered its name: *Zonotrichia leucophrys*—the White-Crowned Sparrow. In the world of birders, the song of this particular bird is thought to be unremarkable. As one commentator notes (disparagingly) of its insistent, even repetitious song: "here is a bird that seems determined that we remember its song."

I never felt that way. Nor did I feel drawn to compare this particular bird's song with that of any others (though I eventually came to cherish the songs of the Western Meadowlark, the Mockingbird, and the Canyon Wren among others). I came to love it simply because it inhabited this particular place, a place that over the next twenty years became so important to me. Its simple, lilting song (rendered in *Sibley's Guide to Birds*: *seeee sitli-sitli te-te-te-te-te-zrrrr*) gradually became a familiar and recognizable part of the music of the place, in particular of the field that ran down from the old ranch house to the cliff above the ocean. [10] I spent many long hours in that field, stretched out on the limbs of an old, bleached eucalyptus tree, gazing up at the sky or out over the ocean, doing nothing in particular. Simply attending to the presence of the life around me. Always, I would hear the song of the sparrow rising up out of the stillness. Then the crashing waves below, the wind in the grass; then, again, that sweet song. It is only now as I reflect on this encounter that I realize how deeply the wild beauty of that song touched me. Here was this tiny being alive in the world, singing, endlessly it seemed—its distinctive song giving voice to the life of that particular place. And I was alive *inside* it, listening.

This little story, while holding real importance for me, might otherwise seem hardly worth relating. It is after all simply a story of learning to notice and listen to a wild being in the natural world; and not even a rare or endangered being, but a very ordinary one. Still, it touches on a question that for me is of central importance, especially in this chapter, namely what does it mean to learn how to listen? And why does it seem to be so difficult to cultivate the habit of deep listening that is at the heart of contemplative practice and of any sustained effort to attend to the life of the world? Perhaps to address these questions it will help to step back a little from this story and say something about the larger context in which it unfolds. This requires returning to the monastery. I came to the Sinkyone Wilderness from Redwoods Monastery; this was the threshold across which I initially passed to enter this wild place. And during my stays at the Sinkyone I regularly returned to the monastery, traveling up the road to sit in that space of silence, to join the community for meditation and prayer and song, to cook with them, to share a meal. Then after a time, I would descend again down that narrow, twisting road to the coast, to the little cabin, to the field overlooking the ocean. This movement from monastery to wilderness and back again became a central part of the rhythm of my life in that place. Learning to live into this rhythm, I understand now, helped initiate me into the practice of listening, of attending to the word that arises out of silence, out of sacred texts, out of the life of wild beings and places. Whether at the monastery or down at the coast, I gradually came to see this practice of contemplative attention as arising out of a common concern: the desire to find a deeper sense of intimacy between Word and world.

Growing up in the Pacific Northwest, I had an intuitive sense of this intimate relationship between Word and world. It was there in the woods and marshes where I played as a boy, in the play of light off of Lake Washington on summer afternoons, in the numinous presence of Salmon, in the place names—Salish, Snohomish, Yakima—that already as a child I understood to express an important part of the older meaning of that place. It was also there in the ritual gestures of the mass in which I served as an altar boy, the Word arising not only through scripture but also in the mysterious gift of bread and wine: the Word made flesh. Here, I came to understand, was a Word that entered into, sanctified, and was expressed through ordinary matter. The world was not mute. It had a voice, a presence. Listening and responding to that voice shaped my early sense of the world profoundly. Still, for reasons that are difficult for me to trace even now, I stopped listening. I turned my attention elsewhere. And my capacity for listening became diminished.

My apprenticeship at the monastery, extending over a period of many years, gradually changed this. More than anything else it was the discipline of sitting in silence that wakened me again to my own capacity for hearing. I was almost entirely unaccustomed to such silence and for a long while I resisted and struggled against it. I was far too restless in myself to bear more than a tiny fragment of such stillness. Yet, over time, it began to seep into me. Not only during the appointed times for meditation and prayer, but also in the spaces between—walking in the woods, eating, sleeping. A space began to open up within me that I came to see as reflective of both the place itself and the silence to which the monastic discipline seeks to create and foster attention and awareness. In the most immediate sense, entering into this space allowed me to feel and sense more fully the life unfolding all around me—the life of the woods and fields and river, as well as the life of the monastic community and of members of the wider community beyond the monastery whose presence and concerns were regularly invoked in our prayers. It also helped me attend more carefully to the life and spirit of the communal liturgy, in which word and silence arose, it seemed, as one. These two processes, I have come to see, are not separate or distinct from one another; rather they inform and illuminate one another. The word arising in the liturgy—including the chanting of psalms, the proclamation of scripture, and the celebration of the eucharist—both participates in and gives meaning to the larger, more capacious voice of the world surrounding us.

Long before this realization enters into your conscious awareness, you feel it in your body. I mean the way it feels to enter into the space of prayer, to bow, to sit in silence, to rise and walk slowly around the chapel between periods of meditation, pausing at each step, to descend again into silence, waiting, listening. To notice your breathing, the beating of your heart, the presence of the others sharing the space, the flickering candle, the altar, the barely perceptible outline of trees and sky just becoming visible through the glass behind the altar. Also to notice and contend with the unceasing flow of thoughts moving through the mind, with the deeply embedded anxieties that seem to surface with particular force in that space. To notice them arising and then letting them go. To notice too the unexpected sense of peace and stillness emerging and taking hold of you. To feel yourself learning little by little to listen and dwell within the rhythms of that silence. And then to feel yourself rising and joining others in listening and giving voice to a word: "O God, come to my assistance; O Lord, make haste to help me."

I have already made reference to the importance of the recitation of this verse from Psalm 70 to the early Christian monastic practice of *prosoche* or attention. John Cassian's perceptive commentary on this practice makes it clear how the simple repetition of this text (and others) helps to focus and still the mind, deepening one's awareness to the presence of the Divine. Here I wish to note something slightly different: the attention to the subtle and delicate relationship between word and silence that exists within monastic contemplative practice. The early Christian monks gave careful and sustained attention to this matter; they came to recognize that whatever power the Word might have in their lives would depend on their capacity to listen to the silence out of which it arose. "Perfect silence alone proclaims [God]," says Maximus the Confessor.[11] An entire spirituality of silence arose in the Christian contemplative tradition in response to this fundamental intuition. For the one who wished to know oneself, and know God, to understand the meaning of one's existence in the world, honoring and maintaining silence was an essential spiritual practice. Cultivating this practice involved, among other things, learning how to live in the space of silence, how to refrain from speaking unnecessarily, and how to allow the shape and gestures of one's life become the principle means of expression. It meant above all learning, as Maximus put it, how "to keep the ear of the mind open."

But for what, or to whom is one listening? The ancient Christian contemplative tradition answered this question in different ways. Certainly, one can say that the contemplative sought through this disciplined silence to learn to hear and know God. But how and by what means? Here one returns again to the centrality in this tradition of the Word of God in this tradition. Attending to the Word in the silence of prayer and meditation, in the communal chanting of the psalms, in the proclamation of the Gospel, or in the Eucharist, always leads one simultaneously inward—toward a recognition of what Meister Eckhart famously described as "the birth of the Word in the soul," and outward—toward an encounter with the Word Incarnate in all creation, all matter. This intuition, whose truth and beauty is supported by witnesses across the Christian tradition, perhaps requires some further elucidation. After all, at a cultural, historical moment in which rhetoric about the Word of God is so often employed, didactically, often angrily, and in terms of its narrowest possible doctrinal meaning, to support ideals and practices that are both exclusive and anthropocentric, it might well seem improbable that this basic Christian idea could be retrieved as a force for healing and reconciliation between the human community and the natural world. But the Christian contemplative tradition bears witness to an older and more encompassing understanding of the Word that invites us to reconsider how it arises and speaks to us in the deepest reaches of the soul and in the endless intricacy of the life of the world.

Nor should we ignore the remarkable resonance between this ancient Christian idea and comparable ways of grappling with the living world's expressive power that arise from a range of sources beyond the Christian tradition. I am thinking here of Henry David Thoreau's still suggestive *gramática parda* or "tawny grammar," and the "the wild and dusky knowledge" that comes from being intimate with wild, living beings.[12] Also of Gary Snyder's reflections on the "ecology of language," especially the way languages, dialects, argots are inescapably bound to particular places, and the way "the stratigraphy of rocks, layers of pollen in a swamp, the outward expanding circles in the trunk of a tree, can be seen as texts."[13] Viewed in this way, it becomes clear that the world's expressive power is bound, inescapably, to its wildness; and, at least implicitly, to the sacred character of the wild. The contemplative work of retrieving the sense of the world as alive and speaking will, in this sense, necessarily involve recovering a sense of the spiritual potency of wildness.

This is precisely what Snyder undertakes in his magnificent essay, "The Etiquette of Freedom." He acknowledges the difficulty, perhaps the impossibility, of defining this term precisely. "The word wild," he says, "is like a gray fox trotting off through the forest, ducking behind bushes, going in and out of sight." Close to the root meaning is something elusive and mysterious. But certain things can be said, mostly in an adjectival voice:

Of animals—free agents, each with its own endowments, living within natural systems.
Of plants—self-propagating, self-maintaining, flourishing in accord with innate qualities.
Of land—a place where the original and potential vegetation and fauna are intact and in full interaction and the landforms are entirely the result of nonhuman forces. Pristine.

One can also speak, as Snyder does, of the wild character of food crops, societies, individuals, and behavior. And of wild language. The wild, in other words, most emphatically includes us, as well as human culture in all its manifold expressions. But it also transcends us, encompasses us, defying our best attempts to limit or circumscribe it or even to say precisely what it is. Perhaps it is the immensity of the idea (Snyder revises Thoreau, saying "Wildness is not just 'the preservation of the world.' It *is* the world.") that leads him to suggest that wild in the sense that he is using the word comes very close to how the Chinese define the *dao*, the *way* of Great Nature: "eluding analysis, beyond categories, self-organizing, self-informing, playful, surprising, impermanent,

insubstantial, independent, complete, orderly, unmediated, freely manifesting, self-authenticating, self-willed, complex, quite simple."

Here, Snyder suggests, "wild" comes close to what we sometimes refer to
as "sacred." Close to the Hindu and Buddhist term *Dharma* and its original senses of "forming and framing."[14] Or, we might add, close to the Jewish
understanding of *Hokmah/Sophia* (Wisdom), understood as the enlivening
life force sustaining the very "structure of the world and the properties of
the elements" (Ws 7:17). Close also to the Christian understanding of *Logos*
(Word), understood as the generative utterance through which the universe
came into being and by which it is sustained.

Dao, Dharma, Hokma/Sophia, Logos: here is language that invites us to
consider again the cosmological sensibilities of our great religious traditions,
and the informing spiritual principles that arise from paying close attention
to the wild. The wild world has its own voice, its own language. Learning how
to listen—whether in a field by the ocean or in a chapel in the Redwood forest, or anywhere—is part of our common task.

The Incarnate Word

[Christ] is Himself the Word of God...who in His invisible form pervades us universally in the whole world,
and encompasses its length and breadth and height and
depth.[15]

IRENAEUS OF LYONS

The *logos* is the order of the *kosmos*, guiding alike the
flight of the sparrow and the life of the sage.[16]

ERAZIM KOHÁK

Everything that exists comes into being and is sustained by the creative power
of the *Logos* or Word. This is the fundamental intuition underlying the
Christian understanding of the Word's power to shape and form the mind of
the one seeking God and to sustain and give meaning to the life of the cosmos.
The roots of this intuition can be traced to the New Testament, where, in
the prologue of John's Gospel and in the Letter to the Colossians especially,
Christ the Word is understood as the utterance of God through whom the
world has come into existence. Creation and redemption are understood as
part of a single, continuous process. The world is incomprehensible apart from
the Word. And the Word cannot be apprehended fully and deeply except in

and through the world. This potent cosmological sense of *Logos* came into Christianity through an eclectic range of influences, including the ancient Jewish understanding of *Hokmah/Sophia* (Wisdom), the feminine creative principle through whom the world is birthed, and *dabar*, the divine Word that always effects what it says. Also present in this unfolding process were traditions of Greek philosophical speculation on *logos* as mediating principle between God and the world. Gradually there emerged a theological intuition that the redemptive power of Christ as *Logos* comes to expression and is experienced not only through the person of Jesus and the scriptures, but also through the varied gestures of the cosmos itself.

This perception of the Word's cosmic significance, while an ancient and enduring part of Christian theology and spiritual practice, has not always been given the attention it deserves—by Christians or by those beyond the Christian tradition. Part of this has to do with the common perception that the soteriological significance of Christ the Word is largely, if not exclusively, personal in character; salvation in this view is understood as an encounter between an individual and Christ, or as it has come to be expressed in our own time, as "personal salvation." Also contributing to this narrowing of the scope of the Word's expressive power is the habit of identifying the Word almost exclusively with scripture. The Word of God in this understanding is a discursive text to be read and a message to be learned, rather than a sacramental reality to be eaten, savored, and absorbed. A further difficulty arises from a tendency, at least in some of the most elaborate theological and philosophical articulations of the *Logos*, to project the Word into a space of radical transcendence, beyond matter, beyond the world, beyond history; in this understanding, the work of beholding the Word has often come to be seen as almost completely disembodied and ahistorical. These particular ways of encountering and interpreting the Word in Christian theology and spirituality have had deep, and often ambiguous, impacts on the way Christians have come to conceive of and respond to the living world. Any honest account of Christian thought will, of necessity, have to grapple with the effects of such perceptions of the Word on the world itself, especially the habit of disregard for the non-human world that has often been part of the legacy of such theological sensibility. Still, this characterization of Christian attitudes toward the Word hardly does justice to the rich and varied cosmologies that Christians developed to account for their understanding of the presence of the Word at the heart of the cosmos, or to the sense of what it means for Christians to inhabit and respond to a world that is fundamentally sacramental. Nor can one appreciate the particular contribution of the Christian contemplative

tradition to the shaping of a contemplative ecology without reckoning seriously with this more capacious Christology.

Still, there is a paradox at the heart of the Christian contemplative response
to the Word that affects how we conceive of its potential for helping us recover
a sense of the world's expressive power. I am referring to the continuous tension
between Word and silence within contemplative practice. There is a strong
and recurring appreciation in Christian contemplative thought and practice
for the revelatory power of the Word—including the sense in which it can be
understood as the enlivening force behind and within every living being. The
contemplative's primary orientation in response to this revelation is to listen
for the Word, to give oneself over to its power and beauty, not least as comes
to expression within created beings. The Word speaks through the world
and it is necessary to learn this language. But there is also the rich ground
of silence in which the contemplative listens, the physical silence of solitude
and the interior condition of *hesychia* or stillness in which the Word can be
apprehended and absorbed. And there is a still-deeper silence—the apprehension of the Divine beyond language, beyond images, in what some of the early
Christian contemplatives referred to as wordless, imageless prayer. A renunciation of all language (including, perhaps, all metaphors of language) for the
sake of a pure, simple apprehension of what Meister Eckhart calls the birth of
the Word in the ground of the soul—a deeply personal experience that is at
the same time an expression of an encompassing unity with all beings.

This renunciation of language for the sake of a silence that can speak
more eloquently of the divine mystery than can any language forms a critical part of the apophatic strain of Christian mystical thought. Paradoxically,
this tradition employs a particular language and vocabulary—darkness,
silence, unknowing, emptiness—to point toward and evoke a kind of knowing that cannot be encompassed, finally, in language. In this view the Word
is ineffable, unknowable. It expresses, it seems, nothing—or nothing that
can be grasped through language and concepts. But this apophatic dimension of Christian thought always stands in creative tension with kataphatic
expressions of thought and experience, which place more confidence than
apophatic traditions do in the expressive power of language, symbols, and
concepts to evoke and make present the Divine mystery. In this kataphatic
tradition, words, images, and things are understood to possess a sacramental
significance, mediating, making present and effecting an encompassing and
transformative awareness of divine mystery. In this tradition, the Word com-
municates—life, meaning, Spirit—in and through incarnate reality. Still,
even here, one often encounters a recognition that language has limits, that

the sheer force of the Word's expressive, revelatory power must eventually yield to silence, unknowing, emptiness.

The tension or paradox that has so often marked the relationship between Word and silence, between apophatic and kataphatic approaches to spiritual experience, has assumed particular importance in discussions about the kind of theological meaning Christians derive from their encounter with the *Logos*.[17] In terms of the central theme of this book, it also helps to account for the ambiguous character of Christian attitudes toward the Word's relationship with the world. Although Christian thought and practice has generally avoided the profound denigration of the living world that characterized gnostic and other radically dualistic systems of thought, the Christian tradition has nevertheless struggled at times with a deep ambivalence regarding how to think about and respond to the world. Even the bedrock theological conviction of the Word's incarnate character has not always been sufficient to overcome the sense, articulated already in the New Testament, that the Christian's true citizenship is in heaven (Phil 3:20); or that the soul's delicate and beautiful encounter with God, while mediated by the body, cannot, ultimately, be contained by it. There are serious theological and existential reasons for this ambivalence, one of the most significant being Christianity's longstanding concern to balance and reconcile the seemingly irreconcilable convictions that God is both radically transcendent (and hence neither fully comprehensible or able to be contained by and known through the world) and radically immanent (and hence sacramentally present in the world). The richly articulated theology of the *Logos* has been crucial to Christian contemplative efforts to maintain a sense of balance and reciprocity between these two convictions, to discover what it means to inhabit a world that is, as Gerard Manley Hopkins memorably expressed it, "charged with the grandeur of God" while also recognizing the limits of all language, all embodied experience to mediate the mystery of God. The Word arises from the very heart of God and comes to expression in the world. It permeates all matter, all living beings, and gives them life. But in its immensity and reach, it also transcends matter and can never be fully encompassed by it.

Somehow, amidst this ongoing tension, the Christian seeks to engage the world with a sensitivity and openness that facilitates a recognition that this is also and always an encounter with the Divine; similarly, one seeks to open oneself so deeply to the presence of the *Logos* in the soul that the full extent of the world's beauty and significance can be apprehended. Historically, the effort to understand and stand within this mystery has involved both theological reflection and concrete, spiritual practice. The theological elaboration of the Word's relationship with the world—both suffusing and transcending it—began very early and unfolded in a remarkable number of different idioms over time. The Christian contemplative communities drew upon these idioms in various ways to shape their own sense of what it meant to listen for and respond to the Word as part of their spiritual practice. A brief consideration of some of the ways Christians imagined the presence of the Word in the world can help to illuminate the distinctively contemplative contributions to the practice of attending to and living within this mystery.

One of the most important expressions of the Christian sense of the Word as permeating the entire cosmos arose from the Stoic philosophical tradition, in particular its attention to the idea of the Word as seed. The Stoics believed that the universe was governed by the divine *Logos*, was in some sense identical with the *Logos*, and must therefore be rational and bound by rules of cause and effect. But how to account for the inexplicable changes and developments that occur in nature, but that are not easily predicted by such rules? The answer the Stoics arrived at was the notion of the *logos spermatikos*, the "seed of the *logos*" which contains within itself the germ of everything it is eventually to become. *Logoi spermatikoi* exist as seeds planted as it were in the divine *logos* waiting to germinate and unfold at some later, divinely ordained moment.[18] Still, the *logos* is not merely an idea, a philosophical principle. It is a kind of palpable substance. Zeno likened it to fire. It is "as it were a seed, possessing the *logoi* of all things and the causes of events, past, present, and future."[19] The cosmos is alive with this word. The metaphor of the word as seed not only helped to address a pressing philosophical question—did the universe cohere? It also suggested the deep and significant continuity between the *logos* as generative principle of the universe and the *logoi* that quickens every human person and the entire living world. It is in this sense that the Stoics could say, as philosopher Erazim Kohák suggests, that: "The *logos* is the order of the *kosmos*, guiding alike the flight of the sparrow and the life of the sage."[20] From such a perspective, the human person is anything but a stranger in the cosmos.

Here is an understanding of the word *logos* that early Christian thinkers found immensely helpful in their own attempts to articulate a theologically and cosmologically meaningful Christology. Tertullian, for example, draws upon the Stoic understanding of the *logos* in responding to those like Hermagoras who claim that God is remote from the created world. To the contrary, he says: the Stoics remind us "that God permeates the world in the same way as honey in the comb."[21] Elsewhere, he addresses the question of how the divine *Logos* can be said to permeate the sensible world without losing its divinity: it is like the sun's relations with its own rays, he says, which are a portion and extension of their source.[22] Both analogies draw upon the idea of *logos* as a generative principle immanent in the cosmos. Tertullian also voices his support for the Stoic idea that everything that exists, including the *logos*, is a kind of body: "All things have one form of simple corporeality, which is a substantial thing."[23]

Other early Christian theologians, such as Clement of Alexandria, would give more attention to the transcendent character of the *Logos*, all the while seeking to discover an understanding of the Word supple enough to encompass both the transcendent reality of God and the immanent particularity of the living world. Drawing upon an eclectic mix of Jewish-Alexandrine philosophy, Stoicism, Middle Platonism, and Neoplatonism, Clement articulates an understanding of the *Logos* capable of reaching into the hidden depths of the transcendent Godhead while also stretching out across the whole universe. According to Clement, the *Logos* has three distinct but related dimensions. It is utterly transcendent, being identical with the totality of the ideas or powers of God. It is also the principle or pattern of everything that has been created. And it is the *anima mundi*, or world soul, the law and harmony of the universe, the power that holds it together and permeates it from the center to its most extreme boundaries.[24]

Subsequent Christian reflection on this idea unfurled like so many seeds scattered by the winds, flowering, cross-pollinating and spilling their seeds again into the dark loam of the earth. The Word's cosmic expressions within the Christian tradition are, to borrow a phrase Paul Ricoeur uses to describe the revelatory character of scripture, irreducibly polyphonous and polysemous.[25] Light, darkness, seed, garden, tree, bread, wine are but some of the palpable realities of the world through which the *Logos* was understood to have gestured forth.[26] So too are the modes of its expression diverse, arising not only within Christian theological discourse, but also in art and architecture, in biblical commentary, in mystical literature, in ascetic practice, in music, in poetry.

Consider how in the *fiat lux* of the Genesis creation account and in the luminous gold background of ancient Christian and later Byzantine mosaics, *Logos* comes to expression through light.[27] Or how the Word that speaks through the cross also gestures forth across the cosmos. According to Irenaeus, "because [Christ] is Himself the Word of God…who in His invisible form pervades us universally in the whole world, and encompasses its length and breadth and height and depth…the Son of God was also crucified in these, imprinted in the form of a cross on the universe." This cosmic cross is given exquisite aesthetic expression in the Mausoleum of Galla Placidia in Ravenna, where a brilliant gold cross floats in a shallow, dark blue dome surrounded by stars arranged in concentric circles, whose diminishing size toward the center gives one the impression of gazing into a heavenly vault.[28] On a more intimate scale, consider the presence of the *Logos* who, according to Origen of Alexandria, rises up to meet one in the biblical text as ardent lover and who kindles within the reader a passionate love for the world: "If a [person] can so extend his thinking as to ponder and consider the beauty and grace of all things that have been created in the Word," he claims, "the very charm of them will so smite him, the grandeur of their brightness will so pierce him as with a chosen dart ... that he will suffer from the dart Himself a saving wound, and will be kindled with the blessed fire of His love."[29] Here is a sensual, palpable Word, present to us, says Origen, as touch, fragrance, sound, vision, and taste.

Rhythm and movement, form and color are also important to the expression of the *Logos* within the long tradition of manuscript illustration, in which the Word was often set—actually and figuratively—within an entire constellation of living beings, suggesting the sense in which the Word is virtually embedded within and arising out of the living world. In the Lindisfarne Gospels, for example, one finds surrounding its illustration of the opening words from John's Gospel, *in principio erat verbum*, "trumpet-patterns, whorls, triangles and lozenges, and birds and animals interlaced, as though foreshadowing the whole wealth of forms and life that was to issue from the Word; and this whole microcosm is highlighted by the interplay of colours used for the illumination ... green, mauve, yellow, red and pink."[30] To gaze upon this intricate dance of word and World is to be drawn more deeply into the mystery of the Word's generative power. It is also to be asked to listen more carefully to the eloquence of the world.

It is to be invited to listen, as twelfth-century mystic and visionary Hildegard of Bingen apparently did, for traces of the *prima vox* or "voice primordial," the animating principle everywhere present in the world and present to the one sensitive enough to notice it and take it in.[31] It is to feel the redemptive, healing transformative power of the incarnation of the Word as "a blossoming of a beautiful flower/that gave fragrance/to all the spices/which had been dry."[32] It is to listen intently for the music in that flowering, a music that is the redemptive power of the Word present at once in the soul and the cosmos. And it is to be invited to respond, in song, to that music. Hildegard's own work does just this, her *symphonia* refracting and giving voice to the celestial harmony that was revealed to her through vision and through the palpable world. So does the work of Francis of Assisi, who praised God in his renowned *Canticle to the Creatures*, not *because* of the elements of the living world but *through* them, his own voice rising, as it were, through theirs: "Praised be You, my Lord, *through* Sister Moon and the stars.... Praised be You, my Lord, *through* Brother Wind and through the air."[33]

These expressions of feeling for the Word's incarnate presence in the life of the world serve as a reminder of how deeply the Christian imagination could respond to the world as a spiritually vital reality. Still, the Christian tradition does not speak with a single or unified voice regarding the presence of the *Logos* at the heart of creation. And one must acknowledge also all the ways that Christians have responded to the force of the Word not as an invitation to listen or respond to the living world, but as a justification for dominating and exploiting it. This tendency to read and respond to the Word through a radically anthropocentric lens, too long a defining feature of Christian thought and practice, has more recently begun to receive critical scrutiny as part of renewed commitment on the part of Christians to understand what it might mean to engage the natural world as part of a serious ethical-spiritual practice. Reckoning with this historical blindness must figure importantly into any contemporary effort at retrieving an awareness of the ways the Word arises and addresses us through the living world.

So too must there be a sustained attention to the diverse idioms through which the Word's expressive presence comes alive within the soul of the practicing Christian contemplative. Certainly, this will involve attending carefully to the Word's presence in the immanent, palpable, reality of the natural world (in mediating realities of light, color, sound, and matter), brought to language in the kind of natural, physical, spatial metaphors and analogies alluded to here—the long-germinating seed, the drenched honeycomb, the permeating warmth of the sun, the lover's embrace, spatial depth and breadth, embodiment. These kataphatic expressions of our encounter with the Word are critical to the work of retrieving a genuinely sacramental feeling for the living world. Nor can one ignore the poetic or theopoetic character of this work. The cultivation of the kind of sensitivity to the Word's presence in the world that led Gerald Manley Hopkins to develop his ideas of "inscape" and "instress"—a way of apprehending and "reading" the presence of the Word in the distinctive shape and texture of particular things—will be essential if we are to learn to inhabit the world fully and deeply. But, it is also necessary to recover a feeling for the eloquence of silence, emptiness, and darkness, for the way in which stillness can provide a ground for hearing the Word's presence at the very limits of language and concepts, in that space that opens up where speech ceases. The Christian contemplative tradition has always been acutely sensitive to this space and its importance for shaping one's capacity for hearing the Word—in the depths of the soul and at the heart of the world. It is to this dimension of the Word's expressive presence and to the contemplative practices that helped bring it to conscious awareness that I now turn.

The Birth of the Word in the Soul

O Mystery exalted beyond every word
and beyond silence.[34]

ISAAC OF NINEVAH

Your face is [now] so fully turned towards this birth that,
no matter what you see or hear, you can get nothing but
this birth from all things. All things become simply God
to you, for in all things you notice only God....[35]

MEISTER ECKHART

Attention to the Word must be cultivated in silence. Indeed the most profound expression of the Word comes to us in silence, *as* silence. Apprehending this Word requires a relinquishment so radical that nothing of one's familiar language and conceptual structures is allowed to remain. Still, entering into this emptiness, this silence enables an apprehension of the expressive power of the Divine so profound that all things are brought to life in a simple, encompassing awareness. Here one encounters one of the strange paradoxes of the Christian contemplative tradition: the Word who reveals God, who reveals the very life and soul of the world, and upon whom Christians are called to ruminate ceaselessly, remains hidden, shrouded in mystery. There is both revelation (speech) and concealment (silence). One is invited to attend to a Word that is at once as close and intimate to us as our own breath and, as Isaac of Ninevah puts it, "beyond every word and beyond silence."

The early Christian contemplatives were immensely sensitive to this rhythm between Word and silence. And the tradition of thought and practice that emerges from their ascetic experiments in the desert reverberated deeply in the subsequent traditions of contemplative thought and practice in the Christian world. Ruminating on the Word in silence became one of the crucial spiritual practices for Christians. And as theological reflection on the meaning of the Word continued to grow and develop, the meaning of such rumination also continued to deepen. Without question, the immediate significance of this practice was felt in the personal life of an individual monk where the primary question was always: what would it mean to listen

for and incorporate the meaning of the Word into one's life? And how could
such careful attention to the Word contribute to the personal transformation
of the monk's life that would enable him or her to learn to live in freedom,
openness and love? The plaintive cry found throughout the early monastic
literature—"Abba, speak to me a word"—reflects the pathos and personal significance of this hunger for a healing word. But this ruminative work also had
a critical communal meaning, for the monk chewing on the Word—whether a
word from Scripture or a word from a spiritual elder—was inevitably brought,
sooner or later, to a recognition that the work of "realizing" or incorporating the Word into one's life had profound significance for the entire community. And while the community meant, in the first instance, those men
and women with whom one shared one's life, it eventually came to mean,
explicitly or implicitly, the wider community of the world and the cosmos.
Learning to listen for and apprehend the voice of the Word—in the world
and in one's soul—became one of the primary means by which the Christian
contemplative learned to cultivate a mindful awareness of the whole and to
live simply and deeply *within* the whole. Still, there was always an acute awareness that even amidst this growing incorporation of the Word into the heart
of one's life, the sheer immensity of the Word (the expressive power of the
Divine) ensured that it could never be apprehended fully and that anything
one might say in response to the Word would eventually need to be unsaid or
transcended. Listening this deeply always meant entering, again, into wordless silence. Learning to listen and respond to the Word, opening oneself to its
transformative power, allowing oneself to become incorporated into the life
of the Word, learning to dwell in the silence from which the Word arises and
toward which it always tends—these are among the most fundamental and
enduring challenges of Christian contemplative life.

The *Life of Antony* remains a paradigmatic early Christian narrative expression of this contemplative rhythm of Word and silence. The entire structure
of the work, from the young man's initial, piercing encounter with the Word,
to his withdrawal and ever-deepening descent into the silence of the desert
(also sustained by the Word), and to his eventual incorporation back into
the community during which he is experienced as a living embodiment of
the Word, turns on this fundamental rhythm. And it gives expression to
questions that would continue to echo in the work of so many subsequent
Christian contemplatives: how can I learn to listen carefully to the Word that
is beckoning to me, from deep within my own soul and from the heart of the
world? And how can I learn to live into that Word? These questions were
fraught with theological meaning for Christians who never ceased to wonder

at the mystery of how God could have become manifest in person of Christ and in the life of the world. But in more practical terms they were questions about how to live, how to open up the mind, indeed the whole of one's life, to receive this great gift.

Athanasius' narrative plunges almost immediately into this fundamental question. Following a few brief comments on Antony's childhood, we encounter a young man, around eighteen to twenty years old, sunk deep in thought, reflecting on the recent death of his parents and on the prospects for his own life in the aftermath of this event. Athanasius depicts Antony as both restless and still, "gathering his thoughts," acutely attentive to the weight and possibilities of this moment. He is pondering not only the loss of his parents but also the witness of those members of the early Christian community, "who forsaking everything, followed the Savior." It is within the space of this loss, this witness, this silence, that he encounters the Word that will change everything. In a village church situated near his home along the Nile River, Antony hears a text from the Gospel being read aloud: "If you would be perfect, go sell what you possess and give it to the poor, and you will have treasure in heaven" (Mt 19:21). Athanasius relates that Antony felt the force of the text as if "the passage were read on his account." Immediately, he gets up, sells his possessions, keeping only a few things for the care of his sister, and gives everything else to the townspeople and to the poor. But this initial encounter with the Word, for all its force, does not free Antony entirely from his attachment to his former life. Once again, he enters the church and again hears a text being read aloud: "do not be anxious about tomorrow" (Mt 6:34). It is in response to this Word that Antony makes the final break, leaving behind his old life in the village forever and embarking on a journey that would take him deep into the heart of the desert.[36]

This highly stylized account of the monk's call and conversion would eventually come to inspire many similar accounts in the Christian hagiographical tradition. Athanasius constructs here a narrative in which the reader can feel, implicitly, the providential hand of God guiding the monk toward his destiny. It is no accident that just as he is walking near the church a particular text is being read, nor that this happens yet a second time in almost the same manner, this time pushing him even further down the path toward the desert. All of this, we are led to understand, has been set in motion by God's providential presence. Still, one can discern within this beautifully choreographed narrative a pattern that would soon come to define the entire Christian contemplative relationship with the Word: there is a hunger, a longing, an openness for a Word; a moment of stillness and attention and silence; a Word arising from the silence that provokes thought, reflection and response; and a descent, again, into a space of silence. The work of living into the Word, of absorbing it into one's life, takes place in silence, stillness. Of course it is not any word. The Gospel passages that inspire Antony to break from his former life and enter the desert have particular significance within the Christian contemplative tradition precisely because of their fierce call to renounce everything that would prevent one from living into and for what another Gospel text described as "the one thing necessary" (Lk 10:42). Why and how these texts came to be read and interpreted in the particular way they were at this historical moment—as a call to enter the desert—cannot be accounted for simply or easily. But the basic pattern described in the *Life of Antony* would become paradigmatic for the Christian contemplative tradition: to listen and respond to the Word fully and deeply, one must enter silence. Indeed the Word beckons one into the silence of the desert.

In time, this call to enter the desert would become part of a rich vocabulary of stillness, emptiness, and darkness that was crucial to the Christian understanding of how the Word mediates the human encounter with the Divine. But in its initial expression in the *Life of Antony*, one encounters a charmingly concrete reading of this experience: the monk, moved by the Word, enters the desert. The Word inspires, even provokes the monk into engaging in that quintessentially monastic act—*anachoresis* or withdrawal into the space of emptiness and silence. This tension between the concrete and metaphorical readings of the Word in the desert is not insignificant in the effort to draw from these ancient monastic sources ideas and practices that can help inform a contemporary contemplative ecology. The idea of the desert would continue to reverberate in the Christian spiritual imagination, profoundly shaping the Christian understanding of what it meant to live in the Word. To listen to the Word one had to be prepared to enter into an inner landscape of such stillness, such encompassing silence that it was itself a kind of desert. It was less important to find an actual desert than a place of emptiness in which the soul could come alive and be reborn in the Word. Still, in this important early Christian monastic narrative, and in much of the early Christian monastic tradition, the actual desert—a vast, mysterious, beautiful terrain—figures significantly into the Christian understanding of what it means to listen and respond to the Word. Antony is provoked by his initial encounter with the Word to enter the desert, and as he learns to dwell in that emptiness, his capacity for hearing and responding to the Word continues to deepen and grow. And this in turn leads him further into the emptiness of the desert, until he reaches the remote place near the Red Sea known as the "Inner Mountain," a place he "fell in love with" at first sight and would come to cherish as "his own home."[37]

There is a beautiful and important arc here: from the initial stillness in which the revelatory power of the Word is first heard, felt, and apprehended; to the long, purifying *ascesis* in which one learns to relinquish all attachments that keep one from hearing and living into the Word; to that endless expanse of emptiness and silence within and beyond the Word into which one gradually learns to dwell. This is the silent land—what the early Christian writer Rufinus described as the *silentium ingens, quies magna* ("huge silence and … great quiet")—within which the ancient monks passed their lives.[38] This is the empty space on the map of Christian contemplative experience, a hidden and secret space that is crucial for understanding what it meant to listen to and live in the Word.

Silence. Stillness. Emptiness. Darkness. Desert. These are among the images that the apophatic tradition employed to grapple with the question of how the Divine is encountered in the space beyond images, beyond language, even beyond the Word. These images describe at once the physical conditions of the contemplative life (the need for space, solitude, and silence), the kinds of ascetic practices and spiritual dispositions the contemplative sought to cultivate, and the particular understanding of the Divine to which contemplative practice seemed inevitably to lead. For Christian contemplatives, this apparent negation of the Word was both necessary and challenging. There was an abiding conviction that the divine mystery—the presence of which the Word was believed to mediate and make present—was so immense and vast that no image, no language could ever encompass or express it; hence the need to fall silent and enter what Gregory of Nyssa and others called "the divine darkness." But there remained the question of how to attend to and cherish the incarnate Word alive at the heart of the world if that Word ultimately recedes into darkness and silence. What kind of silence is this? And what knowledge of the Word, and the world, is possible in such silence?

Addressing this question honestly requires one to confront a tension that arose early on in the Christian contemplative tradition, regarding how to think about and respond to the created world. I am referring to the tension between the impulse to honor and value the living world by virtue of its having been brought into being sustained by the Word, and the impulse to detach oneself from the world for the sake of the eternal Word that exists both within and beyond the created world. In the Christian contemplative tradition, one rarely encounters the radical world-denying dualism that characterized certain forms of Gnostic or Manichean thought. But one does encounter an ongoing struggle to reckon with what it means to respond to an incarnate and eternal Word, through whom embodied, material existence is suffused with the divine presence, and in whom one is called to live forever in God. "The grass withers and the flower fades; but the Word of God endures forever" (Is 40:8). The world is precious but ephemeral; the Word, through whom the world exists, is eternal. Can one attend, carefully, to both? Can one cultivate a contemplative awareness sensitive and subtle enough to encompass the whole?

Consider this saying from the *Apophthegmata Patrum*: "Once Abba Arsenius came to a place where there was a bed of reeds shaken by the wind. He said to the brothers, 'What is this rustling noise?' They said, 'It is the reeds.' He said to them, 'If a man sits in silence and hears the voice of a bird, he does not have quiet in his heart; how much more difficult is it for you, who hear the sound of these reeds?'"[39] It would be difficult to imagine an attitude less open to the work of cultivating genuine sensitivity and care toward the created world than the one expressed in this saying. Here, it seems, one encounters a very different kind of sensitivity, in which the inner silence cultivated by the contemplative is perceived as so delicate and precious that even the faintest trace of life in the created world is enough to disturb and compromise it. The Word arises in silence; everything else is distraction. What then of the Word at the heart of the world—birdsong, the rustling of reeds—whose discourse and presence the contemplative seeks to attend and respond to with ever deepening care? Is this apparent paradox resolvable? Addressing this question requires grappling with the particular understanding the Christian contemplative tradition developed regarding the need for detachment in helping one learn to see and apprehend reality (including the reality of the created world) truly and honestly. Of particular importance for learning to apprehend the Word and the world in this way was cultivating a capacity for what the early Christian contemplatives referred to as *hesychia* or stillness.

The practice of *hesychia* was part of the larger, more encompassing project of ascetic relinquishment through which the contemplative's mind could be cleansed and freed from the attachments that prevented one from seeing the true character of things. For the monks, this was the work of an entire lifetime. They realized that stillness was both an *end* to be sought—what John Climacus called "the very center of the mysteries"—and the *means* by which one might gradually come to this end, that is, a *practice*. Stillness belonged at the beginning of contemplative life and practice (Evagrius of Pontus believed it to be the foundation of everything else); but it was also something one would expect to encounter at the deepest levels of contemplative experience. In his work *The Foundations of the Monastic Life: A Presentation of the Practice of Stillness,* Evagrius offers this exhortation to those who would learn to live in stillness: "Leave behind the concerns of the world, the principalities and powers set over them (Eph 6:12); that is, stand free of material concerns and passions, beyond all desire, so that as you become a stranger to the conditions deriving from these you may be able to cultivate stillness properly."[40] With this simple reminder of the need to "stand free of material concerns and passions," Evagrius signals what for him is the heart of the matter: to the extent that one is attached to things through the passions, one's perception of these things and one's relationship with them will be distorted, leaving one unable to respond to them freely and openly. But the work of *hesychia* ultimately goes deeper still, for Evagrius believed it was only by cultivating stillness that one could begin to experience the freedom from anxieties, worries and obsessions that obscure the true character of existence. As he notes in another of his works, *Exhortation to the Monks:* "As it is impossible to purify water once troubled unless it remains undisturbed, so too it is impossible to purify the state of a monk unless he practice stillness with all rigor and perseverance."[41] Only by rooting out the deep sources of obsessive thoughts and concerns, Evagrius believed, could one learn to see things for what they are. This is what stillness makes possible. This is what it means to see all things in the Word and the Word in all things.

The early Christian contemplative tradition developed its own distinctive vocabulary for expressing this integrated, whole way of seeing reality in and through the Word, rooted in a sense of the intimate relationship that exists between the *Logos* (the divine, creative principle through whom all of creation came into being) and the *logoi* or "inner essences" of created things. Contemplative practice meant acquiring, through ever-greater detachment and inner stillness, a capacity to discern the *logoi* of created things and so come to know them in and through the *Logos.* In his treatise *On Prayer,* Evagrius articulates it in these terms: "We pursue the virtues for the sake of the inner essences (*logoi*) of created beings, and these we pursue for the sake of the Word (*Logos*) who gave them being, and [who] usually manifests himself in the state of prayer."[42] Here one finds the principal rationale for the conviction within early Christian contemplative thought and practice that all created beings are worthy of our most careful attention: in their *logoi* they carry traces of divine life (the *Logos*) within them, and as one learns to attend to them, one is brought to a profound knowledge of God that is also a knowledge of these created beings. There is a fundamental theological intuition underlying this vision of reality that reflects one of the most cherished convictions of the early Christian contemplative tradition: the created world can truly be apprehended only in and through God. Vladimir Lossky, the great twentieth-century Russian Orthodox theologian, expressed it this way: "When we examine the nature of created things, seeking to penetrate into the reason of their being, we are led finally to the knowledge of the Word, causal principle and at the same time end of all beings. All things were created by the *Logos* who is as it were a divine nexus, the threshold from which flow the creative outpourings, the particular *logoi* of creatures, and the centre towards which in their turn all created beings tend, as to their final end."[43] In the contemplative tradition, this intuition became woven into a *practice* through which one was brought, little by little, to a felt sense of this unity and wholeness. According to Maximus the Confessor, the seventh-century theologian and mystic: "... when after practicing the virtues [the contemplative] attains the state of dispassion, he culls the inner principles (*logoi*) of created beings and devoutly nourishes himself with the divine knowledge they contain."[44]

Such observations regarding the contemplative practice of attending to the *logoi* of created beings can be found throughout the contemplative tradition represented in the *Philokalia* and other ancient Christian texts, and reflect the sustained effort on the part of Christian contemplatives to understand what it might mean to live with an awareness of the created world as alive in God. Still, there is a paradox at the heart of this tradition, namely the presence of an equally strong conviction that the very *Logos* whose life is manifest and made present through the *logoi* of created beings so radically transcends them that it can never fully be known through them. The "divine knowledge" that Maximus describes being mediated through the *logoi* is limited. There is a further, more encompassing, more mysterious knowledge that one comes to only through unknowing. It is in this sense that Maximus can say: "the divine *Logos* is eternally made manifest in different modes of participation, and yet remains eternally invisible to all in virtue of the surpassing nature of his hidden activity."[45] The hidden character of the Word's activity is, for Maximus, due to the immensity of the mystery of which it partakes. And it is this fundamental mystery that leads one to a practice of silence, or to a language of negation regarding the Word. "The one who speaks of God negatively through negations is making the Word spirit," says Maximus, "as in the beginning he was God and with God. Using absolutely nothing which can be known he knows in a better way the utterly Unknowable."[46] Thus Maximus encourages his readers to cultivate a capacity for a "simple

encounter with the Word without the veils of the mind covering him... ";
to develop an ability to "behold with the naked mind the pure Word ... the
incorporeal Word"; to pay attention to and dwell in the presence of what he
calls the "naked Word."[47]

There is an undeniable beauty in the severity of this negation, an eloquence
in this silence. Still, one wonders how attention to this "naked Word" could
ever facilitate a feeling of intimacy and kinship with the living world. Can
one's affection or regard for any particular thing—any living being, any physical place, any fragrance or shade of color—withstand such a fierce emptiness?
It seems more likely that one will end up, with Arsenius, refusing the sound
of birdsong, of wind rustling through the reeds. The things of the world, seen
from this perspective, are not enough to hold us. Only the *Logos*, only God,
can do that. And yet, this is not the only way to read the contemplative tradition's commitment to radical negation. One is, after all, invited by this same
tradition to attend to the "hidden activity" of the *Logos* at the heart of all
reality. There is nothing in this invitation to suggest the need to refuse the
things of this world. To the contrary, the impulse to preserve a wide margin of silence, to prescind from filling up the space of emptiness, has always
been understood as rooted in a desire to know and encounter the *Logos* in
its purest, its most diffuse, and its most varied expressions. Nowhere in the
Christian contemplative tradition has this vision of the Word encountered
in radical emptiness and unknowing been expressed more powerfully than in
the sermons of the great Dominican mystic Meister Eckhart. Here, especially
in Eckhart's vision of "the birth of the Word in the soul," one begins to see
how the most profound negation opens up a space in which everything and
everyone can be beheld in God.

Eckhart employs a range of images—nakedness, emptiness, darkness,
unknowing, barrenness—to get at this central idea, namely that we must be
free to receive God, that there must be *space* within us if we are to respond
to and live in God. "[A]t this birth," he says, "God needs and must have a
vacant free and unencumbered soul, containing nothing but Himself alone,
and which looks to nothing and nobody but him."[48] Eckhart is commenting
here on one of the great New Testament texts of renunciation, where Jesus
warns his followers: "Whoever loves anything but me, whoever loves father
and mother or many other things is not worthy of me" (Mk 10:34). Like the
early Christian monks, whose single-minded response to these "hard sayings"
earned them the name *apotaktikoi*, or "renunciants," Eckhart gives sustained
and pointed attention to these texts of renunciation. He recognizes, as the
desert monastics did, that a willingness to let go of everything that is less than

God must exist at the very foundation of the soul. It is the posture of openness that makes everything else possible.

It is precisely this openness that can and often does trigger the sudden upwelling or birth of the Word in the soul. "God must enter into your being and powers," says Eckhart, "because you have bereft yourself of all possessions, and become a desert, as it is written: 'The voice of the one crying in the wilderness' (Mt 3:3). Let this eternal voice cry out in you as it listeth, and be a desert in respect of yourself in all things."[49] To "become a desert"—for Eckhart, this image of the contemplative life points to the immense space that opens up within us when we let go of things, become "bereft of all possessions." Not simply material possessions, but anything and everything that we substitute for God, including our images of God: "God needs *no* image and has no image," says Eckhart: "without any means, likeness or image God operates in the soul—right in the ground where no image ever got in, but only He Himself with His own being."[50] This is what it means to enter the desert, to keep oneself "empty and bare." "As for what it profits you to pursue this possibility, to keep yourself empty and bare," says Eckhart, "just following and tracking this darkness and unknowing without turning back—it contains the chance to gain Him who is all things. And the more barren you are of self and unwitting of all things, the nearer you are to him. Of this barrenness it is said: 'I will lead my beloved into the wilderness and will speak to her in her heart.' [Hos. 2:14] The true word of eternity," Eckhart insists, "is spoken only in solitude, where a man is a desert and alien to himself and multiplicity."[51] The language here is suggestive of the immense shift in self-awareness that Eckhart believes is necessary if one is to make room for God in one's life: keep yourself empty and bare; follow and track this darkness without turning back; become barren of self, unwitting of all things; become a desert, alien to yourself. Only then will you have hope of gaining the God who is "all things."

One must increasingly relinquish, Eckhart suggests, the sense that one's activity, one's thought, one's ideas of God and the self are what really matters. To the contrary, what matters is letting go of one's attachment to such ideas, allowing oneself to be empty and still and attentive. Such stillness is necessary if one is to enter the desert and become alien to oneself for the sake of God. "Here," Eckhart says, "[one] must come to a forgetting and an unknowing. There must be a stillness and a silence for this word to make itself heard. We cannot serve this word better than in stillness and in silence: *there* we can hear it, and there too we will understand it aright—in the unknowing. To [the one] who knows nothing it appears and reveals itself."[52]

The end of this process of relinquishment, for Eckhart, is an experience of union so profound that one can no longer imagine or sense one's own existence as separate or distinct from the existence of anyone or anything—including God. It is here that one begins to see how the work of detachment contributes to one's growing awareness of the unity of all life in God. It is a matter, Eckhart, says of learning to "grieve for nothing." "The child [the Word] is fully born when a [person's] heart grieves for nothing: *then* a [person] has the essence and the nature and the substance and the wisdom and the joy and all that God has. *Then* the very being and the Son of God is ours and in us and we attain to the very essence of God."⁵³ What does it mean, to grieve for nothing? For Eckhart, it seems to be one of the key signs that the "breakthrough," or birth has really happened, an indication that one's identity is now so deeply bound up in God that it is no longer possible to make any distinction between the self and God. One now lives completely and utterly *in* God. This sense of living from one's deepest center, from the deepest center of God, has practical consequences. For example, no longer is one concerned to detach oneself from "creatures" or "images" or other things that are less than God. This posture of renuncia-tion, necessary at an earlier time when the self was still inordinately attached to all manner of things and blind to God, is no longer necessary. Eckhart says, "… your face is [now] so fully turned towards this birth that, no matter what you see or hear, you can get nothing but this birth from all things. All things become simply God to you, for in all things you notice only God.…"⁵⁴

"All things become simply God to you." Here is the simple and staggering realization toward which rumination on the Word in the Christian tradition leads. By cultivating a capacity for silence, for stillness, by entering deeply into a space of emptiness in which the Word can be born in the soul, one arrives little by little at this sense of God alive in everything. The voice, the Word, at the heart of reality can be known and apprehended, though paradoxically one can arrive at this knowledge fully only by way of unknowing. One can learn to live in the presence of this Word, live *in* this Word, and in this way truly come to inhabit and cherish the living world.

Lingua Vernacula *and the Spirit of Place*

I heard the forlorn but melodious note of a hooting owl indefinitely far; such a sound as the frozen earth would yield if struck with a suitable plectrum, the very *lingua vernacula* of Walden Wood.⁵⁵

HENRY DAVID THOREAU

Voice. Come out of the silence.
Say something.
Appear in the form of a spider.
Or a moth beating the curtain.[56]

THEODORE ROETHKE

Can we learn this language? Can we recover the capacity to hear the subtle music, the voice of the world? The silence in the music? One way to begin thinking about how we might do so is by cultivating what Barry Lopez calls a "more particularized understanding" of place—an awareness and sensitivity to the infinitely subtle, delicate and varied life of particular places.[57] In the ancient pictographs of the Southwest, in the myths, stories, and songs of so many indigenous peoples of this continent, and in the literature and poetry of nature that has flourished in North America and beyond during the past hundred and fifty years, one finds language deeply rooted in particular places, responsive to the life and movements of plant and animal species through those places, intricately woven into the patterns of sky, rock, and wind.[58] One finds vivid traces, that is, of an incarnate Word. To listen to this Word is to hear a language arising from the shape and texture of the living world, a Word as old as the world itself. It is to be brought around to dwell in a silence beyond and beneath all language, from which language and the world itself arise.

This more particularized understanding of place arises, as does all understanding, through language. And through the silence from which language arises and to which it always returns. Which is why the careful attention to language (and silence) that one finds in the literature of nature is so significant. Through an extraordinary range of literary forms and strategies, language here acts as a medium through which the voice of particular places can come to expression. But language is not only a medium; it is also a potent metaphor that brings with it its own challenging questions. Does the natural world itself speak a kind of language? Can we learn to hear and understand this language, allow it to permeate our awareness? Can we begin to discover our own voices inflected with the language of the living world? Also, can we learn to still our own minds and dwell in the silence that is the ground of all speech, all language? Can we humble ourselves enough to attune ourselves to this silence, allow it (and all that lives within it) to open up and expand within and around us?

Such questions seem to have been much on the mind of Henry David Thoreau during his sojourn at Walden Pond. To listen, to learn the language of the place—these were among his central concerns. "We are in danger," he says in

Walden, "of forgetting the language which all things and all events speak without metaphor, which alone is copious and standard." This is the fundamental language, of which the language of books is but a pale reflection. Which is why, he says, he spent his first summer at Walden not reading books but hoeing beans, giving himself over to what he called "the bloom of the present moment," to "the discipline of looking always at what is to be seen." He sought to open himself, with his whole being, to whatever was unfolding before him, to give himself over to the place without prejudice, without expectation. To drift, to float, to feel. "Sometimes, in a summer morning," Thoreau writes, "having taken my accustomed bath, I sat in my sunny doorway from sunrise till noon, rapt in a revery, amidst the pines and hickories and sumachs, in undisturbed solitude and stillness, while the birds sang around or flitted noiseless through the house, until by the sun falling in at my west window, or the noise of some traveler's wagon on a distant highway, I was reminded of the lapse of time."[59] Here, as throughout his work, the language of consciousness or awareness seems to occupy Thoreau's interest every bit as much as the language of the world. What does it mean to pay attention? To abandon oneself so fully to observing the world that one is no longer a "a reader, a student merely, but a seer?" Such questions haunt the pages of *Walden*, and remind us how intent Thoreau was not only on listening to the language emerging in and through the texture of the world but also on attending to that profoundly interior moment when "a fact flowered into a truth." At times, the language of the world, the particular distinctive music of things, seems to become absorbed into and even eclipsed by the language of awareness.

Still, one catches hints elsewhere, in *Walden*, in the *Journal*, and in other late works, that Thoreau never lost interest in trying to hear and respond to the distinctive voice of his own place. In *Walden's* "Winter Animals" chapter, he notes: "For sounds in winter nights, and often in winter days, I heard the forlorn but melodious note of a hooting owl indefinitely far; such a sound as the frozen earth would yield if struck with a suitable plectrum, the very *lingua vernacula* of Walden Wood, and quite familiar to me at last, though I never saw the bird while it was making it."[60] Here, again, the metaphor of the word mediates the terms of the encounter. It is language Thoreau is listening for, a language rooted in, arising from, particular to, this place. And he hears it in the cry of the owl, which speaks in "the very *lingua vernacula* of Walden Wood." It is not clear why the owl is seen as being the quintessential voice of this place. But the precise reason for this choice is less important here than the fact that Thoreau thinks of the owl's sounding presence as a kind of "vernacular language." A local language or dialect. And that he notes that this language has become "quite familiar to me at last." It takes time to learn the language of a place, time and careful attention to the intricate patterns of the place.

There is a paradoxical tension between the local and universal character of this *lingua vernacula*. At times, Thoreau's attention to the particular sounds of the local landscape lead to an awareness of something more encompassing, more universal, what he calls "the general earth-song." On June 13, 1851, he records in his journal: "As I climbed the hill again toward my old bean-field, I listened to the ancient, familiar, immortal, dear cricket sound under all others, hearing at first some distant chirps; but when these ceased I was aware of the general earth-song, which my hearing had not heard amid which these were only taller flowers in a bed, and I wondered if behind or beneath this was not some other chant more universal."[61] There is something poignant and beautiful in the connection Thoreau draws between the familiar music of crickets and the larger more universal chant that he senses arising within it. There is no accounting for the intuition that enables him to feel and sense this connection. Nor can it be proven. But this feeling of the musicality of the world becomes for Thoreau a fundamental means of experiencing its particular voice and of exploring the way it comes to expression in this or that place. It deepens his capacity to receive and respond to it. Still, it is more than an occasional intuition, for his sustained attention to the universal chant is also part of a practice, a way of living that he actively seeks to cultivate. Two weeks later, he reflects on this question: "All the world goes by and is reflected in our deeps. Such clarity! Obtained by such pure means! By simply living, by honesty of purpose. We live and rejoice. I awoke to a music which no one about me heard. Whom shall I thank for it? The luxury of wisdom! the luxury of virtue!... To the sane man the world is a musical instrument. The very touch affords an exquisite pleasure."[62] There is a relationship, Thoreau suggests, between our capacity to hear and take in the music of the world and the condition of our soul, our mind. We do not always hear this music; but the capacity to do so is within us. "Pure means...honesty of purpose." These are the fundamental moral or spiritual qualities required for awakening to such music, to feel it coursing through our veins. Nor, suggests Thoreau, is our relationship to this music merely passive. The world itself is a musical instrument. We play upon it, create our own music, and through it come to know an "exquisite pleasure."

Is such exquisite pleasure still possible for us, especially those of us who spend our lives in densely populated, noisy, urban places—where, if we pause to listen, we will more likely hear the roar of freeway traffic, the cry of sirens or ringing gunshots than birdsong or crickets? Perhaps we can only read

Thoreau's account as a reminder of what once was possible in a simpler (and quieter) time but is now no longer available to us. I wonder, as I move through my days in the immense metropolis of Los Angeles that has been my home for many years, what it might mean to learn to listen with such intense attention in this place, in this historical moment. There is an immense gulf between the world Thoreau knew and the one I (and I suspect most of us) inhabit. Nor is it easy to comprehend his rare, even peculiar experiment at Walden Pond; it feels so far removed from the lives that most of us live. Sometimes I wonder whether we can we even begin to imagine, in light of these immense differences, what it might mean to emulate Thoreau's practice of attentive listening? Or the kind of music we would hear if we did so? These questions and others like them arise almost inevitably for anyone seeking to retrieve and reinterpret elements of contemplative practice arising from other times and places, whether it be from Thoreau's nineteenth-century Walden Pond or Antony's fourth-century Egyptian desert. Are such practices really adaptable to our own very different situations?

Many of the personal stories in this book arise from my experiences in remote places—especially in monasteries and wild places. These experiences have taught me much of what I know about what it means to pay attention, to listen for the still small voice within and without, and over time I have learned to incorporate them into the larger patterns of my life, most of which unfold in this urban place. It is here, amidst the shifting and always-complex responsibilities of work and family life and the needs of the wider community of which I am a part, that the challenge of learning to listen takes hold most forcefully. Many different voices beckon to me and call for my attention, and in each moment I strive to open myself to them, to listen with a pure heart. So too, I continue to listen for the silence that, even if in its often-attenuated form, underlies and unfolds beyond them here in this place. And I consider, daily, what it might mean, here in this intense urban environment, to listen for the voices of those beings amidst whom we continuously live and move and without whom our own lives would be so much poorer. I commit myself, in a simple gesture of respect and love, to trying to notice them. It is not much, I admit. But it is something. So: early one morning, I walk out the front door of my home to take my daughter to the airport, and pause for a moment before getting in the car to listen with her to the sweet sound of the mockingbird on the telephone wire. Another day, riding along the bike path next to Ballona Creek, I am surprised by a sudden whoosh nearby and look up to see a Great White Egret passing just overhead. Walking to class one day with a student, I hear the cry of a Red-Tailed Hawk somewhere nearby; we pause and scan the sky until we see it circling high above us, floating on the thermals. I am always (my friends tell me) stopping to listen for something. I am? I say. Yes, you are, they say, smiling.

It has taken me a long time to learn how to become this insistently distractible, this habitually attentive. But I have begun to realize how much this music means to me, how essential it is to my life—especially as an increasing number of voices in the living world fall silent. I have begun also to see how infectious the habit of listening can become, how the more you listen the more you long to hear. Still, the question how and where such habits of attention can be deepened most effectively arises often in the present moment. Established forms of contemplative living surely have an important role to play here, and the number of those who continue to choose these forms, whether in one of its classical expressions or in one of the many improvised forms of contemplative living that are emerging in contemporary life, testifies to their enduring power. But, it is important I think not to identify the work of cultivating contemplative awareness too closely with the specific forms. Neither monastic life nor solitude is necessary for this work. Nor do certain places (for example, wilderness places) have any particular claim on those who would give themselves to this work. Rather, it is quality of attention and deepening awareness that matters most. And these can be achieved anywhere and by anyone willing to commit himself or herself to the work of listening.

It is in this sense that one can say that the primary value to us of Thoreau's contemplative witness is to be found less in his particular form of life (especially his much-celebrated but brief sojourn at Walden Pond) than in the quality of awareness he assiduously cultivated over his entire lifetime. His experiment at Walden Pond has its own enduring value of course, and can perhaps be considered as having a comparable value to certain forms of monastic living: important but open-ended symbols of what it can mean to open one's awareness to the subtle currents that bind one more deeply to the world, to God, and to the wider community. These forms are important, and the commitment to solitude and detachment that gives them so much of their meaning is also important. But it is the cultivation of deepening contemplative awareness that is of greatest significance. And such work cannot and should not be thought of as the prerogative of solitaries and monks only. Indeed the force of Thoreau's vision of contemplative practice, or that of the ancient monks, is felt nowhere more strongly than when it is adapted, as it so often is, to the utterly different circumstances of the contemporary world. The world we inhabit is paradoxically more cacophonous and more eerily silent than the worlds they knew. In the midst of a continuous flow of information and white noise, we struggle to find space to think, to listen, to be. And we also recognize that the world is gradually growing silent, bereft of the music of other living beings. Learning to listen to the song of the world, we are coming to realize, is a moral and spiritual act of the greatest significance.

The language of nature, Thoreau suggests, comes to us as a kind of music into which we enter more and more fully and whose harmonies fill and move us. It also comes to us intimately and incrementally, through our growing familiarity with a particular place. Which is why he gave himself over, with ever-greater acuteness and precision, to the study of Concord's botanical, zoological, and geological forms. This is particularly apparent in his great study of seed dispersal, a study Thoreau hoped would reveal to him the true language of the forest. This study led him, as one commentator has noted, to move "past the mere naming of trees—the nouns of the forest—to track its verbs: the birds, rodents, and insects that pollinate flowers or disperse seeds, and all other agents that shape the forest's structure."[63] He was intent on uncovering the subtle dynamism of his home place in all its complexity, not only as it presented itself in a given moment but also as it unfolded across time. Careful observation, scientific precision, and literary expression converged to create a powerful and compelling poetics of nature. Consider this description of maple keys, part of a much longer account of the life of maple trees within the local ecosystem:

About the middle of May, the red maples along the edges of swamps, their fruit being nearly ripe, are among the most beautiful objects in the landscape, especially if seen in a favorable light with respect to the sun. The keys are high colored, a sort of pink scarlet commonly, dangling at the end of peduncles three inches or more in length and only a little darker shade than themselves. The lit masses of these double samarae, with their peduncles gracefully arching upward and outward a little before they curve downward in order to spread the fruit and give it room, are unequally disposed along the branches, where they tremble in the wind and are often tangled by it. Like the flower of the shadbush, this handsome fruit is seen for the most part against bare twigs, it is so much in advance of its own and other leaves.[64]

There is a sense here, in this spare, lyric language, of drawing closer to the language of the forest itself. Thoreau himself seemed to think so, seemed to feel he was gradually moving toward a more adequate means of evoking and encompassing the life of the place he called home. As his language grew both more precise and more intricate, the complex dynamism of the entire life world around him gradually came into clearer focus.

Not that he ever stopped believing in the transcendentalist idea of correspondence, in which the truth of the physical world is understood as always corresponding to a hidden, transcendent truth. But as Daniel Peck has shown so clearly, the patterns of correspondence that most interested Thoreau toward the end of his life were less vertical ones, between the seen and unseen world, than horizontal ones, between one thing and another in the natural world.[65] Thoreau's sense of transcendence became increasingly grounded, increasingly focused on the unfolding relationships *within* the natural world. The language of his later work, which can seem plain and relatively lacking in literary style compared with the higher flights found in *Walden*, may in fact reflect a more difficult and sharply focused literary accomplishment: the simple evocation of the world as it is. By 1857, already deep into his study of seed dispersal, Thoreau could declare confidently but also with humility, "If a man is rich and strong anywhere, it must be on his native soil. Here I have been these forty years of learning the language of these fields that I may better express myself."[66]

Language, World, Spirit

Voices last only for their moment of sound, but they originate in life.[67]

PAUL SHEPARD

Language. World. Spirit. The connection and relationship between them is strong and deep. And yet in this particular historical moment that bond feels increasingly tenuous. We struggle to hear the music of the living world, or the silences between the music. Even so, we retain an awareness of our capacity to do so. There are moments when, amidst the cacophony of noise in which we are continuously engulfed, the faint traces of this music can still be heard. But must this remain only an occasional, sporadic occurrence? Or can the capacity to hear and enter into the music of the world be deepened and extended? Again, we return to the question of practice. Thoreau recognized that cultivating the capacity to hear the music of the world must become part of a sustained practice, that one must learn to orient oneself and become sensitive to the myriad ways the world is always expressing itself. For the early Christian monks, the contemplative practices of *ruminatio* and *lectio*—through which one learned to become more and more sensitive to the voice of the Word arising both within and without—had a similar purpose. In our own time, we are rediscovering these practices and giving new expression to them as part of our effort to come home to the world.

The great Provençal writer Jean Giono spent most of his life listening to the music of the world in his native place and working to give imaginative expression to its varied moods and to the human capacity to hear and respond to it. In the opening pages of his novel *The Song of the World*, we meet Antonio, a man of the forest; he has just embarked on a dangerous journey to help find the son of his friend Sailor who has gone missing somewhere upriver. Giono takes care to locate Antonio in his home place and to help us feel what it means for him to listen and enter into the life of the forest.

> Antonio heard the sound of the forest. They had left the region of silence, and from where they stood, they could hear the night teeming with life in the forest. It came and touched the ear like a cold finger. It was a long, muffled breath, a throaty purr, a deep noise, a long, monotonous song from an open mouth. It filled all the tree-clad hills with its wide presence. It was in the sky and on earth like rain; it came from all sides at once and it surged up slowly like a heavy wave, rumbling in the narrow corridors of the dales. In the depths of the noise, slight patterings of leaves scampered away like rats. Off they went and shot to one side, then slipped away down the stairs of the branches, and one heard the pit-path of a light noise, clicking and soft like a raindrop dripping through a tree. Moanings rose from the earth and went heavily up through the sap of the trunks to the forking-off of the big branches.
>
> Antonio leaned against a beach. He heard a slight whistling close to his ear. He felt it with his finger. It was the sap dripping from a split in the bark. It had just opened. He felt under his fingers the lips of the green wood which were slowly widening.[68]

The forest singing: a long, muffled breath, a throaty purr, a deep noise, a long, monotonous song from an open mouth, rumbling, pattering, moaning, whistling. These are sounds that could easily be missed; or even if they were not missed, they could seem meaningless or inconsequential. Background noise. But this is not how it is for Antonio. He notices everything, misses nothing. He opens himself to this music and allows himself to be stirred, seduced by it. He wants to know where he is in the world and this means listening carefully to all that is emerging around him and entering into him. He carefully distinguishes one sound from another, even as he listens for the music that encompasses and moves through everything. And there are sounds so faint and subtle that one has to draw close to hear them at all: the slight whistling of sap just beginning to drip from the bark of a tree, for example. *The still small voice.* Here Giono invites us to consider what it is to live with such sensitivity, with the capacity to hear and notice everything, not for any particular purpose, but simply because this music is unfolding around us all the time and because we can, if we are alert and awake, notice it, take it in, cherish it.

One cannot help but wonder whether such sensitivity, the ability to listen with careful attention and awareness to the world, is still possible for us. Or whether it has become so atrophied from disuse that we simply cannot hear such music any more. Paul Shepard argues that we do in fact retain this capacity and that it is woven into our own evolutionary history, part of a memory we carry of how we once inhabited the world. It is most evident, he suggest, in the childhood imagination where the sense of the world as expressive, as filled with "voices" remains forcefully alive. "[The child] has been bathed in voices of one kind or another always," Shepard observes. "Voices last only for their moment of sound, but they originate in life. The child learns that all life tells something and that all sound—from the frog calling to the sea surf—issues from a being kindred and significant to himself, telling some tale, giving some clue, mimicking some rhythm that he should know."[69] What happens to this knowledge as we move from childhood into our more mature lives? Must it be lost to us? Must we fall from this condition of graced awareness of the world as alive and beckoning to us to a sense of the world as cold and mute? More importantly, what would it mean for us to enter into a kind of "second naïveté" in which the world might again become a place full of voices? Much of the value of our contemporary imaginative literature lay in its capacity to conjure into being just such a world—where it becomes possible to imagine what it would feel like to sense the presence of these voices and to listen for them.

I think here of the figure of old Ku'oosh in Leslie Marmon Silko's *Ceremony,* a Laguna Pueblo elder who seeks to keep alive in himself and his community not only a feeling for the world's distinctive voice, but also a sense of the care we must take in speaking of it. He has been asked to help Tayo, a Laguna man who has returned from war damaged and lost, unable to maintain a thread of connection with his community, his history and his land. Ku'oosh and Tayo begin to work together on a ceremony that will, they hope, bring about some measure of healing in Tayo. But Tayo soon realizes that Ku'oosh has long been working toward a much deeper and wider work of reparation, oriented toward the healing of the fragmentation of the Laguna Pueblo people and of the whole world. Tayo's own rehabilitation will of necessity be bound up with this larger work of healing. No small part of the ceremony is rooted in the recovery of language and in particular of the intimate connection between language and world. "… [O]ld Ku'oosh … spoke softly, using the old dialect full of sentences that were involuted with explanations of their own origins, as if nothing the old man said were his own but all had been said before and he was only there to repeat it. Tayo had to strain to catch the meaning, dense with place names he had never heard." Places have been lost, along with the names and stories that anchored them to the cultural memory of the people. The simple utterance of these place-names is already a gesture toward recovering a relationship with these lost places and stories. And Tayo begins to see that he must re-learn this language if he is to return to himself and to this place, if he is to participate in and facilitate the larger healing of his community and the damaged land upon which they live. He must become more sensitive to the particular meaning of words and how they bear upon our understanding of the world. Old Ku'oosh begins with a lesson about fragility.

> "But you know, grandson, this world is fragile."
>
> The word he chose to express "fragile" was filled with intricacies of a continuing process, and with a strength inherent in spider webs woven across paths through sand hills where early in the morning the sun becomes entangled in each filament of web. It took a long time to explain the fragility and intricacy because no word exists alone, and the reason for choosing each word had to be explained with a story about why it must be said this certain way. That was the responsibility that went with being human, old Ku'oosh said, the story behind each word must be told so there could be no mistake in the meaning of what had been said; and this demanded great patience and love.[70]

The language we use to reflect upon and respond to the living world has its own ecology. And the recovery—through artful storytelling and the simple recitation of names—of places that have been lost, contributes not only to the retrieval of ancient cultural traditions tied to the land but also to the healing of the world. This is why it is so important not to be careless or forgetful about the language we use to evoke and express the world, and why this contemplative work must be informed by all the patience and love of which we are capable.

The recovery of a *lingua vernacula* may in fact depend on nothing so much as a rekindling of our ability and willingness to speak openly of what we most love. And on our deepened understanding of the relationship between our love for the world and our ability express its particular beauty. What else do we really wish to speak of, after all, other than love? And how can we speak of the world honestly and deeply if not out of love? "It seems as if the right words can come only out of the perfect space of a place you love," says Ellen Meloy. "In canyon country they would begin with three colors: blue, terra cotta, green. Sky, stone, life." But the process of naming and describing is hardly static, for it moves as the world moves, as one's love for the place moves and deepens. One begins with what is elemental. But then, Meloy notes, something more inevitably emerges: "some feather or pelt or lizard's back, the throat of a flower or ripple or sunlit river, would enter the script and I would have to leap from three colors to uncountable thousands, all in some exquisite combination of Place, possessed by this one and no other."[71] The way we speak of the places we love will always be characterized by this feeling for the utter particularity and endlessness of the life unfolding there.

This is one of the reasons the poetics of place emerging both in North America and elsewhere is so significant. Here we find a sustained and varied effort to listen carefully to the *lingua vernacula* of particular places, and to give voice to it in language that evokes the life of these places. In the late work of Denise Levertov, for example, one can hear the voice of the Pacific Northwest, and of Mt. Rainier in particular: "clear gold/of late summer, of opening autumn,/the dawn eagle sunning himself on the highest tree,/ the mountain revealing herself unclouded, her snow/tinted apricot as she looked west,/tolerant, in her steadfastness, of the restless sun/forever rising and setting."[72] For Alaska writer Richard Nelson, the song of his place can be discerned in the "shrill voices" of oystercatchers "punishing but beautiful, a pure incantation of this northern shore, arising from the dark rocks, the chill gray waters, and the slick fronds of kelp."[73] For Robert Hass, a Californian, it is in the intricate delicacy of a Sierra Nevada mountain meadow on a late afternoon that one senses the local language: "So many wildflowers/tangled in the grass. So many grasses—reedgrass, the bentgrass and timothy, little quaking grass, dogtail, rip-gut brome—the seeds flaring from the stalks/ in tight chevrons of green and purple-green/but loosening."[74] To name and describe with such care and precision is to open up a space within the self in which the minute particularities of the living world can sound and reverberate. Mary Oliver describes this contemplative work as a process of self-emptying: "To learn something by being nothing/A little while but the rich lens of attention."[75]

But attention here means more than looking and listening. It means working to cultivate empathy, trying, as Oliver says elsewhere, "to enter the long black branches of other lives—/to imagine what the crisp fringes, full of honey,/hanging/from the branches of the young locust trees, in early summer,/feel like."[76] It means working to discover within oneself the capacity for deep engagement, for encounter, working to kindle a sense of relationship between one's own life and those "other lives." It means learning to give oneself over, unstintingly, to these other lives, dwelling among them, ardently seeking and listening. "Only last week I went out among the thorns and said/to the wild roses:/deny me not,/but suffer my devotion./Then, all afternoon, I sat among them. Maybe//I even heard a curl or two of music, damp and rouge-red,/hurrying from their stubby buds, from their delicate watery bodies."[77]

Is this not the language of prayer, the most intimate and probing of all languages? Certainly the audacity of the direct address—"I ... said/to the wild roses"—and the boldness of the imperative voice—"Deny me not"—suggest something akin to prayer. So does the note of humility: "*suffer* my devotion," the poet implores. "Allow me," that is, "permit me." Such language reflects a reverential respect, even awe, a sense that one is approaching the numinous Other. As does the language of "devotion." To *devote* oneself is to vow oneself, consecrate oneself to the Holy One. And if the object of one's devotion should turn out to be wild roses? Then seek there the voice, the presence of the numinous. Significantly, the most eloquent expression of devotion here comes not through spoken words, but through an extravagant, deeply contemplative gesture: "all afternoon I sat among them." Saying nothing at all, apparently. Listening rather for the voice of these wild roses, hearing— "maybe"—a kind of music, "damp and rouge-red," arising from their "delicate watery bodies."

Poetry here becomes a kind of prayer, a response to a word arising in and through the living world. The language of prayer, it turns out, is necessary and integral to the contemporary experience and poetic expression of the word incarnate. But this poetic expression, like so much of our experience of the natural world, is fraught with uncertainty and doubt. We are not sure whether we hear and understand the voice of the living world. "*Maybe*/I ... heard a curl or two of music," says the poet. Prayer, and the poetry of prayer become a means of probing this uncertain terrain, of asking the most difficult questions. Like whether the world speaks at all, whether we can discern the meaning of its signs and whether we possess the capacity and courage to respond.

Few places in contemporary literature have seen these questions subjected to a more searching inquiry than in Annie Dillard's *Pilgrim at Tinker Creek*. Signs abound in the natural world, she suggests, including signs hinting at a transcendent presence. There is a language speaking in and through the world. But this language is ambiguous and immensely difficult to read. She describes waking one morning to discover her cat has kneaded her chest while she slept and left her covered in blood, as though she had been painted with roses. But she wonders: "what blood was this, and what roses? It could have been the rose of union, the blood of murder, or the rose of beauty bare and the blood of some unspeakable sacrifice or birth."[78] And so it continues, the universe speaking now as an "inrush of power and light," now as a "thick darkness"; now as an Osage orange tree lighting up as though kindled from within by fire, now as a tiny frog suddenly imploding, its muscles and organs dissolved by the venom of a giant water bug; now as the gratuitous free fall of a mockingbird, now as the grotesque pressure of fecundity. To attend to such a world, to inquire into its meaning requires the courage and devotion of a pilgrim, Dillard suggests. It also requires the capacity to live with ambiguity, to respond to the world with something like faith. Not blind faith, for the world is not utterly bereft of signs. But a naked faith, able to carry us deep into the darkness of a *via negativa*, beyond signs, beyond language where the world and the word speaking through the world are encountered, as mystics have always understood, in both knowing and unknowing.

But perhaps we are lacking in faith. Perhaps we do not really believe the world speaks to us or that we know how to listen. These troubling questions form the heart of Louise Glück's remarkable book-length collection of prayer-poems, *The Wild Iris*. More than a third of the fifty-four poems in this collection are set within the ancient ritual context of Matins and Vespers, are themselves prayers. Filled with profound longing and an often-painful sense of uncertainty, they address a God who may or may not be listening, who may not even exist. But the world exists and it is the world that speaks, that responds to these prayers, mostly in the language of flowers—trillium, lamium, snowdrops, scilla, violets, clover, a red poppy, a white rose—but also in the language of a clear morning, retreating wind, early darkness, September twilight. Each has its own subjective presence, its own distinctive voice. Each calls out to the lonely supplicant, seeking though a gesture of some kind (itself a kind of word) to touch, perhaps to heal. Glück invites us to enter imaginatively into the life of these beings, to consider what their voices might sound like, what they might be saying to us. Or simply to open ourselves to the idea that the world is full of speech and that we ourselves are being addressed continuously. As in this case by a sunset:

> My great happiness
> is the sound your voice makes
> calling to me even in despair; my sorrow
> that I cannot answer you
> in speech you accept as mine.

Prayer does not always know what or whom it seeks, or even that it is seeking at all. Here, the supplicant calls out in despair, but to whom? We are invited to consider that it is perhaps the sun, or the fading light of sunset, whose voice we now hear addressing the one who has called out. There is no judgment; the sound of the supplicant's voice, even in despair, is received in "great happiness." Still, there is a gulf that separates them from one another and that prevents the intimacy and reciprocity that is at the heart of prayer from taking hold: the one crying out cannot hear, or cannot accept the voice of the Other, at least not on its own terms. But it is not only that we cannot hear the voice of the Other; we do not even trust our own speech, our own capacity to reach beyond ourselves and touch the life of another.

> You have no faith in your own language.
> So you invest
> authority in signs
> you cannot read with any accuracy.

There is, it seems, a supple, fluid, expansive language, shared by all. But there is an inclination to mistrust it, to close the space, to reduce the scope of what can be spoken and heard—the "signs that can be read"—to something small and poor. This is not the field in which prayer lives and moves, which remains open, alive, undetermined. The poet invites us to consider what it would mean to enter this space, to trust the exchange of speech that emerges there.

> And yet your voice reaches me always.
> And I answer constantly,
> my anger passing
> as winter passes. My tenderness
> should be apparent to you

in the breeze of the summer evening
and in the words that become
your own response.[79]

Here Glück gives expression to one of the most fundamental questions of prayer, indeed of all theology: do we share the same language with the Other whom we seek? Can we hear and understand what the Other is saying to us? Can we respond? There is a profound sense of brokenness at the heart of this exchange. The sunset here speaks as a lover longing for intimacy with her beloved, an intimacy mediated through an exchange of voices. But there is no exchange. A voice calls out, its despair-tinged sound sufficient to fill the Other with happiness. It is our voice. But we do not hear the voice of the Other. We do not know how to listen, or are perhaps unwilling to listen. Which is why the the one calling out to us also feels sorrow, why the voice of the Other cannot be heard: "I cannot answer you/in speech you accept as mine." So the world falls silent—because we lack faith in our own language. Because we don't believe we are heard when we call out. But the silence is only apparent: "your voice reaches me always,/and I answer constantly." Perhaps we already believe this. Perhaps we already hear the tenderness, the voice of the Other: "in the breeze of the summer evening/and in the words that become/[our] own response."

Words Beneath the Water

If you listen carefully you will hear that the words are
underneath the water.[80]

NORMAN MACLEAN

This exchange catches well the pathos and ambiguity at the heart of so much contemporary writing about the natural world. One finds there expressions of profound fear, that the world itself has gone silent, or that something in us has died, leaving us unable to hear the world's subtle and delicate music. But one also finds here myriad expressions of faith: faith in the presence of a voice beckoning to us in and through the living world, and faith in power of "our own responses"—that is, our own poetic evocations of the living world—to bring this voice to clear and vivid expression. In its honest exploration of this rich and troubling ambiguity and in its careful attention to the intricate relationship between word and world, the contemporary literature and poetry of nature can help us recover a sense of the Word as incarnate in every living being—as creative, renewing presence in the world, as the source of all language, all storytelling, community, the cosmos itself.

It can also help us recover the inescapably poetic character of Christian theological reflection on the Word incarnate. More than thirty years ago, poet and New Testament critic Amos Wilder called for Christian theology to overcome its "long addiction to the discursive, the rationalistic, and the prosaic ... [and do more] justice to the role of the symbolic and ... mythopoetic dimension[s] of faith."[81] To retrieve, that is, a sense of the *theopoetic*. If we listen carefully to the literature and poetry of nature, we will discover, I think, the elements of a theopoetics of the natural world. To be drawn into the spell of this literature is to find oneself beckoned to listen to the language, the idiom of the natural world, to discern how the Word comes to expression through particular places, in the stories, poems, and living communities that take root in those places. It is to be brought to a heightened awareness of what it might mean to live more deeply into the truth of the Word and the living world.

This means learning to remythologize the Word in the idiom of our own native places. As the Priest of the Sun does in N. Scott Momaday's *House Made of Dawn*, reimagining the Christian creation story in light of ancient Kiowa myth:

In the beginning was the Word ... there was nothing. There was *nothing!* Darkness. There was no end to it ... there was only the dark infinity in which nothing was. And something happened, and everything began. The Word did not come into being, but *it was*. It did not break upon the silence, but *it was older than the silence and the silence was made of it* .... And from that day the Word has belonged to us, who have heard it for what it is, who have lived in fear and awe of it. In the Word was the beginning; *In the beginning was the Word* ....[82]

Or as father and son do in Norman Maclean's *A River Runs Through It*, perched at the edge of the Big Blackfoot River in Montana, listening:

Then [my father] told me, "In the part I was reading it says the Word was in the beginning, and that's right. I used to think water was first, but if you listen carefully you will hear that the words are underneath the water."

"That's because you are a preacher first and then a fisherman," I told him. "If you ask Paul, he will tell you that the words are formed out of the water."

"No," my father said, "you are not listening carefully. The water runs over the words. Paul will tell you the same thing."[83]

Are we listening carefully enough? Can we discern this Word, older than the silence, deeper than the water, woven into both?

I think of that unknown artist at the bottom of Barrier Canyon and of that old man on the island of Patmos. Did they know that deep, archaic silence woven into the very fabric of the world? Did they stand, trembling, in that silence, listening to the world, before finally giving voice, in word, in song, to what they had heard? Can we recover a sense of world so pregnant with Word, a sense of Word so intimately bound up with the very life of the world? Such attentive listening promises a deeper sense of relationship with the places we inhabit. It may also be necessary to the long-term survival of those places.

7

Eros: *Exchange, Intimacy, Reciprocity*

Ardor: the earth's fervent song, which we answer with
our own, imperfect song.[1]

ADAM ZAGAJEWSKI

The sun shines not on us, but in us. The rivers flow not
past, but through us, thrilling, tingling, vibrating every
fiber and cell of the substance of our bodies.[2]

JOHN MUIR.

ON THIS LATE summer afternoon in California's Santa Lucia Mountains in
Big Sur, a thick fog from the Pacific Ocean pours up the steep narrow canyon
where I sit. The pearl gray mist catches in the redwood and fir trees and drifts
through them, creating its own weather. The temperature drops. It is dark,
quiet. In the silence I can hear tiny droplets of water hitting the ground. The
moss glistens. Just above me I notice the blue sky appearing and disappearing. I catch glimpses of sage and scrub oak in the burnt ochre chaparral just
beyond the edge of the mist. The fog clears and I feel the heat of the summer sun on my back. Then after a moment, I am again plunged into the cool
mist. It envelops me, holds me. I stand and raise my hands and feel it moving
through me. I am right at the edge, at the meeting point of these two worlds
where they mingle and dance together. I am beyond the edge. I am inside.

In biology, a transitional area between two different communities is called
an ecotone. It is, as Barry Lopez notes, "a special meeting ground, like that of
a forest's edge with a clearing; or where the fresh waters of an estuary meet
the saline tides of the sea; or at a river's riparian edge. The mingling of animals from different ecosystems charges such border zones with evolutionary
potential." One becomes alert, in such a place, to the movement of species
across conventional habitats and to unexpected changes in the evolution of
species. Lopez observes how at Admiralty Inlet in the Arctic for example,

"flying creatures walk on ice. They break the pane of the water with their dives to feed. Marine animals break the pane of water coming the other way to breathe."[3] To engage and respond to such a world means learning to accept its vital, insistent dynamism and its organic evolutionary developments as basic features of the landscape. To inhabit such a world means learning to dwell in a landscape where borders are fluid and permeable, where life unfolds in unexpected ways in a continuous exchange across borders. It is easy to miss these subtle movements. Yet to do so is to risk missing the very life of a place.

So it is with other ecotones we inhabit, those fluid, often-contested imaginative spaces between the human and the "more-than-human" worlds, between matter and spirit, body and soul, heaven and earth, humanity and divinity. It is not easy to move across the borders that distinguish these worlds from one another, or to inhabit that charged liminal space that sometimes joins them together. Contemplative practitioners have long sought to cultivate a sensitivity to those places of exchange where the possibility of reciprocity and intercourse with the Other can be felt and realized, where one can learn to enter into the life of the Other and feel its presence deep within one's own being—whether this Other be conceived of as the Divine or another living being or the world itself. But spiritual traditions have also contributed in their own way to our inability to imagine ourselves as participating in a larger whole or as capable of intimate exchange with another. Old habits of dualistic thinking have created boundaries that are too rigid, categories of thought that are too narrow, too limiting. In such a constricted world, it has become increasingly difficult even to imagine real exchange or reciprocity, much less embody it. Yet the hunger for such exchange remains strong. It seems clear, for the sake of the world as well as for the sake of our own souls, that we must discover again the kind of expansive, fluid categories of thought and practice that can help us understand what it is to feel the touch of the other, to enter into the life of another. Unless we can imagine this possibility, unless we can sense and feel the movement of life across boundaries, and come to know ourselves as participating in this mysterious exchange, we will be condemned to live a thin, impoverished existence, bereft of intimacy, empty of feeling and spirit. And we will almost surely continue to visit our own sense of alienation upon the living world.

Is it possible to recover a capacity for intimacy that can help us overcome this profound alienation and contribute to a more thoughtful, tender response to the living world? Can we discover a language for the intimacy we seek that honors the earthy, embodied reality of our physical, material existence without ignoring the less visible, more hidden dimensions of our affections rooted in the life of the soul? Can we, in other words, overcome the old habits of dualistic thinking and rediscover a means of expressing and embodying our longing for intimacy and reciprocity with the world that is whole, undivided, and spacious, that allows a free exchange of life across boundaries, a deeper sense of participation within the beautiful pulsing whole?

These questions have emerged with increasing urgency within the contemporary discourse about our place in the natural world, often focusing attention on the role of *eros* or desire in rekindling a relationship with the other. *Eros*, as understood in contemporary ecological discourse and as it has often been employed in the Christian contemplative tradition, refers to the longing to share in the life of another, whether that "other" be understood as a person, a place, a non-human species, or God. Its increasing prominence in contemporary thought and practice points to growing recognition of the centrality of desire—often expressed as feeling, affection, tenderness, or ardor—for helping us understand who we are in the world. E. O. Wilson's "biophilia hypothesis" which he describes as "the innate tendency to focus on life and lifelike processes"—is perhaps the most prominent example of this to have emerged within contemporary ecological discourse.[4] The particular meaning and significance of this hypothesis continues to be debated. But its emergence in the present moment has already helped give renewed attention to the question of how our feelings and affections shape our relationship with the natural world, our very sense of self within the world. And it has enabled us to listen more carefully to the testimony of many others for whom the work of cultivating a feeling for the living world has become critical to our understanding of it and our capacity to tend to it. Edward Abbey has eloquently expressed the kind of erotic sensibility that he believes is necessary in the present moment for anyone wishing to engage the natural world fully and deeply: "sympathy for the object under study, and more than sympathy, love. A love based on prolonged contact and interaction. Intercourse if possible. Observation informed by sympathy, love, intuition."[5] The naked vulnerability expressed here reflects a widespread and growing sense of the need for greater and deeper intimacy with the living world.

It also points to an increasing awareness of the need for such intimacy to become part of a sustained practice, both personal and communal. It is here that the presence of *eros* in contemplative traditions can contribute something important to our understanding of what it means to approach and cross over the seemingly impermeable boundaries between one life and other. Within ancient Christian contemplative thought and practice, the language of *eros* has always occupied a central if ambiguous place. Christianity's well-documented ambivalence, even hostility toward human sexuality, the body, and the physical world points to the very real sense in which desires (or passions) have been viewed within this tradition with intense suspicion and have been seen as antithetical to the life of the Spirit. But there is also rich discourse within the Christian contemplative tradition that honors *eros* as critical to the human person's deepening awareness of divine presence. Here, the charged borderlands between the human person and the divine Other are often negotiated nowhere else than through the mysterious and dynamic reality of desire—which is endless. This is the significance of Gregory of Nyssa's famous formulation of what it is to seek and know the Divine: "And so every desire for the beautiful which draws us on this ascent is intensified by the soul's very progress towards it. And this is the real meaning of seeing God: never to have this desire satisfied."[6] It is significant, I think, that in this particular formulation of the quest for the Divine, the one who seeks to know God through the kindling of desire must travel far into an impenetrable darkness where all knowing ceases, where only desire can show the way. Also that the horizon of one's desire is infinite and that the distance into which one yearns only increases the yearning.[7]

That the object of such contemplative yearning is conceived of as so radically transcendent is of course significant. Nor can one ignore the sometimes-dualistic thought that informs this contemplative vision or the language of ascent that stands as its central metaphor. If we are to develop what one scholar has described as a Christian "asceticism of *eros*," we will have to undertake a critical reexamination of the deep ambivalence that has for so long characterized the Christian spiritual tradition's attitudes toward the body, human sexuality, and the world. Such a process has already begun and is helping to reveal the full complexity of *eros* in the Christian spiritual tradition.[8] In particular, it is helping point the way toward understanding what it might mean to incorporate the particular sense of desire found in ancient Christian contemplative practice into a larger vision of contemplative ecology. It is becoming increasingly clear that there are important resources here that can help us to understand what it means to search out and inhabit those charged borderlands between oneself and another, those places of encounter where longing gives way to relationship, communion, intimacy. Still there are significant challenges. One of the most formidable of these challenges will be learning how to incorporate *eros* deeply within the world of Spirit without succumbing to the temptation to spiritualize it. It is also crucial that we consider what it might mean to embrace the fully embodied reality of the erotic without falling prey to the brutalizing tendencies of a culture in which *eros* has often become separated from simple expressions of tenderness and affection. It will mean learning to retrieve the fundamental sense of exchange and reciprocity and intimacy at the heart of erotic experience.

Here, in this liminal space, it may yet become possible again to imagine the apparently impermeable boundaries that separate one place from another, Spirit from matter, ourselves from other living species, ourselves from God, as *permeable*. It may become possible to imagine ourselves not as standing aloof and distant from the world, but as caught up into, transformed by the intimate presence of the living world within and around us—by, as Robert Hass puts it: "all this life going on about my life, or living a life about all this life/ going on."[9] Such simple, radical relationality—everything understood and experienced as being in relationship with everything else—lies at the heart of the emerging contemplative vision of *eros* I wish to consider here. Within this vision, it becomes possible to imagine again a profound and lasting intimacy with the living world, with our own embodied selves, and with the Spirit who lives and breathes among us.

Exchange: Navigating the Penumbral

We exist because we exchange.[10]

SUSAN GRIFFIN

One of the great virtues of Susan Griffin's *The Eros of Everyday Life* is how it draws our attention once again to the fundamentally relational sense of the word *eros* and resituates it at the center of the intricate web of relationships within which we live. Drawing on Hesiod's ancient cosmogonic sense of the word, she considers *eros* as that which draws us toward those highly charged meetings, encounters with the "other," that which makes possible the fluid, dynamic exchanges that take place in such encounters, and the very life that emerges from them. Such meetings are immensely complex, and move toward ever-greater complexity. They are inclusive of the biological, the emotional, the linguistic, the socio-political and the spiritual dimensions of our lives. To inhabit the world of *eros* means recognizing that borders—between oneself and another, between human beings and the more-than-human world, between matter and spirit—are permeable, that life emerges nowhere else so fully and deeply as it does in the exchange across these borders. But we create and perpetuate, says Griffin, a world of impermeable borders, a world marked by divisions and obstructions, a world where such exchanges become unimaginable.

This is not how we came into the world, nor is it how we first came to know about our world. Consider, says Griffin, how easily a newly born child turns toward the mother's body. "Groping with cheeks and mouth, the infant burrows over the mother's breast in search of her nipple. Finding this, her tiny lips must explore at the same time both the contours of the mother's nipple and their own movement, new, uncharted. With his first small acts the child finds nourishment, knowledge and love all in the same efforts." Only later, Griffin suggests, does the child learn to divide these things. And with this division comes an impoverishment of experience and awareness: "Eating, [the child] is no longer aware of taking life into his body. Even if she takes sensual pleasure in a meal, she has lost the memory of the mouth as an instrument of intelligence. He has forgone a deeper knowledge of his own existence as part of a continual process of transubstantiation, *bodies becoming bodies*; she loses the *eros* at the heart of becoming." Such a division, claims Griffin, "is not really possible." It is not, ultimately, sustainable. "All that is severed returns."[11] Providing of course that we learn to open ourselves to this world of intimacy, exchange, and encounter.

Such openness can only come from a more supple, generous, and wide-ranging imagination. It is precisely this capacity to imagine ourselves as entering continuously into transformative exchanges with an "other" that interests Lewis Hyde and leads him to explore the ancient tradition of gift-giving. His book, *The Gift*, contains the odd-sounding subtitle, *Imagination and the Erotic Life of Property*. Its oddness comes at least partly from our habitual sense of property as something inert, something that comes into our possession through a payment of some kind, an exchange, to be sure, but one with fairly strict rules and mechanisms. Certainly each of us knows, if not personally then at least at second hand, the frenzied desire to possess that often fuels buying and selling in our culture. Still, to suggest that property itself has an erotic character seems a strange kind of anthropomorphism. Hyde, however, draws an important distinction in his book between two kinds of property, the commodity and the gift. A commodity is bought and sold in a relatively dispassionate way according to rules agreed upon by the two sides. Once purchased, a commodity comes into the possession of the one who has paid for it. And there it remains. The exchange is over. A gift, however, operates on a completely different principle.

The key difference, Hyde says, is this: "the gift must always move." And it must always be used up, consumed, eaten. "The gift is property that perishes." Yet, in perishing, life comes into being.[12] These two principles, which Hyde arrives at on the basis of extensive research into traditional folk tales and into the cultural patterns of ancient indigenous peoples, suggest a life and dynamism that, while not inherent in the property itself, is mediated, kindled by the "economy" of gift giving, by the movement of property through the human community.

How does this happen? One can see it at work most clearly, Hyde suggests, when the gift exchange is not merely reciprocal (that is involving just two people) but moves into the circle of a larger community. Circular giving is richer and more complex than reciprocal giving. When the gift moves in a circle, no one ever receives a gift from the same person she gives it to. "[I]ts motion is beyond the control of the personal ego, and so each bearer must be part of the group and each donation is an act of social faith."[13] This relinquishment of the personal ego is a fundamental dimension of authentic gift exchange. It is also one of the sources of its creative power. Within this dynamic of exchange, one gradually transcends the hardened patterns of what Hyde calls the "ego-of-one" or even the "ego-of-two," that constellation of identity that forms when we fall in love. As one is drawn into the life of the gift-giving-and-receiving community, conventional ego boundaries begin to dissolve. It becomes easier and easier to say "we" instead of "me," to know oneself as bound up intimately within the life of the community. As this process deepens and grows, the understanding of community itself can expand to include the more-than-human community. "The ego's firmness has its virtues," says Hyde, "but at some point we seek the slow dilation...in which the ego enjoys a widening give-and-take with the world and is finally abandoned in ripeness."[14]

To allow oneself to be "dilated" in this way, taken up in the life of a larger community, requires imagination. It requires us to relinquish our imaginative attachment to boundaries and hierarchies that keep things distinct and separate and to reimagine a world that is fluid, relational, organic. It demands that we discover a new language, supple enough to evoke and draw us into this dynamic world. This is why David Abram, in his book *The Spell of the Sensuous*, devotes so much attention to the influence of language upon the way we perceive and experience the world. The roots of our current sense of alienation from the living world, he suggests, are linguistic and philosophical. Drawing upon the research into oral culture conducted in recent years by scholars such as Eric Havelock, Jack Goody, and Walter Ong, Abram suggests that cultures that have developed within a predominantly written language tradition tend to divide the world more clearly and easily between the human and the more-than-human, the interior and the exterior, spirit and matter. In oral cultures, on the other hand, language mediates these worlds, joins them, creates a climate in which one can pass back and forth between them. The philosophical impasse, which can be traced back at least to the time of Descartes has, Abram argues, bequeathed to us a conception of the material world as almost completely mechanical and inanimate and an understanding of the human person as a detached, objective, isolated ego. The phenomenological philosophical tradition of Husserl and Merleau-Ponty, Abram suggests, offers a more fluid way of understanding the self, the material world, and the relationship between them, a way that is more open to the sensual as a medium of consciousness and more attentive to the possibilities for "intersubjective" communication between human beings and the living world.

The implications of this way of speaking and seeing are profound and far-reaching: "As we return to our senses," says Abram, "we gradually discover our sensory perceptions to be simply our part of a vast, interpenetrating web work of perceptions and sensations borne by countless other bodies—supported, that is, not just by ourselves, but by icy streams tumbling down granite slopes, by owl wings and lichens, and by the unseen, imperturbable wind." Further, Abram notes, "this intertwined web of experience," which Husserl referred to in his later writings as the "life-world," "has been disclosed as a profoundly *carnal* field, as this very dimension of smells and tastes and chirping rhythms warmed by the sun and shivering the seeds. It is, indeed, nothing other than the biosphere—the matrix of earthly life in which we ourselves are embedded." Still, it is not a biosphere that we can conceive of as somehow detached from us, viewed from the objective distance of science. It is, says Abram, "the biosphere as it is experienced and *lived from within*, by the intelligent body—by the attentive human animal who is entirely a part of the world that he, or she, experiences."[15]

To inhabit such a world is to transcend the old dualisms, to know oneself as an embodied subject dwelling within a world of other embodied subjects, subjects who are capable of speaking and responding to us. It is to dwell in a living world of "multiple subjectivities, a collective landscape, constituted by other experiencing subjects as well as oneself."[16] It is to inhabit a world charged with *eros*, where momentous encounters and exchanges are endlessly unfolding before us, among us, and within us.

What does it feel like to inhabit the world in this way, to relinquish the habitual tendency to stand against the world, to see the world as somehow existing outside of or beyond oneself, and instead allow oneself to become immersed in the world, suffused with its life and spirit? How does it happen? Certainly it sometimes occurs simply and easily, an awareness of the vibrant presence of the world in one's being arising in a sudden flash of intuition. But there is also a dimension of such awareness that requires time and effort to grasp and apprehend, that reveals itself slowly and must be cultivated through assiduous practice. This paradox has long been recognized as critical and necessary within traditions of contemplative practice—the moment of ecstasy, when one is suddenly taken out of oneself into a larger field of being, always standing in tension with the long, slow work of stillness through which the life of the other gradually comes to be seen and felt as part of the fabric of one's own being. And it has also come to inform the discourse about what it is to know and feel the touch of the natural world. This is the work of the boundaries, where the porousness of the membrane between the life of one thing and another becomes palpable, and the potential for exchange within and across that space can begin to be realized. Or perhaps we should speak, as anthropologist Michael Jackson does, of the "penumbral" region as the space we enter and inhabit in moments of intense and expansive awareness.[17]

A sensitivity to the penumbral, Jackson suggests, with its connotations of a "phenomenologically indeterminate zone 'between regions of complete shadow and complete illumination,' 'an area in which something exists to a lesser or uncertain degree' and 'an outlying or peripheral region,'" can help deepen our awareness of the fluid, mysterious, open space between things, and of the relations between them. But it is not only the indeterminate character of the penumbral that recommends its use here; it is also its immensity, its abundance, its always-emerging, ever-unfinished and mysterious character. In these and other ways, it is kindred to William James's notion of "the more," an idea that informs Jackson's own sense of what it is to grapple with any rich and complex experience. In his *Essays on Radical Empiricism,* James observed: "Our fields of experience have no more definite boundaries than have our fields of view. Both are fringed forever by a more that continuously develops, and that continuously supersedes them as life proceeds. The relations, generally speaking, are as real as the terms are."[18] Our fields of experience, James suggests, are fundamentally unbounded, open, endless; so too the boundaries we assign to them are and must understood to be provisional, partial and porous. Cultivating an awareness of this unbounded space enables one to perceive the *primacy of the relations* between and among things, the intricate connections that bind them to one another and to the encompassing whole. Our awareness of this fundamental reality and of ourselves as existing within the flow of this relational field can alter completely the sense of what it is to be a subject acting in the world. "To speak of the penumbral," Jackson suggests, "is to invoke this hazy and indeterminate region between a world where we experience ourselves as actors and a world where we experience ourselves as acted upon."[19] Learning to open oneself to the penumbral, to the more, learning to experience oneself as "acted upon" in this way requires vulnerability, openness, receptivity. It means relinquishing control and allowing oneself to feel and be touched by the presence of the life that is continuously emerging around and within us; to be absorbed into it in a kind of ecstasy.

Ekstasis—to stand outside of oneself, to be drawn beyond oneself into some larger reality. These are the primary meanings associated with the term *ekstasis* in the world of ancient Greek thought, and subsequently in the discourse of ancient Greek Christian thinkers. In the early Christian monastic tradition, John Cassian used the phrase *excessus mentis* (evoking the feeling of being drawn beyond or outside the boundaries of one's mind) to express that particular sense of overflowing that often accompanies intense spiritual experience, the strange sensation of being taken out of oneself, of floating in an endless expanse. Something comparable can be felt in William James's less explicitly religious formulation: "Reality, life, experience, concreteness, immediacy, use what word you will, exceeds our logic, overflows and surrounds it.[20]" Ecstasy. Here the recognizable boundaries between the self and other, sense and nonsense, dissolve. Such experience "exceeds our logic" says James. As surely it must.

It is precisely at this point, when logic or language or conceptual structures fail, that other, often-richer possibilities of understanding and engagement emerge. Both the Christian contemplative tradition and the traditions of ecological discourse under consideration here share the view that such moments of ecstatic awareness offer important insight into the possibilities for inhabiting the world more fully and deeply. But they offer no simple explanation regarding the meaning of such expansive experience or its genesis. Nor is it always possible to discern the religious character of such experience. Sometimes the language and imagery of the Divine signals a theistic orientation that is clear and unambiguous. However, even within avowedly religious texts, the immensity and reach of the Divine underlying the experience often exceeds the ability of the one bearing witness to find language in which to express it. It is unsayable. In other cases, the sense of the larger reality into which one is being drawn eludes any simple religious or theological classification and must be alluded to and grasped more obliquely. Instead one hears of a sense of the All. The Whole. The Cosmos. Such distinctions are or can be significant. But often the feeling of being drawn out of and beyond oneself remains so fundamentally mysterious and potent that the ability to stand within that mysterious reality becomes more important than naming or classifying it. The indeterminate, porous, penumbral character of the experience turns out to be inescapable and fundamental, and a large part of its value. Allowing oneself to be touched by this mysterious reality, to be drawn into this rich field of being in a movement of ecstatic wonder becomes crucial to the task of coming to know the world. For this reason, it is helpful to look to the particular and varied testimony of those for whom the sense of overflowing into the penumbral region has come to occupy the center of their experience.

One often encounters this sense of overflowing in Thoreau's journals. The sense of being drawn into the world, of feeling one's desire quickened by its sensual beauty, its music, its touch, spills over into a language of excess that reflects the density and encompassing intensity of the experience. Here, self and world can no longer be easily distinguished from one another; there is a feeling of immersion, of disappearing into a world of boundless immensity. Thoreau's careful and assiduous attention to these moments of ecstatic awareness is, as Allan Hodder has demonstrated, central to his emerging understanding of how we come to know ourselves in relation to the living world.[21] Ecstasy begets intimacy, an intimate knowledge that can come to us only through relinquishment of a narrow, bounded self and an openness to an ever-emerging sense of participation in a larger whole. Attention to those moments when such ecstatic expansion occurs can quicken and deepen one's sensitivity to the world, can open one to the possibility of a continuous exchange, an ever-more encompassing exchange. Still, what kind of exchange is this? And who is acting upon whom? Consider these two passages from Thoreau's early journals:

> Drifting in a sultry day on the sluggish waters of the pond, I almost cease to live—and begin to be. A boat-man stretched on the deck of his craft, and dallying with the noon, would be as apt an emblem of eternity for me, as the serpent with his tail in his mouth. I am never so prone to lose my identity. I am dissolved in the haze.[22]
>
> The eaves are running on the south side of the house—The titmouse lisps in the poplar—the bells are ringing for the church—while the sun presides over all and makes his simple warmth more obvious than all else.—What shall I do with this hour so like time and yet so fit for eternity? Where in me are these russet patches of ground—and scattered logs and chips in the yard?—I do not feel cluttered.—I have some notion what the johnswort and life-everlasting may be thinking about—when the sun shines on me as on them—and turns my prompt thought—into just such a seething shimmer—I lie out indistinct as a heath at noon-day—I am evaporating airs ascending into the sun.[23]

These journal entries reveal a similar concern—one that Thoreau never lost—to describe and understand that particular moment when a previously-clear boundary between the self and the wider world begins to dissolve and become permeable; but they touch on different dimensions of this experience. In the earlier passage, suggests Hodder, "[A]ll of matter, the creation itself, is subsumed in an ocean of consciousness; here, on the contrary, subjectivity is almost entirely subsumed in matter."[24] The distinction is significant, especially as one tracks the changes in Thoreau's sensibilities over time, from a transcendental idealism that favors human consciousness as the primary subject (into which the natural world is absorbed) to what Hodder describes as a "mindful naturalism" in which the natural world begins to emerge as the primary subject, or in any case as a rich, complex reality with its own claims on the human subject. Gradually, the idealism that is so prominent in Thoreau's early work gives way to a vivid sense of the primacy of matter and of the relationships between and among all living beings. Thoreau's unfinished Kalendar project, which represents his most intense and sustained effort to catalogue the intricate relations among and between species across time, reveals the extent of his commitment to understanding what would later come to be known as the ecological character of the natural world. But his steady and growing attention to this concrete ecological reality never led him to abandon his fundamental concern with that mysterious boundary region across which the self is sometimes drawn in its encounter with the living world. "I lie out indistinct as a heath at noon-day—I am evaporating airs ascending into the sun." For Thoreau, this indeterminate ever-shifting space between the self and the world and the mysterious ecstatic movement by which one is drawn into and beyond it possesses an almost endless significance. This is in no small measure because it is here above all that one learns to open oneself to the touch of love.

In November, 1850, thirteen years into the regular and assiduous process of engaging in what he called his "morning work," Thoreau boldly declared: "My Journal should be the record of my love. I would write in it only of the things I love, my affection for any aspect of the world, what I love to think of. I have no more distinctness or pointedness in my yearnings than an expanding bud, which does indeed point to flower and fruit, to summer and autumn, but is aware of the warm and spring influence only." This is clearly a statement of aspiration, an effort to describe something he hopes to realize in himself more fully as time unfolds. But the intense feeling for the world is already present, already coming alive in him. Even so, there is also something lacking: "I feel ripe for something, yet do nothing, can't discover what that thing is. I feel fertile merely. It is seedtime with me. I have lain fallow long enough."[25] The sense of uncertainty about what he is seeking is striking. There is a restlessness in him, a growing sense of ripeness, fertility. But for what? He cannot say, at least not precisely. He is like a budding plant, his yearning is indistinct and without clear purpose. But he *feels* intensely; he is all feeling—like the budding plant that feels the warm and spring influence only. Here one encounters one of Thoreau's strongest statements regarding the centrality of love to one's ability to apprehend and know the world; also his sense of the inevitable difficulties that arise when such intense feeling is lacking or weak.

It is not easy to reconcile these dreamy, affective musings on the experience of being taken out of oneself into a larger world with the pattern of clear-eyed attention to particular places and beings and the ecological systems that sustain their life that one finds increasingly present in Thoreau's journals. Still, one senses that for Thoreau there is no contradiction; both are integral to the mindful naturalism he was continually seeking to cultivate and deepen. And both depend on the consistent willingness to allow oneself to be aroused and stirred by the natural world, susceptible to its potent beauty. The next summer, in an entry dated July 11, 1851, Thoreau records this observation concerning his "susceptibility" to the sound emanating from Heywood's Brook as it falls into Fair Haven Pond. It is, he says, "inexpressibly refreshing to my senses. It seems to flow through my very bones. I hear it with insatiable thirst. It allays some sandy heat in me. It affects my circulations; methinks my arteries have sympathy with it. What is it I hear but the pure waterfalls within me, in the circulation of my blood, the streams that fall into my heart?"[26] Thoreau's acute sensitivity to sound has been well-documented and has already been noted in the earlier discussion on the idea of the Word. Here, one senses the particular importance of sound for evoking the fluidity and interpenetrating character of the experience of being alive in the natural world. And for kindling desire. "I hear it (Heywood's Brook) with insatiable thirst," he says. In this moment at least, that thirst is satisfied: he notes that the sound of the brook "allays some sandy heat" in him. But the cooling, calming, satisfying effect of the experience does nothing to stop the flow of the sound in him, through him: "It seems to flow through my very bones... it affects my circulations." This is an utterly embodied experience. But in penetrating the body, it also quickens something in his awareness, his affections. "What is it I hear," he asks, "but the pure waterfalls within me, in the circulation of my blood, the streams that fall into my heart?" Everything moves together here—the sound of the water touching his senses, quickening his soul and continuing to pulse and flow who knows where? Language itself circles and flows from one dimension of experience to another. It is the relations between and among things that one feels here, relations that have no simple or fixed boundaries. And Thoreau, in his effort to describe the experience, stands and moves within those relations and facilitates their deeper interpenetration even as he opens himself to their powerful, stirring effect on him.

Is this a kind of ecstasy? Perhaps. But the profound intermingling of self and world expressed here makes it difficult to say who or what the subject of the ecstatic experience is, or where it begins or ends. Heywood Brook moves endlessly down, down, down, tumbling into Fair Haven Pond, where it is lost within that larger body. The sound of the moving water moves up and out and into the listening ears of the one standing nearby, and continues to move further still, down into the arteries, affecting the circulation, quickening the heart. What kind of reciprocity is this? What kind of exchange? Hasn't the brook now become entwined with the very life of the listener? Hasn't the listener become lost in those waters? Here is an ecstasy that simultaneously takes one beyond the senses and draws one more deeply into the physical world. Thoreau leaves little doubt about the immersive force of this experience: "The sound of this gurgling water, running thus by night as by day, falls on all my dashes, fills all my buckets, overflows my floatboards... makes me a flume, a sluice-way, to the springs of nature. Thus I am washed; thus I drink and quench my thirst. Where the streams fall into the lake, if they are only a few inches more elevated, all walkers may hear"[27] The primary note here is one of celebration—at being capable of such immersion, at the sheer vastness of this experience, at the wonder of how far into the world one can be drawn, how far into oneself the world can penetrate. But what is the meaning and significance of such experience? Here and elsewhere, Thoreau seems to acknowledge that its mysterious and fundamentally ephemeral character make it difficult to determine its meaning or its enduring value. But, in a journal entry from September of that year, he returns to this question and offers an important comment about his understanding about why such experiences matter. "Our ecstatic states, which appear to yield so little fruit, have this value at least" he notes; they are "an experience of infinite beauty on which we unfailingly draw."[28]

Already during this time Thoreau demonstrates his clear and growing interest in the particular character of things and places in the natural world that can provoke such a response. Over time, his cataloguing of these natural facts will become more precise, more detailed, more oriented toward describing and understanding how natural systems work. But even as his skills as a naturalist become more refined and his understanding of ecological relationships more complex and nuanced, he retains his strong sense of the significance of ecstatic experience for understanding the natural world. Unless one is open to being taken up into the living world and immersed in it—loving it—he suggests again and again, one can hardly hope to cultivate an enduring relationship with it. Ecstasy kindles intimacy, regard for, and knowledge of the living world. Much later, Aldo Leopold would call attention to the practical meaning of this insight, declaring: "We can be ethical only in relation to something we can see, feel, understand, love, or otherwise have faith in."[29] Few ideas have had such strong and enduring resonance in contemporary ecological thought. But in reflecting on its significance for helping us engage in thoughtful and effective environmental action, we are drawn back again and again to Thoreau's witness regarding the fundamental importance of cultivating a feeling for the living world, of allowing ourselves to be drawn ecstatically across the farthest horizon into a new awareness of our lives as immersed in and flowing forth from the life of the world.

Desire and Darkness

Longing we say, because desire is full
of endless distances.[30]

ROBERT HASS

He or she is a mystic who cannot stop walking and, with the certainty of what is lacking, knows of every place and object that it is *not that;* one cannot stay *there* nor be content with *that.* Desire creates an excess. Places are exceeded, passed, lost behind it. It makes one go further, elsewhere. It lives nowhere.[31]

MICHEL DE CERTEAU

The Christian contemplative tradition has always maintained its own intense interest in navigating the penumbral regions where the soul, kindled by desire, feels itself drawn ecstatically out beyond all known boundaries of the self and into the divine mystery. It has taken a variety of forms, from the intense eroticism of the commentary tradition on the Song of Songs found in the work of Origen of Alexandria, Bernard of Clairvaux, and many others, to the mysterious unfolding of desire amidst the divine darkness found in the writing of Gregory of Nyssa, Dionysius the Areopagite, the *Cloud of Unknowing* and John of the Cross, to Augustine's profound if complicated sense that the kindling of desire and delight is fundamental to our capacity to know and experience God, to the embodied eucharistic devotion found in the writing of medieval woman mystics such as Mechthild of Madgeburg, to the utter vulnerability of ecstasy in prayer found in the writings of the sixteenth-century Spanish mystic Teresa of Avila (and memorably reimagined in Bernini's famous sculpture in the Cornaro Chapel of Santa Maria della Vittoria in Rome), and beyond. The consistent refrain in this tradition is that there can be no true knowledge of the Divine apart from a kindling of desire within the soul. Contemplative practice at its deepest is oriented toward creating the conditions in which this kindling of feeling and intimacy between the human person and the divine Other can unfold and deepen. Love becomes the very climate of prayer. Here, the boundaries between the self and God begin to dissolve and the contemplative makes bold to claim, with Meister Eckhart: "In love I am more God."[32]

Still, what is the character of this love and where does it take hold and express itself? Also, how can attention to this dimension of contemplative practice contribute to the work of rekindling a feeling for the living world? Regarding the first question, it must be acknowledged that the role of desire in spiritual experience has long been a subject of debate among Christians, mirroring in significant ways the fundamental ambivalence within the Christian tradition toward the body and human sexuality. It was the Swedish theologian Anders Nygren who, in the 1930s, gave forceful and enduring expression to the idea that *agape* and *eros* should be seen as distinct from and even antithetical to one another—*agape* or selfless love being understood as the characteristically Christian expression of love and *eros* being understood as largely drawn from Greek thought, too deeply bound to the "lower" impulses, and as fundamentally alien to the Christian sensibility.[33] This view has come to be seen by many as too simple, too dichotomous. In light of subsequent work on the part of theologians and historians, we can now grasp more fully than we did before the complexity and diversity of attitudes toward love found in the Christian tradition: different expressions and manifestations of love, not always consistent, not always compatible with one another, often arose and existed together in Christian spiritual practice. It is important to bear this in mind in what follows.

As to the question of where such love takes hold and how it comes to expression, one must face squarely the question that has often been raised about the Christian contemplative tradition: are articulations of desire found in this tradition the expressions of a soul whose life touches and is touched hardly at all by the material world? Are they mostly symbolic or allegorical expressions of yearning for a divine Other so radically transcendent that they can only be realized beyond the body, beyond the world? An honest response to this question would require one to say: sometimes, though not always. Or even: it depends on what you mean by a radically transcendent Other. One of the most complex questions one faces in understanding the meaning of desire in this tradition is precisely its endless or infinite character. The insistence on the unknowability or radical transcendence of God in this tradition is often connected closely to the sense of the infinite character of the *eros* that draws us and binds us to the divine Other. It is the endlessness of desire that leads contemplatives to guard and preserve with such fierceness the endlessness, the utter transcendence of God. And vice versa. This can and often has led to a strong renunciation of the claims of the body, of human sexuality, and of the world. But one encounters a much more complex and ambiguous reality among Christian contemplatives: an embodied subject seeking to immerse himself or herself in a desire so profound and encompassing, so deeply woven into the fabric of existence, that the experience of immersion yields a sense of unity and integration with everyone and everything. This unitive experience has been described and understood in many different ways. But often it is simply understood as the experience of dwelling in and beholding the world and everything in love.

It is just such an enfolding experience of love that has long been celebrated within the Jewish and Christian traditions through their commentaries on the Song of Songs. The rabbis early on recognized the power of the imagery of the two lovers drawn toward one another in an erotic embrace; they described this book as the "holy of holies," the most sacred text in all of scripture. Yet, its erotic power has been consistently redirected, sublimated by the tradition. The palpable and highly-charged physical attraction of the lovers to one another has been allegorized—first to stand for the relationship between God and Israel, then for the relationship between Christ and the Church, and finally, from Origen of Alexandria onwards, for the relationship between Christ and the soul. But to say that the text has been allegorized and spiritualized does not mean that its erotic power was lost completely. The commentary tradition stretching from Origen to Gregory of Nyssa, to Gregory the Great, to Hugh of St. Victor, to William of St. Thierry, to Allan of Lille, to Denys the Carthusian and beyond reveals the fecundity of this metaphor for helping early and medieval Christians articulate the soul's deepest and most subtle yearnings for God, yearnings that retained, in spite of the allegorizing tendency, much of the palpable, erotic power of the Song itself.

This is one of the central arguments of Denys Turner's book, *Eros and Allegory: Medieval Exegesis of the Song of Songs*. Turner suggests that "the Song offered the mediaeval commentator something which only the Song could supply; and that that something was precisely what was most specific to and characteristic of it: its exuberant celebration of *eros*."[34] When one considers the reality of sexual abstinence that characterized the lives of the figures Turner is describing here, and the insistence on the need for sexual purity (of mind and body) that marked the teaching of this tradition, it is difficult to know how *eros* could have appeared as anything other than a distraction or a temptation. But this is to think of *eros* too narrowly, too exclusively in terms of its explicit sexual connotations. Clearly, for these medieval writers, *eros*, while never losing entirely its highly-charged sexual connotations, also took on larger meanings that had to do their understanding of what it meant for them to inhabit a kind of borderlands region. Turner puts it this way:

> [T]he reasons why the erotic model of the love of God so appealed to the monastic commentators of the middle ages...had to do with very fundamental preoccupations of the monastic theologian and...these, in turn, were intimately connected with the monks' perception of their *Sitz im leben*...[they] are rooted in the monks' theological eschatology, in their sense that their life of partial withdrawal from the world situated them at a point of intersection between this world and the next, between time and eternity, between light and dark, between anticipation and fulfillment. This meant that the concept of love as a "yearning" or "longing"—as an *amor desiderium*, or, in Greek, *eros* exactly expressed what they wanted by way of a language of love.[35]

Still, it was not this biblical, eschatological monastic theology *alone* that accounts for the vibrancy and dynamism of this commentary tradition, according to Turner. It was the fusion or cross-fertilization of this eschatological theology with Christian neo-platonic metaphysical eroticism—exemplified in the work of Origen, Gregory of Nyssa, and Pseudo-Dionysius and mediated to the West through John Scotus Eriugena—that gave the medieval monastic commentary on the Song its particular character and force.

Two aspects of this argument are particularly worth noting in the present context. First, it is the contemplative's consciousness of occupying a liminal space, a physical, cultural, theological "ecotone," that makes the language of *eros* so attractive to them. They understand themselves as standing between worlds, as knowing the kingdom to be "already" present and "not yet" fully realized, knowing their beloved to be now present, now absent. One might say that their consciousness of standing at the border between worlds makes them particularly attentive to the possibility of encounter, to an exchange between those worlds. *Eros* in this sense expresses a longing, not to leave one world for another but to draw them together in a tender embrace. A rich vocabulary emerged to express this subtle and beautiful intermingling of lives and worlds: the idea of *perichoresis* or coinherence perhaps captures best the sense of deep interpenetration of one life in another so cherished by these figures. The second point is that the medieval contemplative tradition absorbed into its theology and spirituality not an eviscerated, completely spiritualized sense of the erotic but a powerful, highly-charged eroticism capable of speaking to the deepest human longing and desire for union with the ultimate.[36]

These reflections on *eros*, nature, and spirit raise important questions about the habitual distinctions we make between ourselves and the living world, between spirit and matter, between the mundane and the holy. If with Griffin and Hyde we understand *eros* as the capacity for communion with another—the capacity to encounter the other, to enter into the life of the other, and to receive life back—then we need to ask whether we are prepared to imagine the boundaries dividing one world from another as perhaps being more porous than we habitually do. If with Abram we consider our imaginative, linguistic life not as disembodied and immaterial, but as part of a fluid, carnal "field," then we need to ask whether we are prepared to dig deeper to fathom the capacity of the living world to "speak" to us, and elicit a response from us, whether we are prepared to consider anew the possibilities for conversation between the human and the more-than-human worlds. And if with Turner and the Christian contemplative tradition, we understand *eros* as a primary, concrete, and encompassing discourse for articulating the deepest human longing for the holy, arising from within our embodied experience, then we need to ask whether we are prepared to ground the language of spiritual longing more firmly in the palpable, particular reality of *eros*?[37]

Such questions lead, in turn, to others. How much intimacy with the living world do we want? How much intimacy can we bear? What are the limits and possibilities of language for articulating our experience of intimacy? What does it mean to speak of "losing oneself," "crossing over," "entering into" the living world, the world of the Other? If we can "cross over," what will happen to us on the other side? Who/what will we become? These are questions that surface repeatedly in the both the Christian contemplative tradition and in contemporary ecological discourse. They comprise part of an ongoing struggle to imagine a fuller, deeper sense of relationship with the transcendent

Other—whether beyond or within the living world. In considering them, we are invited to risk participating in that most demanding of contemplative, erotic practices: to imagine one thing as another, even oneself as another.

To consider these questions in greater depth, I want to return once again to the desert, and to the sense of yearning expressed among the early desert monks. Also to the work of certain other Christian contemplatives for whom the language of desire became central for understanding and expressing the feeling of being drawn *out of and into* themselves in an intimate encounter with the Divine. Their effort to describe such ecstatic, unitive experience yielded a remarkably diverse range of expressions: the meeting of the lover and the beloved, certainly, but also the enkindling of sparks and flames, the sense of being pierced by an arrow, being drawn into the steady rhythm of tides, immersion in torrential rain, the gentle touch of dew, night. In spite of the real differences of experience evoked by such images, they point to a widely shared, and often ineffable sense of what it is to pass beyond oneself and be drawn into a mysterious, wild, boundless immensity. In almost every instance, both the passing beyond and the drawing into are understood as grounded in and enabled by love; they are part of a continuous movement of love within the soul. But it is a love of such reach and depth that it cannot be contained, cannot be conceptualized, cannot even be spoken or understood. One must relinquish every effort to do so. Hence the frequent convergence of desire and darkness in this tradition. To love in this way is to be drawn beyond oneself into the unknown, into the cloud, into the endless darkness. Only, there, in the mysterious depths of the night can the lover and beloved lose themselves, find one another, feel the kindling of desire, experience intimacy and exchange. *Eros* comes alive in the penumbral.

This is the key insight of Gregory of Nyssa's great fourth-century work, *The Life of Moses*. Gregory offers one of the earliest and most enduring expressions in the Christian tradition of the notion that true contemplation can only be realized through the renunciation of all vision and knowledge: "This is the true knowledge of what is sought," he says: "the seeing that consists in not seeing, because that which is sought transcends all knowledge, being separated on all sides by incomprehensibility as by a kind of darkness."[38] This insight had a history: the sense of God's incomprehensibility and inaccessibility owed much to the earlier tradition of Jewish and Christian thought found in the work of Philo and Clement of Alexandria.[39] But Gregory extended and deepened it in important ways, not least by fusing the notion of divine incomprehensibility with the centrality of desire. The darkness that surrounds the

Divine was understood to be immense and total. But one could enter into the darkness and encounter God there, if not through knowledge, then through desire. But in Gregory's understanding, desire was endless, as deep and extensive as the night into which it carried one. The kindling of desire was the crucial work of the soul necessary for allowing one to live endlessly into God.[40]

Epectasis is the name usually given to this idea of endless spiritual progress rooted in desire. It suggests the notion of an endless straining forward for that which has not yet been realized, and owes its presence in the *Life of Moses* to an idea found in Paul's letter to the Philippians. Gregory takes this idea and turns it to his own ends, noting: "If nothing comes from above to hinder its upward thrust (for the nature of the Good attracts to itself those who look to it), the soul rises ever higher and will always make its flight yet higher, by its desire of the heavenly things straining ahead for what is still to come, as the Apostle says"(Phil 3:13).[41] This notion of "straining ahead," which in the early Christian monastic tradition is often employed to express the character of ascetic exertion, here gives expression to the fundamental desire of the soul for God ("heavenly things") that rises "ever higher" and "yet higher." This desire cannot end because what kindles it and moves the soul to "strain ahead" is itself without end, boundless. Still, how does one move? And why? Gregory makes some effort to describe the phenomenology of this experience, enabling the reader to feel, even amidst this highly stylized account of Moses's itinerary, the urgency and pathos of this movement and all that lay behind it. "Made to desire and not to abandon the transcendent height by the things already attained, [the soul] makes its way upward without ceasing, ever through its prior accomplishments renewing its intensity for the flight."[42] One senses here the dynamic and fluid character of such experience. "The things already attained," and the "prior accomplishments" have themselves been made possible through the movement of desire in the soul. But there is no sense of satiety here. Rather, they serve to quicken an even deeper desire that yearns forward further into the divine mystery. Each experience of proximity made possible by the movement of desire in the soul opens a new horizon, a new sense of distance between the soul and God. Which only deepens the intensity with which the soul, through renewed desire, seeks to reach further into the mystery.

This sense of perpetual dissatisfaction, born of endless yearning, is central to the experience of *epectasis* as Gregory understands it. Vision and its satisfactions always vie with what has not and cannot be seen or known. And this tension can only kindle deeper desire. Gregory seems to anticipate objections to this approach. He reminds us, in a clear reference to Moses's encounter with God in the burning bush that he "saw the brilliance of the light." He "shone

with glory." How could this not satisfy? But for Gregory, it did not and cannot fulfill the intense longing that draws Moses ever deeper. "Although lifted
up through such lofty experiences, he is still unsatisfied in his desire for more.
He still thirsts for that with which he constantly filled himself to capacity,
and he asks to attain as if he had never partaken, beseeching God to appear
to him, not according to his capacity to partake, but according to God's true
being."[43] Gregory's language here suggests the utterly paradoxical character
of the experience. Moses is lifted up, filled to capacity. And yet he remains
thirsty. He asks to be emptied still further, "as if he had never partaken." He
wants to behold God, but not according to his own limited capacities. He
asks, if not directly, then by implication, to be taken up into the very life of
God.

The boundaries of this space keep expanding, dilating. They are porous,
permeable. The space into which the soul is drawn by desire is endless. Nor,
it seems, is there any limit to the soul's capacity to know God. But the movement across and into this infinite space is made possible only through a
deepening of desire. And this leads always to a loss of knowledge, to a deeper
obscurity. "Such an experience," Gregory notes, "seems to me to belong to
the soul which loves what is beautiful. Hope always draws the soul from the
beauty which is seen to what is beyond, always kindles the desire for the hidden through what is constantly perceived."[44] The soul, even as it responds to
and is drawn forth from itself by beauty, knows there is more and still more.
Beauty kindles "desire for the hidden," drawing the soul always beyond what
is seen, always beyond. The soul must again enter the darkness. Desire and
darkness, it seems, are bound to one another, endlessly.[45]

Endless desire: "This is truly the vision of God," says Gregory, "never to be
satisfied in the desire to see [God]. But one must always, by looking at what he
can see, rekindle his desire to see more. Thus, no limit would interrupt growth
in the ascent to God, since no limit to the Good can be found nor is the
increasing of desire for the Good brought to an end because it is satisfied."[46]
Endless darkness: "For leaving behind everything that is observed, not only
what sense comprehends but also what intelligence thinks it sees, it keeps on
penetrating deeper until by the intelligence's yearning for understanding it
gains access to the invisible and the incomprehensible, and there it sees God.
This is the true knowledge of what is sought; this is the seeing that consists
in not seeing, because that which is sought transcends all knowledge, a being
separated on all sides by incomprehensibility as by a kind of darkness."[47]
Desire requires darkness, it seems, to express itself fully and deeply. And the
meaning of darkness as a medium for kindling intimacy between the human

person and the divine Other can only be apprehended through the exercise of desire.

What kind of intimacy is kindled in this space of endless darkness and desire? What effect does this endless yearning have on the soul, on its capacity to know and engage the divine Other? The very terms of the discourse Gregory employs in the *Life of Moses* would seem to preclude any clear response to these questions. The paradoxical relationship of proximity and distance found throughout this text suggests still a further challenge: how can the soul be drawn ever beyond itself, toward an infinite and ever-expanding horizon, and not become lost in the immensity? How can intimacy be maintained when there is only immensity, when the movement of desire seems to lead relentlessly toward an absorption, an eclipsing of the self that is utter and total? Perhaps one cannot avoid this altogether. In fact, as many witnesses in the Christian contemplative tradition attest, the movement of love in the soul leads one inexorably toward such absorption. To open oneself to this love is to risk becoming lost in its immensity.

Still, there is not only an endlessly receding horizon. There is also an intimate, hidden space of encounter, a space that, at least in imaginative terms, is closer to hand and more contained. Gregory explores this intimate space more fully in his *Homilies on the Song of Songs*. But already here in the *Life of Moses*, amidst the soul's ever-expanding itinerary into the immensity of the desert, one catches a glimpse of this more intimate space. It arises particularly in his reflections on the image of the *adyton* or sanctuary. "When, therefore, Moses grew in knowledge," Gregory says, "he declared that he had seen God in the darkness, that is, that he had then come to know what is divine is beyond all knowledge and comprehension, for the text says, 'Moses approached the dark cloud where God was.' What God? He who made darkness his hiding place, as David says, who also was initiated into the mysteries in the same inner sanctuary (*adyton*)."[48] The image of the *adyton* or sanctuary refers to the deepest, and most inaccessible part of the ancient Jewish tabernacle (Ex 26:1. ff), and Gregory draws upon the image here to evoke the sense of deep interiority that for him is critical to understanding the soul's experience in prayer. The *adyton* is a hidden place, like the deep darkness into which the soul is continuously moving. And it is in its own way immense. But it is also, at least in the way Gregory imagines it here, an intimate space, a hidden part of a person's own soul, that for all its closeness to the person is not entirely accessible or knowable. This is what he means when, in *Commentary on the Lord's Prayer*, he calls the *adyton*, "the hidden inner chamber of our heart...."[49] Or, when, in his treatise *On the Beatitudes*, he says: "Whatever was contained within the sanctuary was pure and sacred; but its inner most part was *adyton* and inaccessible and was called the Holy of Holies."[50]

His commentary *On the Beatitudes* in particular offers important insight into Gregory's understanding of the way contemplative practice—even as one is being drawn into the most hidden, inaccessible parts of one's own soul—can contribute to the work of healing the torn fabric of the whole. And it offers an important complement to and commentary on the radically apophatic vision of contemplative practice seen in *The Life of Moses*. For Gregory, as for many other Christian contemplatives, this healing work can take hold only through the unfolding of love in the soul. But the cultivation of the capacity to love, to develop genuine and enduring regard for another, requires a willingness to confront and struggle with all those disordered desires—what the Christian ascetic tradition calls the passions—that, when left unattended, undermine and weaken love's hold on the soul. Nor are the effects of these disordered desires felt only in isolated, individual souls; they manifest themselves in the body of the community and tear at the communal fabric of life. Only through assiduous contemplative practice can a person hope to transform these passions; but the effects of such transformation are felt not only in the life of the person but also in the life of the wider community. Gregory's attention to the particular experience of entering the intimate space of the *adyton* or sanctuary in contemplative prayer is for this reason bound inextricably to his sense of its healing effects on the community as a whole. Here, he limits his observations to the healing effects of contemplative practice on the human community; but it is clear from remarks he makes elsewhere that he believes the healing power of contemplative practice—born of love—ultimately extends to every living being.[51]

It is the mysterious experience of wakening to love in the soul and the effects of such experience in the life of the community that interests Gregory most here. The point of departure for his reflections is a text from the Beatitudes: "Blessed are the peacemakers, for they shall be called sons of God" (Mt 5:9). Gregory is especially concerned to understand the reciprocal, interdependent relationship between the experience of kinship with God and the work of peacemaking, and the tightly woven fabric of existence to which this relationship points. How, he wonders, does the sense of intimacy born of kinship with God (represented here by the promise of becoming a child of God) shape the human capacity for ethical action within the community (peacemaking)? And how does the *practice* of peacemaking, especially the practice of regarding another with love, enable the promise of kinship with God to be realized, within the person and the community? How, in other words, can the pattern of pervasive violence, isolation, and alienation from others that characterizes so much of human existence come to be transformed into an abiding sense of living in and for others? How can intimacy and communion be restored? On a personal level, the possibility of realizing this transformative, communal vision of existence in one's life depends, Gregory suggests, on one's willingness and capacity to see oneself as partaking in the life of God. But this recognition of kinship with God is more than personal, for it opens up and makes possible a new awareness of one's kinship with others. It is this utterly improbable and incomparable transformation—the realization that one is a child of God and partakes in the divine nature—that Gregory has in mind when he speaks of entering the *adyton* or holy of holies. The only thing it can be likened to at all is the experience of beholding God; but it surpasses even this. "For if the blessedness of seeing God cannot be surpassed," he says, "to become the [child] of God transcends bliss altogether."[52]

Gregory reminds his readers that this transcendent experience of entering the *adyton*, and discovering there in the secret chamber of the heart one's kinship with God, is beyond understanding, beyond language. It cannot be named. In this sense, entering this intimate hidden place is like being drawn out into the immense darkness. But here in this immensity there is also an awareness of love, a sense of kinship with God that is experienced as pure gift. This simple, encompassing awareness of being held and known in love is, for Gregory, what allows community itself to be reimagined and reconstituted. Peace, he says, "is nothing else but a loving disposition towards one's neighbor." It is the embodied practice of love that keeps all those impulses that would undermine and overwhelm its presence in the larger community— "hate and wrath, anger and envy, harboring resentment as well hypocrisy and calamity of war"—from doing so.[53] Much of the rest of the sermon is devoted to a psychologically astute examination of how these and other habits of mind enter into and colonize the soul and how in this way they contribute to the fragmentation and destruction of relationships and community. For Gregory, there is a profound connection between one's capacity to live into the mystery of one's kinship with the Divine and one's ability to embody love in the world. The same desire that draws one ever deeper into the divine darkness, into an awareness of one's life as rooted in the mystery of love, draws one into a relationship of genuine and enduring regard for others.

Here one encounters one expression of an idea whose importance would only continue to deepen and grow in Christian contemplative experience: that all beings are bound together in a single, unbroken fabric and that the work of reknitting the torn fabric requires opening oneself to the healing presence of desire in the soul. Arriving at an awareness of this truth is but one moment in a larger process of renewal. But it is a critical moment. Living into this desire more fully means allowing the soul to be remade in love, with all the risk and relinquishment that this entails. Only through this transformative work can the boundaries separating oneself from God and others begin to dissolve. Only then can true exchange and reciprocity become possible. Only in this way can the torn fabric that binds everything together begin to be repaired. The Christian contemplative tradition devotes continuous attention to the work of understanding what it might mean to live into this transformative vision of existence. Following upon Gregory of Nyssa's sensitive and subtle evocation of the soul's journey into the immense intimacy of darkness, *eros* emerges again and again at this heart of this vision.

Immanent Transcendence and the Rekindling of Intimacy

> They loved each other because everything around them
> willed it, the trees and the clouds and the sky over their
> heads and the earth under their feet.... This compatibil-
> ity of the whole was the breath of life to them.[54]
>
> BORIS PASTERNAK

The compatibility of the whole—realized though a response to and participation in the erotic force of the living world. This vision of existence may well feel like a relic of some other, simpler time, before the fabric of the world began unraveling, before we stopped believing in the possibility of our own intimate embrace of the world. But the tenacity of this vision in the contemporary imagination and the refusal to abandon entirely the sense of the compatibility of the whole suggests something important, I think, about its enduring significance for us. It is fundamentally an imaginative gesture, born of an intuitive sense of the kind of relationship with the living world that is still possible for us. And this is where its power lay: in helping us reimagine who we are in the world and what it might mean to know ourselves as alive inside the world, even as the world courses deeply through our lives. Still, learning to live into this vision of the whole will also mean, at least in the present moment, confronting the stark fact of loss, and the patterns of destruction created by a distorted, acquisitive, grasping *eros*. It will mean considering deeply and carefully how the healing of desire can contribute to the work of repairing the torn fabric of the world. The temptation in the present moment to abandon all hope of cultivating an intimate exchange with the living world is real. But the work of reparation will require an ongoing effort to imagine and give expression to our sense of the possibility of this intimate exchange—especially the cultivation of sensitivity to the porous boundaries across which life insistently moves and across which we ourselves are continuously drawn.

What will it mean to cultivate a sensitivity to these porous boundaries, to those penumbral spaces where desire is always drawing us toward an ecstatic exchange, an intimate touch with the Other? What kind of contemplative practice is this and how can it be deepened? The testimony of the Christian contemplative tradition suggests a range of particular practices and modes of thought that can help to deepen one's awareness of others in and across this porous space. At the root of these practices is a willingness to allow oneself to become open and vulnerable to the touch, voice, fragrance, taste, and vision of the Other. A willingness to risk, through the exercise of the imagination or through the relinquishment of all imaginative and linguistic constructs, being drawn into the life of the Other: a particular person or being, the world, God. One of the striking features of the present moment, something that is itself perhaps a comment on the need for a dissolving of old boundaries, is how often these seemingly distinct realities flow together in experience and imagination. And how many different names—and, paradoxically, how many refusals of names—we require for articulating the ultimate end of our desires. Also the increasing extent to which the proximate, the particular, the embodied and material are called upon to bear the weight of these ultimate desires. In this context, the contemplative practice of *eros*—the opening of oneself to the possibility of an ecstatic experience of transcendence, in which one comes to know oneself as participating in and touched by the life of the Other, has tremendous potential significance. But increasingly, it is coming to be understood in terms of what Luce Irigiray calls *extase instante*—a flowing outward that is always also a flowing inward, an immanent transcendence or a sensibility transcending itself.[55] Within such an ecstatic encounter, especially when it is characterized by what Irigiray calls a "letting be transcendence"—a way of loving that refrains from defining or categorizing the other but leaves open a space for the other to define and express himself or herself—the possibility for authentic and meaningful exchange remains open and alive.[56] When transposed onto our relationship with living beings in the natural world, this sense of ecstatic exchange suggests the possibility for a kind of communion, an exchange of life between the so-called inner and outer worlds. We can trace our yearning for this communion to the womb, suggests Paul Shepard. It is there that the feeling for our participation in things takes hold of us, where the fluid sense of exchange begins to live and move in us: "The outdoors is also in some sense another inside, a kind of enlivenment of that fetal landscape which is not so constant as once supposed. The surroundings are also that-which-will-be-swallowed, internalized, incorporated as the self."[57]

This conception of the self is expansive, open, unfinished. It is fundamentally and intrinsically relational, ecological, contemplative. The "outdoors" here functions imaginatively not unlike the endless darkness found in the writings of Christian contemplatives. It has a substantial presence. Yet, it is open, mysterious, not-completely-knowable. And yet it is consumed and in being consumed transformed. So too with the self: if it can be said to possess the capacity to swallow up and incorporate its surroundings, it can also be swallowed up and incorporated by them. *Eros* enables and facilitates such intimate exchange, opens us to it. But the very possibility of such exchange also serves as a continuous reminder of the distance that remains, of the broken bonds that separate us from and inhibit our capacity to attend to and participate in the life of the other. Paradoxically, our awareness of this chasm and distance often only serves to deepen our desire for connection and intimacy. It is this perhaps that helps to account for the powerful presence of desire, and the longing for exchange in so much modern and contemporary writing about the natural world. At its most thoughtful, such work opens up an imaginative space where we can begin to feel both the acuteness of loss and the possibility of a restored intimacy with the living world. It helps restore our own capacity for sensitivity and tenderness toward the life of things.

The longing for intimacy certainly includes and is affected by loss; but often it is kindled by intimacy itself, by a sudden awareness of how fluid and porous the boundaries between and among things in the world are; and by an awareness of how permeable the boundaries of our own consciousness are, how we can come to know ourselves as living within and touched by the life of another. It is not easy to grasp or express the experience of this fluid, shifting movement of life around and within us. To say anything at all is already to risk putting into language something that can never be contained or encompassed by it—not only because of its ephemeral character but also because of its endlessness. But the act of imagining what cannot be fully or completely imagined is still a worthy gesture. And it can help us cultivate sensitivity to those boundary regions where life insistently emerges and moves, where light and wind and birdsong course together and enter into us and where one thing cannot be separated from another. I think here, for example, of Mary Austin's account of the subtle, reciprocal exchange of light and sound in the vast, beautiful landscape of California's Owens Valley:

> In quiet weather mesa days have no parallel for stillness, but the night silence breaks into certain mellow or poignant notes. Late afternoons the burrowing owls may be seen blinking at the doors of their hummocks with perhaps four or five elfish nestlings arow, and by twilight begin a soft *whoo-ooing,* rounder, sweeter, more incessant in mating time. It is not possible to disassociate the call of the burrowing owl from the late slant light of the mesa. If the fine vibrations which are the golden-violet glow of spring twilights were to tremble into sound, it would be just that mellow double note breaking along the blossom tops.[58]

This account is noteworthy for its reticence regarding the effect of such subtle movements on us. All of Austin's attention is on the shifting movement of life within the place itself. Yet there is tremendous delicacy in her observation, especially regarding the way stillness and light and song move and flow into and through one another. The stillness is itself something palpable. But it is open, dynamic, receptive to sound, to which it occasionally yields. That "soft *whoo-ooing*" of burrowing owls whose song can hardly be distinguished from the "late slant light of the mesa." There seems to be something kindred between them. Or perhaps it is simply how they rise and move together, how difficult it is to discern where one begins and the other ends, how light and sound coalesce and resonate continuously in the senses and in the imagination.

Austin makes no attempt here to suggest what it might mean for us to notice and feel this rich movement of life around and within us. But it is difficult to miss the sense of intimacy and participation that her account of the dance of light and sound and stillness on the mesa invites and makes possible. Nor can one easily miss her sense of the porousness of the imagination through which the life of things enters into us and takes hold of our affections, lifting and carrying us out beyond ourselves into the immensity. What is perhaps only implicit here is expressed more explicitly in other accounts: the struggle to open oneself to this immensity and allow oneself to be absorbed into it. Often such relinquishment is indeed a struggle, as one begins to reckon with the kind of surrender it will entail for this to happen. But sometimes it comes as a relief to know that the self is not so constrained, that it is capable of living within a larger, more capacious reality. Perhaps this comes most easily for children. That at least is true in Michael Ondaatje's rendering of a moment in a young boy's life when the old boundaries gradually disappear and the sense of separation between himself and the immensity beyond dissolves. Rafael and his mother Aria are traveling through southern France by horse and caravan making their way slowly toward a place where they hope to settle for a time. They are Romany and are accustomed to the rhythms of endless movement and to the intimacy with the earth that comes from sleeping in forests and fields. Still, the experiences of this particular journey touched Rafael and woke something in his imagination.

> There were evenings when Aria and Rafael stood on the dry night-grass with a hundred layers of stars above them. Uncountable. A million orchestras. The boy could scarcely store the delirious information. That journey south with his mother and the return north broke his heart again and again with happiness. It was when he felt most clearly that there was no distinction between himself and what was beyond him—a tree's sigh or his mother's song, could, it seemed, have been generated by his body. Just as whatever gesture he made was an act performed by the world around him.[59]

There is too much delirious information. It cannot be "stored" or contained in the imagination or the affections. It spills forth in heartbreaking happiness. Heartbreaking. Here meaning: *everything* lives and moves through and within me, everything moves me; even as *I* live and move within everything around me. And this is happiness. This is the heart opening out and taking in everything and being taken in by everything. Happiness. Ecstasy. Communion.

And what if one begins elsewhere, not under those uncountable layers of stars, but in the arms of one's beloved? How far out can this embrace carry one? Can anything contain it? Does not everything move within it? Is not everything moved by it? This was the implicit starting point for all those in the Christian contemplative tradition who were drawn to comment upon the Song of Songs. And if one considers the intuition that lay beneath so many of these commentaries, it seems to be rooted almost always in the realization that only here in this intimate embrace can one touch the deepest, strongest, most fundamental elements of experience. "Let him kiss me with the kisses of his mouth" (Sg 1:2). Only here in this most intimate exchange can one be drawn out of oneself and into the life of the other. Only within this embrace can one begin to imagine an embrace that encompasses everything and everyone. But this intuition also arises frequently in literature and poetry, where the embrace of the lover and the beloved becomes a fulcrum through which the power of everything that exists moves. The lovers' intensely focused gaze paradoxically moves out and beyond itself—to find that everything can be seen and known in the eyes of one's beloved.

A beautiful expression of this idea is found in Boris Pasternak's great novel *Dr. Zhivago*. Toward the end of a story that has already seen the lives of almost every figure in the novel uprooted and exiled by the cataclysmic events of 1917—including Zhivago himself—Pasternak pauses to consider the fate of his two protagonists, Lara and Yuri. For a brief time, they had found refuge together beyond the reach of the brutal civil war that was tearing the country apart and which would soon enough tear them from one another. They had given themselves to one another in love. In the official narrative that would eventually come to be told of this time and this struggle, their meeting and their love would be rendered trivial and insignificant; they would simply disappear in the sweep of history. But Pasternak resists this reductive narrative and offers his own imaginative response to their brief, hidden exchange of love. Yuri Zhivago has now died. Lara stands next to his coffin. This is the first time she has seen him since their enforced separation years earlier at Varykino. Suddenly, she is brought once again into the presence of that time and of the love they shared.

> It was not out of necessity that they loved each other, "enslaved by passion," as lovers are described. They loved each other because everything around them willed it, the trees and the clouds and the sky over their heads and the earth under their feet. Perhaps their surrounding world, the strangers they met in the street, the landscapes drawn up for them to see on their walks, the rooms in which they lived or met, were even more pleased with their love than they were themselves.
>
> Well, of course it had been just this that had united them and had made them so akin! Never, never, not even in their moments of richest and wildest happiness, had they lost the sense of what is highest and most ravishing—joy in the whole universe, its form, its beauty, the feeling of their own belonging to it, being part of it.
>
> This compatibility of the whole was the breath of life to them.[60]

This account may seem too personal or even sentimental to help us in this age of environmental catastrophe. But it is worth remembering that Pasternak's vision of cosmic joy emerged amidst the depth of the Cold War, as the dream in the Soviet Union of industrial and military supremacy overran all other considerations, including the idea that human kinship with the natural world might be worth cultivating or celebrating. Pasternak seems to have been intent on calling attention to the severe shortcomings of this way of seeing and inhabiting the world. It is Lara who gives voice to this skepticism: "They were unattracted to the modern fashion of coddling man, exalting him above the rest of nature and worshipping him. A sociology built on this false premise and served up as politics, struck them as pathetically homemade and amateurish beyond their comprehension."[61] That Soviet system Pasternak critiqued has now disappeared. But the tendency to marginalize and denigrate the importance of kinship with the living world has hardly diminished at all. Which is why Pasternak's vision, of the "compatibility of the whole"—the sense of belonging to, and an openness to being ravished by, the universe—remains compelling and important. That this sense of the whole was then and continues now to be bound up with an awareness of the extensive fragmentation and loss that afflicts the natural world only deepens its potential significance for us. It serves as an important reminder of how the work of cultivating vulnerability and openness to the living world may yet help us resist the growing tendency to see ourselves as dominant over and alienated from the world.

What is it that kindles in us the desire to enter into and become part of this living, vibrant whole? Can the kindling of desire itself become part of a sustained contemplative practice? In the present moment, addressing this question will require us to attend not only to the mysterious process through which we are drawn into that porous space where we can sense and feel the life of the other, but also to the harsh, sometimes brutal hardening of the boundaries as the very fabric that sustains living beings becomes torn and frayed. Often these two experiences move together within us. And while it is difficult, especially in light of this deepening loss, to avoid closing oneself off to all feeling, the continuous presence of *eros* in our shared cultural and spiritual imagination asks something else of us: to remain open and attentive and tender toward all living beings, even in their compromised and degraded condition.

Almost inevitably, this means turning one's attention to those particular beings, those particular places that have already taken hold of one's affections. This does not mean that feeling and affection cannot be expansive. They can be. It only means that it is in our relation to particular things, often those things closest to us, that we begin to feel desire rise up within us, where we feel the intricacy and strength of the fabric that binds us to these things; and where we also feel the tearing of the fabric most deeply. This is where affection takes hold, where desire lives in us, and helps to create a space where the life of the other can meet and flow together with our own lives. I think again of those old-growth redwoods in the Headwaters Forest in Northern California, part of a fragile and threatened web of living beings that extends south to the land where Redwoods Monastery sits. And of the shared efforts to feel and imagine the particular character of their lives more deeply, to prevent them from falling into the category of the generic or merely useful, to stand with and for these trees. Through long hours spent gazing up at one of these ancient trees outside of the monastery chapel, I have come to feel its utterly particular and distinctive life. Nor can I separate my feeling for the life of this particular tree from my feeling for the lives of those who make up this monastic community, or from the lives of those visitors who come here seeking refuge and solace. Or from the lives of all those struggling souls far from this place for whom we regularly pray. We "hold them in prayer." And in this holding, in the strength of our ardor, we bind ourselves and are bound to one another. This contemplative work is largely hidden. And its effects can never be calculated. Still, such work can serve to deepen our feeling for and our sense of participation in the mysterious life of things. And in this way it can help to help kindle in us a deeper concern for all that is being lost to us, all that we love.

I think sometimes about a small stand of poplars that once stood along a river near Oxford, England. I never saw them, for they were cut down over a hundred years ago. But ever since I first read Gerard Manley Hopkins's poem "Binsey Poplars," I have never been able to forget them. Hopkins knew these trees well and often walked near them[62]. In the poem, he gives voice to the feeling of realizing suddenly that they were gone: "My aspens dear, whose airy cages quelled,/Quelled or quenched in leaves the leaping sun./All felled, felled, are all felled." One hardly needs to read further to sense all that has been lost here. Those three opening words—"My aspens dear"—an utterly unguarded expression of feeling for these trees, made all the more pathetic by the realization that they have all been felled. The repetition only deepens this realization, and with it the reality of what has been lost. But even this is not sufficient to express the loss. It must be said again: "Not spared, not one/that dandled a sandalled/Shadow that swam or sank/On meadow and river and wind-wandering weed-winding bank." Language here evokes and gives imaginative expression to an immensely complex and delicate reality: the shape and texture and movement and life of those trees, as well as the whole movement of life in and through and around them. Nor can the poet's deep affection for the trees or his grief at their loss be separated from that life; it has all already entered into and seized hold of his feeling and affection. The miracle of poetic expression here is how it holds and expresses this entire rich field, and the continuous movement and exchange between and among all the elements within it—the trees (those "airy cages"), the sunlight, the shadows (now swimming, now sinking), the meadow and river and "wind-wandering weed-winding bank." Also the poet's imaginative engagement with and participation in the field, including his feelings of affection, grief, loss. Nothing stands still, everything moves—inside of, between, and through everything else. There are no firm borders, only porous spaces of exchange. One feels here the intricate seamlessness of the whole. But one also feels the raw tearing of the fabric, what Hopkins, in one of his most audacious claims, calls the "unselving" of the whole.

There is risk involved in cultivating such sensitivity and tenderness. One becomes vulnerable to the life of things, allowing them to gain purchase on one's imagination and affections. One begins to feel them living inside and oneself as living in them. Such vulnerability was integral to Hopkins's poetic practice and had deep spiritual significance for him. The ideas of "instress" and "inscape," which he coined to describe how the particular and utterly singular form and life of things manifest themselves to us and take hold in our imaginations, became critical to his own practice of attending to the world with vulnerability. The disciplined practice of attending to things in this way yielded an utterly distinctive poetics that expresses and embodies the power of *eros* to join the life of one thing with the life of another. It creates a space where one can imagine living inside of things and feeling the life of things penetrating deeply into one's own life, and where one can also begin to feel and reckon seriously with all that has been lost.

These are among the central concerns that occupy Robert Hass in his 1996 collection of poems, *Sun Under Wood*.[63] Here, intimations of intense intimacy and exchange are nested within and shaped by losses and alienation so profound that language itself cannot contain it. Nor are these exchanges and these losses merely personal, for they touch upon, provide a way into, and are in turn shaped by a much larger landscape of loss. The poet asks: what language can I find to describe the loss of my mother, through alcoholism and mental illness, to some far distant place I cannot now reach? Or to account for that tangled web of other losses that seem bound, as if by invisible threads, to this original one? Like the loss of a cherished mountain meadow, "the deep-rooted bunchgrass/and the wet alkali-scented earth...pushed aside/or trucked someplace out of the way," replaced by concrete slabs for a housing development? Or the disappearance of all those indigenous peoples, decimated by influenza and syphilis, who inhabited this land before us, and who "also loved these high meadows on summer mornings?"

How are we to understand the cumulative effect of such losses upon the soul, upon the human community, upon the natural world? They are at once personal (the loss of one's mother), geographic-ecological (the loss of those mountain meadows) and historical-cultural (the loss of indigenous peoples through genocide and disease). To hold them together as part of a single, complex whole is an immensely challenging imaginative and moral task. And yet, they are so clearly part of a whole. They participate in and express, each in a different way, the loss of relationship, in some cases the violent suppression of relationship. Yet, in each case, there is a memory of some intimacy, some deep connection that lingers in our emotional, spiritual lives. Everything that is severed returns.

But does it, can it return? Can that which has been lost or discarded be reclaimed and reincorporated? Restored? Susan Griffin recognizes, as Hass also seems to do in these poems, that such a "return" is anything but simple or assured. Retrieving the lost parts of ourselves, the sense of "the *eros* at the heart of becoming," involves a long, difficult struggle, a willingness to probe the gaps and rifts as well as the possible avenues of return. In the terms in which these questions are posed in Hass's poem, this means facing up to and giving careful attention to the effects of a mother's alcoholism and emotional instability upon a child's own emerging feeling for the world. It also means describing the particular shape and texture of his displacement, and struggling to situate the most particular and personal experiences of displacement and loss within a larger, more inclusive frame.

In the poem, "My Mother's Nipples," Hass describes a boy coming home from school one day, finding his mother missing, and going to the park to look for her.

> She had passed out under an orange tree, curled up. Her face, flushed, eyelids swollen, was a ruin. Though I needed urgently to know whatever was in it, I could hardly bear to look. When I couldn't wake her, I decided to sit with her until she woke up. I must have been ten years old: I suppose I wanted for us to look like a son and mother who had been picnicking, like a mother who had fallen asleep in the warm light and scent of orange blossoms and a boy who was sitting beside her daydreaming, not thinking about anything in particular.[64]

It is difficult to imagine a deeper, more painful, more pervasive displacement than this. It is utterly personal, and yet encompasses the young boy's entire cosmos that in this very moment is being rent from end to end. He himself is divided. He cannot bear to look. But he cannot look away—even though he is afraid to look, has always been afraid: "Mothers in the nineteen forties didn't nurse./I never saw her naked. Oh! yes, I did,/once, but I can't remember. I remember/not wanting to."[65] But now he looks, gazing upon her ruined face, needing urgently to know where she has gone, hoping he might yet get her back. And he looks away, pretending she has fallen asleep, struggling to create a make-believe world less brutal than the one he actually inhabits, trying to find a way to fill the longing created by her absence.

"They're where all displacement begins." One can hardly help from pausing here to consider the force of this assertion. The beginning. Of all displacement. Is it true? An argument can certainly be made for the primordial and fundamental character of the child's passage from the womb into the harsh light of the world; or from his mother's breast into an unsteady and always-fragile autonomy. But this is not really an argument. It is a feeling about the pain of an absence that has never ceased to wound. And about an inchoate knowledge of how far from that tender embrace our lives unfold. It is inevitable, inescapable, necessary. But it damages us. As do the many other losses that separate us from the world. There is an ecology of loss that must be accounted for, which is why as the poet meditates upon this fundamental displacement, he also looks beyond it, or rather to all that is included within it. For there are so many other losses, extensive in their reach but intimate and particular as they enter our experience, all bound mysteriously to this primordial loss. There is, for instance, the gap created by the bulldozing of the upper meadow at Squaw Valley, which the poet remembers as a place: "where horses from the stable, two chestnuts, one white,/grazed in the mist and the scent of wet grass on summer mornings/and moonrise threw the owl's shadow on voles and wood rats."[66] It is all gone now. So are "The people who lived here long before us," whom Hass recalls in the poem, "Dragonflies Mating." They "also loved these high mountain meadows on summer mornings./They made their way up here in easy stages/when heat began to dry the valleys out,/following the berry harvest probably and the pine buds:/climbing and making camp and gathering,/then breaking camp and climbing and making camp and gathering." They are gone too, with hardly a trace of their presence remaining in our collective memory. Nor do we seem to carry much feeling of responsibility for this loss. Which is why, Hass suggests, it is crucial to recall and reckon with another facet of this complex ecology, the historical fact of our incursion onto this continent and our systematic disregard for those whom we encountered here. In California, Hass observes, this included: "The Franciscan priests who brought their faith in God/across the Atlantic," but also: "influenza and syphilis and the coughing disease.// Which is why we settled an almost empty California."[67]

What conflicted, distorted *eros* created this emptiness? Hass does not even attempt an answer. Still the juxtaposition of these images itself suggests a pattern. The silence of that eviscerated California landscape also haunts the meadow destroyed by the bulldozer and the heart of that young boy under the orange tree. The accumulation of loss creates its own pattern.

But these poems are not only about loss. They are also about the longing that stretches across the empty spaces created by loss. They are about the possibility of recovering what has been lost, of rediscovering our capacity for intimacy with the living world. Chicasaw writer Linda Hogan suggests that we remember that part of us that is still "deep and intimate with the world" by "feel." "We experience it," she says, "as a murmur in the night, a longing and restlessness we can't name, a yearning that tugs at us."[68] One senses this longing, this "feel" for the world in the very language Hass uses to describe life unfolding before him. There is this careful recollection of the intricate life of that lost meadow: "So many grasses—/reedgrass, the bentgrass and timothy, little quaking grass,/dogtail, rip-gut brome—the seeds flaring from the stalks/in tight chevrons of green and purple-green/but loosening." Or, in another poem, the recounting of: "rainbow perch/ . . . reeled in gleaming from the cliffs, the black rockbass,/scales like polished carbon, in beds of kelp/ along the coast,"—the sudden memory of which helped pull a friend back from the brink of suicide.[69]

There is such tenderness, delicacy, and precision in this language, a sense that the shimmering beauty of the world always comes to us through particular things. Also a sense that the effort to name and describe these particular things might itself contribute to a healing of the rift that has grown up between us and the natural world. That learning to open ourselves to this porous space where the life of things can be felt as an intimate part of our own embodied lives might prove to be indispensable to our efforts to love and tend to the world.

Increasingly, this means learning to open ourselves in love to places that are damaged and to beings who cling to existence amidst a deepening assault on their habitats. I think often of those salmon from my childhood, the ones whose presence I hardly acknowledged and whose lives meant so little to me then. Also about how long it has taken me to feel my way back into relationship with them. I understand more clearly now than I did then how my own limited imagination contributed to this blindness. And it has made me sensitive to those who have learned to see and feel the world more deeply and fully. In the communities around Redwoods Monastery and the Headwaters Forest in Northern California there is an ongoing effort underway to help revive diminished salmon populations in local rivers and streams. There have been some successes; but there have also been significant set backs, as heavy logging continues to fill fragile streambeds with silt and runoff. Freeman House chronicles some of these efforts in his book *Totem Salmon*. But just as importantly, he also reflects on what it feels like to draw close to such beautiful, mysterious, and increasingly rare beings. What it feels like to allow oneself to be taken up into their lives.

> King salmon and I are together in the water. The basic bone-felt nature of this encounter never changes, even though I have spent parts of a lifetime seeking the meeting and puzzling over its meaning, trying to find for myself the right place in it. It is a *large* experience, and it has never failed to contain these elements, at once separate and combined: empty-minded awe; an uneasiness about my own active role both as a person and as a creature of my species; and a looming existential dread that sometimes attains the physicality of a lump in the throat, a knot in the abdomen, a constriction around the temples.[70]

Together in the water: a *large* experience. Here is a simple, direct evocation of an encompassing, immersive experience. The language House uses is revealing: it is analogous to the terms often used to describe a momentous spiritual experience. It is an "encounter," a "meeting," a "*large* experience," whose immensity evokes in him a deep sense of humility as he struggles to find his "right place in it." It pervades his entire being. Later, at some remove from the immediacy of this experience, he reflects on its meaning: "Each fish brought up from the deep carries with it implications of the Other, the great life of the sea that lies permanently beyond anyone's feeble strivings to control or understand it.... True immersion in a system larger than oneself carries with it exposure to a vast complexity wherein joy and terror are complementary parts."[71]

Who is this Other whom we meet in such moments? Is it the "world" of these luminous beings ("a system larger than oneself...a vast complexity"—a world that will forever elude our understanding and because of this remains fundamentally mysterious and alluring)? The beings themselves? God? An encounter with salmon, or any living species, or the entire fabric of life, invites us to consider all of these possibilities, to open ourselves and respond to the mysterious Other with honesty and imagination and, perhaps, faith. Learning to live with such openness toward the Other, to become immersed in the "vast complexity" of the world is a profoundly erotic, contemplative work, and a fundamental part of our learning to inhabit the world and take responsibility for it.

Immersion, Love, Healing

> The dreams had been terror at loss, at something lost forever; but nothing was lost; all was retained between the sky and earth, and within himself. He had lost nothing. The snow-covered mountain remained...love had outdistanced death. The mountain could not be lost to them, because it was in their bones...nothing was ever lost as long as love remained.[72]
>
> LESLIE MARMON SILKO

> Lean into me.
> The universe
> sings in quiet meditation.[73]
>
> SIMON ORTIZ

The desire to be immersed within an immensity—to become endlessly, hopelessly lost in it, tumbling down, out, into a vast space, born along, carried ever deeper by love—is itself endless. And yet, the dissolving of the boundaries and intimate exchange that are at the very heart of such immersion provoke ambivalent responses in us. We want to be drawn out of ourselves into this larger field, to know ourselves as embracing and embraced by the mysterious Other. But we also fear it, especially the threat of annihilation that we sense is always part of such experience. Who and what will we become when we disappear into the immensity? Do we have the will and the courage to open ourselves to a relinquishment of the self that is, after all, a kind of death? Such questions, long familiar to contemplatives and visionaries, are increasingly surfacing in contemporary discourse about our relationship with the natural world. Can we open ourselves to the life of the other so that the distance that so often separates us from other beings gradually begins to diminish and we come to know and feel ourselves united to and living within the whole? Can the renewed sense of intimacy with other beings that comes from such recognition contribute to a greater capacity to care for them?

Such questions reveal the fundamental importance of the relationship between the simple contemplative gesture of opening oneself to the other and the ethical imperative to care for the other. The Christian contemplative tradition insists that the longing to open oneself to the immensity of the divine mystery can never be separated from the practical work of tending to the life of the community—something that is often expressed as a form of accompaniment. Still, this tradition also affirms that the only way of under-standing one's place within and responsibility for the larger community is through a deep and abiding sense of participation in the mystery of the whole. It is this knowledge of oneself as participating in the life of the Divine, or of the whole intricate web of existence—as fundamentally inseparable from every other living being—that enables one to live on behalf of the whole. The contemplative practice of attending to the desire that draws us out of the nar-row confines of a guarded, fearful self and into a condition of vulnerability and openness to the Other can be costly. But it is also precisely this intense vulnerability that allows the contemplative practice of *eros* to become a heal-ing work, and to contribute something important to the work of reweaving the torn fabric of the world.

One of the most significant contributions the Christian contemplative tradition makes to this healing work is its insight that desire itself must be healed. Or educated. The ascetic practice of attending to, analyzing, and struggling to confront the myriad ways that desire becomes distorted and damaged is oriented toward precisely this healing work. Certainly there are parts of this tradition that are more pessimistic about the prospects and pos-sibility of such healing. But in the work of many Christian contemplatives, we encounter a sustained attempt to understand how we can learn to face and purify the distorted and ambiguous desires that are at the root of so much per-sonal and communal suffering. This is certainly true of the tradition in which Gregory of Nyssa stands. His articulation of how the healing and deepening of desire can help one to move ever deeper into the divine darkness and into an awareness of one's existence as indistinguishable from that immensity is an important reminder of the unifying, healing power of *eros*. In a similar way, the purification of desire known in the earliest monastic tradition as *apatheia* was understood as critical to the possibility of learning to live in that lumi-nous, encompassing awareness of the whole Evagrius called the blue sapphire of the mind. Similarly, one begins to realize that Antony's response of ecstatic love when he first arrives at the inner mountain, and his subsequent immer-sion in the vast emptiness of that desert landscape can only be understood as the outpouring of a soul gradually made whole through the cleansing work of prayer. The hope of being able to relinquish oneself, of being drawn by desire into the immensity of the Divine, is always bound up with the recognition that desire itself must be healed. And that this healing can and must open out onto a larger process of healing that includes everyone and everything.

The language we use to describe both the desire that draws us into an intimate embrace with the Other, and the very character of that Other, is almost endlessly diverse and cannot be contained within neat boundaries. So too with the silence out of which such language arises and into which it endlessly opens. The very richness of such expression and of the ground out of which it arises reminds us of how many different ways there are to imagine and perform the dream of entering into and participating in the life of the whole. And of how many paths there are to the work of reconstituting of the whole. We are coming home to the recognition that for this larger healing to occur, we have to participate in it, allow ourselves to be made whole. Which means allowing ourselves to become vulnerable, open to the Other, willing to relinquish our narrow, confined identities for the sake of entering into something larger, more encompassing, more capacious.

The imaginative work of opening ourselves to mystery of the whole will require risking everything. But the meaning and possible efficacy of such relinquishment cannot always be accounted for or known. Sometimes there is only the gesture of allowing oneself to become vulnerable; and the hope that this gesture will somehow create possibilities for healing within the larger community. I think often in this regard of the courageous vision of healing expressed in Leslie Marmon Silko's novel *Ceremony*. Much of the power of Silko's novel arises from her clear-eyed attention to the immense damage that has been done to the community through our chronic and long-standing refusal to acknowledge the deep reciprocity through which life is sustained. Nothing has been left untouched by this refusal. Everything—individuals, the life of the community, the entire natural world—has been degraded, sometimes beyond all recognition. For the Laguna Pueblo people among whose life and history the novel unfolds, this degradation has taken a very particular form, bound to the larger story of their oppression at the hands of those who overran their ancestral lands. The intense social fragmentation, environmental degradation, and cultural and spiritual alienation that have taken hold in the aftermath of this terrible history reveal the story of the Laguna to be a "limit case"—a place where the very possibility of healing and reintegration feels utterly remote, impossible to imagine. But this is precisely why Silko's effort at imagining it remains so compelling. If healing can happen here, even if it requires an unimaginably painful journey of reintegration, it might be possible to imagine a wider, deeper healing of the whole.

It is not insignificant that this struggle for healing should be embodied in the figure of Tayo, a member of the Laguna Pueblo community in whose life and history the trauma of war, the cumulative force of chronic political and cultural disenfranchisement, and loss of place have become so intensely concentrated. Tayo has become lost to himself, undone by alcohol addiction and by nightmares of loss and destruction so fierce and wild they seem to touch the very bottom of the world. He cannot overcome his afflictions by himself and his efforts to do so are continuously thwarted. The poison of distorted desires—embodied in forces Silko refers to as "witchery"—running though him is too strong. He is drawn toward the very edge of himself in helplessness and despair. It is only here, amidst this dark and painful undoing of his soul, that he finally risks opening himself to the older wisdom embodied in the ceremonies of the Laguna Pueblo traditions. This is the only medicine that is strong enough to heal him.

Everything, we realize, depends on Tayo's healing. His is the story of the broken world, and his longing to rediscover in himself a tenderness and vulnerability toward the world is emblematic of everything we seek in this moment. It matters that he has suffered so much, that he has been so severely reduced, that his need is so great. His story invites us to consider again the damage we have inflicted on the world, our own impaired condition and the possibility for healing that may yet exist. Silko's beautiful evocation of Tayo's struggle and his gradual return to himself can be seen as part of a larger story of a possible return to ourselves and to the world. For Tayo himself, there is a particular moment when everything he seeks for himself, for his people and for the world, becomes clear. Still, he must decide whether he will yield himself to what is unfolding within him, what he senses the world itself is asking of him, or hold back; whether he will seek the security of known boundaries or let himself go across the numinous threshold to be embraced again by "the center."

Black pebbles and the ancient gray cinders the mountain had thrown poked into his backbone. He closed his eyes but did not sleep. He felt cold gusts of wind scattering dry oak leaves in the grass.... He was aware of the center beneath him; it soaked into his body from the ground through the torn skin on his hands, covered with powdery black dirt. The magnetism of the center spread over him smoothly like rainwater down his neck and shoulders; the vacant cool sensation glided over the pain like feather-down wings. It was pulling him back, close to the earth, where the core was cool and silent and mountain stone, and even with the noise and pain in his head he knew how it would be: a returning rather than a separation...lying above the center that pulled him down closer felt more familiar to him than any embrace he could remember; and he was sinking into the elemental arms of mountain silence. Only his skull resisted; and the resistance increased the pain to a shrill whine. He visualized each piece of his own skull, fingering each curve, each hollow, testing its thickness for a final thin membrane worn thin by time and the witchery of dead ash and mushroomed bullets. He searched thin walls, weak sutures of spindle bones above the ear for thresholds. He knew if he left his skull unguarded, if he let himself sleep, it would happen: the resistance would leak out and take with it all barriers, all boundaries; he would seep into the earth and rest with the center, where the voice of the silence was familiar and the density of the dark earth loved him. He could secure the thresholds with molten pain and remain; or he could let go and flow back. It was up to him.[74]

These questions arise from the depth of the imagination and reveal the challenge of reimagining the world and our place within it. Yet, they also live in the body and cannot be engaged fully except through our embodied existence in the actual world. In Tayo's case, this means reckoning not only with the accumulated sense of loss and fragmentation that has made its home in the collective memory of his community and in his own soul, but also with the residual trace-memories of "the center" that grounds all of existence and his own life. In this moment, that mysterious center beckons to him not only through his memory and imagination, but also through the particular place on the earth where he now lies—the black pebbles and gray cinders pressing into his back, the cold gusts of wind buffeting his body, the sound of the scattering dry oak leaves, the torn skin of his hands covered with powdery black dirt. This is where the work of healing, if it is to happen, will take place.

Here one encounters a particular expression of the challenge facing us in this historical moment: whether or not we are able and willing to yield to the immensity of which we are a part. "*Lean into me.*/The universe/sings in quiet meditation." What could be simpler than this? Yet, it seems increasingly clear that this simple gesture of relinquishment requires a depth of vulnerability to which we are afraid to open ourselves. We long to "let go and flow back" to the center of all things. But we also resist this gesture of wild abandon. It is too costly.

Still, it is difficult to know how we can learn again to imagine ourselves as part of the immensity we long for and how we can learn to care for it without risking such relinquishment. There is no assurance that such risk will yield the healing we seek. But without it, without a willingness to open ourselves to the contemplative practice of *eros*, and the deep, reciprocal exchange with the world to which such practice opens us, what possibilities for healing remain? Our language for love, for desire, for longing, has become so debased that it often feels pointless to try to speak of these things at all. Yet, one senses that we have hardly begun the work of reimagining *eros* as a healing force in our lives and in the world. Silko imagines our long-dormant love for the world as powerful enough to overcome the forces of death that continuously threaten to destroy it: "The dreams had been terror at loss, at something lost forever; but nothing was lost; all was retained between the sky and earth, and within himself. He had lost nothing. The snow-covered mountain remained...love had outdistanced death. The mountain could not be lost to them, because it was in their bones...nothing was ever lost as long as love remained."[75] This is an audacious and in some ways incomprehensible vision of the whole grounded and sustained by love. Haven't we seen too much of the power of death—all those destructive forces unleashed by our own distorted desires—to believe this could really be true? Perhaps. But this vision of the whole, and the persistent and varied testimony to the power of love to draw us into and kindle concern for the world, endures. Love endures.

8

Kenosis: *Empty, Emptied*

Now the moment has come when we too must measure
ourselves against silence, against all that, within us, has
spoken, acted and fallen silent for good.[1]

EDMUND JABÈS

He spoke of the broad dryland barrial and the river and
the road and the mountains beyond and the blue sky
over them as entertainments to keep the world at bay,
the true and ageless world. He said that the light of the
world was in men's eyes only for the world itself moved
in eternal darkness and darkness was its true nature and
true condition and that in this darkness it turned with
perfect cohesion in all its parts but that there was naught
there to see. He said that the world was sentient to its
core and secret and black beyond men's imagining and
that its nature did not reside in what could be seen or
not seen.[2]

CORMAC MCCARTHY

I AWAKE EARLY in order to be at the Unterlinden Museum when it opens.
It rained overnight and the streets of Colmar glisten in the morning light. It
is quiet. The museum is nearly empty when I arrive. Slowly, I make my way
through room after room, not paying much attention to what is on the walls. I
am strangely empty of thought, though I feel some anxiety at what lies before
me. I am still not sure what has brought me here or what I am looking or hoping for. But I walk on, until finally I turn the last corner and find myself gazing
down at Grünewald's great altarpiece. I hesitate, uncertain about whether I
want to move closer. It is so dark, so awful, even from this distance. I have
travelled so far to stand in the presence of this painting, and now I am not
sure I can bear it. So I wait, pausing to gather myself in the silence.

I had first seen this altarpiece years earlier in a college art history class. The sight of the gaunt, lifeless Christ, the full weight of his body tearing at the nails in his hands and feet, his flesh torn to shreds by what appeared to be staples, his head hanging limp like a thing hardly attached to his body, had stirred me deeply. I hardly remember anything that was said about the image, its history, its context. But I do remember feeling disturbed, bewildered, and finally appalled at the sight of that broken body. I remember wanting to avert my gaze. I simply had no way of taking in the enormity and profundity of this image. I suspect I already knew that I wanted no part of it. It was too heavy, too sad. It seemed to speak of a world almost completely devoid of hope. So I put it from my mind, as well as I could. But, now, more than twenty-five years later, it had unexpectedly reemerged as an image with which I needed to reckon. In some ways, I felt no more prepared to face this disturbing image now than I had been years earlier. But something had shifted in me. Now I needed to face it.

My mother was dying of cancer. The disease had first appeared several years earlier. On three different occasions, under treatment, it had gone into remission. But it had recently returned and had advanced to the point where further treatment was no longer viable. This knowledge weighed heavily on me that day in Colmar. I knew I would soon be returning home to be with her. But I was full of apprehension about what lay ahead. I was trying to find a way to face what was happening to her, to summon the courage to accompany her in her struggle and, soon enough I knew, her death.

I still carried within me the memory of sitting with my mother at the dinner table the night her hair began to fall out from her first chemotherapy treatment. Brushing her hand along her scalp, a large clump of hair came loose. She sat there for a moment looking at it, as though not quite comprehending what she was seeing. Then she got up and left the room. I remained sitting there with my father, neither of us knowing what to do or say. Her chemotherapy treatment had begun a few weeks earlier. I had understood that once the treatment commenced, she would very soon begin experiencing its effects. But up until that moment, this had been an idea, in the same way the cancer had been an idea. Suddenly, though, here it was before me, her hair, soft and wispy, resting in her hand. Here was an undeniable and unambiguous sign of the reality and power of the disease with which she was struggling. I knew I should pay careful attention to this. Yet in that moment I was seized by a perverse impulse to look away, to put what I had seen far from my mind. I was like a small child who believes that covering his eyes will make him invisible to the adults in the room. Maybe if I imagined it gone, this terrible thing would simply disappear. What foolishness. Yet, fear has that kind of power. In that moment, it had me by the throat. My mother was sick and would likely die from that sickness and there was nothing I could do about it. I was afraid to look at her. I did not want to acknowledge the reality of her sickness. It was too painful. But neither did I want to turn my gaze away. In that moment, when the truth of my mother's disease became palpable, when the depth of her fragility and vulnerability became so plain to me, I found myself wanting to look at her carefully, tenderly, honestly, to stand with her and accompany her in her struggle. Still, I could not entirely overcome the impulse I felt to look away, to deny what was happening to her. I was not sure I could bear the weight of it.

It is painful for me even now to acknowledge how much my own anxiety and fear weighed on me during that time, and how ashamed I felt at my seeming inability to accompany my mother in a simple, honest way. But her impending death, and my feelings of helplessness in the face of the capricious, malevolent disease that was killing her, were too potent, too painful for me to take in. They threatened to eclipse everything I had ever known of my life. So I shut them out. Or tried to. But I could not do it. I knew I was being invited to accompany her—in the whole, painful, ambiguous reality of her experience. Learning to do so, I was gradually coming to realize, would mean letting go of my own sense of what that experience meant—or even that it meant anything at all—and descending with her into the place of emptiness and unknowing through which she was now travelling.

It was this realization more than anything else, I think, that helped draw me again to the Isenheim Altarpiece. It also opened me to an encounter with a dimension of contemplative practice that had until then mostly eluded me: the practice of facing and learning to stand within the most abysmal suffering, including the apparent loss of meaning and hope that so often accompanies that suffering. It was the discovery of the figure of St. Antony of Egypt embedded within the Isenheim Altarpiece—mercilessly attacked and nearly torn asunder by demons—that really brought this home for me. Here, I saw, was a powerful image of that most difficult and painful dimension of contemplative experience, known in the tradition by many different names: the dark night, the desert, the abyss, the void, emptiness, impasse. I knew well enough how important this part of contemplative experience was to the mysterious process of purgation and renewal in the lives of the monks: to enter the desert meant letting go of everything, allowing oneself to become completely undone. Still, I had not fully reckoned with the depths to which the one called into this empty place often had to descend. I had always attended carefully to the hope of transformation that accompanies the descent into the desert, to the sense that one is eventually drawn out of the place of emptiness to an awareness of the world's luminous beauty and one's life in God. But I had given less attention to the contemplative tradition's acute recognition that for the person caught in such a place, the experience can be utterly opaque, dark, and heavy; and that the possibility of movement and transformation often remains obscured from view, impossible to imagine. In this place, there is only the weight of one's experience, the weight of the world itself, and the struggle to bear that weight.

The betrayal of one's body through the pain of sickness or disease is only one of the many ways we feel such weight bear down upon us. But in its immediacy and force, it is surely one of the most profound. Such experience is of course utterly personal and particular; still, it has a way of touching into and opening out onto the vast, incomprehensible horizon of suffering, loss, and death. Which is perhaps why it is precisely here that the most difficult questions about the trustworthiness of the cosmos—and of God—tend to emerge. Theologically, such questions often arise in response to what is classically referred to as the issue of "theodicy," how evil—one of the names we give to unbearable and inexplicable suffering—can exist in a universe called into being and sustained by an all-loving, all-powerful God. Or in response to the simple, brute fact of death, unrelieved by the hope of transformation or renewal. Such questions should not be conceived of as narrowly theological, as accessible, or meaningful only to those with a particular belief in God. They have a much wider and deeper resonance that arises from the nearly universal sense of betrayal we feel at the sudden failure of the world to work or function or, as we see it from our perspective, to care for us; or from the anxiety we feel about the possibility that the world may ultimately turn out to be inhospitable, unreliable, even hostile to our concerns.

It is tempting to think of such questions as expressions of a skeptical, post-enlightenment, scientific age. In fact, they have always figured importantly within the discourse of the great spiritual traditions of the world. Within the Jewish and Christian spiritual traditions, such questions have tended to find their most forceful expression within wisdom literature, the part of the biblical canon most open to skepticism and doubt about God's providential care for the universe, and most attentive to the beauty and mystery of the cosmos. Here, as well as in the subsequent contemplative traditions that have also reflected deeply upon these mysteries, one encounters an ancient and enduring concern about what it is to exist in a living world, what that existence means, and what kind of response to the world is possible for us in light of the seemingly boundless convergence of beauty and cruelty that meets us at every turn. Such concern is not, strictly speaking, ecological in the sense that we have come to understand that term today. But to the extent that attention to this concern invites a serious reckoning with the nature and character of the cosmos in which we find ourselves living, it can complement and give meaning to those more fundamentally ecological questions regarding our relationship with the living systems through which the world itself is sustained. And the contemplative traditions that have created space for attending to this concern have a particularly important contribution to make to our common effort to locate ourselves meaningfully within the living world: their habit of careful, sustained attention to the utter ambiguity of embodied existence, to the ephemeral character of things, and especially to the fact of death.

Attention to mortality has always figured importantly in traditions of contemplative practice, usually as a means of deepening and expanding one's awareness of the simple, precious reality of existence in the present moment. I have noted earlier the importance of the practice of *memento mori* for the early Christian monks: only by bearing in mind the day of one's death can one hope to live with full awareness of the present moment, to notice one's life and the life around one. But there is more to it than this. There is also the call to attend to the reality of death itself, to descend into the mystery of death. Is such a gesture possible? Meaningful? It is difficult to know for certain. But traditions of contemplative thought and practice can, I believe, help us face these questions, especially the question of what it means to face the empty, broken places of experience where all sense of meaning evaporates and one is left naked and alone and vulnerable. As happens, for example, when one gazes upon or looks out onto the world from a fragile, broken body. Or when one begins to become aware of the fractured character of the world itself. One of the distinctive contributions of the Christian contemplative tradition is found precisely in its commitment to enter into the places of the greatest vulnerability and fragility, to dwell there, and to see them as places of particular, if also mysterious, value.

Nowhere is this idea more powerfully expressed than in the idea of *kenosis* or self-emptying. In Christianity this idea is understood as manifested principally in God's radical gesture of *kenosis* (the relinquishment of divinity) in becoming human in Christ (Phil 2:5–11). But in terms of the questions being raised in this book, this gesture of self-emptying can be seen as having wider meaning, leading to an understanding of what it might mean to become so small, to enter so deeply into the fragile places of existence that the very life of the world seems to have receded beyond the point where we can see or feel or imagine it. Simone Weil names this abyss affliction (*malheur*) and suggests that we are called not to flee from it but to embrace it and learn to dwell within it. In this way, the affliction of others, and of the world itself becomes our own; we do not observe it from afar, but participate in it. This emptiness, this dark place, this desert—utterly desolate and seemingly bereft of hope— becomes a kind of home, a place in which to dwell and apprehend the mystery of the world.

Affliction

The great enigma of human life is not suffering but affliction.[3]

SIMONE WEIL

Three images converge in my imagination: Grünewald's awful, broken Christ; Antony alone in the crucible of the desert; and Job, lost in his affliction. Nor can I easily separate these images from the poor, shrinking figure of my mother, diminished and diminishing under the force of her disease, or from the looming presence at the edge of my awareness of the fraying fabric of the world. They have become necessary to me in the work of attending to and standing within the immensity of loss that washes over the world continuously. Not in order to resolve it, but simply to face it, to learn somehow how to bear it. Grünewald himself saw and felt the connection between the crucified Christ, emptied out and forsaken, and the figure of Antony groaning under the assault of the demons. And these two forlorn figures were themselves bound intimately to others, especially those hollowed-out victims of the disease known as St. Antony's Fire. They were the principal inhabitants of the hospital at Isenheim and it was for their sake that the altarpiece was originally commissioned by the Anthonite order; precious few of them left the hospital alive. As for Job, one need not look long at Grünewald's work or meditate on Antony's story to feel his broken presence. Indeed, his story stands at the origin of almost all subsequent attempts to confront the apparently patternless character of the cosmos.

What does it mean to descend into the abyss, to dwell in emptiness and unknowing? What does it mean for the person seeking to live in the world with meaning and hope to reckon honestly with such experience? What kind of response is possible when existence and the cosmos seem to have become bereft of both meaning and hope? Attention to these questions have long formed a central part of both the Jewish and Christian spiritual traditions. In the Hebrew scriptures, such questions surface most sharply in Wisdom literature, where nature and the cosmos are often experienced as radically ambiguous and where the hope of God's benevolent presence in the world is anything but assured.[4] It is a relentlessly honest literature that gives particular attention to the need to stand in and face one's experience, however harsh and unyielding it may be, and to prescind from forcing such experience into preexisting categories of divine justice. In the Christian tradition, one encounters such questions already in the New Testament, especially in those places where the Gospel message of hope and renewal confronts the abysmal and seemingly intractable realities of disease, despair and death. The subsequent contemplative tradition took this struggle deeply to heart, in its insistent affirmation of the fundamental goodness of the material world and its belief in the possibility of renewal and transformation, but also in its awareness of and attention to the fragility and dark terror of existence and the profound uncertainty that always haunts those who seek such renewal.[5]

In its careful attention to *experience* and its commitment to stand within it, no matter how anomalous or difficult the experience may be, the Christian contemplative tradition stands firmly within this older wisdom tradition; and it also bears a striking resemblance to the way Czeslaw Milosz understands the work of poetry, which he describes in one place simply as "a passionate pursuit of the Real."[6] Milosz shares with many contemporary writers the sense that poetry has a moral obligation to hew as closely as possible to the very grain of existence—to those places in our experience where the simple beauty shines forth and to those places where the brutal force of nature and history threatens to undo or destroy us. Attending to this ambiguous reality, he argues, will almost inevitably compel us to grapple with the question of God's justice or, as it is sometimes framed, the question of evil. These are old questions, and their contemporary expressions echo with the same numbing pain and anxiety found in the Book of Job. The questions arise in different ways. But the central question is surprisingly consistent: when we look out onto the natural world or into our own bodies and find there a reality that is ambiguous, shifting, and possibly even hostile to our own hopes, what kind of response is possible? Is there any discernible pattern to be found in such a world? To consider the acuteness with which such questions emerge in the traditions of contemplative thought and practice and within contemporary discourse is to be brought close to the texture and feeling of heaviness that so often marks the human experience of the natural world. It is also to find oneself invited to participate in the struggle of making sense of such experience and to consider again one of the oldest and primordial spiritual questions: can we behold and take in the whole of our experience of the world?

The root of this question, certainly among the traditions that have shaped the Western imagination, is found in the Book of Job. Nowhere are the questions concerning the ambiguous character of embodied existence, the trustworthiness of the world, and of God's possible absence from our experience expressed as starkly and honestly as they are here. Yet Job's bewilderment, terror, and sense of affliction have often been obscured from view. In part this is due to his longstanding reputation for patience, for the ability to endure every kind of calamity and still keep faith in God. But it is also due to the literary structure of the book. The prologue provides us with an explanation of his plight that Job himself never receives—God has entered into a contest with the Accuser to see how deep Job's faithfulness actually runs. Job's immense and incomprehensible suffering—the loss of all his possessions, the death of his children, the wretched and debilitating illness that comes over him—all of this is accounted for in the prologue as part of an elaborate test. It is given an explanation, a particular meaning. And the Job we meet in the prologue accepts his plight. Without understanding what has befallen him, he accepts that his fortunes have now changed. He actually blesses God.

Yet the serene, accepting Job of the prologue is not the same person we meet in the long, tumultuous body of the book. Here is a person who knows one thing only: he has been stripped of everything and left to die. No explanation has been given nor, one suspects, could any explanation ever suffice. The cosmos has become a dark, tangled place, absent of meaning or purpose. Job finds himself plunged into a deep, aching silence: Finally, though, he speaks. Or rather he howls. This is how Stephen Mitchell's magnificent translation renders Job's initial response to his plight:

> God damn the day I was born
>   And the night that forced me from the womb.
> On that day—let there be darkness;
>   Let it never have been created;
>   Let it sink back into the void.
> Let chaos overpower it;
>   Let black clouds overwhelm it;
>   Let the sun be plucked from its sky.

Here we encounter not the patient, longsuffering Job, but a person so lost in grief at what has befallen him that he wishes his life, the very life of the cosmos would cease to exist. But this is more than a mere wish; it is a curse. In ancient Jewish thought such language was potent and dangerous; the curse was a form of speech charged with power to work for its own fulfillment. Once uttered, it passed beyond the power of the one uttering it and went forth to do its evil work. Here Job wishes for the unthinkable: that the day of his birth would somehow be undone. If that day remains, if it is allowed to stand and be recreated every year, then his existence will continue until death. But if somehow the memory of that day can be extinguished, if every trace of his ever having existed can be erased, then his present agony will disappear. Because *he* will disappear.

Job wants the day of his birth returned to the primordial chaos. He wants to become totally nonexistent. But he seems in fact to want even more than this: he wants the cosmic order itself to be returned to the primordial chaos. He wants the world never to have existed.

> On that night—let no child be born,
> No mother cry out with joy.
> Let sorcerers wake the Serpent
> To blast it with eternal blight.
> Let its last stars be extinguished;
> Let it wait in terror for the daylight;
> Let its dawn never arrive.
> For it did not shut the womb's doors
> To shelter me from this sorrow.[7]

What kind of agony lay beneath such a protest? Philippe Nemo, in *Job and the Excess of Evil*, argues that at its root is a very particular kind of suffering, one that is not reducible to any other kind and is the progenitor of them all: anxiety.[8] One hears the language of anxiety and dread everywhere in the book of Job. "In the anguish of my spirit I must speak" (7:11) Job says. And: "No longer make me cower from your terror" (13:21). And still later: "I am full of fear before him, and the more I think, the greater grows my dread of him" (23:15). This anxiety, suggests Nemo, arises from a very specific scenario: "the long approach of death." Initially the whole of humanity is drawn into this scenario; then Job the individual man is drawn in; ultimately the cosmos itself.

The human being, says Job, passes away like a plant: "He blossoms and he withers, like a flower" (14:2). Human life is insubstantial, "a leaf chased by the wind" (13:25). It is "fleeting as a shadow, transient" (14:2). This sense of human existence as something that suffers what Nemo calls "a vegetal evanescence" is pervasive and inescapable in the Book of Job. But what gives this universal sense of dismay at the brevity of life its purchase on our imagination is what Nemo describes as Job's acute and utterly personal "experience of enfeeblement, aging, deterioration, of pain in the flesh." At the heart of this experience and at the heart of Job's anxiety, suggests Nemo, is:

> the idea of a "never-again-as-before" that throws light—or perhaps a new shadow on existence.... Because the end is henceforth *envisaged,* it is already *present,* even if it is far off in the future. What characterizes the subjective situation here is the impossibility of *forgetting* a truth that, although it has always been true, emerges only now from a sleep wherein it abides in normal time. From the moment this truth emerges, "normal" time becomes inaccessible time, time of what was before, irreparable and un-restorable time. The impossibility of forgetting the truth is the first characteristic of anxiety.

Memory, once an aid in calling to mind signs of life's goodness, of God's goodness, now becomes an affliction. What one *is* able to remember is life's apparent meaninglessness, its emptiness, its cruelty. These feelings of overwhelming anxiety haunt the questions about the nature of Wisdom and the possibility of finding it that emerge so strongly in the Book of Job.

"Where is wisdom to be found? Where, then, does wisdom come from (Job 28:12,20)?" These questions, part of a Wisdom hymn found at the very heart of the Book of Job, seem at first glance to be innocent, optimistic, even hopeful. It is almost as though the questioner believes an answer to be forthcoming. Yet they arise directly out of Job's devastating experience of suffering and loss and are in fact suffused with dread and anxiety. They come toward the end of the long, painful struggle between Job and his so-called comforters, who have offered every kind of explanation for Job's suffering. But their explanations of his suffering fall miserably short, as all explanations must; they cannot account for or provide a sense of the meaning of what has happened to him. The way of Wisdom, a moral and spiritual path whose course was once well known to all, has now come to be shrouded in darkness. The virtuous are no longer rewarded; indeed they are punished and made to suffer, apparently without reason. The wicked meanwhile go unpunished. The moral shape of the universe appears no longer to hold. To ask about the locus of Wisdom in this context is to express a profound anxiety about the trustworthiness of God and the world. It is to ask not simply where God, or the meaning of one's own experience of the world, are to be found. It is to ask *whether* they can be found. The author of the hymn seems not at all sure that they *can* be discovered: "[Wisdom]" says the writer, "lies outside the knowledge of every living thing" (Job 28:13).

It is difficult to overstate the sense of terror that lies at the heart of that statement. To say that Wisdom is beyond the grasp of human beings is tantamount to declaring that the world is for us a place without pattern or meaning. In religious terms, it also carries the suggestion that God—or at least God's design for human lives—is fundamentally elusive, unknowable. Given the climate of crisis out of which the Book of Job arose—arising as it did from the ashes of the Jewish people's devastating exile to Babylon—such deep pessimism is hardly surprising. But it is disturbing nonetheless. It seems to undermine the promises expressed throughout the Jewish scriptures concerning God's accessibility and presence within human experience, God's faithfulness. Indeed it *does* undermine these promises, or at the very least calls them into question. But in doing so, it offers us something else: a fierce resistance to the kind of certitudes about God and the world that one finds elsewhere in the biblical tradition and that simply cannot be maintained amidst the kind of crushing loss described in the Book of Job. At least not by Job. It also makes clear the kind of intimate and intricate connection that exists between the annihilation of the self and the undoing of the cosmos. And it raises pointed questions, questions that are still very much with us, about what it means to exist in the world in the face of such uncertainty, doubt, and affliction.

Writing in the 1940s, French philosopher Simone Weil made the question of *malheur* (affliction) central to her inquiry into the meaning of suffering in human experience. There is a Jobian fierceness to her meditations on this question and an equally fierce commitment to learn what it might mean to stand within the reality of affliction, to resist the temptation to flee from it or evade it. Her reflections contain valuable insight into the character of the abyss into which human beings sometimes fall and why it matters to pay attention to this experience. In her essay, "The Love of God and Affliction," she makes clear from the outset her sense that affliction has a unique and incomparable character. "In the realm of suffering," she says, "affliction is something apart, specific, and irreducible...."[9] But what is it exactly and what distinguishes it from ordinary suffering? Her sense that affliction "is inseparable from physical suffering and yet quite distinct" reveals what for her is at the very heart of the matter: affliction is embodied, and it is the force of prolonged, embodied suffering and its acute impact on the soul that gives suffering the character of affliction. She is even prepared to argue that suffering that is not bound up with physical pain is "artificial, imaginary, and can be eliminated by a suitable adjustment of the mind." This statement, which might seem to suggest a certain insubstantiality to purely mental or emotional suffering, is in fact oriented primarily toward something else: underlining the particular force of suffering rooted in embodied experience. The existential weight and reach that such experience possesses, its capacity to engulf the person completely is, for Weil, critical and central to understanding this kind of suffering. It is this that leads her to suggest that affliction can be understood as "the uprooting of life, a more or less attenuated equivalent of death, made irresistibly present to the soul by the attack or immediate apprehension of physical pain."[10]

One of the reasons the Book of Job compels our attention in the way it does is precisely because of its unambiguous attention to the embodied character of Job's suffering. Certainly Job suffers from a sense of moral and spiritual disorientation. The classic categories for accounting for his abysmal experience do not apply; they illuminate and clarify nothing. But this mental disorientation cannot be separated from his acute and protracted physical pain. "I am in agony," he declares. "Pain pierces my skin; suffering gnaws my bones ... my innards boil and clamor ... my flesh blackens and peels; all my bones are on fire."[11] Nemo is right, I think, to point to the sense of anxiety to be found throughout the Book of Job. But it is a certain kind of anxiety, acute and far-reaching, born of physical suffering so deep and chronic that it seems to partake of death itself. Here, anxiety is very close to what Weil means by affliction. And it cannot be understood apart from the tearing apart of the body. In fact, one could argue that it cannot be understood at all. Such suffering reaches so far into the person that it feels as if one's very soul were being emptied out. "Affliction makes God appear to be absent for a time," Weil says, "more absent than a dead man, more absent than light in the utter darkness of a cell. A kind of horror submerges the whole soul."[12]

What kind of response can one make to such experience? What meaning, if any, can one draw from it? Or, if there is no meaning to be found in it, is there a way of meeting the experience, and standing in it? These questions are almost impossible to answer; but they are still worth asking and struggling with, not least because of the potential dangers inherent in not doing so. One of the greatest dangers is losing entirely the capacity to live in and respond to a fundamentally ambiguous world. The kind of affliction described in the Book of Job and in Simone Weil's writings is so ubiquitous that one can hardly conceive of existence in the world without it. And yet, what is one to make of this? Is the world itself (at least our experience of it) fundamentally and inherently capricious, even malicious? Or, in spite of everything, is it still possible to affirm the presence of beauty and goodness in the world? Part of what makes the Book of Job so valuable to us even now is its refusal to offer any simple response to such questions. There is affliction. And there is the beautiful, mysterious cosmos. Job encounters and experiences both of them. There is no effort to offer any resolution to what has befallen him (other than that offered by the editor who supplied the epilogue). Nor is it easy to interpret Job's silence at the end, following his astonishing encounter with the Voice from the Whirlwind. Is it acquiescence? Resignation? Or perhaps acceptance? And if it is acceptance, what sort of acceptance is it? Here, again, Simone Weil can help us feel something of the force of what it might mean to accept even such awful affliction, to stand in it and refuse the temptation to flee from it.

> To accept what is bitter. The acceptance must not be reflected back on to the bitterness so as to diminish it, otherwise the acceptance will be proportionately diminished in force and purity, for the thing to be accepted is that which is bitter in so far as it is bitter; it is that and nothing else. We have to say like Ivan Karamozov that nothing can make up for a single tear from a single child, and yet to accept all tears and the nameless horrors which are beyond tears. We have to accept these things, not in so far as they bring compensations with them, but in themselves. We have to accept the fact that they exist simply because they do exist.[13]

The stark, uncompromising character of this statement is unnerving. To accept what is bitter ... in so far as it is bitter. To seek no compensation from such acceptance. To accept the fact that all the "nameless horrors" exist "simply because they exist." This sounds very close to fatalism; but it could not be more different. It is rather, I think, a profound form of engagement, a way of entering into, participating in, the affliction of others that refuses the dubious comforts of distance or of resolutions. It is a form of accompaniment.

Into a Dark and Chilly Valley

> Such words as "God" and "Death" and "Suffering" and
> "Eternity" are best forgotten. We have to become as
> simple and as wordless as the growing corn or the falling
> rain. We must just be.[14]

ETTY HILLESUM

What one of us lives through, each must, so that this, of
which we are part, will know itself.[15]

CAROLYN FORCHÉ

What does such accompaniment look like in practice? For Simone Weil herself, living in exile in England during World War II, it meant participating
to the fullest extent possible in the affliction of all those in France suffering from cold and hunger and sickness amidst the German occupation—a
commitment that almost certainly led to her own early death. But there is
another case I want to consider here, that of Etty Hillesum, a Dutch Jew and
contemporary of Simone Weil's. Her diaries, first published in English in
1983 as *An Interrupted Life,* provide a remarkable commentary on the kind of
inner transformation required to live into such a commitment.[16] The affliction she herself experienced and witnessed was of course shared by Jews all
across Europe during this period, and her account is but one of the many
testimonies to have emerged from the Holocaust. Still, her diaries provide
real insight into the moment-by-moment experience of a person struggling
to face the most severe affliction and learn to stand in it. This was for Etty
Hillesum a critical spiritual task, a form of contemplative practice—not in
the sense of always seeking a spiritual meaning for her experience, for such
meaning too often receded into the shadows. Rather it was about learning
to face and stand in her experience of affliction—to *accept* it—and to stand
with others in their experience. It was also about struggling to maintain a
sense of the whole in the midst of the apparent destruction of everything
and everyone.

In April 1942, Dutch Jews were forced to wear the Star of David and
wholesale deportations began that spring. Hillesum went to work for the
Jewish Council in Amsterdam and in part because of this was not selected for
the earliest deportations. But in August of that year, she volunteered to go to
Westerbork, the transport camp in the eastern part of the Netherlands near
the German border from which Jews were sent to the extermination camps in
Poland. It was from Westerbork that Etty Hillesum herself was transported to
Auschwitz where she was sent to her death on November 30, 1943. Her diaries
from the spring and summer of 1942 are especially important for helping us
feel the extent and depth of Hillesum's struggle to absorb the full force of
what was happening to her and her fellow Jews. And, in light of this shared
affliction, to reimagine her own life in the world. On May 26, she records, in
the form of a prayer, this entry:

It is sometimes hard to take in and comprehend, oh God, what those created in Your likeness do to each other in these disjointed days. But I no longer shut myself away in my room, God, I try to look things straight in the face, even the worst crimes, and to discover the small, naked human being amidst the monstrous wreckage caused by man's senseless deeds. I don't sit here in my peaceful flower-filled room, praising you through your poets and thinkers. That would be too simple, and in any case I am not as unworldly as my friends so kindly think. Every human being has his own reality, I know that, but I am no fanciful visionary, God, no schoolgirl with a "beautiful soul". I try to face up to Your world, God, not to escape from reality into beautiful dreams—though I believe that beautiful dreams can coexist beside the most horrible reality—and I continue to praise Your creation, God, despite everything.[17]

One feels here the immense challenge of what it is to look honestly and carefully at the world, "to look things straight in the face, even the worst crimes." Also how tempting it is to look away, to avert one's gaze. We catch a glimpse here of a significant shift in perspective, amidst the most harrowing circumstances, that will contribute to a radical reorientation of her entire life. There is a profound moral commitment implied here—to stand within and face reality as it exists; a commitment also to refrain from fleeing into the world of dreams and fantasies. But in spite of everything, amidst the undeniable harshness of all that is unfolding, there remains a defiant, even quixotic commitment to affirm the reality and importance of dreams, especially of the beauty of the world. Hillesum's contemplative gaze seeks to hold all of this altogether.

Learning to live within such a vision of reality does not happen all at once, but requires a sustained attention, a deepening apprehension of something that often remains maddeningly beyond one's ability to grasp. One senses in Hillesum's journal entries from the summer of 1942 a growing commitment to see and name things for what they are, as well as a deepening sense of dread at what it will mean for her to do so. On June, 19, 1942, she records this entry: "I am sometimes afraid to call a spade a spade. Because nothing will then be left to the imagination? No, things ought to be called by their proper name. If they can't stand it, then they have no right to be. We try to save so much in life with a vague sort of mysticism. Mysticism must rest on crystal-clear honesty, can only come after things have been stripped down to their naked reality."[18] No vague mysticism (the employment of spiritual language to soften or evade the force of what is unfolding). No evading of the truth. One must call things by their proper names. Engage things in their "naked reality." Stand within them—a mysticism of clear-eyed honesty. Ten days after writing these words, she is given the opportunity to face more fully the truth of what is happening: "The latest news is that all Jews will be transported out of Holland through Drenthe Province and then on to Poland. And the English radio has reported that 700,000 Jews perished last year alone, in Germany and the occupied territories." She registers her own response to these brutal facts, and it is very mixed: "[E]ven if we stay alive we shall carry the wounds with us throughout our lives," she says. "And yet I don't think life is meaningless ... I have already died a thousand deaths in a thousand concentration camps. I know about everything and am no longer appalled by the latest reports. In one way or another I know it all. And yet I find life meaningful and beautiful. From minute to minute." She has already begun her own descent into the hell of the camps; and yet she refuses to succumb to the temptation to despair, at least in this moment. Instead there is her audacious affirmation of life. But less than a week later, on July 3, she writes: "They are out to destroy us completely, we must accept that and go on from there. Today I was filled with terrible despair, and I have to come to terms with that as well."[19]

What can it mean, morally and spiritually, to try to *accept* such bitterness? No one other than the person groaning under the weight of it can possibly answer such a question. And Hillesum herself does not tell us what it means for her, at least not directly. But one does catch glimpses of her attempts to meet and stand within this experience. She acknowledges: "The reality of death has become a definite part of my life; my life has, so to speak, been extended by death, by looking death in the eye and accepting it, by accepting destruction as part of life and no longer wasting my energies on fear of death or the refusal to acknowledge its inevitability."[20] There is no attempt here to give a "greater meaning" to death, to suggest the good that might come after or what might come of sacrificing oneself to it in the present, awful circumstances. Nor does she make any distinction between the simple, reality of human mortality and the mass death being inflicted upon the Jewish people by the Nazis (except perhaps in her allusion to "destruction" as part of life). It is the whole complex reality of death that she confronts here, its inevitability here being both bitter and double-edged: it is her fate as a human being born into this world, and also as a Jew caught in the deadly snare of a brutal genocide. Yet, even here she can say her life has been "extended by death." How and in what way she does not explain; but there is a simple, clear-eyed conviction that her increasingly naked confrontation with death has illuminated her existence, her feeling of what it is to exist in the world.

There is nothing instrumental about this conviction—no sense that her own impending death or the growing number of dead all around her are somehow "good for" something. She refuses to turn this experience into an instrument for anything. Still, the transformation taking place within her is real, and has altered her own capacity to enter into and participate in the wider reality of the world, including the reality of suffering and affliction. Strikingly, it is the fragility of her body that opens her to this sense of participation in a wider whole. "My body is a home for many pains; they lie hidden in every corner with first this one making itself felt and then the next ... then I thought, or rather I didn't really think it, it welled up somewhere inside me: throughout the ages people have been tired and have worn their feet out on God's earth, in the cold and the heat ... I am not alone in my tiredness or sickness or fears, but at one with millions of others from many centuries and it is all part of life."[21] One can hear an echo in this statement of Simone Weil's sense of the embodied character of affliction, of the particular despondency that can take hold of the soul when it is subjected to sustained physical pain. We have no account of Hillesum's experiences at Auschwitz and only a few brief sketches from her time at Westerbork. But even here, in this account from the relative freedom of occupied Amsterdam, one can sense the corrosive effects of the daily humiliations and the increasing deprivations—the body's fragility and the growing loss of hope. Still, there is also an unexpected expansion of soul, a growing awareness of her participation in the larger reality of embodied human suffering. What this means to her she does not say. But one feels the importance, the luminous beauty of her growing awareness of this whole of which she is a part.

The question of how to dwell within that whole, how to continue looking things "straight in the face," how to *accept* the bitterness that has befallen her and her people haunts so many of her diary entries from the summer of 1942. And in spite of her continual affirmation that life "still has meaning"—so necessary to her survival—there is a growing reckoning with the inescapable fact that she is descending into an abyss from which she will never return. On July 6, she writes: "From all sides our destruction creeps up on us and soon the ring will be closed and no one at all will be able to come to our aid. All the little loopholes that are still left will soon be stopped up. Life is so strange: it is cold and wet just now. As if you had suddenly been thrown down from the peaks of a sultry summer night down a steep drop into a dark and chilly valley."[22] It has now become clear: there is no way out of this place, no hope of rescue.

No meaning to be derived from this experience. There is only this dark and chilly valley. Hillesum's refusal to seek any such meaning, or try to make sense of what is happening to her can be understood in different ways; she herself does not try to explain what it feels like to find herself thrown suddenly into this dark and chilly valley. But a few days later, in what can be taken as a comment on this reality and a striking expression of her oft-stated commitment to look reality in the face, she declares: "Such words as 'God' and 'Death' and 'Suffering' and 'Eternity' are best forgotten. We have to become as simple and as wordless as the growing corn or the falling rain. We must just be."[23]

This stark refusal of language—especially language normally used to account for the strongest and deepest elements of human experience—in favor of wordless silence surely reflects the extreme character of the plight in which Hillesum now found herself. But it is an ambiguous silence that shares much in common with the refusal of language that has long characterized apophatic spiritual traditions. These traditions have always been characterized by a fierce commitment to silence, to a deep skepticism toward all linguistic expressions, especially those that claim to say something meaningful about the Divine. Silence allows things to be known and cherished that can never be encompassed in language; which is perhaps why these traditions are returning with such force in late twentieth and early twenty-first centuries. One of the reasons for this, surely, is our growing recognition of how little we can say about certain crucial experiences, how easily language can betray the truth of such experience, and how often we must rely instead on naked silence and emptiness to be the bearers of whatever meaning an experience might hold. This late diary entry, written shortly before Hillesum's departure for Westerbork, reflects her own acute awareness of how far short all language falls, and must fall—even language as precious and necessary as this—from being able to express the immensity of what is unfolding around and within her. Her refusal to name what is happening stands in paradoxical tension with her insistence on naming and facing everything. "Ultimately," she says, "what matters most is to bear the pain, to cope with it and to keep a small corner of one's soul unsullied, come what may."[24]

Hillesum wrote these words near the end of her life, in a moment of profound reckoning with the irrevocable fact of her own descent into death. They bear an uncanny resemblance to Simone Weil's thoughts on affliction. "To accept what is bitter," Weil wrote. "We have to accept these things, not in so far as they bring compensations with them, but in themselves. We have to accept the fact that they exist simply because they do exist." Hillesum's diaries reveal one person's attempt, through immense struggle and doubt, to live into this harsh truth. Still, it is difficult to know what it meant for her in these circumstances to try to "bear the pain" of this reality. Or what it meant for her to try to keep a small corner of her soul "unsullied." Or why this mattered so much, sensing all that was coming and how helpless she was to stop it. But *that* it mattered she does not seem to have questioned. Her commitment to call things by their proper names—to face reality as it presents itself and refuse the comforts of a "vague mysticism"—remains one of the most moving and important dimensions of her contemplative witness. But even when she could no longer do this, when the extent of the horrors overtaking her exceeded her capacity to name or comprehend, silence became a means of meeting and standing in the truth of her affliction.

Still, even amidst the obvious courage of Hillesum's (and Weil's) testimony, questions remain. Why open oneself so fully to affliction? Why allow oneself to be drawn into the very depths of suffering, with so little hope of respite or restitution? To respond that it is unavoidable, that no one can escape affliction, offers only part of an answer. For one must also try to reckon with what it means to turn and *face* affliction—whether unavoidable or not—and to struggle daily to stand within it, both for one's own sake and as a means of participating in and expressing solidarity for the suffering of others. Even when it does no apparent good nor effects any meaningful change. Such an orientation can easily be misconstrued as a kind of fatalism, or defeatism. But understood as a form of contemplative practice, as an expression of a fundamental commitment to face and attend to the Real as it presents itself, it can be seen to have a very different character than this. Rooted in acceptance, in the way that both Weil and Hillesum understand this idea, such contemplative practice becomes a means of standing in and reckoning with the full extent of the embodied suffering visited upon us and the world. Because these things exist. Because acknowledging their existence and opening oneself to them is already a significant and courageous gesture of solidarity. "The capacity to give one's attention to a sufferer," Simone Weil notes, "is a very rare and difficult thing; it is almost a miracle; it *is* a miracle." This is in no small measure because of the radical character of the relinquishment required to give one's attention to another in this way. "The soul empties itself of all its own contents in order to receive into itself the being it is looking at, just as he is in all his truth."[25]

Healing and renewal and hope can issue forth from such contemplative practice; but the practice itself cannot be predicated upon expectation of them. One is called to remain empty, open, alert, always attentive to the presence of the other, particularly the suffering other. Still, there is also the hope that even as one learns to open oneself to affliction, one might succeed in keeping a small corner of the soul unsullied—a place where the light and beauty of the world can continue to live amidst the nameless horrors. We catch a glimpse of such an unsullied place in one of Hillesum's diary entries from March of 1942. It reflects the deep vitality that informs so much of her writing during this period, even as the grim presence of death and destruction are gathering force all around her. It is the simplest of experiences, riding a bicycle to see her lover on a warm spring evening. But it evokes so much. "[A]s I rode dreamily along, over the asphalt of Lairessestraat, looking forward to seeing him, I suddenly felt the caress of the balmy spring air. Yes, I thought, that's how it should be. Why shouldn't one feel an immense, tender ecstasy of love for the spring, or for all humanity.... I well remember a wine-red beech tree from my youth. I had a very special relationship with that tree. At night, filled with a sudden longing, I would bicycle for half-an-hour to reach it, then dance around it, captivated and bewitched by its blood-red look."[26] Emptiness can also yield ecstasy: the tender, felt presence of a wine-red beech tree from one's childhood, the memory of seeking and finding it, of dancing in the darkness around its bewitching beauty. An unexpected consolation amidst affliction that mysteriously radiates out to touch and hold everything.

St. Antony's Fire

Horror could not be painted more ruthlessly.[27]

NIKOLAUS PEVSNER

[The demons'] aim—and here one senses that the fourth
century, when Athanasius wrote, was one of those periods
when the world grows old and an age approaches its
end—is to sow cosmic anxiety and despondency.[28]

GEORG SCHEJA

Hour after hour I drove, through the changing French countryside. Finally, toward evening, I crested a small hill and saw Colmar before me, lovely and still, in the distance. It seemed strange to me to imagine that dark and forbidding image situated amidst such beauty. But by then I had already begun to question whether I really understood what kind of image it was and where its particular beauty lay. Perhaps there was beauty even in that tormented figure.

Was Grünewald's painting beautiful to those who first gazed upon it, especially those suffering from the terrible, painful and often fatal bacterial disease known as St. Antony's Fire? I wonder. This disease had been ravaging Europe for almost five hundred years by the time the altarpiece was commissioned by the Antonite order. When it was completed, it came to stand as part of a hospital complex where victims of the disease were treated. The hospital setting, with its countless suffering souls, helps to account for the distinctive and dark imagery of the altarpiece. This is true not only of its depiction of Christ, but also of its rendering of two other figures who are central to the altarpiece. One of them, appearing on a side panel, is a hideous figure whose flesh is covered with putrid sores; his stomach is distended and his limbs appear about to fall from his body altogether. He is suffering, in all likelihood, from the dreaded disease. The other is St. Antony of Egypt, after whom the Antonites were named, a saint who was believed to have a particular power to secure healing for those suffering from the disease. He is depicted as enduring his own torment, being pummeled, clawed and torn at by a host of gruesome, demonic beings.

The confluence of these three figures—Christ, St. Antony, and the anonymous victim of St. Antony's Fire—in Grünewald's altarpiece creates an almost overwhelming vision of human suffering. Yet the precise meaning of this vision of suffering is not easy to grasp. The resurrection is also represented prominently within the larger tableau of the altarpiece; it is inconceivable that this central Christian image of hope should have been ignored or underplayed. In this sense, one can fit the image of the suffering Christ into the classic Christian paradigm of the paschal mystery: suffering is redemptive; death is a passage through which one must move in the mysterious process leading to rebirth. But the suffering Grunewald depicts in his altarpiece is so deep and intense, the gaunt, bloody, torn figure of Christ is so awful, so grotesque, so *lifeless*, that one hesitates to venture any thought about his possible rebirth. It is difficult to avoid entirely a feeling of uncertainty about whether relief from this suffering is possible at all. More than anything else, one feels here the pure force of death.

In the context in which the altarpiece was first created, it was crucial that neither Christ nor St. Antony be seen as aloof from the suffering and anxiety that marked the lives of those afflicted by the disease. Rather they needed to be seen as empathizing with, even participating in it. A description of the disease from a medieval source helps to show why this must have mattered so much: "The intestines [are] eaten up by the force of St. Antony's Fire, with ravaged limbs, blackened like charcoal; [victims] either die miserably, or they

live more miserably seeing their feet and hands develop gangrene and separate from the rest of the body; and they suffer muscular spasms that deform
them."[29] It is in light of such pathetic, gruesome scenes that Grunewald's altarpiece must be seen.

"Horror could not be painted more ruthlessly."[30] So comments Nikolaus
Pevsner on the Christ figure of the crucifixion. But this comment could
apply equally to Grünewald's rendering of Antony or of the anonymous
figure suffering from the disease who also appears in the painting: all are
plunged into the horror of this debilitating, incurable disease. None of them
emerges unscathed. This is part of the power of the altarpiece. The Christ
of the Isenheim altarpiece, suggests J.K. Huysmans, "personifies...the religious piety of the sick and poor...[and] would seem to have been made in the
image of the [victims of the disease] who prayed to him; they must surely have
found consolation in the thought that this God they invoked had suffered the
same torment as themselves, and had become flesh in a form as repulsive as
their own; and they must have felt less forsaken, less contemptible."[31] This is
a beautiful idea and may well reflect something of what victims of the disease
felt as they gazed upon the images of the altarpiece. But in fact we do not
really know what they felt about their condition, any more than we can ever
know what another human being afflicted by suffering feels. Still, gazing at
this magnificent altarpiece, one senses its insistent question, a question whose
disturbing force we still feel five hundred years later: is it possible to look into
the darkest places of affliction and find hope there?

The Christian spiritual tradition has always responded to this question,
at least in its formal dogmatic and liturgical formulations, with an unequiv-
ocal affirmation: the resurrection of Christ represents a total and ultimate
triumph over death. In the ancient prayer of Melito of Sardis one senses the
force and meaning of this affirmation for believers: "The Lord has risen from
among the dead,/and Death itself He crushed with valiant foot./Behold the
cruel tyrant bound and chained, And [all] made free by Him who rose!"
Without this hope, Christianity is unrecognizable. Still, the iconographic
tradition presents us with images of the death of Christ that are so stark, so
bleak and uncompromising that it is difficult to avoid the sense that one is
being asked to attend to the pure force of death on its own terms, without
recourse to the hope of the resurrection—at least not as an "answer" to the
"problem" of death. Instead there is a kind of descent into death itself. Much
of the enduring value of these representations, not only Grünewald's altarpiece, but also Andrea Mantegna's "Lamentation of Dead Christ" and Hans
Holbein the Younger's "The Body of Dead Christ in the Tomb," lay precisely

in their insistence on gazing into the dark reality of death. To confront these images, to gaze upon them is to find oneself drawn into an encounter with death so intimate, so harsh, and so unrelenting that the possibility of hope becomes muted, if not altogether absent. In part because it becomes nearly impossible to imagine an end to death. It threatens to engulf everything.

It was this very fear, or something close to it, that seems to have provoked Fyodor Dostoevsky's remarkable response to Hans Holbein's "The Body of Dead Christ in the Tomb" in his novel *The Idiot*. Dostoevsky himself had seen the painting in Basel during a trip to Europe in 1867; from accounts left by his wife Anna, it is clear that his encounter with the painting had a profound impact upon him. In the novel, it is Prince Myshkin who first gives voice to this: upon seeing a copy of the painting in Rogozhin's apartment, the Prince recalls a trip he had taken some years earlier when he had seen the original. He declares to Rogozhin, "Why, that picture might make some people lose their faith."[32] This is a strange response to a painting that can be and often has been understood very differently and more hopefully.[33] Still, Dostoevsky captures something fundamental about Holbein's bleak portrait of Christ's dead body: it is difficult to think of another image in the history of Western art that conveys so uncompromising and potent a vision of Christ's death, and of death itself. It feels, as Julia Kristeva has noted, "inaccessible, distant, and without a beyond."[34] For Dostoevsky, who was so preoccupied with what he perceived to be the relentless force of death then manifesting itself in an increasingly secularized and nihilistic Europe and Russia, the painting evoked something terrifying: an end with no hope of renewal of transformation. Here one feels the utter finality of death, that well of darkness from which no one emerges.

It is the character Ippolit, one of Dostoevsky's "underground men," who expresses the full weight of this idea, and who senses its potential impact on the soul. Considering the figure in the tomb, Ippolit declares:

It is in every detail the corpse of a man who has endured infinite agony before the crucifixion; who has been wounded, tortured, beaten by the guards and the people when He carried the cross on His back and fell beneath its weight, and after that has undergone the agony of crucifixion, lasting for six hours at least (according to my counting)… it is simply nature, and the corpse of a man, whoever he might be, must really look like that after such suffering. I know that the Christian Church laid it down, even in the early ages, that Christ's suffering was not symbolical but actual, and that His body was therefore fully and completely subject to the laws of nature on the cross. In the picture the face is fearfully crushed by blows, swollen, covered with fearful, swollen and blood-stained bruises, the eyes are open and squinting: the great wide-open whites of the eyes glitter with a sort of deathly, glassy light.... The question instinctively arises: if death is so awful and the laws of nature so mighty, how can they be overcome? How can they be overcome when even He did not conquer them? He who vanquished nature in his lifetime, who exclaimed, "Maiden, arise!" and the maiden arose—"Lazarus, come forth!"[35]

Here, as he will do again in *The Brothers Karamozov,* Dostoevsky pushes the question of faith to its most extreme expression. If Christianity is to mean anything, it must somehow be capable of absorbing and responding to the full weight of this reality. Not the idea of death. Or death as a temporary antechamber. But its full, awful finality. Still, as we encounter Holbein's painting in *The Idiot*, it reveals and invites a reckoning not only with the stark fact of Christ's death, but also with what Ippolit describes as the mighty "laws of nature."

Looking at such a picture, one conceives of nature in the shape of an immense, merciless, dumb beast, or more correctly, much more correctly, speaking, though it sounds strange, in the form of a huge machine of the most modern construction which, dull and insensible, has aimlessly clutched, crushed and swallowed up a whole earth, which was created perhaps solely for the sake of the advent of that Being. This picture expresses and unconsciously suggests to one the conception of such a dark, insolent, unreasoning and eternal Power to which everything is in subjection.[36]

This image torments Ippolit and leaves him living a kind of waking nightmare in which he himself is continuously threatened with annihilation from this dumb beast. In Dostoevsky's novel, it evokes a sense of reality that seemed to him to be growing increasingly prevalent in the late nineteenth century: the world as mechanized, soulless, and empty of meaning.

This was not, of course, Dostoevsky's final word on this subject. But the unflinching honesty with which he represents Holbein's painting, and his articulation of the devastating effects that such a serious reckoning with death can have upon the soul, remains a singular contribution to our efforts to understand what it means to gaze upon and stand within affliction. As an imaginative act, his reflections can be seen as a significant gesture of empathy for souls who have descended into the very abyss of fear, who feel intensely the threat of the dumb beast of death. Dostoevsky makes it clear here and elsewhere that he believes it is possible to live without being consumed by this fear. Still, he never wavers from his conviction of the need to attend honestly and carefully to that fear, and from his sense that any meaningful affirmation of life and hope can only emerge from a serious reckoning with the abyss of death. Here the abyss becomes identified, as it was for many during this period and would continue to be into the twentieth and twenty-first centuries, with nature itself. Not the luminous, healing beauty of the night sky or of the earth to which Alyosha so fully opens himself in *The Brothers Karamazov*, but "a dark, insolent, unreasoning and eternal Power to which everything is in subjection." The image of that poor, lonely figure in Holbein's painting evokes and captures the force and terror of this fearful Power—which perhaps helps to account for why Dostoevsky and his characters find themselves so conflicted about how to respond to it. Can one gaze upon this image without feeling the presence of that awful Power and its threat of annihilation? But is it really possible to look away, to avoid the challenge of this gaze?

Considering these questions can help one begin to understand the significance of *kenosis* as a contemplative practice, especially within the context of our efforts to learn how to stand within and reckon with the deeply ambiguous character of the natural world. The sense of existential dread before "the dark, insolent, unreasoning Power" that Dostoevsky identified so closely with nature itself has continued to surface in Western literature and art. Yet, it remains maddeningly difficult to describe what it is that lay at the source of this dread or to distinguish it in any simple way from the equally insistent feeling for life that so often accompanies such dread. Rilke notes this in a letter written to Lotte Hepner in 1915 concerning Tolstoy's long struggle with these questions.

> Tolstoy's enormous experience of Nature (I know hardly anyone who had so passionately entered inside Nature) made him astonishingly able to think and write out of a sense of the whole, out of a feeling for life which was permeated by the finest particles of death, a sense that death was contained everywhere in life, like a peculiar spice in life's powerful flavor. But that was precisely why this man could be so deeply, so frantically terrified when he realized that somewhere there was pure death, the bottle full of death or the hideous cup with the handle broken off and the meaningless inscription "Faith, love, hope," out of which people were forced to drink a bitterness of undiluted death.[37]

Pure, undiluted death. One senses here something akin to Holbein's rendering of Christ Dead in the Tomb, or Grünewald's stark crucifixion, or Dostoevsky's dumb beast. Terror before this brute reality overwhelms everything. Nor is it easy to say how faith, or in Tolstoy's case a "sense of the whole," can stand in the face of such bitterness. Yet somehow it does. To say that death is "contained everywhere in life, like a peculiar spice in life's powerful flavor," as Rilke says of Tolstoy's work, comes perilously close to cliché. Perhaps the only thing keeps it from becoming so is the very honesty with which the terror before death is represented here. This honesty in the face of the Real, or what Milosz calls "the passionate pursuit of the Real," comprises a critical part of the practice of *kenosis*. Still, Rilke's observation leaves unanswered the question of how much reality we can bear; or what it might mean in the face of such an honest, uncompromising reckoning with death to maintain a sense of the whole, or a feeling for life.

Seeking to address these questions for ourselves will require thinking carefully about what kind of attention we are capable of giving the anomalous, ambiguous force of reality in our own historical moment. Not only personal feelings of terror in the face of death, but also unchecked disease, historical genocide, and the death of nature. Can honest attention to these painful realities make any difference, contribute to any lasting change? And even if one cannot be certain that it does, is there still value in such contemplative practice?

In response to these questions, I want to return to Grünewald's Isenheim Altarpiece and to the witness of St. Antony and the early monks. In particular, I want to consider the significance of the simple gesture of entering into and attending to the most severe and abysmal suffering that one encounters in both the altarpiece and in the monastic tradition. Not as a substitute for serious, ethical engagement with such suffering but as an exercise for opening up a space where one's awareness of its weight and significance can be deepened. Consider, for example, the account of Grünewald's Altarpiece found in W. G. Sebald's *The Emigrants*. Here, in one of his many penetrating explorations into the kind of existence that is still possible for us in the aftermath of the Holocaust, Sebald's narrator reflects on his own encounter with the Isenheim Altarpiece:

The extreme vision of that strange man, which was lodged in every detail, distorted every limb, and infected the colours like an illness, was one I had always felt in tune with, and now I found my feeling confirmed by the direct encounter. The monstrosity of that suffering, which, emanating from the figures depicted, spread to cover the whole of Nature, only to flood back from the lifeless landscape to the humans marked by death, rose and ebbed within me like a tide. Looking at those gashed bodies and at the witnesses of the execution, doubled up by grief like snapped reeds, I gradually understood that, beyond a certain point, pain blots out the one thing that is essential to its being experienced—consciousness—and so perhaps extinguishes itself; we know very little about this. What is certain, though, is that mental suffering is effectively without end. One may think one has reached the very limit, but there are always more torments to come. One plunges from one abyss into the next.[38]

One's response to this extreme and pessimistic reading of Grünewald's Altarpiece will depend in no small measure on one's feeling for the ground out of which it arises—the immensity of suffering and death that eclipsed the lives of untold millions of human beings during the Holocaust. This is the long shadow that hangs over all of Sebald's work, and one senses its presence here in the narrator's sympathetic response to Grunewald's crucifixion. The narrator's feeling of relief at his direct encounter with Grunewald's work seems strange, especially given how deeply it opens him to the reality of suffering. But it *confirms* something in him—an inchoate feeling that he had long carried within him about the crushing weight of such suffering. It enables him to acknowledge it, and stand more fully in the mystery of it, even as its meaning remains elusive, incomprehensible.

At the heart of this aesthetic intuition is the growing awareness that such suffering is endless. Not only can one never adequately express it in language, but neither can one determine any precise boundaries: "The monstrosity of that suffering, which, emanating from the figures depicted, spread to cover the whole of Nature, only to flood back from the lifeless landscape." The whole of nature. Here, one begins to feel the true power of these artistic representations: nothing escapes the reach of such suffering. Everything is engulfed, distorted, destroyed by it. The broken body holds and draws to itself every other broken thing, which empowers the image still further. "There are always more torments to come." We know this catalogue of torments; and we recognize the immense difficulty of facing up to it. The narrator risks such a gaze. In doing so he descends, if only for a moment, into the dark space occupied by all those suffering souls.

The power of many of these images derives in no small part from their close imaginative relationship to actual executions and rituals of punishment.[39] It is

not only our own violence-stunned time that leads us to respond to the painting so forcefully; it is all the blood and violence that lay behind these works.
At Isenheim, there were all those suffering from St. Antony's Fire; but there
were also countless other souls, mostly nameless, including all those hauled to
the scaffolds and subjected to long, painful deaths. Sebald's narrator in *The
Emigrants* seems to feel all of this intuitively as he gazes at the torn body of
Grünewald's Christ. But there is even more that is amiss, much more. In his
work *After Nature*, Sebald considers the question of what this image tells us
about the character of the world itself.

> The panic-stricken
> kink in the neck to be seen
> in all of Grünewald's subjects,
> exposing the throat and often turning
> the face towards a blinding light,
> is the extreme response of our bodies
> to the absence of balance in nature
> which blindly makes one experiment after another
> and like a senseless botcher
> undoes the thing it has only just achieved.[40]

One hears echoes here of Dostoevsky's "dark, insolent, unreasoning and eternal Power." And of Job's unknowable and, possibly, malevolent Wisdom.
The universe cannot be found out. And it is, in any case, set against us. The
"absence of balance in nature" is written on the broken bodies of the afflicted.
It is senseless. Because of it the world is continuously unmade.

One recoils against such a relentlessly pessimistic reading of our embodied
condition and of the cosmos itself. But in truth there is no argument that can
entirely refute this vision of existence. It is an intuition born of long, fierce
attention to the reality of affliction. And if it does not reflect the whole of
reality, it reveals a baffling, ambiguous dimension of reality that seems to run
through almost everything. But what to call it? Death? Nature? The ephemeral character of everything that exists? And how can one situate it in relation
to the equally powerful intuition that the world is, was, and always will be
endlessly beautiful and grace-filled, that somehow existence matters and has
meaning? Such questions lead one almost inevitably to a place of humility,
even silence: the mystery to which they point is unfathomable. Still, they call
for our attention. And it is here that contemplative traditions can be so helpful. Their fundamental commitment to the work of noticing, describing, and

standing within experience allows everything, however ambiguous or painful, to be held, for its own sake. There is a consistent trajectory of hope here, a sense that affliction and death are not the final words. But there is also a remarkable willingness to face affliction, to stand in it and seek to understand what it is and what it has to teach.

Grünewald discovered and gave expression to a dark, wounded, all-but-defeated Christ who has been plunged into the most abysmal human suffering. The portrait of Antony that emerges in the Isenheim altarpiece reflects and embodies this awful struggle. This saint is not so much a heroic as a sympathetic figure, intimately connected both to the crucified Christ and to the lonely, anonymous figure suffering from the terrible fire. Grünewald's depiction of Antony's descent into that fire and his willingness to stand with the victims of that awful disease, says something important about the contemplative act of *kenosis*. And it is consistent with what we know from the earliest traditions of Christian contemplative practice. There, one witnesses the monk struggling, often amidst loneliness and near-despair, with the temptation to give up hope; also with the temptation to flee to a place of safety, where he can avoid facing his own and the world's emptiness and affliction. But the question always arises: is this really possible? Is there anywhere to go?

If one considers the testimony of the early monastic literature concerning Antony's experience, it becomes clear how familiar he was with this sense of emptiness and what it meant to struggle with it. Knowing this helps to account for Antony's significance in Grünewald's Altarpiece and for the pathos of the Altarpiece as a whole. Athanasius, for his own theological and ecclesial reasons, insists on the ultimate triumph of his ascetic hero.[41] But not without giving us glimpses of the profound uncertainty and anxiety Antony experiences in the face of the assaults of the demons. The range and subtlety of the assaults—confronting the ascetic where he is most uncertain and insecure at any given moment (around concerns about family, money, food, sexuality, and the threat of death)—suggest the depth at which they took hold within Antony's psyche. But beneath or within these particular temptations lay something even more disturbing—the sense of being subjected to suffering so painful that one is brought to the very limits of one's capacity to describe or explain it. There is a telling moment in the *Life of Antony* when one catches a glimpse of the kind of anxiety and pain that were woven deep into the ascetic's experience. It is just after Antony has moved to the tombs seeking greater solitude. Athanasius relates that "... approaching one night with a multitude of demons [the enemy] whipped [Antony] with such force that he lay on the earth, speechless from the tortures. He contended that the pains were so severe as to lead one to say that the blows could not have been delivered by humans, since they caused such agony."[42] One reads this statement with a sure knowledge of what Antony (and Athanasius) means us to grasp: these are demonic assaults. The pain they inflict is far more potent than anything human beings alone are capable of. But this realization only brings us to the threshold of the experience. It does not really help us to understand it or encompass it. It points rather to the unfathomable character of such pain. Neither its origin nor its reach can be described or accounted for, not completely anyway.

At another point, Athanasius tells us that Antony was assaulted with such ferocity that the place where he was dwelling "seemed to be shaken by a quake. The demons, as if breaking through the building's four walls, and seeming to enter through them … struck and wounded" him.[43] The sense of psychological vulnerability in this image is palpable. The ascetic experiences the boundaries of the space he occupies as porous, completely open to the demonic forces. There is no protection, no safe place to dwell, at least not in this moment. He is exposed and fragile. Here, as with the image of Antony lying alone, on the bare earth, unable to speak, we encounter the monk as utterly vulnerable. The outcome of his struggle remains, in this moment at least, uncertain.

This portrayal of vulnerability in the ascetic's experience is consistent with that depicted in the sayings of Antony found in the *Apophthegmata Patrum*. There one sees a monk who displays uncertainty in the face of affliction; who expects temptation to the last breath; who groans at the thought of the "snares that the enemy spreads out over the world"; who seems near despair at the recognition of how difficult it can be for the ascetic to actually change; and who expresses profound anxiety about the reality of death, and grief at the injustice that seems to reign over the world.[44] The feeling of anxiety one encounters in these sayings is cosmic in its dimensions. Certainly, the social and political tensions within which early Christian monasticism took root contributed to this anxiety. But they are not sufficient in themselves to account for its scope and intensity. It was fundamental, elemental. It was the power of death.[45]

Certainly hope was not absent from the experience of the early Christian monks. However, it is clear that anxiety and struggle and pain were abiding elements of their lives, and that this pain was embodied. The image of the monk lying alone and in pain on the bare earth, rendered helpless from the relentless attacks of the demons and uncertain whether help will ever arrive, is crucial to any understanding of early monastic experience. It is this willingness to make oneself vulnerable, to descend into the place of the greatest doubt and uncertainty, perhaps even hopelessness, that enabled Antony and the other early Christian monks to emerge as the bearers of compassion they became.

Matthias Grünewald's depiction of Antony in the Isenheim altarpiece, surrounded and hounded and being torn to pieces by a host of gruesome creatures, reveals a figure who is nothing if not exposed, vulnerable, helpless. And when one places this image, as Grünewald himself did, in proximity to the bruised, pierced, degraded corpse that is Grünewald's crucified Christ, and in the company of all those victims of the disease known as St. Antony's Fire, for whom the altarpiece was commissioned and who suffered the most terrible and painful and debilitating wasting away of their bodies and of their very beings, one begins to get a sense of the compelling power of his witness for those in danger of losing all hope. Like Christ, Antony ultimately triumphs over disease and death and pain, but not before having descended deep into a place of affliction.

"Through fire everything changes," says Gaston Bachelard. "When we want everything to be changed we call on fire."[46] This observation suggests one way of understanding the enduring power of the suffering figures in the Isenheim altarpiece. In the ancient monastic tradition, fire meant ecstasy, purification, judgment—all significant images of transformation. By the time this altarpiece was painted, fire had come to mean affliction, desolation, loss. But here is Antony, together with Christ and the nameless victim of disease, descending into the inferno. The fire that ravaged the bodies and perhaps the very souls of countless victims of that terrible disease also burned in the saint and in the redeemer. Abba Sisoes once said: "If I had one of Antony's thoughts, I should become all aflame." A thousand years later, we see Antony himself aflame, and with him the suffering Christ, joined with all those anonymous souls destined to die an early, painful death. It is a haunting image of solidarity—much of whose power comes from the refusal to evade or look away from the harsh realities of embodied suffering and loss.

The Beauty of the Earth and the Law of Necessity

How to cope with beauty and at the same time with the
mathematical cruelty of the universe?[47]

CZESLAW MILOSZ

My darkness was very tolerable when it was only dark
night, something spiritually approved. But it is rapidly

> becoming an "exterior" darkness. A nothingness in one-
> self into which one is pressed down further and fur-
> ther ... [though] perhaps here in this nothingness is
> infinite preciousness, the presence of a God who is not
> an answer, the God of Job, to Whom we must be faithful
> above all, beyond all.[48]
>
> THOMAS MERTON

How to face such immense suffering and loss—whether arising from the action of human beings in history or from what Czeslaw Milosz calls "the mathematical cruelty of the universe?" How to summon the necessary courage to take it in, make it part of the fabric of one's own moral life—even when it seems to elude every attempt to place it within a meaningful moral framework? How to behold it as part of a whole that also acknowledges and cherishes the enduring beauty of the world? These are old questions and are by almost every measure insoluble. But this does not mean we are free to set them aside or avoid them. Indeed, within much contemporary reflection on the natural world, they are returning with renewed force. The most fundamental questions about the character of the world itself—whether there is any kind of pattern within the seemingly capricious and cruel shape of things, whether we can trust in the world, whether we can face the ambiguous reality of death itself—continue to press down upon us, even as we seek meaningful ways to respond to the deepening environmental catastrophe. Often reflection on these questions arises in the most hidden, personal form; yet for all this, they resonate widely and deeply.[49] A significant contribution to this shared work can be found in the correspondence of Thomas Merton and Czeslaw Milosz published in the slim volume *Striving Towards Being* in 1997.[50]

Thomas Merton first wrote to Czeslaw Milosz In December, 1958 to thank Milosz for his book *The Captive Mind*. Merton was amazed and heartened to discover how deeply Milosz's analysis of the political and cultural malaise of cold war Poland resonated with his own sense of the situation in the United States and wanted to express his appreciation for what he felt to be Milosz's courageous and honest critique. His letter initiated an exchange that would continue off and on until Merton's death in December, 1968. The correspondence is remarkable, not only for the honesty with which the two men grapple with their shared anguish over the deepening crisis settling over twentieth-century political and cultural life, but also for the tenacity with which they search out the underlying roots of this crisis and a possible way forward. Their letters reveal a growing and shared conviction that doing so will mean reckoning honestly with the pervasive sense of lostness, exile, darkness, emptiness that has come to characterize so much contemporary experience, and opening themselves to the awful potency of such affliction wherever it surfaces; also grappling with the cost of such openness, and with the question of whether it is possible to become that vulnerable to affliction without becoming overwhelmed, perhaps even consumed by it. The sense of fragility and uncertainty they express to one another reveals that these were for them not abstract intellectual questions, but deeply felt existential realities. This is also true of their struggle to articulate what it might mean to try to stand in the place of affliction and unknowing as part of a sustained contemplative practice, and to somehow do so without sacrificing their sense of the enduring beauty and goodness of the whole. For both Merton and Milosz, maintaining a sense of the whole meant somehow learning to see and stand within the radical ambiguity of both nature and history, and responding to it as an exercise of moral and spiritual responsibility. Their effort to engage one another and help one another understand what it might mean to respond to an anguished and beautiful world with integrity and honesty remains a significant witness to the meaning of such contemplative practice in our own time.

Merton and Milosz not only established a quick and easy rapport. They also discovered significant differences between them relating to some of their most fundamental concerns. In a letter dated February 28, 1960, Milosz writes to Merton: "Every time you speak of Nature, it appears to you as soothing, rich in symbols, as a veil or a curtain. You do not pay much attention to torture or suffering in Nature ... I am far from wishing to convert you to Manicheism. Only it is so that the palate of your readers is used to very strong sauces and *le Prince de ce monde* is a constant subject of their reflections. That ruler of Nature and of History ... does not annoy you enough—in your writings."[51] Here, in this gentle reproach, Milosz signals not only his dissatisfaction with what he feels to be Merton's overly optimistic reading of nature and history, but also his own longstanding struggle to understand how to affirm the beauty of the world amidst its seemingly endless cruelty. Milosz adds, a little teasingly it seems: "I think you would be more effective if you did not avoid a certain Manichean touch."[52] Merton's response is intriguing. He notes that the works of his to which Milosz is responding (especially Merton's often-lyrical *Sign of Jonas*, which Milosz appreciated) come mostly from the "Edenic" period of his life, and that a different, more critical sense of things emerges in his later work. But he cannot accept Milosz's more pessimistic sense of nature and of the world. He tells him: "I find it difficult to be sincerely bitter in the way you describe." Nevertheless, Merton acknowledges to Milosz that, ironically, he is often accused, in both America and in England, of being "too Manichean"; he also confesses his own difficulties with the "fake optimism" that permeates both American life and American religion; and he struggles to balance his basic feelings of hope (and, at times, optimism) with his recognition of the need to embrace the affliction of the world. Merton decides to share with Milosz a work in progress, "Notes for a Philosophy of Solitude," which for him captures much of his own emerging thought on the subject of what it means for the contemplative to enter into the darkness and suffering of his own time, and a poem, "A Message from the Horizon," which he acknowledges may (again) be too optimistic. "But you see," he says, concluding his letter, "for me emptiness is fullness, not mere vacuum. But in tribute to the seriousness of this happy void, I ought to make it more empty and not be so quick to say positive things about it. This I agree."[53]

One can sense in this exchange the shared concerns that drew Milosz and Merton toward one another. Also their mutual respect. Each defers to the other on occasion—Milosz to Merton because of what he perceives to be Merton's real gifts as a contemplative practitioner and thinker; and Merton to Milosz because of the deep moral seriousness and gravity of his poetic and philosophical vision. But their differences are real too. Most importantly, perhaps, Milosz's Manichean sensibility—his sense of the world as inescapably fallen, hopelessly under the sway of *le Prince de ce monde*—stands in sharp tension with Merton's more sacramental vision of reality, his sense of the world as blessed and luminous. Still, even these differences are in some ways deceptive. In an earlier letter, written on May 21, 1959, Merton notes what he perceives to be a significant divide in Milosz's thought and sensibility, a perception that has the effect of softening in some ways Milosz's more trenchant pessimism. "I suppose it is not strange," Merton notes, "that your younger, earthly and cosmic self should be so sharply divided from the late political self. *Sur les bords de l'Issa* [*The Issa Valley*] is admirably alive, rich in all kinds of archetypal material with a deep vegetative substratum that gives it a great fertility of meanings … It [strikes] me that this element of your being is very essential to you and that you will not produce your greatest work without it." This comment concerning both the tone and spirit of *The Issa Valley*, Milosz's lyrical reflection on his childhood in Lithuania, goes to the heart of a tension that pervades almost all of his work. Merton seems to feel intuitively the difficulty Milosz faces in integrating these different elements of his experience: "It is hard to see," Merton comments, "how ancient pagan naturalistic remnants from archaic Lithuanian peasant culture could be fitted into the tragic story of Warsaw."[54] Still, those ancient remnants persist in Milosz's work and

Merton senses the importance of this "deep vegetative substratum" for his continuing efforts to articulate a vision of the whole.

The larger story of how these tensions came to exist in Milosz's life and thought is, principally in *The Issa Valley* and *The Native Realm*. In 1918, with Europe still reeling from the shock of war, Milosz had returned with his family to his native Lithuania. There, he says, "I found an earthly paradise...I entered into a stunning greenness, into choruses of birds, into orchards bent low with the weight of fruit, into the enchantment of my native river ...."[55] Nature was, initially anyway, a gift, simple and beautiful, to be cherished. His early education did nothing to change this fundamentally sacramental outlook. "The lakes and forests that surrounded the town gave one a sense of being constantly in touch with nature ... so I was initiated early into the habits of animals and birds, into the species of trees and plants, and as a supplement I had my textbooks on ornithology and botany."[56] Milosz became part of a "circle of nature lovers," and delivered his first talk on Darwin and natural selection, settling confidently on his future profession as a naturalist. However, he notes that it was at just this time that his "religious crisis" began.

The crisis had its roots in a growing awareness of an inherent tension between the world known to science and that known to faith. "If nature's law is murder," Milosz observes, "if the strong survive and the weak perish, and it has been this way for millions and millions of years, where is there room for God's goodness? Why must man, suspended on a tiny star in the void, no more significant than the microbes under a microscope, isolate his own suffering as though it were different from that of a bird with a wounded wing or a rabbit devoured by a fox? ... such questions plunged me, sometimes for weeks, into a state bordering on physical illness."[57] The growing sense of the "law of necessity" that governs nature led Milosz eventually to embrace certain ideas from the Gnostics, Manicheans, and Albigensians. Milosz notes with some relief that "They at least did not take refuge behind some vague will of God in order to justify cruelty. They called necessity, which rules everything that exists in time, the work of an evil Demiurge opposed to God." It was this sense of nature as "an abode of evil" that Milosz believed helped account for his "propensity for Manicheanism." In his 1974 collection of poems, *From the Rising of the Sun*, Milosz writes, reflecting on this propensity: "Indeed, quite early you were a gnostic, a Marcionite,/A secret taster of Manichean poisons./From our bright homeland cast down to the earth,/Prisoners delivered to the ruin of our flesh,/Unto the Archon of Darkness."[58] This propensity would resurface continuously during Milosz's life and manifest itself in both his prose and poetry, though an equally strong propensity, to see the world as beautiful and sweet and a source of the deepest joy, never left him.

What does it mean to be caught in such a dilemma, to feel one's very being stretched taut between nature's cruel "law of necessity," and the beauty of the earth? For Milosz, this was not an abstract question, but was rather a profound and ongoing spiritual challenge. His willingness to open himself to this challenge, to live and work within that radically ambiguous space where necessity and beauty make their respective claims upon us, gives his work a depth and gravity worthy of the stark questions the past century has put before us. But what is the nature of the challenge, precisely? Is it a matter of trying to live with and reconcile two opposing attitudes—an optimism and pessimism—arising in response to an ambiguous world? Perhaps this is part of it. However, I think it goes deeper. There are serious theological and religious questions at the heart of Milosz's poetic struggle that have to do with the *experience* of living in such a world. It is this experience that shapes the particular theological questions that emerge in his work, the brute shape of experience for which simple or clear responses seem both inadequate and dishonest. He describes one such moment, in 1939, as Hitler's armies were gathering force and Europe readied itself for the inevitable cataclysm. "My state of mind in those days could be described as the same dream over and over: we want to run but cannot because our legs are made of lead. I had come up against the powerlessness of the individual involved in a mechanism that works independently of his will."[59] Here one encounters that feeling of heaviness, of being unable to move, that shows up everywhere in Milosz's writing. The source of the heaviness in this instance is the cruel necessity of history, not nature. But one soon begins to realize that the heaviness is one, that the world itself is a heavy place and that this heaviness is beyond our control. It is perhaps because of this sense that Milosz finds himself drawn into the company of those for whom the sense of the world's heaviness was integral to their spiritual experience. "I felt a certain affinity with these sectarians [of Eastern Christianity] who, from the ruthlessness of nature and human society, drew the conclusion that the world is in the undivided power of Satan."[60]

Here is an extreme, and perhaps idiosyncratic formulation of what is nevertheless a common and long-held suspicion, found among both believers and non-believers, that there is no pattern or meaning to be discovered in the universe. Or worse, that there is a malevolent force that controls both nature and history. In Milosz's letters to Merton, he articulates his own anxiety about these matters in terms of the old question of providence. He cannot subscribe to the idea of a God who guides and directs the universe, he tells Merton. It is simply impossible for him.[61] Merton's response to Milosz on the question of providence is long, complex, and empathetic. He feels the truth of Milosz's complaint and offers no defense of it. To the contrary, he acknowledges the utter inadequacy of "glib clichés" that are so often offered in place of careful thought on the question of providence (simplistic ideas about why suffering, death, or other horrors befall people "for their good") and the need for a deeper engagement with the question. At the heart of the matter for Merton is the need to shift from a purely external understanding of providence—a guiding hand that controls and guides persons and events—to a more hidden, internal understanding. And for a Christian, this means somehow reckoning with the hidden presence of Christ amidst everything, not least our experience of suffering and loss.

> Providence is not *for* this hidden Christ. He Himself is His own Providence. In us. Insofar as we are Christ, we are our own Providence. The thing is then not to struggle to work out the "laws" of a mysterious force alien to us and utterly outside us, but to come to terms with what is inmost in our own selves, the very depth of our own being. No matter what our "Providence" may have in store for us, on the surface of life (and this inner Providence is not really so directly concerned with the surface of life) what is within, inaccessible to the evil-will of others, is always good unless we deliberately cut ourselves off from it.[62]

Perhaps it is not surprising to learn, even given Milosz's intense aversion to the idea of Providence in history, of his enthusiastic agreement with Merton's formulation of the question. It is, after all, so different from the often-deterministic, even mechanical articulations of the idea toward which Milosz rightly expresses such deep moral revulsion. Here is an understanding of Providence that seeks no explanation or justification (theological or otherwise) for the pervasive and often incomprehensible violence in both history and nature. Rather, it seeks a way of *being with* the ambiguity of experience that accepts the inscrutable character of so much of our experience, that acknowledges the inviolable character of each human person, and that understands Providence as something that is always being worked out mysteriously in "the very depth of our being."

This distinctively contemplative approach to Providence seems to come as an immense relief to Milosz; by his own admission, he has grown weary, as Merton has, with what he sees as a tendency toward theological (and moral) evasion, toward offering answers to questions that have no answer. This is something very different. This is about learning to stand in the midst of and give one's serious and careful attention to the most anomalous and ambiguous dimensions of existence, both in one's own experience and in the experience of others. For Merton, this reflects his own long-standing commitment to make of his own contemplative practice a sustained gesture of solidarity. And to do so in no small measure through opening himself to the reality of emptiness and darkness. Not only his own darkness but the darkness of everyone and everything. Here Merton reveals himself to be the true heir to St. Antony of Egypt and to all those for whom the desert, sometimes described as the *via negativa,* the way of darkness, or the way of emptiness, has proven the most alluring and fruitful way of attending to God and the world. Merton knew this path well and for some years already his writing on contemplative prayer had reflected a more apophatic sensibility. Increasingly, he was also finding himself drawn to the language and practice of emptiness to help him grapple with the seemingly intractable challenges emerging in his life and in the world. Silence and unknowing, a refusal to say what things mean or might mean, became increasingly necessary and important to him. In May, 1960, Merton had written to Milosz regarding the emptiness that is "not mere vacuum," and of the need to make the "happy void" more empty as he struggled to meet and face the suffering of the world. The way of emptiness, long cherished by teachers of the contemplative path, now became a means of engaging and descending into the darkness of the world.

In a letter dated May 30, 1961, without question Milosz's most honest and personally involving contribution to the correspondence to date, he tells Merton: "nothing is more important than to find a common language with those who 'search in despair,' through poetry, prose, any means." Milosz identifies himself as one of them and notes the presence, especially evident to him in the work of young Polish poets he knows, of "a metaphysical torment of a seriousness unknown in preceding decades."[63] Merton's response, sent less than a week later, suggests the deep significance of Milosz's words for him personally. He expresses his regret for the many facile affirmations he has made, especially regarding those things "that cannot be said"; and acknowledges that he has more of Charles Péguy and Simone Weil in him than he has ever before realized. But he goes further, acknowledging a sense of awful emptiness that has become part of his present experience: "There are times," he says, "when I feel spiritually excommunicated. And that it is right and honest for me to be so." In the end, he notes: "I will end up on your side, in metaphysical torment." A remarkable confession, but one that seems to reflect Merton's growing sense of what it means to "search in despair." Much of this has to do with his growing feeling of alienation from his own faith community, especially its "absurd optimism" and its attachment to the security of "right answers." But it also has to do with his sharpened awareness of how deeply his own efforts to attend and respond to the suffering of the world have affected him. "One is left without answers, without comfort, without companionship, without a community of saints … exterior darkness. That is the thing that has finally hit me. My darkness was very tolerable when it was only dark night, something spiritually approved. But it is rapidly becoming 'exterior' darkness. A nothingness in oneself into which one is pressed down further and further … perhaps here in this nothingness is infinite preciousness, the presence of the God Who is not an answer, the God of Job, to Whom we must be faithful above all, beyond all."[64]

This intense evocation of darkness clearly reflects the apophatic tradition that Merton knew well. But it also complicates and deepens it, locating it firmly in the present moment when darkness has begun to take on new and unexpected meanings. This is a darkness, Merton suggests, whose meaning cannot be accounted for solely by reference to the classic spiritual vocabulary of the dark night, at least not if this means evading its gritty, embodied manifestations in the actual world. Whatever spiritual emptiness means now, it will have to include sustained attention to the sense of lostness and despair—the "metaphysical torment"—that is increasingly shaping the contemporary experience of the world. The force of despair in that particular historical moment was, for Merton and many others, palpable and at times overwhelming. Earlier that year, he had written to his friend Etta Gullick in England: "Everybody is suffering emptiness. All that is familiar to us is being threatened and taken away … there may be little or nothing left and we may all have evaporated. Surely one cannot feel comfortable or at ease in such a world. We are under a sentence of death, an extinction without remembrance or memorial, and we cling to life and to the present. This causes bitterness and anguish."[65] The particular sources of anguish in that moment were many and varied: the threat of nuclear annihilation, the pernicious effects of racism, the crushing cynicism of cold war politics, and the dawning awareness of widespread environmental destruction. The year 1961 saw a flood of poems, articles and books reflecting Merton's own efforts to grapple with this anguish and with what he perceived to be our persistent and deepening complicity in a culture of death. His stark anti-poem, "Chant to Be Used in a Procession Around a Site with Furnaces," chronicled the horrors of the concentration camps (in language taken directly from letters from German manufacturers of lethal gas and crematorium equipment to camp authorities). The urge among some Americans to seek protection from nuclear destruction in the pathetic form of fallout shelters provoked Merton's essay "The Shelter Ethic" which appeared in *The Catholic Worker* in 1961. His sense of the enduring significance of the catastrophic bombings of Hiroshima and Nagasaki on our collective moral awareness led him to compose one his most haunting and disturbing works, *Original Child Bomb*, which also appeared in the fall of 1961. And his "A Letter to Pablo Antonio Cuadra Concerning Giants," which Michael Mott notes "frightened even the author with its bitterness," painted a bleak picture of the impending war between God and Magog, the two huge power structures of the world.

This literary outpouring reflects Merton's own deepening conviction that the contemplative vocation requires one to face and enter into the darkness and emptiness of the world and to stand in solidarity with all those struggling and suffering in darkness. This echoes in significant ways Milosz's sense of the poet's vocation. And while Milosz consistently refused to identify himself as a contemplative (he associated this ideal with the capacity to enter into spiritual depths that he felt he did not possess), his understanding of what it means to see stands as a courageous and important complement to the long tradition of contemplative reflection on this question. This is how he describes that understanding in his 1980 Nobel Lecture:

> "To see" means not only to have before one's eyes. It may mean also to preserve in memory. "To see and describe" may also mean to reconstruct in imagination. A distance achieved thanks to the mystery of time must not change events, landscapes, human figures into a tangle of shadows growing paler and paler. On the contrary, it can show them in full light, so that every event, every date becomes expressive and persists as an eternal reminder of human depravity and human greatness. Those who are alive receive a mandate from those who are silent forever. They can fulfill their duties only by trying to reconstruct precisely things as they were by wrestling the past from fictions and legends.[66]

Here, we sense more fully what Milosz means by the "passionate pursuit of the Real." And what it means to give one's attention to the Real as a deeply involving moral gesture, as part of a sustained contemplative practice. Those events, landscapes, and human figures from the past—"those who are silent forever"—have a moral claim on us, suggests Milosz. They beckon to us, asking not to be forgotten, not to be allowed to disappear into the fog of "fictions and legends." In responding to this call, in striving to see things, to reconstruct "things precisely as they were," in all their expressive particularity, the poet makes a wager on transcendence, on the belief that these things will persist, in our imaginations, in our work and in our lives, will become "an eternal reminder." This engagement with the Real, at once an existential choice and a work of the imagination, is in its own way an expression of *kenosis*, a way of entering into and participating in the beautiful, ambiguous whole. And perhaps also a gesture toward redemption.

Exile, Redemption

> Even the divine is estranged from itself; the Shekinah—
> the divine presence—is in exile from Elohim, the being
> of God, just as the Jews were in exile in Palestine.

> Only redemption—restoration, tikkun—can return
> the sparks of light to their source in the primeval soul;
> only redemption can restore God's exiled presence to his
> being in eternity. Only redemption can reunite an exiled
> soul with its root. The holy person, however, can hasten
> redemption and help mend heaven and earth.[67]

ANNIE DILLARD

> Your cold mornings are filled with the heartache about
> the fact that although we are not at ease in this world,
> it is all we have, that it is ours but that it is full of strife,
> so that all we can call our own is strife; but even that
> is better than nothing at all, isn't it? And as you split
> frost-laced wood with numb hands, rejoice that your
> uncertainty is God's will and His grace toward you and
> that *that* is beautiful, and part of a greater certainty, as
> your own father always said in his sermons and to you at
> home. And as the ax bites into the wood, be comforted
> in the fact that the ache in your heart and the confusion
> in your soul means that you are still alive, still human,
> and still open to the beauty of the world, even though
> you have done nothing to deserve it.[68]

PAUL HARDING

Is redemption possible? Or does the cruel law of necessity, the seemingly endless night, the bitter emptiness of existence, eventually crush everything, including hope? Even to open oneself to these questions is to feel the pathos and immense challenge of attending so fully to the whole of reality—especially the reality of emptiness, affliction, darkness. How and whether one chooses to engage these questions at all will of course depend on one's sense of the reality toward which these ideas point—as a space into which one is invited to encounter and grapple with mystery, or simply as a void. The metaphysical torment to which Czeslaw Milosz refers perhaps reflects anxieties particular to our age; but it can also be understood as yet another expression of the "cosmic anxiety and despondency" that has never been absent from our experience. And whether born of historical atrocity or the cruelty of nature, it contributes to our uncertainty about how to respond to our still-beautiful yet fractured existence. It may seem that in an age of rampant environmental destruction, such questions are a luxury. Perhaps. But without an honest attempt to locate ourselves in this beautiful, ambiguous universe, to face the Real as it presents itself in nature and history, is a meaningful and sustained engagement with the world really possible? I wonder.

I return in my mind to that moment with my mother, when she pulled those wispy strands of hair from her scalp. And to the moment when I first turned the corner in the Unterlinden Museum in Colmar and beheld that afflicted body. These two images are forever bound together in my imagination, as is my memory of how, in both moments, I hesitated to look closer. Or look at all.

It was some time later that I found myself sitting at my mother's bedside as she lay dying. Neither of us spoke. In fact, she had been silent for much of the previous two weeks. She seemed to be descending deep into herself, into a place where I could not follow her. I had come to accept this. Now, I simply wanted to accompany her. The end came quickly. Her breathing became ragged. Her chest heaved as she struggled for air. Then she grew quiet. One breath. Then another. Then the last breath. Gone.

We scattered her ashes in the Wood River Valley near her home beneath the Sawtooth Mountains in Idaho. The aspens shimmering gold in the breeze of that cold autumn day. The river beneath our feet, those jagged mountains reaching into the luminous blue sky above. Stories of her life carried into the wind along with her ashes, lifting, soaring, drawn out and into the mysterious whole.

The emptiness remains. But so does a mysterious sense of presence. I cannot separate them from one another. Nor can I pretend somehow that I did not see my mother's final breath leave her body, or that I did not gaze upon her lifeless corpse. I did. And I am glad I did. That image will remain seared into me forever. Whatever sense I carry within me of her enduring presence somehow has to include that reality. I think again of Holbein's painting and of the awful finality of that image. And of these words of Dostoevsky: "The people surrounding the dead man, not one of whom is shown in the picture, must have experienced the most terrible anguish and consternation on that evening, which had crushed all their hopes, and almost their convictions. They must have parted in the most awful terror, though each one bore within him a mighty thought which could never be wrested from him."[69] Yes, this seems right to me. Awful terror at the absolutely inescapable reality of death. And a mighty thought, never to be wrested from them, of what they had come to know from his life. Bound together. Within Christian faith, it is the doctrine of the resurrection that is most often called upon to resolve this paradox. But in truth this doctrine is sometimes invoked too readily, without sufficient attention to the brute fact of death. One is able in a sense to evade death, to skirt it. The idea of *kenosis*—the self-emptying of God into human form, into fragile, impermanent flesh, does not allow for such evasion. Which is why, for me, it is more helpful in this context to call upon another ancient and beautiful idea within Christianity: *apokatastasis panton*—the renewal of all things.

We do not know what endures. We do not know how to orient ourselves to a world in which death seems always to have the final word, in which it seems everything is ultimately lost to us. Still, the hope of redemption and restoration persists. Honesty in the face of the endless ambiguity of existence will necessarily mean living with some measure of uncertainty and doubt about whether it is possible to even imagine such restoration. Nor can we any longer afford to distinguish so easily between personal redemption and the redemption of the world; they are bound together. But it is crucial that we make an effort to articulate and live into such a vision of redemption.

Czeslaw Milosz refers in several places in his work to the idea of *apokatastasis panton*, or "the renewal of all things." It is a vision of eschatological hope rooted in the conviction that in the end nothing, not even the tiniest fragment of life will ever be lost, that everything that ever was will be transformed and renewed, will somehow endure. Milosz, like many of his contemporaries as well as his forbears, never ceases struggling with the radical ambiguity of existence, with the sense that nature is at once sacrament and harbinger of death. But he also stands within a tradition that is tenacious in trying to discover the ground for an authentic hope in the face of this ambiguous reality.

Thus it is not entirely surprising that Milosz should be able make this confession: "Yet I belong to those who believe in *apokatastasis.*/That word promises reverse movement, ... /It means restoration. So believed: Gregory of Nyssa,/ Johannes Scotus Erigena, Ruysbroeck, and William Blake."[70]

Here among these Christian mystics and poets, Milosz gives an expression to a beautiful and hopeful vision of the world, one that contends fiercely with that of the gnostics' demiurge, where death and loss have the final word. It recognizes the need for attention to the real, for honesty in the faith of loss and death. But it remains open to the possibility of a mysterious renewal. When will this restoration commence? Perhaps, says Milosz, it already has begun. Perhaps signs of this reversal are already to be found among us.

> Though not for certain, perhaps in some other year.
> It shall come to completion in the sixth millennium, or next
>   Tuesday.
> The demiurge's workshop will suddenly be stilled. Unimaginable
>   silence.
> And the form of every single grain will be restored in glory.[71]

Telos: *Practicing Paradise*

> The whole world has risen in Christ … if God is "all in
> all," then everything is in fact paradise, because it is filled
> with the glory and presence of God, and nothing is any
> more separated from God.[1]
>
> THOMAS MERTON

> So from the ground we felt that virtue branch
> Through all our veins till we were whole, our wrists
> As fresh and pure as water from a well,
> Our hands made new to handle holy things,
> The source of all our seeing rinsed and cleansed
> Till earth and light and water entering there
> Gave back to us the clear unfallen world.[2]
>
> EDWIN MUIR

THE CHRISTIAN TRADITION has long cherished a vision of the world as paradise, a simple, harmonious whole made manifest in creation and renewed in Christ. From the garden in Genesis to the peaceable kingdom in Isaiah to the heavenly city in the Book of Revelation, one encounters recurring images of this unbroken whole that is paradise. But what kind of place is it and where is it to be found? Is it part of a world that once was but is no longer? Is it part of a dream that can only be realized in the world to come? Or does it perhaps exist here and now, for those with eyes to see and ears to hear? The persistent presence of violence, suffering, and death makes it difficult if not impossible to believe in the idea that in the world as we know it, "everything is in fact paradise." It seems more honest to acknowledge that paradise is simply lost to us, that if it exists at all it must be as part of a future hope, never to be fully realized in our current existence. Still, there is a recurring dream that, in fact, paradise is somehow knowable, graspable, inhabitable in this present reality. If this seems quixotic, as indeed it almost surely must seem to any sober observer, one must nevertheless ask what the cost would be to us were we ever to stop believing in this possibility. That is, is the dream of paradise, still mysteriously present and alive to us even in the midst of suffering and loss and grief, necessary to the work of healing the broken world? Must we be able to imagine the world as whole in order to learn again to inhabit it with tenderness and care, to contribute toward its renewal?

I would argue that it is indeed necessary—for the sake of our own happiness and well-being and for the sake of our increasingly threatened world—for us to be able to imagine paradise. What is more, I would suggest that we must learn to *practice* paradise, to learn how to incorporate an awareness of this mysterious reality into the heart of our contemplative practice. Learning to do so can have a profound transformative effect on the life of the person who undertakes such a practice; but it also has the potential to effect a wide and deep transformation in society and the world. It is the connection between these two forms of transformation that I wish to consider here. In particular, I want to consider how the contemplative practice of paradise might help us address the growing fragmentation and degradation of the living world.[3] For those of us living at this particular moment of history, the loss of paradise is increasingly coming to be experienced through the loss of biological diversity, the extinction of species, the erosion of the very structure of the ecological web through which life is maintained. We are losing not simply our feeling for the world; we are losing the world itself. Yet, it is nevertheless true that our own deepening alienation from the living world—the increasing difficulty we experience in knowing how to see and feel its presence as intimately woven into the fabric of our lives—is part of the larger loss and contributes to it directly. Addressing this loss and engaging it, in terms of both its personal and its larger ecological meaning, has now become central to the work of contemplative practice.

There is a strange paradox at the heart of this challenge. Nothing, it seems, could be simpler or easier than waking up to and embracing the glorious, transcendent reality of one's life in the natural world. It is, or should be, something that comes naturally to us, like breathing: our original innocence. Yet it seems not to come naturally to us at all. We experience instead a profound and persistent alienation from the world. In theological terms, this is sin, an expression of our own estrangement from a place that we know (or once knew) to be our home. It is primordial in its force and its sweep. In practical terms, this alienation arises from our conscious or unconscious attachment to myriad problematic ideas about our life in the world, such as our susceptibility to the allure of power and security, to a freedom without constraints. The work of reimagining paradise will require an honest, critical examination of the patterns of thought and practice that contribute to the perpetuation of these attachments (and the destructive practices that arise from them). Only by struggling to become free from their overweening power will it be possible for us to learn again how rekindle a simple awareness of the power and beauty of the living world: our life in paradise. This work has an inescapably personal dimension; but it is affected by and opens out onto larger social, political, ecological realities. It will be necessary to learn to imagine them together if we are to envision and live into the task of healing the whole.

Here, I want to consider the question of what it might mean to practice paradise as part of the critical task of contemplative awakening to the living world in the present moment. The language of paradise has long figured significantly into the Christian understanding of what it means to live "free from care." At its root, the idea of paradise expresses the conviction that one can learn, through assiduous spiritual practice and openness to grace, to overcome the anxieties and fears (our condition outside of or beyond paradise) that prevent us from opening ourselves to simple, open loving relationship with God and with all beings (human and non-human). The recovery of what is sometimes described as an "original innocence" has tremendous significance for those who realize it in their lives, creating a capacity for renewed intimacy and reciprocity with all living beings. But there has always existed a strong conviction within the paradise tradition of Christianity that the personal work of reimagining and reinhabiting paradise has the potential to effect a transformation that touches every dimension of the cosmos. The hope for a final integration or transfiguration of all living beings—often expressed in the language of *apokatastasis panton* or renewal of all things—is a critical part of this paradise tradition. As the depth and extent of our destruction of the natural world becomes increasingly evident, the language of paradise has gained renewed significance within contemporary cultural and ecological discourse. Much of this clearly has to do with the extent of the loss we have experienced and the ache to be part of a world that is less fragmented, more whole. And if the language of paradise within such discourse often has a less explicitly religious charge than it once did, it continues to haunt the contemporary imagination and retains a potency that few other ideas have for helping us reimagine our relationship to and responsibility for the world. In that sense the dream of paradise remains crucial for the broader work of ecological-spiritual renewal.

It is in this sense that I wish to locate these reflections on the Christian contemplative idea of paradise among the growing chorus of contemporary

voices who are calling for an utterly fundamental rethinking of our relationship with the natural world in terms of a recovery of paradise. One of the
common features of this wider, shared discourse, and something that marks
it as distinctively contemplative, is the growing sense that the transformation
we need must go beyond a merely instrumental approach to dealing with
environmental concerns and touch on the very depths of what the world is
and who we are in the world. Reflection on the meaning of paradise as an
integral part of contemplative practice can, I believe, help us reach a more
thoughtful understanding of the kind of relationship with the living world
we are seeking to cultivate, and perhaps help us develop a shared language
for doing so. Still, a word of caution is necessary here. The language of paradise has been frequently employed, after all, to express very different and
often diametrically opposed ideas about what it means to live in the world—
supporting not only the hope of a more whole, reciprocal way of living, but
also an acquisitive, exploitive, and destructive ethos that seeks a paradise that
leaves the world and those living in it diminished. The contemplative practice of paradise will need to retain a critical awareness of and response to the
tendency to seek a paradise that serves only our needs. Only such a critical
retrieval of the dream of paradise will be sufficient to help us heal our own
increasingly fragmented world.

"Everything Is in Fact Paradise"

A sweet summer afternoon. Cool breezes and a clear sky
This day will not come again.
The young bulls lie under a tree in the corner of their field.
Quiet afternoon. Blue hills. Day lilies nod in the wind.
This day will not come again.[4]

THOMAS MERTON.

To dwell in paradise: this is one of the oldest and most enduring images of
spiritual longing to have emerged from the ancient Christian contemplative
tradition. Its precise meaning shifted and developed over time; but never far
from the center of this longing is the hope that it might be possible to learn
to live in the world with a simple awareness of the whole. At its root, this is
an eschatological vision, born of a recognition that the world as we know
it is broken and frayed but that it is possible to discern even in the midst of
such brokenness what Thomas Merton described as a "hidden wholeness"—
the true, unbroken character of the world that is always mysteriously present.

The capacity to cultivate an awareness of this "hidden wholeness" and to live within and on behalf of it is one of the contemplative tradition's primary contributions to the work of healing of the world. One catches a compelling glimpse of this contemplative vision of the whole in Thomas Merton's correspondence with the Japanese Zen Buddhist teacher and philosopher D. T. Suzuki. Beginning in 1959, Merton and Suzuki exchanged several letters over the next several years, and eventually met one another in New York City in 1964. At the heart of their dialogue and friendship was a shared sense that it was in fact possible to learn to see and respond to the simple fact of existence free of the distorting force of egoic concerns, that it was possible to live as though "everything is in fact paradise."

Thomas Merton wrote those hopeful words in a letter to D.T. Suzuki In April, 1959. It is a remarkable letter, full of deep feeling about Merton's growing awareness of how profoundly his contact with Zen Buddhism had transformed his awareness of his own Christian identity. Also full of hope that the Christian tradition as a whole might recover its own deepest intuition about what it means to live in God and that Christians might join with those from other traditions—such as Suzuki himself—in turning this transformed awareness into a force for healing in the world. At the center of these reflections, indeed occupying the symbolic center of Merton's thought, is the idea that when one learns to penetrate into the heart of one's life, learns to let go of attachments, fears, ideologies—all those unhealed elements of one's life that leave one trapped and lost and fearful and unable to apprehend oneself and the world as graced and whole—then "everything is in fact paradise." This is a strange and bewildering claim. Affirming its truth would seem to require one to remain willfully blind to the persistent presence of suffering, death, and evil in the world. Merton does not skirt these difficulties. Indeed, he acknowledges that the effort to learn what it might mean to inhabit paradise must include a sober reckoning with all those elements of existence that prevent its realization in our midst. Still, he refuses to succumb to the possibility that it is beyond our reach, that we cannot know paradise. In this, he gives expression to an eschatological vision of hope that was widely shared in the early church and in a particular way by the ancient Christian monastic tradition in which he himself stood. This vision has always held in tension the idea that paradise is both a future and a present reality—only fully realizable in eternity, but always breaking through in the present moment. Here, in his correspondence with Suzuki, it is the present moment, the taste of paradise that is the heart and soul of contemplative living, that interests Merton most. It is a vision of paradise that has the potential to transform our very sense of what it is to be alive in the world.

In Merton's first letter to Suzuki, dated March 12, 1959, he expresses the sense of "profound and intimate agreement" he feels in reading the teachings of Zen Buddhism—especially what he describes as "its beautiful purposelessness."[5] I will return to this theme a bit later, for I believe it holds great significance for understanding what the contemplative tradition means when it speaks of inhabiting paradise. For now, I simply wish to acknowledge the deep sense of kinship between this idea of "beautiful purposelessness" and what the Gospel tradition refers to as living "free from care," or what Meister Eckhart will later describe as "living without a why." Merton himself affirms this kinship in one of his characteristically exuberant outbursts to Suzuki: "It seems to me that Zen is the very atmosphere of the Gospels," he says, "and the Gospels are bursting with it."[6] It is precisely this deep, mutually illuminating kinship that he seeks to understand and express in his letter of April 1959. And it is here that the idea of paradise comes more clearly into play. Three ideas are central here: transfiguration, identity, and grace.

It is intriguing to note that Merton's reflections on transfiguration arise directly from what he describes as Suzuki's "deeply moving and profoundly true intuitions on Christianity." Suzuki had written to Merton: "God wanted to know Himself, hence the creation," prompting Merton to acknowledge the importance of this idea in Christianity, especially among Russian Orthodox thinkers such as Sergius Bulgakov and Nicholas Berdyaev. "The Russian view," Merton says, "pushes very far the idea of God 'emptying himself' (*kenosis*) to go over into His creation, while creation passes over into a divine world—precisely a new paradise. Your intuition about paradise is profoundly correct and patristic," he tells Suzuki. "In Christ the world and the whole cosmos has been created anew (which means to say restored to its original perfection and beyond that made divine, totally transfigured). The whole world has risen in Christ, say the fathers. If God is 'all in all,' then everything is in fact paradise, because it is filled with the glory and presence of God, and nothing is any more separated from God."[7] Here one encounters a staggeringly beautiful vision of Christian faith in which one is invited to behold the Divine as encompassing, indeed transfiguring the entire living cosmos. It is a very old vision and has been expressed and celebrated almost from the beginning of the Christian tradition—in the cosmological Christologies found in the prologue to the fourth Gospel, in the letters to the Colossians and Ephesians, and throughout patristic thought.[8]

The force and reach of this vision is astounding: nothing is separated from God; everything is transfigured. And we dwell within this transfigured world. Is it possible to live as though this were true? It seems not: we live instead with a continuous awareness of the vast gulf that separates our intuition of the truth of this vision from our capacity to embody and practice it in our lives. Still, it is precisely here, in response to the question of what kind of awareness is possible for us, that the contemplative tradition has the most to contribute to helping us heal this gulf. Merton's letter to Suzuki takes up this question directly, posing the question of "whether or not the Resurrection of Christ shows that we had never really been separated from [God] in the first place. Was it only that we *thought* we were separated from [God]?" he asks. Perhaps. Even so, he concludes "that thought was a conviction so great and so strong that it amounted to separation." Here, set in the mythic time of the first paradise, Merton reflects on the poignant question of how any sense of separation from God ever arises in our consciousness, and why it is that knowing ourselves to be inseparable from God, we nevertheless separate ourselves continuously. This is, he suggests, an indisputable and unavoidable existential fact. In theological terms, it is the expression of Original Sin. "In this sense," Merton acknowledges, "there is exclusion from paradise. But yet," he insists, "we are in paradise, and once we break free from the false image, we find ourselves what we are: and we are 'in Christ.'"[9]

We find ourselves. We are "in Christ." We are in paradise. Here is a central paradox of Christian faith: we experience ourselves as separated and alienated from God and the world. But we also know, on a deeper level, that there is no separation. The great challenge is unearthing and living into this deeper identity in Christ and through it to a deeper identity with everything.

The question of identity, and whether it is possible for us to discover and live into a more authentic and less superficial and egoic identity than the one we habitually fall prey to, preoccupied Merton his entire monastic life. Here, in his correspondence with Suzuki, he engages this question with particular force. He seeks to express to Suzuki what Christian identity has come to mean to him in light of his contact with Zen Buddhism and his understanding of how the paradise tradition in Christianity contributes to authentic Christian living. But he first makes clear what it cannot mean: reducing Christ to particular social and conventional images, to a projection, a "symbol of a certain sector of society, a certain group, a certain class, a certain culture." This, he says, is "fatal," and is inimical to any honest attempt to open oneself and live into the mystery of Christ. Instead, he says, "The Christ we seek is within us, in our inmost self, *is* our inmost self, and yet infinitely transcends ourselves.

We have to be 'found in Him' and yet be perfectly ourselves and free from the domination of any image of Him other than Himself."[10]

How simple and beautiful this vision of spiritual life is—with its intimate sense of being found, of knowing and being known by the Other. Yet, to become aware of this truth in one's life requires risk, vulnerability. It means letting go completely of all images and ideas about God, allowing oneself to be drawn into the desert. This is what Merton means when he says to Suzuki: "Christ Himself is in us as unknown and unseen. We follow Him, we find Him (it is like the cow-catching pictures) and He must vanish and we must go along without Him at our side. Why? Because He is even closer than that. *He is ourself.*"[11] Merton would elaborate further upon these insights in his formal dialogue with D.T. Suzuki found in *Zen and the Birds of Appetite*. But it is difficult to think of another place in his writings where he speaks so personally and passionately of his own felt sense of what it means to walk this pathless path. Something about being in conversation, about feeling the deepest thing within him called forth by the discerning mind of his esteemed interlocutor, stirred him. "Oh, my dear Dr. Suzuki," he exclaims with disarming openness, "I know you will understand this so well."

And what of paradise? Merton concludes these reflections with a promise to Suzuki to have someone at the monastery copy out for him the *Exultet*—explaining to him that it is sung on Easter night in celebration of the mystery of the Resurrection. "You will see what the Church really thinks about the 'new creation' and new paradise in Christ," he tells him. "Right after the *Exultet*, the first chapter of Genesis is sung, with obvious implications."[12]

Here in this simple primer of faith offered to a friend from another spiritual tradition, one begins to see the connections between the theological vision underlying Christianity's idea of the new creation—the transfiguration of the living world imagined as new paradise—and the contemplative's commitment to live out this vision in personal terms. "Life in Christ," the gift given to every Christian through the resurrection and in baptism, is life in paradise. And while it is deeply personal, it is not merely personal. It touches on and includes everything, every fiber of the cosmos, every person living and dead, everything. To inhabit paradise is to feel oneself participating deeply in this mysterious whole, living in it, loving it. All of this, claims Merton, comes to us through grace.

Merton defines the Christian doctrine of grace for Suzuki simply as "the gift of God's life to us." But he makes it clear that for all its simplicity, grace is fundamental and is at the heart of what it means to live in paradise. "The realization, the finding of ourselves in Christ and hence in paradise," he says, "has a special character from the fact that this is all a free gift from God. With us, this stress on freedom, the *indeterminateness* of salvation, is the thing that corresponds to Zen in Christianity ... there is always this sudden irruption, this breakthrough of God's freedom into our life, turning the whole thing upside down so that it comes out, contrary to all expectation, right side up."[13] Grace here is nothing more or less than the means by which one wakes up to oneself, to God and to the world. As such, it is critical to any understanding of what it might mean to live in the world as if it were paradise.

The End of the World

When I was a child, I had a recurring dream. It was a mild summer's day. I was walking barefoot through an open field full of tall grass. An expansive feeling enveloped me as my body arched to meet the curve of the hill. Suddenly there appeared before me a large metallic cylinder embedded in the earth. My curiosity got the better of me: I reached out and pressed it. In an instant, the whole universe imploded.

I think about this dream often and, even though it has been many years since I last experienced it, it haunts me still. I will not try to offer an interpretation of it here. Rather I simply want to convey the kinds of feelings it provoked in me, and the associations it conjures up in me even now. I remember the feeling of intense well-being walking through that field, the sense that this was a place of endless peace, that there was nothing here that could harm me. The earth was tender and embraced me. I could have walked through those fields forever. When I saw that metal cylinder, I instinctively recoiled. I thought: this should not be here. I sensed the threat, the danger that it held. But I could not resist the impulse to touch it. There was something too about the moment just before I pressed it, that brief instant before the world disappeared, that I remember strongly: I knew what this meant. I knew this was the end. And I was suddenly engulfed in a wave of sadness. Then everything was gone.

I grew up under the shadow of the bomb. Air raid drills were a regular part of my school life. Climb down under your desks, children, keep your heads down (and, as some acerbic commentators later added to this scenario: kiss your ass goodbye). Was I conscious of the depth of this threat at the time? I am not sure. But it seems clear that the awful prospect of the world's imminent destruction had seeped into my subconscious mind and that, along with myriad other threats, became incorporated into my dream life. One of the worst aspects of that dream was the feeling of helplessness: I *had* to touch that cylinder. It *had* to explode. The world *had* to end. And each time I found myself on that hillside, the whole process was mercilessly repeated. Reflecting on the dream now, I find myself thinking more about the field, about the grass swaying in the breeze and how it felt to walk through it. It was not like any place I knew in my actual life, but it was easy enough to associate it with other places I had come to know and love near my home in the Pacific Northwest: the weeping willow tree in my backyard I would climb and hide away in, swaying by myself under the deep blue sky for endless hours; the abandoned field across the street from my house filled with huge gnarled cherry trees that was for me and my friends a place of secret enchantment; the marsh down the hill where I would search for frogs and tadpoles with my brother; and in the distance, Lake Washington, every summer welcoming us into its cool waters. I already knew what paradise felt like. That it should reappear in my dream was really not so surprising. But that it should be destroyed so suddenly and completely was appalling and terrible, a loss beyond my capacity to describe even now.

At the center of the dream is a sense that violence—an impersonal mechanized violence—dominates the world, and that there is nothing I or anyone else can do to prevent its destructive force from laying waste to everything. Certainly the threat of the bomb contributed to this sense. But I realize now that there were other threats, closer to home, that may also have entered into this terrible dream. There was the chronic damming of the Columbia River and the consequent decimation of the salmon population. There was the systematic clear-cutting of the ancient forests, hidden from view behind the so-called "vista corridors" that were left intact along the interstate highways we traveled (I still remember the pungent smell of the pulp mills near my grandparents' house in Tacoma, though at the time I did not connect this with the destruction of the forests). And far off the coast, the hunting and killing of whales continued unabated.

All of this constituted the fraying and fragmented field of being in which my childhood unfolded. In a sense, there is nothing remarkable about it. Indeed the scope and extent of violence which many children face coming into the world far exceeds anything I have described here. Still, I mention it because I think it is useful to pause and consider how deeply the fragmentation and violence of the world we inhabit penetrates into our souls, and how painful it can be to reckon with this loss and with the terrible wasteland that seems increasingly to be taking its place.[14] And because it raises the question of whether in light of such loss, the paradise tradition can still have meaning for us. What I have described from my own experience is, after all, but one instance of a much larger pattern of loss and destruction within which we increasingly find ourselves living. The particular character of this loss in North America and beyond has been well-documented in recent years.[15] This research makes clear what we have long suspected: that we once inhabited a very different and more abundant world than the one we live in now. It also makes clear our own complicity in this diminishment, and our awareness, not only recently but relatively early, of what we were doing. This growing awareness of the tearing of the fabric of the living world and of how our own attitudes toward it and way of living in it have contributed to its erosion marks a significant change in human consciousness. It may be that we still carry within us faint traces of memory of what it felt like to live in a world that is whole; but these traces are growing increasingly faint. In light of this, one wonders, is it still possible to affirm that "everything is in fact paradise," or is this is an illusion, a dream that is no longer possible for us?

I do not pretend to have any clear answer to this question. But I think it is important for us to face up to it honestly and carefully if we are to have any hope of recovering a world that is ecologically whole. I believe the dream of paradise, so cherished within the Christian contemplative tradition, is still viable and has something significant to contribute to this work—not least in its insistence that the world is, has been, and will again be whole. The eschatological character of this vision of the whole is one of its chief virtues, for it invites us to invest hope in both the present and the future, insisting that we can come to know the world as eternal and whole (even if partially and provisionally) in the present moment, while also acknowledging that the ultimate transfiguration of all things is yet to be realized. But the very hope of such a transfiguration can inspire a deeper level of attention to and care for the world we now inhabit. This, I believe, is a crucial part of what it means to "practice" paradise: to learn to see and cherish the world, even in its degraded condition, as whole.

The Purposeless Life

> I am especially struck with the idea of the purposeless
> life, "filling the well with snow." I suppose all life is just
> that anyway, but we are obsessed with purpose.[16]

THOMAS MERTON

I want to return here to the idea of the purposeless life, something that figures prominently in Merton's correspondence with Suzuki and finds many echoes

in the Christian contemplative tradition, in ecological thought, and in contemporary discussions about the relative weight and value we place on utility,
productivity, and purposefulness in our culture. The ancient Christian contemplative tradition gave considerable attention to the question of whether it
was possible to learn to live "free from care." This idea traces its origins to the
teachings of Jesus in the Sermon on the Mount on the importance of learning
to live free from anxiety and is expressed most eloquently in reference to the
"birds of the air" and the "lilies of the field" (Mt 6:19-34). These images had
tremendous potency for the early monks, for they captured precisely the character of the life they believed they were called to live: free, open, alive, unbur-
dened by the debilitating power of anxiety and fear. The ascetic practices they
undertook—both the practical, embodied practices involving detachment
and simplification of their lives as well as the more hidden, interior practices involving the reckoning with and gradual healing of their own obsessive
thoughts—were all oriented toward helping them realize within themselves
an authentic and enduring freedom. The notion of *amerimnia*—which can
be translated variously as "insouciance" or "freedom from anxiety" or "freedom from care"—figured critically into the monks' understanding of what it
meant to live with true contemplative simplicity. And it was bound closely to
the question of what it meant to recover or learn to reinhabit paradise.

The longing to live "free from care," or to live what Merton in his letter
to Suzuki calls "the purposeless life," should not be mistaken for a simple
disregard for others or for the world, or a willingness to live "without care"
for persons or things. Rather, it expresses a hunger to discover a more honest, free, and open way of living in the world that enables one to see and
respond to the other without succumbing to the temptation to think of such
relationships only in terms of their utility and purpose. Indeed, one of the
fundamental questions raised by the contemplative tradition has to do with
how best to understand purpose and utility in human life, and whether the
meaning of things depends on their having a purpose or a use. Also, whether
an insistence on the fundamental value of utility and purposefulness undermines our very capacity to see and notice and respond to the world on its
own terms. At its root, these are also questions about what kind of value we
attribute to things like play, imagination, attention, and prayer; and whether
they can be understood, at least in conventional or economic terms, as having any purpose at all.

Echoes of such questions can be heard in contemporary debates, certainly
in North America, about the relative weight and value we place on purpose
and utility in our culture, our economic lives, and even our spiritual practice.[17]

And about how little patience we have for allowing the deeper kinds of knowledge and understanding acquired through long, slow contemplative practice—what environmental philosopher David Orr refers to as "slow knowledge," and what others are addressing through renewed attention to "slow living" and "slow food"—to grow and develop within us.[18] I will return to this question below. For the moment, I want simply to note the resonance between this understanding of knowledge and the kind of knowing that contemplative traditions have long advocated and to suggest that it is precisely this kind of knowledge or sensibility that will be necessary if we are to develop a capacity for examining critically the assumptions that govern our way of living in the world.[19] Especially important in this regard is the cultivation of the kind of capacious awareness that can help us learn to feel and take in the beauty and power of the world for its own sake and refrain from evaluating it purely in terms of its utility. Here the contemplative tradition can be seen as deeply sympathetic to a strain of thought within ecological literature and poetry that places great value on the practice of noticing, describing, and feeling the simple pleasure of the physical world for its own sake. And while the cultivation and practice of such awareness may not be sufficient in itself to help us redress the pernicious effects of our utilitarian and acquisitive culture, the recovery of such capacity will almost certainly be necessary to the kind of sustained imaginative, ecological, and spiritual renewal that we need.

So, there is a paradox: contemplation is useless; it partakes of a dimension of living that cannot be given a precise utilitarian value. Indeed, at its deepest level, it resists being forced into such categories. At the same time, it is necessary and important (that is, useful) to the task of renewing human culture and healing a fragmented and degraded natural world. Contemplation has no end or purpose beyond itself. It seeks only to become more aware of, more alive to everything and everyone. And yet it has a *telos* or end toward which it moves and which it helps to facilitate: the great consummation or recapitulation of all things in God, the new heaven and new earth long dreamed of by prophets and mystics. Contemplative practice invites one to enter into this paradoxical space and be mindful of the mysterious presence of God always radiating forth in the present moment and yearning toward the fulfillment of all things in the age to come. This relinquishment of purpose can thus be understood and experienced as having a profound meaning and even, paradoxically, a kind of purpose.

Still, there is always present in the contemplative tradition a suspicion of purpose that is too narrowly conceived, that threatens to undermine the upwelling of the free and spontaneous response to life that is the soul's true freedom. Even amidst the kind of necessary and helpful distinctions that sometimes arose in ancient monastic literature—such as John Cassian's well-known differentiation between the *scopos* or immediate aim of the contemplative life (purity of heart) and the *telos* or ultimate end (the reign of heaven) of that life—there is a sense that contemplative living cannot be reduced to means and ends. It always transcends them, reaches past them into the space of pure freedom—the reign of heaven.[20] In spite of this, one encounters in the ancient monastic literature a persistent anxiety over whether or how to measure and quantify progress. A trace of this anxiety is found in a story from the *Apophthegmata Patrum*: "Abba Sisoes said to a brother, 'How are you getting on?' and he replied: 'I am wasting my time, father.' The old man said, 'If I happen to waste a day, I am grateful for it.'"[21] It is not easy to know what particular concern underlay this brother's response to Abba Sisoes, or to be certain of the meaning of Abba Sisoes's expression of gratitude for his own occasional experiences of simple, profligate living. But seen in the context of the monks' consistent expression of hope that they might learn to live "free from care," Sisoes's response takes on a very particular meaning: it expresses the value the ancient monks attributed to relinquishing all plans, all projects, all designs for one's life and resting instead in the beneficent abundance of God's providence.

Such freedom from care was not acquired simply or easily. Indeed the entire literature of Christian contemplative thought can be understood as a sustained attempt to learn how to relinquish those habits of mind that prevent one from realizing it in one's life. The very difficulty of realizing such freedom from care perhaps helps to account for the recurring attention in this literature to the meaning of detachment, to learning to live with an awareness of the kingdom of heaven, and to cultivating true "insouciance." It also helps to account for the importance attached to those images of transformed existence—often envisioned as a wild, unfettered life—that appear from time to time in this literature. Both the teachings and the images reflect a fundamental tension that was ever present in ancient monastic literature—between a sense that paradise was something only fully realizable at the end of all things (the future kingdom of heaven) and a sense that it was possible, even in this life, to acquire a foretaste of this ultimate reality, to learn to live against the horizon of eternity here and now. This tension is never fully resolved. Indeed, there is a clear sense in the literature that it never *can be* fully resolved, that the contemplative is one who cultivates a consciousness of eternity in the present moment precisely through an assiduous attention to the end of all things. Such contemplative practice was at once utterly simple and an expression of a complex and sustained effort at self-knowledge and relinquishment of fear and anxiety. Learning to live into this space became critical to the contemplative practice of seeing and inhabiting the world as whole and alive.

The gesture of relinquishment or detachment often lay at the heart of early monastic narratives. And for good reason. The monk's gesture—often expressed as a willingness to leave behind home, possessions, ties to family and society—was dramatic and compelling and signaled in clear, unambiguous terms a shift of allegiance from "the world" to "the kingdom of heaven." Still, as the monk struggled to live into this gesture, its complexity, difficulty, and ambiguity soon became clear: letting go of things, places, or persons was only the beginning of a much more challenging process of relinquishment that entailed learning to live free of the obsessive thoughts that fuel fear and anxiety. And this involved not merely a struggle with what we would consider "personal" concerns, but a reckoning with one's relationship with the whole of reality. Athanasius's reference to the "great dust cloud of considerations" that clouded Antony's mind not long after he made his initial break from life in the village is but one indication of the true scope of these concerns in the lives of the early monks. Family, home, financial security, the fragility of embodied existence, mortality: these are but a few of the concerns that figured into Antony's understanding of what it meant to relinquish his old life for the sake of the new one emerging before him. One can see these concerns expressed in more systematic terms in Evagrius's painstaking taxonomy of the "eight principal thoughts" found in the *Praktikos* and elsewhere. Learning to become "free from care," the monks believed, involved a life-long commitment to probe and grapple with precisely those thoughts, memories and feelings that prevented one from grasping and accepting the true character of one's existence in eternity. The concrete gestures of detachment, then, contained within them the seeds of a much deeper process of relinquishment through which the monk entered into and facilitated renewal of the self and the wider community.

Few gestures expressed this longing for freedom more eloquently than the willingness to abandon the security of a sheltered dwelling for a more itinerant and precarious form of "open-air living." It is not easy to determine how many early monks lived this way; nor can one be certain how accurately the stories of such living reflect the way such monks actually lived. Still, these stories give us access to at least part of what it meant for the early monks to live free from care. And they point to an element of this life that seems to have had particular meaning and significance for some of them: the wildness at the heart of such living. One sees vivid expressions of this form of monastic living, especially in the Syrian monastic tradition where the presence of wild ascetics known as "grazers" appears to have been particularly prominent. Theodoret of Cyrrhus's *History of the Monks of Syria* opens with an account of a certain James of Nisbis, who we are told: "embraced the eremitical and quiet life, and gaining the tops of the highest hills lived upon them. In spring, summer, and autumn, he used the thickets, with sky for a roof; in the winter season a cave received him and provided scanty shelter. He had food not sown and produced with labor but that which grows by itself: it was by gathering the natural fruits of wild trees and edible plants and vegetables that he provided his body with the bare necessities of life, rejecting the use of fire."[22] Another important figure, Maron, who may well have been the first of the open-air hermits in the region of Cyrrus, is described as "embracing the open-air life, [repairing] to a hill-top formerly honored by the impious [and] ... pitching a small tent which he seldom used."[23] And Theodoret tells of yet another monk, Eusebius of Asihka, who followed a similar way of life, "repairing to a mountain ridge ... and using a mere enclosure whose stones he did not even join together with clay, [continuing] for the rest of his life to endure the hardship of the open-air, covered in clothing of skins, feeding on chick peas and beans soaked in water."[24]

There is an undeniably idealized, romantic, even heroic character to such accounts. The "open-air" ascetics are portrayed as being so advanced in their ascetic practice as to have become impervious to the usual human concern with food, clothing, and shelter. Yet even within this idealized portrayal of their life, one can discern more than a trace of the harshness and wonder of what it must have meant actually to live this way. Living in the open air was a form of serious ascetic practice, a way of living close to the pulse of things, simply and humbly and in a condition of openness and vulnerability. It also had a social meaning, helping to locate those who lived in this way in a particular, often critical, relationship to the wider world around them; living in the open allowed one to see and understand things that could not be seen and understood amidst the stifling pressure of towns and villages. And it brought into bold relief the needs of the body and the uncontrollable, indeed wild character of the world through which monks moved; contemplative practice meant allowing oneself to be shaped by the wild world. And while these particular accounts do not always reflect a great degree of self-awareness concerning what this life meant, they remain important for what they reveal about the kind of intimate contact with the physical world that was such a regular part of early monastic experience.

Still, early monastic literature also bears witness to a running conversation about the *meaning* of such ascetic relinquishment, especially as it relates to the fundamental question of what it meant to live free from care. A story told of Abba Bessarion from the Egyptian monastic tradition contained in the *Apophthegmata Patrum* reveals how the particular shape of a life could also come to be understood in relation to a governing idea about that life. Abba Bessarion's disciples testified that: "his life had been like that of a bird of the air, or a fish, or an animal living on earth, passing all the time of his life without trouble or disquiet. The care of a dwelling did not trouble him, and the desire for a particular place never seemed to dominate his soul, no more than the abundance of delights, or the possession of houses or the reading of books... he lived in patience ... always suffering cold and nakedness, scorched by the sun. He always lived in the open air, afflicting himself on the edge of the desert like a vagabond."[25] There is a striking similarity here to the stories about open-air living found in the Syrian ascetic tradition—both in its idealization of a certain kind of unencumbered existence and in its recognition of how difficult it could be to live this way. But one senses something else also: an interest in the inner character of the monk's life, a concern to understand how and why he lives this way. Part of the response to this question comes from the vocabulary used to describe the monk's way of life: Bessarion is said to be *autarkos* (without trouble) and *amerimnos* (without disquiet or worry). Both of these terms figured importantly into the early monastic understanding of what it meant to achieve true freedom. In the world in which Abba Bessarion moved, to be characterized as *amerimnos* would almost inevitably have called to mind the Gospels' repeated insistence on the futility of worry, in which the very same word is employed to express Jesus's conviction that those who wish to inhabit the kingdom of God must learn to cease worrying about things beyond their control and in so doing emulate the insouciance of the birds of the air and the lilies of the field.

Within ancient Christian ascetic culture, the call to practice *amerimnia* implied an invitation to engage in a deep cleansing of the mind, a purging of every thought that held one captive to anxiety and worry. It was a profoundly intimate and personal work of reckoning with the self. Still, such practice unfolded within the context of the wider community and also had a significant social meaning. This wider meaning is implied in the characterization of Bessarion as *autarkos*—without trouble. The apparent disregard or lack of concern for others implied in this term is, in fact, deceptive. The ascetic's struggle to cultivate such freedom unfolded within an immensely complex social reality and drew its meaning precisely in response to that reality. As

Peter Brown has noted, the monk's "powers and his prestige came from acting out, heroically, enmeshed in oppressive obligations and abrasive relationships, the role of the utterly self-dependant, autarkic man."[26] It is difficult for us to read this and not hear echoes of the kind of radical individualism—with its refusal of participation in and responsibility for community—that has taken such deep hold in contemporary North American culture and beyond. But the meaning of *autarkos* in the world of early Christian monasticism was significantly different than this. To have achieved in one's life an authentic freedom from the "oppressive obligations and abrasive relationships," did not mean abandoning one's relationships with others. It meant rather cultivating a critical awareness of the claims such relationships could and could not make upon one's life and learning to free oneself from illegitimate claims in order to engage the world from a place of authentic detachment and freedom. To have achieved the kind of radical insouciance implied in the story told of Bessarion and the other wild ascetics of the early monastic tradition suggested the possibility of a different kind of life in which one's relationships with others—indeed with the whole of existence—could be reimagined as rooted not in oppressive and arbitrary obligation but rather in freedom and reciprocity. The hope of realizing this possibility in one's life had meaning not only for the individual monk, but for the entire community. Indeed, it was in the context of communal living that the dream of freedom from care took hold most deeply.

One sees vivid expression of this in the many teachings and stories about what it meant to inhabit the kingdom of heaven. While the hope for a fulfillment of all things in a mysterious still-to-be-revealed future was part of what the monks meant when they spoke of heaven, this was also their preferred language for expressing what it meant to live every moment, and perceive every element of one's existence, with an awareness of eternity. Learning to live with an awareness of heaven, of paradise, meant struggling to overcome those practices and habits of thought that prevented one from realizing in one's life the qualities of detachment, humility, simplicity, and love. Only in this way could one learn to see things truly, to inhabit the world fully and deeply. It is this mysterious convergence of ascetic struggle and luminous knowledge to which Evagrius refers when he describes the kingdom of heaven as "*apatheia* of the soul along with true knowledge of existing things."[27] This strange saying of Evagrius points to a fundamental tension in the monks' understanding of what it was to see and know the world truly. Only by struggling daily to become free from the debilitating power of the passions (the word *apatheia* can be roughly translated as "passionlessness" or "beyond the passions") could one acquire what Evagrius calls the "true knowledge of existing things." This knowledge, what the monastic tradition refers to elsewhere as *theoria physike* or "natural contemplation," was itself understood as an expression of a deep inner freedom. The capacity to see, feel, and know the world as the kingdom of heaven or paradise was only possible for those who allowed themselves, through a long process of spiritual transformation, to be drawn gradually into the possession of such freedom.

The monks seemed aware that every moment, including those moments when their ascetic struggle was most acute, held within it the possibility of an awareness of heaven. "Let your thoughts be ever in the kingdom of heaven," said Abba Hyperchius, "and soon you will possess it as a heritage."[28] Evagrius held a similar view of the monks' capacity to live with a continuous awareness of eternity even amidst the struggles of their lives. "Those who hold the land of heaven as their own by means of ascetic labors," says Evagrius, "participate in a nourishing light from the highest realities."[29] How and where is this light to be found? When "the mind ... gazes upwards towards its inner heaven..." says Evagrius.[30] Such language points to a sense that was ever present in early monastic literature—that heaven was not a temporally and spatially remote region, distinct from and unknowable in this world, but somehow woven into the very fabric of human, earthly existence. The monks experienced heaven as a nourishing presence; they participated in it, felt it within them, around them. But they also recognized how easily one could lose hold of this awareness. It is because of this that they gave such careful attention to the *means* by which consciousness of heaven—within and without—could be cultivated. This is the significance of the relationship between what Evagrius calls "ascetic labors" and the gradual possession of the "land of heaven." To inhabit paradise, one had to learn to practice it, allowing it to take hold of and transform one's entire existence.

One of the most remarkable aspects of early monastic teaching on heaven is its careful attention to the entire range of habits and dispositions through which anxiety came to dominate the soul and through which freedom from anxiety could be attained. Learning to live free from care meant rooting out not only the sources of anxiety that arose over basic concerns with food, clothing, and other bodily needs, but also those that manifested themselves in the continuing presence in the monk's soul of pride, resentment, and anger. Inhabiting the kingdom of heaven meant learning to live instead in a deepening condition of trust, humility, and love.

The value of basic detachment from material things is often expressed in terms of its capacity to help the monk live with consciousness of eternity.

Abba Hyperchius said: "'A monk's treasure is voluntary poverty. Lay up treasure in heaven ... for there are the ages of quiet and bliss without end.'"[31] It is not easy to determine the meaning of this saying. One reading of it, a reading that has dominated thinking about the meaning of heaven in much Christian thought, suggests an orientation to a world beyond this one, and to a treasure that transcends ordinary earthly experience. However, another possible reading, which is consistent with so much early monastic teaching, points to an understanding of treasure in heaven—here: quiet and bliss without end—as a quality that pervades one's current existence. This is how Evagrius understands the value of detachment in a monk's life. "The person without possessions," he says, "enjoys the pleasure of a life free from cares."[32] There is no sense that this is a reward to be enjoyed in some other life. Yet, what did it mean in practice? And why did the monks believe detachment from things yielded such freedom? Evagrius addresses these questions in a comment on how the monk ought to think about and deal with clothing. "In the case of clothes," he says "entertain no desire for extra clothing; make provision for those sufficient to meet the needs of the body. Rather 'Cast your cares upon the Lord and he will provide for you' (Ps 54:23)... when tomorrow has arrived, that time will provide what is needed, as long as you are seeking above all for the kingdom of heaven ...."[33] This teaching points to the complex and demanding character of the practice of detachment in the life of the monk. Its fundamental value is rooted in the possibility that one might learn to live in a condition of radical trust—neither calculating or planning for one's needs beyond the present moment. The realization of this possibility, Evagrius suggests, depends on a certain intentionality—"seeking above all for the kingdom of heaven." And it affects not only one's own well-being, opening up a space in one's soul where freedom from care can take root; a monastic economy based on such detachment understands possessions as gifts that are always to be shared with the larger community.

Something of this concern is reflected in a story told by Abba Gelasius about: "an old man of very great simplicity and poverty, living in a single cell to the end... [whose] particular acts of asceticism had been to guard against having two tunics (Luke 9:3) and till the day of his death not to think of the morrow (Mt 6:34) whilst he was with his companions."[34] Here one comes close to the heart of what living "free from care" meant for the early Christian monks. The simplicity and poverty of the monk's life clearly mattered; his fulfillment of the call to renounce everything for the sake of the kingdom, even to the point of maintaining vigilance against possessing two tunics, would have been recognizable and compelling to his contemporaries. But it is difficult to avoid the sense that it is his other ascetic practice—"not thinking about the morrow whilst he was with his companions"—that has the greater significance. Was it really possible to practice such simple attention, such that care and worry did not cloud one's capacity to be present to another? This is what is implied in this saying. And while there is no clear sense of whether the monk ever achieved pure insouciance, this image of a steady, disciplined practice of presence reveals much about what the early monks valued most: a freedom from care that manifested itself in simple, loving attention to the life of another. Anxiety about food, possessions, and money was harmful not because of anything inherently problematic in the things themselves but because of how the anxiety that arose in response to them undermined one's capacity for living in joyful freedom. It is no doubt with something like this in mind that Abba Euprepius commented: "If we happen to lose something, we must accept this with joy and gratitude, realizing that we have been set free from care."[35]

Ultimately acquiring such freedom meant learning to open a space in one's soul where love could come to full and luminous expression: "If we have indeed acquired love," says Evagrius, "we have extinguished the passions and have let our light shine into the heavens."[36] It is perhaps this conviction that accounts for Evagrius's sense of the "heavenly" character of the one whose life has come to be so suffused by love. "When the mind has put off the old self and shall put on the new one born of grace (Col 3:9-10)," he says, "then it will see its own state in the time of prayer resembling sapphire or the color of heaven; this state scripture calls the place of God that was seen by the elders on Mt. Sinai (Ex 24:9-11)."[37] The blue sapphire of the mind is a pure, luminous space unencumbered by anxiety and fear, pulsing with love. A kind of paradise.

A haunting, mirage-like image of this paradise and of the freedom enjoyed by the monks who inhabited it is conveyed in a story told by Abba Macarius. He had been prompted by the Spirit to go out in the remotest part of the desert. "There," he recounts, "I found a sheet of water and an island in the midst, and the animals of the desert came to drink there. In the midst of these animals I saw two naked men … they said, 'It is God who has made this way of life for us. We do not freeze in the winter, and the summer does us no harm.'"[38] Macarius was shaken by this image and, looking upon these two figures, was pierced with the realization that he had not yet become a true monk. But it also spoke to his deepest aspirations about what the contemplative life could be: an unfettered, graced existence, like our ancestors in paradise had enjoyed before us. Macarius's encounter with these ghostly figures in the remotest region of the desert served as a reminder that the recovery of paradise was not merely a dream, but could be realized in one's life. As Peter Brown notes: "The monk['s] ... decision to 'sit alone' in the desert gave reality to a long tradition of speculation on the lost simplicity of Adam: 'the glory of Adam' was summed up in his person."[39]

Adam (and Eve) in the garden; here we have what is perhaps *the* archetypal image of "the purposeless life" within the Jewish and Christian religious traditions. The particular contribution of the contemplative reading of this story is its suggestion that the original innocence or simplicity known to our ancestors in the ancient garden can—through a gradual process of healing and renewal of the mind—be recovered and made manifest in our own lives. The concrete character of this life as it is described in the monastic literature, especially the descent into the wild, trackless places of the desert, should not be ignored. Those who embarked upon this life did so with the full hope of realizing the ideals of contemplative living in the most practical, embodied terms. And the physical character of their lives in those wild places has real significance for understanding what contemplative living meant to them. But I think it would be a mistake to literalize these images or identify them too closely with a particular gesture (such as withdrawal into solitude) or a particular place (such as the desert). The greatest miracle of this way of life and its greatest value to us, after all, is its witness to the transformation that can take place in the imagination, the freedom and simplicity that can take hold in one's soul and the depth of engagement with the world that can result from it. If the contemplative tradition has anything to offer to us in this moment of acute loss and fragmentation, it is the conviction that this vision of the whole can be restored to our world.

Innocence

I remember the vast wastes of the Mojave, but much more than that, I recall a baby ground squirrel that I came upon suddenly sunning himself in some fresh-turned earth beside the family burrow. His mother must have been careless, for here was her little waif blissfully lying on his back and patting his stomach. He looked up at me without a trace of fear as I stood over him. There the image stays, yet close to fifty years have passed: one ground squirrel patting his paunch.

I think, you know. It is the innocence. A violent dog-eat-dog world, a murderous world, but one in which the very young are truly innocent. I am always amazed at this aspect of creation, the small Eden that does not last, but recurs with the young of every generation. I can remember when I was just as innocent as that baby ground squirrel and expected good from everyone, as a puppy might. We lose our innocence inevitably, but isn't there some kind of message in this innocence, some hint of a world beyond this fallen one some place where everything was otherwise? Why else do infants peer up with such humorous, arch visages, as when I briefly scratched the ground squirrel's belly and saw him wriggle?[40]

LOREN EISELY

Is such innocence still possible for us? Or must this image, along with those images of monks traversing the wild places in blissful insouciance, be recognized for what they are—hopelessly quixotic, exercises in nostalgia or wishful thinking about a world that once was but can no longer be? Perhaps they cannot help but appear to be so. The loss of innocence—in ourselves and in the world—seems so complete and pervasive. Still, the dream of paradise persists, not only among those contemplatives who devote themselves to practices of renunciation and stillness, who live in the hope of realizing in their own lives a more simple and yes, innocent, way of responding to God and the world, but also among those who seek through their own practices of deepening attention and awareness to discover a more intimate and reciprocal relationship with the living world. Can the idea of paradise found in these diverse but kindred forms of spiritual practice help us in the work of healing a broken world? It seems to me that it can. But if paradise is to have meaning for us and contribute to the work of ecological restoration, we will need to examine carefully and critically not only the possible benefits of retrieving this ancient idea but the dangers inherent in its ongoing distortions and misappropriations. It will have to be integrated into a critical discourse of spiritual and political resistance.

Such a renewal, for example, will require us to rethink (and perhaps reject once and for all) our persistent tendency to imagine the living world only in terms of its usefulness to us and to open ourselves instead to its presence as pure gift. The idea of the "purposeless life," or a "life free from care" arising from contemplative traditions of spiritual practice can contribute to this renewal—not only by inspiring a more free, open-hearted response to the natural world, but also by creating an imaginative space from which we might begin to conceive of alternatives to the ideas and practices that have contributed most significantly to its abuse and destruction. If the idea of paradise is to be for us something more than an escapist fantasy, which in its blindness to the ongoing destruction of the world only perpetuates it, it will have to help us engage the question of how our own acquisitive, utilitarian ideals have undermined our inability to regard and cherish the world for its own sake. Paradise—as we learn to imagine and inhabit it anew—will need to become a site of resistance.

But there is another, more complex and subtle task, both imaginative and practical in character, for which a more capacious understanding of paradise will be indispensable. I am referring to the need to reimagine the world as whole. This apparently simple task remains one of the most elusive and challenging dimensions of the contemplative ecological project. This is in no small part because of our longstanding tendency to separate and divide dimensions of the whole that in fact belong together. Our inability to think of paradise as part of our present existence or to imagine our embodied, earthly existence as deepened by an awareness of the mystery of paradise is but one expression of a much more widespread tendency to reduce the world to something small and poor. Imagining paradise as a realm utterly beyond this world has led inevitably to a heedless flight from or even denigration of this present earthly existence, undermining our ability to see and cherish the world for its own sake; imagining paradise as an utterly terrestrial realm of our own making has only exacerbated our tendency toward conquest and exploitation; not imagining paradise at all, an increasingly common impulse in the scientific age, has led to the elimination of an essential dimension of mystery from the world. If the renewal of contemporary ecological discourse is to be as deep and far-reaching as possible, it will somehow have to account for the entire range of relationships that bind us to the world: the moral or spiritual ecology within which we live and move and have our being. The language of paradise can help us reintegrate those dimensions of the whole that belong together but have too long been conceived of as separate and distinct; it can help us navigate the fluid space that binds heaven and earth, learn again to see them *together,* as part of a single mysterious reality. The recovery of paradise that I have in mind remains firmly grounded in this world, though it also acknowledges the beauty and imaginative significance of a realm beyond this world and perhaps beyond anything we can imagine, sometimes called heaven or what Czeslaw Milosz calls simply "the second space."[41]

There is one other consideration of a very different character that must be included here before proceeding: there can be no meaningful retrieval of the idea of paradise that fails to acknowledge the pervasive presence of violence, suffering, and anguish in the world or the poignancy of unaccountable loss; a paradise for the few is no paradise at all, which is why the hope for a final reconciliation of all things (the tradition of *apocatastasis panton)* has retained its importance within reflections on the meaning of paradise, especially in the Christian tradition. This vision of hope, long cherished in the Christian theological tradition, has resurfaced in the present moment as part of the effort to understand how we might conceive of the ultimate significance of all living things. This too is part of the meaning of paradise: the hope of reconciliation of all things in God.

The simple awareness of the goodness and beauty of the living world seems to lodge itself in the mind most deeply in childhood—in that time of innocence and purity before a mature consciousness of the self emerges, a consciousness that inevitably brings with it an awareness of one's own divided self and of the profound ambiguity and brokenness of existence. I do not think it is a coincidence that reflections on paradise so often arise from memories of this cherished, mysterious place. Here, in memory at least, one lives in the wild world fully and unambiguously, with feelings of tenderness and regard for other living beings whose rightness and truth are unquestioned. That this feeling somehow becomes more elusive as time proceeds is one of the great sources of sadness we carry into our adult lives. What meaning we attach to such memory and to the residual feeling of being alive in the world that continues to pulse within us is a question that I think deserves our most careful attention. For here one senses a kind of golden thread that can perhaps open one to the world again—not in that same childlike simplicity, but in the form of a second childhood, no less valuable and maybe even more so. "Unless you become like little children you cannot enter the kingdom" (Mt 18:3).

How to think about, imagine such innocence amidst such pervasive degradation? Perhaps one must begin simply by describing what it feels like to be alive in the world, those fleeting moments of awareness—of particular things and of the magic that binds us to them—that remain within us long afterwards, as a purchase on the reality and truth of what we increasingly find to be incredible: the idea of the world whole and complete. I think of the children whom I have been given to tend and care—one nearly grown, the others still in earlier stages of blooming—and their own still-tender feeling for the world. They have not yet "outgrown" this feeling. The world for them is still alive and alluring and woven deeply into their own sense of self.

The hard boundaries of identity that seem inevitably to rise up and distance us from the world have not yet appeared. But they will. We do not yet possess the cultural and spiritual resources to keep alive in us this feeling of unbroken intimacy. It must be acknowledged as lost, then reclaimed, reimagined. Which is why the images of innocence (lost or regained) one encounters so often on contemporary reflections on the natural world remain so poignant, even irresistible. There is no question about the depth of the loss that is the ground of such reflections. But it is precisely because of this that the possibility of a return, a rekindling of a feeling of intimacy with the living world carries such weight and poignancy for us. Our hopes for a recovery of our own "lost simplicity" are increasingly bound up with our hopes for the renewal of the world itself.

Still, there is first of all the task of remembering, reimagining the innocence that has been lost and in the work of imagining it perhaps coming to an awareness that it has never been lost to us altogether. This is an essential part of our common work, without which it is difficult to imagine how we will ever learn again what it is to live in paradise. Let me cite some examples.

The Spanish poet, Luis Cernuda, forced to flee from Franco's Spain, spent long years in exile conjuring up places and experiences now lost to him. He recalls with particular tenderness his childhood wonder at what it meant for him to participate in creating the world.

> The child took pleasure in following patiently, day after day, the mysterious sprouting of plants and their flowers. The appearance of a leaf, in translucent green still folded and scarcely visible next to the stem where yesterday it wasn't there, filled him with astonishment, and with attentive eyes, for hours at a time, he loved catching its movement, its invisible growing, the way others love to catch, in flight, the flapping wings of a bird.
>
> To take a tender cutting from a mature plant and root it apart, with a touch he wished to be soft and smooth as air, the care it then required, keeping it shaded the first days watering its thirst each morning and evening when the weather was warm, absorbed him in a selfless expectation.
>
> What joy when he saw the leaves break out at last, and their tender color, which in their transparency seemed luminous, revealing in relief the veins, darkening little by little with the stronger sap. He felt as if he himself had worked the miracle of giving life, of awakening out of the basic earth, like a god, the form until then asleep in the dream of nonexistence.[42]

There is no sense here of the kind of lust for power that has so often come to dominate our contemporary dreams of "making the world." The child here simply notices and tends to the life already bursting forth from the earth. For its own sake. With joy.

The writer Jean Giono, who spent most of his life documenting and imagining the vibrant life of his native Provence, recalls in his autobiographical novel *Blue Boy* a moment from his own childhood:

> The sap came up from the root hairs and pushed through the trees to the very tips of the leaves. It passed between the claws of the roosting birds. The bark of the tree, the scale of the food, that was all there was between the blood of bird and tree. There were only these barriers of skin between. We were all like sacks of blood one touching the other. We were the world. I was against the earth with my whole body, the palms of my hands. The sky was pressing on my back, it was touching the birds that were touching the trees; the sap came from the rocks; the big snake yonder in the wall was rubbing against the stones. The foxes were touching the earth; the sky was pressing on their fir. The wind, the birds, the swarming ants in the earth, the villages, the families of trees, the forests, the flocks, we were all pressed, atom against atom, in an enormous pomegranate, thick with our juice.[43]

To see and feel the world so fully and deeply; is this the child's prerogative alone? Or does it belong to those who have passed on from this place of innocence as well? Giono's work probes these questions endlessly, asking whether it is possible for those who have long since stopped believing the world is alive in this way to be reborn, reawakened to themselves and to the wild world.

The American writer Willa Cather, in her novel *My Ántonia,* imagines a moment in the life of a young boy living in a frontier settlement on the American plains. For a moment there is only the world and the boy *in* the world, not separate but moving together in some mysterious whole:

> I sat down in the middle of the garden, where snakes could scarcely approach unseen, and leaned my back against a warm, yellow pumpkin. There were some ground-cherry bushes growing along the furrows, full of fruit. I turned back the papery triangular sheaths that protected the berries and ate a few. All about me giant grasshoppers, twice as big as any I had ever seen were doing acrobatic feats among the dried vines. The gophers scurried up and down the ploughed ground. There

in the sheltered draw-bottom the wind did not blow very hard, but I could hear it singing its humming tune up on the level, and I could see the tall grasses wave. The earth was warm under me, and warm as I crumbled it through my fingers. Queer little red bugs came out and moved in slow squadrons around me. Their backs were polished vermilion, with black spots. I kept as still as I could. Nothing happened. I did not expect anything to happen. I was something that lay under the sun and felt it, like the pumpkins, and I did not want to be anything more. I was entirely happy. Perhaps we feel like that when we die and become a part of something entire, whether it is sun and air, or goodness and knowledge. At any rate, that is happiness; to be dissolved into something complete and great. When it comes to one, it comes as naturally as sleep.[44]

The uncanny sense of being inside of the world, even as you are noticing and feeling it all around you. You are not it and it is not you. But neither is the distinction between you and the world entire and complete. There is a dissolving of each into the other. Is this happiness? It is for this boy, in this moment.

We have long ago been warned of the "pathetic fallacy," the danger of allowing ourselves to trust what we learn about ourselves and about the world through our felt sense of things. And close to the danger of too much feeling, it is argued, is the risk of sentimentality. True knowledge of the world does not come to us in this way. One could make the objection, certainly, that the witness of these writers is too sentimental, too much affected by nostalgia for a world long gone or never real in the first place. Or that even if such moments exist, they do not last and cannot be sustained in any meaningful way. Being in reality requires coming to the recognition that such childish moments must finally be put away.

But this in fact is precisely the question: what are we to make of such vivid, unforgettable parts of our experience? And must they be put away? Or is there a way to deepen and extend them so that the imagination becomes alive with the beautiful liveliness of the world? Can the wonder of disappearing into the world become, not simply a shard of memory from a lost time, but an ever-present possibility? Becoming a child again. Recovering our lost simplicity. Living free from care. It is this dream that stands at the heart of the ancient Christian contemplative tradition's idea of what it is to see and know the world as paradise. The echoes of this dream found in the accounts of these writers come to us from diverse geographies and cultural traditions. And they are, indeed, utterly personal in character. But at a moment when we are struggling to understand whether such a vision and experience of the world is still possible for us, they resonate with wider significance. They serve as important reminders that the dream of living in the world with openness, tenderness, and feeling, and allowing the world to enter and transform us, remains alive in us. Also that cherishing this dream will always retain a certain purposelessness. "I kept as still as I could. Nothing happened. I did not expect anything to happen. I was something that lay under the sun and felt it, like the pumpkins, and I did not want to be anything more."

Here, in this radical relinquishment of aspiration, purpose, and utility, lies one of the most significant contributions of contemplative thought to our efforts to reimagine our place in the natural world. The capacity and willingness to become small, to acknowledge the primacy of the living world, to open oneself completely to the life of the world, and to do so without any aim beyond the simple pleasure of the gesture itself: such unselfconscious simplicity and innocence can become the foundation of a more responsive and reciprocal way of being in the world. It can also help us to articulate an understanding of what our life in the world means when it is not defined narrowly by the values of utility and purpose. The fact that such a sensibility comes so easily to children suggests the kind of reversal that anyone who has passed beyond childhood must now undergo if it is to have an enduring purchase on one's life. It also helps to account for why the contemplative tradition speaks so often of the importance of acquiring simplicity and innocence. This open, receptive consciousness becomes the ground from which one learns again how to apprehend the world and live in it without calculation or purpose. It also enables one to formulate an alternative vision of life that can serve as a source of spiritual, political, and ecological renewal.

The Bloom of the Present Moment

I must live above all in the present.[45]

My first thoughts are azure; there is a bloom and a dew on them; they are papillary-feeders which I put out, tender, innocent.[46]

HENRY DAVID THOREAU

This remains one of the most enduring contributions of Henry David Thoreau's experiment at Walden Pond and of the tradition of ecological writing that has flowed forth from it. Thoreau's *Walden*, together with his *Journals*, have long been recognized as expressing one of the most arresting visions of life in the natural world to have appeared in the American canon. And in spite of the criticisms that continue to be leveled at Thoreau—his seemingly intractable misanthropy, his continuous flights into the transcendental realm—that have led many to wonder how valuable he can be to us in the context of our own struggles to reimagine our relationship with the natural world, certain aspects of his thought remain both compelling and helpful. In the context of these reflections on paradise, it is Thoreau's vision of the "purposeless life" and the powerful social critique such a vision of life makes possible that call in a particular way for our attention.

In the chapter, "What I Came For," which comprises Thoreau's most careful articulation of his philosophical or spiritual vision, he offers this comment about the life he had come to live: "Every morning was a cheerful invitation to make my life of equal simplicity, and I may say innocence with Nature herself." This observation, so crucial to understanding Thoreau's vision of life at Walden Pond, has received a great deal less attention than his famous statement of purpose that comes just a little bit further on: "I went to the woods," he says, "because I wished to live deliberately, to front only the essential facts of life, and see if I could not learn what it had to teach and not, when I came to die, discover that I had not lived."[47] This latter comment locates Thoreau's experiment clearly and self-consciously within a long (if unspecified) tradition of spiritual practice aimed at transforming one's consciousness in order to arrive at a fuller and more capacious awareness of existence. It also illuminates the meaning of his earlier comment in a helpful way, revealing it also to be a kind of statement of intention marked by the same fundamental seriousness of purpose. But there is a noticeable playfulness and lightness to the earlier comment that suggests something important about the character of Thoreau's contemplative work at Walden Pond: it is aimed at a recovery of simplicity and innocence... "with Nature herself." He does not elaborate upon the particular meaning of this work here. But one is left in no doubt about its importance, especially when viewed in the light of other related reflections on the same subject.

Some of these reflections are found in Thoreau's long opening chapter "Economy," whose very prominence at the beginning of *Walden* suggests the importance he attached to the practical work of detachment within the larger process of moral and spiritual transformation and coming alive to the world. Here one encounters the seeds of Thoreau's trenchant critique of the kind of social, cultural, and economic values that he believes have contributed so significantly to the erosion of our capacity for living with simplicity and innocence. His careful and minute calculations of his expenses, his obvious delight in his frugality, and his proud declarations of how little he requires to live are all laid out in service of a larger argument about the severe limitations inherent in the values and assumptions that drive the lives of so many of his contemporaries. "Even in this comparatively free country," he says, "through mere ignorance and mistake, [we] are so occupied with the factitious cares and superfluously coarse labors of life that its finer fruits cannot be plucked ... I think that we can safely trust a good deal more than we do."[48] At the root of Thoreau's critique in "Economy" is his sense of the high cost to both persons and the larger community of allowing ourselves to become consumed with "factitious cares." We miss the "finer fruits" of life (one of the ways Thoreau expressed his feeling for the subtle beauties of the life of the world), he suggests, not because we are unaware of their existence, but because our feeling for their value and importance has become atrophied through long, habitual preoccupation with lesser—"coarser"—realities. But it is not only the focus of our concerns ("fine" vs. "coarse") that matters, he seems to say; it is the character and depth of the concern itself. "We can safely trust a good deal more than we do" he notes, surely one of the most piercing and perceptive of Thoreau's observations regarding our inability to give ourselves freely and openly to what has been given to us, especially in the living world.

It is the lack of trust above all that prevents us from living in simplicity and innocence, suggests Thoreau. That is because beneath this mistrust are myriad fears that can never be allayed, and misplaced ideas about security that can never be satisfied. As long as one insists on trying to address them through the "coarser" means of incessant work, striving and acquisition, there can be only deepening care and anxiety. This is why Thoreau's ideas about the importance of detachment and relinquishment, as severe as any monk's, loom so large in the early sections of *Walden*. Simplicity and innocence, he suggests, are only possible for those who are prepared, both inwardly and outwardly, to relinquish the striving and the time and care necessary for acquiring the particular kind of security things offer. Thoreau argues for the importance of *insecurity*, for the wide-ranging freedom that comes from being ready and willing to relinquish everything for the sake of those "finer fruits." What does this mean in practical terms? Thoreau's brief meditation on clothes suggests why the simple practice of detachment held so much significance for him; without it, he believed, one could hardly begin to make the critical judgments necessary for determining the kind of work one was prepared to do, and to whom and to what one was prepared to give one's allegiance. "I say beware of all enterprises—that require new clothes, and not rather a new wearer of clothes. If there is not a new man, how can the new clothes be made to fit?"

Here, one encounters one of the most common refrains in Thoreau's work—the need for a radical transformation of identity. But in this instance, he links it directly and specifically to the question of work ("enterprise") and how profoundly the time and energy one devotes to work can shape (and distort) one's identity. Hence, his ironic reference to clothes, and to the danger of mistaking the "coarser" things (the outer role) for the "finer fruit" (one's inner identity). Underlying these reflections is a deep suspicion of our tendency to give ourselves uncritically to "enterprises" of all kinds and in the process sacrifice the possibility that a new person might come into being.

It is this fundamental concern that leads Thoreau to make a further comment on clothes that is also, at least indirectly, about the tyrannical force of "enterprises" upon our lives, especially the constraints that our unquestioned allegiance to them place upon us. In contrast to such a deeply compromised existence, he says: "It is desirable that a man be clad so simply that he can lay his hands on himself in the dark, and that he live in all respects so compactly and unpreparedly, that, if an enemy take the town, he can, like the old philosopher, walk out the gate empty-handed without anxiety."[49] It is not difficult to imagine how extreme such an image would have seemed to many of Thoreau's contemporaries; nor has its resonance weakened over time. Such radical relinquishment is, at least when expressed in such pure terms, simply unimaginable for most of us. Yet, one is close here to the heart of Thoreau's vision of what it means to live with simplicity and innocence, that is, in paradise. His vision, undeniably radical, remains powerful precisely because of this. And because of how skillfully he weaves together the practical dimensions of such simple living with sense of the interior disposition required to give it meaning. Also because of how well he understands the critical, political meaning of such a choice: the one who lives this way (simply clad) is unencumbered, and not beholden to those who would determine the shape of his existence for him, able to formulate a different way of thinking about and living in the world.[50] But it also has a meaning that is more personal, or hidden in character: the "simply clad" person lives not only "compactly" but "unpreparedly." Thoreau never tells us precisely what he means by this strange idea. But it is hard not to feel that this is one of the interior expressions of the choice to live simply clad and compactly: a heightened alertness to one's existence that is also a kind of insouciance. There is so little to tend to and care for that the need to prepare for this or that eventuality (to live preparedly) finally disappears. One simply lives. Because of this, in a moment of crisis, one is able to "walk out the gate empty-handed without anxiety."

One might well object, and many have objected, that Thoreau's paradisal vision is so fundamentally solitary and personal that it lacks value and meaning for the larger community. Or that its ascetic character is simply too severe. However, I think that it is possible to understand his vision of an innocent and simple life, a life free of anxiety, differently—as leading to a way of living that is open and responsive to the larger whole. Much like the early Christian monks, for whom *anachoresis* became part of a critical response to an acute social crisis, Thoreau understood his experiment at Walden Pond not simply as a personal gesture but as an effort to think through and work out in practice a different, and more sustainable way for society as a whole to live. His profound examination of the sources of care and anxiety that prevent us from seeing and living in the world in innocence and simplicity was at the heart of this project. And like the monks before him, his alternative vision of the self in the world undercut many of the prevailing assumptions of what it meant to live in the world with meaning and purpose. In particular, he articulated what it might mean to live in a way that was at once less acquisitive, less anxious, and more open and attentive to the life of the world. This is a truly contemplative practice that seeks, through a steady relinquishment of attachment to "things" and of the anxiety that such attachment breeds, to discover what it means to live openly and responsively to the gift of the world.

Paradoxically, this meant for Thoreau cultivating an awareness of the "heavenly" character of the world. This is part of what simplicity had come to mean for him: an awareness of the true character of existence free of anxiety and unwanted attachments that amounted to a continuous awareness of heaven on earth. This is one of the qualities Thoreau admires in certain older ways of living: "The very simplicity and nakedness of man's life in the primitive ages," he notes, "imply this advantage at least, that they left him still but a sojourner in nature ... we now no longer camp as for a night, but have settled down on earth and forgotten heaven."[51] It is strange to hear this most earthy of men regret the loss of heaven, but one feels intuitively the significance of this idea for his larger vision of our life in the world. Remembering heaven, Thoreau seems to suggest, is necessary for fully inhabiting our embodied, earthly existence. It is this that enables us to see and feel the world as luminous and precious. We are always in danger of "settling down on earth," of succumbing to what he calls our "low and primitive condition," and losing sight of the "higher and more ethereal life" to which we are called.[52] There is no denigration of material reality implied here; rather, there is simply a call to feel the life of the world more deeply. This requires not only the practice of detachment and the cultivation of the capacity to pay attention, but *time*. The ethereal or heavenly life Thoreau imagines is, among other things, spacious, empty, free. It is purposeless.

In the chapter entitled "Sounds," Thoreau offers what may be one of his most important and enduring accounts of what it means to dwell in such spaciousness. Yet, it is utterly and, at the same time, deceptively, simple. He proudly recounts:

> I did not read books the first summer; I hoed beans. Nay, I often did better than this. There were times when I could not afford to sacrifice the bloom of the present moment to any work, whether of the head or the hands. I love a broad margin to my life. Sometimes, in a summer morning, having taken my accustomed bath, I sat in my sunny doorway from sunrise till noon, rapt in a revery, amidst the pines and hickories and sumachs, in undisturbed solitude and stillness, while the birds sang around or flitted noiseless through the house, until by the sun falling in at my west window, or the noise of some traveller's wagon on the distant highway, I was reminded of the lapse of time.[53]

The entirety of Thoreau's vision of the contemplative life can be seen in this passage. One senses too its importance for helping us understand what it means for him to notice and respond to the living world. At the heart of his account is a simple refusal of the demands of work; not only did he eschew reading, but sometimes he even abandoned the necessary work of tending to his beans. He did nothing. Or rather sat in his doorway for long hours "rapt in a revery." He is not so far lost to the "ethereal life" that he fails to notice the trees, the birds, or the movement of the sun; indeed, he is profoundly alive to the world. But so rich and deep is his participation in the moment that he is in a sense lost to himself, and to any cares that would cloud his awareness of its simple beauty. His language for this spaciousness—"the bloom of the present moment," a "broad margin to my life" suggests his own awareness of its value and meaning for him personally. But he also recognizes the utter futility of trying to explain it or account for it in any definitive way. "For the most part," he says, "I minded not how the hours went. The day advanced as if to light some work of mine; it was morning, and lo, now it is evening, and nothing memorable is accomplished.... This was sheer idleness to my fellow-townsmen...."[54] It is difficult to miss the sense of whimsy in these remarks. But there is also something serious and unsettling in this vision of contemplative living: "Nothing memorable is accomplished ... Sheer idleness." Only in such an empty, purposeless space, Thoreau suggests, can the life of the world begin to enter into us again, can we learn to come alive to the world and care for it.

Practicing Paradise

> It's time we gave something back to the natural systems of order that have supported us, some care and tenderness, which is the most operative notion, I think—tenderness. Our isolations are gone in the West and everywhere. We need to give some time to the arts of cherishing the things we adore, before they simply vanish. Maybe it will be like learning a skill: how to live in paradise.[55]

> WILLIAM KITTREDGE

Learning how to live in paradise: it seems like an almost unimaginable prospect at the present moment. Yet it is also difficult to imagine how we will be able to participate in the work of repairing the world without seriously grappling with the question of what kind of world we hope to discover and live within—without reimagining paradise. Too often we have imagined ourselves as living in and creating a paradise of our own making that only serves our own narrow concerns; this has resulted in a chronic and pervasive alienation from the living world and has had disastrous effects on the living world itself. But we can (and must) learn to imagine paradise differently. The contemplative tradition, with its careful attention to the art of moral and spiritual transformation that enables us to understand ourselves as participating in the life of a larger whole, can contribute significantly to this work. In particular, it can help us see paradise not as a realm separate from (and superior to) the earth, but as woven deeply into everything that exists. The contemplative practice of learning to become detached from the grasping, acquisitive habits of a corrupt, materialistic culture and live with a simple awareness of the heavenly character of things can help us recover a sense of the enduring value of the palpable things of this world. But it seems increasingly clear that whatever personal meaning such renewed awareness of paradise may have for us as individuals, it will also need to inform a larger and more encompassing transformation of our spiritual, political, and cultural values. It is here that the emerging vision of contemplative ecology has something of genuine importance to contribute to the work of reimagining and repairing the world. A contemplative vision of paradise, whether it is rooted in a particular spiritual tradition or in a simple awareness of the world's beauty, is always grounded in the hope that we might yet learn to retrieve and learn to live within an unbroken whole. Even amidst our continued and frenzied assault upon the living world, we dream of the whole. The tenacity of the dream itself has healing power.

It is perhaps this that helps account for the persistence of this dream in our own ongoing discourse about the life of the world. It seems increasingly clear that we need the language of paradise to help us feel and understand the enormity of what we have lost and what we might yet recover. Which is why the personal accounts of engagement with paradise—lost, broken, renewed— remain so important to the larger work of healing the world. Among the many testimonies of this kind to emerge in contemporary American discourse, few are as compelling to me as that found in the work of Montana writer William Kittredge. In his haunting memoir *A Hole in the Sky*, Kittredge recounts his own encounter with paradise growing up in Oregon's Warner Valley. It is an emblematic tale, for he and his family arrived there at a moment when the place had not yet been worked to death, when its fecund beauty and power seemed to well up everywhere, when it was possible to live with a sense of intimacy with the natural world. But the way of living and responding to the land that he and his family chose took them down another path. "We tried to manage our ranchlands with efficiency we thought of as scientific, but our actual model was industrial," Kittredge relates. "The places around us were not alive with history but they could be useful. It was another way for the world to be dead … we thought we were doing God's work. We were cultivating, creating order and what we liked to think of as a version of Heaven on Earth."[56] Even his education in the way of animals was marred by a singular lack of attention to their utterly particular and mysterious way of being in the world. "My father was trying to give me something essential about the world as he knew it, which was horsemanship, but what I was learning, ultimately, was the art of keeping intimacy at some distance, and living with power."[57]

These observations are, of course, utterly personal and are distinctive to the time and place that Kittredge is describing. It is one child's memory of what it meant to come to know and ultimately lose the world. But these particular recollections of a childhood in Eastern Oregon resonate more widely and deeply; and they touch on patterns of thinking and living that have become endemic in our time and that have contributed, directly or indirectly, to our seemingly endless capacity for keeping the living world at a distance. It is this loss of intimacy and feeling for the world that lay at the heart of Kittredge's own narrative and his own sense of what it has meant for us to lose paradise. "Not long ago in the American West," Kittredge notes, "it was easy to think we were living in harmony with an inexhaustible paradise … but aspects of our paradise have been worked to death. The old growth timber has been mostly logged; the great salmon runs have vanished; cattle and sheep tromp streamsides to dust and dust again; hard metals percolating up from mine-shafts abandoned decades ago poison our mountain waters."[58] This of course is only one part of a much larger story of how our carelessness and inattention to the living world, as well as our willingness to choose distance and control over intimacy, have helped wreck the world. It seems important to recognize that an honest account of the particular ways this has happened, the particular places and beings we have lost, must be part of the story we tell ourselves of our life in the world. But have we really lost paradise? Is it useful or necessary, as we try to come to terms with our predicament, to speak in such terms?

I find it noteworthy that Kittredge, who elsewhere in his narrative describes himself as "irreligious as a stone," should find the language of paradise so indispensable to his own efforts to reimagine the world. Nor do I believe he is using it loosely or casually. It speaks to the tremendous potency that the dream of paradise still possesses for us—even at a cultural moment when the working out of religious identity has become so contentious and problematic and the meaning of many religious symbols has become so opaque or empty. But paradise itself will have to be reimagined, Kittredge suggests, if we are to reinvest it with all the meaning it is capable of, if we are to reinhabit it honestly and deeply. In a creative and whimsical gesture toward such renewal, he wonders whether we might need to rethink the meaning of the fall, that mythical moment when we lost our innocence in paradise and came to inhabit a broken, sinful world. What if we thought of ourselves instead as falling *into paradise*, falling into the endless beauty and mystery of the living world? And not abstractly, but in all the concrete particularity of our actual lives. Such an orientation would give added power to the work of imagining our place in the world, including the world we knew as children. This is precisely where Kittredge finds himself as he nears his sixtieth year: "I want to be like the child for whom it was so simple to let himself go into affection for what we are ... what a release it might be, falling back into the world as if through some gate that was reopened, into that time in which we felt ourselves seamlessly wedded to every thing, and every other thing, getting closer." Simplicity and innocence; the distinctive characteristics of a child turn out to be the essential "skills" for learning how to live in paradise.

Here, it seems to me, the ancient Christian contemplative insight about what it means to acquire purity of heart, to inhabit the kingdom of heaven, resonates deeply with a longing that is welling up in our own time to discover how to live again with a true simplicity and innocence in the natural world.

It is of course a "second naïveté" that we are seeking; we must become *again* as little children. We must learn to see differently, see everything as alive, part of a single fabric. Kittredge bears witness to his own longing for such a transformed existence:

> I want to see if the light is really burning. I want to see the Lombardy poplars and apple trees and the posts supporting the woven-wire fence around the house where I lived in that boyhood, I want to see if they are glowing in the luminous world. I want *things* to be radiant and permeable. I want to be welcome inside these memories if nowhere else, and I think I was welcome as a child. I want the child who thought about the world and understood that he was welcome to have been correct. I want to have had that; I want the world to be that good.[59]

The sheer force of such wanting is difficult to deny. Yet it is not easy to say what it means or might mean for our efforts to learn how to reinhabit the world. One part of its meaning, I think, is the notion that the feeling for the world as radiant, permeable, and welcoming that is so accessible to our childhood selves can in fact be recovered and reinhabited. In Kittredge's narrative, this is expressed through a self-conscious exercise of the imagination and will, born of a recognition that this sense of things must be rediscovered and reconstructed—not through an exercise in nostalgia for a simpler time, but through something more akin to an act of faith. It will require real risk to believe in and inhabit the world in this way, a willingness to be foolish, like a child. The practical value of such risk will only become clear in time, as we work at learning to live in the world this way. But we should not underestimate the importance of recovering this capacity for opening ourselves to the living world in simplicity and innocence.

Heaven on earth. Can this idea, and the *practice* of this idea, still have value and meaning for us? Not if it continues to be associated in our minds primarily with the desire to dominate and control the earth. But the contemplative tradition reminds us that it can mean something altogether different and can serve as an inspiration for helping us imagine ourselves and the living world as part of a whole, unbroken fabric. The correspondence between Thomas Merton and D.T. Suzuki with which this chapter began points to one crucial element of this practice: the gradual opening up of the mind to the simple reality of the living world, not in terms of its usefulness to us, but for its own sake. The "purposeless life" is nothing more or less than the creation of a transparent, open space in which the full reality of the world can enter. But this is also what is so often meant in the contemplative tradition by the idea of paradise or heaven. On April 23, 1964, during a period in his life when he had begun to spend an increasing amount of time in his hermitage, Thomas Merton found himself reflecting in his journal on the meaning of "heavenliness":

> All the trees are fast beginning to be in leaf, and the first green freshness of a new summer is all over the hills.... Mixture of heavenliness and anguish. Seeing "heavenliness" suddenly, for instance, in the pure white of the mature dogwood blossoms against the dark evergreens in the cloudy garden. "Heavenliness" too of the song of the unknown bird that is perhaps here for only these days, passing through, a lovely, deep, simple, song. Pure—no pathos, no statement, no desire, pure heavenly sound. Seized by this "heavenliness" as I if I were a child—a child's mind I have never done anything to deserve to have and that is my own part in the heavenly spring. Not of this world, or of my making. Born partly of physical anguish (which is really not there, though. It goes quickly). Sense that "heavenliness" is the real nature of things, *not* their nature, not *en soi*, but the fact that they are a gift of love and freedom.[60]

Merton's late journals are filled with simple, delicate descriptions of the natural world, expressions of his deepening capacity to see and feel the simple, luminous beauty of the world. In spite of critiques from Czeslaw Milosz and Rosemary Radford Ruether that his view of the natural world was too romantic, not sufficiently attentive to the presence of inexplicable suffering and death found everywhere in nature, Merton held fast to his own sense of its fundamentally sacramental, paradisal character.[61] Still, at this particular moment, one senses a more complex and ambiguous feeling for the natural world taking hold within him. Heavenliness and anguish exist together. As the ancient Jewish and Christian wisdom traditions affirm, they are bound together eternally. But they do not cancel each other out—at least not completely. If "heavenliness," something Merton elsewhere describes in terms of "the transformation of life and of human relations by Christ *now*,"[62] is to have meaning and significance for us in our present existence, it must somehow take account of the enduring and painful presence of anguish—both the inexplicable pain and suffering that are part of the brute reality of our embodied lives in the natural world as well as the anguish manifested in the myriad distortions and abuses of paradise that we ourselves visit upon the world. And more than this, it must lead to a willingness to stand within that anguish and to seek meaningful forms of resistance to the patterns of thought and ways of living that continue to diminish and impoverish the world.

In much of Merton's later writing, one sees the effort to identify and retrieve a meaningful idea of paradise joined to a fierce resistance to the increasing presence of "false paradises" within contemporary thought and practice. This is particularly clear in two important late essays, "Rain and the Rhinoceros," and "Day of a Stranger," which frame the ideal of contemplative living as being both utterly "purposeless" and necessary to the work of social criticism and political resistance.[63] His correspondence from this period also reveals his continued attention to this theme and his growing suspicion of the kind of secular expressions of hope that promised an illusory paradise on earth. See, for example, his letter to Mary Childs Black, January 24, 1962, in which he notes the continuing importance of the Shakers' vision of eternity present on earth, and the danger of new secular versions of paradise: "The Shakers ... saw the deceptiveness of the secular hope, and their eyes were open, in childlike innocence, to the evil, the violence, the unscrupulousness that too often underlay the secular vision of the earthly paradise. It was a paradise in which the Indian had been slaughtered and the Negro was enslaved." In a letter to Madame Camille Drevet, dated July 1, 1965, he calls attention to the problematic character of "the ancient American myth of rejuvenation, justification, and a totally new start. By definition this is the land not only of 'liberty' but also of primeval innocence and indeed complete impeccability;" he notes ruefully the patterns of blindness and exploitation that have issued forth from this particular vision of paradise. And in a letter to Leslie Dewart, dated September 1962, he comments on the tremendous harm that has been done by what he describes as "The illusion of America as the earthly paradise, in which everyone recovers original goodness: which becomes in fact a curious idea that prosperity itself justifies everything, is a sign of goodness, is a carte blanche to continue to be prosperous in any way feasible ... we are entitled to defend ourselves by any means whatever, without any limitation, and all the more so because what we are defending is our illusion of innocence."[64]

It is chilling to read these comments today and to feel how little has changed and how deeply attached we remain to our own profoundly destructive visions of paradise. It serves as a reminder of the need to continue to cultivate our own contemplative critique, one that can address the ongoing patterns of our destructive presence in the world and our anguish over this. But such a critique must also help us find language for affirming that even amidst such anguish, heavenliness is real, and is woven deeply into our present experience.

"We already have everything, but we don't know it and don't experience it. Everything has been given to us in Christ. All we need is to experience what we already possess."[65] This is how Thomas Merton expressed his sense of the contemplative life during his visit with the community at Redwoods monastery in 1968. Here again, one hears an echo of the ancient monastic conviction that, as Columba Stewart expresses it, "contemplation and prayer are a kind of participation in heavenly beatitude."[66] In Merton's conference at the Redwoods, as in so much of his later work, it is the realization of this beatitude in the life of the person of prayer that concerns him most. One senses here a reflection of his own long struggle to simplify contemplative practice, to allow it to take hold on a deep level beyond the usual concern with means and ends. "We have been indoctrinated so much into means and ends," he said, "that we don't realize that there is a different dimension in the life of prayer." It is mostly a matter of "giving ourselves in prayer a chance to realize that we have what we seek. We don't have to rush after it. It is there all the time, and if we give it time, it will make itself known to us."[67]

"We have what we seek." Here, in its simplest form, is how the Christian contemplative tradition understands the mystery of paradise. It is present to us always—in "the mature dogwood blossoms against the dark evergreens in the cloudy garden." In the "song of the unknown bird." In everything that exists. It is accessible to all of us. All we have to do to encounter it, to feel the heavenliness of things, is to open our eyes or ears. "Live in each season as it passes; breathe the air, drink the drink, taste the fruit, and resign yourself to the influences of each."[68] That is Henry David Thoreau's advice, and it is not far from what we sense in Merton's journal entry from April, 1964 or in his earlier correspondence with Suzuki or in the ancient monastic teaching on contemplative practice. The simple reality of existence is deeply graced. It is our growing awareness of this truth, the recovery of our original innocence, what Merton calls our "child mind," that accounts for our capacity to experience the world—even amidst the anguish we feel at its brokenness—as luminous, revelatory, and whole. If we are to participate in the healing and renewal of the world, we will need to risk inhabiting and embodying in our own lives the truth that "everything is in fact paradise, because it is filled with the glory and presence of God, and nothing is any more separated from God."

Notes

FRONT MATTER

1. Evagrius, *On Thoughts* 39. *Evagrius of Pontus: The Greek Ascetic Corpus*, trans. Robert E. Sinkewicz (New York: Oxford University Press 2003), 180.
2. Rebecca Solnit, *A Field Guide to Getting Lost* (New York: Penguin, 2005), 29.

CHAPTER I

1. Gary Snyder, "By Frazier Creek Falls," *Turtle Island* (New York: New Directions, 1974), 41.
2. Thomas Merton, *The Hidden Ground of Love: The Letters of Thomas Merton on Religious Experience and Social* Concerns, ed. William H. Shannon (New York: Farrar, Straus and Giroux, 1985), 115 [letter to Amiya Chakravarty, April 13, 1967].
3. Simone Weil, *Waiting for God*, trans. Emma Craufurd (New York: Putnam's, 1952), 58.
4. The broad and varied phenomenon sometimes described as the "greening of religion" has emerged with particular force during the past twenty-five years and has taken many different forms—both in terms of its scholarly expressions and its practical applications (often integrated). The *Forum on Religion and Ecology* [FORE], under the leadership of Mary Evelyn Tucker and John Grim, has been at the forefront of this work and has helped facilitate the emergence of much of the best scholarship in the field. One of the most significant accomplishments of the FRE to date has been the remarkable series of conferences held at Harvard's Center for the Study of World Religions during the late 1990s and the volumes of essays that emerged subsequently. This initiative resulted in groundbreaking work on the role of nature in Hinduism, Jainism, Buddhism, Christianity, Judaism, Islam, Indigenous traditions, Shinto traditions, Daoism, and Confucianism. See http://fore.research.yale.edu/publications/books/book_series/cswr/index.html.

Increasingly, religious traditions are figuring in the public debate over the fate of the natural world.

For an early and influential analysis of the relationship between religion and ecology as part of the larger public debate about the environmental crisis, see the special issue of *Daedulus: Journal of the American Academy of Arts and Sciences* on "Religion and Ecology" (Fall 2001). Also important to the growing awareness of the relationship between ecology and religion has been the "Ecology and Religion" group at the American Academy of Religion, which has helped to bring ecological concerns to the center of scholarship on religion in North America. The journals *Worldviews: Global Religions, Culture and Ecology* (Brill) and *The Journal for the Study of Religion, Nature and Culture* (Equinox) have offered important fora for emerging scholarship in this area. *The Encyclopedia of Religion and Nature*, ed. Bron Taylor (New York: Continuum, 2005), remains the single most encompassing reference work in the field.

5. The terms "spiritual ecology" or "ecological spirituality," which have come to occupy an increasingly important place in contemporary thinking about the natural world, point to a growing recognition that there is a dimension of the human experience of nature, perhaps a dimension of the natural world itself, that transcends simple, materialistic explanations, that requires an honest attempt to create a wider field of discourse in which natural phenomena and the experience of the spiritual or transcendent (however it is construed), can be understood as part of a single, unbroken reality. Among the most significant works touching on these questions are Catherine Albanese, *Nature Religion in America from the Algonkian Indians to the New Age* (Chicago: University of Chicago Press, 1990); David Kinsley, *Ecology and Religion: Ecological Spirituality in Cross-Cultural Perspective* (Englewood Cliffs, NJ: Prentice Hall, 1995); Thomas R. Dunlop, *Faith in Nature: Environmentalism as Religious Quest* (Seattle: University of Washington Press, 2004); Sarah McFarland Taylor, *Green Sisters: A Spiritual Ecology* (Cambridge, MA: Harvard University Press, 2007); Fikret Bekes, *Sacred Ecology,* 2nd ed. (London: Routledge, 2008); Bron Taylor, *Dark Green Religion: Nature, Spirituality and Our Planetary Future* (Berkeley: University of California Press, 2009); William Gibson, *A Reenchanted World: The Quest for a New Kinship with Nature* (New York: Metropolitan, 2009); *The Oxford Handbook of Religion and Ecology*, ed. Roger Gottlieb (New York: Oxford University Press, 2010); Whitney Bauman, Richard Bohannon, and Kevin O'Brien, eds., *Grounding Religion: A Field Guide to the Study of Religion and Ecology* (London: Routledge, 2010); Celia Deane-Drummond, ed., *Religion and Ecology in the Public Sphere* (Edinburgh: T&T Clark, 2011); Leslie Sponsel, *Spiritual Ecology: A Quiet Revolution* (Santa Barbara, CA: Praeger, 2012).

Thomas Berry's work occupies a distinctive place in the emerging field of religion and ecology. His book *The Dream of the Earth* gave early and important expression to the idea that religion and spiritual practice could not be meaningfully understood without reference to the natural world in general and to ecological concerns in particular. Nor should one underestimate the influence of his thought among those who have subsequently extended and deepened his work. See Thomas Berry, *The Dream of the Earth* (San Francisco: Sierra Club, 1990); *The Great Work: Our Way into the Future* (New York: Bell Tower, 1999); Thomas Berry and Brian Swimme, *The Universe Story From the Primordial Flaring Forth to the Ecozoic Era: A Celebration of the Unfolding of the Cosmos* (San Francisco: HarperOne, 1994); Brian Swimme and Mary Evelyn Tucker, *The Journey of the Universe* (New Haven: Yale University Press, 2011). For a thoughtful theological critique of Berry and Swimme's work, see J. Matthey Ashley, "Reading the Universe Story Theologically: The Contribution of a Biblical Narrative Imagination," *Theological Studies* 71:4 (2010): 870–902.

For work that takes up these questions from an explicitly Christian perspective, see Sallie McFague, *Super, Natural Christians: How We Should Love Nature* (Minneapolis: Fortress Press, 1997); Mark I. Wallace, *Finding God in the Singing River: Christianity, Spirit, Nature* (Minneapolis: Augsburg Fortress, 2005); Steven Chase, *Nature as Spiritual Practice* (Grand Rapids, MI: Eerdmans, 2011); Timothy Hessel-Robinson and Ray Maria McNamara, eds., *Spirit and Nature: The Study of Christian Spirituality in a Time of Ecological Urgency* (Eugene, OR: Pickwick, 2011).

6. Gregory Bateson, *Steps to an Ecology of Mind: Collected Essays in Anthropology, Psychiatry, Evolution, and Epistemology* (Chicago: University of Chicago Press, 1972).

7. The field of ecology itself remains diverse and variegated, providing many different means by which a dialogue with history, social science, philosophy, and spirituality can be engaged. One of the most fruitful areas to examine for a possible engagement with traditions of spiritual practice is phenomenological ecology or human ecology. See, for example, David Seamon, ed., *Dwelling, Seeing, and Designing: Toward a Phenomenological Ecology* (Albany: State University of New York Press, 1993); John Llewelyn, *Seeing through God: A Geophenomenology* (Bloomington: Indiana University Press, 2004); Frederick Steiner, *Human Ecology: Following Nature's Lead* (Washington: Island Press, 2002). There are also more synthetic attempts to understand how ecological thought and practice can be situated in relation to a wider context of shared cultural and political life. See, for example, Stephen Harrison, Steve Pile, and Nigel Thrift, eds., *Patterned Ground: Entanglements of Nature and Culture* (London: Reaktion Books, 2004); Robert Thayer, *LifePlace: Bioregional Thought and Practice* (Berkeley: University of California Press, 2003). For a primarily scientific account of ecology that gives careful attention to the increasingly fragmented character of ecological communities while also attending to the application of this analysis to conservation of biological diversity, ecological restoration, and ecological planning, see Sharon E. Collinge, *Ecology of Fragmented Landscapes* (Baltimore: Johns Hopkins University Press, 2009). And there is also growing attention to the political meaning of ecological thought and practice. Muhamed Suliman, ed., *Ecology, Politics and Violent Conflict* (London: Zed Books, 1999); Rob Nixon, *Slow Violence and the Environmentalism of the Poor* (Berkeley: University of California, 2011).

8. On the idea of the "spiritual senses" in Christianity, see Paul Gavrilyuk and Sarah Coakley, eds., *The Spiritual Senses: Perceiving God in Western Christianity* (Cambridge: Cambridge University Press, 2011); Stephen Fields, "Balthasar and Rahner on the Spiritual Senses," *Theological Studies* 57 (1996): 224–241.

9. Joseph Wood Krutch, *The Desert Year* (Tucson: University of Arizona Press, 1985), 37–38.

10. Denise Levertov, *New and Selected Essays* (New York: New Directions, 1992), 4–6 On the significance of apophatic traditions of thought and practice, in both ancient and contemporary contexts, see: Michael Sells, *Mystical Languages of Unsaying* (Chicago: University of Chicago Press, 1994); Denys Turner, *The Darkness of God: Negativity in Christian Mysticism* (Cambridge: Cambridge University Press, 1995); Thomas A. Carlson, *Finitude and the Naming of God* (Chicago: University of Chicago Press, 1999); Michael Kessler and Christian Sheppard, eds. *Mystics: Presence and Aporia* (Chicago: University of Chicago Press, 2003); William Franke, *On What Cannot Be Said: Apophatic Discourse in Philosophy, Religion, Literature and the Arts. Vol. 1. Classic Formulations* (Notre Dame: University of Notre Dame Press, 2007); William Franke, *On What Cannot Be Said: Apophatic Discourse in Philosophy, Religion, Literature and the Arts. Vol. 2: Modern and Contemporary Transformations* (Notre Dame: University of Notre Dame Press, 2007).

Levertov's allusion to the feeling of immersing oneself in a "larger whole" is emblematic of the oblique way many contemporary writers express the sense of how the experience of the natural world becomes woven into a larger fabric of meaning that also includes what we often refer to as the sacred. Still, she is careful in her language and leaves open the question of what precisely the whole refers to, what it is know oneself as drawn into it, and what particular practices (poetic, meditative, contemplative) are most conducive to facilitating openness to such immersion. In this, she echoes the work of many ancient spiritual writers who also sought to understand what it meant to immerse oneself in a larger whole and what spiritual practices could help open the mind and heart to this possibility. But how to understand the character of this whole? How should one (or should one even try to) name it? Often, during the course of writing this book, I have struggled with the question of how to speak adequately and honestly about the reality at the heart of contemplative practice, especially as it relates to the experience of knowing and caring for the natural world. Specifically, I have wondered how, when and whether to speak of *God* as the central focus of this work, especially in the face of the seemingly endless diversity of responses to the idea of God that inform both the historical traditions of Christian spiritual practice and the various efforts to reimagine the meaning of spiritual practice in the modern and postmodern worlds. Finding the right language is challenging, for while some historical traditions (including the ancient Christian contemplative tradition) of spiritual practice use God language to articulate the center of their concerns, others do not. And even among those that do employ theistic language, the meanings arising from such discourse are often so varied and ambiguous as to defy any simple categorization. Something similar applies in the contemporary moment, in which many continue to find the language of God meaningful to describe the source and end of their ultimate concerns, indeed the source and end of life itself. But increasingly, as old certitudes give way to a more open, searching feeling for the sacred, one encounters ambivalence about how to express this reality, as well as a greater level of trust in language that is oblique or allusive. The growing range of terms used to express the center of ultimate concern reflects these changes. One still hears reference to God and the Divine of course. But also: the sacred, the other, the ultimate, the all, the real, the whole, mystery. These are but a few of the terms employed to speak of the source and end of all things that engages, envelops and sustains us (terms that are sometimes capitalized, sometimes not, depending on a variety of considerations). And while they do not necessarily refer to the same thing or have the same meaning (differences of meaning arising from distinctive historical, cultural, religious and literary contexts matter), there are often striking resonances among and between them. Their prominent presence in contemporary discourse about spiritual experience and the natural world present us with certain undeniable challenges and opportunities, not least of which is the question of whether, amidst such diversity of expression (and, one presumes, experience), we can find a shared language for our deepest concerns. But there is also something promising and hopeful about these developments: the opportunity that this open, unfinished and allusive discourse gives us for expanding and deepening the way we imagine our relationship with the living world.

I make an effort in these pages to attend carefully to the diverse expressions for the mystery at the heart of our experience of the world without delimiting either their meaning or their possible relationships with one another too closely. I also give careful attention to the recurring refusal on the part of many, including many in the Christian contemplative tradition, to name this mystery at all, and to their commitment to dwell instead in silence, darkness and emptiness--even absence. The sense of humility about how or whether to speak of God remains one of the central contributions of apophatic traditions of spiritual practice, and is a large part of what makes them resonate so strongly in the present moment. We want to find ways of expressing what it means to us exist within an encompassing, mysterious whole. But we also recognize the need for reticence in speaking about a mystery that will always remain hidden beyond language, beyond images, beyond thought. On the significance of apophatic traditions of thought and practice, in both ancient and contemporary contexts, see: Michael Sells, *Mystical Languages of Unsaying* (Chicago: University of Chicago Press, 1994); Denys Turner, *The Darkness of God: Negativity in Christian Mysticism* (Cambridge: Cambridge University Press, 1995); Thomas A. Carlson, *Finitude and the Naming of God* (Chicago: University of Chicago Press, 1999); Michael Kessler and Christian Sheppard, eds. *Mystics: Presence and Aporia* (Chicago: University of Chicago Press, 2003); William Franke, *On What Cannot Be Said: Apophatic Discourse in Philosophy, Religion, Literature and the Arts. Vol. 1.*

Classic Formulations (Notre Dame: University of Notre Dame Press, 2007); William Franke, *On What Cannot Be Said: Apophatic Discourse in Philosophy, Religion, Literature and the Arts. Vol. 2: Modern and Contemporary Transformations* (Notre Dame: University of Notre Dame Press, 2007).

11. Attention to the spiritual character of contemporary literary evocations of the natural world—part of the larger ecocritical project—is growing, especially in relation to the North American literary tradition. See Scott Slovic, *Seeking Awareness in American Nature Writing: Henry Thoreau, Annie Dillard, Edward Abbey, Wendell Berry, Barry Lopez* (Salt Lake City: University of Utah Press, 1992); John P. O'Grady, *Pilgrims to the Wild: Everett Ruess, Henry David Thoreau, John Muir, Clarence King, Mary Austin* (Salt Lake City: University of Utah Press, 2002); John Gatta, *Making Nature Sacred: Literature, Religion, and Environment in America from the Puritans to the Present* (New York: Oxford University Press, 2004).

For my own efforts to map this phenomenon, worked out in a number essays published during the past several years, see Douglas Burton-Christie, "A Feeling for the Natural World: Spirituality and the Appeal to the Heart in Contemporary Nature Writing," *Continuum* 2, nos. 2–3 (Spring 1993); "Mapping the Sacred Landscape: Spirituality and the Contemporary Literature of Nature," *Horizons* 21, no. 1 (Spring 1994): 22–47; "The Literature of Nature and the Quest for the Sacred," *The Way Supplement* 81 (1994): 4–14; "Living between Two Worlds: Home, Journey and the Quest for Sacred Place," *Anglican Theological Review* 79, no. 3 (Summer 1997): 413–432; "The Sense of Place," *The Way* 39, no. 1 (January 1999): 59–72; "Into the Body of Another: *Eros*, Embodiment and Intimacy with the Natural World," *Anglican Theological Review* 81, no. 1 (Winter 1999): 13–37; "The Immense Call of the Particular: Czeslaw Milosz on Nature, History and Hope," *Interdisciplinary Studies in Literature and Environment* 7, no. 1 (Winter 2000): 115–129; "Words beneath the Water: Logos, Cosmos and the Spirit of Place," in *Christianity and Ecology*, ed. Dieter T. Hessel and Rosemary Radford Ruether (Cambridge: Harvard University Press, 2000), 317–336; "The Wild and the Sacred," *Anglican Theological Review* 85, no. 3 (Summer 2003): 493–510; "The Spirit of Place: The Columbia River Watershed Letter and the Meaning of Community," *Horizons* 30, no. 1 (Spring 2003): 7–24; "Nature," in *The Blackwell Companion to Christian Spirituality*, ed. Arthur Holder (Oxford: Blackwell, 2005), 478–495; "The Weight of the World: The Heaviness of Nature in Spiritual Experience," in *Exploring Christian Spirituality: Essays in Honor of Sandra M. Schneiders*, ed. Bruce Lescher and Elizabeth Liebert (New York: Paulist, 2006), 142–160; "Spirituality in an Age of Ecological Loss," *Ascent* 31, no. 1 (Fall 2007): 27–43; "Darwin's Contemplative Vision," *Spiritus* 9, no. 1 (Spring 2009): 89–95; "Place-Making as Contemplative Practice," *Anglican Theological Review* 91, no. 3 (Summer 2009): 347–372; "The Blue Sapphire of the Mind: Christian Contemplative Practice and the Healing of the Whole," *Sewanee Theological Review* 54, no. 3 (June 2011); "Practicing Paradise: Contemplative Awareness and Ecological Renewal," *Anglican Theological Review* 94, no. 2 (Spring 2012): 281–303.

12. Denise Levertov, "Settling," in *Evening Train* (New York: New Directions: 1992), 3.

13. Robert Finch, "Being at Two with Nature," *Georgia Review* 45, no. 1 (Spring 1991): 101 (emphasis mine).

14. Paul Shepard, "The Ark of the Mind," in *Traces of an Omnivore* (Washington, DC: Island Press, 1996).

15. Krutch, *The Desert Year*, 37–38.

16. Edith Cobb, *The Ecology of Imagination in Childhood* (Dallas: Spring Publications, 1993), 27–28.

17. Thomas Merton, *Contemplative Prayer* (New York: Herder and Herder, 1969), 112.

18. Rainer Maria Rilke, *Sonnets to Orpheus*, trans. Edward Snow (New York: North Point, 2004), 101.

19. On the practice of *prosoche* or attention within ancient philosophical practice and early Christian monasticism, see Pierre Hadot, *Philosophy as a Way of Life,* ed. Arnold I. Davidson, trans. Michael Chase (Oxford: Blackwell, 1995), 126–144.

20. Athanasius's *The Life of Antony* is perhaps the most significant of the early Christian monastic texts to reflect on this question. Athanasius of Alexandria, *The Life of Antony and the Letter to Marcelinus*, trans. Robert C. Gregg (New York: Paulist, 1980). For a thoughtful historical analysis of the monk's role in reconstituting society, see Peter Brown, *The Making of Late Antiquity* (Cambridge, MA: Harvard University Press, 1978); "The Rise and Function of the Holy Man in Late Antiquity," *Journal of Roman Studies* 61 (1971): 80–101; reprinted in *Society and the Holy in Late Antiquity* (London: Faber and Faber, 1982). On the significance of communal living within early monastic experience, see Graham Gould, *The Desert Fathers on Monastic Community* (Oxford: Oxford University Press, 1993).

21. David Tracy, *Blessed Rage for Order: The New Pluralism in Theology* (Chicago: University of Chicago Press, [1975], 1995), 45. Michel de Certeau helpfully points to the "poetic ways of 'making do,'" the "artisan-like inventiveness" that so often characterizes the work of *bricolage* in everyday life. The result of such improvisation, he observes, is often the emergence of a new "network of relations" among and between things whose kindred character may well have gone unrecognized before the work of *bricolage* brought it to light. See Michel de Certeau, *The Practice of Everyday Life*, trans. Stephen Rendall (Berkeley: University of California Press, 1984), xv, xviii. For an illuminating discussion of the role of *bricolage* in shaping religious identity, especially in the fluid contemporary cultural context, see Vincent Miller, *Consuming Religion: Christian Faith and Practice in a Consumer Culture* (New York: Continuum, 2005), 172.

22. Robert A. Orsi, *Between Heaven and Earth: The Religious Worlds People Make and the Scholars Who Study Them* (Princeton: Princeton University Press, 2005), 144.

23. See William Cronon, *Uncommon Ground: Rethinking the Human Place in Nature* (New York: Norton, 1996); also Jennifer Price, *Flight Maps: Adventures with Nature in Modern America* (New York: Basic Books, 2000).

24. Samuel M. Scheiner and Michael R. Willig, eds., *The Theory of Ecology* (Chicago: University of Chicago Press, 2011), 10.

25. Daniel Botkin, *Discordant Harmonies: A New Ecology for the Twenty-First Century* (New York: Oxford University Press, 1990), 7–9.

26. Timothy Morton, *The Ecological Thought* (Cambridge: Harvard University Press, 2010), esp. 33–38.

27. Aldo Leopold, *A Sand County Almanac. And Sketches Here and There* (New York: Oxford University Press, 1949), 207–201.

28. On the distinction between spirituality and religion (especially in the North American context), and the tensions and relationship between them in contemporary experience, see Robert Fuller, *Spiritual but not Religious: Understanding Unchurched America* (New York: Oxford University Press, 2001); Sandra Schneiders, "Religion vs. Spirituality: A Contemporary Conundrum," *Spiritus* 3 (2003): 163–185; Wade Clark Roof, "Religion and Spirituality: Toward an Integrated Analysis," in Michelle Dillon, ed., *Handbook of the Sociology of Religion* (Cambridge: Cambridge University Press, 2003), 137–148; Brian J. Zinnbauer, Kenneth Pargament, et al., "Religion and Spirituality: Unfuzzying the Fuzzy," *Journal for the Scientific Study of Religion*, 36, no. 4 (1997): 549–564; Paul Heelas, Linda Woodhead, et al., *The Spiritual Revolution: Why Religion Is Giving Way to Spirituality* (Oxford: Blackwell, 2005); Jeremy Carrette and Richard King, *Selling Spirituality: The Silent Takeover of Religion* (New York: Routledge, 2005). On the broader question of spirituality's increasing prevalence in contemporary life, see Robert Wuthnow, *After Heaven: Spirituality in America since the 1950s* (Berkeley: University of California Press, 1998); Wade Clark Roof, *Spiritual Marketplace: Baby Boomers and the Remaking of American Religion* (Princeton: Princeton University Press, 1999); Leigh Eric Schmidt, *Restless Souls: The Making of American Spirituality* (San Francisco: HarperSanFrancisco, 2005).

    Allan D. Hodder, in his book, *Thoreau's Ecstatic Witness* (New Haven: Yale University Press, 2001) offers a caution about the usefulness of this contemporary distinction when it comes to analyzing the work of certain figures from the historical past. In the case of Thoreau's work, Hodder notes: "It is as a somewhat grudging concession to the contemporary popular connotations of 'spiritual' and 'spirituality' that I have employed the terms in [this] study. I say grudging because while I see the need for terms such as these that center upon personal inward experience, I do not on historical grounds accept the privileging of the 'spiritual' over the 'religious' that this usage now often implies—the view is that to be spiritual is somehow more authentic, more natural, less historically motivated than to be religious in the more conventional, collective, or institutional sense" (p. 4).

29. Sandra M. Schneiders, "The Study of Christian Spirituality: Contours and Dynamics of a Discipline," in Elizabeth Dreyer and Mark Burrows, eds., *Minding the Spirit: The Study of Christian Spirituality* (Baltimore: Johns Hopkins University Press, 2005), 5–6.

30. Increasingly one is encountering attempts to articulate a secular or even atheistic spirituality. See, for example, Peter H. Van Ness, ed., *Spirituality and the Secular*

Quest (New York: Crossroad, 1996); Robert C. Solomon, *Spirituality for the Skeptic: The Thoughtful Love of Life* (New York: Oxford University Press, 2006); Andre Compte-Sponville, *The Little Book of Atheistic Spirituality* (New York: Viking, 2007).

For an important example of how the distinction between religion and spirituality can signify meaning, especially in relation to contemporary scientific thought and practice, see Elaine Howard Ecklund, *Science vs. Religion: What Scientists Really Think* (New York: Oxford, 2010). Her study, based on an in-depth survey of contemporary scientists, reveals that nearly a quarter of atheists and agnostics describe themselves as "spiritual." And while the precise meaning of such self-identification cannot be simply or easily determined, it suggests that the very categories of "science" and "religion" may well be too narrow to account for the range of feelings about spirituality commonly found among scientists.

For an eloquent example of the effort to move "beyond religion" toward a more encompassing idea of the spiritual that can inform a broadly shared ethic of concern for the world, see the Dalai Lama, *Beyond Religion: Ethics for a Whole World* (New York: Houghton Mifflin Harcourt, 2011).

31. On the shifting contexts in which contemporary persons experience and express spiritual meaning, and the growing importance of lived religion as a category of interpretation, see Meredith B. McGuire, *Lived Religion: Faith and Practice in Everyday Life* (New York: Oxford University Press, 2008); Ruth Frankenburg, *Living Spirit, Living Practice: Poetics, Politics, Epistemology* (Durham: Duke University Press, 2004); Kelly Besecke, "Speaking of Meaning in Modernity: Reflexive Spirituality as a Cultural Resource," *Sociology of Religion* 62, no. 3 (2001): 365–381; David D. Hall, ed., *Lived Religion in America: Toward a History of Practice* (Princeton: Princeton University Press, 1997); Orsi, *Between Heaven and Earth*; Nancy T. Ammerman, ed., *Everyday Religion: Observing Modern Religious Lives* (New York: Oxford University Press, 2007).

32. On contemplative spirituality in a contemporary, inter-religious context, see Mirabai Bush, ed., *Contemplation Nation: How Ancient Practices Are Changing the Way We Live* (New York: CreateSpace, 2011); Patrick Henry, ed., *Benedict's Dharma: Buddhists Reflect on the Rule of St. Benedict* (New York: Riverhead, 2001).

33. Of particular importance in the contemporary retrieval of ancient Christian contemplative thought has been the work of the American Trappist writer, Thomas Merton. His classic work *New Seeds of Contemplation* (New York: New Directions, 1961) offers a simple, clear, but intellectually sophisticated articulation of the Christian contemplative vision that has had an enduring impact on contemporary thought, not least because of its spirit of openness and expansiveness, its understanding of contemplative experience as arising from and touching into the heart of life: "Contemplation is the highest expression of [our] intellectual and spiritual life. It is that life itself, fully awake, fully active, fully aware that it is alive. It is spiritual wonder. It is spontaneous awe at the sacredness of life, of being. It is gratitude

for life, for awareness and for being. It is a vivid realization of the fact that life and being in us proceed from an invisible, transcendent and infinitely abundant Source" (1). The importance of Merton's witness also owes much to his continuing effort to develop this contemplative vision in relation to art, culture, politics, and in dialogue with a wide range of seekers beyond the Christian tradition.

One of the most notable examples of the growing contemporary interest in contemplative practice in the Christian tradition can be seen in the "centering prayer" movement, rooted in ancient contemplative thought and practice and given contemporary reinterpretation through the work of Thomas Keating, OCSO of Snowmass Monastery in Colorado. See Thomas Keating, *Intimacy with God: An Introduction to Centering* Prayer (New York: Crossroad, 2009). For a recent effort to rethink the meaning of these traditions in light of contemporary experience, see Martin Laird, *Into the Silent Land: A Guide to the Christian Practice of Contemplation* (New York: Oxford, 2006); and *A Sunlit Absence: Silence, Awareness and Contemplation* (New York: Oxford, 2011). In the Eastern Christian tradition, the *Philokalia* remains the single most important compilation of contemplative teaching. See the recent collection of essays on this important text: *The Philokalia: A Classic Text of Orthodox Spirituality,* ed. Brock Bingaman and Bradley Nassif (New York: Oxford, 2012).

34. See, for example, Gustavo Gutierrez, *We Drink from Our Own Wells: The Spiritual Journey of a People* (Maryknoll, NY: Orbis, 1984); Jon Sobrino, *Spirituality of Liberation: Toward a Political Holiness* (Maryknoll, NY: Orbis, 1988); Barbara Ann Holmes, *Joy Unspeakable: Contemplative Practices of the Black Church* (Minneapolis: Augsburg Fortress, 2004); Philip Sheldrake, *Explorations in Spirituality: History, Theology and Social Practice* (New York: Paulist, 2010); "Christian Spirituality as a Way of Living Publicly: A Dialectic of the Mystical and Prophetic," *Spiritus* 3 (2003); Janet Ruffing, ed., *Mysticism and Social Transformation* (Syracuse, NY: Syracuse University Press, 2001); Claire Wolfteich, *Lord Have Mercy: Praying for Justice with Conviction and Humility* (San Francisco: Jossey-Bass, 2006); J. Matthew Ashley, "Contemplation in the Action of Justice: Ignacio Ellacuría and Ignatian Spirituality," in *Love that Produces Hope: The Thought of Ignacio Ellacuría,* ed. Kevin F. Burke and Robert Lasalle-Klein (Collegeville: Liturgical Press, 2006), 144–164. For a thoughtful reassessment of the Christian contemplative tradition from a critical, feminist perspective, see Sarah Coakley, *Powers and Submissions: Spirituality, Philosophy and Gender* (Oxford: Blackwell, 2002).

35. Certeau, *The Practice of Everyday Life*, xix–xx.

36. For an important recent discussion of the fundamentally participatory character of spirituality as a discipline, see: Jorge N. Ferrer and Jacob H. Sherman, eds., *The Participatory Turn: Spirituality, Mysticism, Religious Studies* (Albany: State University of New York Press, 2008).

37. Orsi, *Between Heaven and Earth,* 145.

38. Meister Eckhart, *Sermons and Treatises*, Vol. 1, trans. and ed. M. O'C. Walshe (Longmead: Element, 1987), 117.

39. Eckhart, *Sermons and Treatises*, Vol. 1, 3, 117.

40. Scott Russell Sanders, *Staying Put: Making a Home in a Restless World* (Boston: Beacon, 1993), chap. 5.

41. William Kittredge, *Who Owns the West?* (San Francisco: Mercury House, 1996), 108.

42. Paul Shepard, *Nature and Madness* (San Francisco: Sierra Club, 1982), 129.

43. Shepard, *Nature and Madness,* 112.

44. Wendell Berry, "How to Be a Poet," *Poetry* 177, no. 3 (January 2001): 269–270.

45. John Muir, *My First Summer in the Sierra* (New York: Penguin, 1987), 51.

46. This is a paraphrase of what then-candidate for governor Ronald Reagan actually said. What he did say was equally damning. "I mean, if you've looked at a hundred thousand acres or so of trees—you know, a tree is a tree, how many more do you need to look at?" And on another occasion, he is reported to have said, of one of the oldest and most magnificent groves of redwoods, "I saw them; there is nothing beautiful about them, just that they are a little higher than the others." See Lou Cannon, *Governor Reagan: His Rise to Power* (New York: Public Affairs, 2003), 299–303.

47. Berry, "How to Be a Poet."

CHAPTER 2

1. Rainer Maria Rilke, *Duino Elegies* (Eighth Elegy). This version is cited by Pierre Hadot in his essay "The Sage and the World," in *Philosophy as a Way of Life*, ed. Arnold I. Davidson, trans. Michael Chase (Oxford: Blackwell, 2005), 258. Hadot draws upon Rilke's intuitive sense of the whole (or the "Open") to illuminate, by analogy, the meaning of the contemplative vision through which some ancient philosophers sought to locate themselves fully within the cosmos. "The contemplation mentioned by Seneca is…a kind of unitive contemplation. In order to *perceive* the world, we must, as it were, perceive our *unity with* the world, by means of an exercise of concentration on the present moment" (261). For another rendering of Rilke's notion of what can come of dwelling in what he calls the "Open," see *Duino Elegies and the Sonnets to Orpheus*, trans. Stephen Mitchell (New York: Vintage, 2009), 50–51: "It sees all time/and itself within all time, forever healed."

2. Marilynne Robinson, *Housekeeping* (New York: Farrar, Straus and Giroux, 1980), 152.

3. Evagrius, *On Thoughts* 39: *Evagrius of Pontus: The Greek Ascetic Corpus*, trans. Robert E. Sinkewicz (New York: Oxford University Press, 2003), 180. See also *Reflections* 2: "If someone would want to behold the state of the mind, let him deprive himself of all mental representations, and then he shall behold himself resembling sapphire or the color of heaven (Exod. 24: 9–11). It is impossible to accomplish this without impassibility, for he will need God to collaborate with him and breathe into him connatural light" (Sinkewicz, *Evagrius*, 211).

See also Columba Stewart, "Imageless Prayer and the Theological Vision of Evagrius Ponticus," *Journal of Early Christian Studies*, 9, no. 2 (2001): 173–204;

Antoine Guillaumont, "La vision de l'intellect par lui-même dans la mystique évagrienne," in *Études su la spiritualité de l'Orient Chrétien, Spiritualité orientale* (Bégrolles-en-Mauges: Abbaye de Bellefontaine, 1996), 143–150; William Harmless and Raymond R. Fitzgerald, "The Sapphire Light of the Mind: The *Skemmata* of Evagrius Ponticus," *Theological Studies* 62 (2001): 493–529; Martin Laird, "The 'Open Country Whose Name Is Prayer': Apophasis, Deconstruction, and Contemplative Practice," *Modern Theology* 21, no. 1 (2005): 141–155; Mette Sophia Bøcher Rasmussen, "Like a Rock or Like God? The Concept of *apatheia* in the Monastic Theology of Evagrius of Pontus," *Studia Theologica* 59, no. 2 (2005): 147–162.

4. See Evagrius, *On Prayer* 56 and 57, where the "place of God" is juxtaposed with the "place of prayer." Sinkewicz, *Evagrius of Pontus*, 198.

5. Evagrius, *Reflections* 20; Sinkewicz, *Evagrius of Pontus: The Greek Ascetic Corpus*, 213. Columba Stewart, "Imageless Prayer and the Theological Vision of Evagrius Ponticus," 197, notes: "The place of God is, by definition, 'unimaged,' meaning that the mind itself, when it becomes the place of God, is free of self-created imagery."

   Julia Konstantinovsky, in her book, *Evagrius of Pontus: The Making of a Gnostic* (London: Ashgate, 2008), offers a thoughtful analysis of one of the fundamental tensions in Evagrius's thought, between the contemplation of the life of created beings (the *logoi*) and the contemplation of God's essence. "Natural contemplation" of creatures or the created world offers us, according to Evagrius, an important but mediated and bounded experience of God. Through this mode of contemplation, Konstaninovsky notes, "The entire created universe becomes transparent to the mind's eye as God's sacred book and God's temple. As well as constituting the identities of created beings, the *logoi* also testify to God's creative and economic power encoded in creation. Natural contemplation, then, also allows knowledge about God through [God's] operations and traces within the universe. Akin to the bodily perception at its inception, natural contemplation involves a refinement and transformation of ordinary sensation into spiritual perception" (65–66). But there is also a higher or deeper mode of contemplative awareness in which the mind transcends all knowledge of created beings and is bathed in the uncreated light of the Trinity. Such knowledge is unmediated, unbounded and can never be exhausted. The question of how much continuity or discontinuity exists between these two modes of contemplation is difficult to address. On the one hand, Evagrius is clear about his sense of the superiority of contemplation that is not bounded or limited by the ephemeral reality of created things and of the desirability of seeking an encounter with God in prayer that is imageless and limitless. However, Evagrius (and here he is joined by many of those who will follow him in the Eastern Christian tradition) views natural contemplation as a significant part of the larger contemplative project. Learning to see the created world this carefully and sensitively is no small part of what it means to become a contemplative.

6. This image and much of the discussion of island biogeography contained in this chapter come from the work of David Quammen, *The Song of the Dodo: Island Biogeography in an Age of Extinction* (New York: Scribner, 1996).

7. *Lives of the Desert Fathers*, trans. Norman Russell (Kalamazoo: Cistercian Publications, 1981), 50.

8. Cited in Kevin Bezner and Kevin Walzer, eds., *The Wilderness of Vision: On the Poetry of John Haines* (Brownsville, OR: Story Line Press, 1996), 28.

9. The question what it might mean in the present moment to value and preserve wildness and wilderness is complex and much disputed. Thoreau's well-known comment, "In wildness is the preservation of the world" (often unhelpfully paraphrased as "In *wilderness* is the preservation of the world") continues to haunt much contemporary debate on this subject. My own thinking about this subject has been much influenced not only by Thoreau's sense of an encompassing wildness at the heart of reality, but also by Gary Snyder's similarly expansive reading of wildness as something that permeates everything and that can become part of a sustained spiritual practice: *The Practice of the Wild* (San Francisco: North Point, 1990). But these important reflections on wildness have been deepened, of late, by questions about the continued meaningfulness of the term in an increasingly degraded and fragmented world. See especially Jack Turner's trenchant *The Abstract Wild* (Tucson: University of Arizona Press, 2006) and Stephen Meyer's *The End of the Wild* (Cambridge: MIT Press, 1996).

10. For an impressive and disturbing analysis of this phenomenon, see Rob Nixon, *Slow Violence and the Environmentalism of the Poor* (Cambridge: Harvard University Press, 2011).

11. E. O. Wilson, "Ecology and the Human Imagination: Dialogue between E. O. Wilson and Barry Lopez," in Edward Lueders, ed., *Writing Natural History: Dialogues with Authors* (Salt Lake City: University of Utah Press, 1989), 26.

12. Harold Searles, "Unconscious Processes in the Environmental Crisis," in *Countertransference and Related Subjects* (New York: International Universities Press, 1979), 237.

13. Shierry Weber Nicholsen, *The Love of Nature and the End of the World: The Unspoken Dimensions of Environmental Concern* (Cambridge, MA: MIT Press, 2002).

14. Michael Ortiz Hill, *Dreaming the End of the World: Apocalypse as a Rite of Passage* (Dallas: Spring, 1994), 68. Cited in Nicholsen, *The Love of Nature and the End of the World*, 131.

15. Nicholsen, *The Love of Nature and the End of the World*, 148.

16. Aldo Leopold, *A Sand County Almanac* (New York: Oxford University Press, 1949), 214.

17. *Verba Seniorum* II. 2. *Patrologica Latina* 73: 858A; also Antony 11, *Patrologia Graeca* 65: 77C. *The Sayings of the Desert Fathers*, trans. Benedicta Ward (Kalamazoo: Cistercian Publications, 2006), 3. The quotation represents a slight conflation of two versions of this saying. The Latin version does not mention the word "desert," while the Greek version does. But the Latin version views solitary life in the desert as a struggle of the heart while the Greek version sees it as a struggle against lust or fornication.

18. Paul Bowles, *Their Heads Are Green and Their Hands Are Blue* (New York: Ecco, 1994), 133–34, 147.

19. Athanasius of Alexandria, *The Life of Antony and the Letter to Marcelinus,* trans. Robert C. Gregg (New York: Paulist, 1980); 50, 68. References to the *Life of Antony* [*VA*] are from Robert Gregg's English translation [Gregg], with chapter number followed by page number. Occasionally I have made my own translations (from the critical edition: Athanase d'Alexandrie, *Vie d'Antoine.* trad. G.J.M. Bartelink. Paris: Cerf, 1994), or have emended Gregg's translations (indicated by [modified translation]).

20. Athanasius, *VA* 50. 2; Gregg, *Life of Antony,* 68.

21. Athanasius, *VA* 59. 6; Gregg, *Life of Antony,* 75.

22. Athanasius, *VA* 51; Gregg, *Life of Antony,* 70.

23. It should be noted that the *Life of Antony* presents a highly stylized portrait of early monastic life. And while it can be described as *emblematic* of a fundamental element of the early monastic quest, it cannot be said to be *representative* of the entire range of experiments in monastic living that emerged in the late antique world. As James Goehring and others have noted, at least one effect of this self-consciously literary and theological portrait was to create a sense of this solitary path as being *the* model of Christian monasticism. Careful historical analysis of early Christian monasticism has revealed a wide range of models and practices and suggests the need for a more subtle and critical reading of monastic origins. See James Goehring, "The Encroaching Desert: Literary Production and Ascetic Space in Early Egyptian Christianity," *Journal of Early Christian Studies* 1 (1993): 281–296. Still, the influence of the *Life of Antony* upon the ideals of early Christian monastic life was formidable. Also, we are now coming to understand much more clearly than we once did the crucial role of women's experience in the early Christian monastic world. See Susanna Elm, *"Virgins of God": The Making of Asceticism in Late Antiquity* (Oxford: Clarendon Press, 1994); Rebecca Krawiec, *Shenoute and the Women of the White Monastery: Egyptian Monasticism in Late Antiquity* (New York: Oxford University Press, 2002); Caroline T. Schroeder, *Monastic Bodies: Discipline and Salvation in Shenoute of Atripe* (Philadelphia: University of Pennsylvania Press, 2007).

24. See James E. Goehring, *Ascetics, Society and the Desert: Studies in Early Egyptian Monasticism* (Harrisburg, PA: Trinity, 1999), 1–72.

25. See Peter Brown, *The Making of Late Antiquity* (Cambridge, MA: Harvard University Press, 1978), 82. Our awareness of the social meaning and function of early Christian monastic practice owes much to Peter Brown's groundbreaking work, especially his early and widely influential essay on the holy man: "The Rise and Function of the Holy Man in Late Antiquity," *Journal of Roman Studies* 61 (1971): 80–101; reprinted in *Society and the Holy in Late Antiquity* (London: Faber and Faber, 1982). There has been much subsequent reflection on and revision of Brown's important work on the holy man in late antiquity. For Brown's own rethinking of his early work on this subject, see Peter Brown, "The Saint as Exemplar in Late Antiquity," *Representations* 2 (1983): 1–25; and "The Rise and Function of the Holy Man in Late Antiquity, 1971–1997," *Journal of Early Christian Studies* 6, no. 3 (Fall

1998): 353–376. For a range of critical scholarly responses to Brown's work, see the special issue of *Journal of Early Christian Studies* 6, no. 3 (Fall 1998), and *The Cult of Saints in Late Antiquity and the Middle Ages,* ed. James Howard-Johnston and Paul Antony Hayward (New York: Oxford University Press, 2000).

26. Keith Basso, *Wisdom Sits in Places: Landscape and Language among the Western Apache* (Albuquerque: University of New Mexico Press, 1996). On the broad application of the idea of "thinking with" things, and the roots of this idea in the work of Claude Lévi-Strauss, see Marjorie Garber, "Good to Think With," *Profession* (2008): 11–20.

27. The sense of place in early Christian monastic experience is a complex and multifaceted reality, touching at once on the concrete specificity of the monk's life within a particular social and geographical reality and on the mysterious and often-elusive inner landscape that arose from but in important ways transcended that concrete reality. On the concrete and symbolic function of place in the *Life of Antony*, see Judith Sutera, "Place and Stability in the *Life of Antony*," *Cistercian Studies Quarterly* 27, no. 2 (1992): 101–114; Douglas Burton-Christie, "The Place of the Heart: Geography and Spirituality in *The Life of Antony*," in *Purity of Heart in Early Ascetical Literature*, ed. Harriet A. Luckman and Linda Kulzer (Collegeville: Liturgical Press, 1999), 45–66.

28. *Apophthegmata Patrum [AP]* Moses 6; Ward, *The Sayings of the Desert Fathers*, 139. See also Dar Brooks-Hedstrom, "The Geography of the Monastic Cell in Early Egyptian Monastic Literature," *Church History* 78 (2009): 756–791.

29. Athanasius, *VA* 3; Gregg, *Life of Antony,* 32; on the practice of *prosoche* within ancient philosophical practice and as crucial to early Christian monasticism, see Hadot, *Philosophy as a Way of Life*, 126–144.

30. Athanasius, *VA* 5; Gregg, *Life of Antony,* 35.

31. Athanasius, *VA* 8; Gregg, *Life of Antony,* 37.

32. Brown, *The Making of Late Antiquity,* 89–90. David Brakke cautions against interpreting the language of the demonic in early Christian monastic life in terms that are too exclusively psychological. David Brakke, *Demons and the Making of the Monk: Spiritual Combat in Early Christianity* (Cambridge, MA: Harvard University Press, 2006), 7–14.

33. *AP* Poemen 67; Ward, *The Sayings of the Desert Fathers*, 176. Cf. Brown, *The Making of Late Antiquity*, 90.

34. Evagrius, *Praktikos 6*; Sinkewicz, *Evagrius of Pontus: The Greek Ascetic Corpus*, 97–98.

35. Peter Brown, *The Body and Society: Men, Women and Sexual Renunciation in Early Christianity* (New York: Columbia University Press, 1988), 167.

36. Antony of Egypt, Letter Seven; Samuel Rubenson, *The Letters of St. Antony: Monasticism and the Making of a Saint* (Minneapolis: Fortress, 1995), 226.

37. Antony of Egypt, Letter Six; Rubenson, *The Letters of St. Antony*, 218–219.

38. Athanasius, *VA* 91; Gregg, *Life of Antony,* 97 [modified translation].

39. Athanasius, *VA* 14; Gregg, *Life of Antony,* 42.

40. Athanasius, *VA* 84. 6; Gregg, *Life of Antony,* 92.

41. Athanasius, *VA* 50. 1; Gregg, *Life of Antony,* 68; See also Athanasius, *VA* 51,1; Gregg, *Life of Antony,* 69.

42. Athanasius, *VA* 50. 1; Gregg, *Life of Antony,* 68; See also Athanasius, *VA* 51.1; Gregg, *Life of Antony,* 69.

43. Athanasius, *VA* 54. 6; Gregg, *Life of Antony,* 71.

44. Athanasius, *VA* 55; Gregg, *Life of Antony,* 72.

45. Athanasius, *VA* 59; Gregg, *Life of Antony,* 75.

46. Athanasius, *VA* 56; Gregg, *Life of Antony,* 73.

47. Different spiritual traditions vary widely in the ways they articulate the meaning of such engaged contemplative practice. Nor should such contemplative practice be seen as limited to explicitly religious formulations. Indeed one of the questions implicit throughout this book has to do with how our understanding of contemplative practice is changing and perhaps expanding in the present historical moment to include forms and expressions that extend and complement those found in classical religious traditions. For a capacious, cross-cultural reading of such contemplative traditions of practice, inclusive of but not limited to its explicitly religious formulations, see Isabel Colegate, *A Pelican in the Wilderness: Hermits, Solitaries and Recluses* (Washington, DC: Counterpoint, 2003). For a thoughtful analysis of the many and varied forms of engaged, socially conscious spiritual practices in North America, see Gregory C. Stanczak, *Engaged Spirituality: Social Change and American Religion* (New Brunswick, NJ: Rutgers University Press, 2006).

48. William Kittredge, *Hole in the Sky: A Memoir* (New York: Knopf, 1992), 8.

49. Stephanie Mills, "The Wild and the Tame," in *Place of the Wild,* ed. David Clarke Burks (Washington DC: Island Press, 1994), 53.

50. Rainer Maria Rilke, *Diaries of a Young Poet,* trans. and ed. Edward Snow and Michael Winkler (New York: Norton, 1997), 47–48.

51. Rilke, *Diaries of a Young Poet,* 48–49.

52. Rilke, *Diaries of a Young Poet,* 49.

53. Rilke, *Diaries of a Young Poet,* 147.

54. Rilke, *Diaries of a Young Poet,* 163.

55. Rainer Maria Rilke, *Sonnets to Orpheus,* trans. Edward Snow (New York: North Point, 2002), Second part, 21, 101.

56. Aldo Leopold, *A Sand County Almanac* 214.

57. Aldo Leopold, *The River of the Mother of God and other Essays,* ed. Susan L. Flader and J. Baird Callicott (Madison: University of Wisconsin Press, 1991), 340.

58. Leopold, *A Sand County Almanac,* 138–139.

59. In this regard, Leopold's sense of what it means to cultivate an "ecological conscience" bears a striking resemblance to the quality of awareness that Rilke describes in terms of the notion of the *Offen* or "Open." In *Duino Elegies* 8, Rilke reflects on

how diminished this fundamental capacity for dwelling *in* the world (or in "Open") has become in us:

> With all its eyes the natural world looks out
> into the Open. Only *our* eyes are turned
> backward, and surround plant, animal, child
> like traps, as they emerge into their freedom.
> We know what is really out there only from
> the animal's gaze; for we take the very young
> child and force it around, so that it sees
> objects—not the Open, which is so
> Deep in Animal's faces

(*Duino Elegies and the Sonnets to Orpheus*, trans. Stephen Mitchell, 49.)

Is this capacity for dwelling in the Open known only to animals and, perhaps, to children? Rilke himself seems uncertain about how to respond to this question, noting simply that our alienation from the world is so profound that knowledge and awareness of the Open is, for most of us, extremely rare. Still, as he suggests in a letter to Lev P. Struve, we may yet possess the capacity to rekindle this awareness in ourselves: "The animal's degree of consciousness is such that it comes into the world without at every moment setting the world over against itself (as we do). The animal is *in* the world; we stand *in front of* the world because of the peculiar turn and heightening which our consciousness has taken. So by the 'Open' it is not sky or air or space that is meant; they too, for the human being who observes and judges, are 'objects' and thus 'opaque' and closed. The animal or the flower presumably is all that, without accounting for itself, and therefore has before itself and above itself that indescribably open freedom which has its (extremely fleeting) equivalent for us perhaps only in the first moments of love, when we see our own vastness in the person we love, and in the ecstatic surrender to God." Cited and translated by Stephen Mitchell in *Duino Elegies and the Sonnets to Orpheus*, 238–239.

For a thoughtful critique of Rilke's notion of the "Open," see Eric L. Santer, *On Creaturely Life: Rilke, Benjamin, Sebald* (Chicago: University of Chicago Press, 2006), 1–41.

60. Leopold, *A Sand County Almanac*, 129–132.
61. Gary Snyder, "Pine Tree Tops," in *Turtle Island* (New York: New Directions, 1974), 33.
62. Mills, "The Wild and the Tame," in *Place of the Wild*, 53.
63. Levertov, "From Below," in *This Great Unknowing: Last Poems* (New York: New Directions, 1999), 3.
64. Denise Levertov, "From Below," in *This Great Unknowing: Last Poems*, 3.
65. See Rowan Williams, *On Christian Theology* (Oxford: Blackwell, 2000), 3–15, who speaks of "A dispossession in respect of what is easily available for religious language.

This dispossession is, at its simplest, the suspension of ordinary categories of 'rational' speech; at a more pervasive level it is a dispossession of the human mind conceived of as central to the order of the world...to use a word like 'dispossession' is to evoke the most radical level of prayer, that of simple waiting on God, contemplation... [especially] *apophasis,* the acknowledgement of the inadequacy of any form, verbal, visual or gestural, to picture God definitively, to finish the business of religious speech...and expression of this recognition in silence and attention" (10–11).

66. Evagrius, *On Prayer* 36; Sinkewicz, *Evagrius of Pontus: The Greek Ascetic Corpus,* 196. See also these sayings: "Make no attempt at all to receive a figure or form or color during the time of prayer." *On Prayer* 114; Sinkewicz, *Evagrius of Pontus: The Greek Ascetic Corpus,* 205; "Blessed is the mind which becomes immaterial and free from all things during the time of prayer." *On Prayer* 119; Sinkewicz, *Evagrius of Pontus: The Greek Ascetic Corpus,* 206.

67. However, see Bernard McGinn, "Ocean and Desert as Symbols of Mystical Absorption in the Christian Tradition," *Journal of Religion* 74, no. 2 (1994): 155–181, for a sense of how deeply the image or idea of the desert resonated in subsequent Christian mystical thought.

68. Henry David Thoreau, *The Maine Woods,* ed. Joseph J. Moldenhauer (Princeton: Princeton University Press, 1972), 71.

69. Allan D. Hodder, *Thoreau's Ecstatic Witness* (New Haven: Yale University Press, 2001); David M. Robinson, *Natural Life: Thoreau's Worldly Transcendentalism* (Ithaca: Cornell University Press, 2004).

70. See David M. Robinson, "Thoreau's 'Ktaadn' and the Quest for Experience," in *Emersonian Circles: Essays in Honor of Joel Myerson,* ed. Wesley T. Mott and Robert E. Burkholder (Rochester: University of Rochester Press, 1997). "By the time Thoreau undertook his excursion toward Ktaadn, he had already lived at Walden Pond for more than a year, in an experiment that was aimed at personal reformation, but also in establishing, despite the seclusion of his life, a stage for a larger message of social transformation. The excursion to Ktaadn is thus heavily conditioned by the imperative of the Walden experiment to search for new beginnings, beginnings conditioned by the hope that the context of nature might prove liberating from social convention" (208).

71. Thoreau, *The Maine Woods,* 4–6.

72. Thoreau, *The Maine Woods,* 16.

73. Thoreau, *The Maine Woods,* 21.

74. Thoreau, *The Maine Woods,* 33.

75. Thoreau, *The Maine Woods,* 36.

76. Thoreau, *The Maine Woods,* 64.

77. Thoreau, *The Maine Woods,* 71.

78. Thoreau's reflections on the meaning and significance of wildness continued to deepen long after his early trip to Mt. Ktaadn. Almost ten years to the day that he first set out for the Maine Woods, Thoreau again returns to this question, although

this time much closer to home. In his journal for August 30, 1856, he writes: "I seem to have reached a new world, so wild a place that the very huckleberries grew hairy and were inedible.... What's the need of visiting far-off mountains and bogs, if a half-hour's walk will carry me into such wildness?... It is vain to dream of a wildness that is distant from ourselves. There is none such. I shall never find in the wilds of Labrador any greater wildness than in some recess in Concord." Henry David Thoreau, *I to Myself: An Annotated Selection from the Journal of Henry David Thoreau*, ed. Jeffrey S. Kramer (New Haven: Yale University Press, 2007), 279–280.

79. Henry David Thoreau, *Walden*, ed. J. Lyndon Shanley (Princeton: Princeton University Press, 1971), 317.

80. We continue to struggle with the question of what it might mean for us in the present moment to both engage and preserve wildness. Jack Turner, in his fierce reflection on the fate and meaning of wildness in the present moment (*The Abstract Wild*), makes a case that the two issues are related, that until we retrieve a sense of wildness as something real, palpable, and meaningful, we will never be able to summon the necessary motivation for preserving and helping to restore the little wildness that is left to us. "We only value what we know and love, and we no longer know or love the wild. So instead we accept substitutes, imitations, semblances, and fakes—a diminished wild." But in a reflection of the maddening circularity that seems to define our current situation, we must acknowledge that a diminished or abstract wild will not be sufficient to motivate us to resist the very diminishment we mourn. "To reverse this situation," he argues, "we must become so intimate with wild animals, with plants and places, that we answer to their destruction from the gut" (25). And not only with wild animals, plants, and places, but also with what he calls (borrowing from Walter Benjamin) the "aura" or quality of presence that wild places and beings express. The growing diminishment of wild places and our increasing sense of distance and alienation from them results, Turner argues, in a profound loss, not only of aura, but also "wildness, spirit, enchantment, the sacred, holiness, magic, and soul... these qualities deserve as much, if not more attention as the decline of wilderness and biodiversity, because the decline of the latter has it root cause in the decline of the former" (15).

CHAPTER 3

1. E. M. Cioran, *Tears and Saints*, trans. Ilinca Zarifopol-Johnston (Chicago: University of Chicago Press, 1995), 62.

2. *Apophthegmata Patrum* [*AP*] Syncletica 3; *The Sayings of the Desert Fathers*. trans. Benedicta Ward (Kalamazoo: Cistercian Publications, 2006), 231.

3. Aldo Leopold, *A Sand County Almanac: And Sketches Here and There* (New York: Oxford University Press, 1949), 48.

4. Pierre Hadot, *Philosophy as a Way of Life*, ed. Arnold I. Davidson, trans. Michael Chase (Oxford: Blackwell, 1995), 81–144.

5. Alexander Mitscherlich and Margarete Mitscherlich, *The Inability to Mourn*, trans. Beverly R. Placzek (New York: Grove Press, 1975).

6. *AP* Poemen 119; Ward, *The Sayings of the Desert Fathers*, 184.

7. Saul M. Olyan, *Biblical Mourning: Ritual and Social Dimensions* (New York: Oxford, 2004).

8. Kimberly Christine Patton and John Stratton Hawley, eds., *Holy Tears: Weeping in the Religious Imagination* (Princeton: Princeton University Press, 2005). On the fundamental importance of emotions within religious experience and understanding, and within recent scholarship on religion, see John Corrigan, ed., *Religion and Emotion: Approaches and Interpretation* (New York: Oxford University Press, 2004); and John Corrigan, ed., *The Oxford Handbook of Religion and Emotion* (New York: Oxford University Press, 2008).

9. Peter Brown, "The Rise and Function of the Holy Man in Late Antiquity," *Journal of Roman Studies* 61 (1971): 80–101; and "A Social Context to the Religious Crisis of the Third Century, A.D." Colloquy 14 (Berkeley, CA: Center for Hermeneutical Studies, 1975).

10. Irénée Hausherr, *Penthos: The Doctrine of Compunction in the Christian East*, trans. Anselm Hufstader (Kalamazoo, MI: Cistercian Publications, 1982). On *compunctio cordis,* see Mary Caruthers, *The Craft of Thought: Meditation: Rhetoric and the Making of Images, 400–1200* (Cambridge: Cambridge University Press, 1998), 96ff. She brings to light the sense of puncturing the skin that became associated with this term in Western Christian experience. For a searching analysis of the tradition of tears in the eastern Christian tradition, see Hanna Hunt, *Joy-Bearing Grief: Tears of Contrition in the Writings of the Early Syrian and Byzantine Fathers* (Leiden: Brill, 2004).

11. F. Nau, *Histoires des solitaires egyptiens 141. Revue de l'Orient Chretien* 13 (1908): 4.

12. *AP* Poemen 69; Ward, *The Sayings of the Desert Fathers*, 176.

13. *AP* Macarius 34; Ward, *The Sayings of the Desert Fathers*, 136.

14. *AP* Antony 33; Ward, *The Sayings of the Desert Fathers*, 8.

15. John Climacus, *The Ladder of Divine Ascent*, trans. Colm Luibheid and Norman Russell (New York: Paulist Press 1992), 140.

16. *AP* Poemen 26; Ward, *The Sayings of the Desert Fathers*, 171.

17. *AP* Poemen 72; Ward, *The Sayings of the Desert Fathers*, 177.

18. *AP* Matoes 26; Ward, *The Sayings of the Desert Fathers*, 145.

19. *AP* Poemen 119; Ward, *The Sayings of the Desert Fathers*, 184.

20. Philip Rousseau, review of *Der Weg des Weinens. Die Tradition des "Penthos" in den Apophthegmata Patrum, Journal of Theological Studies* 53, no. 2 (2002), 720.

21. Leopold, *A Sand County Almanac*, 48

22. Margarete Mitscherlich-Neilson, "The Inability to Mourn—Today," trans. Beverly R. Placzek, in *The Problem of Loss and Mourning: Psychoanalytical Perspectives,* ed. David Dietrich and Peter Shabad (Madison, CT: International Universities Press, 1990), 407.

23. Leopold, *A Sand County Almanac*, 44–50.

24. Leopold, *A Sand County Almanac*, 109.

25. Leopold, *A Sand County Almanac*, 109.

26. Leopold, *A Sand County Almanac*, 110.

27. Alexander Mitscherlich and Margarete Mitscherlich, *The Inability to Mourn*, trans. Beverly R. Placzek (New York: Grove Press, 1975).

28. Mitscherlich-Nielson, "The Inability to Mourn—Today," 407.

29. W. G. Sebald, *On the Natural History of Destruction*, trans. Anthea Bell (New York: Modern Library, 2004).

30. Sebald, *On the Natural History of Destruction*, 3–4.

31. Sebald, *On the Natural History of Destruction*, 10.

32. Sebald, *On the Natural History of Destruction*, 23.

33. Sebald, *On the Natural History of Destruction*, 89.

34. Michael Jackson, "The Prose of Suffering and the Practice of Silence," *Spiritus* 4, no. 1 (2004): 44–59.

35. Sebald, *On the Natural History of Destruction*, 25.

36. Sebald, *On the Natural History of Destruction*, 11.

37. Sebald, *On the Natural History of Destruction*, 53.

38. Henry David Thoreau, *A Week on the Concord and Merrimack Rivers* (New York: Penguin, 1998), 284.

39. Leo Tolstoy, *War and Peace,* trans. Constance Garnett (New York: Modern Library, 2002), 1122.

40. *AP* Evagrius 4, Ward, *The Sayings of the Desert Fathers,* 64.

41. For much of the discussion that follows, I am indebted to the brilliant and perceptive analysis in David M. Robinson, *Natural Life: Thoreau's Worldly Transcendentalism* (Ithaca: Cornell University Press, 2004), esp. 32–76.

42. Henry David Thoreau, *Collected Essays and Poems*, ed. Elizabeth Hall Witherall (New York: Library of America, 2001), 22.

43. Robinson, *Natural Life*, 41.

44. Thoreau, *Collected Essays and Poems*, 22.

45. Thoreau, *Collected Essays and Poems*, 22.

46. Robinson, *Natural Life*, 41.

47. See H. Daniel Peck, *Thoreau's Morning Work: Memory and Perception in* A Week on the Concord and Merrimack Rivers, *the* Journal, *and* Walden (New Haven: Yale University Press, 1990): "while *A Week* is, for Thoreau, peculiarly retrospective, the elegiac memorializing dimension of this work is not unique to this book. His mature *Journal* of the 1850's is a profound attempt to 'hold' experience, and *Walden*, for all its buoyancy, has its own deeply elegiac character" (12).

48. Thoreau, *A Week on the Concord and Merrimack Rivers,* 284.

49. Thoreau, *A Week on the Concord and Merrimack Rivers*, 286–287.

50. Robinson, *Natural Life*, 60.

51. Thoreau, *A Week on the Concord and Merrimack Rivers*, 285.

52. Thoreau, *A Week on the Concord and Merrimack Rivers*, 304.

53. Thoreau, *A Week on the Concord and Merrimack Rivers*, 307.

54. Bartolomé de las Casas, *A Short Account of the Destruction of the Indies*, ed. and trans. Nigel Griffin (London: Penguin, 1992), 50–51.

55. Victor Hugo, *Les Miserables*, trans. Charles Wilbour (1862; reprint, New York: Random House, 1992). Book V, ch. 13.

56. Harold Searles, "Unconscious Processes in Relation to the Environmental Crisis," in *Countertransference and Related Subjects* (New York: International Universities Press, 1979), 237.

57. Gary Snyder, *Turtle Island* (New York: New Directions, 1974), "Introductory Note," n.p.

58. Las Casas, *A Short Account of the Destruction of the Indies*, 23.

59. Las Casas, *A Short Account of the Destruction of the Indies*, 96–97.

60. The accuracy of some of Las Casas's accounts has been called into question by historians. It is also important to note that his work contributed to the growth of La Leyenda Negra or the Black Legend, the depiction of Spain and Spaniards as cruel, intolerant, and fanatical in anti-Spanish literature, starting in the sixteenth century. Even so, his work is widely regarded as providing an honest and clear-eyed view of the violence and brutality that characterized at least part of the European incursion into the Americas.

61. Barry Lopez, *The Rediscovery of North America* (New York: Vintage, 1992).

62. Lopez, *Rediscovery of North America*, 15.

63. Lopez, *Rediscovery of North America*, 32–34.

64. See, for example, the sustained reflections on loss and grief found in works such as Leslie Marmon Silko, *Ceremony* (New York: Viking Penguin, 1977); William Kittredge, *Hole in the Sky: A Memoir* (New York: Knopf, 1992); Linda Hogan, *Solar Storms* (New York: Scribner, 1995); Robert Hass, *Sun under Wood* (New York: Ecco, 1998); Diane Ackerman, *The Rarest of the Rare: Vanishing Animals, Timeless Worlds* (New York: Random House, 1995).

65. Richard Nelson, *The Island Within* (New York: Vintage, 1991), 53.

66. Nelson, *The Island Within*, 55.

67. Nelson, *The Island Within*, 56.

68. Nelson, *The Island Within*, 57.

69. Cioran, *Tears and Saints*, 55.

70. Clifton R. Spargo, *The Ethics of Mourning: Grief and Responsibility in Elegiac Literature* (Baltimore: Johns Hopkins University Press, 2004).

71. Judith Butler, *Precarious Life: The Powers of Mourning and Violence* (London: Verso, 2004), 20.

72. Elizabeth Kolbert, *Field Notes from a Catastrophe: Man, Nature and Climate Change* (New York: Bloomsbury, 2006).

73. Shierry Weber Nicholsen, *The Love of Nature and the End of the World: The Unspoken Dimensions of Environmental Concern* (Princeton: Princeton University Press, 2002), 179–182.

74. *AP* Arsenius 41; Ward, *The Sayings of the Desert Fathers*, 18.

75. Cioran, *Tears and Saints*, 55.

CHAPTER 4

1. Novalis, *Henry of Ofterdingen,* trans. Petery Hilty (Long Grove, IL: Waveland Press, 1990), 159. [Translation adapted].

2. *Apophthegmata Patrum [AP]* Agathon 1; *The Sayings of the Desert Fathers,* trans. Benedicta Ward (Kalamazoo: Cisterican Publications, 1987), 20.

3. *AP* Moses 6; Ward, *The Sayings of the Desert Fathers*, 139.

4. *AP* Agathon 6; Ward, *The Sayings of the Desert Fathers*, 21; *AP* Agathon 1; Ward, *The Sayings of the Desert Fathers*, 20.

5. Elie Wiesel, "Longing for Home," in *The Longing for Home,* ed. Leroy S. Rouner (Notre Dame, IN: University of Notre Dame Press, 1996), 19.

6. Joseph O'Neill, *Netherland* (New York: Pantheon, 2008), 121.

7. Simone Weil, *The Need for Roots: Prelude to a Declaration of Duties toward Mankind*, trans. Arthur Wils (New York: Harper, 1952), 43.

8. Wiesel, "Longing for Home," 19.

9. Marc Augé, *Non-Places: Introduction to the Anthropology of Supermodernity*, trans. John Howe (London: Verso, 1995).

10. Peter Berger, Brigitte Berger, and Hansfried Kellner, *The Homeless Mind* (New York: Vintage, 1974), 82.

11. The classic work of Yi-Fu Tuan continues to exert considerable influence over contemporary discussions of the significance of place and space for human and environmental well-being. See *Topophilia: A Study in Environmental Perceptions, Attitudes, and Values* (New York: Columbia University Press, 1974); *Space and Place: The Perspective of Experience* (Minneapolis: University of Minnesota Press, 1977); *Cosmos and Hearth* (Minneapolis: University of Minnesota Press, 1996). Tuan's work often expresses a subtle and discerning attempt to balance the respective goods of place (security) and space (freedom). However, in a recent work [Yi-Fu Tuan and Martha Strawn, *Religion: From Place to Placelessness* (Chicago: University of Chicago Press, 2010)], he has argued for the particular significance of "placelessness" for understanding religious experience.

    For a strong defense of *place* and a critique of the ascendency of a "placeless" sense of *space* in the Western philosophical tradition, see Edward Casey, *Getting Back into Place,* 2nd ed. (Bloomington: Indiana University Press, 2009), and *The Fate of Place: A Philosophical History* (Berkeley: University of California Press, 1997). Also important to this discussion are E. V. Walter, *Placeways: A Theory of the Human Environment* (Chapel Hill: University of North Carolina Press, 1988); J. Nicholas Entriken, *The Betweenness of Place: Towards a Geography of Modernity* (Baltimore: Johns Hopkins University Press, 1991); John B. Jackson, *A Sense of Place, a Sense of Time* (New Haven: Yale University Press, 1994); and Lucy R.

Lippard, *The Lure of the Local: Senses of Place in a Multicentered Society* (New York: New Press, 1997).

There is growing awareness, in our increasingly globalized world, of the need to give critical attention to the often-ambiguous meaning of *both* space and place. A crucial dimension of this work is the quest for a way of valuing place that does not become reduced to provincialism or nationalism; and for a way of valuing the possibilities inherent in the idea of space (especially as it contributes to a more vibrant sense of global responsibility) without succumbing to an uncritical acceptance of "placelessness." See Doreen B. Massey, *For Space* (Thousand Oaks, CA: Sage, 2005); Harm de Blij, *The Power of Place: Geography, Destiny, and Globalization's Rough Landscape* (New York: Oxford University Press, 2010); Ursula Heise, *Sense of Place and Sense of Planet: The Environmental Imagination of the Global* (New York: Oxford University Press, 2008). Heise shares with many contemporary observers a recognition of how devastating the growing phenomeonon of "deterritorialization" is to persons and communities. But she offers an important caveat: "Deterritorialization also implies possibilities for new cultural encounters and a broadening of horizons that environmentalists as well as other politically progressive movements have welcomed, sometimes without fully acknowledging the entanglements of such a cultural unfolding with globalization processes that they otherwise reject. The challenge that deterritorialization poses for the environmental imagination, therefore, is to envision how ecologically based advocacy on behalf of the nonhuman world as well as on behalf of greater socioenvironmental justice might be formulated in terms that are premised no longer primarily on ties to local places but on ties to territories and systems that are understood to encompass the planet as a whole" (10).

12. See Miles Richardson, ed., *Place: Experience and Symbol; Geoscience and Man*, Vol. 24 (Baton Rouge: Geoscience Publications, Department of Geography and Anthropology, Louisiana State University, 1984).

13. See W. J. T. Mitchell, ed., *Landscape and Power,* 2nd ed. (Chicago: University of Chicago Press, 2002); Stephen Richard Higley, *Privilege, Power and Place: The Geography of the American Upper Class* (Lanham, MD: Rowman and Littlefield, 1995); Barbara Ching and Gerald W. Creed, eds., *Knowing Your Place: Rural Identity and Cultural Hierarchy* (New York: Routledge, 1997).

14. Steven Feld and Keith Basso, eds., *Senses of Place* (Santa Fe, NM: School of American Research Press, 1996), 4.

15. See Eric Hirsch and Michael O'Hanlon, eds., *The Anthropology of Landscape: Perspectives on Place and Space* (Oxford: Clarendon Press, 1995). For a work dealing with similar questions but rooted more in the fields of literary and culture studies, see Smadar Lavie and Ted Swedenburg, eds., *Displacement, Diaspora, and Geographies of Identity* (Durham: Duke University Press, 1994).

16. Keith H. Basso, *Wisdom Sits in Places: Landscape and Language among the Western Apache* (Albuquerque: University of New Mexico Press, 1996).

17. Anne Fadiman, *The Spirit Catches You and You Fall Down: A Hmong Child, Her American Doctors, and the Collision of Two Cultures* (New York: Farrar, Straus and Giroux, 1997), 203–204.

18. Fadiman, *The Spirit Catches You and You Fall Down*, 187–188.

19. Fadiman, *The Spirit Catches You and You Fall Down*, 203–204.

20. William Dietrich, *Northwest Passage: The Great Columbia River* (Seattle: University of Washington Press, 1995), 187–195. Dietrich cites an account of the English explorer Adolph Baillie-Groham, who at the end of the nineteenth century spoke with nostalgia for a world of abundant salmon runs that was already disappearing: "Forty years ago the number of fish who reached these beds was so great that the receding waters would leave millions of dead salmon strewn along the banks, emitting a stench that could be smelled miles off, and which never failed to attract a great number of bears. Though I have never performed the feat of walking across a stream on the backs of fish, which many an old timer will swear he has done, I have certainly seen fish so numerous near their spawning grounds that nowhere could you have thrown a stone into the water without hitting a salmon." Dietrich, *Northwest Passage*, 188.

21. Blaine Harden, *A River Lost: The Life and Death of the Columbia* (New York: Norton, 1997), 105–116. Harden documents the harsh treatment of the Colville Indians, especially in the aftermath of the construction of the Grand Coulee Dam. "None of the irrigation water diverted from the river by the Grand Coulee Dam has ever been made available to the Indians.... As the non-Indian side of the Columbia...attracted industry and farmers with its subsidized power and water, the economy of the reservation withered. Unemployment hovered around 50 percent for decades. A chart of income distribution on the reservation in the early 1990's showed no middle class.... Electricity generated by the Grand Coulee Dam earns the federal government more than four hundred million dollars a year. Since the dam went on line in 1942, it has earned the government more than five billion dollars. Although half of the dam sits on reservation property, none of the power earnings was allotted to the Colvilles."

22. Anne Michaels, *The Winter Vault* (New York: Knopf, 2009), 47.

23. *The Delicacy and Strength of Lace: Letters between Leslie Marmon Silko and James Wright*, ed. Anne Wright (Saint Paul, MN: Graywolf, 1986), 28.

24. O'Neill, *Netherland*, 121.

25. Basso, *Wisdom Sits in Places*, 7.

26. Basso, *Wisdom Sits in Places*, 7. The literature on place and place-making has burgeoned in recent years, something that seems to reflect, at least to a degree, the pervasive sense of displacement and longing for place (often expressed as a spiritual longing) in contemporary culture. See, for example, Michael Jackson, *At Home in the World* (Durham, NC: Duke University Press, 1995); Deborah Tall, *From Where We Stand: Recovering a Sense of Place* (New York: Knopf, 1993; reprint, Baltimore: Johns Hopkins University Press, 1997); Robert Root, ed., *Landscapes with Figures:*

The Nonfiction of Place (Lincoln: University of Nebraska, 2007); Belden C. Lane, *Landscapes of the Sacred: Geography and Narrative in American Spirituality* (Baltimore: Johns Hopkins University Press, 2001); Philip Sheldrake, *Spaces for the Sacred: Place, Memory and Identity* (Baltimore: Johns Hopkins University Press, 2001).

27. Basso, *Wisdom Sits in Places,* 121.

28. Basso, *Wisdom Sits in Places,* 107.

29. Keith Basso, "Wisdom Sits in Places: Notes on a Western Apache Landscape," in *Senses of Place,* 79.

30. Robert Adams, *Beauty in Photography* (New York: Aperture, 1996), 14.

31. Seamus Heaney, *Preoccupations: Selected Prose 1968–1978* (New York: Farrar, Straus and Giroux, 1980), 132.

32. Lawrence Buell, *The Environmental Imagination: Thoreau, Nature Writing, and the Formation of American Culture* (Cambridge: Harvard University Press, 1995), 261, 268–279.

33. Adams, *Beauty in Photography,* 15–16.

34. *AP* Antony 3; Ward, *The Sayings of the Desert Fathers,* 2.

35. *AP* Bessarion 12; Ward, *The Sayings of the Desert Fathers,* 42–43.

36. Thomas Merton, *The Other Side of the Mountain: The End of the Journey. The Journals of Thomas Merton,* Vol. 7, *1967–1968,* ed. Brother Patrick Hart (San Francisco: HarperSanFrancisco, 1998), 323.

37. He expressed this most memorably in his 1967 essay, "Day of a Stranger," *Hudson Review* 20, no. 2 (Summer 1967): 211–218. The idea of becoming an exile or stranger shows up continuously in his later work.

38. *The Rule of St. Benedict in English,* edited by Timothy Fry (Collegeville, MN: Liturgical Press, 1982), especially chap. 58.

39. For a thoughtful examination of how these tensions played out in the Apophthegmata Patrum, see Graham Gould, "Moving On and Staying Put in the *Apophthegmata Patrum,*" *Studia Patristica* 25 (1989): 231–237. On the life of Antony, see Judith Sutera, "Place and Stability in *The Life of Antony,*" *Cistercian Studies Quarterly* 28 (1993): 101–114; Douglas Burton-Christie, "The Place of the Heart: Geography and Spirituality in *The Life of Antony,*" in *Purity of Heart in Early Ascetic and Monastic Literature,* ed. Harriet A. Luckman and Linda Kulzer (Collegeville: Liturgical Press, 1999), 45–66.

   The role of travel and pilgrimage in late antique ascetic culture has been the subject of renewed scholarly attention. See Daniel Folger Caner, *Wandering, Begging Monks: Spiritual Authority and the Promotion of Monasticism in Late Antiquity* (Berkeley: University of California Press, 2002); Maribel Dietz, *Wandering Monks, Virgins, and Pilgrims: Ascetic Travel in the Mediterranean World, A.D. 300–800* (Philadelphia: Pennsylvania State University Press, 2005); Brouria Bitton-Ashkelony, *Encountering the Sacred: The Debate on Christian Pilgrimage in Late Antiquity* (Berkeley: University of California Press, 2005); Georgia Frank,

The Memory of the Eyes: Pilgrimage to Living Saints in Christian Late Antiquity (Berkeley: University of California Press, 2000); David Frankfurter, ed., *Pilgrimage and Holy Space in Late Antique Egypt* (Leiden: Brill, 1998).

40. For a masterly analysis of the material reality of the early Christian monastic world, with a particular focus on the Judean desert, see Yizhar Hirschfeld, *The Judean Desert Monasteries in the Byzantine Period* (New Haven: Yale University Press, 1992); also John Binns, *Ascetics and Ambassadors of Christ: The Monasteries of Palestine, 314–631* (Oxford: Clarendon, 1994), especially chap. 5, "The Desert," 99–120.

41. On the concrete character as well as the symbolic meaning of the monk's dwelling place, see Caroline T. Schroeder, "'A Suitable Abode for Christ': The Church Building as Symbol of Ascetic Renunciation in Early Monasticism," *Church History* 73, no. 3 (2004): 472–521; Darlene Brooks-Hedstrom, "The Geography of the Monastic Cell in Early Egyptian Monastic Literature," *Church History* 78, no. 4 (2009): 756–791; Brooks-Hedstrom, "Divine Architects: Designing the Monastic Dwelling Place," in *Egypt in the Byzantine World, 300–700*, ed. Roger Bagnall (Cambridge: Cambridge University Press, 2007), 368–389. Elizabeth R. O'Connell, "Transforming Monumental Landscapes in Late Antique Egypt: Monastic Dwellings in Legal Documents from Western Thebes," *Journal of Early Christian Studies* 15, no. 2 (2007): 239–273.

42. Dietz, *Wandering Monks, Virgins and Pilgrims,* 11.

43. Dietz, *Wandering Monks, Virgins and Pilgrims,* 23.

44. *AP* Poemen 191; Ward, *The Sayings of the Desert Fathers,* 194.

45. *AP* Longinus 1; Ward, *The Sayings of the Desert Fathers,* 122.

46. *AP* Theodora 7; Ward, *The Sayings of the Desert Fathers,* 84.

47. *AP* Syncletica 6; Ward, *The Sayings of the Desert Fathers,* 231.

48. *AP* Antony 3; Ward, *The Sayings of the Desert Fathers,* 2.

49. *AP* Isaac of Cells 11; Ward, *The Sayings of the Desert Fathers,* 101.

50. Thomas Merton, *The Wisdom of the Desert* (New York: New Directions, 1970), 45.

51. *The Philokalia: The Complete Text,* Vol. 1, ed. G. E. H. Palmer, Philip Sherrard, and Kallistos Ware (London: Faber and Faber, 1979), 33.

52. *The Philokalia,* Vol. 1, 34.

53. *AP* Ammonas 4; Ward, *The Sayings of the Desert Fathers,* 26.

54. *AP* Bessarion, 12; Ward, *The Sayings of the Desert Fathers,* 42–43.

55. Thomas Merton, *The Other Side of the Mountain: The End of the Journey. The Journals of Thomas Merton,* Vol. 7, *1967–1968* (San Francisco: HarperSanFrancisco, 1998), 174–175.

56. Renée Daumal, *Mount Analogue* (Woodstock, NY: Overlook, 2004), 56.

57. Merton reflected often on solitude, the solitary life, and the "work of the cell" during the last few years of his life as his own eremetical practice deepened. See Thomas Merton, *Contemplation in a World of Action* (Garden City, NY: Image, 1973), especially "The Cell," 265–272; "Notes for a Philosophy of Solitude," in Thomas Merton,

Disputed Questions (New York: Farrar, Straus and Giroux, 1960), 163–193. See also Isabel Colegate, *A Pelican in the Wilderness: Hermits, Solitaries and Recluses* (Washington, DC: Counterpoint, 2002), who makes a compelling case for seeing "the work of the cell" as a fundamental and near universal (if also immensely varied) phenomenon in human culture, and one not at all limited to explicitly religious expressions.

58. A complex and delicate sense of relationship between place and movement, the interior and exterior landscapes, can be seen, for example, in the Laguna Pueblo tradition (Leslie Marmon Silko, *Yellow Woman and Beauty of the Spirit* [New York: Simon and Schuster, 1996], especially, "Interior and Exterior Landscapes: Pueblo Migration Stories," 25–47); in the Buddhist tradition (expressed memorably in Matsuo Basho, *Narrow Road to the Interior,* in *The Essential Basho*, trans. Sam Hamill [Boston: Shambala, 1999]); among the Walpiri people of Australia, see Michael Jackson, *At Home in the World*; in the work of Henry David Thoreau, whose reflections on the spiritual significance of movement—in *Walking* (Boston: Beacon, 1991) and *A Week on the Concord and Merrimack Rivers*, ed. Carl F. Hovde, William L. Howarth, and Elizabeth Hall Witherell (Princeton: Princeton University Press, 2004)—stand juxtaposed to his call to dwell deeply in place, expressed most powerfully in *Walden,* ed. Jeffrey S. Kramer (New Haven: Yale University Press, 2004) and *The Journals—I to Myself: An Annotated Selection from the Journal of Henry David Thoreau* (New Haven: Yale University Press, 2007).

59. Thomas Merton, *Turning toward the World: The Pivotal Years. The Journals of Thomas Merton*, Vol. 4, *1960–1963*, ed. Victor Kramer (San Francisco: HarperSanFrancisco, 1996), 63.

60. Merton, *Turning toward the World*, 73.

61. Merton, *Turning toward the World*, 80.

62. Merton, *The Other Side of the Mountain*, 34

63. Merton, *The Other Side of the Mountain,* 51.

64. Merton, *The Other Side of the Mountain*, 172.

65. Merton, *The Other Side of the Mountain*, 3.

66. Merton, *The Other Side of the Mountain*, 46, 47.

67. Merton, *The Other Side of the Mountain*, 23–64.

68. Merton, *The Other Side of the Mountain*, 8.

69. Merton, *The Other Side of the Mountain*, 15.

70. Merton, *The Other Side of the Mountain*, 33.

71. Merton, *The Other Side of the Mountain*, 135.

72. On Merton's efforts to offer a distinctively contemplative response to the growing threat of technological culture, especially to the environment, see Donald P. St. John, "Technological Culture and Contemplative Ecology in Thomas Merton's *Conjectures of a Guilty Bystander*," *Worldviews* 6, no. 2 (2002): 159–182.

73. Thomas Merton, *The Hidden Ground of Love: The Letters of Thomas Merton on Religious Experience and Social Concerns*, ed. William Shannon (New York: Farrar, Straus and Giroux, 1985), 47–48.

74. Thomas Merton, *Learning to Love: Exploring Solitude and Freedom. The Journals of Thomas Merton*, Vol. 6, *1966–1967*, ed. Christine M. Bochen (San Francisco: HarperSanFrancisco, 1997), 303–304, 324.

75. Merton, *The Other Side of the Mountain*, 112, 110.

76. Michel de Certeau argues that the dialectical tension between rootedness and homelessness, place and departure, is fundamental to Christian spiritual practice. "Within the Christian experience, the boundary or limit is a place for the action which ensures the step from a particular situation to a progress (opening a future and creating a new past), from a being 'there' to a being 'elsewhere', from one stage to another. . . . A particular place—our present place—is required if there is to be a departure. Both elements, the place and the departure, are interrelated, because it is the withdrawal from a place that allows one to recognise the enclosure implicit in the initial position, and as a result it is this limited field which makes possible a further investigation. Boundaries are the place of the Christian work, and their displacements are the result of this work." See Michel de Certeau, "How Is Christianity Thinkable Today?" in *The Postmodern God*, ed. Graham Ward (Oxford: Blackwell, 1997), 151. For an illuminating discussion of the importance of this idea in de Certeau's work, with particular attention to the influence of Ignatian spiritual practice, see Philip Sheldrake, "Unending Desire: Certeau's 'Mystics,' " *The Way Supplement* 102 (2001): 38–48.

77. Merton, *The Other Side of the Mountain*, 103.

78. Much of Merton's most compelling writing during the final years of his life concerned the question of what it meant to belong. In this sense, his writing about place and his writing about love should be seen as related to each other. See "Rain and the Rhinoceros," *Raids on the Unspeakable* (New York: New Directions, 1966), 9–26; "Day of a Stranger"; "Love and Need: Is Love a Package or a Message," in *Love and Living,* ed. Naomi Burton Stone and Brother Patrick Hart (New York: Bantam, 1980; reprint, New York: Harcourt Trade, 2002), 25–37. See also Douglas Burton-Christie, "The Work of Loneliness: Thomas Merton's Experiments in Solitude," *Anglican Theological Review* 88, no. 1 (Winter 2006): 25–46; Burton-Christie, "Place-Making as Contemplative Practice," *Anglican Theological Review* 91, no. 3 (Summer 2009): 347–372.

79. Merton, *The Other Side of the Mountain*, 205.

80. Merton, *The Other Side of the Mountain*, 174–175.

81. Merton's final journey to Asia had a particular and personal significance for him insofar as it enabled him to enter more deeply into a landscape and culture within which he felt himself so surprisingly at home. But it also represented a complex and delicate work of cultural and religious exchange, an experience of dislocation and reorientation that was, in itself, a crucial part of his work of place-making. For a critical assessment of Merton's final trip to Asia within this context, see John D. Barbour, "The Ethics of Intercultural Travel: Thomas Merton's Asian Pilgrimage and Orientalism," *Biography* 28, no. 1 (2005): 15–26.

82. Merton, *The Other Side of the Mountain*, 278.

83. Merton, *The Other Side of the Mountain*, 205.

CHAPTER 5

1. Simone Weil, *The Notebooks of Simone Weil*, Vol. I, trans. Arthur Wills (London: Routledge, 2004), 515.

2. Evagrius, *On Prayer*; *The Philokalia: The Complete Text*, Vol. I, trans. and ed. G. E. H. Palmer, Philip Sherrard, and Kallistos Ware (London: Faber and Faber, 1979), 71.

3. For a thoughtful analysis of the problematic character of much contemporary "parascientific" thinking, see Marilynne Robinson, *Absence of Mind: The Dispelling of Inwardness from the Modern Myth of the Self* (New Haven: Yale University Press, 2010).

4. See William Gibson, *A Reenchanted World: The Quest for a New Kinship with Nature* (New York: Metropolitan, 2009).

5. Samuel Taylor Coleridge, *Notebooks: A Selection*, ed. Seamus Perry (New York: Oxford University Press, 2002), 20.

6. William Blake, *Complete Writings with Variant Readings*, ed. Geoffrey Keynes (New York: Oxford University Press, 1966), 158 [paraphrased for inclusive language].

7. Coleridge, *Notebooks*, 35.

8. William Wordsworth, "Lines Written a Few Miles above Tintern Abbey," in *Oxford Poetry Library* (Oxford: Oxford University Press, 1994), 58.

9. For a thoughtful discussion of the significance of the notion of the "penumbral" for interpreting liminal experiences, see Michael Jackson's *The Palm at the End of the Mind: Relatedness, Religiosity and the Real* (Durham, NC: Duke University Press, 2009).

10. Athanasius of Alexandria, *The Life of Antony and the Letter to Marcelinus*, trans. Robert C. Gregg (New York: Paulist, 1980) [*VA*] 91; 97.

11. Seneca, *Letters to Lucilius* 64: 6; cited in Pierre Hadot, *Philosophy as a Way of Life*, ed. Arnold I. Davidson, trans. Michael Chase (Malden, MA: Blackwell, 1995), 257.

12. *Apophthegmata Patrum* [*AP*] Poemen 35; *The Sayings of the Desert Fathers*, trans. Benedicta Ward (Kalamazoo: Cistercian Publications, 2006), 172 [modified translation].

13. Athanasius, *VA* 3; Gregg, *The Life of Antony*, 32. [modified translation].

14. Athanasius, *VA* 91; Gregg, *The Life of Antony*, 97. [modified translation].

15. Hadot, *Philosophy as a Way of Life*, 84.

16. Marcus Aurelius, *Meditations* 7, 54. cited in Hadot, *Philosophy as a Way of Life*, 84.

17. Athanasius, *VA* 7; Gregg, *The Life of Antony*, 37. See also *VA*, 16: "as though making a beginning daily, let us increase our dedication. For the entire life span of men is very brief when measured against the ages to come" (Gregg, *The Life of Antony*, 43). And *VA*, 91: "Be watchful and do not destroy your lengthy discipline, but as if you

were making a beginning now, strive to preserve your enthusiasm" (Gregg, *The Life of Antony,* 97).

18. Evagrius, *On Prayer*; *The Philokalia: The Complete Text,* Vol. 1, trans. and ed. G. E. H. Palmer, Philip Sherrard, and Kallistos Ware (London: Faber and Faber, 1979), 71.

19. Seneca, *Letters to Lucilius* 64: 6; cited in Hadot, *Philosophy as a Way of Life,* 257.

20. Evagrius, *Eight Thoughts* 3: 7; *Evagrius of Pontus: The Greek Ascetic Corpus*, trans. Robert E. Sinkewicz (New York: Oxford University Press, 2003), 79.

21. Evagrius, *Praktikos* 10; Sinkewicz, *Evagrius of Pontus: The Greek Ascetic Corpus*, 98.

22. Evagrius, *Eight Thoughts* 22; Sinkewicz, *Evagrius of Pontus: The Greek Ascetic Corpus*, 83.

23. On early Christian monastic reading of scripture, see Douglas Burton-Christie, *The Word in the Desert: Scripture and the Quest for Holiness in Early Christian Monasticism* (New York: Oxford University Press, 1993); "Hearing, Reading, Praying: Orality, Literacy and the Shape of Early Monastic Spirituality," *Anglican Theological Review* 83, no. 2 (Spring 2001): 5–25; Luke Dysinger, *Psalmody and Prayer in the Writings of Evagrius Ponticus* (Oxford: Oxford University Press, 2005); Steven D. Driver, *John Cassian and the Reading of Egyptian Monastic Culture* (New York: Routledge, 2002), esp. 111–117 on prayer in relation to reading; Elizabeth Clark, *Reading Renunciation: Asceticism and Scripture in Early Christianity* (Princeton: Princeton University Press, 1999).

24. *Apophthegmata Patrum,* Anonymous 146. F. Nau, "Histoires des solitaires égyptiens," *Revue d'orient Chrétien* 13 (1908): 50. English translation: Benedicta Ward, *Wisdom of the Desert Fathers*: *The "Apophthegmata Patrum" (The Anonymous Series)* (Oxford: SLG Press, 1986), 4.

25. *AP* Theodore of Enaton 3; Ward, *The Sayings of the Desert Fathers*, 79.

26. Cassian, *Collationes* 10: 10; For a critical edition, see E. Pichery, *Jean Cassien, Conférences, Sources chrétiennes* [*SC*] 42, 54, 64 (Paris: Éditions du Cerf, 1955, 1958, 1959); English translations: *Western Asceticism*, ed. Owen Chadwick (Louisville, KY: Westminster John Knox, 1979); John Cassian, *The Conferences. Ancient Christian Writers* 57, ed. and trans. Boniface Ramsey (New York: Paulist Press, 1997); John Cassian, *The Conferences*. Classics of Western Spirituality, trans. Colm Luibéid (New York: Paulist Press, 1985); *A Select Library of Nicene and Post-Nicene Fathers*, n.s. no. 11, trans. Edgar C. S. Gibson (Oxford: Parker and Co., 1894; reprint, Grand Rapids, MI: Eerdmans, 1973). Pichery, *SC* 54, 86; Chadwick, *Western Asceticism*, 240–242.

27. Cassian, *Collationes* 10: 10; Pichery, *SC* 54, 91; Chadwick, *Western Asceticism*, 243. A fascinating commentary on this disposition can be found in the dialogue between Thomas Merton and D. T. Suzuki contained in Thomas Merton, *Zen and the Birds of Appetite* (New York: New Directions, 1968). Suzuki associates the idea of innocence with the Buddhist idea of "Anabhoga-Carya," roughly translated as "effortless" or "no striving." It connotes a kind of openness and transparency of mind that enables one to apprehend and stand in "the original light of Suchness

which is Emptiness" (104–105). Merton's response, most of which is rooted in the language and thought of the ancient desert tradition, points to a similar notion crucial to the early Christian monks.

28. Cassian, *Collationes* 10: 10; Pichery, *SC* 54, 90; Chadwick, *Western Asceticism*, 243.

29. Cassian, *Collationes* 14: 13; Pichery, *SC* 54, 201; Gibson, *A Select Library of Nicene and Post-Nicene Fathers*, 442.

30. Cassian, *Collationes* 10: 10; Pichery, *SC* 54, 86; Chadwick, *Western Asceticism*, 242.

31. Cassian, *Collationes* 10:11; Pichery, *SC* 54, 86; Chadwick, *Western Asceticism*, 243.

32. *The Philokalia: The Complete Text*, Vol. 1, 62.

33. Cassian, Abba Moses, *The Philokalia: The Complete Text*, Vol. 1, 97.

34. St. Peter of Damaskos, *The Philokalia: The Complete Text*, Vol. 3, trans. and ed. G.E.H. Palmer, Philip Sherrard, and Kallistos Ware (London: Faber and Faber, 1984), 136–137.

35. Lyanda Lynn Haupt, *Pilgrim on the Great Bird Continent: The Importance of Everything and Other Lessons from Darwin's Lost Notebooks* (New York: Little Brown, 2006), 15–16.

36. Richard Holmes's book, *The Age of Wonder: How the Romantic Generation Discovered the Beauty and Terror of Science* (New York: Pantheon, 2008), offers a thoughtful and nuanced discussion of how the deeply enmeshed work of scientists and romantic poets and writers in the eighteenth century created the conditions for the kind of play of ideas and movement among and between different modes of thought that is increasingly difficult for us to imagine.

37. For a thoughtful analysis of the distinctively *contemplative* dimension of contemporary scientific thought, see Allan Wallace, *Contemplative Science: Where Buddhism and Neuroscience Converge* (New York: Columbia University Press, 2007).

38. Holmes, *The Age of Wonder*, 249.

39. Coleridge, *Notebooks*, 39.

40. Haupt, *Pilgrim on the Great Bird Continent*. Haupt is particularly sensitive to the way Darwin looked at things in the natural world and to the importance of this way of looking for our own understanding of what it means to behold the world. See also Adam Gopnik, *Angels and Ages: A Short Book about Darwin, Lincoln, and Modern Life* (New York: Vintage, 2009): "More than anything else in life, Charles Darwin liked to look at things. He liked to look at things the way an artist likes to draw, the way a composer likes to play the piano, the way a cook likes to chop onions: it is the simple root physical activity that makes the other, higher order acts not just possible but pleasurable" (72).

41. Charles Darwin, "Darwin's Ornithological Notes," ed. Emma Nora Barlow, *Bulletin of the British Museum* (Natural History) Historical Series 2 (1963): 201–278; Charles Darwin, *Charles Darwin's Beagle Diary*, ed. Richard Darwin Keynes (Cambridge: Cambridge University Press, 2001). Charles Darwin, *Charles Darwin's Zoology Notes and Specimen Lists from H.M.S. Beagle*, ed. Richard Darwin Keynes (Cambridge: Cambridge University Press, 2000).

42. Haupt, *Pilgrim on the Great Bird Continent,* 11–12.

43. Haupt, *Pilgrim on the Great Bird Continent,* 14.

44. See Janet Browne, *Charles Darwin: A Biography.* Vol. 1, *Voyaging* (New York: Knopf, 1995), 325–327, 396–399, 438–439, for an illuminating discussion of Darwin's complex and shifting relationship to the Church of England and his struggle to reconcile orthodox Christian belief with his emerging understanding of the principles of evolution. Brown suggests that "the religious sentiment was never strongly developed in [Darwin]" (325) and that his continued adherence to the teachings of the Church of England may well have owed as much to his temperamental aversion to confronting doubt and to the conventions of his class as it did to any particular conviction Darwin had regarding the truth of those teachings. Still, there is little doubt that he did ultimately find it impossible to reconcile his emerging scientific understanding with the teachings of Christianity. Even so, this leaves unanswered the question of how best to understand the potential spiritual significance of Darwin's work as a naturalist, in particular his deep devotion to paying attention to the world. It is here that Haupt's work is especially helpful, for it opens up a space that allows us to distinguish Darwin's struggles with religion from the contemplative character of his work as a naturalist.

45. Haupt, *Pilgrim on the Great Bird Continent,* 15–16.

46. Haupt, *Pilgrim on the Great Bird Continent,* 49–50.

47. Darwin, *Charles Darwin's Zoology Notes,* February 29, 1832, 65,

48. Darwin, *Charles Darwin's Beagle Diary,* 42.

49. Darwin, "Darwin's Ornithological Notes," 250.

50. Haupt, *Pilgrim on the Great Bird Continent,* 86.

51. Haupt, *Pilgrim on the Great Bird Continent,* 86.

52. Haupt, *Pilgrim on the Great Bird Continent,* 186.

53. Haupt, *Pilgrim on the Great Bird Continent,* 187.

54. Haupt, *Pilgrim on the Great Bird Continent,* 244.

55. Charles Darwin, *On the Origin of Species* (New York: New York University Press, 2010), 314.

56. Henry David Thoreau, *I to Myself: An Annotated Selection from the Journal of Henry David Thoreau,* ed. Jeffrey S. Cramer (New Haven: Yale University Press, 2007), 86.

57. Vincent van Gogh, *The Letters of Vincent van Gogh,* ed. Ronald de Leeuw, trans. Arnold Pomerans (London: Penguin, 1997), 470.

58. Adrienne Baxter Bell, *George Inness and the Visionary Landscape* (New York: Braziller, 2003), 28.

59. Bell notes: "Innes was not especially engaged by the challenge of capturing, through his art, the fleeting, physical appearances of scenes in nature, of representing nature according to information derived through physical sight. He attempted, instead, to express something far more difficult to discern: a sense of nature's "inner life," a sense of those invisible forces—those divine forces of influx—that generated nature's 'living motion.'" (*George Inness and the Visionary Landscape,* 29–30).

60. See Marc Simpson, ed., *Like Breath on Glass: Whistler, Inness, and the Art of Painting Softly* (New Haven: Yale University Press, 2008).

61. Paul Cezanne, *Letters,* ed. John Rewald, trans. Marguerite Kay (New York: Da Capo Press, 1995), 327.

62. Cezanne, *Letters,* 316–317. He also comments on his sense of the importance of optics: "Optics, which are developed in us by study, teach us to see," 317.

63. Van Gogh, *Letters,* 193–194.

64. Aldo Leopold, *A Sand County Almanac: And Sketches Here and There* (New York: Oxford, 1949), 149–150.

CHAPTER 6

1. John 1:1.

2. N. Scott Momaday, *House Made of Dawn* (New York: Harper and Row, 1968), 97.

3. N. Scott Momaday, "The Native Voice in American Literature," in *The Man Made of Words: Essays, Stories, Passages* (New York: St. Martin's, 1997), 14.

4. An underlying assumption throughout this chapter is that there much to be gained from considering together the various ways in which the idea of 'the Word' has been employed to connote the expressive power of the world (and our experience of this expressive power). However, the sheer range of ways in which the idea of 'the Word' (and related metaphors) has been employed to evoke the sense of the expressive, numinous power of the natural world presents certain challenges. One of these is how to denote the particular meaning of this idea in any given context. The high theological meaning of Logos or Word associated with the idea of the Divinity of Christ came into being gradually within the Christian tradition. Also, it drew upon a more diffuse set of meanings associated with logos arising from Greek philosophical thought and from the Hebrew Scriptures (particularly the Septuagint or Greek translation of those scriptures), many of which had no particular association with God or the divinity of Christ (several of these are detailed in this chapter). Nor should one make simple comparisons between the explicitly theological meaning the term has in the Christian theological tradition and the more wide-ranging and open-ended meanings the metaphor of language and speech has come to possess in contemporary poetic and ecological discourse. Still, there are resonances between and among these different uses of this metaphor that can be illuminating for our efforts to consider how the living world speaks to us. Yet, because of the diffuse meanings and usages of this idea in both ancient and contemporary discourse, it is almost impossible to be consistent in determining the simple matter of whether or when to capitalize Logos or Word. The usage of these terms in this chapter reflects this difficulty. In broad terms, I capitalize Logos or Word to express the intuition, found in ancient Christian and Greek philosophical texts as well as in the work of many contemporary writers, that the expressive power of the world is numinous and powerful, or has a divine character or source. In other cases, when the context

seems to suggest something more like 'reason' or 'purpose', though without explicitly reference to God, I use word or logos. But this idea arises in so many different ways and such different contexts that it is not always easy to know how to interpret its meaning. For example, while it might seem safer or more respectful in the case of the work of certain contemporary poets and writers, to use the term in its lower case form, the appropriateness of such a choice is not always clear. For here also one often encounters a sense of the world's expressive power that so numinous and powerful that one can hardly avoid speaking of 'the Word.' It seems important to acknowledge the complexity and ambiguity of this idea (and our use and understanding of it) and how it mirrors in significant ways the complexity and ambiguity of our own cultural-religious moment.

5. It is easy for us to forget the force of these words at the time the book was published. Hearing of the possibility that the book might in fact carry this title (instead of the working title *The War against Nature* or *War against Nature)*, Carson's close friend Dorothy Freeman wrote to her: "I shudder at the thought of a 'Silent Spring.'" Rachel Carson, *Always Rachel: The Letters of Rachel Carson and Dorothy Freeman, 1952–1964,* ed. Martha Freeman (Boston: Beacon, 1995), 379–380.

6. Recent reflections on this question include Garret Keizer, *The Unwanted Sound of Everything We Want: A Book about Noise* (New York: Public Affairs, 2010); George Prochnik, *In Pursuit of Silence: Listening for Meaning in a World of Noise* (New York: Doubleday, 2010); George M. Foy, *Zero Decibels: The Quest for Absolute Silence* (New York: Scribner, 2010).

7. Anne D. Leclaire, *Listening below the Noise: A Meditation on the Practice of Silence* (New York: Harper, 2009); Sara Maitland, *A Book of Silence* (Washington, DC: Counterpoint, 2010).

8. Cited in Kevin Bezner and Kevin Walzer, eds., *The Wilderness of Vision: On the Poetry of John Haines* (Brownsville, OR: Story Line Press, 1996), 28.

9. Maximus the Confessor, "Various Texts on Theology, the Divine Economy, and Virtue and Vice," *The Philokalia: The Complete Text,* Vol. 2, trans. and ed. G. E. H. Palmer, Philip Sherrard, and Kallistos Ware (London: Faber and Faber, 1981), 271.

10. David Allen Sibley, *The Sibley Guide to Birds* (New York: Knopf, 2000), 495. For an unusually sensitive reflection on the language of birds, see John Bevis, *Aaaaw to Zzzzzd: The Words of Birds. North America, Britain and Northern Europe* (Cambridge: MIT Press, 2010). Nearly half of this remarkable little book comprises a list of phrases used to denote the distinctive idiom of birdsong. See also Bernie Krause, *Into a Wild Sanctuary: A Life in Music and Natural Sound* (Berkeley: Heyday Books, 1998), and *The Great Animal Orchestra: Finding the Origins of Music in the World's Wild Places* (New York: Little, Brown, 2012); David Rothenberg, *Why Birds Sing: A Journey into the Mystery of Birdsong* (New York: Basic Books, 2005).

11. Maximus the Confessor, "Various Texts on Theology," 271.

12. Henry David Thoreau, *Walking* (Boston: Beacon, 1991), 112.

13. Gary Snyder, *The Practice of the Wild* (San Francisco: North Point, 1990), especially "Tawny Grammar," 48–77. See also Robert Bringhurst, *The Tree of Meaning: Language, Mind and Ecology* (Berkeley: Counterpoint, 2008), especially "Wild Language," 257–276. Anne Whiston Spirn, *The Language of Landscape* (New Haven: Yale University Press, 1998), makes a compelling case for the always-bound-up character of language and landscape.

14. Snyder, *The Practice of the Wild*, 9–10.

15. Cited in Gerhard Ladner, *God, Cosmos, and Humankind: The World of Early Christian Symbolism,* trans. Thomas Dunlap (Berkeley: University of California Press, 1995), 99.

16. Erazim Kohák, *The Embers and the Stars: A Philosophical Inquiry into the Moral Sense of Nature* (Chicago: University of Chicago Press, 1984), 10.

17. On this question, see Oliver Davies and Denys Turner, eds., *Silence and the Word: Negative Theology and Incarnation* (Cambridge: Cambridge University Press, 2002).

18. Marcia L. Colish, *The Stoic Tradition from Antiquity to the Early Middle Ages I: Stoicism in Classical Latin Literature.* Second Impression with Addenda and Corrigenda (Leiden: E. J. Brill, 1990), 31–35.

19. J. van Arnim, *Stoicorum Veterum Fragmenta* (Leipzig, 1903–1905), 1.98; cited in David E. Hahm, *The Origins of Stoic Cosmology* (Columbus: Ohio State University Press, 1977), 60.

20. Kohák, *The Embers and the Stars,* 10.

21. Tertullian, *Adv. Herm.* 44.1; in Marcia L. Colish, *The Stoic Tradition from Antiquity to the Early Middle Ages 2. Stoicism in Christian Latin Thought through the Sixth Century.* Second Impression with Addenda and Corrigenda (Leiden: E. J. Brill, 1990), 19.

22. Tertullian, *Apol.* 18, 11–13, 21, 10–14; cited in Colish, *The Stoic Tradition*, 2, 19.

23. Tertullian, *Adv. Herm.* 36.4; cited in Colish, *The Stoic Tradition*, 2, 20.

24. Salvatore R. C. Lilla, *Clement of Alexandria: A Study in Christian Platonism and Gnosticism* (Oxford: Oxford University Press, 1971), 199–212.

25. Paul Ricoeur, *Essays on Biblical Interpretation*, ed. Lewis S. Mudge (Philadelphia: Fortress, 1980), 92.

26. Ladner, *God, Cosmos, and Humankind*, 65–154.

27. Ladner, *God, Cosmos, and Humankind*, 84.

28. Ladner, *God, Cosmos, and Humankind*, 99.

29. Origen of Alexandria, *The Song of Songs: Commentary and Homilies*, trans. R. P. Lawson (New York: Newman Press, 1956), 29.

30. Donald Nicholl, *The Beatitude of Truth* (London: Darton, Longman and Todd, 1997), 18.

31. Hildegard of Bingen, *Symphonia*, trans. Barbara Newman (Ithaca: Cornell University Press, 1988), 102–103: "O Pastor animarum" (Antiphon for the Redeemer).

32. Hildegard of Bingen, *Symphonia*, 126–127: "O viridissima virga" (Song to the Virgin) [translation adapted].

33. Francis of Assisi, "Canticle of the Creatures," in *Francis and Clare: The Complete Works,* ed. and trans. Regis J. Armstrong and Ignatius C. Brady (New York: Paulist Press, 1992), 38–39. The theological-ecological significance of the Canticle has long been appreciated by commentators. The very language of the Canticle, especially the force of the Italian *"per,"* suggests the kind of intimate reciprocity between Word and world embodied in the Franciscan vision of creation. The editors of the Paulist volume comment: "[*per*] may be translated 'for,' suggesting an attitude of thanksgiving; 'by,' expressing a sense of instrumentality; or 'through' indicating instrumentality as well as a deeper sense of mysticism in perceiving God's presence in all creation" (p. 38). For a perceptive commentary on the meaning of the Franciscan "creation tradition," with particular attention to the importance of the Eucharist—the incarnate Word, ingested and absorbed into the fabric of one's being—to the Franciscan understanding of creation, see Timothy J. Johnson, "Francis and Creation," in *The Cambridge Companion to Francis of Assisi*, ed. Michael J. P. Robson (Cambridge: Cambridge University Press, 2012), 143–158.

34. Isaac of Ninevah, *'The Second Part,' Chapters IV–XLI. Corpus Scriptorum Christianorum Orientalum*, 225, trans. Sebastian Brock (Louvain: Peeters, 1995), 8.

35. Meister Eckhart, *Sermons and Treatises*, Vol. I, trans. and ed. M. O'C. Walshe (Shaftesbury, Dorset: Element, 1987), 45.

36. Athanasius, *The Life of Antony and the Letter to Marcelinus*, trans. Robert C. Gregg (New York: Paulist, 1980), 1–4; 30–32.

37. Athanasius, *Life of Antony* 50; 68.

38. Rufinus, *Historia Monachorum in Aegypto, Patrologia Latina* 21, 443C, 444C; English translation: *The Lives of the Desert Fathers*, trans. Norman Russell (London: Cistercian Publications, 1980), XX, 7, 106; see also Benedicta Ward's introduction, 3.

39. *AP*, Arsenius 25, Benedicta Ward, *The Sayings of the Desert Fathers* (Kalamazoo: Cistercian Publications, 2006), 13.

40. Evagrius, *Foundations* 3; *Evagrius of Pontus: The Greek Ascetic Corpus*, trans. Robert E. Sinkewicz (New York: Oxford University Press 2003), 5.

41. Evagrius, *Exhortation to Monks* 7; Sinkewicz, *Evagrius of Pontus: The Greek Ascetic Corpus*, 218.

42. Evagrius of Pontus, *On Prayer* 51; Sinkewicz, *Evagrius of Pontus: The Greek Ascetic Corpus*, 198. This translation has been slightly adapted. Sinkewicz translates *logoi* as "reasons"; other translators, especially those responsible for translating the *Philokalia* into English, use the phrase "inner essences" to translate *logoi*. Both translations are accurate. However, "inner essences" seems to me to more accurately reflect the sense of the inner life and purpose of created beings to which Evagrius and other early Christian writers refer. Vladimir Lossky, in his classic work, *The Mystical Theology of the Eastern Church* (Cambridge: James Clarke, 1957), 98–99, refers to the *logoi* as the divine "willings" or "thought-wills"—the will of God manifest in the created world.

43. Lossky, *The Mystical Theology of the Eastern Church*, 99. Italics for Logos added.

44. Maximus the Confessor, "Two Hundred Texts on Theology and the Incarnate Dispensation of the Son of God," # 32 (First Century); *The Philokalia. The Complete Works*, Vol. 2, trans. and ed. G. E. H. Palmer, Philip Sherrard, and Kallistos Ware (London: Faber and Faber, 1981), 120. On the idea of the *logoi* (and their relationship to the logos) in Maximus's work, see Adam G. Cooper, *The Body in St. Maximus the Confessor: Holy Flesh, Wholly Deified* (Oxford: Oxford University Press, 2005), especially 92–95: "In Maximus' cosmology, the *logoi* are God's original ideas or intentions for creation: the unifying, ordering, determinative and defining principles in accordance with which God institutes created natures. A thing's being—what it is—is determined by its *logos*, by what God intends it to be. As constitutive of relation and definition, the *logoi* define the essential qualities and purpose of creaturely being and at the same time disclose the divine Word and Wisdom operative within the cosmic economy" (92).

45. Maximus the Confessor, "Various Texts on Theology, the Divine Economy, and Virtue and Vice," #8 (First Century); *The Philokalia: The Complete Text*, Vol. 2, 166.

46. Maximus the Confessor, "Chapters on Knowledge," #39 (Second Century); in Maximus the Confessor, *Selected Writings*, trans. George C. Berthold (New York: Paulist, 1985), 156. Italics (for Logos) added.

47. Maximus the Confessor, *Selected Writings*, #61 (160); #73 (163); #60 (160).

48. Eckhart, *Sermons and Treatises*, Vol. I., 20. On the central place of this idea in Meister Eckhart's thought, see Karl G. Kertz, "Meister Eckhart's Teaching on the Birth of the Divine World in the Soul," *Traditio* 15 (1959): 327–363. See also Bernard McGinn, *The Mystical Thought of Meister Eckhart: The Man from Whom God Hid Nothing* (New York: Herder and Herder, 2001), 53–70. On the intimate relationship between birthing and detachment in Eckhart, see Reiner Schürmann, *Wandering Joy: Meister Eckhart's Mystical Philosophy* (Great Barrington, MA: Lindisfarne Books, 2001), 18–37.

49. Eckhart, *Sermons and Treatises*, Vol. I, 33.

50. Eckhart, *Sermons and Treatises*, Vol. I, 5.

51. Eckhart, *Sermons and Treatises*, Vol. I, 42.

52. Eckhart, *Sermons and Treatises*, Vol. I, 20–21.

53. Eckhart, *Sermons and Treatises*, Vol. I, 67.

54. Eckhart, *Sermons and Treatises*, Vol. I, 45.

55. Henry David Thoreau, *Walden* (Princeton: Princeton University Press, 1971), 271–272.

56. Theodore Roethke, *Selected Poems* (New York: Library of America, 2005), 23.

57. Barry Lopez, *Arctic Dreams: Imagination and Desire in a Northern Landscape* (New York: Bantam, 1986), 11.

58. Reflections on the role of language (storytelling, narrative, poetry) in facilitating a more encompassing awareness of the living world have long held a central place within the literature of nature and within the critical discourse of eco-criticism. One important strain of contemporary eco-critical thought involves the call to

rethink the character of language itself and what it means to conceive of the living world itself has having a "voice." Christopher Manes, "Nature and Silence," in *The Ecocriticism Reader,* ed. Cheryl Glotfelty and Harold Fromm (Athens: University of Georgia Press, 1996), 15–29, gives eloquent expression to the growing awareness of how silent nature has become in our culture ("[silent] in the sense that the status of being a speaking subject is jealously guarded as an exclusively human prerogative," 15) and calls for "a new language free from the directionalities of humanism, a language that incorporates a decentered, postmodern, post-humanist perspective…[a] language of ecological humility" (17). Only such humility, Manes suggests, will enable us to begin hearing and responding to voices other than our own. David Abram's work, both *The Spell of the Sensuous: Perception and Language in a More-Than-Human World* (New York: Pantheon, 1996), and *Becoming Animal: An Earthly Cosmology* (New York: Pantheon, 2012), reflects a similar sensibility, giving assiduous attention to the experience of deep reciprocity that can begin to emerge between us and the world when we learn to attune ourselves to the voices everywhere discernible within the living world.

Karl Kroeber, *Ecological Literary Criticism: Romantic Ecology and the Biology of Mind* (New York: Columbia University Press, 1994), argues, especially in chap. 5, "Discovering Nature's Voice" (67–81), for the fundamentally ecological (i.e., reciprocal, interdependent) characracter of the romantic literary tradition and for the importance of its intensely "ecological vision, a vision of cultured humankind with its imaginings as an integral part of a natural scene, in which 'works and days,' humanizing ritual and nonhuman natural process in both expansion and diminishment, are 'felt in the blood and felt along the heart,' so that even the passing through fulfillment of natural loveliness becomes transfigured into the enduring beauty of a singular linguistic expression" (77–78). Lawrence Buell, in *The Environmental Imagination: Thoreau, Nature Writing and the Formation of American Culture* (Cambridge: Harvard University Press, 1995) argues, especially in chap. 3, "Representing the Environment" (83–114), for a similarly robust understanding of the possibilities of linguistic representation to both express and kindle in the reader a sense of the living world's complex ecological character. Drawing upon Francis Ponge's notion of *adéquation* (the notion that verbal expressions are not simply replicas but equivalents of the world of objects), Buell notes that such writing can "in some measure bridge…the abyss that inevitably yawns between language and the object world," and can inspire "environmental bonding" (98). Still, others have observed that the abyss between language and world cannot always be bridged, at least not completely. See Rebecca Raglon and Marion Sholtmeijer, "Heading off the Trail: Language, Literature and Nature's Resistance to Narrative," in *Beyond Nature Writing: Expanding the Boundaries of Ecocriticism,* ed. Karla Ambruster and Kathleen R. Wallace (Charlottesville: University Press of Virginia, 2001), 248–262.

On the fundamental theoretical challenges of arriving at a truly ecocentric understanding of language, see Alwin Fill and Peter Mühlhäusler, eds., *The Ecolinguistics Reader: Language, Ecology and Environment* (New York: Continuum, 2001). On the always politically and culturally particular (and charged) character of discourse about the natural world, see Elizabeth DeLoughrey and George B. Handley, eds., *Postcolonial Ecologies: Literatures of the Environment* (New York: Oxford University Press, 2011), and Helen Tiffin and Graham Huggan, eds., *Postcolonial EcoCriticism: Literature, Animals, Environment* (London: Routledge, 2010).

59. Thoreau, *Walden*, 111.

60. Thoreau, *Walden*, 271–272.

61. Henry David Thoreau, *I to Myself: An Annotated Selection from the Journal of Henry D. Thoreau* (New Haven: Yale University Press, 2007), 70–71.

62. Thoreau, *I to Myself*, 72.

63. Gary Paul Nabhan, "Foreword," in Henry David Thoreau, *Faith in a Seed* (Washington, DC: Island Press, 1993), xvi.

64. Thoreau, *Faith in a Seed*, 51.

65. H. Daniel Peck, *Thoreau's Morning Work: Memory and Perception in* A Week on the Concord and Merrimack Rivers*, the* Journal*, and* Walden (New Haven: Yale University Press, 1990), 39–114. See also David M. Robinson, *Natural Life: Thoreau's Worldly Transcendentalism* (Ithaca: Cornell University Press, 2004).

66. Cited by Nabhan in "Foreword," *Faith in a Seed*, xvi.

67. Paul Shepard, *Nature and Madness* (San Francisco: Sierra Club, 1982), 11.

68. Jean Giono, *The Song of the World*, trans. Henry Fluchère and Geoffrey Myers (San Francisco: North Point, 1981), 9–10.

69. Paul Shepard, *Nature and Madness* (San Francisco: Sierra Club, 1982), 11.

70. Leslie Marmon Silko, *Ceremony* (New York: Viking Penguin, 1977), 35–36.

71. Ellen Meloy, *The Anthropology of Turquoise: Meditations on Landscape, Art, and Spirit* (New York: Pantheon, 2002), 15.

72. Denise Levertov, *Evening Train* (New York: New Directions, 1992), 3.

73. Richard Nelson, *The Island Within* (New York: Vintage, 1991), 150.

74. Robert Hass, *Sun under Wood* (New York: Ecco, 1996), 18–19.

75. Mary Oliver, "Entering the Kingdom," *New and Selected Poems*, Vol. 1 (Boston: Beacon, 2005), 190.

76. Mary Oliver, "Have You Ever Tried to Enter the Long Black Branches," *West Wind* (Boston: Houghton Mifflin, 1997), 61.

77. Oliver, *West Wind*, 62.

78. Annie Dillard, *Pilgrim at Tinker Creek* (New York: Harper, 1974), 1.

79. Louise Glück, "Sunset," in *The Wild Iris* (New York: Ecco, 1992), 57.

80. Norman Maclean, *A River Runs through It* (Chicago: University of Chicago Press, 1976), 95–96.

81. Amos Wilder, *Theopoetic: Theology and the Religious Imagination* (Philadelphia: Fortress, 1976), 1–2.

82. Momaday, *House Made of Dawn*, 97.

83. Maclean, *A River Runs through It*, 95–96.

CHAPTER 7

1. Adam Zagajewski, *A Defense of Ardor*, trans. Clare Cavanagh (New York: Farrar, Straus and Giroux, 2004), 16.

2. John Muir, *John of the Mountains: The Unpublished Journals of John Muir*, ed. Linnie Marsh Wolfe (Boston: Houghton Mifflin, 1938), 92.

3. Barry Lopez, *Arctic Dreams: Imagination and Desire in a Northern Landscape* (New York: Bantam, 1987), 109–110.

4. E. O. Wilson, *Biophilia* (Cambridge, MA: Harvard University Press, 1984), 1.

5. Edward Abbey, "Down the River with Henry Thoreau," in *Words from the Land,* ed. Stephen Trimble (Reno: University of Nevada Press, 1995), 62.

6. Gregory of Nyssa, *The Life of Moses*, trans. Abraham Malherbe and Everett Ferguson (New York: Paulist, 1978). Critical edition with French translation: *La Vie de Moïse*, trans. Jean Daniélou (Paris: Cerf, 1987), II, 239, 2.4.7: 116.

7. On the idea of distance and the horizon as a defining feature of the Western intellectual and spiritual tradition, see Didier Maleuvre, *The Horizon: A History of Our Infinite Longing* (Berkeley: University of California Press, 2011).

8. A work of particular importance for shedding light on early Christian understanding of *eros* is Catherine Osborne, *Eros Unveiled: Plato and the God of Love* (Oxford: Clarendon Press, 1994). On the broad effort to reexamine the meaning of eros within the Christian theological tradition, see Margaret Kamitsuka, ed., *The Embrace of Eros: Bodies, Desire, and Sexuality in Christianity* (Philadelphia: Fortress, 2010); Virginia Burrus and Catherine Keller, eds., *Toward a Theology of Eros: Transforming Passion at the Limits of a Discipline* (New York: Fordham University Press, 2006); Mark D. Jordan, *The Ethics of Sex* (Malden, MA: Blackwell, 2002). We are also witnessing a sustained if varied effort to better understand the meaning of *eros* within a fully embodied Christian *spiritual* practice. See, for example, Wendy Farley, *The Wounding and Healing of Desire: Weaving Heaven and Earth* (Louisville: Westminster John Knox, 2005); Belden C. Lane, *Ravished by Beauty: The Surprising Legacy of Reformed Spirituality* (New York: Oxford University Press, 2011); James D. Whitehead and Evelyn Easton Whitehead, *Holy Eros: Recovering the Passion of God* (Maryknoll, NY: Orbis, 2008); Margaret R. Miles, *Practicing Christianity: Critical Perspectives for an Embodied Spirituality* (Eugene, OR: Wipf and Stock, 2006); Ronald Rolheiser, *The Holy Longing: The Search for a Christian Spirituality* (New York: Doubleday, 1999).

9. Robert Hass, "Iowa City: Early April," in *Sun under Wood* (New York: Ecco, 1996), 35.

10. Susan Griffin, *The Eros of Everyday Life: Essays on Ecology, Gender and Society* (New York: Doubleday, 1995), 150.

11. Griffin, *The Eros of Everyday Life,* 69.

12. Lewis Hyde, *The Gift: Imagination and the Erotic Life of Property* (New York: Vintage, 1979), 4, 8.

13. Hyde, *The Gift,* 16.

14. Hyde, *The Gift*, 16.

15. David Abram, *The Spell of the Sensuous: Perception and Language in a More-Than-Human World* (New York: Pantheon, 1996), 65.

16. Abram, *The Spell of the Sensuous*, 37.

17. Michael Jackson, *The Palm at the End of the Mind: Relatedness, Religiosity and the Real* (Durham: Duke University Press, 2009), xii, xiii.

18. William James, *Essays on Radical Empiricism* (Cambridge, MA: Harvard University Press, 1976), 35.

19. Jackson, *The Palm at the End of the Mind*, 39.

20. William James, A Pluralistic Universe (Cambridge, MA: Harvard University Press, 1977), 96–97.

21. Allan D. Hodder, *Thoreau's Ecstatic Witness* (New Haven: Yale University Press, 2001). Much of my analysis here draws on Hodder's fine opening chapter, "My Life Was Ecstasy" (28–69), especially 60–69.

22. Henry David Thoreau, *Journal*, Vol. I, ed. John C. Broderick, et. al. (Princeton: Princeton University Press, 1981), 69–70.

23. Thoreau, *Journal*, I. 256.

24. Hodder, *Thoreau's Ecstatic Witness*, 65.

25. Henry David Thoreau, *I to Myself: An Annotated Selection from the Journal of Henry D. Thoreau*, ed. Jeffrey S. Kramer (New Haven: Yale University Press, 2007), 60.

26. Thoreau, *I to Myself*, 75.

27. Thoreau, *I to Myself*, 75.

28. Thoreau, *I to Myself*, 97.

29. Aldo Leopold, *A Sand County Almanac* (New York: Oxford University Press, 1949), 214.

30. Robert Hass, "Meditations at Lagunitas," in *Praise* (New York: Ecco, 1979), 4–5.

31. Michel de Certeau, *The Mystic Fable*, trans. Michael B. Smith (Chicago: University of Chicago Press 1992), 299.

32. I am indebted to Charlotte Radler for this insight into Eckhart's thought. See her essay, " 'In Love I Am More God': The Centrality of Love in Meister Eckhart's Mysticism," *Journal of Religion* 90, no. 2 (2010): 171–198.

33. Anders Nygren, *Agape and Eros* (Chicago: University of Chicago Press, 1982).

34. Denys Turner, *Eros and Allegory: Medieval Exegesis of the Song of Songs* (Kalamazoo, MI: Cistercian Publications, 1995), 41.

35. Turner, *Eros and Allegory*, 20.

36. For a fuller development of this encompassing theological understanding of eros, see Osborne, *Eros Unveiled: Plato and the God of Love*.

37. For a lucid account of how the language of the erotic and the language of prayer and mysticism can mutually inform one another, see Mark D. Jordan, *The Ethics of Sex*, especially 164–169.

38. Gregory of Nyssa, *Life of Moses*, II, 163, 95.

39. See Henry Fiska Hägg, *Clement of Alexandria and the Beginnings of Christian Apophaticism* (New York: Oxford University Press, 1996).

40. Gregory's reflections on the *Song of Songs* are also critical to his thinking about the relationship between desire and darkness. See Martin Laird, "The Fountain of His Lips: Desire and Divine Union in Gregory of Nyssa's *Homilies on the Song of Songs*," *Spiritus* 7 (2007): 40–57; "Under Solomon's Tutelage: The Education of Desire in the *Homilies of the Song of Songs*," *Modern Theology* 18 (2002): 507–525.

41. Gregory of Nyssa, *Life of Moses*, II, 225; 113.

42. Gregory of Nyssa, *Life of Moses*, II, 226, 113.

43. Gregory of Nyssa, *Life of Moses*, II, 230, 2, 114.

44. Gregory of Nyssa, *Life of Moses*, II, 231, 5, 114.

45. Martin Laird has argued that the image of Gregory of Nyssa as a radically (and perhaps exclusively) apophatic thinker needs to be revised, especially given the significant attention in his work to the experience of illumination. See Martin Laird, *Gregory of Nyssa and the Grasp of Faith: Union, Knowledge, and Divine Presence* (Oxford: Oxford University Press, 2004), esp. 174–212.

46. Gregory of Nyssa, *Life of Moses*, II, 239, 2.4.7, 116.

47. Gregory of Nyssa, *Life of Moses*, II, 163.

48. Gregory of Nyssa, *Life of Moses*, II, 164, 95.

49. Gregory of Nyssa, *The Lord's Prayer, The Beatitudes*, trans. Hilda C. Graef (Mahwah, NJ: Paulist Press, 1978) [*The Lord's Prayer*], 3, 46.

50. Gregory of Nyssa, *The Lord's Prayer, The Beatitudes* [*The Beatitudes*, 7, 154].

51. Gregory's intense interest in the idea of *apocatastasis panton* should be seen as one important expression of his larger concern for how spiritual practice can contribute to a renewal and healing of all things. See John R. Sachs, "Apocatastasis in Patristic Theology," *Theological Studies* 54 (1993): 617–640, esp. 632–638.

52. Gregory of Nyssa, *The Lord's Prayer, The Beatitudes* [*The Beatitudes*, 7, 154].

53. Gregory of Nyssa, *The Lord's Prayer, The Beatitudes* [*The Beatitudes*, 7, 159].

54. Boris Pasternak, *Doctor Zhivago*, trans. Manya Harari and Max Hayward (New York: Knopf, 1986), 528–529.

55. For an illuminating discussion of the notion of ecstasy in Luce Irigiray's thought, see Fergus Kerr, *Immortal Longings: Versions of a Transcending Humanity* (Notre Dame: University of Notre Dame Press, 1997), ch. 5, esp. p. 99. See also Christopher Cohoon, "Coming Together: The Six Modes of Irigirayan Eros," *Hypatia* 26, no. 3 (Summer 2011): 478–496.

56. See Luce Irigiray, *The Way of Love,* trans. Heidi Bostic and Stephen Pluhécek (New York: Continuum, 2004).

57. Paul Shepard, *Nature and Madness* (San Francisco: Sierra Club, 1982), 7.

58. Mary Austin, *Land of Little Rain* (Albuquerque: University of New Mexico Press, 1974), 96–97.

59. Michael Ondaatje, *Divisadero* (New York: Knopf, 2007), 184.

60. Pasternak, *Doctor Zhivago*, 528–529.

61. Pasternak, *Doctor Zhivago*, 529.

62. Gerard Manley Hopkins, Poems and Prose, ed. W/H. Gardner (London: Penguin, 1953). 39–40.

63. Robert Hass, *Sun under Wood* (New York: Ecco, 1996).

64. Hass, *Sun under Wood*, 21–22.

65. Hass, *Sun under Wood*, 15.

66. Hass, *Sun under Wood*, 12.

67. Hass, *Sun under Wood*, 6, 8.

68. Linda Hogan, *Dwellings: A Spiritual History of the Living World* (New York: Norton, 1995), 83.

69. Hass, *Sun under Wood*, 18–22.

70. Freeman House, *Totem Salmon: Life Lessons from Another Species* (Boston: Beacon, 1999), 13.

71. House, *Totem Salmon*, 70.

72. Leslie Marmon Silko, *Ceremony* (New York: Viking Penguin, 1977), 219–220.

73. Simon Ortiz, "Culture and the Universe," *Out There Somewhere* (Tucson: University of Arizona Press, 2002).

74. Silko, *Ceremony*, 201–202.

75. Silko, *Ceremony*, 219–220.

CHAPTER 8

1. Edmund Jabès, *The Book of Resemblances*. 2. *Intimations of the Desert,* trans. Rosmarie Waldrop (Hanover: Wesleyan University Press, 1991), 113.

2. Cormac McCarthy, *The Crossing* (New York: Knopf, 1994), 283.

3. Simone Weil, *Waiting for God,* trans. Emma Craufurd (New York: Harper Perennial, 2009), 69.

4. While these questions surface throughout ancient Jewish Wisdom literature, it is in the Book of Job that the full weight of the moral and spiritual challenge they present can be felt most acutely. Three studies that probe the questions arising out of Job's predicament with particular depth and clarity are Carol A. Newsom, *The Book of Job: A Contest of Moral Imaginations* (New York: Oxford, 2003), Philippe Nemo, *Job and the Excess of Evil* (Pittsburgh: Duquesne University Press, 1998), and Bruce Zuckerman, *Job the Silent: A Study in Historical Counterpoint* (New York: Oxford, 1991). Also helpful to my reading of the Book of Job has been Steven Chase, "Re-reading Job: Entertaining Spiritualities of Suffering," *Spiritus* 11, no. 1 (Spring 2011): 104–120.

5. This struggle has had a wide and deep purchase on the Christian imagination, surfacing, for example, in the debates between Christians, Manicheans, and Gnostics over the nature of material reality. While Christian writers involved in these debates almost uniformly affirmed the goodness of creation and the natural world in light of the doctrine of the incarnation, one also encounters among Christian thinkers a continuous struggle to grapple with the anomalous and seemingly capricious dimensions of material, embodied existence. Although the question of how much influence Manichean thought has had on Christian spirituality has been much

debated, there is little question that it had an enormous influence upon Augustine's thinking and through Augustine on much of the subsequent Christian spiritual tradition. The sense of the heaviness of material existence pervades much of Augustine's thinking about the meaning of sin. For Augustine, sin is often imagined as an experience of being "weighed down," unable to move. This is utterly consistent with the Manichaean understanding of embodied existence and their insistent attention on what one scholar has described as the "battle for the body," which was believed to be congenitally antagonistic to good. For a probing discussion of the Manichean understanding of human physiology, see Jason BeDuhn, "The Metabolism of Salvation: Manichaean Concepts of Human Physiology," in *The Light and The Darkness: Studies in Manichaeism and Its World,* ed. Paul Mirecki and Jason BeDuhn (Leiden: Brill, 2001), 3–37.

The issue of how much or little Christianity has been shaped by Manichean or Gnostic thought impinges on a wider set of questions concerning whether the Christian tradition has fully embraced the doctrine of the incarnation and its insistence on the inherent and enduring value of material reality. For a thoughtful examination of this question, see Wendell Berry, "Christianity and the Survival of Creation," in *Sex, Economy, Freedom and Community* (New York: Pantheon, 1993), 93–116.

This struggle has come to form a crucial part of the Christian theological tradition, especially in the effort to understand what it might mean to imagine God as somehow both shining through the world in its endless beauty and participating in its suffering, bearing its weight. For a lucid examination of the old question of whether God can be known and trusted amid a world that seems not at all trustworthy, see John G. Stackhouse, *Can God Be Trusted? Faith and the Challenge of Evil* (New York: Oxford, 1998).

6. Czeslaw Milosz, *The Witness of Poetry* (Cambridge: Harvard University Press, 1983), 25.
7. *The Book of Job*, trans. Stephen Mitchell (San Francisco: North Point Press, 1987), 13.
8. Nemo, *Job and the Excess of Evil.* The following quotations are taken from 17–23.
9. Weil, *Waiting for God*, 68.
10. Weil, *Waiting for God*, 68.
11. *The Book of Job*, trans. Stephen Mitchell, 72–73.
12. Weil, *Waiting for God*, 70. For a perceptive analysis of the meaning of affliction in Simone Weil's thought and its intimate relationship to the reality of necessity, see Vance C. Morgan, *Weaving the World: Simone Weil on Science, Mathematics and Love* (Notre Dame: University of Notre Dame Press, 2005), especially 171–186.
13. Simone Weil, *Gravity and Grace,* trans. Emma Crawford and Mario von der Ruhr (London: Routledge, 2002), 80.
14. Etty Hillesum, *An Interrupted Life*, trans. Arno Pomerans (New York: Pantheon, 1983), 145.
15. Carolyn Forché, *Blue Hour* (New York: HarperCollins, 2003), 7.

16. Hillesum's diaries record the period from March 1942 to October 1943. She died in Auschwitz on November 30, 1943.

17. Hillesum, *An Interrupted Life,* 114.

18. Hillesum, *An Interrupted Life,* 121.

19. Hillesum, *An Interrupted Life,* 127, 130.

20. Hillesum, *An Interrupted Life,* 131–132.

21. Hillesum, *An Interrupted Life,* 133.

22. Hillesum, *An Interrupted Life,* 141.

23. Hillesum, *An Interrupted Life,* 145. For a searching analysis of Hillesum's work as a gesture of resistance, see Rachel Brenner Feldhay, *Writing as Resistance: Four Women Confronting the Holocaust* (University Park: Penn State University Press 1997). On the distinctive, mystical character of Hillesum's work, see Frans Maas, *Spirituality as Insight: Mystical Texts and Theological Reflections* (Leuven: Peeters, 2004), 112–145.

24. Hillesum, *An Interrupted Life,* 146. Sarah Coakley's reflections on *kenosis* and contemplative practice are particularly helpful here. See "*Kenosis* and Subversion: On the Repression of Vulnerability in Christian Feminist Writing," in Sarah Coakley, *Powers and Submissions: Spirituality, Philosophy and Gender* (Oxford: Blackwell, 2002), 3–39, especially 32–39, in which she works to retrieve the notion that silent attention to God in prayer—long understood as the heart of *apophatic* spiritual practice—can be understood as a means of participating in or performing *kenosis.* Bearing in mind the challenges raised by feminist scholars regarding the potential danger (for women in particular) in adopting uncritically attitudes and practices of self-abnegation, Coakley observes that the practice of *kenosis* she has in mind is a "special form of vulnerability [that] is not an invitation to be battered...nor is its silence a silen*cing.*... This special self-emptying is not a negation of self, but the place of the self's transformation and expansion into God" (35–36).

25. Simone Weil, *Waiting for God*, trans. Emma Craufurd (New York: Putnam's, 1952), 64–65.

26. Hillesum, *An Interrupted Life,* 74–75.

27. Nikolaus Pevsner and Michael Meier, *Grünewald* (New York: Harry N. Abrams, 1958), 14.

28. Georg Scheja, *The Isenheim Altarpiece,* trans. Robert Erich Wolf (New York: Henry N. Abrams, 1969), 28.

29. Sigebert de Gembloux, cited in Andreé Hayum, *The Isenheim Altarpiece: God's Medicine and the Painter's Vision* (Princeton: Princeton University Press, 1989), 21.

30. Pevsner and Meier, *Grünewald,* 14.

31. J-K. Huysmans, "The Grünewalds in the Colmar Museum," in *Grünewald* (Oxford: Phaidon, 1976), 12.

32. Fyodor Dostoevsky, *The Idiot,* trans. Constance Garnett (New York: Barnes and Noble, 2004), 201.

33. See Derek Wilson, *Hans Holbein: Portrait of an Unknown Man* (London: Weidenfeld and Nicolson, 1996), 94–95. He accuses Dostoevsky of having "missed

the point entirely" of the painting; in Wilson's view, its uncompromising depiction of death was in fact oriented toward expressing "what Incarnation is about."

34. Julia Kristeva, "Holbein's Dead Christ," in *Fragments for a History of the Human Body, Part One,* ed. Michael Feher (New York: Zone Books, 1989), 243. See also Nigel Spivey, *Enduring Creation: Art, Pain, and Fortitude* (Berkeley: University of California Press, 2001), who situates Holbein's and Grünewald's works within a long history of efforts within Western art to represent the most extreme experiences of pain and suffering. He describes Holbein's panel as expressing "a true limit of representation: the absolute sacrifice of divinity to flesh" (p. 101).

35. Dostoevsky, *The Idiot,* 374–375.

36. Dostoevsky, *The Idiot,* 375. On these passages in *The Idiot,* seen within their broader historical, cultural, and religious contexts, see Konstantin Mochulsky, *Dostoevsky: His Life and Work,* trans. Michael A. Minihan (Princeton, NJ: Princeton University Press, 1967), 334–381, especially 362–365.

37. *Letters of Rainer Maria Rilke, 1910–1926,* trans. Jane Bannard Greene and M. D. Herter Norton (New York: Norton, 1947, 1948), 148. I am grateful to my colleague Steven Chase for drawing my attention to this correspondence.

38. W. G. Sebald, *The Emigrants,* trans. Michale Hulse (New York: New Directions, 1996), 170.

39. Valentin Groebner, *Defaced: The Visual Culture of Violence in the Late Middle Ages,* trans. Pamela Selwyn (New York: Zone Books, 2004). See especially ch. 4: "The Crucified and His Doubles," 87–123.

40. W. G. Sebald, *After Nature,* trans. Michael Hamburger (London: Hamish Hamilton, 2002), 27.

41. See Robert C. Gregg and Dennis E. Groh, *Early Arianism: A View of Salvation* (Philadelphia: Fortress, 1981); and David Brakke, *Athanasius and the Politics of Asceticism* (Oxford: Clarendon, 1995), 201–265.

42. Athanasius, *VA* 8; The *Life of Antony and the Letter to Marcellinus,* trans. Robert G. Gregg (New York: Paulist, 1980), 37.

43. Athanasius, *VA* 9; Gregg, *The Life of Antony,* 38.

44. *AP* Antony, 1, 3, 7, 19, 2; *The Sayings of the Desert Fathers,* trans. Benedicta Ward (Kalamazoo: Cistercian Publications, 2006), 1–5.

45. See Brakke, *Athanasius and the Politics of Asceticism,* 148–50; 217–227.

46. Gaston Bachelard, *The Psychoanalysis of Fire* (Boston: Beacon, 1987), 57.

47. Milosz, *Native Realm: A Search for Self-Definition* (New York: Doubleday, 1968; reprt., Berkeley: University of California Press, 1981), 86.

48. *Striving Towards Being. The Letters of Thomas Merton and Czeslaw Milosz,* ed. Robert Faggen (New York: Farrar, Straus and Giroux, 1997), 120, 122.

49. There is a growing number of works within the contemporary literature and poetry of nature that grapple seriously with the ambiguity of the human experience of the natural world, several of which articulate these questions in theological or religious terms. Those that have shaped my own thinking in significant ways include Annie

Dillard, *Pilgrim at Tinker Creek* (New York: Harper and Row, 1974), and *For the Time Being* (New York: Knopf, 1999); Norman Maclean, *A River Runs through It* (Chicago: University of Chicago Press, 1976), and *Young Men and Fire* (Chicago: University of Chicago Press, 1992); Pattiann Rogers, *Firekeeper* (Minneapolis: Milkweed, 1994); D. J. Waldie, *Holy Land* (New York: St. Martin's Press, 1996); Terry Tempest Williams, *Refuge: An Unnatural History of Family and Place* (New York: Pantheon, 1991); Ellen Voight, *Kyrie* (New York: Norton, 1995); Jeanette Winterson, *Weight* (New York: Canongate, 2005).

For a probing analysis of this question, with a particular focus on Annie Dillard's *Pilgrim at Tinker Creek*, see Lynn Ross-Bryant, "The Silence of Nature," *Religion and Literature* 22, no. 1 (Spring 1990): 79–94. For a thoughtful theological analysis, with a particular focus on the ethical implications, see Lisa H. Sideris, *Environmental Ethics, Ecological Theology, and Natural Selection* (New York: Columbia University Press, 2003).

50. *Striving Towards Being*, 120, 122.
51. *Striving Towards Being*, 64–65. The question of "blind necessity" in nature and history shows up continuously in Milosz's work. See, for example, his essay, "On the Effects of the Natural Sciences," in Czeslaw Milosz, *Visions from San Francisco Bay*, trans. Richard Lourie (New York: Farrar, Straus and Giroux, 1982), 21–25. Attending honestly to this question became for Milosz a matter of intellectual and theological integrity, something that helps to account for the deep affinity he felt for Simone Weil in whose work the question of necessity also figured centrally. See "On the Importance of Simone Weil," in Czeslaw Milosz, *Emperor of the Earth: Modes of Eccentric Vision* (Berkeley: University of California Press, 1977), 85–98. For a more in-depth analysis of Milosz's efforts to grapple with the paradoxical presence of necessity and grace in nature and history, see Douglas Burton-Christie, "The Immense Call of the Particular: Czeslaw Milosz on Nature, History and Hope," *Interdisciplinary Studies in Literature and Environment* 7, no. 1 (Winter 2000): 115–129.
52. *Striving Towards Being*, 66–67.
53. *Striving Towards Being*, 69–78.
54. *Striving Towards Being*, 37.
55. Milosz, *Native Realm*, 47.
56. Milosz, *Native Realm*, 64.
57. Milosz, *Native Realm*, 77.
58. Czeslaw Milosz, *The Collected Poems* (New York: Ecco, 1988), 303.
59. Milosz, *Native Realm*, 120.
60. Milosz, *Native Realm*, 143.
61. Milosz to Merton: "I do not understand the notion of Providence and am very much on the side of Simone Weil who preferred to leave as much as possible to necessity ruling the world. I do not know whether by using the highest name we do not commit an act against piety." (*Striving Towards Being*, 22).

62. *Striving Towards Being*, 39.

63. *Striving Towards Being*, 119.

64. *Striving Towards Being*, 120–122.

65. Thomas Merton, *The Hidden Ground of Love: The Letters of Thomas Merton on Religious Experience and Social Concerns*, ed. William H. Shannon (New York: Farrar, Straus and Giroux, 1985), 350.

66. Czeslaw Milosz, *Beginning with My Streets: Essays and Recollections* (New York: Farrar, Straus and Giroux, 1991), 280–281.

67. Annie Dillard, *For the Time Being*, 52.

68. Paul Harding, *Tinkers* (New York: Bellevue Literary Press, 2009), 72.

69. Dostoevsky, *The Idiot*, 375.

70. Milosz, *Collected Poems*, 310.

71. Milosz, *Collected Poems*, 314. Merton adds a fascinating coda to his reflections on Providence cited earlier that echoes some of Milosz's thinking on *apokatastasis panton* or final reconciliation: "As for those who are too shattered to do anything about it one way or the other, they are lifted, in pieces, into heaven and find themselves together there with no sense of how it might have been possible" (*Striving Towards Being* 39–40).

CHAPTER 9

1. Thomas Merton, *The Hidden Ground of Love: The Letters of Thomas Merton on Religious Experience and Social Concerns*, ed. William H. Shannon (New York: Farrar, Straus and Giroux, 1985), 563–564.

2. Edwin Muir, "The Transfiguration," *Collected Poems* (London: Faber and Faber, 1963), 198.

3. The growing attention to the paradise motif in contemporary thought and the effort to retrieve and reinterpret ancient Jewish, Christian, and Muslim understandings of this important theme are striking. Among the works that have informed my own thinking are Rebecca Ann Parker and Rita Nakashima Brock, *Saving Paradise: How Christianity Traded Love of this World for Crucifixion and Empire* (Boston: Beacon, 2008); Alesandro Scafi, *Mapping Paradise: A History of Heaven on Earth* (Chicago: University of Chicago Press, 2006); Jean Delumeau, *History of Paradise: The Garden of Eden in Myth and Tradition*, trans. Matthew O'Connell (New York: Continuum, 1995); Milad Doueihi, *Earthly Paradise: Myths and Philosophies*, trans. Jane Marie Todd (Cambridge, MA: Harvard University Press, 2009); Markus Bockmuel and Guy S. Stroumsa, eds. *Paradise in Antiquity: Jewish and Christian Views* (Cambridge: Cambridge University Press, 2010); Carolyn Muessig and Ad Putter, eds., *Envisaging Heaven in the Middle Ages* (New York: Routledge, 2007); Carolyn Merchant, *Reinventing Eden: The Fate of Nature in Western Culture* (New York: Routledge, 2003). Two older treatments that are still useful are John Armstrong, *The Paradise Myth* (London: Oxford University Press, 1969) and Louis

L. Martz, *The Paradise Within: Studies in Vaughan, Traherne, and Milton* (New Haven: Yale University Press, 1964).

4. Merton, *Conjectures of a Guilty Bystander* (Garden City, NY: Image, 1968), 45.

5. Merton, *The Hidden Ground of Love*, 561.

6. Thomas Merton, *The Hidden Ground of Love*, 561; see also Merton's comment in his letter of April 11, 1959: "We have very much the same views, and take the same standpoint, which is, it seems to me, so truly that of the New Testament." *The Hidden Ground of Love*, 563.

7. Merton, *The Hidden Ground of Love*, 563–564.

8. See, for example, Aloys Grillmeier, *Christ in the Christian Tradition, I: From the Apostolic Age to Chalcedon* (451), trans. John Bowden, 2nd ed. (Atlanta: John Knox, 1987); Rebecca J. Lyman, *Christology and Cosmology: Models of Divine Activity in Origen, Eusebius, and Athanasius* (Oxford: Clarendon Press, 1993).

9. Merton, *The Hidden Ground of Love*, 564–565.

10. Merton, *The Hidden Ground of Love*, 564.

11. Merton, *The Hidden Ground of Love*, 564.

12. Merton, *The Hidden Ground of Love*, 564.

13. Merton, *The Hidden Ground of Love*, 565.

14. For an account of how such traumatic experience affects the human capacity to encounter, take in, and respond to the world, see Shierry Weber Nicholsen, *The Love of Nature and the End of the World: The Unspoken Dimensions of Environmental Concern* (Cambridge, MA: MIT Press, 2002), especially 129–160.

15. Mark V. Barrow Jr., *Nature's Ghosts: Confronting Extinction from the Age of Jefferson to the Age of Ecology* (Chicago: University of Chicago Press, 2009); Steve Nicholl, *Paradise Found: Nature in America at the Time of Discovery* (Chicago: University of Chicago Press, 2009); William MacLeash, *The Day Before America: Changing the Nature of a Continent* (Boston: Houghton Mifflin, 1994). For an account of critical episodes of environmental collapse at even earlier moments of human history, see Ian Whyte, *World without End? Environmental Disaster and the Collapse of Empires* (London: I. B. Tauris, 2008).

16. Merton, *The Hidden Ground of Love*, 569.

17. Rick Warren's wildly popular *The Purpose Driven Life* and the recent documentary film on the American education *Race to Nowhere* reveal, albeit in very different ways, both the high cultural value we continue to place on purposefulness and productivity, and the high costs of not addressing the unforeseen consequences of our often-obsessive preoccupation with these ideals. Rick Warren, *The Purpose Driven Life* (Grand Rapids, MI: Zondervan, 2002). *Race to Nowhere*, www.racetonowhere.com/.

18. David Orr, *The Nature of Design: Ecology, Culture and Human Intention* (New York: Oxford University Press, 2002), 35–42. See also Carl Honoré, *In Praise of Slowness: Challenging the Cult of Speed* (New York: HarperOne, 2005); Carlo Petrini, *Slow Food Nation: Why Our Food Should Be Good, Clean, Fair* (New York: Rizzoli, 2007).

Similar concerns are also expressed, albeit in different ways, in Nicholas Carr's analysis of the increasingly fragmented (and often) superficial character of knowledge being acquired in the digital age; and in Sherry Turkle's investigation of the increasing speed and brevity of our communications through digital media, something she argues is contributing to an erosion of community. Nicholas Carr, *The Shallows: What the Internet Is Doing to Our Brains* (New York: Norton, 2011); Sherry Turkle, *Alone Together: Why We Expect More from Technology and Less from Each Other* (New York: Basic Books, 2011). For a thoughtful assessment of the complex and often ambiguous relationship between "fast" and "slow" knowledge, see Daniel Kahneman, *Thinking, Fast and Slow* (New York: Farrar, Straus and Giroux, 2011).

19. The fundamental question of how and why we place such a strong value on "utility" and "purpose" and why alternative modes of being, rooted in idleness, play, and prayer, have such a difficult time being accepted and cultivated in contemporary American culture have been examined, albeit from different perspectives, by Mark Slouka, "Quitting the Paint Factory: On the Virtues of Idleness," *Harpers* (2004): 57–65; and Walter Burghardt, "Contemplation: A Long, Loving Look at the Real," *Church* (Winter, 1989): 14–18.

20. John Cassian, *Conference* I. For a discussion of the background of this distinction, see Columba Stewart, *Cassian the Monk* (New York: Oxford University Press, 1998), 38–39. This distinction had already been made by Clement of Alexandria and it is likely that it was from Clement that it came to be used in Evagrius's works and from there to Cassian. As Columba Stewart notes, "the two fundamental themes of 'purity of heart' and 'reign of heaven' . . . underlie the whole of [Cassian's] theology" (38).

21. *Apophthegmata Patrum* [*AP*] Sisoes 54; *The Sayings of the Desert Fathers,* trans. Benedicta Ward (Kalamazoo: Cistercian Publications, 2006), 222.

22. Theodoret of Cyrrhus, *A History of the Monks of Syria,* trans. R. M. Price (Kalamazoo: Cistercian Publications, 1985), I.2, 13. The translator, R. M. Price, makes reference to another account of the ascetics of Nisibis found in Sozomen's *Ecclesiastical History*: "They are called 'Grazers,' since they neither have houses nor eat bread or cooked food nor drink wine, but living on the mountains praise God in prayers and hymns . . . when it is time for nourishment, they wander over the mountain, like animals driven to pasture, each with a sickle, and feed on plants" (Sozomen, *Eccl. Hist.* VI. 33); cited in *A History of the Monks of Syria,* 21.

23. Theodoret, *A History of the Monks of Syria*, XVI, 1; 117.

24. Theodoret, *A History of the Monks of Syria*, XVIII, 126. One hears an echo of this same sensibility in an account of James of Cyrrhestica: "This man, bidding farewell to all these things, tent and hut and enclosure, has the sky for roof," Theodoret, *A History of the Monks of Syria*, XXI, 3, 134.

25. *AP* Bessarion 12; Ward, *The Sayings of the Desert Fathers,* 42.

26. Peter Brown, *The Making of Late Antiquity* (Cambridge: Harvard University Press, 1978), 86.

27. Evagrius, *The Praktikos and Chapters on Prayer*, trans. John Eudes Bamberger (Kalamazoo: Cistercian Publications, 2006), 15.

28. *AP* Hyperchius 7; Ward, *The Sayings of the Desert Fathers*, 239.

29. Evagrius, *Eulogios* 1; *Evagrius of Pontus: The Greek Ascetic Corpus*, trans. and introd. Robert E. Sinkewicz (New York: Oxford University Press, 2003), 29.

30. Evagrius of Pontus, *Thoughts* 34: Sinkewicz, *Evagrius of Pontus: The Greek Ascetic Corpus*, 177.

31. *AP* Hyperchius 6; Ward, *The Sayings of the Desert Fathers*, 238.

32. Evagrius, *Eulogios* 12:11; Sinkewicz, *Evagrius of Pontus: The Greek Ascetic Corpus*, 38.

33. Evagrius, *Foundations* 4; Sinkewicz, *Evagrius of Pontus: The Greek Ascetic Corpus*, 6.

34. *AP* Gelasius 5; Ward, *The Sayings of the Desert Fathers*, 49.

35. *AP* Euprepius 3; Ward, *The Sayings of the Desert Fathers*, 62.

36. Evagrius, *Eulogios* 30:32; Sinkewicz, *Evagrius of Pontus: The Greek Ascetic Corpus*, 57.

37. Evagrius, *Thoughts* 39; Sinkewicz, *Evagrius of Pontus: The Greek Ascetic Corpus*, 180. See also these related statements: "If someone should want to behold the state of his mind, let him deprive himself of all mental representations, and then he shall behold himself resembling sapphire or the color of heaven" (Sinkewicz, *Evagrius of Pontus: The Greek Ascetic Corpus,* 211). "The state of the mind is an intelligible height resembling the color of heaven" (Sinkewicz, *Evagrius of Pontus: The Greek Ascetic Corpus,* 211).

38. *AP* Macarius 2; Ward, *The Sayings of the Desert Fathers*, 125–126.

39. Brown, *The Making of Late Antiquity*, 86.

40. Loren Eiseley, *All the Strange Hours: The Excavation of a Life* (New York: Scribner, 1975), 154.

41. Czeslaw Milosz, *Second Space: New Poems*, trans. by the author and Robert Hass (New York: Ecco, 2004). See especially the title poem, 3.

42. Luis Cernuda, *Written in Water*, trans. Stephen Kessler (San Francisco: City Lights, 2004), 4.

43. Jean Giono, *Blue Boy*, trans. Katherine A. Clarke (San Francisco: North Point, 1981), 134–135.

44. Willa Cather, *My Ántonia* (Boston: Houghton Mifflin, 1918), 14.

45. Henry David Thoreau, *I to Myself: An Annotated Selection from the Journal of Henry D. Thoreau,* ed. Jeffrey S. Cramer (New Haven: Yale University Press, 2007), 62.

46. Thoreau, *I to Myself,* 164.

47. Henry David Thoreau, *Walden*, ed. J. Lyndon Shanley (Princeton: Princeton University Press, 1971), 88; 90.

48. Thoreau, *Walden*, 6, 11. Thoreau's essay, "Paradise (To Be) Regained," which appeared in the November 1943 issue of *The Democratic Review* [now included in *The Essays of Henry D. Thoreau*, ed. Lewis Hyde (New York: North Point Press, 2002), 43–60] reflects how fiercely Thoreau resisted the identification with what he understood to be a dangerous and misguided idea of unlimited "progress." In this particular essay, he was responding to the recent book by J. A. Etlzer, *The Paradise within the*

Reach of all Men, without Labor, by Powers of Nature and Machinery, in which the author celebrated, among other things, the hope that we might soon come to "level mountains, sink valleys, create lakes, drain lakes and swamps, and intersect the land everywhere with beautiful canals, and roads for transporting heavy loads of many thousand tons, and for traveling one thousand miles in twenty-four hours." But it was not only the vision of progress contained in the book that Thoreau resisted. It was the vision of labor it contained, with its boundless optimism regarding what could be achieved through technological wizardry. Nowhere, Thoreau noted, does the author inquire about the degradation—of self or world—that might result from such "progress" or whether the world that emerges from this vision will be worth inhabiting.

49. Thoreau, *Walden*, 23, 24.

50. For an insightful analysis of Thoreau's integration of the work of solitude with the work of social, political engagement, see Rebecca Solnit, "Prisons and Paradises," in *Storming the Gates of Paradise: Landscapes for Politics* (Berkeley: University of California Press, 2007), 1–11.

51. Thoreau, *Walden*, 37.

52. Thoreau, *Walden*, 41.

53. Thoreau, *Walden*, 111.

54. Thoreau, *Walden*, 112.

55. William Kittredge, *Who Owns the West?* (San Francisco: Mercury House, 1996), 35.

56. William Kittredge, *Hole in the Sky: A Memoir* (New York: Knopf, 1992), 27, 29.

57. Kittredge, *Hole in the Sky,* 69.

58. Kittredge, *Who Owns the West?* 4.

59. Kittredge, *Hole in the Sky,* 8.

60. Thomas Merton, *Dancing in the Waters of Life: Seeking Peace in the Hermitage. The Journals of Thomas Merton,* Vol. 5, 1963–1965, ed. Robert E. Daggy (San Francisco: HarperSanFrancisco, 1997), 99.

61. For Merton's correspondence with Rosemary Radford Ruether, see *The Hidden Ground of Love,* 497–516, esp. 504–508. For the correspondence between Thomas Merton and Czeslaw Milosz, see *Striving Towards Being: The Letters of Thomas Merton and Czeslaw Milosz,* ed. Robert Fagen (New York: Farrar, Straus and Giroux, 1997), 37, 50, 64–73. The subject of "nature"—its meaning in Merton's writings in general and in the context of his understanding of contemplative practice in particular—is complex. His correspondence with Ruether and Milosz points to a certain ambivalence in his thinking about the natural world. While he resists what he perceives as a certain strain of Manicheism in Milosz' attitudes toward nature and insists, by contrast, that "I am in complete and deep complicity with nature" (*Striving Towards Being,* 69), he nevertheless admits to both Milosz and Ruether that his "Edenic" sensibility needs to be qualified by a more sober assessment of the ambiguity of the natural world and by a recognition that whatever else para-

dise might mean for the Christian contemplative, it cannot be separated from true
engagement with a suffering world.

62. Merton, *Dancing in the Waters of Life*, 87.

63. Thomas Merton, *Raids on the Unspeakable* (New York: New Directions, 1964),
9–23; "Day of a Stranger," *Hudson Review* 20: 2 (Summer, 1967): 211–218..

64. Thomas Merton, *Witness to Freedom: Letters in Times of Crisis,* ed. William H.
Shannon (New York: Farrar, Straus and Giroux, 1994), 31, 99, 282–283. David
Oates's *Paradise Wild: Reimagining American Nature* (Corvallis: Oregon State
University Press, 2003) offers a brilliant and necessary critique of the paradise myth
that is consistent with many of Merton's observations. But there is relatively little
attention in his work to the question of what it might mean to retrieve and reinterpret this myth.

65. Cited in David Steindl-Rast, "Man of Prayer," in *Thomas Merton Monk: A Monastic
Tribute*, ed. Patrick Hart (Kalamazoo: Cistercian Publications, 2005), 80.

66. Stewart, *Cassian the Monk*, 60.

67. Steindl-Rast, "Man of Prayer," 80–81.

68. Thoreau, *I to Myself,* 200, August 23, 1853.

Selected Bibliography

Abbey, Edward. "Down the River with Henry Thoreau." *Words from the Land*. Edited by Stephen Trimble, 48–76. Reno: University of Nevada Press, 1995.

Abram, David. *Becoming Animal: An Earthly Cosmology*. New York: Pantheon, 2012.

————. *The Spell of the Sensuous: Perception and Language in a More-than-Human World*. New York: Pantheon, 1996.

Ackerman, Diane. *The Rarest of the Rare: Vanishing Animals, Timeless Worlds*. New York: Random House, 1995.

Adams, Robert. *Beauty in Photography*. New York: Aperture, 1996.

Albanese, Catherine. *Nature Religion in America from the Algonkian Indians to the New Age*. Chicago: University of Chicago Press, 1990.

Ammerman, Nancy T., ed. *Everyday Religion: Observing Modern Religious Lives*. New York: Oxford University Press, 2007.

Armstrong, John. *The Paradise Myth*. London: Oxford University Press, 1969.

Ashley, J. Matthew. "Contemplation in the Action of Justice: Ignacio Ellacuría and Ignatian Spirituality." In *Love that Produces Hope: The Thought of Ignacio Ellacuría*. Edited by Kevin F. Burke and Robert Lasalle-Klein, 144–165. Collegeville: Liturgical Press, 2006.

————. "Reading the Universe Story Theologically: The Contribution of a Biblical Narrative Imagination." Theological Studies 71, no. 4 (2010): 870–902.

Athanase d'Alexandrie. *Vie d'Antoine*. Edited by G. J. M. Bartelink. Paris: Cerf, 1994.

Athanasius of Alexandria. *The Life of Antony and the Letter to Marcelinus*. Translated by Robert C. Gregg. New York: Paulist Press, 1980.

Augé, Marc. *Non-Places: Introduction to the Anthropology of Supermodernity*. Translated by John Howe. London: Verso, 1995.

Austin, Mary. *Land of Little Rain*. Albuquerque: University of New Mexico Press, 1974.

Bachelard, Gaston. *The Poetics of Space*. Boston: Beacon, 1959.

———. *The Psychoanalysis of Fire*. Boston: Beacon, 1987.

Barbour, John D. "The Ethics of Intercultural Travel: Thomas Merton's Asian Pilgrimage and Orientalism."*Biography* 28, no.1 (2005): 15–26.

Barrow, Mark V. Jr. *Nature's Ghosts: Confronting Extinction from the Age of Jefferson to the Age of Ecology*. Chicago: University of Chicago Press, 2009.

Bartalomé de las Casas. *A Short Account of the Destruction of the Indies*. Edited and translated by Nigel Griffin. London: Penguin, 1992.

Basho, Matsuo. "Narrow Road to the Interior." In *The Essential Basho*. Translated by Sam Hamill. Boston: Shambala, 1999.

Basso, Keith. *Wisdom Sits in Places: Landscape and Language among the Western Apache*. Albuquerque: University of New Mexico Press, 1996.

Bateson, Gregory G. *Steps to an Ecology of Mind: Collected Essays in Anthropology, Psychiatry, Evolution, and Epistemology*. Chicago: University of Chicago Press, 1972.

Bauman, Whitney, Richard Bohannon, and Kevin O'Brien, eds. *Grounding Religion: A Field Guide to the Study of Religion and Ecology*. London: Routledge, 2010.

BeDuhn, Jason. "The Metabolism of Salvation: Manichaean Concepts of Human Physiology." In *The Light and the Darkness: Studies in Manichaeism and Its World*. Edited by Paul Mirecki and Jason BeDuhn, 3–37. Leiden: Brill, 2001.

Bekes, Fikret. *Sacred Ecology*. 2nd ed. London: Routledge, 2008.

Berger, Peter, Brigitte Berger, and Hansfried Kellner. *The Homeless Mind*. New York: Vintage, 1974.

Berry, Wendell. "Christianity and the Survival of Creation." *Sex, Economy, Freedom and Community*, 93–116. New York: Pantheon, 1993.

———. "How to Be a Poet." *Poetry* 177, no. 3 (January 2001).

Berry, Thomas. *The Dream of the Earth*. San Francisco: Sierra Club, 1990.

———. *The Great Work: Our Way into the Future*. New York: Bell Tower, 1999.

———. and Brian Swimme. *The Universe Story From the Primordial Flaring Forth to the Ecozoic Era: A Celebration of the Unfolding of the Cosmos*. San Francisco: HarperOne, 1994.

Besecke, Kelly. "Speaking of Meaning in Modernity: Reflexive Spirituality as a Cultural Resource." *Sociology of Religion* 62, no. 3 (2001): 365–381.

Bevis, John. *Aaaaw to Zzzzzd: The Words of Birds. North America, Britain and Northern Europe*. Cambridge: MIT Press, 2010.

Bezner, Kevin, and Kevin Walzer, eds. *The Wilderness of Vision: On the Poetry of John Haines*. Brownsville, OR: Story Line Press, 1996.

Bingaman, Brock, and Bradley Nassif, eds. *The Philokalia: A Classic Text of Orthodox Spirituality*. New York: Oxford University Press, 2012.

Binns, John. *Ascetics and Ambassadors of Christ: The Monasteries of Palestine, 314–631*. Oxford: Clarendon, 1994.

Bitton-Ashkelony, Brouria. *Encountering the Sacred: The Debate on Christian Pilgrimage in Late Antiquity*. Berkeley: University of California Press, 2005.

Blake, William. *Complete Writings with Variant Readings*. Edited by Geoffrey Keynes. New York: Oxford University Press, 1966.

de Blij, Harm. *The Power of Place: Geography, Destiny, and Globalization's Rough Landscape*. New York: Oxford University Press, 2010.

Bockmuel, Markus, and Guy S. Stroumsa, eds. *Paradise in Antiquity: Jewish and Christian Views*. Cambridge: Cambridge University Press, 2010.

Botkin, Daniel. *Discordant Harmonies: A New Ecology for the Twenty-First Century*. New York: Oxford University Press, 1990.

Bowles, Paul. *Their Heads Are Green and Their Hands Are Blue*. New York: Ecco, 1994.

Brakke, David. *Athanasius and the Politics of Asceticism*. Oxford: Clarendon, 1995.

———. *Demons and the Making of the Monk: Spiritual Combat in Early Christianity*. Cambridge: Harvard University Press, 2006.

Bringhurst, Robert. *The Tree of Meaning: Language, Mind and Ecology*. Berkeley: Counterpoint, 2008.

Brooks-Hedstrom, Darlene. "Divine Architects: Designing the Monastic Dwelling Place." In *Egypt in the Byzantine World, 300–700*. Edited by Roger Bagnall. Cambridge: Cambridge University Press, 2007.

———. "The Geography of the Monastic Cell in Early Egyptian Monastic Literature." *Church History* 78, no. 4 (2009): 756–791.

Brown, Peter. *The Body and Society: Men, Women and Sexual Renunciation in Early Christianity*. New York: Columbia University Press, 1988.

———. *The Making of Late Antiquity*. Cambridge, MA: Harvard University Press, 1978.

———. "The Rise and Function of the Holy Man in Late Antiquity," *Journal of Roman Studies* 61 (1971): 80–101.

———. "The Rise and Function of the Holy Man in Late Antiquity, 1971–1997." *Journal of Early Christian Studies* 6, no. 3 (Fall 1998): 353–376.

———. "The Saint as Exemplar in Late Antiquity." *Representations* 2 (1983): 1–25.

———. "A Social Context to the Religious Crisis of the Third Century, A.D." Colloquy 14. Center for Hermeneutical Studies, Berkeley, CA, 1975.

Browne, Janet. *Charles Darwin: A Biography*. Vol. 1, *Voyaging*. New York: Knopf, 1995.

Buell, Lawrence. *The Environmental Imagination: Thoreau, Nature Writing, and the Formation of American Culture*. Cambridge: Harvard University Press, 1995.

Burghardt, Walter. "Contemplation: A Long, Loving Look at the Real." *Church* (Winter 1989): 14–18.

Burrus, Virginia, and Catherine Keller, eds. *Toward a Theology of Eros: Transforming Passion at the Limits of a Discipline*. New York: Fordham University Press, 2006.

Burton-Christie, Douglas. "The Blue Sapphire of the Mind: Christian Contemplative Practice and the Healing of the Whole." *Sewanee Theological Review* 54, no. 3 (June 2011): 238–253.

———. "Darwin's Contemplative Vision." *Spiritus* 9, no.1 (Spring 2009): 89–95.

————. "A Feeling for the Natural World: Spirituality and the Appeal to the Heart in Contemporary Nature Writing." *Continuum* 2, nos. 2–3 (Spring 1993): 229–252.

————. "Hearing, Reading, Praying: Orality, Literacy and the Shape of Early Monastic Spirituality." *Anglican Theological Review* 83, no. 2 (Spring 2001): 5–25.

————. "The Gift of Tears: Loss, Mourning and the Work of Ecological Restoration." *Worldviews: Global Religions, Culture, and Ecology* 15, no.1 (2011): 29–48.

————. "The Immense Call of the Particular: Czeslaw Milosz on Nature, History and Hope." *Interdisciplinary Studies in Literature and Environment* 7, no. 1 (Winter 2000): 115–129.

————. "Into the Body of Another: *Eros*, Embodiment and Intimacy with the Natural World." *Anglican Theological Review* 81, no. 1 (Winter 1999): 13–37.

————. "The Literature of Nature and the Quest for the Sacred." *The Way Supplement* 81 (1994): 4–14.

————. "Living between Two Worlds: Home, Journey and The Quest for Sacred Place." *Anglican Theological Review* 79, no. 3 (Summer 1997): 413–432.

————. "Mapping the Sacred Landscape: Spirituality and the Contemporary Literature of Nature." *Horizons* 21, no. 1 (Spring 1994): 22–47.

————. "Nature." *The Blackwell Companion to Christian Spirituality*. Edited by Arthur Holder, 478–495. Oxford: Blackwell, 2005.

————. "Place-Making as Contemplative Practice." *Anglican Theological Review* 91, no. 3 (Summer 2009): 347–372.

————. "Geography and Spirituality in *The Life of Antony*." *Purity of Heart in Early Ascetical Literature*. Edited by Harriet A. Luckman and Linda Kulzer, 45–66. Collegeville: Liturgical Press, 1999.

————. "Practicing Paradise: Contemplative Awareness and Ecological Renewal." *Anglican Theological Review* 94, no. 2 (Spring 2012): 281–303.

————. "The Sense of Place." *The Way* 39, no. 1 (January 1999): 59–72.

————. "The Spirit of Place: The Columbia River Watershed Letter and the Meaning of Community." *Horizons* 30, no. 1 (Spring 2003): 7–24.

————. "Spirituality in an Age of Ecological Loss." *Ascent* 31, no. 1 (Fall 2007): 27–43.

————. "The Weight of the World: The Heaviness of Nature in Spiritual Experience." In *Exploring Christian Spirituality: Essays in Honor of Sandra M. Schneiders*. Edited by Bruce Lescher and Elizabeth Liebert, 142–160. New York: Paulist, 2006.

————. "The Wild and the Sacred." *Anglican Theological Review* 85, no. 3 (Summer 2003): 493–510.

————. *The Word in the Desert: Scripture and the Quest for Holiness in Early Christian Monasticism*. New York: Oxford University Press, 1993.

————. "Words beneath the Water: Logos, Cosmos and the Spirit of Place." In *Christianity and Ecology*. Edited by Dieter T. Hessel and Rosemary Radford Ruether, 317–336. Cambridge: Harvard University Press, 2000.

Bush, Mirabai, ed. *Contemplation Nation: How Ancient Practices Are Changing the Way We Live*. New York: CreateSpace, 2011.

Butler, Judith. *Precarious Life: The Powers of Mourning and Violence*. London: Verso, 2004.

Caner, Daniel Folger. *Wandering, Begging Monks: Spiritual Authority and the Promotion of Monasticism in Late Antiquity*. Berkeley: University of California Press, 2002.

Cannon, Lou. *Governor Reagan: His Rise to Power*. New York: Public Affairs, 2003.

Carlson, Thomas A. *Finitude and the Naming of God*. Chicago: University of Chicago Press, 1999.

Carr, Nicholas. *The Shallows: What the Internet Is Doing to Our Brains*. New York: Norton, 2011.

Carrette, Jeremy, and Richard King. *Selling Spirituality: The Silent Takeover of Religion*. New York: Routledge, 2005.

Caruthers, Mary. *The Craft of Thought: Meditation: Rhetoric and the Making of Images, 400–1200*. Cambridge: Cambridge University Press, 1998.

Casey, Edward S. *The Fate of Place: A Philosophical History*. Berkeley: University of California Press, 1997.

―――. *Getting Back into Place*. 2nd ed. Bloomington: Indiana University Press, 2009.

Cassian, John. *The Conferences*. Ancient Christian Writers 57. Edited and translated by Boniface Ramsey. New York: Paulist Press, 1997.

―――. *The Conferences*. Edited and translated by Colm Luibéid. Classics of Western Spirituality. New York: Paulist Press, 1985.

―――. *Conférences. Sources chrétiennes*, 42, 54, 64. Edited by E. Pichery. Paris: Éditions du Cerf, 1955, 1958, 1959.

Cather, Willa. *My Ántonia*. Boston: Houghton Mifflin, 1918.

Cernuda, Luis. *Written in Water*. Translated by Stephen Kessler. San Francisco: City Lights, 2004.

de Certeau, Michel. *The Mystic Fable*. Translated by Michael B. Smith. Chicago: University of Chicago Press, 1992.

―――. *The Practice of Everyday Life*. Translated by Stephen Rendall. Berkeley: University of California Press, 1984.

Cezanne, Paul. *Letters*. Edited by John Rewald. Translated by Marguerite Kay. New York: Da Capo Press, 1995.

Chadwick, Owen, ed. *Western Asceticism*. Louisville, KY: Westminster John Knox, 1979.

Chase, Steven. *Nature as Spiritual Practice*. Grand Rapids, MI: Eerdmans, 2011.

―――. "Re-reading Job: Entertaining Spiritualities of Suffering." *Spiritus* 11, no. 1 (Spring 2011): 104–120.

Ching, Barbara, and Gerald W. Creed, eds. *Knowing Your Place: Rural Identity and Cultural Hierarchy*. New York: Routledge, 1997.

Cioran, E. M. *Tears and Saints*. Translated by Ilinca Zarifopol-Johnston. Chicago: University of Chicago Press, 1995.

Clark, Elizabeth. *Reading Renunciation: Asceticism and Scripture in Early Christianity*. Princeton: Princeton University Press, 1999.

Climacus, John. *The Ladder of Divine Ascent.* Translated by Colm Luibheid and Norman Russell. New York: Paulist Press 1992.

Coakley, Sarah. *Powers and Submissions: Spirituality, Philosophy and Gender.* Oxford: Blackwell, 2002.

Cobb, Edith. *The Ecology of Imagination in Childhood.* Dallas: Spring Publications, 1993.

Cohoon, Christopher. "Coming Together: The Six Modes of Irigirayan Eros." *Hypatia* 26, no. 3 (Summer 2011): 478–496.

Colegate, Isabel. *A Pelican in the Wilderness: Hermits, Solitaries and Recluses.* Washington, DC: Counterpoint, 2002.

Coleridge, Samuel Taylor. *Notebooks: A Selection.* Edited by Seamus Perry. New York: Oxford, 2002.

Colish, Marcia L. *The Stoic Tradition from Antiquity to the Early Middle Ages 1: Stoicism in Classical Latin Literature.* Second Impression with Addenda and Corrigenda. Leiden: E. J. Brill, 1990.

———. *The Stoic Tradition from Antiquity to the Early Middle Ages 2. Stoicism in Christian Latin Thought through the Sixth Century.* Second Impression with Addenda and Corrigenda. Leiden: E. J. Brill, 1990.

Collinge, Sharon E. *Ecology of Fragmented Landscapes.* Baltimore: Johns Hopkins University Press, 2009.

Compte-Sponville, Andre. *The Little Book of Atheistic Spirituality.* New York: Viking, 2007.

Cooper, Adam G. *The Body in St. Maximus the Confessor: Holy Flesh, Wholly Deified.* Oxford: Oxford University Press, 2005.

Cooper, David D. *Thomas Merton's Art of Denial: The Evolution of a Radical Humanist.* Athens: University of Georgia Press, 1989.

Corrigan, John, ed. *The Oxford Handbook of Religion and Emotion.* New York: Oxford University Press, 2008.

———, ed. *Religion and Emotion: Approaches and Interpretation.* New York: Oxford University Press, 2004.

Cronon, William. *Uncommon Ground: Rethinking the Human Place in Nature.* New York: Norton, 1996.

Dalai Lama, *Beyond Religion: Ethics for a Whole World.* New York: Houghton Mifflin Harcourt, 2011.

Darwin, Charles. *Charles Darwin's Beagle Diary.* Edited by Richard Darwin Keynes. Cambridge: Cambridge University Press, 1988.

———. *Charles Darwin's Zoology Notes and Specimen Lists from H.M.S. Beagle.* Edited by Richard Darwin Keynes. Cambridge: Cambridge University Press, 2000.

———. "Darwin's Ornithological Notes." Transcribed and edited by Emma Nora Barlow. *Bulletin of the British Museum* (Natural History) Historical Series 2 (1963): 201–278.

———. *On the Origin of Species.* New York: New York University Press, 2010.

Daumal, Renée. *Mount Analogue.* Woodstock, NY: Overlook, 2004.

Davies, Oliver, and Denys Turner, eds. *Silence and the Word: Negative Theology and Incarnation.* Cambridge: Cambridge University Press, 2002.

Deane-Drummond, Celia, ed. *Religion and Ecology in the Public Sphere.* Edinburgh: T&T Clark, 2011.

DeLoughrey, Elizabeth, and George B. Handley, eds. *Postcolonial Ecologies: Literatures of the Environment.* New York: Oxford University Press, 2011.

Delumeau, Jean. *History of Paradise: The Garden of Eden in Myth and Tradition.* Translated by Matthew O'Connell. New York: Continuum, 1995.

Dietrich, William. *Northwest Passage: The Great Columbia River.* Seattle: University of Washington Press, 1995.

Dietz, Maribel. *Wandering Monks, Virgins, and Pilgrims: Ascetic Travel in the Mediterranean World, A.D. 300–800.* Philadelphia: Pennsylvania State University Press, 2005.

Dillard, Annie. *For the Time Being.* New York: Knopf, 1999.

———. *Pilgrim at Tinker Creek.* New York: Harper, 1974.

Dostoevsky, Fyodor. *The Idiot.* Translated by Constance Garnett. New York: Barnes and Noble, 2004.

Doueihi, Milad. *Earthly Paradise: Myths and Philosophies.* Translated by Jane Marie Todd. Cambridge, MA: Harvard University Press, 2009.

Driver, Steven D. *John Cassian and the Reading of Egyptian Monastic Culture.* New York: Routledge, 2002.

Dunlop, Thomas R. *Faith in Nature: Environmentalism as Religious Quest.* Seattle: University of Washington Press, 2004.

Dysinger, Luke. *Psalmody and Prayer in the Writings of Evagrius Ponticus.* Oxford: Oxford University Press, 2005.

Ecklund, Elaine Howard. *Science vs. Religion: What Scientists Really Think.* New York: Oxford University Press, 2010.

Eiseley, Loren. *All the Strange Hours: The Excavation of a Life.* New York: Scribner, 1975.

Elm, Susanna. *"Virgins of God": The Making of Asceticism in Late Antiquity.* Oxford: Clarendon Press, 1994.

Entriken, J. Nicholas. *The Betweenness of Place: Towards a Geography of Modernity.* Baltimore: Johns Hopkins University Press, 1991.

Evagrius. *Evagrius of Pontus: The Greek Ascetic Corpus.* Translated by Robert E. Sinkewicz. New York: Oxford University Press, 2003.

———. *The Praktikos and Chapters on Prayer.* Translated by John Eudes Bamberger. Kalamazoo: Cistercian Publications, 2006.

Fadiman, Anne. *The Spirit Catches You and You Fall Down: A Hmong Child, Her American Doctors, and the Collision of Two Cultures.* New York: Farrar, Straus and Giroux, 1997.

Farley, Wendy. *The Wounding and Healing of Desire: Weaving Heaven and Earth.* Louisville: Westminster John Knox Press, 2005.

Feld, Steven, and Keith Basso, eds. *Senses of Place*. Santa Fe, NM: School of American Research Press, 1996.

Feldhay, Rachel Brenner. *Writing as Resistance: Four Women Confronting the Holocaust*. University Park: Pennsylvania State University Press 1997.

Ferrer, Jorge N., and Jacob H. Sherman, eds. *The Participatory Turn: Spirituality, Mysticism, Religious Studies*. Albany: State University of New York Press, 2008.

Fields, Stephen. "Balthasar and Rahner on the Spiritual Senses." *Theological Studies* 57 (1996): 224–241.

Fill, Alwin, and Peter Mühlhäusler, eds. *The Ecolinguistics Reader: Language, Ecology and Environment*. New York: Continuum, 2001.

Finch, Robert. "Being at Two with Nature." *Georgia Review* 45, no. 1 (Spring 1991): 567–574.

Forché, Carolyn. *Blue Hour*. New York: HarperCollins, 2003.

Foy, George M. *Zero Decibels: The Quest for Absolute Silence*. New York: Scribner, 2010.

Francis and Clare: The Complete Works. Edited and translated by Regis J. Armstrong and Ignatius C. Brady. New York: Paulist Press, 1992.

Frank, Georgia. *The Memory of the Eyes: Pilgrimage to Living Saints in Christian Late Antiquity*. Berkeley: University of California Press, 2000.

Franke, William. *On What Cannot Be Said: Apophatic Discourse in Philosophy, Religion, Literature and the Arts. Vol. 1. Classic Formulations*. Notre Dame: University of Notre Dame Press, 2007.

————. *On What Cannot Be Said: Apophatic Discourse in Philosophy, Religion, Literature and the Arts. Vol. 2: Modern and Contemporary Transformations*. Notre Dame: University of Notre Dame Press, 2007.

Frankenburg, Ruth. *Living Spirit, Living Practice: Poetics, Politics, Epistemology*. Durham, NC: Duke University Press, 2004.

Frankfurter, David, ed. *Pilgrimage and Holy Space in Late Antique Egypt*. Leiden: Brill, 1998.

Freeman, Martha, ed. *Always Rachel: The Letters of Rachel Carson and Dorothy Freeman, 1952–1964*. Boston: Beacon, 1995.

Fry, Timothy, ed. *The Rule of St. Benedict in English*. Collegeville, MN: Liturgical Press, 1982.

Fuller, Robert. *Spiritual but not Religious: Understanding Unchurched America*. New York: Oxford University Press, 2001.

Garber, Marjorie. "Good to Think With." *Profession* (2008): 11–20.

Galvin, James. *The Meadow*. New York: Henry Holt, 1992.

Gatta, John. *Making Nature Sacred: Literature, Religion, and Environment in America from the Puritans to the Present*. New York: Oxford University Press, 2004.

Gavrilyuk, Paul, and Sarah Coakley, eds. *The Spiritual Senses: Perceiving God in Western Christianity*. Cambridge: Cambridge University Press, 2011.

Gibson, William. *A Reenchanted World: The Quest for a New Kinship with Nature*. New York: Metropolitan, 2009.

Giono, Jean. *Blue Boy*. Translated by Katherine A. Clarke. San Francisco: North Point, 1981.

———. *The Song of the World*. Translated by Henry Fluchère and Geoffrey Myers. San Francisco: North Point, 1981.

Glück, Louise. *The Wild Iris*. New York: Ecco, 1992.

Gregg, Robert C., and Dennis E. Groh. *Early Arianism: A View of Salvation*. Philadelphia: Fortress, 1981.

Griffin, Susan. *The Eros of Everyday Life: Essays on Ecology, Gender and Society*. New York: Doubleday, 1995.

Grillmeier, Aloys S. J. *Christ in the Christian Tradition, I: From the Apostolic Age to Chalcedon (451)*. 2nd ed. Translated by John Bowden. Atlanta: John Knox, 1987.

Goehring, James E. *Ascetics, Society and the Desert: Studies in Early Egyptian Monasticism*. Harrisburg, PA: Trinity, 1999.

———. "The Encroaching Desert: Literary Production and Ascetic Space in Early Egyptian Christianity." *Journal of Early Christian Studies* 1 (1993): 281–296.

Gopnik, Adam. *Angels and Ages: A Short Book about Darwin, Lincoln, and Modern Life*. New York: Vintage, 2009.

Gottlieb, Roger, ed. *The Oxford Handbook of Religion and Ecology*. New York: Oxford University Press, 2010.

Gould, Graham. *The Desert Fathers on Monastic Community*. Oxford: Clarendon Press, 1993.

———. "Moving on and Staying Put in the *Apophthegmata Patrum*." *Studia Patristica* 25 (1989): 231–37.

Gregory of Nyssa. *The Life of Moses*. Translated by Abraham Malherbe and Everett Ferguson. New York: Paulist Press, 1978.

———. *The Lord's Prayer. The Beatitudes*. Translated and annotated by Hilda C. Graef. New York: Newman Press, 1954.

———. *La Vie de Moïse*. Translated by Jean Daniélou. Paris: Cerf, 1987.

Groebner, Valentin. *Defaced: The Visual Culture of Violence in the Late Middle Ages*. Translated by Pamela Selwyn. New York: Zone Books, 2004.

Guillaumont, Antoine. "La vision de l'intellect par lui-même dans la mystique Évagrienne." In *Études su la spiritualité d l'Orient Chrétien*, 143–150. Bégrolles-en-mauges: Abbaye de Bellefontaine, 1996.

Gutierrez, Gustavo. *We Drink from Our Own Wells: The Spiritual Journey of a People*. Maryknoll, NY: Orbis, 1984.

Hadot, Pierre. *Philosophy as a Way of Life*. Edited by Arnold I. Davidson. Translated by Michael Chase. Oxford: Blackwell, 1995.

Hägg, Henry Fiska. *Clement of Alexandria and the Beginnings of Christian Apophaticism*. New York: Oxford University Press, 1996.

Hahm, David E. *The Origins of Stoic Cosmology*. Columbus: Ohio State University Press, 1977.

Hall, Adrienne Baxter. *George Inness and the Visionary Landscape*. New York: Braziller, 2003.

Hall, David D, ed. *Lived Religion in America: Toward a History of Practice*. Princeton: Princeton University Press, 1997.

Harden, Blaine. *A River Lost: The Life and Death of the Columbia*. New York: Norton, 1996.

Harding, Paul. *Tinkers*. New York: Bellevue Literary Press, 2009.

Harmless, William, and Fitzgerald, Raymond R. "The Sapphire Light of the Mind: The *Skemmata* of Evagrius Ponticus." *Theological Studies* 62 (2001): 493–529.

Harrison, Stephen, Steve Pile, and Nigel Thrift, eds. *Patterned Ground: Entanglements of Nature and Culture*. London: Reaktion Books, 2004.

Hart, Patrick, ed. *Thomas Merton Monk: A Monastic Tribute*. Kalamazoo: Cistercian Publications, 2005.

Hass, Robert. *Praise*. New York: Ecco, 1979.

———. *Sun Under Wood*. New York: Ecco, 1998.

Haupt, Lyanda Lynn. *Pilgrim on the Great Bird Continent: The Importance of Everything and Other Lessons from Darwin's Lost Notebooks*. New York: Little, Brown, 2006.

Hausherr, Irénée. *Penthos: The Doctrine of Compunction in the Christian East*. Translated by Anselm Hufstader. Kalamazoo: Cistercian, 1982.

Hayum, Andreé. *The Isenheim Altarpiece: God's Medicine and the Painter's Vision*. Princeton: Princeton University Press, 1989.

Heaney, Seamus. *Preoccupations: Selected Prose 1968–1978*. New York: Farrar, Straus and Giroux, 1980.

Heelas, Paul, Linda Woodhead, et al. *The Spiritual Revolution: Why Religion Is Giving Way to Spirituality*. Oxford: Blackwell, 2005.

Heise, Ursula. *Sense of Place and Sense of Planet: The Environmental Imagination of the Global*. New York: Oxford, 2008.

Henry, Patrick, ed. *Benedict's Dharma: Buddhists Reflect on the Rule of St. Benedict*. New York: Riverhead, 2001.

Hessel-Robinson, Timothy, and Ray Maria McNamara, eds. *Spirit and Nature: The Study of Christian Spirituality in a Time of Ecological Urgency*. Eugene, OR: Pickwick, 2011.

Higley, Richard. *Privilege, Power and Place: The Geography of the American Upper Class*. London: Rowman and Littlefield, 1995.

Hildegard of Bingen. *Symphonia*. Introduction, translation, and commentary by Barbara Newman. Ithaca: Cornell University Press, 1988.

Hill, Michael Ortiz. *Dreaming the End of the World: Apocalypse as a Rite of Passage*. Dallas: Spring, 1994.

Hillesum, Etty. *An Interrupted Life*. Translated by Arno Pomerans. New York: Pantheon, 1983.

Hirschfeld, Yizhar. *The Judean Desert Monasteries in the Byzantine Period*. New Haven: Yale University Press, 1992.

Hirsh, Eric, and Michael O'Hanlon, eds. *The Anthropology of Landscape: Perspectives on Place and Space.* Oxford: Clarendon Press, 1995.

Hodder, Allan D. *Thoreau's Ecstatic Witness.* New Haven: Yale University Press, 2001.

Hogan, Linda. *Dwellings: A Spiritual History of the Living World.* New York: Norton, 1995.

———. *Solar Storms.* New York: Scribner, 1995.

Holmes, Barbara Ann. *Joy Unspeakable: Contemplative Practices of the Black Church.* Minneapolis: Augsburg Fortress, 2004.

Holmes, Richard. *The Age of Wonder: How the Romantic Generation Discovered the Beauty and Terror of Science.* New York: Pantheon, 2008.

Honoré, Carl. *In Praise of Slowness: Challenging the Cult of Speed.* New York: HarperOne, 2005.

Hopkins, Gerard Manley. *Poems and Prose.* Edited by W.H. Gardner. London: Penguin, 1953.

House, Freeman. *Totem Salmon: Life Lessons from Another Species.* Boston: Beacon, 1999.

Howard-Johnston, James, and Paul Antony Hayward, eds. *The Cult of Saints in Late Antiquity and the Middle Ages.* New York: Oxford University Press, 2000.

Hugo, Victor. *Les Miserables,* Translated by Charles Wilbour. New York: Random House, 1992.

Hunt, Hanna. *Joy-Bearing Grief: Tears of Contrition in the Writings of the Early Syrian and Byzantine Fathers.* Leiden: Brill, 2004.

Hyde, Lewis. *The Gift: Imagination and the Erotic Life of Property.* New York: Vintage, 1979.

Irigiray, Luce. *The Way of Love.* Translated by Heidi Bostic and Stephen Pluhécek. New York: Continuum, 2004.

Isaac of Ninevah. "The Second Part," Chapters IV–XLI. *Corpus Scriptorum Christianorum Orientalum.* 225. Translated by Sebastian Brock. Louvain: Peeters, 1995.

Jabès, Edmund. *The Book of Resemblances. Vol. 2. Intimations of the Desert.* Translated by Rosmarie Waldrop. Hanover: Wesleyan University Press, 1991.

Jackson, John B. *A Sense of Place, a Sense of Time.* New Haven: Yale University Press, 1994.

Jackson, Michael. *At Home in the World.* Durham, NC: Duke University Press, 1995.

———. *The Palm at the End of the Mind: Relatedness, Religiosity, and the Real.* Durham, NC: Duke University Press, 2009.

———. "The Prose of Suffering and the Practice of Silence." *Spiritus* 4, no. 1 (2004): 44–59.

James, William. *Essays on Radical Empiricism.* Cambridge, MA: Harvard University Press, 1976.

———. *A Pluralistic Universe.* Cambridge, MA: Harvard University Press, 1977.

Johnson, Timothy J. "Francis and Creation." In *The Cambridge Companion to Francis of Assisi*, edited by Michael J. P. Robson, 143–158. Cambridge: Cambridge University Press, 2012.

Jordan, Mark D. *The Ethics of Sex*. Malden, MA: Blackwell, 2002.

Kamitsuka, Margaret, ed. *The Embrace of Eros: Bodies, Desire, and Sexuality in Christianity*. Philadelphia: Fortress, 2010.

Kahneman, Daniel. *Thinking, Fast and Slow*. New York: Farrar, Straus and Giroux, 2011.

Keizer, Garret. *The Unwanted Sound of Everything We Want: A Book about Noise*. New York: Public Affairs, 2010.

Kerr, Fergus. *Immortal Longings: Versions of a Transcending Humanity*. Notre Dame: University of Notre Dame Press, 1997.

Kertz, Karl. "Meister Eckhart's Teaching on the Birth of the Divine World in the Soul." *Traditio* 15 (1959): 327–363.

Kessler, Michael and Christian Sheppard, eds. *Mystics: Presence and Aporia*. Chicago: University of Chicago Press, 2003.

Kinsley, David. *Ecology and Religion: Ecological Spirituality in Cross-Cultural Perspective*. Englewood Cliffs, NJ: Prentice Hall, 1995.

Kittredge, William. *Hole in the Sky: A Memoir*. New York: Knopf, 1992.

———. *Who Owns the West?* San Francisco: Mercury House, 1996.

Kohák, Erazim. *The Embers and the Stars: A Philosophical Inquiry into the Moral Sense of Nature*. Chicago: University of Chicago Press, 1984.

Konstantinovsky, Julia. *Evagrius of Pontus: The Making of a Gnostic*. London: Ashgate, 2008.

Krause, Bernie. *The Great Animal Orchestra: Finding the Origins of Music in the World's Wild Places*. New York: Little, Brown, 2012.

———. *Into a Wild Sanctuary: A Life in Music and Natural Sound*. Berkeley: Heyday Books, 1998.

Krawiec, Rebecca. *Shenoute and the Women of the White Monastery: Egyptian Monasticism in Late Antiquity*. New York: Oxford University Press, 2002.

Kristeva, Julia. "Holbein's Dead Christ." In *Fragments for a History of the Human Body, Part One*. Edited by Michael Feher, 238–269. New York: Zone Books, 1989.

Krutch, Joseph Wood. *The Desert Year*. Tucson: University of Arizona Press, 1985.

Kolbert, Elizabeth. *Field Notes from a Catastrophe: Man, Nature and Climate Change*. New York: Bloomsbury, 2006.

Kroeber, Karl. *Ecological Literary Criticism: Romantic Ecology and the Biology of Mind*. New York: Columbia University Press, 1994.

Ladner, Gerhard. *God, Cosmos, and Humankind: The World of Early Christian Symbolism*. Translated by Thomas Dunlap. Berkeley: University of California Press, 1995.

Laird, Martin. "The Fountain of His Lips: Desire and Divine Union in Gregory of Nyssa's *Homilies on the Song of Songs*." *Spiritus* 7 (2007): 40–57.

————. *Gregory of Nyssa and the Grasp of Faith: Union, Knowledge, and Divine Presence.* Oxford: Oxford University Press, 2004.

————. *Into the Silent Land: A Guide to the Christian Practice of Contemplation.* New York: Oxford, 2006.

————. "The 'Open Country' Whose Name Is Prayer': Apophasis, Deconstruction, and Contemplative Practice." *Modern Theology* 21, no. 1 (2005): 141–155.

————. "Under Solomon's Tutelage: The Education of Desire in the *Homilies of the Song of Songs.*" *Modern Theology* 18 (2002): 507–525.

————. *A Sunlit Absence: Silence, Awareness and Contemplation.* New York: Oxford, 2011.

Lane, Belden C. *Landscapes of the Sacred: Geography and Narrative in American Spirituality.* Baltimore: Johns Hopkins University Press, 2001.

————. *Ravished by Beauty: The Surprising Legacy of Reformed Spirituality.* New York: Oxford University Press, 2011.

Lavie, Smadar, and Ted Swedenburg, eds. *Displacement, Diaspora, and Geographies of Identity.* Durham, NC: Duke University Press, 1994.

Leclaire, Anne D. *Listening below the Noise: A Meditation on the Practice of Silence.* New York: Harper, 2009.

Leopold, Aldo. *The River of the Mother of God and Other Essays.* Edited by Susan L. Flader and J. Baird Callicott. Madison: University of Wisconsin Press, 1991.

————. *A Sand County Almanac: And Sketches Here and There.* New York: Oxford University Press, 1949.

Levertov, Denise. *Evening Train.* New York: New Directions, 1992.

————. *New and Selected Essays.* New York: New Directions, 1992.

————. *This Great Unknowing: Last Poems.* New York: New Directions, 1999.

Lilla, Salvatore. *Clement of Alexandria: A Study in Christian Platonism and Gnosticism.* Oxford: Oxford University Press, 1971.

Lippard, Lucy R. *The Lure of the Local: Senses of Place in a Multicentered Society.* New York: New Press, 1997.

Lives of the Desert Fathers. Translated by Norman Russell. Kalamazoo: Cistercian Publications, 1981.

Llewelyn, John. *Seeing through God: A Geophenomenology.* Bloomington: Indiana University Press, 2004.

Lopez, Barry. *Arctic Dreams: Imagination and Desire in a Northern Landscape.* New York: Bantam, 1987.

————. *The Rediscovery of North America.* New York: Vintage, 1992.

Lossky, Vladimir. *The Mystical Theology of the Eastern Church.* Cambridge: James Clarke, 1957.

Lueders, Edward, ed. *Writing Natural History: Dialogues with Authors.* Salt Lake City: University of Utah Press, 1989.

Lyman, Rebecca J. *Christology and Cosmology: Models of Divine Activity in Origen, Eusebius, and Athanasius.* Oxford: Clarendon Press, 1993.

Lyon, Thomas, ed. *This Incomperable Lande: A Book of American Nature Writing*. New York: Houghton Mifflin, 1989.

Maas, Frans. *Spirituality as Insight: Mystical Texts and Theological Reflections*. Leuven: Peeters, 2004.

Maclean, Norman. *A River Runs through It*. Chicago: University of Chicago Press, 1976.

————. *Young Men and Fire*. Chicago: University of Chicago Press, 1992.

MacLeash, William. *The Day Before America: Changing the Nature of a Continent*. Boston: Houghton Mifflin, 1994.

Maitland, Sara. *A Book of Silence*. Washington, DC: Counterpoint, 2010.

Maleuvre, Didier. *The Horizon: A History of our Infinite Longing*. Berkeley: University of California Press, 2011.

Manes, Christopher. "Nature and Silence." In *The Ecocriticism Reader*. Edited by Cheryl Glotfelty and Harold Fromm, 15–29. Athens: University of Georgia Press, 1996.

Martz, Louis L. *The Paradise Within: Studies in Vaughan, Traherne, and Milton*. New Haven: Yale University Press, 1964.

Massey, Doreen B. *For Space*. Thousand Oaks, CA: Sage, 2005.

Maximus the Confessor. *Selected Writings*. Translation and Notes by George C. Berthold. New York: Paulist, 1985.

McCarthy, Cormac. *The Crossing*. New York: Knopf, 1994.

McFague, Sallie. *Super, Natural Christians: How We Should Love Nature*. Minneapolis: Fortress Press, 1997.

McGinn, Bernard. *The Mystical Thought of Meister Eckhart: The Man from Whom God Hid Nothing*. New York: Herder and Herder, 2001.

————. "Ocean and Desert as Symbols of Mystical Absorption in the Christian Tradition." *Journal of Religion* 74, no. 2 (1994): 155–181.

McGuire, Meredith B. *Lived Religion: Faith and Practice in Everyday Life*. New York: Oxford University Press, 2008.

Meister Eckhart, *Sermons and Treatises*. Volumes 1–3. Translated and edited by M. O'C. Walshe. Longmead: Element, 1987.

Meloy, Ellen. *The Anthropology of Turquoise: Meditations on Landscape, Art, and Spirit*. New York: Pantheon, 2002.

Merchant, Carolyn. *Reinventing Eden: The Fate of Nature in Western Culture*. New York: Routledge, 2003.

Merton, Thomas. *Conjectures of a Guilty Bystander*. Garden City, NY: Image, 1968.

————. *Contemplation in a World of Action*. Garden City, NY: Image, 1973.

————. *Contemplative Prayer*. New York: Herder and Herder, 1969.

————. *Dancing in the Waters of Life: Seeking Peace in the Hermitage. The Journals of Thomas Merton*, Vol. 5, 1963–1965. Edited by Robert E. Daggy. San Francisco: HarperSanFrancisco, 1997.

————. "Day of a Stranger." *Hudson Review* 20, no. 2 (Summer 1967): 211–218.

————. *Disputed Questions*. New York: Farrar, Straus and Giroux, 1960.

————. *Entering the Silence: Becoming a Monk and Writer. The Journals of Thomas Merton*. Vol. 2, 1941–1952. Edited by Jonathan Montaldo. San Francisco: HarperSanFrancisco, 1995.

————. *The Hidden Ground of Love: The Letters of Thomas Merton on Religious Experience and Social Concerns*. Edited by William H. Shannon. New York: Farrar, Straus and Giroux, 1985.

————. *Learning to Love: Exploring Solitude and Freedom. The Journals of Thomas Merton*, Vol. 6, 1966–1967. Edited by Christine M. Bochen. San Francisco: HarperSanFrancisco, 1997.

————. *Love and Living*. Edited by Naomi Burton Stone and Brother Patrick Hart. New York: Bantam, 1980; reprint: New York: Harcourt Trade, 2002.

————. *The Other Side of the Mountain: The End of the Journey. The Journals of Thomas Merton*, Vol. 7, 1967–1968. Edited by Brother Patrick Hart. San Francisco: HarperSanFrancisco, 1998.

————. *Raids on the Unspeakable*. New York: New Directions, 1966.

————. *Run to the Mountain: The Story of a Vocation. The Journals of Thomas Merton*, Vol. 1, 1939–1941. Edited by Patrick Hart. San Francisco: HarperSanFrancisco, 1995.

————. *A Search for Solitude: Pursuing the Monk's True Life: The Journals of Thomas Merton*, Vol. 3, 1952–1960. Edited by Lawrence S. Cunningham. San Francisco: HarperSanFrancisco, 1997.

————. *Sign of Jonas*. New York: Image, 1956.

————. *Turning toward the World: The Pivotal Years. The Journals of Thomas Merton*, Vol. 4, 1960–1963. Edited by Victor Kramer. San Francisco: HarperSanFrancisco, 1996.

————. *The Wisdom of the Desert*. New York: New Directions, 1970.

————. *Witness to Freedom: Letters in Times of Crisis*. Selected and edited by William H. Shannon. New York: Farrar, Straus and Giroux, 1994.

————. *Zen and the Birds of Appetite*. New York: New Directions, 1968.

Merton, Thomas, and Czeslaw Milosz. *Striving Towards Being: The Letters of Thomas Merton and Czeslaw Milosz*. Edited by Robert Fagen. New York: Farrar, Straus and Giroux, 1997.

Meyer, Stephen. *The End of the Wild*. Cambridge: MIT Press, 1996.

Michaels, Anne. *The Winter Vault*. New York: Knopf, 2009.

Miles, Margaret R. *Practicing Christianity: Critical Perspectives for an Embodied Spirituality*. Eugene, OR: Wipf and Stock, 2006.

Miller, Vincent. *Consuming Religion: Christian Faith and Practice in a Consumer Culture*. New York: Continuum, 2005.

Mills, Stephanie. "The Wild and the Tame." In *Place of the Wild*. Edited by David Clarke Burks, 43–57. Washington, DC: Island Press, 1994.

Milosz, Czeslaw. *Beginning with My Streets: Essays and Recollections*. New York: Farrar, Straus and Giroux, 1991.

————. *Emperor of the Earth: Modes of Eccentric Vision*. Berkeley: University of California Press, 1977.

————. *Native Realm: A Search for Self-Definition*. New York: Doubleday, 1968; reprint: Berkeley: University of California Press, 1981.

————. *Second Space: New Poems*. Translated by the author and Robert Hass. New York: Ecco, 2004.

————. *Visions from San Francisco Bay*. Translated by Richard Lourie. New York: Farrar, Straus and Giroux, 1982.

————. *The Witness of Poetry*. Cambridge, MA: Harvard University Press, 1983.

Mitchell, W. J. T., ed. *Landscape and Power*. 2nd ed. Chicago: University of Chicago Press, 2002.

Mitscherlich, Alexander, and Margarete Mitscherlich. *The Inability to Mourn*. Translated by Beverly R. Placzek. New York: Grove Press, 1975.

Mitscherlich-Neilson, Margarete. "The Inability to Mourn—Today." Translated by Beverly R. Placzek. Edited by David Dietrich and Peter Shabad, 405–426. Madison: International Universities Press, 1989.

Mochulsky, Konstantin. *Dostoevsky: His Life and Work*. Translated by Michael A. Minihan. Princeton, NJ: Princeton University Press, 1967.

Momaday, N. Scott. *House Made of Dawn*. New York: Harper and Row, 1968.

————. *The Man Made of Words: Essays, Stories, Passages*. New York: St. Martin's Press, 1997.

Morgan, Vance C. *Weaving the World: Simone Weil on Science, Mathematics and Love*. Notre Dame: University of Notre Dame Press, 2005.

Muessig, Carolyn, and Ad Putter, eds. *Envisaging Heaven in the Middle Ages*. New York: Routledge, 2007.

Muir, Edwin. *Collected Poems*. London: Faber and Faber, 1963.

Muir, John. *John of the Mountains: The Unpublished Journals of John Muir*. Edited by Linnie Marsh Wolfe. Boston: Houghton Mifflin, 1938.

————. *My First Summer in the Sierra*. New York: Penguin, 1987.

Nabhan, Gary Paul, and Stephen Trimble. *The Geography of Childhood*. Boston: Beacon, 1994.

Nau, F. "Histoires des solitaires égyptiens 141." *Revue de l'Orient Chretien* 13 (1908): 47–57.

Nelson, Richard. *The Island Within*. New York: Vintage, 1991.

Nemo, Philippe. *Job and the Excess of Evil*. Translated by Michal Kigel. Pittsburgh: Duquesne University Press, 1998.

Newsom, Carol A. *The Book of Job: A Contest of Moral Imaginations*. New York: Oxford, 2003.

Nicholl, Donald. *The Beatitude of Truth*. London: Darton, Longman and Todd, 1997.

Nicholl, Steve. *Paradise Found: Nature in America at the Time of Discovery*. Chicago: University of Chicago Press, 2009.

Nicholsen, Shierry Weber. *The Love of Nature and the End of the World: The Unspoken Dimensions of Environmental Concern*. Cambridge, MA: MIT Press, 2002.

Nixon, Rob. *Slow Violence and the Environmentalism of the Poor.* Berkeley: University of California, 2011.

Novalis. *Henry of Ofterdingen.* Translated Petery Hilty. Long Grove, IL: Waveland Press, 1990.

Nygren, Anders. *Agape and Eros.* Chicago: University of Chicago Press, 1982.

Oates, David. *Paradise Wild: Reimagining American Nature.* Corvallis: Oregon State University Press, 2003.

O'Connell, Elizabeth R. "Transforming Monumental Landscapes in Late Antique Egypt: Monastic Dwellings in Legal Documents from Western Thebes." *Journal of Early Christian Studies* 15, no. 2 (2007): 239–273.

O'Grady, John P. *Pilgrims to the Wild: Everett Ruess, Henry David Thoreau, John Muir, Clarence King, Mary Austin.* Salt Lake City: University of Utah Press, 2002.

Oliver, Mary. *New and Selected Poems,* Vol. 1. Boston: Beacon, 2005.

———. *West Wind.* Boston: Houghton Mifflin, 1997.

Olyan, Saul M. *Biblical Mourning: Ritual and Social Dimensions.* New York: Oxford University Press, 2004.

Ondaatje, Michael. *Divisadero.* New York: Knopf, 2007.

O'Neill, Joseph. *Netherland.* New York: Pantheon, 2008.

Origen of Alexandria. *The Song of Songs: Commentary and Homilies.* Translated and annotated by R. P. Lawson. New York: Newman Press, 1956.

Osborne, Catherine. *Eros Unveiled: Plato and the God of Love.* Oxford: Clarendon Press, 1994.

Orr, David. *The Nature of Design: Ecology, Culture and Human Intention.* New York: Oxford University Press, 2002.

Orsi, Robert A. *Between Heaven and Earth: The Religious Worlds People Make and the Scholars Who Study Them.* Princeton: Princeton University Press, 2005.

Ortiz, Simon. *Out There Somewhere.* Tucson: University of Arizona Press, 2002.

Palmer, G. E. H., Philip Sherrard and Kallistos Ware, eds. *The Philokalia: The Complete Text, Volumes 1–4.* London: Faber and Faber, 1979–1995.

Parker, Rebecca Ann, and Rita Nakashima Brock. *Saving Paradise: How Christianity Traded Love of this World for Crucifixion and Empire.* Boston: Beacon, 2008.

Pasternak, Boris. *Doctor Zhivago.* Translated by Manya Harari and Max Hayward. New York: Knopf, 1986.

Patton, Kimberly Christine, and John Stratton Hawley, eds. *Holy Tears: Weeping in the Religious Imagination.* Princeton: Princeton University Press, 2005.

Peck, H. Daniel. *Thoreau's Morning Work: Memory and Perception.* New Haven: Yale University Press, 1990.

Petrini, Carlo. *Slow Food Nation: Why Our Food Should Be Good, Clean, Fair.* Translated by Clara Furlan and Jonathan Hunt. New York: Rizzoli, 2007.

Pevsner, Nikolaus, and Michael Meier. *Grünewald.* New York: Harry Abrams, 1958.

Price, Jennifer. *Flight Maps: Adventures with Nature in Modern America.* New York: Basic Books, 2000.

Prochnik, George. *In Pursuit of Silence: Listening for Meaning in a World of Noise.* New York: Doubleday, 2010.

Quammen, David. *The Song of the Dodo: Island Biogeography in an Age of Extinction.* New York: Scribner, 1996.

Radler, Charlotte. "'In Love I Am More God': The Centrality of Love in Meister Eckhart's Mysticism." *Journal of Religion* 90, no. 2 (2010): 171–198.

Raglon, Rebecca, and Marion Sholtmeijer. "Heading Off the Trail: Language, Literature and Nature's Resistance to Narrative." In *Beyond Nature Writing: Expanding the Boundaries of Ecocriticism,* edited by Karla Ambruster and Kathleen R. Wallace, 248–262. Charlottesville: University of Virginia Press, 2001.

Ricoeur, Paul. *Essays on Biblical Interpretation.* Edited with an Introduction by Lewis S. Mudge. Philadelphia: Fortress, 1980.

Rasmussen, Mette Sophia Bøcher. "Like a Rock or Like God? The Concept of *apatheia* in the Monastic Theology of Evagrius of Pontus." *Studia Theologica* 59, no. 2 (2005): 147–162.

Richardson, Miles, ed. *Place: Experience and Symbol; Geoscience and Man,* Vol. 24. Baton Rouge: Department of Geography and Anthropology, Louisiana State University, 1984.

Rilke, Rainer Maria. *Diaries of a Young Poet.* Edited and translated by Edward Snow and Michael Winkler. New York: Norton, 1997.

———. *Duino Elegies and the Sonnets to Orpheus.* Translated by Stephen Mitchell. New York: Vintage, 2009.

———. *Letters of Rainer Maria Rilke, 1910–1926.* Translated by Jane Bannard Greene and M. D. Herter Norton. New York: Norton, 1947, 1948.

———. *Sonnets to Orpheus.* Translated by Edward Snow. New York: North Point, 2002.

Robinson, David M. *Natural Life: Thoreau's Worldly Transcendentalism.* Ithaca: Cornell University Press, 2004.

———. "Thoreau's 'Ktaadn' and the Quest for Experience." In *Emersonian Circles: Essays in Honor of Joel Myerson.* Edited by Wesley T. Mott and Robert E. Burkholder, 207–223. Rochester: University of Rochester Press, 1997.

Robinson, Marilynne. *Absence of Mind: The Dispelling of Inwardness from the Modern Myth of the Self.* New Haven: Yale University Press, 2010.

———. *Housekeeping.* New York: Farrar, Straus and Giroux, 1980.

Roethke, Theodore. *Selected Poems.* New York: Library of America, 2005.

Rogers, Pattiann. *Firekeeper.* Minneapolis: Milkweed, 1994.

Rolheiser, Ronald. *The Holy Longing: The Search for a Christian Spirituality.* New York: Doubleday, 1999.

Roof, Wade Clark. "Religion and Spirituality: Toward an Integrated Analysis." In *Handbook of the Sociology of Religion.* Edited by Michelle Dillon, 137–148. Cambridge: Cambridge University Press, 2003.

Root, Robert, ed. *Landscapes with Figures: The Nonfiction of Place.* Lincoln: University of Nebraska, 2007.

Ross-Bryant, Lynn. "The Silence of Nature." *Religion and Literature* 22, no. 1 (Spring 1990): 79–94.

Rothenberg, David. *Why Birds Sing: A Journey into the Mystery of Birdsong.* New York: Basic Books, 2005.

Rousseau, Philip. Review of *Der Weg des Weinens. Die Tradition des 'Penthos' in den Apophthegmata Patrum. Journal of Theological Studies* 53, no. 2 (2002): 719–722.

Rubenson, Samuel. *The Letters of St. Antony: Monasticism and the Making of a Saint.* Minneapolis: Fortress Press, 1995.

Sachs, John R. "Apocatastasis in Patristic Theology." *Theological Studies* 54 (1993): 617–640.

Sanders, Scott Russell. *Staying Put: Making a Home in a Restless World.* Boston: Beacon, 1993.

Santer, Eric L. *On Creaturely Life: Rilke, Benjamin, Sebald.* Chicago: University of Chicago Press, 2006.

The Sayings of the Desert Fathers. Edited and translated by Benedicta Ward. Kalamazoo: Cistercian Publications, 2006.

Scafi, Alesandro. *Mapping Paradise: A History of Heaven on Earth.* Chicago: University of Chicago Press, 2006.

Scheiner, Samuel M., and Michael R. Willig, eds. *The Theory of Ecology.* Chicago: University of Chicago Press, 2011.

Scheja, Georg. *The Isenheim Altarpiece.* Translated by Robert Erich Wolf. New York: Henry N. Abrams, 1969.

Schmidt, Leigh Eric. *Restless Souls: The Making of American Spirituality.* San Francisco: HarperSanFrancisco, 2005.

Schneiders, Sandra. M. "Religion vs. Spirituality: A Contemporary Conundrum." *Spiritus* 3 (2003): 163–185.

——. "The Study of Christian Spirituality: Contours and Dynamics of a Discipline." In *Minding the Spirit: The Study of Christian Spirituality.* Edited by Elizabeth Dreyer and Mark Burrows. Baltimore: Johns Hopkins University Press, 2005.

Schroeder, Caroline T. *Monastic Bodies: Discipline and Salvation in Shenoute of Atripe.* Philadelphia: University of Pennsylvania Press, 2007.

——. "'A Suitable Abode for Christ': The Church Building as Symbol of Ascetic Renunciation in Early Monasticism." *Church History* 73, no. 3 (2004): 472–521.

Schürmann, Reiner. *Wandering Joy: Meister Eckhart's Mystical Philosophy.* Great Barrington, MA: Lindisfarne Books, 2001.

Seamon, David, ed. *Dwelling, Seeing, and Designing: Toward a Phenomenological Ecology.* Albany: State University of New York Press, 1993.

Searles, Harold. "Unconscious Processes in the Environmental Crisis." *Countertransference and Related Subjects.* New York: International Universities Press, 1979.

Sebald, W. G. *After Nature.* Translated by Michael Hamburger. London: Hamish Hamilton, 2002.

———. *The Emigrants*. Translated by Michale Hulse. New York: New Directions, 1996.

———. *On the Natural History of Destruction*. Translated by Anthea Bell. New York: Modern Library, 2004.

A Select Library of Nicene and Post-Nicene Fathers, n.s. no. 11. Translated by Edgar C. S. Gibson. Oxford: Parker and Co., 1894; reprint: Grand Rapids, MI: Eerdmans, 1973.

Sells, Michael. *Mystical Languages of Unsaying*. Chicago: University of Chicago Press, 1994.

Sheldrake, Philip. *Spaces for the Sacred: Place, Memory and Identity*. Baltimore: Johns Hopkins University Press, 2001.

———. "Unending Desire: Certeau's 'Mystics'. *The Way Supplement* 102 (2001): 38–48.

Shepard, Paul. *Nature and Madness*. San Francisco: Sierra Club, 1982.

———. *Traces of an Omnivore*. Washington, DC: Island Press, 1996.

Sibley, David Allen. *The Sibley Guide to Birds*. New York: Knopf, 2000.

Sideris, Lisa H. *Environmental Ethics, Ecological Theology, and Natural Selection*. New York: Columbia University Press, 2003.

Silko, Leslie Marmon. *Ceremony*. New York: Viking Penguin, 1977.

———. *Yellow Woman and Beauty of the Spirit*. New York: Simon and Schuster, 1996.

Silko, Leslie Marmon, and James Wright. *The Delicacy and Strength of Lace: Letters between Leslie Marmon Silko and James Wright*. Edited by Anne Wright. St. Paul, MN: Graywolf, 1986.

Simpson, Marc, ed. *Like Breath on Glass: Whistler, Inness, and the Art of Painting Softly*. New Haven: Yale University Press, 2008.

Slouka, Mark. "Quitting the Paint Factory: On the Virtues of Idleness." *Harpers Magazine*, November 2004: 57–65.

Slovic, Scott. *Seeking Awareness in American Nature Writing: Henry Thoreau, Annie Dillard, Edward Abbey, Wendell Berry, Barry Lopez*. Salt Lake City: University of Utah Press, 1992.

Snyder, Gary. *The Practice of the Wild*. San Francisco: North Point, 1990.

———. *Turtle Island*. New York: New Directions, 1974.

Spirn, Anne Whiston. *The Language of Landscape*. New Haven: Yale University Press, 1998.

Spivey, Nigel. *Enduring Creation: Art, Pain, and Fortitude*. Berkeley: University of California Press, 2001.

Solnit, Rebecca. *Storming the Gates of Paradise: Landscapes for Politics*. Berkeley: University of California Press, 2007.

Solomon, Robert C. *Spirituality for the Skeptic: The Thoughtful Love of Life*. New York: Oxford University Press, 2006.

Spargo, Clifton R. *The Ethics of Mourning: Grief and Responsibility in Elegiac Literature*. Baltimore: Johns Hopkins University Press, 2004.

Sponsel, Leslie. *Spiritual Ecology: A Quiet Revolution*. Santa Barbara, CA: Praeger, 2012.

St. John, Donald P. "Technological Culture and Contemplative Ecology in Thomas Merton's *Conjectures of a Guilty Bystander*." *Worldviews* 6, no. 2 (2002): 159–182.

Stanczak, Gregory. *Engaged Spirituality: Social Change and American Religion*. New Brunswick, NJ: Rutgers University Press, 2006.

Steiner, Frederick. *Human Ecology: Following Nature's Lead*. Washington: Island Press, 2002.

Stewart, Columba. *Cassian the Monk*. New York: Oxford University Press, 1998.

————. "Imageless Prayer and the Theological Vision of Evagrius Ponticus." *Journal of Early Christian Studies* 9, no. 2 (2001): 173–204.

Suliman, Muhamed, ed. *Ecology, Politics and Violent Conflict*. London: Zed Books, 1999.

Sutera, Judith. "Place and Stability in the *Life of Antony*." *Cistercian Studies Quarterly* 27, no. 2 (1992): 101–114

Swimme, Brian, and Mary Evelyn Tucker. *The Journey of the Universe*. New Haven: Yale University Press, 2011.

Tall, Deborah. *From Where We Stand: Recovering a Sense of Place*. Baltimore: Johns Hopkins University Press, 1997.

Taylor, Bron. *Dark Green Religion: Nature, Spirituality and Our Planetary Future*. Berkeley: University of California Press, 2009.

Taylor, Sarah McFarland. *Green Sisters: A Spiritual Ecology*. Cambridge, MA: Harvard University Press, 2007.

Thayer, Robert. *LifePlace: Bioregional Thought and Practice*. Berkeley: University of California Press, 2003.

Theodoret of Cyrrhus, *A History of the Monks of Syria*. Translated by R. M. Price. Kalamazoo, MI: Cistercian Publications, 1985.

Thoreau, Henry David. *Collected Essays and Poems*. Edited by Elizabeth Hall Witherall. New York: Library of America, 2001.

————. *The Essays of Henry D. Thoreau*. Selected and annotated by Lewis Hyde. New York: North Point Press, 2002.

————. *Faith in a Seed*. Washington, DC: Island Press: 1993.

————. *I to Myself: An Annotated Selection from the Journal of Henry David Thoreau*. Edited by Jeffrey S. Kramer. New Haven: Yale University Press, 2007.

————. *Journal*. Edited by John C. Broderick et. al. Princeton: Princeton University Press, 1981.

————. *The Maine Woods*. Edited by Joseph J. Moldenhauer. Princeton: Princeton University Press, 1972.

————. *Walden*. Edited by J. Lyndon Shanley. Princeton: Princeton University Press, 1971.

————. *Walking*. Boston: Beacon, 1991.

————. *A Week on the Concord and Merrimack Rivers*. Edited by Carl F. Hovde, William L. Howarth, and Elizabeth Hall Witherell. Princeton: Princeton University Press, 2004.

Tiffin, Helen, and Graham Huggan, eds. *Postcolonial EcoCriticism: Literature, Animals, Environment*. London: Routledge, 2010.

Tracy, David. *Blessed Rage for Order, the New Pluralism in Theology*. Chicago: University of Chicago Press, 1995.

Tuan, Yi Fu. *Cosmos and Hearth*. Minneapolis: University of Minnesota Press, 1996.

———. *Space and Place: The Perspective of Experience*. Minneapolis: University of Minnesota Press, 1977.

———. *Topophilia: A Study in Environmental Perceptions, Attitudes, and Values*. New York: Columbia University Press, 1974.

Tuan, Yi Fu, and Martha Strawn. *Religion: From Place to Placelessness*. Chicago: University of Chicago Press, 2010.

Turkle, Sherry. *Alone Together: Why We Expect More from Technology and Less from Each Other*. New York: Basic Books, 2011.

Turner, Denys. *Eros and Allegory: Medieval Exegesis of the Song of Songs*. Kalamazoo, MI: Cistercian Publications, 1995.

———. *The Darkness of God: Negativity in Christian Mysticism*. Cambridge: Cambridge University Press, 1995.

Turner, Jack. *The Abstract Wild*. Tucson: University of Arizona Press, 2006.

Van Gogh, Vincent. *Letters*. Selected and Edited by Ronald de Leeuw. Translated by Arnold Pomerans. London: Penguin, 1996.

Van Ness, Peter H, ed. *Spirituality and the Secular Quest*. New York: Crossroad, 1996.

Voight, Ellen. *Kyrie*. New York: Norton, 1995.

Waldie, D. J. *Holy Land*. New York: St. Martin's Press, 1996.

Wallace, Mark I. *Finding God in the Singing River: Christianity, Spirit, Nature*. Minneapolis: Augsburg Fortress, 2005.

Walter, E. V. *Placeways: A Theory of the Human Environment*. Chapel Hill: University of North Carolina Press, 1988.

Ward, Graham, ed. *The Postmodern God*. Oxford: Blackwell, 1997.

Warren, Rick. *The Purpose Driven Life*. Grand Rapids, MI: Zondervan, 2002.

Weil, Simone. *Gravity and Grace*. Translated by Emma Crawford and Mario von der Ruhr. London and New York: Routledge, 2002.

———. *The Need for Roots: Prelude to a Declaration of Duties toward Mankind*. Translated by Arthur Wils. New York: Harper, 1952.

———. *The Notebooks of Simone Weil*, Vol. I. Translated by Arthur Wills. London: Routledge, 2004.

———. *Waiting for God*. Translated by Emma Craufurd. New York: Putnam's, 1952.

Whitehead, James D., and Evelyn Easton Whitehead. *Holy Eros: Recovering the Passion of God*. Maryknoll, NY: Orbis, 2008.

Whyte, Ian. *World without End? Environmental Disaster and the Collapse of Empires*. London: I. B. Tauris, 2008.

Wiesel, Elie. "Longing for Home." Edited by Leroy S. Rouner. *The Longing for Home*, 17–29. Notre Dame: University of Notre Dame Press, 1996.

Wilder, Amos. *Theopoetic: Theology and the Religious Imagination*. Philadelphia: Fortress, 1976.

Williams, Rowan. *On Christian Theology*. Oxford: Blackwell, 2000.

Williams, Terry Tempest. *Refuge: An Unnatural History of Family and Place*. New York: Pantheon, 1991.

Wilson, Derek. *Hans Holbein: Portrait of an Unknown Man*. London: Weidenfeld and Nicolson, 1996.

Wilson, E.O. *Biophilia*. Cambridge, MA: Harvard University Press, 1984.

Winterson, Jeanette. *Weight*. New York: Canongate, 2005.

Wisdom of the Desert Fathers: The "Apophthegmata Patrum" (The Anonymous Series). Edited and translated by Benedicta Ward. Oxford: SLG Press, 1986.

Wordsworth, William. *Poems. Selections. Oxford Poetry Library*. Edited by Stephen Gill and Duncan Wu. Oxford: Oxford University Press, 1994.

Wuthnow, Robert. *After Heaven: Spirituality in America since the 1950s*. Berkeley: University of California Press, 1998.

Zagajewski, Adam. *A Defense of Ardor*. Translated by Clare Cavanagh. New York: Farrar, Straus and Giroux, 2004.

Zinnbauer, Brian J., Kenneth Pargament, et al. "Religion and Spirituality: Unfuzzying the Fuzzy." *Journal for the Scientific Study of Religion*, 36, no. 4 (1997): 549–564.

Zuckerman, Bruce. *Job the Silent: A Study in Historical Counterpoint*. New York: Oxford, 1991.

Index